SOCIOLOGY

The Study of Human Relationships

Fifth Edition

SOCIOLOGY

The Study of Human Relationships

Fifth Edition

W. LaVerne Thomas

HOLT, RINEHART AND WINSTON
Harcourt Brace & Company
Austin • New York • Orlando • Chicago • Atlanta
San Francisco • Boston • Dallas • Toronto • London

THE AUTHOR

W. LaVerne (Verne) Thomas has taught courses in the behavioral sciences at Wheat Ridge High School, Wheat Ridge, Colorado, since 1960. He received his B.A. education at Nebraska Wesleyan University and earned his M.A. in sociology at the University of Denver. He is active in several professional organizations, including the American Sociological Association and the National Education Association.

CRITICAL READERS AND CONSULTANTS

Scott Beck
Department of Sociology
East Tennessee State University
Johnson City, Tennessee

John Cochran
Department of Sociology
University of Oklahoma
Norman, Oklahoma

Nancy Conway
Wheat Ridge Senior High School
Wheat Ridge, Colorado

Shelley Gulley
Eastern High School
Pekin, Indiana

Tim Harshman
Jefferson Alternative High School
Toledo, Ohio

Dewey Hinderman
Hopkins Senior High School
Minnetonka, Minnesota

Gerald Leslie
Department of Sociology, Emeritus
University of Florida
Gainesville, Florida

James C. Matiya
Carl Sandburg High School
Orland Park, Illinois

Barbara Moore
Center for Economic Education
University of Central Florida
Orlando, Florida

Cynthia Rexroat
Center for Research on Women
Memphis State University
Memphis, Tennessee

William Schwab
Department of Sociology
University of Arkansas
Fayetteville, Arkansas

Constance Shehan
Department of Sociology
University of Florida
Gainesville, Florida

Debralee Stauffer
Wheat Ridge Senior High School
Wheat Ridge, Colorado

W. Clinton Terry, III
Department of Criminal Justice
Florida International University
North Miami, Florida

Buff Yelton
Williston-Elko High School
Williston, South Carolina

ACKNOWLEDGMENTS

For permission to reprint copyrighted material, grateful acknowledgment is made to the following sources:

Academic Press, Inc. and Susan Curtiss: From *Genie: A Psycholinguistic Study of a Modern-Day ''Wild Child''* by Susan Curtiss. Copyright © 1977 by Academic Press, Inc.

Addison-Wesley Publishing Company, Inc.: From ''Communications: Working the Cultural Network'' from *Corporate Cultures* (Retitled: ''The Rites and Rituals of Corporate Life'') by Terrence Deal and Allan Kennedy. Copyright © 1982 by Addison-Wesley Publishing Company, Inc.

Continued on page 551

Printed in the United States of America

ISBN 0-03-097589-1

3 4 5 6 7   071   97 96 95

CONTENTS

UNIT 2 THE INDIVIDUAL IN SOCIETY 96

UNIT 3 SOCIAL INEQUALITY

UNIT 4   SOCIAL INSTITUTIONS

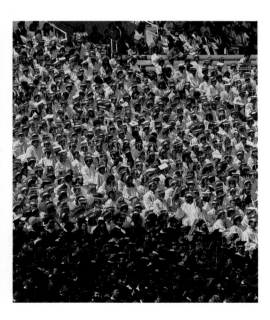

UNIT 5 THE CHANGING SOCIAL WORLD

DEVELOPING SOCIOLOGICAL IMAGINATION

INTERPRETING PRIMARY SOURCES

CASE STUDIES

APPLYING SOCIOLOGY

ACROSS SPACE AND TIME

CHARTS, GRAPHS, TABLES, AND MAPS

The sociological imagination, I remind you, in considerable part consists of the capacity to shift from one perspective to another, and in the process to build up an adequate view of a total society and of its components. It is this imagination, of course, that sets off the social scientist from the mere technician.

C. WRIGHT MILLS

CULTURE AND SOCIAL STRUCTURE

The Sociological Point of View

1 **Examining Social Life**

The Sociological Perspective
Sociology's Place in the Social Sciences

2 **Sociology: Then and Now**

The Early Years
Current Perspectives

Chapter Focus

Chapter 1 examines the nature and focus of sociology. A brief overview of sociology's early years and current theoretical perspectives also is presented.
  As you study the chapter, look for the answers to the following questions:

1. What is sociology, and how does having a sociological imagination help us to understand society and ourselves?
2. What is sociology's place in the social sciences?
3. How did early sociologists view society and the role of the sociologist?
4. How do the three main theoretical perspectives in sociology differ in their focus?

KEY TERMS

The following terms, while not the only terms emphasized in the chapter, are basic to your understanding of sociology. Determine the meaning of each term, either by using the Glossary or by watching for context clues as you read the chapter.

sociology	function	theory
social interaction	*Verstehen*	dysfunction
social sciences	ideal type	symbolic interaction

- While drug use among high school students has been declining over the past several years, a survey of members of the class of 1991 found that about 37 percent had tried marijuana or hashish, 88 percent had used alcohol, and slightly more than 61 percent had smoked cigarettes.

- In 1992, Republican George Bush, Democrat Bill Clinton, and Independent Ross Perot campaigned for election to our nation's highest office—President of the United States. Although election results gave the presidency to Clinton, Perot received more of the popular vote than any other third-party candidate since Theodore Roosevelt in 1912.

- Since AIDS was first reported to the national Centers for Disease Control and Prevention in 1981, more than 150,000 people have died from the disease in the United States alone. The World Health Organization estimates that by the year 2000, up to 40 million people worldwide will be infected with the virus that is believed to cause AIDS.

- The average age at which people in the United States first marry has been rising steadily for decades. As a result, single people are a rapidly growing segment of our population. In 1991, there were over 41 million American adults who had never been married.

- Nearly 23 million American households were victimized by crime in 1991. On average, there was one violent crime every 17 seconds in 1991, one property crime every 2 seconds, and one murder every 21 minutes.

1 EXAMINING SOCIAL LIFE

As the introduction above indicates, we live in a complex social environment. For some of us, life is full of opportunities. For others, life often consists simply of surviving from day to day. For most of us, however, it is a mixture of both—good and bad, achievements and disappointments.

Our view of the world is shaped by our daily lives. The values, beliefs, life-styles, and experiences of those around us, as well as historic events, help to mold us into unique individuals who have varied outlooks on social reality. The fact that we do not all view things in exactly the same way is what gives society its rich diversity. At the same time, however, all of us in society share many of the same perceptions and characteristics. It is this combination of diversity and similarity that is of primary interest to sociologists.

Sociology is the science that studies human society and social behavior. Sociologists are mainly interested in **social interaction**—how people relate to one another and influence each other's behavior. Consequently, sociologists tend to focus on the group rather than on the individual. Sociologists do this by examining social phenomena. A social **phenomenon** is an observable fact or event.

The Sociological Perspective

Studying sociology can help us gain a new view, or perspective, for looking at ourselves and the world. Rather than relying on common sense, which often turns out to be incorrect, sociology teaches us to look at social life in a scientific, systematic way. By adopting a sociological perspective, we are able to look beyond commonly

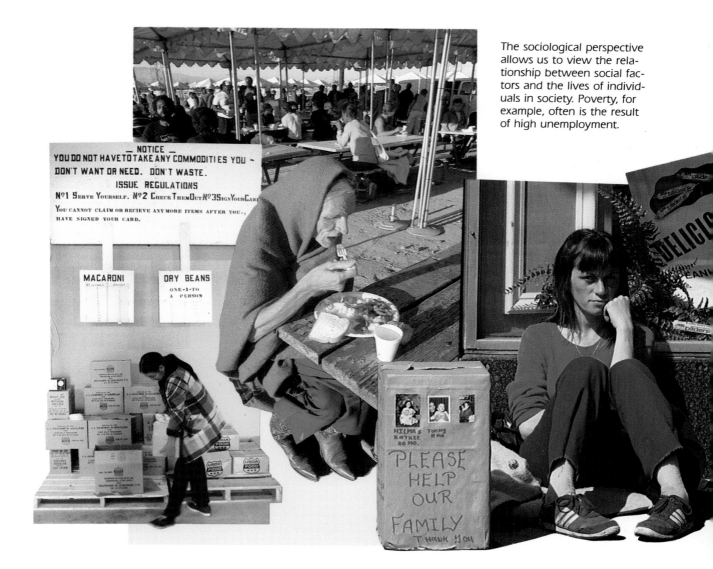

The sociological perspective allows us to view the relationship between social factors and the lives of individuals in society. Poverty, for example, often is the result of high unemployment.

held beliefs to the hidden meanings behind human actions.

The sociological perspective helps us see that we are social beings. It tells us that our behavior is the result of social factors and that we have learned our behavior from others. By using the sociological perspective, we can look at ourselves and the world more objectively. We also can use the sociological perspective to research areas of great importance in our own lives.

The sociological perspective can help us broaden our view of the social world. It tells us that there are many different perceptions of social reality. We can see beyond our own day-to-day world by viewing the world through others' eyes.

Sociology also can help us find an acceptable balance between our personal desires and the demands of our social environment. If we always do what we want to do, we are likely to conflict with others a great deal of the time. On the other hand, if we always do what others demand of us, we will not grow very much as individuals. A knowledge of sociology can help us decide the most acceptable point between these two extremes.

Sociology also can help us view our own lives within a larger social and historical context. It can give us insights into how our social environment shapes us and how we in turn can shape our social environment. This ability to see the connection between the larger world and our personal lives

The same behavior can be studied from a variety of social science perspectives.

is what C. Wright Mills termed the **sociological imagination.** According to Mills, all good sociologists and students of society possess such imagination. An excerpt from Mills's book *The Sociological Imagination* is presented in the Interpreting Primary Sources feature on page 21. In this excerpt, Mills describes what it means to have a sociological imagination.

Sociology's Place in the Social Sciences

Sociology is only one of the disciplines that studies human social behavior in a scientific, systematic manner. The related disciplines that study various aspects of human social behavior are called the **social sciences**. In addition to sociology, the social sciences include anthropology, psychology, economics, political science, and history.

Anthropology—the comparative study of various aspects of past and present cultures—is the social science closest to sociology in its subject matter. Anthropologists traditionally have concen-

trated on examining past cultures and present simple societies. Sociology, on the other hand, is most interested in group behavior in complex societies. Today, however, many anthropologists also concentrate on complex societies. Urban anthropologists, for instance, examine such things as the cultural characteristics of neighborhoods and communities in Western nations.

The social science that deals with the behavior and thinking of organisms is **psychology.** Psychology differs from sociology primarily in that it focuses on individual behavior rather than on group behavior and draws more heavily on the tools of the natural sciences. Areas of interest to psychologists include personality, perception, motivation, and learning. Despite differences in emphasis, sociology and psychology are related, particularly in the area of social psychology. **Social psychology** is the study of how an individual's behavior and personality are affected by the social environment. Social psychology courses are taught both in psychology departments and in sociology departments and people in both disciplines claim the title of social psychologist.

The American Sociological Association

The American Sociological Association (ASA) was founded in 1905 by a small group of social scientists interested in the science of society. Prior to the founding of this national organization, most American sociologists were members of the American Economics Association or the American Association for the Advancement of Science.

When the founders of the ASA first met to discuss the possibility of organizing an association of sociologists, they were unsure whether the association should exist under the umbrella of one of the established organizations or whether it should stand alone. Intense debate followed, but finally a motion was passed to form an organization of sociologists that was separate and independent from all other organizations. A later meeting established the constitution of the organization, elected the officers, and set the dues and membership requirements. Thus the ASA, then called the American Sociological Society, was born.

The establishment of a national association geared specifically to the concerns of sociologists was an important step in the development of sociology as a distinct discipline in the United States. When the organization held its first annual meeting in 1906, membership stood at 115. Since that early time, the role of the American Sociological Association in the lives of professional sociologists has expanded along with its skyrocketing membership.

The ASA is today the largest professional organization of sociologists in the United States. With a current membership roll of more than 13,000 scholars, researchers, teachers, and college students, the ASA serves as an important vehicle for the sharing of new research and new ideas in the field of sociology.

One of the important functions of the ASA is to plan the annual convention, which brings together sociologists from across the nation and throughout the world. At each annual convention, sociologists meet to present papers outlining their most current research and to discuss the problems and issues of the discipline. Each of the specialty areas of sociology, such as family sociology, criminology, theory, and medical sociology, is represented at the convention. The annual meeting is an important means through which sociologists can share their knowledge and build toward the future.

Another way that the American Sociological Association serves to further the knowledge-building quest of sociology is through the sponsoring and publishing of a number of professional journals. Some of the ASA's most influential journals are the *American Sociological Review, Sociological Theory, Journal of Health and Social Behavior,* and *Teaching Sociology.* By publishing articles in these journals, sociologists can share with their colleagues the very latest findings from their research studies. In addition, the ASA publishes *Contemporary Sociology,* a journal containing book reviews of recent publications in the many specialty areas of sociology.

The American Sociological Association also is actively involved in developing materials to assist in the teaching of sociology. The ASA Teaching Services Program, established in 1980, operates a teaching resources center and organizes workshops for sociology teachers. In addition, the ASA provides funds for teacher development and training and presents awards to outstanding teachers.

For additional information on the American Sociological Association, write to the following address:

American Sociological Association
1722 N Street, N.W.
Washington, DC 20036

Hitler's rise to power has been of interest to all of the social sciences.

Economics is the study of the choices people make in an effort to satisfy their wants and needs. Economists examine the processes by which goods and services are produced, distributed, and consumed. They also examine the effects of government policies on economic growth and stability. Sociologists share many areas of interest with economists. The effect of economic factors on the lives of various groups in society, for instance, has attracted the attention of sociologists since the earliest days of the discipline.

The examination of the organization and operation of governments is the focus of **political science.** The interests of sociology and political science often overlap. Areas of mutual interest include voting patterns, the concentration of political power, and the formation of politically based groups.

History is the study of past events. Sociologists also are interested in the past. Like many social historians, sociologists study past events in an effort to explain current social behaviors and attitudes.

Over time, the divisions between the social sciences have become less distinct. Many modern social scientists borrow freely from the various social sciences in an effort to better understand the social forces that help to shape our lives.

SECTION 1 REVIEW

DEFINE sociology, anthropology, psychology, economics, political science, history

1. ***Analyzing Ideas*** Why do sociologists focus on groups rather than on individuals?

2. ***Comprehending Ideas*** ***(a)*** According to C. Wright Mills, what is the sociological imagination? ***(b)*** How can having a sociological imagination assist people in their daily lives?

3. ***Comparing Ideas*** ***(a)*** How does the focus of sociology differ from the focus of the other social sciences? ***(b)*** In what ways is the focus of sociology similar to the focus of the other social sciences?

SOCIOLOGY: THEN AND NOW

The nature of social life and human interaction has been of interest to scholars throughout history. Not until the nineteenth century, however, did a separate academic discipline dedicated to the analysis of society develop.

Several factors led to the development of sociology as a distinct field of study. Of primary importance were the rapid social and political changes that took place in Europe during the seventeenth and eighteenth centuries. At the root of these changes was the Industrial Revolution.

During the Industrial Revolution the rural economy of the Middle Ages, with its farms and cottage industries, gave way to an economy based on large-scale production. Factories replaced the home as the main site for manufacturing. With the growth of factories came the growth of cities, as people left their homes in the countryside in search of paid employment.

The rapid explosion of the urban population produced a multitude of social problems. The number of people seeking work outpaced available jobs. Housing shortages developed, crime increased, and pollution became a major problem. People who had been raised in small rural communities where interactions were based on close personal relationships found themselves faced with the impersonal surroundings of cities and factories.

As the situation worsened, it became more difficult to ignore the impact of society on the individual. Individual liberty and individual rights became the focus of a wide variety of political movements. Out of this period came the American and French revolutions.

Added to these political and social changes were developments in the natural sciences. The Middle Ages had produced methods for studying the physical world in a systematic and scientific manner. Early sociologists applied many of these methods to the study of society.

The Early Years

Sociology took root in the nineteenth century, primarily in France, Germany, and England. These nations had most strongly felt the effects of the Industrial Revolution. Most influential among the early sociologists were Auguste Comte, Karl Marx, Herbert Spencer, Emile Durkheim, and Max Weber.

Auguste Comte. The French philosopher Auguste Comte (1798–1857) usually is considered the founder of sociology. The title of founder is given to Comte because he was the first person to use the term *sociology* to describe the study of society.

Like most French scholars of his day, Comte was concerned with finding solutions to the chaos created by the French Revolution. He believed that his philosophy of society was the key to bringing stability to the world. Heavily influenced by the scientific methods of the natural sciences, Comte argued that sociologists could use similar methods to uncover the laws that govern the operation of society.

The Granger Collection, New York

Auguste Comte lived in France during a period of great social upheaval. He believed his new science could give stability to society.

Comte believed that sociologists should be concerned with two basic problems—order and change. He used the term *social statics* to describe the processes by which the overall structure of a society remains relatively stable, or unchanged, over time. He applied the term *social dynamics* to the processes by which elements within the society change in a systematic fashion to allow for social development.

Although he never completed his college education, Comte wrote and lectured for many years, gaining a considerable following in France as well as in other countries. Throughout his life, however, Comte suffered from depression and other emotional problems. At one point, he began to practice what he called "cerebral hygiene," refusing to read the works of other writers in order to keep his mind pure. Despite this, his ideas concerning the scientific value of sociology influenced the lives of many young scholars. Sociologists today, more than 150 years later, still are concerned with the issues of order and change.

The writings of Karl Marx largely were a reaction to the harsh social conditions produced by industrialization.

Karl Marx. Karl Marx (1818–1883) was born in Germany to middle-class parents. He received his doctorate degree from the University of Berlin, but never held a regular teaching position. Instead, he worked as a writer and then served as editor for a radical newspaper, which later was closed down by the government for its political views. After the newspaper folded, Marx moved to the more liberal atmosphere of Paris, but soon was expelled by the French at the request of the German government. He journeyed onward to Brussels and finally to London, where he earned a scanty living from his writings. Marx died in poverty, following the deaths of his wife and last-surviving child. Nevertheless, his writings have influenced generations of scholars and social critics worldwide.

Marx believed that the overall structure of society is heavily influenced by how the economy is organized. According to Marx, society is divided between those who own the means of production—the materials and methods used to produce goods and services—and those who own only their labor. The people who own the means of production control society. This imbalance in power leads to conflict between owners and laborers. The exact nature of the conflict varies depending on the historical period under consideration.

Although Marx devoted much attention to the changing nature of social relations throughout history, he was most interested in capitalist society. Marx was deeply troubled by the social conditions produced by the capitalist system of his day. These social conditions included long hours, low pay, and harsh working conditions. Thus, unlike many contemporary sociologists, Marx did not believe that social scientists should be passive observers of society. He saw as the task of social scientists—and of ill-treated workers—the transformation of society. According to Marx, the ills of the capitalist system would not be solved until the workers overthrew those in power.

Marx did not really consider himself a sociologist, and relatively few modern sociologists consider themselves Marxists. Nevertheless, his belief that the economic basis of society strongly influences social structure has had a lasting influence on sociology. Similarly, his emphasis on conflict as the primary cause of social change has influenced generations of sociologists.

Herbert Spencer.

Herbert Spencer (1820–1903), an English contemporary of Comte, started his working life as a civil engineer for a railway. A large inheritance received when he was in his thirties freed him from the need to earn a living and allowed him to pursue his interest in the workings of society.

Spencer was strongly influenced by the views of Charles Darwin, the nineteenth-century evolutionist. The influence of Darwin led Spencer to adopt a biological model of society. In a living organism, the biological systems work together to maintain the health of the organism. Spencer attributed a similar process to society, viewing society as a set of interdependent parts that work together to maintain the system over time.

Spencer also used Darwin's notion of the evolution of biological organisms to describe the nature of society. He considered social change and unrest to be natural occurrences in a society's evolution toward stability and perfection. Because he believed that the best aspects of society would survive over time, Spencer thought that no steps should be taken to correct social ills. Although it is often credited to Charles Darwin, the phrase "survival of the fittest" was coined by Herbert Spencer in reference to this weeding-out process. Spencer also believed that the fittest societies would survive over time, leading to a general upgrading of the world as a whole. Because of the strong evolutionary orientation of Spencer's brand of sociology, it came to be known as **social Darwinism.**

Herbert Spencer, like Comte, refused to read the writings of scholars whose ideas differed from his own. As a result, he disregarded the rules of careful scholarship and made unproven claims about the workings of the world. As social problems grew more severe during the nineteenth century, Spencer's social Darwinism fell out of favor.

Emile Durkheim.

The Frenchman Emile Durkheim (1858–1917) gained a teaching position at the University of Bordeaux when he was in his twenties. Although he was deeply interested in the science of society, Durkheim initially taught in the philosophy department because there were as yet no departments of sociology in France. Durkheim later was to offer the first university social science course available in France.

Both Herbert Spencer (top) and Emile Durkheim (bottom) compared society to a living organism. Unlike Spencer, however, Durkheim used scientific methods to test his views of the ways in which society works. For example, Durkheim devoted considerable time to the scientific study of the social causes of suicide and the social functions of religion.

Durkheim was the first sociologist to systematically apply the methods of science to the study of society. Like Spencer, Durkheim was concerned with the problem of social order. Also like Spencer, he saw society as a set of interdependent parts that maintain the system over time. Durkheim, however, viewed the role of these parts in terms of functions. A **function** is the positive consequence that an element of society has for the maintenance of the social system. This idea has been very influential in modern American sociology. Durkheim saw shared beliefs and values as the glue that holds society together. He was particularly interested in the function of religion in maintaining the social order.

At the basis of Durkheim's scientific analysis of society was his belief that sociologists should study only those aspects of society that are directly observable. He did not consider the thoughts and feelings of individuals within society to be the proper subject matter of the discipline. In addition to applying scientific methods to the study of sociology, Durkheim was the first sociologist to test his theories through statistical analysis.

Unlike other sociologists of his day, Max Weber thought it important to understand the individual.

Max Weber. Max Weber (VAY-ber) (1864–1920) was born in Germany to middle-class parents. He received his doctoral degree from the University of Berlin and later was given a teaching position at the university. His impressive level of productivity led in 1896 to a position as Professor of Economics at the University of Heidelberg, where he was to produce some of his most important writings. Among Weber's many accomplishments was the founding in 1910 of the German Sociological Society.

Unlike Comte, Marx, Spencer, and Durkheim, Weber was interested more in groups within society than in the social whole. This emphasis on groups led Weber to analyze the effects of society on the individual.

Weber thought that sociologists should go beyond studying what can be directly observed. He believed that sociologists must try to uncover the feelings and thoughts of individuals. Weber proposed doing this through the method of *Verstehen* (fehr-SHTAY-en). **Verstehen** is the empathetic understanding of the meanings others attach to their actions. In essence, the sociologist puts himself or herself in the place of others and attempts to see situations through their eyes.

In addition to *Verstehen,* Weber employed the concept of ideal type in much of his work. An **ideal type** is a description of the essential characteristics of some aspect of society. An ideal type is constructed by examining many different examples of a phenomenon and then describing the essential features. Thus any particular example of the phenomenon might not contain all of the characteristics described in the ideal type. For instance, the ideal type school might not be a perfect representation of your school, but you would recognize it as a general description of an educational institution.

Current Perspectives

A **theory** is a systematic explanation of the relationships among phenomena. Sociologists develop theories to guide their work and help interpret their findings. Sociologists not only develop theories to explain specific phenomena, they also adopt broad theoretical perspectives to provide a foundation for their inquiries. A **theoretical perspective** is a general set of assumptions about

the nature of phenomena. In the case of sociology, a theoretical perspective outlines certain assumptions about the nature of social life.

Three broad theoretical perspectives form the basis of modern sociology. These perspectives are the functionalist perspective, the conflict perspective, and the interactionist perspective. Each perspective presents a slightly different image of society or focuses on different aspects of social life.

Functionalist Perspective. People who employ the **functionalist perspective** view society as a set of interrelated parts that work together to produce a stable social system. According to functionalists, society is held together through consensus. In other words, most people agree on what is best for society and work together to ensure that the social system runs smoothly. Sociologists who adopt this perspective follow in the tradition of Herbert Spencer and Emile Durkheim. Some of the topics of interest to functionalist sociologists include the division of work in the family and the functions served by education in society.

Like Durkheim, functionalists view the various elements in society in terms of their functions— their positive consequences for society. Recognizing that not everything in society operates smoothly, functionalists also label certain elements as dysfunctional. A **dysfunction** is the negative consequence an element has for the stability of the social system. Dysfunctional elements, such as crime, disrupt society rather than stabilize it.

In addition to being either positive or negative, functions can be either manifest or latent. A **manifest function** is the intended and recognized consequence of some element of society. A manifest function of the automobile, for example, is to provide speedy transportation from one location to another. A **latent function,** on the other hand, is the unintended and unrecognized consequence of an element of society. A latent function of the automobile is to gain social standing through the display of wealth.

Conflict Perspective. People who employ the **conflict perspective** focus on those forces in society that promote competition and change. Following in the tradition of Karl Marx, conflict theorists are interested in how those who possess more power in society exercise control over those with less power. Conflict theorists do not limit their attention to acts of violent conflict. They also are interested in nonviolent competition between various groups in society, such as men and women or people of different ages or racial or national backgrounds. Some of the research topics that conflict sociologists pursue include decision making in the family, relationships among racial groups in a society, and labor disputes between workers and employers.

According to conflict theorists, competition over scarce resources is at the basis of social conflict. Because resources such as power and wealth are in limited supply, people must compete with one another for them. Once particular groups gain control of society's resources, they tend to establish rules and procedures that protect their interests at the expense of other groups. This inequality between groups leads to social conflict as those with less power attempt to gain access to desired resources and those with power attempt to keep it. Conflict, in turn, leads to social change. Thus conflict theorists see social change as an inevitable feature of society.

Text continues on page 16.

APPLYING SOCIOLOGY

Using Sociological Methods

As you learned in this chapter, sociologists study how people interact with one another and with their social environment. There are four broad categories of research methods that sociologists employ to collect **data**, or scientific information, on society and human behavior. These categories are surveys, experiments, observational studies, and the analysis of existing sources. Under these broad headings fall a series of more specific research techniques, such as the historical method or content analysis. Sociologists also employ various techniques to analyze their data once the collection process is completed. The most common of these techniques involve some form of statistical analysis.

Following is a brief description of some of the methods employed in social research. A more detailed discussion of sociological research methods can be found in the Appendix, which begins on page 485. The information presented in the Appendix will be helpful for your understanding of the science of sociology.

The Historical Method

The historical method is one of the techniques used to analyze existing sources. It involves examining any materials from the past that contain information of sociological interest. These materials can include such things as toys, clothes, pictures, tools, or furniture. More often, however, they consist of written documents, such as diaries, newspapers, magazines, government records, laws, and letters.

The historical method enables researchers to learn about events that happened in the recent past or long ago. It also provides a way to study trends. In the case of personal material, such as letters and diaries, the historical method allows researchers to view the private, unguarded feelings of individuals who lived at another point in time.

Content Analysis

Content analysis is another technique used to analyze existing sources. The process involves counting the number of times a particular word, phrase, idea, event, symbol, or other element appears in a given context. Content analysis can be used to analyze any form of recorded communication. Common sources of information include television, radio, sound recordings, movies, photographs, art work, newspapers, magazines, books, and personal or government documents.

Content analysis is a popular research technique because it is easy to use and inexpensive. Researchers merely have to count the number of times the characteristics of interest appear in the source. In recent years, computer programs have further simplified the evaluation of data collected through content analysis.

The Survey Method

The survey method allows sociologists to collect data on attitudes and opinions from large numbers of people. Two techniques are commonly used to gather survey data—questionnaires and interviews.

A questionnaire is a list of questions or statements to which people are asked to respond in writing. Questionnaires can be administered in person or sent through the mail. This technique has the advantage of making it possible to collect information from a large number of people in a relatively short period of time. Questionnaires, however, also have several disadvantages. They do not, for example, enable sociologists to know if the respondents have interpreted the questions correctly. Furthermore, researchers must rely solely on survey answers in drawing conclusions.

An interview is much like a questionnaire, except that respondents are asked to respond orally to questions. Interviews can be administered in person or over the telephone. This technique has the advantage of making it easier for researchers to determine whether respondents understand the questions. It also makes it possible for researchers to ask for clarifications and to note various context clues, such as facial expressions, hesitations, or side comments. One disadvantage of using interviews is that they are much more time consuming and expensive to administer than are questionnaires.

Observation

In observational studies, researchers observe the behavior of individuals in actual social settings. Data can be collected through either detached observation or participant observation.

In detached observation, researchers observe the situation under study from a distance. Because researchers do not participate in the situation being studied, individuals often do not realize that they are being observed. This has the advantage of making it less likely that behavior will be affected by the known presence of a researcher. Detached observation, however, is not always an effective technique. By remaining outside of the situation being studied, social researchers sometimes miss important details.

A more accurate picture of a situation often can be achieved through participant observation. In participant observation, researchers become directly involved in the situation under investigation. Sometimes researchers make their identities known to the people being studied. At other times, researchers remain anonymous. The latter technique has the advantage of increasing the chances that the subjects of the study will act naturally.

The Case Study

A case study is an intensive analysis of a person, group, event, or problem. Although case studies tend to rely heavily on observational techniques, researchers often use survey methods and the analysis of existing source material in their investigations. Thus it is not so much the technique that distinguishes case studies, but rather the intense focus of the investigation.

Case studies are particularly useful in analyzing infrequent or temporary events such as riots or natural disasters. Like observational studies, case studies have the advantage of providing an indepth picture of a real-life situation. Researchers must be careful, however, not to generalize on the basis of one case.

Statistical Analysis

Statistical analysis involves the use of mathematical data. Provided the data can be translated into numbers, statistical analysis can be used with any of the research methods we have discussed. Statistical analysis involves analyzing data that have already been collected to determine the strength of the relationship that may exist between two or more variables. A **variable** is a characteristic that can differ from one individual, group, or situation to another in a measurable way. Examples of variables include income, age, and level of education.

In the computer age, statistical analysis has become the preferred method for interpreting data. The computer allows large amounts of information to be processed in a relatively short amount of time. Many statistical packages are available to assist sociologists in analyzing their data. Sociology, like many of the social sciences, is becoming increasingly dependent on the use of statistics.

The methods described above are only some of the research methods used by sociologists to collect and evaluate data. It is important to note that sociologists often will use more than one method in the research process. In the remainder of the Applying Sociology features, you will have a chance to put these methods to work analyzing information of interest to sociologists. Thus you will have an opportunity not only to read about sociology but also to sharpen your sociological skills.

Interactionist Perspective. Functionalists and conflict theorists tend to focus on society in general or on groups within society. Sociologists who adopt the **interactionist perspective,** on the other hand, focus on how individuals interact with one another in society. Such sociologists are interested in the ways in which individuals respond to one another in everyday situations. They also are interested in the meanings that individuals attach to their own actions and to the actions of others. Many sociologists who adopt an interactionist perspective label themselves as social psychologists. Interactionist theorists are heavily indebted to the work of Max Weber.

Of particular interest to interactionist theorists is the role that symbols play in our daily lives. A **symbol** is anything that stands for something else. In order for something to be a symbol, however, members of society must agree on the meaning that is attached to it. Such things as physical objects, gestures, words, and events can serve as symbols. The United States flag, the bald eagle, Fourth of July celebrations, and Uncle Sam, for instance, are examples of symbols used to represent the United States. In the case of a gesture, a salute is a sign of respect for authority.

Interactionists focus on the interaction between people that takes place through the use of symbols. This process is referred to as **symbolic interaction.** The interactionist perspective is used to study topics such as child development, relationships within groups, and mate selection. This theoretical perspective has been particularly influential in the United States.

The functionalist, conflict, and interactionist perspectives all would focus on different aspects of this strike by workers. While functionalists might be most concerned with how the strike is disrupting production, conflict sociologists would more likely focus on the economic disputes between workers and management. Interactionists, on the other hand, might be most interested in learning how the strike is affecting the family lives of the workers.

Sociologists who follow the interactionist perspective study the ways in which individuals interact through the use of symbols. This military salute, for example, is a symbol through which soldiers show their respect for authority.

SECTION 2 REVIEW

IDENTIFY   Auguste Comte, Karl Marx, Herbert Spencer, Emile Durkheim, Max Weber

1. **Summarizing Ideas   (a)** Why is Auguste Comte considered the founder of sociology?   **(b)** What did Comte mean by the terms *social statics* and *social dynamics?*

2. **Comparing Viewpoints**   How did the views of Karl Marx and Herbert Spencer differ concerning the role of conflict in society?

3. **Contrasting Ideas**   How did Emile Durkheim's view of the proper subject matter of sociology differ from the view of Max Weber?

4. **Understanding Ideas   (a)** What is a theoretical perspective?   **(b)** What are the basic characteristics of the functionalist perspective, the conflict perspective, and the interactionist perspective?

CHAPTER 1   SUMMARY

Sociology is the science that studies human society and social behavior. Because sociologists are primarily interested in social interaction, they tend to focus on groups rather than on individuals.

Sociology is only one of the social sciences—the group of disciplines that study various aspects of human social behavior. The other social sciences include anthropology, psychology, economics, political science, and history.

The field of sociology grew out of the social turmoil of eighteenth- and nineteenth-century Europe. It did not, however, emerge as a separate discipline until the middle of the nineteenth century when Auguste Comte coined the term *sociology* to describe the study of society. Other influential early sociologists include Karl Marx, Herbert Spencer, Emile Durkheim, and Max Weber.

Through their work, the early sociologists established the groundwork for the development of the discipline's three major theoretical perspectives—the functionalist perspective, the conflict perspective, and the interactionist perspective. The functionalist perspective views society as a set of interrelated parts that work together to produce a stable social system. The conflict perspective focuses instead on the forces in society that promote competition and change. The interactionist perspective, on the other hand, focuses on how individuals interact with one another in everyday situations.

DEVELOPING SOCIOLOGICAL

READING ABOUT SOCIOLOGY: Using Textbook Features

Within any textbook that you read, there is a vast amount of information that you have to make your own. To help you understand and remember this information, this textbook has been divided into many parts, each of which has its own function. Some parts of the textbook help you preview the information you are about to study. Other parts help you study that information. Still other parts help you review what you have just studied. Learning to use the textbook and its parts wisely is an important first step in your study of sociology.

Studying the discipline of sociology involves the use of more than one set of tools. The sociology textbook itself is just one of these sets. In succeeding chapters, you will read and learn about other sets of tools that will help you in your study of sociology.

How to Use the Textbook

To get the most from the textbook, use these guidelines.

1. Use the Table of Contents. Start by familiarizing yourself with the textbook's Table of Contents, which begins on page v. Reading the Table of Contents will give you an overview of the topics that are covered in the textbook and an idea of how the book is organized.

2. Study each unit's opening pages. Begin the study of each unit by taking time to look at the unit's opening pages. For example, review the opening pages of Unit 1 (page 1). Read the title of the unit and the titles of each of the chapters found in the unit. Consider what the unit title says about the chapters in the unit.

3. Begin at the beginning. Turn to pages 2–3 for the opening of Chapter 1. Look at the chapter title, the section and subsection headings, and the full-page illustration. What do these items say about the theme of the chapter?

Next, read the Chapter Focus feature. The questions listed in this feature are designed to provide a guide to assist you in studying the chapter material. Then, examine the words listed in the Key Terms feature. Knowing the meaning of these terms will help you understand many of the chapter's key concepts and ideas.

4. Preview the chapter. Skim the chapter, noting the section titles (pages 4 and 9). In each section, note the subheadings that give you clues about the details supporting the section's main ideas. Note the charts, photographs, and other visuals in each section. Take time to read the captions that accompany each of the photographs. Glance at the first Section Review (page 8). Previewing gives you an idea of the framework around which the chapter is constructed.

5. Read the chapter carefully. Use the textbook's clues to help you get the most out of your reading of the chapter. First, use the headings and the subheadings as clues to main ideas and supporting details.

Second, pay close attention to the words printed in bold black type. These **boldfaced terms** are highlighted in the text to indicate their importance to the study of sociology. The meaning of a boldfaced term can be determined from the sentences surrounding it. Third, review each page's illustrations and the captions that accompany these illustrations before moving on to the next page. Relate the information in the illustrations to the chapter content. Finally, use the Section Review at the end of each section to check your understanding of the material.

6. Study the special features. Each chapter has several special features that will add to your knowledge of sociology. When you read the chapter features depends on your learning style. *When* you read them is not as important as making sure that you do read them at some point during the time you are studying the chapter.

7. Summarize the chapter. Each chapter ends with a Chapter Summary (page 17). The Chapter Summary helps you to recap the main ideas of the chapter.

8. Review the chapter. The textbook contains two-page Chapter Reviews (pages 20–21) and one-page Unit Reviews (page 95). These reviews will help you to check your understanding of the important information contained in the chapter.

9. Use the end-of-book material. The Appendix on sociological research methods, the Careers in Sociology, The Sociologist's Bookshelf (a list of suggested readings and references), the Glossary, and the Index are included at the end of the textbook to assist you in understanding the subject matter of sociology. These helpful resources can be used at any time you wish during the study process. Familiarize yourself with this material now so that you may utilize it as needed. The material begins on page 485.

Applying the Skill

Complete the following activities.

1. Turn to the Table of Contents. Use it to find the answers to these questions. **(a)** How many units and chapters are contained in the textbook? **(b)** What is the title of the Interpreting Primary Sources feature found on page 199 in Chapter 8?

If you answered that the textbook has 5 units and 18 chapters and that the title of the Chapter 8 primary source reading is "Crime and American Business," then you have used the Table of Contents correctly.

2. Turn to the Glossary beginning on page 507 and answer the following questions. **(a)** What is the second entry under "F"? **(b)** What is the definition of the term ***norms?*** If you discovered that the second entry under "F" is the term **fad** and that **norms** are the *shared rules of conduct that tell people how to act in specific situations,* you have made good use of the Glossary.

Practicing the Skill

The titles, headings, and subheadings of Chapter 1 can be used to formulate a working outline. Study the sample outline on this page. Compare the outline items with the headings and subheadings of Chapter 1. Then on a separate sheet of paper, make a copy of the outline, filling in the missing parts.

The Sociological Point of View
  I. Examining Social Life
    A. The Sociological Perspective
    B.
  II. Sociology: Then and Now
    A. The Early Years
      1. Auguste Comte
      2. Karl Marx
      3.
      4.
      5. Max Weber
    B.
      1. Functionalist Perspective
      2. Conflict Perspective
      3.

CHAPTER 1 REVIEW

Reviewing Sociological Terms

On a separate sheet of paper, supply the term that correctly completes each sentence.

1. The _____ _____ are related disciplines that study various aspects of human social behavior.

2. _____ is the study of the choices that people make in an effort to satisfy their wants and needs.

3. The empathetic understanding of the meanings others attach to their actions is called _____.

4. An _____ _____ is a description of the essential characteristics of some aspect of society.

5. How people relate to one another and influence each other's behavior is referred to as _____ _____.

6. A _____ _____ is the intended and recognized consequence of some element of society.

Thinking Critically about Sociology

1. **Interpreting Ideas** *(a)* To what was Herbert Spencer referring when he spoke of the "survival of the fittest"? *(b)* How did Spencer's belief in the survival of the fittest influence his view of social conflict?

2. **Contrasting Ideas** How do functional elements in society differ from dysfunctional elements?

3. **Comprehending Ideas** *(a)* What is a theory? *(b)* How might a sociologist's theoretical perspective influence the types of problems he or she chooses to study?

4. **Seeing Relationships** *(a)* List the characteristics of sociology's three main theoretical perspectives. *(b)* Indicate which early sociologists had an influence on each perspective and what that influence was.

5. **Organizing Ideas** What social and political factors led to the emergence of sociology as a separate discipline?

6. **Summarizing Ideas** According to your textbook, how can adopting a sociological perspective help you in your daily life?

7. **Drawing Conclusions** How do manifest functions differ from latent functions?

Exercising Sociological Skills

1. **Using Sociological Imagination** *(a)* List and describe the sociological research methods discussed in the Applying Sociology feature on pages 14–15. *(b)* Suppose that you were asked to study the importance of school sports in the lives of students. Which of the research methods could you use to collect and analyze data, and why are these methods applicable?

2. **Understanding Ideas** Reread the Case Study feature on page 7. *(a)* What is the main purpose of the professional conventions sponsored by the American Sociological Association? *(b)* How does the American Sociological Association help teachers?

3. **Using Textbook Features** Turn to the Table of Contents. Use it to find the titles and locations of the special features in Chapter 1.

Extending Sociological Imagination

1. Suppose that you are a member of a panel studying homelessness in America. The panel also includes an economist, a psychologist, and an anthropologist. As a sociologist, what aspects of this issue would be of interest to you? What aspects would most likely be of interest to each of the other panel members?

2. Attend three different types of sporting events and take notes on the behavior of the spectators and the athletes. Based on your observations, analyze what effect the nature of a sporting event has on group behavior.

INTERPRETING PRIMARY SOURCES
The Sociological Imagination

C. Wright Mills was an American sociologist who was very concerned with sociology's application to the real world and the daily lives of individuals in society. He believed that it is the task of sociologists and students of society to develop a sociological imagination. The sociological imagination allows the individual to understand history and biography and to grasp the relationship between the two in society. Mills believed that it is the exercise of the sociological imagination that truly marks the social analyst.

In the following excerpt from his classic book entitled *The Sociological Imagination*, Mills outlines the types of questions sociologists must ask if they are to fulfill the promise of sociology and exercise their sociological imaginations. While reading the excerpt, consider how developing your own sociological imagination might help you in your daily life.

No social study that does not come back to the problems of biography, of history and of their intersections within a society has completed its intellectual journey. Whatever the specific problems of the classic social analysts, however limited or however broad the features of social reality they have examined, those who have been imaginatively aware of the promise of their work have consistently asked three sorts of questions:

(1) What is the structure of this particular society as a whole? What are its essential components, and how are they related to one another? How does it differ from other varieties of social order? Within it, what is the meaning of any particular feature for its continuance and for its change?

(2) Where does this society stand in human history? What are the mechanics by which it is changing? What is its place within and its meaning for the development of humanity as a whole? How does any particular feature we are examining affect, and how is it affected by, the historical period in which it moves? And this period—what are its essential features? How does it differ from other periods? What are its characteristic ways of history-making?

(3) What varieties of men and women now prevail in this society and in this period? And what varieties are coming to prevail? In what ways are they selected and formed, liberated and repressed, made sensitive and blunted? What kinds of 'human nature' are revealed in the conduct and character we observe in this society in this period? And what is the meaning for 'human nature' of each and every feature of the society we are examining?

Whether the point of interest is a great power state or a minor literary mood, a family, a prison, a creed—these are the kinds of questions the best social analysts have asked. They are the intellectual pivots of classic studies of man in society—and they are the questions inevitably raised by any mind possessing the sociological imagination. For that imagination is the capacity to shift from one perspective to another—from the political to the psychological; from examination of a single family to comparative assessment of the national budgets of the world; from the theological school to the military establishment; from considerations of an oil industry to studies of contemporary poetry. It is the capacity to range from the most impersonal and remote transformations to the most intimate features of the human self—and to see the relations between the two. Back of its use there is always the urge to know the social and historical meaning of the individual in the society and in the period in which he has his quality and his being.

Source Review

1. What does C. Wright Mills mean when he states that no social study has completed its intellectual journey until it comes back to the problems of biography, of history, and of their intersections?

2. What are the three types of questions sociologists who possess a sociological imagination must ask?

Cultural Diversity

 The Meaning of Culture

What Is Culture?
The Components of Culture
Examining Culture

 Cultural Variation

What Do We Have in Common?
Variation among Societies
Dealing with Variation
Variation within Societies

Chapter Focus

Chapter 2 examines the basic components of culture, how culture is transmitted, and how cultural practices vary among and within groups or societies. Fieldwork conducted by anthropologist Margaret Mead among the Arapesh and Mundugumor in the early 1930s is used to illustrate variations in cultural practices among societies.

As you study the chapter, look for the answers to the following questions:

1. What is culture, and what is the difference between material and nonmaterial culture?
2. What are the five basic components of culture?
3. What are cultural universals and why do they exist?
4. What is meant by ethnocentrism and cultural relativism?
5. What factors account for variations among and within cultures?

KEY TERMS

The following terms, while not the only terms emphasized in the chapter, are basic to your understanding of sociology. Determine the meaning of each term, either by using the Glossary or by watching for context clues as you read the chapter.

culture	society	folkways
material culture	values	ethnocentrism
nonmaterial culture	norms	cultural relativism

23

The !Kung Bushmen of Botswana in southern Africa live in the harsh environment of the Kalahari Desert. [The exclamation point before "Kung" represents a clicking sound at the beginning of the word. Clicks are a common feature of all Bushman languages.] During the spring and summer months, temperatures reach as high as 108° F in the shade. In the winter, the temperature drops as low as 30° F. Faced with little water and a barren land, the !Kung do not attempt to grow crops or raise animals for food. Instead, they hunt for meat and gather plants, camping wherever there is enough water. When the plants and animals in an area are used up, the !Kung move to new locations.

!Kung camps are small, consisting of approximately 20 people per group. With the exception of the very young and the very old, all camp members are expected to hunt for food. Although individuals generally hunt alone or in pairs, the day's take always is shared with everyone in the group. In spite of the harsh environment, the !Kung have survived in the Kalahari Desert for at least a thousand years. During that time, their culture has changed very little.

In the United States, on the other hand, less than 3 percent of the civilian labor force is engaged in food production. Yet United States farmers grow approximately 51 percent of the soybeans, 39 percent of the corn, and 10 percent of the wheat produced in the entire world. On average, each person in the United States consumes over 112 pounds of red meat, approximately 16 pounds of fish, over 49 pounds of chicken, approximately 92 pounds of fresh fruit, and around 111 pounds of fresh vegetables every year. Mastering the environment through the application of scientific knowledge has helped people in the United States to produce a society rich in cultural variation.

1 THE MEANING OF CULTURE

Unlike other animals, humans are not controlled by natural instincts. The fact that humans are not locked into a set of predetermined behaviors means that they are able to adapt to and change their environment in a variety of ways. The methods by which collections of people—be they small groups or entire societies—deal with their environment form the foundation of their culture.

What Is Culture?

For many of us, the word *culture* produces images of fine art and literature, dining in expensive restaurants, wearing designer clothes, and having all of the money we could possibly need. Sociologists, however, use the term in a much broader sense. To sociologists, **culture** consists of all the shared products of human groups. These products include both physical objects and the beliefs, values, and behaviors shared by a group.

The physical objects that people create form a group's **material culture.** Examples of material culture include automobiles, clothing, books, buildings, cooking utensils, and computers. Sociologists and anthropologists use the term *artifacts* to refer to the physical objects of material culture. Abstract human creations form a group's **nonmaterial culture.** Examples of nonmaterial culture include language, ideas, beliefs, rules, skills, family patterns, work practices, and political and economic systems.

Although people in everyday speech use the terms *society* and *culture* interchangeably, sociologists distinguish between the terms. A **society** is

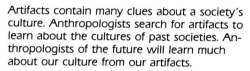

Artifacts contain many clues about a society's culture. Anthropologists search for artifacts to learn about the cultures of past societies. Anthropologists of the future will learn much about our culture from our artifacts.

a group of mutually interdependent people who have organized in such a way as to share a common culture and feeling of unity. In simple terms, society consists of people, and culture consists of the products that people create.

The Components of Culture

Culture is both learned and shared. This does not mean that everyone in the United States dresses the same way, belongs to the same church, or likes the same types of music. It does mean, however, that most people in the United States choose from among the same broad set of material and nonmaterial elements of culture in dealing with and making sense of their environment.

Specific examples of the material and nonmaterial elements of culture vary from society to society. All cultures, however, consist of five basic components. In addition to physical objects, these components are symbols, language, values, and norms.

Symbols. The use of symbols is the very basis of human culture. It is through symbols that we create our culture and communicate it to group members and future generations. A **symbol** is anything that stands for something else. By "stands for," we mean that the symbol has a shared meaning attached to it. Any word, gesture, image, sound, physical object, event, or element of the natural world can serve as a symbol as long as people recognize that it carries a particular meaning. A church service, a class ring, the word *hello,* the Lincoln Memorial, and a handshake are examples of common symbols in the United States. Specific examples vary from culture to culture. Nevertheless, all cultures communicate symbolically through a variety of methods.

Language. The most obvious aspect of any culture probably is its language. **Language** is the organization of written or spoken symbols into a standardized system. Words, when organized according to accepted rules of grammar, can be used to express any idea. In the United States, we learn to speak an American form of English. We use this language as our primary means of communicating with one another. Although there are members of our society who do not speak English, English is the principal language used in schools, in books and magazines, on radio and television, and in business dealings. Anyone who has ever

When people living in an area do not share a common language, the provision of basic services can become quite complicated. To solve this problem, many government agencies and private businesses provide information in a variety of languages.

visited a foreign country and has been unable to speak the language realizes how important the use of language is in daily life.

Values. Language and other symbols are important partly because they allow us to communicate our values to one another and to future generations. **Values** are shared beliefs about what is good or bad, right or wrong, desirable or un-

desirable. The types of values held by a group help to determine the character of its people and the kinds of material and nonmaterial culture they create. A society that values war and displays of physical strength above all else will be very different from one that places the most emphasis on cooperation and sharing. The contemporary Yanomamö of southern Venezuela and Brazil and the eighteenth- and nineteenth-century Kwakiutl of the Pacific Northwest provide examples of how different value systems produce different cultures.

The Yanomamö are horticulturalists (plant growers) who live along the border between Brazil and Venezuela. Warfare and feats of male strength play such an important role in the Yanomamö way of life that anthropologist Napoleon Chagnon named them the Fierce People. Warfare is so common that approximately 30 percent of all deaths among Yanomamö males result from wounds received in battle.

Even though horticultural villages normally can support between 500 to 1,000 people, Yanomamö villages rarely have as many as 200 people. Long before a village's population reaches 200, conflicts within the village cause groups to split off and form new settlements. Hostilities, however, do not end with the splitting up of the village. Most instances of warfare occur between villages that were originally part of the same settlement.

Among the eighteenth- and nineteenth-century Kwakiutl, on the other hand, sharing was a central feature of society. Through ceremonial feasts called "potlatches," Kwakiutl chiefs redistributed the community's food and wealth. By giving away food and material objects, chiefs were able to make up for variations in productivity among group members. In addition, potlatches served as nonaggressive forms of competition. Individuals could increase their standing in the group by holding larger potlatches than their rivals.

Norms. All groups create norms to enforce their cultural values. **Norms** are the shared rules of conduct that tell people how to act in specific situations. The value of democracy, for example, is reinforced through norms governing respect for the flag, political participation, and the treatment of elected officials. It is important to keep in mind that norms are *expectations* for behavior, not *actual* behavior. The fact that a group has norms governing certain behaviors does not necessarily mean that the actions of all individuals will be in line with those norms. In the United States, for example, there are norms concerning financial responsibility; nevertheless, some people do not pay their bills.

There are a tremendous number of norms in our society. These norms range from the unimportant (cover your mouth when you yawn) to the very important (do not kill a human being). Some norms apply to everyone in society; others are applied selectively. For example, no one in American society is allowed to marry more than one person at a time. But only selected groups of people, such as children and the clergy of some religious orders, are forbidden from marrying at all.

Even important norms sometimes are applied selectively. The norm against taking another person's life, for example, is applied differently to military personnel and police officers acting in the line of duty than it is to most members of society. Norms also vary in the strictness with which they are enforced. In recognition of this fact, sociologists distinguish between two types of norms: folkways and mores.

Folkways are norms that do not have great moral significance attached to them. They are the common customs of everyday life: Do not eat peas with your fingers. Take down the American flag before nightfall. Shake hands when you are introduced to someone. Do your homework. Do not crowd people waiting in line. Get to class on time. Some degree of nonconformity to these norms is permitted because their violation by limited numbers of people does not endanger the well-being or stability of society.

Mores (MORE-ayz), on the other hand, have great moral significance attached to them. Unlike nonconformity to folkways, the violation of mores endangers the well-being and stability of society. If people go about killing one another, for example, society is greatly threatened. Similarly, it is difficult for people to acquire property if others are continually stealing it or setting it on fire.

Norms that are important to the stability or well-being of society often are formalized as laws. A **law** is a written rule of conduct that is enacted and enforced by the government. Laws range from simple folkways (no parking) to very strict mores (such as laws against murder, arson, and rape).

Text continues on page 30.

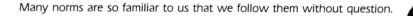

Many norms are so familiar to us that we follow them without question.

Daily Life among the Nacirema

How do sociologists and anthropologists study other cultures? How do they study behaviors and habits different from their own? Social scientists often use the historical method to learn about the cultures of various people. By studying historical documents and records, social scientists can piece together many aspects of a culture. They then can get a fairly complete picture of how people live or lived.

In the 1950s, anthropologist Horace Miner published an article about a people called the Nacirema. In the article, he examined some of the rituals, beliefs, and behaviors of Nacirema society. Following is an excerpt from his article, "Body Ritual Among the Nacirema," which originally appeared in the *American Anthropologist*.

The Nacirema are a North American group living in the territory between the Canadian Cree, the Yaqui and Tarahumare of Mexico, and the Carib and Arawak of the Antilles. Little is known of their origin, although tradition states that they came from the east. According to Nacirema mythology, their nation was originated by a culture hero, Notgnihsaw, who is otherwise known for two great feats of strength—the throwing of a piece of wampum across the river Pa-To-Mac and the chopping down of a cherry tree in which the Spirit of Truth resided.

Nacirema culture is characterized by a highly developed market economy which has evolved in a rich natural habitat. While much of the people's time is devoted to economic pursuits, a large part of the fruits of these labors and a considerable portion of the day are spent in ritual activity. . . .

The fundamental belief underlying the whole system appears to be that the human body is ugly and that its natural tendency is to debility and disease. Incarcerated in such a body, man's only hope is to avert these characteristics through the use of the powerful influences of ritual and ceremony. Every household has one or more shrines devoted to this purpose. . . .

The focal point of the shrine is a box or chest which is built into the wall. In this chest are kept the many charms and magical potions without which no native believes he could live. These preparations are secured from a variety of specialized practitioners. The most powerful of these are the medicine men, whose assistance must be rewarded with substantial gifts. However, the medicine men do not provide the curative potions for their clients, but decide what the ingredients should be and then write them down in an ancient and secret language. This writing is understood only by the medicine men and by the herbalists who, for another gift, provide the required charm. . . .

The Nacirema have an almost pathological horror of and fascination with the mouth, the condition of which is believed to have a supernatural influence on all social relationships. Were it not for the rituals of the mouth, they believe that their teeth would fall out, their gums bleed, their jaws shrink, their friends desert them, and their lovers reject them. . . .

The daily ritual performed by everyone includes a mouth-rite. . . . The ritual consists of inserting a small bundle of hog hairs into the mouth, along with certain magical powders, and then moving the bundle in a highly formalized series of gestures.

In addition to the private mouth-rite, the people seek out a holy-mouth-man once or twice a year. These practitioners have an impressive set of paraphernalia, consisting of a variety of augers, awls, probes, and prods. The use of these objects in the exorcism of the evils of the mouth involves almost unbelievable ritual torture of the client. The holy-mouth-man opens the client's mouth and, using the above mentioned tools, enlarges any holes which decay may have created in the teeth. Magical materials are put into these holes. If there are no naturally occurring holes in the teeth, large sections of one or more teeth are gouged out so that the supernatural substance can be applied. In the client's view, the purpose of these ministrations is to arrest decay and to draw friends. The extremely sacred and traditional character of the rite is evident in the fact that the natives return to the holy-mouth-man year after year, despite the fact that their teeth continue to decay.

Based on the excerpt from the article, answer the following questions:

1. Many references in the article may seem familiar to you. Can you figure out which culture Miner has studied? (Hint: If not, read the word *Nacirema* backwards.)

2. Who does Notgnihsaw represent? What is the Pa-To-Mac?

3. To what is Miner referring in his discussion of the shrine? What does the box or chest stand for?

4. What is the daily mouth-rite that Miner has observed? Who is the holy-mouth-man that people seek out?

5. What did you learn about American culture from this article?

You might wish to consider some other aspects of American culture that lend themselves to being mocked. You can then choose some of these aspects and write an article similar to the one written by Miner.

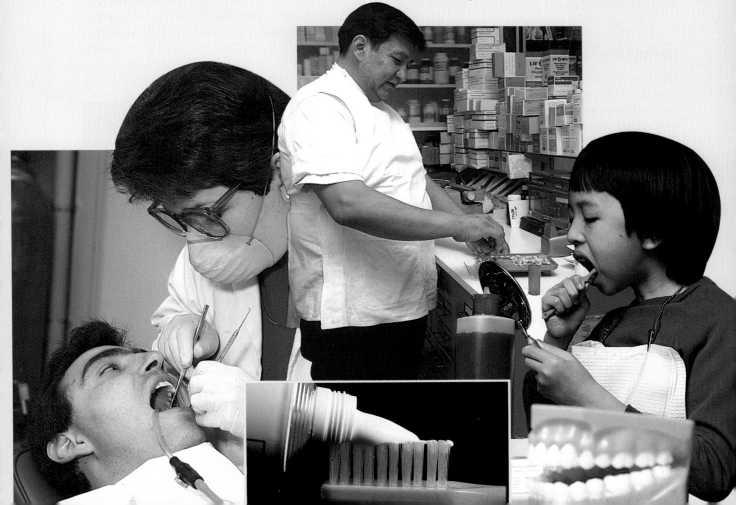

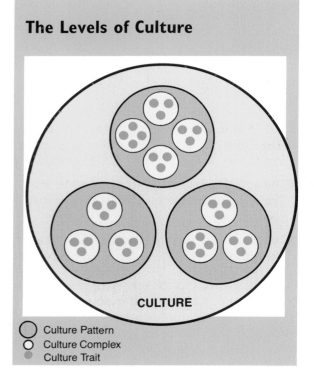

The Levels of Culture

CULTURE

○ Culture Pattern
○ Culture Complex
● Culture Trait

Examining Culture

Culture is continually changing. In sociological terms, it is *dynamic* rather than *static*. New material objects constantly are being introduced, as are new words, expressions, and ideas. If cultures are so vast and complicated and are constantly changing, how do sociologists study them? Sociologists examine a culture by breaking it down into levels and studying each level separately. From the standpoint of complexity, culture can be divided into traits, complexes, and patterns.

Culture Traits. The smallest unit of culture is the culture trait. A **culture trait** is an individual tool, act, or belief that is related to a particular situation or need. Our use of forks, knives, and spoons when eating is a culture trait. Another trait is the specific way in which we greet people. When you walk down the hall at school and meet a good friend, you are likely to say "hi." If you were greeting the personnel manager at a job interview, however, you probably would not be as informal. The greeting you use is related to the particular situation or need.

Culture Complexes. Individual culture traits combine to form culture complexes. A **culture complex** is a cluster of interrelated traits. For example, the game of football is a culture complex that involves a variety of traits. Among the material traits are the football, the measuring chain, cleated shoes, helmets, pads, first-aid kits, and warm-up benches. Specific acts include kicking, passing, catching, running with the ball, blocking, and tackling. There also are specific beliefs related to the game, such as the belief that the players should be good sports, that certain rules should be followed in playing the game, that penalties should be given for rule violations, and that "our" team should win. In industrial societies, there are thousands of culture complexes.

Culture Patterns. Culture complexes combine to form larger units called culture patterns. A **culture pattern** is the combination of a number of culture complexes into an interrelated whole. For example, the complexes of sports such as basketball, softball, swimming, tennis, soccer, and track combine to form the American athletic pattern. Other patterns are related to such aspects of society as agriculture, manufacturing, education, religion, and family life.

SECTION 1 REVIEW

IDENTIFY !Kung, Kwakiutl, Yanomamö, Napoleon Chagnon

1. *Comparing Ideas* What is the difference between culture and society?

2. *Summarizing Ideas* What are the five basic components of culture?

3. *Using Sociological Imagination* *(a)* How do the values of the Kwakiutl differ from those of the Yanomamö of Brazil? *(b)* Why might different values produce different cultures?

4. *Seeing Relationships* *(a)* What are the three levels of culture that sociologists study? *(b)* How are they related?

2 CULTURAL VARIATION

Suppose you take a trip to Melbourne, Australia. You meet an Australian who says to you, "Come over to me house for tea tonight."

You say, "Fine. What time should I come?"

"Oh, 'bout 7 or so," is the reply.

Would you know what time to arrive and what to expect when you got there? Should you eat dinner before you go? If, being an American who always tries to be punctual, you arrived precisely at 7 P.M., your host would be shocked. Preparations for your visit would not even have started. When Australians say 7 P.M., they do not expect you until 7:30 at the earliest, and 8 P.M. would be about right. If you have eaten dinner before you arrive, you will wish you had not. You will find that "tea" includes lamb chops and snags (sausages), chips (french-fried potatoes), a "veggie" (such as peas or beans), a salad, and dessert. After you finish all of this, you will be asked if you are ready for tea, and whether you want it black or white (without or with milk).

The cultures of the world are very different. Consider, for example, the variety of world languages. If we count only the languages that have more than one million users, there are approximately 240 different languages in the world today. If we include all the local languages, the number is enormous. In addition, because often there are many dialects of the same basic language, even people who speak the same language may have difficulty understanding one another. In the English language, for example, British English, American English, Canadian English, and Australian English are just a few of the possible variations.

Societies often can be distinguished by the foods they enjoy. Nevertheless, food is one of the culture traits most readily passed from society to society.

What Do We Have in Common?

You may be wondering how cultures can be so different when all human beings have similar basic needs. The answer is that human beings have the ability to meet these needs in a vast number of ways. We are limited only by our biological makeup and our physical environment. Nevertheless, some needs are so basic that all societies must develop culture traits, complexes, and patterns to ensure their fulfillment. These features, common to all cultures, are called **cultural universals.**

In the 1940s, anthropologist George Murdock examined hundreds of different cultures in an attempt to determine what types of general traits are common to all cultures. Based on his research, Murdock compiled a list of over 60 cultural universals. Among these universals are cooking, feasting, toolmaking, body adornment, religion, myths and folklore, sports, forms of greeting, medicine, dancing, family, housing, music, funeral ceremonies, gift giving, and language.

As is obvious from a quick look at Murdock's list, although survival may dictate the need for cultural universals, the specific nature of these traits can vary widely. The need to care for young children, for example, gives rise to families. The makeup of a family, however, varies from culture to culture.

In most of the Western world, a family consists of one or both parents and their children. In the case of three-generation families, grandparents may be included in this definition. In some parts of the world, however, a family may include a man, his several wives, and their children. Similarly, in the United States, marriages generally take place between two people who choose to get married. In some other societies, marriages are arranged at

birth. In all cases, however, the purpose is the same—to ensure that new members will be added to society and that they will be cared for until they are old enough to fend for themselves. In addition, it is the family that is assigned the task of first introducing children to the components of their culture.

Variation among Societies

In the 1930s, anthropologist Margaret Mead conducted a now-classic study of cultural variation among several small societies in New Guinea. Her purpose in the study was to determine whether differences in basic temperament (the fundamental emotional disposition of a person) result mainly from inherited characteristics or from cultural influences. To find out, she made firsthand observations of the shared, learned behaviors of several New Guinea societies. The desire for an in-depth understanding of cultural variation led Mead to live among the people in these societies and to participate in their activities.

Two of the societies that Mead studied were the Arapesh and the Mundugumor. Both groups lived in the northern part of what is now the nation of Papua New Guinea. Mead found that although the two societies lived only about 100 miles (160 kilometers) apart and shared many social traits, their cultures were vastly different. While reading the following descriptions of the Arapesh and Mundugumor, keep in mind that their cultures have changed greatly since the time of the study. The use of the present tense to describe past cultures simply is a method employed by some anthropologists to improve the clarity of their findings.

The Arapesh. The Arapesh are gentle, warm, receptive, nonaggressive, contented, and trusting people. Their society is one of complete cooperation. They live in close-knit villages consisting of clans (families with a common ancestor). The women bring in the firewood and water, prepare the daily meals, carry goods from place to place, and weed the gardens. The men clear and fence the land, build and repair the houses, carry pigs and heavy logs, hunt, plant and care for the yams, and cook and carve ceremonial food. Both men and women make ornaments and take care of the children. The fathers are very much involved in child care. If the mother's work at the moment is more pressing (if there is no water or firewood, for example), the father minds the children while the mother completes her task.

The children grow up in a very loving and friendly social environment. The babies always are tended to when they cry, and they spend much of their time being held by someone. Children often are "lent out" to relatives, thereby increasing the number of people the children trust. Children are raised in a large circle of warm, friendly people. The young also are encouraged to join in the activities of their elders.

Children are discouraged from displaying any aggression toward others. When they feel aggressive, they are taught to express it in a way that will not harm others, such as by throwing stones on the ground or by hitting a palm tree with a stick. They are taught consideration and respect for the feelings and property of others.

When a girl is about seven or eight years old, she is promised to a boy who is approximately six years her senior. The boy's father makes the match. In choosing a wife for his son, the father considers several factors. For convenience, he might choose a girl close to home. Or he might prefer to widen his circle of relatives by selecting a girl from far away. If the group is in need of specific skills (such as pottery making), the father might choose a girl with the desired skills from another group. In any event, the father wants a girl who is responsible (does she help her mother?) and who has many relatives. The Arapesh view marriage as an opportunity to increase the warm family circle in which one's descendants may live. Therefore, the more relatives a girl has, the more marriageable she is.

Mead's study of societies in New Guinea provided evidence that human behavior is influenced by culture. She found that among the Arapesh, for example, men and women behaved the same way. Both sexes were nonaggressive, warm, caring, and supportive. People in Arapesh society exhibited these traits because they had been taught from infancy that aggression is unacceptable.

After the selection is made, the girl goes to live with the boy's family and works with her mother-in-law. She relates to her husband and his brothers and sisters as if she were a sister in the family. After five years or so, with no pressure and in their own time, the girl and her husband begin to live as a true married couple.

Most Arapesh marriages consist of one husband and one wife. Sometimes, however, a man has two wives. When a woman's husband dies, she usually marries a man who already has a wife.

Mead found people in the Mundugumor society to be very different from the Arapesh. Men and women alike in Mundugumor society exhibited aggressive and jealous behavior. This tendency toward aggression was first learned in childhood. Even infants in Mundugumor society were treated with little warmth. For instance, they seldom were comforted even when they cried.

The Mundugumor. Unlike the Arapesh, the Mundugumor are an aggressive group of people. Men and women alike are violent, competitive, and jealous. They are ready to recognize and avenge any insult. They delight in showing off and fighting. Until the government banned such activities, the Mundugumor were headhunters. Open

hostilities among all members of the same sex force the Mundugumor to scatter their residences throughout the bush. Brothers do not speak to one another and are ashamed to sit together. There is great hostility between fathers and sons. Similarly, hostility exists between sisters and between mothers and daughters.

The only ties between members of the same sex are through members of the opposite sex. These occur through a form of social organization called the "rope." One rope consists of the father, his daughters, his daughters' sons, his daughters' sons' daughters, and so on. Another rope consists of the mother, her sons, her sons' daughters, and so forth. When a person dies, his or her property passes down the line according to the rope. Daughters, for example, inherit their father's property, while sons inherit their mother's property.

For a Mundugumor male, wealth and power mainly come from having a large number of wives. The more wives a man has, the more help he can get in growing tobacco. Not only does he get the assistance of his wives, he also can demand help from the brothers of his wives. Many Mundugumor males have as many as 8 to 10 wives. Wives are obtained by trading sisters.

Children tend to push parents apart rather than unite them. The father wants a daughter to trade for a wife. The mother, on the other hand, wants a son to work with her and be her heir.

The child-rearing practices of the Mundugumor are very different from those of the Arapesh. The Mundugumor infant is carried in a rigid basket that gives no contact with the mother. When the mother works outdoors, she leaves the child hanging in the basket in the house. The mother feeds the child when she is ready. Children are not picked up or comforted. The child faces a world full of prohibitions: Do not wander out of sight, do not cling to your mother, do not go to the houses of your father's other wives. For violating these prohibitions, the child is slapped.

Comparing the Two Societies. What factors might account for the vast cultural differences between these two societies? At the time of Mead's study, the Arapesh lived in the mountains and the Mundugumor lived in the river valley. The Arapesh planted gardens, while the Mundugumor basically were food gatherers. For the Arapesh, food

CASE STUDY

The Israeli Kibbutz: How Culture Shapes Personality

In an effort to shed some light on the question of how culture influences personality development, much sociological attention has been paid to the kibbutz movement in Israel. Kibbutzim (the plural form of kibbutz) are of special interest to sociologists because they provide a natural laboratory in which to study the relationship between culture and the psychological and social characteristics of individuals.

A **kibbutz** is a collective farm or settlement in Israel. Kibbutzim originated in the early 1900s as a method of establishing Jewish settlements in the Palestinian area of the Middle East. The first kibbutzim were agricultural settlements and were founded on the principles of complete equality among members and a strong commitment to group goals.

The collective nature of these settlements meant that individualism—the belief that the individual is more important than the group—was considered an undesirable quality. In an attempt to reduce individualism, the founders of the kibbutzim adopted group child-rearing practices. Rather than living with their parents, children lived in separate houses from birth through adolescence. Each house was occupied by children of the same age group. Contact with parents and brothers and sisters was primarily limited to nightly visits, weekends, and holidays.

Kibbutz founders thought that the family promoted individualism by reducing the influence of the group over the individual. Thus the founders reasoned that less contact between parents and children would strengthen commitment to group goals. In addition, they believed that housing children according to age would result in a close bond between members of the same age group, thereby strengthening group unity.

Since the 1960s, the role of the family in child rearing has increased dramatically in many kibbutzim. It now is common for children—particularly young children—to live with their parents.

In kibbutzim that have adopted family-based sleeping arrangements, the children's houses resemble the day-care centers found in many parts of the world. From a sociological perspective, however, the group-based child-rearing arrangement of the past remains of particular interest.

In an effort to determine the long-term consequences of group-based child-rearing practices, A. I. Rabin and his associates compared a group of 92 kibbutz members with 79 individuals from traditional families. The individuals were first studied as children and then were reexamined 20 years later when they reached adulthood. Both groups were rural, agricultural, and of the same income level. They differed only in how they were raised (group versus family) and in whether farming was done on a collective (kibbutz) or individual (non-kibbutz) basis.

The first comparison was conducted in 1955 when the subjects of the study ranged in age from 8 months to 17 years. Among the findings was that kibbutz infants developed more slowly than nonkibbutz infants but caught up by early childhood. In addition, the researchers found kibbutz children to be less attached to their parents and friends, less aggressive, slightly more anxious, and less clear on career goals.

When Rabin and his associates looked at the two groups 20 years later (1975), they found that the kibbutz-raised group evidenced slightly more anxiety and psychological distress, were less productive and less satisfied with their marriages, and remained less attached to their parents and friends. On the positive side, however, kibbutz-raised adults were equally as satisfied with their jobs, ranked higher in the military, and were more athletic.

Although the differences between the two groups were not great, Rabin's research and the research of others would seem to support the idea that personality development is influenced by cultural factors.

usually was scarce. The Mundugumor, on the other hand, had an abundance of food, and life was relatively easy. Mead's research led her to question what influence environmental conditions might have on basic temperament.

Mead concluded that temperament is mainly the result of culture rather than biology. She based this on the fact that differences in temperament were much greater between the two societies than between males and females in the same society. Among the Arapesh, men and women alike were gentle and cooperative. Among the Mundugumor, everyone was hostile and competitive. Although Mead's research methods have been criticized in recent years, her study nonetheless suggests that culture does affect personality. The Case Study on page 35 further explores this issue.

Dealing with Variation

Variations in cultural practices have both positive and negative consequences for social scientists. On the positive side, cultural variations are what make different societies interesting to study. On the negative side, however, diversity gives rise to the problem of ethnocentrism.

Ethnocentrism. Even anthropologists and sociologists cannot always keep from reacting negatively to cultural traits that differ drastically from their own. Napoleon Chagnon, the anthropologist who first studied the fierce Yanomamö of southern Venezuela and Brazil, admits that he initially was horrified by the appearance and the behavior of the Yanomamö. Everything about the Yanomamö culture contradicted Chagnon's expectations of how people should look and act. Chagnon's first impression of the Yanomamö was filtered through the standards of his own culture. This tendency to view one's own culture and group as superior is called **ethnocentrism**.

Anthropologists and sociologists are not the only people faced with the problem of ethnocentrism. People in all societies are at times ethnocentric. The belief that the characteristics of one's group or society are right and good helps to build group unity. When ethnocentrism becomes extreme, however, culture can stagnate. By limit-

According to Marvin Harris, the Orthodox Jewish prohibition against eating pork and the Indian prohibition against killing cows grew out of practical concerns. In the case of Orthodox Jews, for instance, Harris argues that the prohibition against eating pork originally was based on the fact that pigs are not suited to a desert environment. Over time, this prohibition found its way into religious law.

Subcultures are a common feature of American society. Two of the numerous subcultures found in the United States are the Amish (left) and the Eskimo (right).

ing the pool of acceptable members, groups and societies run the risk of excluding new influences that might prove beneficial.

Cultural Relativism.   Social scientists attempt to keep an open mind toward cultural variations. To do this, many adopt an attitude of cultural relativism. **Cultural relativism** is the belief that cultures should be judged by their own standards. Rather than applying the standards of their own culture, researchers who practice cultural relativism attempt to understand cultural practices from the point of view of the members of the society being studied.

Cultural relativism helps sociologists and anthropologists make sense of many practices that seem strange or illogical. Anthropologist Marvin Harris, for example, notes that the seemingly illogical prohibition in India against killing cows even though people are starving can be explained in relation to the economy of the nation. Cows play a vital role in feeding the Indian people, even though cows themselves are not eaten. Few Indian farmers have tractors, and most planting is done with plows pulled by cattle. Therefore, a large

number of cows are needed to ensure that the fields can be planted. In addition, cows provide milk, which is an important part of the Indian diet. When viewed from this perspective, it is possible to see that the prohibition in the Hindu religion against killing cows is rooted in practical environmental concerns.

Variation within Societies

Cultural variations exist not only among societies, they also exist within societies. Among the major sources of variation within a society are the unique cultural practices of various subgroups.

As citizens of the United States, we share a common culture. American culture is a collection of traits, complexes, and patterns that basically are distinct from those of other societies. In addition to these broad cultural features, however, some groups in society share values, norms, and behaviors that are not shared by the entire population. The unique cultural characteristics of these groups form a **subculture.**

Most subcultures do not reject all of the values and practices of the larger society. Residents of

San Francisco's Chinatown, for example, share many broad American cultural traits, such as the English language (for most), public schools, toys and games, radios and televisions, jobs, and many basic American customs. But the culture of the Chinatown residents also includes another language (Chinese), specific foods, a style of dress, beliefs, customs, and celebrations that are not shared by most people in the United States. The residents of Spanish Harlem and the Navajo people also have their own languages, foods, style of dress, beliefs, customs, and celebrations that are not shared by the larger society. Similarly, soldiers on a military base share many subcultural characteristics, such as a rigid ranking system (military rank), extreme regulation of activities, and dormitory-style living arrangements.

Most subcultures do not present a threat to society. In fact, modern society is dependent on various subcultures—such as the military, the police, lawyers, physicians, teachers, and religious leaders—for many important functions. In addition, subcultures—particularly subcultures based on nationality—help to make a society more interesting and open to change.

In some instances, however, subcultural practices are consciously intended to challenge the values of the larger society. When a group rejects the values, norms, and practices of the larger society and replaces them with a new set of cultural patterns, the subculture that emerges is called a **counterculture.** The Hare Krishna religious movement, punkers, and the youth movement of the 1960s are examples of countercultures in the United States.

As is true in the case of cultural variation among societies, cultural variation within a society gives rise to ethnocentric feelings. Sociologists must maintain the same attitude of cultural relativism when studying subcultures and countercultures that they maintain when studying the cultures of other societies.

During the 1960s, social conditions in the United States ignited a youth counterculture. Many young people expressed their dissatisfaction with existing conditions by participating in peace rallies, civil rights marches, and women's rights demonstrations.

Punkers are an example of a contemporary counterculture.

IDENTIFY George Murdock, Margaret Mead, Arapesh, Mundugumor

1. ***Summarizing Ideas*** ***(a)*** What are cultural universals? ***(b)*** Why do they exist? ***(c)*** List some examples of cultural universals.

2. ***Comprehending Ideas*** ***(a)*** What is ethnocentrism? ***(b)*** What are some of the negative consequences of ethnocentrism? ***(c)*** Are there any positive consequences and, if so, what are they?

3. ***Drawing Inferences*** ***(a)*** What is cultural relativism? ***(b)*** What effect does it have on sociological inquiry?

4. ***Seeing Relationships*** ***(a)*** What is a subculture? ***(b)*** What distinguishes a counterculture from a subculture?

CHAPTER 2   SUMMARY

Culture consists of all of the shared products of human groups. Sociologists distinguish between two types of culture—material culture and nonmaterial culture. Material culture consists of the physical objects people create. Abstract human creations form a society's nonmaterial culture.

In addition to physical objects, there are four other basic components of culture: symbols, language, values, and norms. Sociologists distinguish between two types of norms—folkways and mores. When norms are enforced by the government, they become laws.

Culture can be divided into three levels—traits, complexes, and patterns. Culture traits are individual tools, acts, or beliefs that are related to a particular situation or need. Related culture traits can be combined to form culture complexes. Culture complexes, in turn, can be combined to form culture patterns.

Some needs are so basic that every society must develop culture traits, complexes, and patterns to ensure their satisfaction. These common features of societies are called cultural universals.

Although there are many similarities among cultures, there are enough differences to give rise to the problem of ethnocentrism. Ethnocentrism is the belief that one's own culture or group is superior. To counteract the tendency toward ethnocentrism, many sociologists and anthropologists adopt the attitude of cultural relativism. Cultural relativism is the belief that cultures should be judged by their own standards.

Cultural variation also exists within societies. The unique cultural characteristics of subgroups within a society form subcultures. When a subculture is based on the rejection of the values, norms, and practices of the larger society, it is called a counterculture.

READING ABOUT SOCIOLOGY: Developing a Structured Overview

A student of sociology often is required to read and remember a great deal of information. One way to help you remember what you have read is to develop a structured overview. A structured overview is a kind of outline that details the major ideas and supporting facts contained in a body of information.

How to Develop a Structured Overview

To develop a structured overview, follow these steps.

1. **Identify the major ideas.** Carefully read the information presented, observing the headings for each of the major ideas or main topics.

2. **Identify the categories and the supporting details.** Now, find the major categories under which the material is organized. Look for the key words that point to the supporting details.

3. **Structure the headings and categories.** Form an overview by structuring the headings and categories as shown in the chart on page 41.

Applying the Skill

Skim Section 1 of this chapter, which begins on page 24. The section examines the meaning of culture, thus that becomes the title of the structured overview on page 41. Note that the section covers three main topics. These three main topics are the definition of culture, the components of culture, and the levels of culture. In a structured overview of Section 1, these three topics would then form the main headings under Meaning of Culture.

Under each of the three main headings would fall a series of subheadings. Read through the discussion of the meaning of culture again. Note that after the definition of culture (which becomes the first subheading under Definition of Culture), two categories of culture are discussed. These two categories of culture are (1) material culture and (2) nonmaterial culture. Material culture and nonmaterial culture then become the subheadings under the definition of culture. In turn, each of these topics is followed by its appropriate definition.

Next, reread the discussion of the components of culture. Note that four main topics are discussed. These four main topics are (1) symbols, (2) language, (3) values, and (4) norms. These topics become the four subheadings under the Components of Culture. In turn, each of these topics is followed by its appropriate definition. In the case of norms, the definition is followed by subheadings for the three types of norms. These three subheadings are Folkways, Mores, and Laws. Each of these three subheadings is then followed by its appropriate definition.

Finally, reread the discussion of the levels of culture. Note that after the definition of levels of culture (which becomes the first subheading under Levels of Culture), three levels of culture are discussed. These three levels are (1) culture traits, (2) culture complexes, and (3) culture patterns. These three topics become the subheadings under the definition of levels of culture. In turn, each of these topics is followed by its appropriate definition. Check the structured overview for Section 1 on page 41 to assist you in understanding these instructions.

The number of headings and subheadings included in a structured overview depends on the amount of information covered in the section. The greater the number of topics and supporting details, the greater the number of headings.

Practicing the Skill

Reread Section 2 of Chapter 1. Then develop a structured overview on a separate sheet of paper.

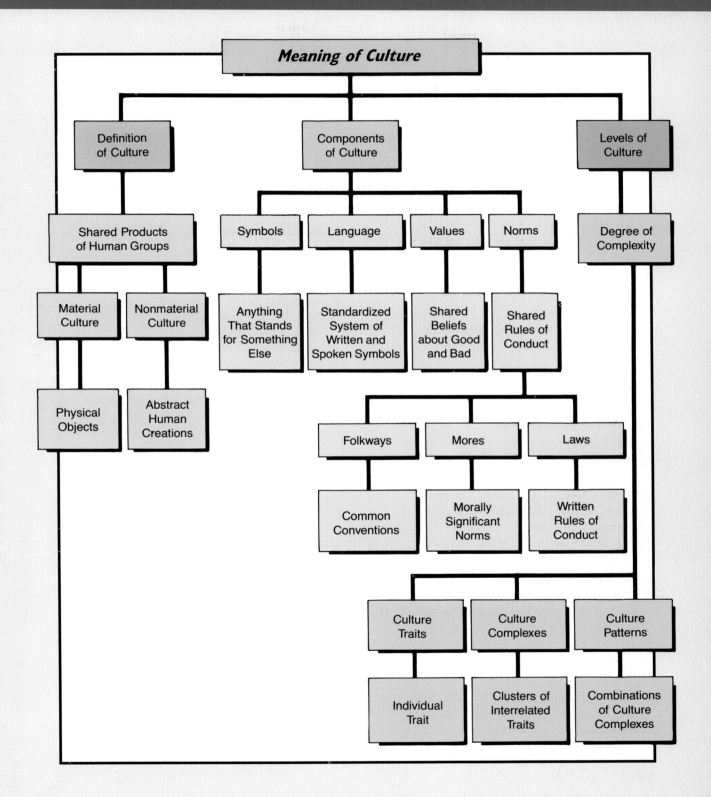

Reviewing Sociological Terms

On a separate sheet of paper, supply the term that correctly completes each sentence.

1. _____ is the term given to objects of material culture.

2. The organization of written or spoken symbols into a standardized system is _____.

3. Abstract human creations are part of a group's _____ _____.

4. _____ is the tendency to view one's own culture or group as superior.

5. Automobiles, clothing, books, cooking utensils, buildings, and computers are examples of _____ _____.

6. A trait that is found in every society is called a _____ _____.

Thinking Critically about Sociology

1. *Seeing Relationships* *(a)* What are values and norms and how are they related? *(b)* What functions do values and norms serve for society?

2. *Comprehending Ideas* *(a)* Adolescents form a subculture in the United States. What are some of the values and norms that are important to the adolescent subculture? *(b)* Which, if any, of these values and norms conflict with those of the larger society?

3. *Summarizing Ideas* *(a)* What is a symbol? *(b)* What types of things can serve as symbols? *(c)* What determines whether something is a symbol?

4. *Using Sociological Imagination* *(a)* According to Marvin Harris, how can environmental factors be used to explain the prohibition in India against killing cattle? *(b)* How might you explain the cultural differences between the Arapesh and Mundugumor in terms of environmental factors?

5. *Comparing Ideas* *(a)* How do folkways, mores, and laws differ? *(b)* List three examples of each type of norm.

6. *Drawing Conclusions* *(a)* What conclusion did Margaret Mead reach concerning the relationship between culture and personality? *(b)* What led her to this conclusion?

Exercising Sociological Skills

1. *Providing Evidence* Reread the Applying Sociology feature on pages 28–29. *(a)* Is Miner's description of the Nacirema an example of cultural relativism? *(b)* Why or why not?

2. *Analyzing Ideas* Reread the Case Study on page 35. Do you think that the comparative study conducted by A.I. Rabin's research group provides evidence supporting the idea that personality development is influenced by culture? Justify your answer.

3. *Developing a Structured Overview* Reread the Developing Sociological Imagination feature on pages 40–41. Then develop a structured overview of Section 2 of this chapter.

Extending Sociological Imagination

1. Research a counterculture. The group may be either contemporary or historical. After examining the data, answer the following questions: *(a)* Against what elements of the larger culture is (was) the group rebelling? *(b)* What are (were) the major norms and values of the group?

2. Research daily life in a foreign society. What are some of the cultural differences and similarities between the foreign society and the United States?

3. Select one example of a specific culture pattern in the United States. List the culture traits and culture complexes that make up the culture pattern.

INTERPRETING PRIMARY SOURCES
Life among Ghosts

When new immigrants to a country settle among others from their old country, a strong subculture often develops. The beliefs and practices of the immigrants and those of the larger society are sometimes at odds.

In the following excerpt from *The Woman Warrior,* Maxine Hong Kingston, a first-generation Chinese American, provides an example of the types of misunderstandings that can occur. The ghosts to which the passage refers are non-Chinese Americans. While reading the excerpt, consider the effects of such misunderstandings on social interaction. Also consider how practicing cultural relativism can help you understand the mother's behavior.

We were working at the laundry when a delivery boy came from the Rexall drugstore around the corner. He had a pale blue box of pills, but nobody was sick. Reading the label we saw that it belonged to another Chinese family, Crazy Mary's family. "Not ours," said my father. He pointed out the name to the Delivery Ghost, who took the pills back. My mother muttered for an hour, and then her anger boiled over. "That ghost! That dead ghost! How dare he come to the wrong house?" She could not concentrate on her marking and pressing. "A mistake! Huh!" I was getting angry myself. She fumed. She made her press crash and hiss. "Revenge. We've got to avenge this wrong on our future, on our health, on our lives. Nobody's going to sicken my children and get away with it." . . .

"Aha!" she yelled. "You! The biggest." She was pointing at me. "You go to the drugstore."

"What do you want me to buy, Mother?" I said.

"But nothing. Don't bring one cent. Go and make them stop the curse."

"I don't want to go. I don't know how to do that. There are no such things as curses. They'll think I'm crazy."

"If you don't go, I'm holding you responsible for bringing a plague on this family."

"What am I supposed to do when I get there?" I said, sullen, trapped. "Do I say, 'Your delivery boy made a wrong delivery'?" . . .

"You get reparation candy." she said. "You say, 'You have tainted my house with sick medicine and must remove the curse with sweetness.' He'll understand."

"He didn't do it on purpose. And no, he won't, Mother. They don't understand stuff like that. I won't be able to say it right. He'll call us beggars." . . .

The druggist leaned way over the counter and frowned. "Some free candy," I said. "Sample candy."

"We don't give sample candy, young lady." he said.

"My mother said you have to give us candy. She said that is the way the Chinese do it."

"What?"

"That is the way the Chinese do it."

"Do what?"

"Do things." I felt the weight and immensity of things impossible to explain to the druggist.

"Can I give you some money?" he asked.

"No, we want candy."

He reached into a jar and gave me a handful of lollipops. He gave us candy all year round, year after year, every time we went into the drugstore. When different druggists or clerks waited on us, they also gave us candy. . . . They thought we were beggars without a home who lived in back of the laundry.

Source Review

1. Why does the delivery of the pills to the wrong house trouble the mother?

2. How do you think the mother's theory of how diseases are spread differs from that of the druggist?

3. The mother was accustomed to Chinese druggists giving customers raisins when they filled a medicine order. The sweetness of the raisins was supposed to ward off the curse of sickness. How would practicing cultural relativism help you explain the mother's reaction to the American druggist?

Cultural Conformity and Adaptation

 1 The American Value System

Traditional American Values
Our Changing Values

 3 Social Change

Sources of Social Change
Resistance to Change

 2 Social Control

Internalization of Norms
Sanctions

Chapter Focus

Chapter 3 examines how culture is maintained and how it changes. An overview of the American value system is presented. This overview sets the stage for an examination of the ways in which society attempts to ensure that its values and norms are upheld. The chapter closes with a look at the sources of social change and why people sometimes resist change.

As you study the chapter, look for the answers to the following questions:

1. What are the basic values that form the foundation for American culture?
2. What is the most significant new American value?
3. What forms of social control exist to help ensure that the norms of society are upheld?
4. What are the main sources of social change?
5. What factors lead individuals to resist social change?

KEY TERMS

The following terms, while not the only terms emphasized in the chapter, are basic to your understanding of sociology. Determine the meaning of each term, either by using the Glossary or by watching for context clues as you read the chapter.

internalization	informal sanction	social movement
sanctions	social control	technology
formal sanction	ideology	cultural lag

As we discussed in the last chapter, values and norms are two of the basic components of culture. We defined values as the shared beliefs about what is good or bad, right or wrong, desirable or undesirable. The values that a society holds help determine the character of its people and the nature of social life. A society's values give rise to a system of norms that guide social interaction. Norms are the shared rules of conduct that tell people how to act in specific situations.

Not all norms in society are of equal importance. Norms that do not have great significance attached to them are called folkways. Folkways are the common customs of everyday life. The well-being and stability of society are not based on a strict upholding of these customs. Thus severe penalties seldom result when limited numbers of people fail to uphold various folkways. Individuals who openly violate many folkways, however, often meet with a negative social response. Nonconformity must be within reasonable limits to be acceptable.

The violation of mores, on the other hand, does meet with serious resistance. This resistance is due to the fact that the stability of society is based on the upholding of mores. Mores are norms that have great moral and social significance attached to them, such as norms against drunk driving or stealing another person's property.

Norms that are important to the stability or well-being of society often are established as laws. A law is a written rule of conduct that is enacted and enforced by the government. Laws are enacted to cover a wide range of behaviors, from simple folkways to strict mores.

In this chapter, we will look at the ways in which society attempts to ensure that its values and norms are upheld. No society can exist without change, however. We therefore also will look at the sources of social change and the reasons why people sometimes resist change. To set the stage for this discussion, we will begin with a look at the American value system and how this system is changing.

1 THE AMERICAN VALUE SYSTEM

Ethnic, racial, religious, and geographical variations in American society make for a culture rich in diversity. Nevertheless, certain values are shared by the majority of Americans. These are the values that we think of when we speak of traditional American culture.

Traditional American Values

In a now-classic 1970 study, sociologist Robin Williams outlined a set of 15 values that are central to the American way of life. Among these basic values are personal achievement, work, morality, humanitarianism, efficiency and practicality, progress, material comfort, equality, democracy, and freedom.

Personal Achievement. Most Americans value personal achievement. This is not surprising considering that we are a nation built on individualism and competition. This belief in personal achievement is most evident in the area of employment, where achievement often is measured in terms of power and wealth.

Work. Most Americans value work, regardless of the rewards involved. Discipline, dedication, and hard work are seen as signs of virtue. People who choose not to work often are viewed as being lazy or even immoral.

Morality and Humanitarianism.

The United States was founded on strong religious faith and on a belief in justice and equality for all and charity toward the less fortunate. Most Americans place a high value on morality and tend to view the world in terms of right and wrong. At the same time, however, they are quick to help those who are less fortunate than themselves.

Efficiency and Practicality.

Americans tend to be practical and inventive people. They believe that every problem has a solution. Problem solving is merely a matter of discovering the most efficient technique for dealing with the situation or determining the most practical response to the issue at hand. Consequently, Americans tend to judge items on the basis of their usefulness and people on their ability to get things done.

Progress and Material Comfort.

Americans have always looked to the future with optimism. They believe that through hard work and determination, living conditions will continue to improve. This belief in progress goes hand-in-hand with a belief in the ability of science to make the world a better and more comfortable place. Both views are important because most Americans also place a high value on material comfort.

Equality and Democracy.

The United States was founded on the principle of human equality. Americans still hold that value in high regard. Today, many Americans believe that human equality means equality of opportunity. At least in principle, most people believe that every individual in the United States should have an equal chance at success. Equality of opportunity, however, does not mean that Americans believe that everyone should be equally successful. The values of hard work and personal achievement lead most Americans to view success as a reward that must be earned.

The belief in equality extends to the form of government that Americans value—democracy. Americans believe that democracy is the best form of government and that citizens everywhere should be allowed to participate freely in choosing the leaders of their governments.

Text continues on page 50.

Achievement in sports is highly valued in American society.

The 100 Percent American?

Have you ever stopped to think about how much our culture has borrowed from other cultures, both past and present? In the 1930s, anthropologist Ralph Linton explored this question in a humorous way. Following is an excerpt from his classic essay on how much Americans owe to other cultures. The essay first appeared in the 1936 edition of his book *The Study of Man: An Introduction.*

Our solid American citizen awakens in a bed built on a pattern which originated in the Near East but which was modified in northern Europe before it was transmitted to America. He throws back covers made from cotton, domesticated in India, or linen, domesticated in the Near East, or wool from sheep, also domesticated in the Near East, or silk, the use of which was discovered in China. All of these materials have been spun and woven by processes invented in the Near East. He slips into his moccasins, invented by the Indians of the Eastern woodlands, and goes to the bathroom, whose fixtures are a mixture of European and American inventions, both of recent date. He takes off his pajamas, a garment invented in India, and washes with soap invented by the ancient Gauls. He then shaves, a masochistic rite which seems to have been derived from either Sumer or ancient Egypt.

Returning to the bedroom, he removes his clothes from a chair of southern European type and proceeds to dress. He puts on garments whose form originally derived from the skin clothing of the nomads of the Asiatic steppes, puts on shoes made from skins tanned by a process invented in ancient Egypt, and cut to a pattern derived from the classical civilizations of the Mediterranean. . . . Before going out for breakfast he glances through the window, made of glass invented in Egypt, and if it is raining, puts on overshoes made of rubber discovered by the Central American Indians and takes an umbrella, invented in southeastern Asia. Upon his head he puts a hat made of felt, a material invented in the Asiatic steppes.

On his way to breakfast he stops to buy a paper, paying for it with coins, an ancient Lydian invention. At the restaurant a whole new series of borrowed elements confronts him. His plate is made of a form of pottery invented in China. His knife is of steel, an alloy first made in southern India, his fork, a medieval Italian invention, and his spoon a derivative of a Roman original. He begins breakfast with an orange, from the eastern Mediterranean, a cantaloupe from Persia, or perhaps a piece of African watermelon. With this he has coffee, an Abyssinian plant, with cream and sugar. Both the domestication of cows and the idea of milking them originated in the Near East, while sugar was first made in India. After his fruit and first coffee he goes on to waffles, cakes made by a Scandinavian technique from wheat domesticated in Asia Minor. Over these he pours maple syrup, invented by the Indians of the Eastern woodlands. As a side dish he may have the egg of a species of bird domesticated in Indo-China, or thin strips of the flesh of an animal domesticated in Eastern Asia which have been salted and smoked by a process developed in northern Europe.

When our friend has finished eating, he reads the news of the day, imprinted in characters invented by the ancient Semites upon a material invented in China by a process invented in Germany. As he absorbs the accounts of foreign troubles he will, if he is a good conservative citizen, thank a Hebrew deity in an Indo-European language that he is 100 percent American.

From your reading of this excerpt, you can see that most "American" culture traits did not originate in the United States. Rather, these culture traits have become part of American culture through the process of diffusion. As you will learn from reading Chapter 3, diffusion is the spreading of culture traits from one society to another. A content analysis of the reading will show just how much diffusion has taken place in the United States over time.

Based on the discussion of content analysis that appears in the Applying Sociology feature in Chapter 1 and in the Appendix, go through the excerpt again and make a list of each culture trait that is mentioned. Then, place each of these traits in one of the following categories: Africa, the Americas, Asia, Europe, and the Near East. You may have to do some library research to categorize some of the unfamiliar regions mentioned in the excerpt.

Now, count up the number of culture traits that appear in each one of the categories. Which one of the categories contains the greatest number of culture traits? Which one of the categories contains the least number of culture traits? What can you conclude from your content analysis about the extent of diffusion that has taken place in the United States?

Some of you may find it enjoyable to consider the origin of some culture traits that you use on a daily basis. Make a list of 10 culture traits not mentioned in the excerpt that originated outside of the United States. Conduct library research to determine where and when these culture traits first appeared. You also might enjoy writing an essay similar to the one written by Linton.

Freedom.   Freedom is an extremely important value for most Americans. This is not surprising in a nation that celebrates individualism. Among the freedoms that Americans value most highly are freedom of personal choice and freedom from direct government interference in people's daily lives and in business dealings.

These are not the only values that help define American culture. Robin Williams included other items such as nationalism and patriotism, science and rationality, and individualism in his list of core values. Other scholars have included values such as educational attainment, religious participation, and romantic love.

Even though values are vital to the stability of society, they also produce conflict. Not everyone agrees on what should be considered acceptable American values. Even when they agree on the importance of a set of values, individuals do not uphold all values to the same degree. The values of personal achievement and material comfort, for example, often weaken values such as morality and equality.

Our Changing Values

The problem of value conflict is complicated by the fact that values, like all aspects of society, change over time. Recent studies of the American value system have uncovered several new values. The most significant of these new American values is self-fulfillment.

Americans are so highly committed to the values of freedom and humanitarianism that they often support the efforts of struggling peoples in other parts of the world. In 1992, for example, American troops were sent to Somalia to help in relief efforts for starving Somalis.

The value of self-fulfillment has encouraged many women to seek careers that will provide economic independence.

lieves this new value affects the economy in a negative way, in that it damages family life and the nation's educational system.

Other social scientists see the new emphasis on personal fulfillment as having positive consequences for individuals and for society. While admitting that current generations of Americans seem to believe less in hard work than did earlier generations, psychologist and survey researcher Daniel Yankelovich views the shift toward self-fulfillment as a beneficial change. He characterizes the new value as an emphasis on self-improvement and a movement away from satisfaction that is based on material gain. Yankelovich believes that this new value will take on added importance if the economy enters a period of low growth or even decline.

Self-fulfillment is a commitment to the full development of one's personality, talents, and potential. Evidence of this new value can be seen in the development of the self-help industry and in the human potential movement. Health clubs, diet centers, seminars, television programs, and books geared toward improving people's looks, health, and personal and professional lives are too numerous to count. Advertisements challenge people to be all that they can be, to grab the gusto, and to experience the good life.

Some social scientists view this growing emphasis on personal fulfillment with alarm. In his book *The Culture of Narcissism,* Christopher Lasch goes so far as to consider it a personality disorder. He terms this disorder **narcissism,** which means extreme self-centeredness. Similarly, sociologist Daniel Bell believes this emphasis on the self weakens the established values of hard work and moderation and threatens the stability of the capitalist system. Sociologist Amitai Etzioni also be-

SECTION 1 REVIEW

DEFINE   self-fulfillment, narcissism

IDENTIFY   Robin Williams, Christopher Lasch, Daniel Yankelovich

1. ***Summarizing Ideas***   List and describe the traditional American values outlined by Robin Williams.

2. ***Comprehending Ideas***   Why do values produce conflict as well as stability?

3. ***Comparing Ideas***   *(a)* What is the new value of self-fulfillment?   *(b)* How do Christopher Lasch and Daniel Yankelovich differ in their views of the effects of self-fulfillment on society?   *(c)* What other criticisms of self-fulfillment have social scientists raised?

2 SOCIAL CONTROL

Every society develops norms that reflect the cultural values its members consider important. For society to run smoothly, these norms must be upheld. There are two basic means through which norms are enforced—through internalization and through sanctions.

Internalization of Norms

When people come to believe that a particular norm is good, useful, and appropriate, they generally follow it and expect others to do the same. They do this because they have internalized the norm. **Internalization** is the process by which a norm becomes a part of an individual's personality, thereby conditioning the individual to conform to society's expectations. We require no thought to eat with a fork, spoon, and knife. We drive on the right side of the road. We stop at stop signs and go when the traffic signal is green. We do not do these things simply because we fear being punished. There would not be enough police to enforce the laws if, for example, everyone conformed to them only out of fear of arrest. Rather, we have internalized the laws.

Sanctions

Most members of society follow norms without conscious thought. Not everyone, however, internalizes all of society's norms. Some people must be motivated by sanctions. **Sanctions** are rewards or punishments used to enforce conformity to norms.

Positive Sanctions. When a sanction is in the form of a reward, it is a **positive sanction.** People are introduced to positive sanctions early in life through interaction in the family. Most parents, for example, praise their children for good behavior. Positive sanctions also are common forms of control outside of the family. Teachers react favorably to students who pay attention in class and who do well in school. Employers often give pay raises to workers who show initiative and dedication. Cheers from team members and the crowd are used to spur athletes on to even greater efforts. And throughout life, ceremonies, ribbons, badges, and awards are used to convince people to meet the challenges of conformity and to continually improve their behavior.

Positive sanctions can range from smiles and nods of the head to public ceremonies and financial rewards. We all like to receive praise and personal recognition, regardless of the form they take. Often the more we get, the more we want. It makes us feel good. At the same time, these

With the exception of the family, the school is the most significant agent through which children come to learn the norms of society. Receiving a gold star from a teacher, for example, is a positive sanction that encourages young children to work hard and to obey instructions.

For much of human history, public humiliation was used as an effective negative sanction. Being confined to the stocks, for example, served both as a punishment for wrongdoers and as a warning to others.

positive sanctions fulfill a vital function by encouraging the upholding of social norms.

Negative Sanctions. Positive sanctions are not always enough to ensure conformity. Society also must employ negative sanctions to bring forth desired behavior. A **negative sanction** is a punishment or the threat of punishment used to enforce conformity. When parents say that coming home late from a date will result in grounding, they are using a negative sanction. The threat of punishment often is enough to ensure conformity. The possibility of having one's car towed away usually is enough to persuade someone not to park in a "no parking" zone. When the threat of punishment fails, however, the actual punishment is there to remind the violator that conformity is expected. Actual punishments can range from frowns, ridicule, rejection, and fines to imprisonment and even death. In general, the more important the norm, the more serious the punishment for nonconformity.

Formal Sanctions. In addition to being positive or negative, sanctions also can be either formal or informal. A **formal sanction** is a reward or punishment that is given by some formal organization or regulatory body, such as the government, the police, a corporation, or a school. Fines, low grades, suspension from school, termination from a job, and imprisonment are examples of negative formal sanctions. Positive formal sanctions include pay raises, promotions, graduation certificates, awards, and medals.

Informal Sanctions. While formal sanctions play an important role in maintaining social stability, the majority of norms are enforced informally. An **informal sanction** is a spontaneous expression of approval or disapproval given by an individual or a group. Positive informal sanctions include standing ovations, compliments, smiles, pats on the back, and gifts. Negative informal sanctions include frowns, gossip, scoldings, insults, and being ignored.

Authority figures set standards for appropriate behavior and thereby reinforce the norms of society. Among the most visible authority figures are political, religious, and social leaders. Contemporary leaders who fulfill this function include (from top to bottom) the Reverend Jesse Jackson, Pope John Paul II, President Bill Clinton, Russian President Boris Yeltsin, the Reverend Billy Graham, and England's Queen Elizabeth II.

The enforcing of norms through either internalization or sanctions is called **social control.** Agents of social control include authority figures, the police, the courts, religion, the family, and public opinion. The principal means of social control in all societies, though, is self-control, learned through the internalization of norms.

When a society's methods for ensuring conformity break down, social stability is lost. If people are killing one another, stealing, and fighting in the streets, then social order is in jeopardy. No society can survive for long without an effective system of social control. Individuals must follow certain rules of behavior if society is to function smoothly.

SECTION 2 REVIEW

DEFINE internalization, sanctions, social control

1. **Summarizing Ideas** What are the two basic ways in which the norms of society are enforced?

2. **Understanding Ideas** *(a)* What is a positive sanction? *(b)* What is a negative sanction? *(c)* Give several examples of positive and negative sanctions.

3. **Contrasting Ideas** *(a)* How does an informal sanction differ from a formal sanction? *(b)* Give several examples of positive and negative formal and informal sanctions.

4. **Analyzing Ideas** Why is it important to enforce norms?

3 SOCIAL CHANGE

All cultures change over time. Some cultures, however, change much faster than do others. The pace of change is closely related to the total number of culture traits in a culture at a particular time. The more culture traits there are, the faster the culture can change, since more possibilities for change exist. The rate of change is further accelerated by the fact that each change brings about other changes. The invention of the automobile, for example, did more than offer us a new form of transportation. In addition to providing employment for millions of people, it affected the way we shop, where we live, how we date, and what we do during our leisure time.

Sources of Social Change

The modern world changes at a rapid rate. Each week brings new material goods, new styles of dress, new ways of doing things, and new ideas to challenge existing ideas. What causes all of these changes? Actually, there are a great number of factors that stimulate change. We will limit our discussion to six factors: values and beliefs, technology, population, diffusion, the physical environment, and wars and conquests.

Values and Beliefs. As functionalist sociologists have noted, society is a system of interrelated parts. A change in one aspect of society produces change throughout the system. Changes in values and beliefs therefore can have far-reaching consequences for society. This is particularly true when new values and beliefs are part of a larger system of ideology.

An **ideology** is a system of beliefs or ideas that justifies some social, moral, religious, political, or economic interests held by a social group or by society. Ideologies often are spread through social movements. A **social movement** is a long-term conscious effort to promote or prevent social change. Social movements usually involve large numbers of people. Examples of social movements include the Prohibition movement, the civil rights movement, the peace movement, the gay rights movement, and the women's movement.

Social movements are an important means through which change is brought about in society. The Reverend Martin Luther King, Jr., was a powerful voice for the civil rights movement until his death in the late 1960s. His life and untimely death still serve as an inspiration in the drive toward justice and equality.

The consequences of shifts in ideology can be seen by examining how the women's movement changed the airline industry. Many years ago, one airline decided to put stewardesses on its flights because it realized that a large number of its passengers were businessmen. The airline hoped to draw passengers away from other airlines and increase its profits by providing better in-flight service. The idea worked, and soon all airline passengers found themselves being greeted by a beautiful young woman as they boarded the plane.

Originally, stewardesses were selected for their looks and youth. They were forced to retire at the age of 30. Today, because of the women's movement, sex discrimination laws, and pressure from the stewardesses themselves, airlines no longer have stewardesses—they have been replaced by flight attendants. These flight attendants are as likely to be over the age of 30 as under the age of 30 and many of them are men.

Technology.   Social change also occurs when people find new ways to manipulate their environment. The knowledge and tools that people use to manipulate their environment for practical purposes is called **technology.** Two ways in which new technologies arise are through discovery and invention.

Discovery occurs when people recognize new uses for existing elements in the world or begin to understand them in new ways. Examples of discoveries include chewing gum, atomic fission, and oil shale. Oil shale, for example, was discovered quite by accident. Along the banks of the Colorado River are many stones that we now know contain rock shale saturated with oil. Story has it that a man used these stones to construct a fireplace in the cabin he was building. When the

cabin was completed, he lit a fire in the fireplace. You can imagine his utter shock when the fireplace itself burst into flames.

Invention occurs when people use existing knowledge to create something that did not previously exist. Inventions can take the form of material objects, ideas, or patterns of behavior. New tools, such as a gadget to take the pits out of cherries or a computer small enough to hold on your lap, are examples of material inventions. Examples of nonmaterial inventions include political movements, religious movements, new hobbies, and business organizations.

Population.   A change in the size of the population may bring about changes in the culture. The population of the United States, for example, has increased rapidly during the twentieth century. This means that more people are living in the same amount of space, thereby creating more crowded conditions. A larger population brings increased demand for housing, energy, schools, stores, transportation, food, and so on.

Population increases and decreases affect the economy. By increasing the demand for goods and services, a growing population may increase employment and stimulate the economy. On the other hand, a community with a declining population needs fewer goods and services, and employment opportunities may become limited for the people who remain.

People also bring about changes by moving from one place to another. Whenever a family moves from one community to another, it stimulates some change both in the community it leaves and in the new community it enters.

Changes in the age structure of a population also bring about social and cultural changes. When

Reprinted by permission of UFS, Inc.

The United States is a highly mobile society. Approximately one in every six families moves each year, often in response to changing occupational opportunities.

fewer babies are being born, for example, the need for schools, recreation centers, and other services geared toward children and young adults is reduced. The need for specialized services geared toward the elderly, on the other hand, increases as more people live to older ages.

Diffusion. People often borrow ideas, acts, beliefs, and material objects from other societies. This process of spreading culture traits from one society to another is called **diffusion.** The Arapesh of what is now Papua New Guinea, for example, learned how to make braided grass skirts from a bride who came from another region. ·

The more contact a society has with other societies, the more ideas it will borrow. Today, with mass transportation and instant communication via radio and television, the number of traits that Americans borrow from other cultures is immense. As a result of contact with other cultures, Americans now eat foods such as pasta from Italy, raw fish dishes called sushi from Japan, Mongolian barbecue, and baklava from Greece. At the same time, other cultures are borrowing many traits from us. American cars and farm machinery, soft drinks, and fast foods, for instance, can be found in many parts of the world.

The Physical Environment. The environment provides conditions that may encourage or discourage cultural change. People in some societies eat only the foods that they can grow locally. Other societies import much of their food. Many societies also adapt new crops to grow in their area. The introduction of new foods or the scarcity of a familiar food can bring about cultural change.

Natural disasters such as droughts, floods, earthquakes, tornadoes, and tidal waves also can produce social and cultural change. Buildings often are destroyed, businesses can be damaged beyond repair, and industries can find themselves so financially burdened that they cannot recover. After such disasters, people often take precautions for the future. Dams may be built to lessen the effects of floods and droughts. Communities may be rebuilt farther from fault lines.

In 1992, Hurricane Andrew devastated large portions of Dade County, Florida. The amount of destruction left in the wake of the hurricane led to an investigation of building practices in the state.

A change in the supply of natural resources also can bring about cultural change. In the 1970s, high fuel prices and fuel shortages created long lines at American gasoline stations. These factors encouraged people to seek long-range alternative sources of energy and to develop smaller, more fuel-efficient cars. When the shortages eased in the 1980s, the search for alternative forms of energy slowed. Similarly, the production of less fuel-efficient cars, such as luxury cars and high-performance sports cars, increased once again.

Wars and Conquests.   Although not as common as other sources of social change, wars and conquests probably bring about the greatest change in a society in the least amount of time. War causes the loss of many lives. It produces broken families, as some family members go off to fight. It brings about the destruction of property and leads to the rise of new cities and towns out of the ruins. It causes changes in the work force, as industry shifts from the production of consumer goods to that of war materials. On the positive side, war also can produce advances in technology and medicine that carry over to civilian life after the fighting has ended.

Conquest results in changes in government, as the new rulers come to power. It often gives rise to new economic policies, too. For example, to gain favor with their subjects, new rulers might increase the wages of workers or reduce taxes.

These are some of the more important causes of cultural change. They are the forces that bring changes in a culture as the people in the society try to adapt to the new situations with which they are faced.

Native Americans: Caught Between Two Worlds

When most high school students go to school, they interact with other people who have backgrounds, interests, and beliefs similar to their own. Their classmates speak the same language, wear similar clothes, hold basically the same beliefs, listen to the same types of music, and watch the same types of movies and television programs. In other words, these students share the same culture.

For some high school students, however, school does not reinforce their cultural beliefs. Instead, school tries to change their beliefs. Students from the Native American Ute tribe of northern Utah have been faced with such a situation. During the 1970s, Betty J. Kramer lived with the Utes and studied their problems with the school system. Kramer also studied the Utes' attempts to maintain their distinct Ute culture in the face of efforts to assimilate the tribe into mainstream American society.

Assimilation is the blending of culturally distinct groups into a single group with a common culture and identity. In theory, assimilation is the blending together of cultures. In practice, however, assimilation usually results in members of the less powerful groups replacing many of their values, beliefs, and practices with those of the larger culture. Schools are among the most important agents of assimilation.

The degree of cultural change involved in assimilation causes many people—particularly members of subcultures—to resist the process. This is true in the case of the Utes. The majority of Utes would prefer to hold on to their own distinct subculture within the framework of the larger American society. This does not mean that they want to reject non-Native American culture. Rather, the Ute resistance to assimilation revolves around the fact that they wish to preserve their Native American traditions and separate identity. The Utes believe that it is important for their children to understand and maintain their cultural

background. Many Utes charge that the school system teaches values that are in direct conflict with traditional Ute culture traits.

There are fundamental differences in the culture traits valued by the school system and those valued by traditional Ute society. The importance of competition is one significant area of disagreement. In general, the school system views competition as a positive feature of American society. One of the goals of education is seen as providing students with the tools necessary to compete in a market economy. In keeping with the competitive model, achievement is measured on the basis of grades, scores on standardized tests, and the winning of athletic events.

Ute society, however, is not based on a competitive model. Rather, the Ute culture is basically cooperative. Thus, the Utes prefer to measure achievement on the basis of effort, commitment, and the degree of satisfaction people receive from the creative process. Most jobs in the Ute community are interchangeable, and people transfer from one job to another with ease. Formal education does not play an important role among the Utes, because jobs are not assigned on the basis of whether or not a person has a high school degree.

Kramer reports that during the 1970s, the Utes resisted the school system's attempts to encourage assimilation. The high school dropout rate for Utes, which ranged from 64 percent to 94 percent, testified to the fact that most Ute children were not being successfully assimilated into the larger culture. Yet the school system, at the direction of the government, continued to stress assimilation. In response, tribal members called for a curriculum that taught aspects of both cultures. The Utes thought that the goal of educating their children should not be assimilation, but rather the teaching of skills needed to live successfully in both the Native American and non-Native American worlds.

Resistance to Change

Cultural change never occurs without some opposition. For each change introduced in society, there are people who strongly oppose it. Thus the changes that actually do take place often are the result of a compromise between opposing forces. This is true both on an interpersonal level and on a societal level. Often a new idea that is strongly resisted at first may be readily accepted by most people some years later. Other people never accept the new idea, but simply put up with it. Although there are numerous reasons why people resist cultural change, we will look at three important factors: ethnocentrism, cultural lag, and vested interests.

Ethnocentrism. Change that comes from outside the group often meets with particularly strong resistance. People tend to believe that their own ideas and ways of doing things are best. This tendency to view one's own culture or group as superior is called **ethnocentrism.** Extreme ethnocentrism can make any type of compromise or borrowing between individuals and groups difficult or even impossible.

The introduction of the Volkswagen Beetle to the United States provides an example of how ethnocentrism can affect the spread of ideas and material objects. In the mid-1950s, an American soldier brought back a Volkswagen Beetle from Germany. It drew a lot of attention, since many people had never seen one before. As a crowd gathered around the strange automobile, someone asked, "What is it?"

"A Volkswagen," the owner responded.

"Where did it come from?" questioned another.

"It was made in Germany," the soldier replied.

"If we allow them to bring those foreign cars into the country, it will put Americans out of work," said a voice from the crowd.

Many people held this view and refused to buy a foreign car, thinking that it somehow was not patriotic. Nevertheless, resistance eventually was overcome, and the little Beetle became a familiar sight on American streets and highways. By the time of the gas shortage of 1979, Americans were running to buy small foreign automobiles, and car lots were full of large domestic cars that no one could sell.

Cultural Lag. People tend to welcome changes in material culture traits much more readily than changes in nonmaterial culture traits. A new technological product is more likely to gain acceptance than is a new religious or social idea. It is much easier to convince a person to buy a new dishwasher for the home, say, than it is to convince him or her to join a new religion or to support environmental causes.

A situation in which some aspects of the culture change less rapidly, or lag behind, other aspects of the same culture is called **cultural lag.** For example, great progress has been made in eliminating the dreaded disease polio. Time was needed, however, for people to accept the polio vaccine. Similarly, the development of computers that can store information about every individual in the United States is far ahead of American laws designed to protect the privacy of citizens.

Vested Interests. The person who is satisfied with the way things are now is bound to resist any effort to change the situation. For some individuals, the present, even if somewhat imperfect, is better than an unknown future. These people have an investment in the present. Workers, for example, may oppose the introduction of a new machine that can do the work of 10 people because they fear it may cost them their jobs. We tend to resist any new idea that threatens our security or standard of living. We have a vested interest to protect.

Large, powerful corporations also have vested interests to protect. Consider, for example, the vested interests of the major American oil companies. In 1973, President Richard Nixon said that one of his goals was to develop a national energy policy. Jimmy Carter ran for president in 1976 stressing the country's need for an energy policy. Yet it was not until 1992, under President George Bush, that the Energy Policy Act was signed. And, even though this plan now is in place, critics charge that it does not focus enough on conservation or the use of renewable fuels.

One reason it has been so difficult to enact a strong national energy policy is that the major oil companies control the petroleum and most of the nuclear fuels we use. To protect their vested interests, oil companies favor voting down or amending energy bills submitted to Congress. Re-

Vested interests lead many people and groups to make their concerns known to politicians.

sistance also comes from private citizens. Even though opinion polls show that Americans generally favor conservation, many people are reluctant to conserve if it means altering their life-styles.

SECTION 3 REVIEW

DEFINE ideology, social movement, technology, diffusion

1. **Organizing Ideas** **(a)** List the six sources of social change discussed in the section. **(b)** Briefly describe how each source brings about social change.

2. **Comparing Ideas** What is the difference between discovery and invention?

3. **Summarizing Ideas** **(a)** What three factors produce resistance to social change? **(b)** How or why do these factors produce resistance?

CHAPTER 3 SUMMARY

The values that a society holds give it its unique character. When we think of American society, certain values come to mind. Chief among these values are personal freedom, work, morality, humanitarianism, efficiency, practicality, progress, material comfort, equality, democracy, and freedom. Recent studies have indicated that several new values are emerging in American society, the most prominent of which is self-fulfillment. Social scientists are divided on whether this new value is positive or negative.

For societies to remain relatively stable, the norms that grow out of values must be enforced. The two basic means through which norms are enforced are internalization and sanctions. Internalization is the process by which norms become a part of an individual's personality. When norms are internalized, people automatically conform to society's expectations. When internalization fails to produce the desired results, people are motivated to conform through the use of sanctions. Sanctions are rewards or punishments used to enforce conformity to norms. In addition to being either positive (rewards) or negative (punishments), sanctions can be formal or informal. The enforcement of norms through internalization or sanctions is called social control.

Regardless of social control, all societies and their cultures change over time. The main sources of social change include values and beliefs, technology, population, diffusion, the physical environment, and wars and conquests. Although social change is inevitable, it does not occur without opposition. Three factors that produce resistance to change are ethnocentrism, cultural lag, and vested interests.

DEVELOPING SOCIOLOGICAL

WRITING ABOUT SOCIOLOGY: Composing an Essay

An essay is a short composition written on a specific topic. You compose an essay when you write a report, answer a thought question on a test, or follow a set of directions that call for a response in your own words.

Here is an example of a directive that demands an essay response.

ESSAY DIRECTIVE: Read the Interpreting Primary Sources feature on page 65. State how the U.S. Department of Agriculture defines hamburger (5 points) and discuss how the definition of hamburger and the rise of the fast-food industry have affected beef consumption (10 points).

How to Compose an Essay
Follow these steps in reading an essay directive and composing an essay.

1. Look for informational terms. As you read the directive, note key terms that give clues to the expected content of the essay. In the above example, key terms include U.S. Department of Agriculture, hamburger, fast-food industry, and beef consumption.

2. Determine the essay's scope. Determine the subject of the essay. Note whether the directive asks you to address one main idea or several main ideas.

3. Note the performance terms. Performance terms are the words in the essay directive that indicate what you are supposed to do. Following are some of the most common performance terms:

- **Discuss:** Tell in some detail; assess the reasons, actions, results, and significance.
- **Identify:** Cite a specific person, group, organization, law, concept, or nation; or name an occurrence such as a specific event, problem, issue, or situation. Relate the piece of information to other information.

- **Describe:** Create a complete word picture of an individual, institution, action, or event.
- **Explain or show:** Determine a process, a sequence, or relationship such as before and after or cause and effect.
- **State:** Make a complete, formal statement consisting of several sentences on the topic.
- **Compare or contrast:** Indicate similarities or differences or differences alone.

4. Develop a structured overview. A structured overview is a kind of outline (see pages 40–41). It is most effective when it is written on a sheet of paper. There are four steps to developing a structured overview.

- **a.** State the subject, or topic. The title often gives clues to the subject.
- **b.** Identify the main ideas. Section titles often give clues to the main ideas.
- **c.** Identify subheadings, or supporting details, of the main ideas.
- **d.** Diagram the information so that it is easily followed.

5. Write the essay. Follow the essay directive in the first column.

Applying the Skill
See Step 1 for the informational terms used in the essay directive on this page. The subject is the increase in beef consumption. An essay based on this directive should provide information on two main points: how the U.S. Department of Agriculture defines hamburger meat and what the connection is between the definition of hamburger meat, the rise of the fast-food industry, and the increase in beef consumption.

The first main point deals with the definition of hamburger. The second main point increases the scope of the essay to include how beef consumption has been affected by the definition of beef and the rise of the fast-food industry.

Note the value assigned to each part of the essay. The part worth the most points should provide the most detail. The sample essay below devotes one paragraph to the U.S. Department of Agriculture's definition of hamburger and one paragraph to the connection between the definition, the rise of the fast-food industry, and increased beef consumption. The introduction states the subject of the essay. The conclusion restates the major points of the essay and reinforces the points made in the introduction.

Practicing the Skill
Read the following essay directive. Then on a separate sheet of paper, complete the activities and answer the questions in the next column.

ESSAY DIRECTIVE: Reread the Case Study feature on page 59. Contrast the school system's view of the role of education and competition with the view held by the Utes. Then discuss how the two groups differ in their measurement of achievement.

1. List the informational terms in the directive.

2. (a) What is the subject of the essay directive?
   (b) List the directive's main ideas.

3. List the performance terms in the essay directive.

4. Develop a structured overview of your response to the essay directive.

5. Write an essay in response to the directive.

SAMPLE ESSAY

INTRODUCTION
Beef consumption has increased dramatically in the United States during this century. Two of the factors that have led to an increase in beef consumption are the U.S. Department of Agriculture's definition of hamburger and the rise of the fast-food industry.

DEFINITION OF HAMBURGER
The U.S. Department of Agriculture defines a hamburger as a ground meat patty that contains no meat or fat other than beef or beef fat. Thus legally there is no such thing as a hamburger that is not all beef.

INCREASED CONSUMPTION
Hamburgers are the most popular convenience food. Fast-food restaurants sell on the order of 6.7 billion hamburgers a year. Fourteen million Americans each day eat at McDonald's alone. Thanks to the U.S. Department of Agriculture's ruling that hamburger must contain only beef and beef fat, all of these hamburgers are made of beef. Thus beef consumption has increased dramatically with the rise of the fast-food industry.

CONCLUSION
In short, by decreeing that hamburger can only contain beef and beef fat, the U.S. Department of Agriculture has guaranteed that beef consumption will increase as the popularity of fast-food restaurants increases.

Reviewing Sociological Terms

On a separate sheet of paper, supply the term that correctly completes each sentence.

1. The use of existing knowledge to create something that did not previously exist is called _____.

2. _____ is the knowledge and tools people use to manipulate their environment for practical purposes.

3. The spreading of culture traits (ideas, acts, beliefs, and material objects) from one society to another is called _____.

4. When people recognize new uses for existing elements in the world or begin to understand them in new ways, it is called _____.

5. _____ is a system of beliefs or ideas that justifies some social, moral, religious, political, or economic interests held by a social group or by society.

Thinking Critically about Sociology

1. *Seeing Relationships*   Make a list of some of the cultural changes brought about by *(a)* the airplane and *(b)* the automobile.

2. *Understanding Ideas*   How does the physical environment affect cultural change?

3. *Drawing Conclusions*   Identify which of the American values discussed in the chapter are contradictory (in that upholding one makes it difficult to uphold another), and explain why they are contradictory.

4. *Organizing Ideas*   In what ways do wars and conquests bring about cultural change?

5. *Applying Ideas*   *(a)* List five negative formal sanctions that the government uses to enforce norms.   *(b)* List five positive formal sanctions used by the government.

6. *Summarizing Ideas*   In what ways do changes in population bring about cultural changes?

7. *Using Sociological Imagination*   Provide real-life examples of the three sources of resistance to change discussed in the chapter.

8. *Comprehending Ideas*   *(a)* What is a social movement?   *(b)* In addition to those mentioned in the textbook, what are some current examples of social movements in the United States?

Exercising Sociological Skills

1. *Investigating Ideas*   Reread the Applying Sociology feature on pages 48–49. List 10 additional American culture traits that originated in other parts of the world and indicate where they originated.

2. *Contrasting Ideas*   Reread the Case Study feature on page 59.   *(a)* What is assimilation?   *(b)* How do the cultural values held by the school system differ from those held by the Utes?

3. *Composing an Essay*   Read the Interpreting Primary Sources feature on page 65. Using the skills presented in the Developing Sociological Imagination feature on pages 62–63, compose an essay answer to the following two-part question: *(a)* What four factors set the stage for the rise of the fast-food hamburger restaurant?   *(b)* What opportunity is provided to two-wage-earner families by such restaurants?

Extending Sociological Imagination

1. Make a list of the sanctions used in your school to control student behavior. Divide the list into four categories: formal positive sanctions, informal positive sanctions, formal negative sanctions, and informal negative sanctions.

2. Watch several weekly family-centered television shows. Using the techniques of content analysis, make a list of the values that are expressed on the shows.

INTERPRETING PRIMARY SOURCES
King Beef, U.S.A.

The process of cultural change is a bit like pushing over the first block in a long row of dominos—each falling domino topples the one next to it. Similarly, change in one area of society produces change in other areas.

In the following excerpt from *The Sacred Cow and the Abominable Pig*, anthropologist Marvin Harris examines the societal factors that led to the emergence of beef as the most popular meat in the United States. While reading the excerpt, consider what social factors led to the emergence of beef as America's favorite meat. Also consider the role played by the fast-food industry in increasing the consumption of beef in the United States and the consequences of this increased consumption.

How did beef finally manage to become king? Through a combination of changes in the beef production and marketing systems which were ideally suited to the emergent life-styles of post-World War II America. . . . Time spent on raising "feeders" (calves that will be sent to feedlots) and the time spent on finishing have grown shorter and shorter. With improved breeds, planted pasture, and scientific management, feeders can now be brought to four hundred pounds in four months. Farmers then sell them for shipment to feedlots where. . . in four more months they have put on another four hundred pounds and are ready for slaughter.

Just as important as the changes in the way beef was produced, were the changes in the way beef was consumed. First came the growth of suburban homeownership and the use of outdoor living space for cooking and entertaining. To the suburban refugees from the central cities, charcoal broiling represented the fulfillment of pent-up recreational and gustatory aspirations. . . . Charcoal-broiled steaks were the favorites, made all the more delectable no doubt because they had once been unaffordable. . . .

The move to suburbia was shortly followed by other social changes that contributed to the beefing of America: the entrance of women into the work force, the formation of families in which both parents work, the rising tide of feminism, and the growing resentment of women against pots, pans, sinks, and stoves. These changes set the stage for an orgy of beef eating outside the home and for the rise of America's most distinctive culinary contribution to world cuisine, the fast-food hamburger. For the new postwar, two-wage-earner families, the fast-food hamburger restaurant provides an opportunity to eat out, to be free of the drudgery of the kitchen—even without homeownership and backyard barbecues—at a cost that is comparable to a medium-budget home-cooked meal. . . .

In the early 1980s, Americans were eating fifty pounds of ground beef per head, mostly in the form of hamburgers. Every second, the fast-food restaurants alone were selling an order of one or two patties on a bun to two-hundred customers to the tune of 6.7 billion per year worth $10 billion. Fourteen million Americans a day eat in McDonald's alone. . . . Beef consumption and the fast-food industry took off together. . . .

Legally, there is no such thing as a hamburger which is not an all-beef hamburger. The statutes of the U.S. Department of Agriculture define hamburger as a ground meat patty which contains no meat or fat other than beef or beef fat. . . . In other words, by government decree, the beef industry holds a kind of patent or trademark on America's most popular convenience food.

Source Review

1. What social factors led to the emergence of beef as America's favorite meat?

2. Why has the fast-food industry played a particularly important role in increasing beef consumption in the United States?

3. What are some of the far-reaching social consequences of increased beef consumption in the United States?

Social Structure

Chapter Focus

Chapter 4 examines the characteristics of social structure, beginning with statuses and roles—the two major components of social structure. The structure of groups and societies then is examined. After looking at social interaction, the chapter closes with a discussion of formal organizations.

As you study the chapter, look for the answers to the following questions:

1. What are the two major components of social structure, and how do they affect human interaction?
2. What is a group, and what features are used to distinguish among groups?
3. What types of societies exist in the world today?
4. What are the five most common types of social interaction?
5. What is a bureaucracy, and how does it function?

KEY TERMS

The following terms, while not the only terms emphasized in the chapter, are basic to your understanding of sociology. Determine the meaning of each term, either by using the Glossary or by watching for context clues as you read the chapter.

social structure	social institution	formal organization
status	group	bureaucracy
role	reference group	voluntary association

Humans are social beings—we live and work in groups and interact in predictable ways. As anthropologists Lionel Tiger and Robin Fox have noted, "we are none of us truly isolated; we are connected to one another by a web of regularities and by a host of shared, deep-seated certainties." In other words, society has a structure that guides human interaction. This structure helps people know what is expected of them in most social situations and what they can expect from others. It also ensures that the general nature of society remains relatively stable from one generation to the next, even though the actual members of society change.

In this chapter, we will examine the nature of social structure. We will see how the social structure provides society with a relatively stable framework that promotes continuity. And because social behavior is by definition group behavior, we will explore the characteristics of groups, from small primary groups such as the family to complex bureaucracies. In the course of the chapter, we also will examine the types of societies that exist in the world today.

1 BUILDING BLOCKS OF SOCIAL STRUCTURE

As the above introduction indicates, social structure is what gives society its enduring characteristics and what makes patterns of human interaction predictable. Although sociologists have viewed society as a system of interrelated parts—as a structure—since the time of Auguste Comte, social structure as a concept often has been very loosely defined. Throughout this textbook, when we speak of **social structure,** we will mean the network of interrelated statuses and roles that guides human interaction. A **status** is a socially defined position in a group or in a society. Each status has attached to it one or more roles. A **role** is the behavior—the rights and obligations—expected of someone occupying a particular status.

Statuses

Regardless of whether a sociologist chooses to focus on small groups or on society as a whole, the concept of status is central to the understanding of social structure. Each individual in society occupies several statuses. An individual can be, for example, a teacher, a father, a husband, an African American, and a church deacon all at the same time. A status is a way of defining the relationships among individuals in society in terms of their rights and obligations.

Ascribed and Achieved Statuses. People do not come to occupy all statuses in the same manner. Some statuses are assigned, while others are gained through effort. A status that is assigned according to standards that are beyond a person's control is called an **ascribed status.** Ascribed statuses are not based on an individual's abilities, efforts, or accomplishments. Instead, ascribed statuses are based on a person's inherited traits or are assigned automatically when a person reaches a certain age. You hold the status of teenager or young adult, for instance, because of your age. You did nothing to earn this status. Neither can you change it. Other examples of ascribed statuses include gender (whether you are male or female), family heritage, and race.

Some statuses are acquired on the basis of a person's direct effort, often through competition.

A status that is acquired by an individual on the basis of some special skill, knowledge, or ability is called an **achieved status.** If you are on the basketball team, you are a member because you have the necessary skills. If you have the lead part in the school play, you hold the status because your acting skills have been judged superior to those of other students who auditioned for the part. Unlike the case of ascribed statuses, people have some control over their achieved statuses. In a complex society such as the United States, the list of achieved statuses is almost endless. For example, all occupations are achieved statuses. Other achieved statuses include being a spouse, parent, high school or college graduate, or athlete.

In addition to being a granddaughter, this girl also is a student, a friend, and a sister. Each of these statuses has a different role.

Master Status. As we have already mentioned, each of us holds many statuses. But for most people, one status is particularly important. The status that plays the greatest role in shaping a person's life and determining his or her social identity is called a **master status.**

A master status can be either achieved or ascribed. In the United States, an adult's master status tends to be assigned on the basis of achieved characteristics. Occupation, wealth, marital status, or parenthood, for example, can serve as a master status.

A person's master status changes over the course of his or her life. During the teenage years, being a student or athlete often serves as a master status. During much of adulthood, on the other hand, master status usually is based on one's occupation. Finally, in late adulthood, volunteer work, hobbies, grandparenthood, or past accomplishments serve as a person's master status.

Roles

Statuses serve merely as social categories. Roles are the component of social structure that bring these statuses to life. You play many different roles every day. At home you play the role associated with the status of son or daughter. At school you play the role associated with the status of student. You may also perform the roles that go along with being a reporter on the school newspaper or a member of the gymnastics team.

All of the roles you perform have reciprocal roles. **Reciprocal roles** are corresponding roles that define the patterns of interaction between related statuses. One cannot, for instance, fulfill the role associated with the status of husband without having someone else perform the role that goes along with the status of wife. Other statuses that require reciprocal roles include doctor–patient, athlete–coach, friend–friend, employee–employer, leader–follower, and sales-clerk–customer.

Role Expectations and Role Performance. Ideally, when people interact with one another, their behavior corresponds to the particular roles they are playing. The socially determined behaviors expected of a person performing a role are called **role expectations.** Doctors, for example, are expected to treat their patients with skill and care. Parents are expected to provide emotional and physical security for their children. Police officers are expected to uphold the law.

In reality, people's **role performance**—their actual role behavior—often does not match the behavior expected by society. Some doctors do not give their patients the best possible care. Some parents mistreat their children. In some cases, the problem arises because role behaviors considered appropriate in a subgroup are considered inappropriate in the larger society. Even when trying to fulfill a role in the manner expected by society, it is often difficult to achieve a close match between actual performance and expectations. This is partly due to the fact that each of us is asked to perform many roles, some of them contradictory.

Role Conflict and Role Strain. Even within a single status, there are many roles to perform. Sociologists call the different roles attached to a single status a **role set.** Each of us, because we hold more than one status, must deal with many role sets in our daily lives. The often-contradictory expectations within and between our role sets can lead to role conflict and role strain.

Role conflict occurs when fulfilling the role expectations of one status makes it difficult to fulfill the role expectations of another status. In other words, role conflict occurs between statuses. Being a good employee, for example, sometimes interferes with being a good parent. **Role strain,** on the other hand, occurs when a person has difficulty meeting the role expectations of a single status. The boss who must maintain the morale of her workers while getting them to work long periods of overtime is likely to experience role strain.

Social Institutions

As we have mentioned, it is possible to examine social structure on either a group level or a societal level. When social structure is examined on a societal level, attention is focused on social institutions. A **social institution** is a system of statuses, roles, values, and norms that is organized to satisfy one or more of the basic needs of society. These basic needs include providing physical and emotional support for members of society, transmitting knowledge, producing goods and services, and maintaining social control.

Sociologists traditionally have recognized five major social institutions: family, economy, politics, education, and religion. In recent years, however, several new social institutions have emerged, among them science and sport. We will examine each of these social institutions in Unit 4.

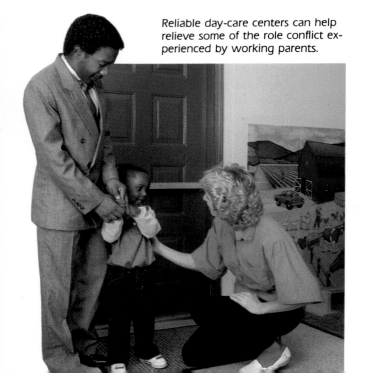

Reliable day-care centers can help relieve some of the role conflict experienced by working parents.

SECTION 1 REVIEW

DEFINE social structure, master status, role, reciprocal roles, role set, social institution

1. *Comprehending Ideas* *(a)* What is a status? *(b)* Describe the difference between an ascribed status and an achieved status.

2. *Comparing Ideas* What is the difference between role expectations and role performance?

3. *Contrasting Ideas* How does role conflict differ from role strain?

2 THE STRUCTURE OF GROUPS AND SOCIETIES

The human interaction that is the focus of role behavior takes place in groups and within the context of a society. In this section, we will examine the features of group structure and the characteristics of the most common types of groups. We also will explore the characteristics of the various types of societies that exist in the world.

What Is a Group?

A **group** is a set of two or more people who interact on the basis of shared expectations and who possess some degree of common identity. A group can be very small—two people on a date, for example. Or it can be very large—500 soldiers at boot camp. A group can be very intimate, as in the case of the family. Or it can be very formal, as in the case of people attending a conference.

Our definition sets forth four requirements for a group. First, there must be two or more people.

Even if you are with just one other person, you are part of a group. Second, there must be interaction. If you exchange greetings with a friend in the hall at school, interaction has taken place. Interaction occurs whenever the actions of one person cause another person or persons to act. Third, the members of the group must have shared expectations. Fourth, the members must possess some sense of common identity.

The last three requirements—interaction, shared expectations, and a common identity—are the factors that distinguish a group from an aggregate or a social category. When people gather in the same place at the same time but lack organization or lasting patterns of interaction, they form an **aggregate.** People waiting to board a plane or standing in a ticket line at the movies are examples of aggregates. In the case of social categories, it is not necessary for the people to interact in any way. A **social category** simply is a means of classifying people according to a shared trait or a common status. Students, women, and the elderly are examples of social categories.

Groups can differ in many ways. Three of the most common ways in which groups differ are in terms of the length of time they remain together, their organizational structure, and their size.

Not only do these girls form a group, but they also are part of the social category of teenagers.

The members of this Native American family make up a primary group. It is within the family that most people first learn about their cultural backgrounds. Because family relationships are long term and intimate, the lessons learned within this primary group are particularly important.

Time. Some groups we participate in meet once and never meet again. Other groups, such as the family, exist for many years. Most groups fall somewhere in between these two extremes. Regardless of the type of group, however, contact is not continuous. Few people spend 24 hours a day with their families, for example. Instead, family members meet as a group during different periods of the day, such as at breakfast or dinner.

Organization. The organization of groups can be either formal or informal. In a formal group, the structure, goals, and activities of the group are clearly defined. In an informal group, on the other hand, there is no official structure or established rules of conduct. The student government in your school is a formal group. All meetings are conducted according to specific rules. The goals of the group are stated in the constitution, and norms for all occasions are listed in the bylaws. A set of officers carries out specific roles in the group. Your circle of friends, on the other hand, would be an example of an informal group.

Size. Groups also can vary in size. Some groups are very small, while other groups are enormous. The smallest group possible, a group with two members, is called a **dyad.** In a dyad, each member of the group has direct control over the group's existence. If one member leaves the group, the group ends. Consequently, decision making in a dyad can be difficult. If the two members fail to agree, one member must convince the other member to change his or her position or the group may cease to exist.

According to sociologist Georg Simmel, a major change occurs in groups when group size increases from two to three members. A three-person group is called a **triad.** In a triad, the group takes on a life of its own, independent of any individual member. No one person can disband the group. Also, decision making in a triad usually is easier than in a dyad, since two-against-one alliances can form in cases of disagreement.

How large can a small group be? Sociologists consider a **small group** to be a group with few enough members that everyone is able to interact on a face-to-face basis. They have found that 15 is about the largest number of people that can work well in one group. When the group is larger than that, the members have a tendency to sort themselves into smaller groups.

Types of Groups

We all are members of different types of groups. Among the most common types of groups are primary groups, secondary groups, reference groups, ingroups, and outgroups.

Primary and Secondary Groups. One of the easiest ways to classify groups is on the basis of the degree of intimacy that occurs among group members. When social scientists study group relationships, they often start with a description of the two opposite extremes. Between the extremes they run a line called a *continuum.* Group relations can then be arranged on this line so that the continuum shows the range of possible relationships. One such continuum shows the range of primary–secondary group relationships.

At the left-hand extreme of the continuum are primary groups. A **primary group** is a small group of people who interact over a relatively long period of time on a direct and personal basis. In primary group relationships, the entire personality of the individual is taken into account. The relationships are intimate and often face to face. Communication is deep and intense, the structure is informal, and personal satisfactions are of primary importance. Family relationships probably are the most primary of all our group relationships.

On the opposite end of the continuum are secondary groups. A **secondary group** is a group in which interaction is impersonal and temporary in nature. Secondary group relationships involve a reaction to only a part of the individual's personality. The person's importance to the group lies in the function that he or she performs in the group. Secondary group relationships also tend to be casual and limited in personal involvement. An individual can be replaced easily by anyone who can carry out the specific tasks needed to achieve the group's goals. This characteristic is particularly important because secondary groups generally are organized around specific goals.

Suppose, for example, an employer hires someone to unload sacks of cement from railroad cars. The employer is not concerned about the person's entire personality, whether he or she attends religious services regularly, has leisure-time activities, or has gleaming white teeth. The employer is interested only in one aspect of the employee's personality—his or her ability to unload the bags of cement. If the person cannot handle the responsibilities of the job, the employer is likely to find someone else who can.

Actually, many of our relationships probably fall closer to the middle than to the ends of the continuum. And this is the purpose of the continuum—to show the degree to which a relationship possesses either of the extreme characteristics. The diagram on this page shows how we can place our various relationships on the primary–secondary continuum.

It also is possible for primary and secondary relationships to exist in the same group. In most secondary groups to which we belong, we develop some primary relationships. On the job, for example, many relationships are quite formal and functional. Employees have specific tasks to perform. Most people, however, form primary relationships with some of the people at work. They do this simply because they enjoy being with these people.

Reference Groups. People usually perform their social roles and judge their own behaviors with reference to the standards set by a particular group or groups. They do not even have to belong to the group. As long as people identify with the group's standards and attitudes, the group influences their behavior. Any group with whom individuals identify and whose attitudes and values they often adopt is called a **reference group.**

Friendship groups or school clubs serve as reference groups for many students. Members of a particular occupation often serve as reference groups for adults. As children grow up, or as adults adjust to changing social conditions, they often change their reference groups. The choice of reference groups is particularly important because groups can have both positive and negative effects on behavior.

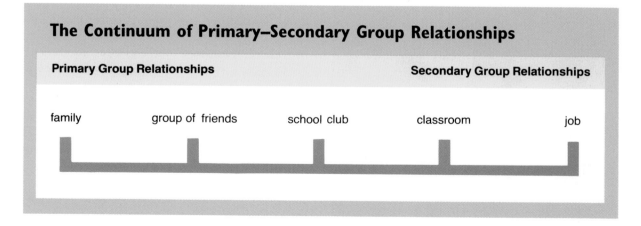

The Continuum of Primary–Secondary Group Relationships

Primary Group Relationships

Secondary Group Relationships

family   group of friends   school club   classroom   job

Ingroups and Outgroups. All groups have boundaries—methods of distinguishing between members and nonmembers. When a group's boundaries are clearly marked, group members tend to think in terms of ingroups and outgroups. The group that a person belongs to and identifies with is called an **ingroup.** Any group that the person does not belong to or identify with is called an **outgroup.** Both primary and secondary groups can serve as ingroups and outgroups.

Most ingroups exhibit three characteristics. First, group members tend to separate themselves from other groups through the use of symbols. For example, groups often use names, slogans, clothing, or badges as forms of identification. Second, members view themselves in terms of positive images, while they view outgroups in terms of negative images. Finally, ingroups generally compete with outgroups, even to the point of engaging in conflict.

Social Networks. We all belong to more than one group and interact with more than one set of people. The web of relationships that is formed by the sum total of a person's interactions with other people is termed a **social network.** Social networks include both direct and indirect relationships. Direct relationships consist of the people we interact with in our primary and secondary group relationships. Indirect relationships include the people we know or who know us but with whom we have little or no interaction, such as friends of a friend.

Unlike actual groups, social networks do not have clear boundaries and do not give rise to a common sense of identity. They do, however, provide us with a feeling of community and with opportunities for career and social advancement. In some instances, knowing the "right" person can mean the difference between getting and not getting a job. Social networks also provide a support system that can help us through stressful periods. The Case Study on page 75 discusses the role of social networks among the elderly.

Types of Societies

Societies can be classified in a variety of ways. One of the most common ways in which sociologists classify societies is by their subsistence strategies. A **subsistence strategy** is the way in which a society uses technology to provide for the needs of its members.

When societies are classified by subsistence strategy, it is possible to place them on a continuum from simple to complex. At the far left of the continuum are those societies in which the majority of the population is engaged in meeting basic needs, particularly the need for food. The **division of labor**—the specialization by individuals or groups in the performance of specific economic activities—is very simple in these societies. As we move toward the right on the continuum, subsistence strategies become more efficient. Consequently, it takes fewer people to provide the necessary food and basic goods. This allows the division of labor to become more complex as individuals pursue new occupations.

Sociologists classify societies as either preindustrial, industrial, or postindustrial on the basis of subsistence strategies. In a **preindustrial society,** food production—which is carried out through the use of human and animal labor—is the main economic activity. Preindustrial societies can be subdivided into hunting and gathering, pastoral, horticultural, or agricultural, depending on

Uniforms are an effective way of expressing ingroup identification.

The Social Networks of the Elderly

We have defined a social network as the web of relationships that is formed by the sum total of an individual's interactions with other people. The people who make up a social network—family, friends, neighbors, business associates, and members of the community—engage in a series of reciprocal exchanges, sometimes offering help and support and at other times receiving it.

The composition of a person's social network changes over time. As an adolescent, family and friends tend to occupy the majority of positions in a person's social network. As an adult, neighbors, business associates, and members of the community play increasingly important roles.

The social networks of the elderly have long been of interest to sociologists. The general public sometimes views the elderly as being dependent on society. Their participation in society is viewed as a one-way receipt of services rather than as a reciprocal exchange. Sociologists have found, however, that as a group the elderly have much to offer. Most of the elderly successfully play out the many roles that are associated with being family members, friends, neighbors, good citizens, and community volunteers.

Strong social networks are extremely important for the elderly. Most elderly people wish to remain independent as long as possible. One way in which independence can be maintained is through establishing reciprocal networks with their families. In this exchange process, the elderly receive affection, comfort, help, and support from their families. In return, the elderly provide help to their children in the form of gifts and money, baby-sitting services, affection, and advice. Furthermore, grandparents, particularly grandmothers, often become the center of family activities, serving to hold the family together.

Another way in which the elderly maintain their independence is through the establishment of social networks with friends and neighbors. These networks are based on a mutual system of exchange. All members of the network socialize with one another, share feelings, and offer mutual support and assistance. Studies have shown that the elderly depend on their friends and neighbors for day-to-day help, turning to their families only in times of emergency or when they need major assistance.

Many elderly people also remain active in community life. For instance, they form networks with many volunteer associations, such as clubs, churches, and synagogues. The Foster Grandparent program is a voluntary association that has proved to be beneficial to children and "grandparents" alike. Research has documented the positive effects that older volunteers can have on the emotional and intellectual development of children.

Community service can play a very important role in the life of the elderly. Community-based social networks can help older people develop new roles when their former roles of workers or full-time parents have ended. The skills that people used on the job, for example, often can be put to valuable use in the community on a volunteer basis. Two organizations that rely on older individuals as a source of volunteers are the Retired Senior Volunteer Program (RSVP) and the Service Corps of Retired Executives (SCORE). RSVP places volunteers in settings such as schools, hospitals, libraries, courtrooms, day-care centers, and nursing homes. SCORE volunteers offer management assistance to small businesses and community organizations.

As we move into the twenty-first century, the social networks of the elderly will take on added importance. Already in some places around the nation, the elderly are serving as a reliable pool of part-time workers. This trend will undoubtedly continue as our population continues to age.

The Fulani of northern Africa are pastoralists who rely on domesticated animals for subsistence.

their level of technology and mode of subsistence. In an **industrial society,** the mechanized production of goods is the main economic activity. In a **postindustrial society,** on the other hand, economic activity centers on the production of information and the provision of services.

Hunting and Gathering Societies.

The main form of subsistence in a **hunting and gathering society** is the daily collection of wild plants and animals. Because hunters and gatherers must move around frequently in search of food, they do not build permanent villages or create a wide variety of artifacts. The need for mobility also serves to limit the size of hunting and gathering societies. Such societies generally consist of fewer than 40 people and almost never exceed 100 people. Statuses within the group are relatively equal and decisions are reached through general agreement. The family forms the main social unit, with most societal members being related by birth or by marriage. This type of organization means that most social functions—including production and education—are carried out by the family.

Pastoral Societies.

Pastoralism represents a slightly more efficient form of subsistence. Rather than searching for food on a daily basis, members of a **pastoral society** rely on domesticated herd animals to meet the bulk of their dietary needs. Because the size of herds can be increased over time, pastoralists are able to produce more food than is immediately needed. Increased food supplies enable pastoral societies to support larger populations. Surplus food also leads to the development of economic and political institutions.

Surplus food gives rise to an economic institution by creating inequalities in wealth and by providing goods that can be traded with other societies. A political institution arises as some individuals acquire power through increased wealth. The transmission of wealth and power from generation to generation within a family forms the basis of hereditary chieftainships, the typical form of government in pastoral societies.

Most pastoral societies move regularly in search of new grazing land for their animals. In some instances, all members of the society move with the herds, trading with other societies for the crops needed to supplement their diets. In other instances, some members of the society remain in villages where they grow their own crops.

Horticultural Societies.

Vegetables grown in garden plots that have been cleared from the jungle or forest provide the main source of food in a **horticultural society.** The most common technique used to clear plots is the "slash and burn" method. In this method, the wild vegetation is cut and burned and the ashes are used as fertilizer. After clearing a plot, horticulturalists cultivate the land for one or more seasons. Cultivation is carried out using human labor and simple tools such as hoes and digging sticks.

When the land becomes barren, the horticulturalists clear a new plot and leave the old plot to revert to its natural state. After several years, they return to the original plot and begin the process again. By rotating their garden plots, horticulturalists can stay in one area for a fairly long period of time. This allows them to build semipermanent or permanent villages. The size of the villages depends on the amount of land available for farming. Villages can range from as few as 30 people to as many as 2,000 people.

Economic and political institutions are better developed in horticultural societies than they are in pastoral societies. This is due in large part to the more settled nature of horticultural life. Surplus food once again leads to the accumulation of wealth and different levels of power within society. Thus hereditary chieftainships also are characteristic of horticultural societies, as is trade. In more advanced horticultural societies, trade and wars between societies serve to strengthen the economic and political institutions.

Food surpluses also mean that some people are freed from the need to produce food. Specialized roles thus are a part of horticultural life. Among the most important roles are traders, shamans (religious leaders), and craftspeople. Role specialization, in conjunction with the relatively permanent village life, allows horticulturalists to create a wide variety of artifacts.

Agricultural Societies. In an **agricultural society,** draft animals and plows are used in the tilling of fields. This technological innovation allows agriculturalists to plant more crops than is possible when only human labor is used. Crop yields are further increased by irrigation. Unlike horticulturalists, who must wait for the rainy season before planting, agriculturalists can plant at various times during the year and bring water to the fields through canals. In addition, irrigation makes it possible for a field to be used year after year. Terracing—the practice of cutting fields into the side of hills—also increases crop yields by making additional lands available for farming.

Higher crop yields mean that agricultural societies can support populations that run into the millions. Higher crop yields also mean that fewer people are needed to work the fields. Consequently, although most people still work in food production, a sizable percentage of the population is able to engage in specialized roles. Specialization, in turn, leads to the development of cities, as individuals engaged in specialized roles come together in central areas.

As the number of cities within a society increases, power often becomes concentrated in the hands of a single individual. This power is transferred from generation to generation, usually in the form of a hereditary monarchy. In more complex agricultural societies, the government appears for the first time as a separate institution. The tendency for agricultural societies to engage in warfare means that a formal military structure also arises. To assist in warfare, agricultural societies often construct roads and build navies.

All of these factors work together to increase trade in agricultural societies. Increased trade, in turn, leads to a number of significant cultural advances. To facilitate trade, for instance, **barter**— the practice of exchanging one good for another— is replaced by the use of money as the medium of exchange. In addition, a system of writing is developed to assist the government, landowners, and traders in keeping records.

It is with agricultural societies that sharp status differences first arise. Most people in an agricultural society fall into one of two groups: landowners or peasants. These two groups are at opposite ends of the social ladder. The small group of landowners controls the wealth and power in society. The large peasant group provides the labor on which the landowners' wealth and power depend.

Industrial Societies. In industrial societies, the emphasis shifts from the production of food to the production of manufactured goods. This shift is made possible by changes in production methods. In preindustrial societies, food and goods are produced using human and animal labor. Production is slow and the number of goods that can be produced is limited by the number of available workers. In industrial societies, on the other hand, the bulk of production is carried out through the use of machines. Thus production can be increased by adding more machines or by developing new technologies.

The use of machines in the production process affects all features of industrial society, beginning with the size of the population and the nature of the economy. Industrialization affects population size by increasing the amount of food that can be produced. The more food that is produced, the more people the society can support. Industrialization changes the nature of the economy by reducing the demand for agricultural laborers. These workers are free to transfer their labors to the production of goods. The size of the industrial work force increases as new technologies make it possible to manufacture a wider variety of goods.

Industrialization also changes the location of work activities. In preindustrial societies, most economic activities are carried out within the bounds of the family setting. With the coming of machines, however, production moves from the home to factories. This, in turn, encourages **urbanization**—the concentration of the population in cities. People move off the farms and to the cities to be near the major sources of employment. As a result, much daily interaction takes place in secondary groups.

In addition to changing the location of work, industrialization changes the nature of work. In preindustrial societies, craftspeople are responsible for manufacturing an entire product. With the rise of machines, however, the goal becomes efficiency. To increase efficiency, the production process is divided into a series of specific tasks, with each task being assigned to a specific person. Thus an individual seldom completes an entire product. Instead, the worker performs the same task over and over. Although this greatly increases productivity, it serves to reduce the level of skill required of most workers and tends to create boredom on the job.

Industrialization also changes the role of the family in society. In preindustrial societies, the family is the primary social institution. Production and education, for instance, are the responsibility of the family. This is not true in industrial societies, however. Not only does production take place outside the bounds of the family, so does education. The need for mass literacy leads industrial societies to establish programs of mandatory education. The role of religion in society also is changed by industrialization. In advanced industrial societies, religious beliefs often must compete with the values and beliefs presented by science, education, and the government.

One of the positive effects of industrialization is the freedom to compete for social position. In preindustrial societies, most social statuses are ascribed. Thus it is difficult for individuals to work their way up the social ladder. In industrial societies, on the other hand, most statuses are achieved. As a result, individuals have more control over their positions in the social structure.

Postindustrial Societies. We usually think of the United States as an industrial society. And without a doubt, the nation does produce a wide range of goods. But in terms of the major emphasis in the economy, the United States, like many Western nations and Japan, actually is a postindustrial society. In a postindustrial society, much of the economy is involved in the production of information and the provision of services. In the United States, for instance, less than 3 percent of

Industrialization increases efficiency, but sometimes can result in worker boredom.

the work force is employed in agriculture and less than 26 percent is employed in the production of goods.

Many significant social changes result from the transition from an industrial society to a postindustrial society. The standard of living, for instance, becomes higher as wages increase for much of the population and as science and technology improve the quality of life. A wider range of employment opportunities and an increased emphasis on education also affect the standard of living by making it easier for people to move up the social ladder through career advancement.

In general, postindustrial societies place strong emphasis on the roles of science and education in society. The future is seen as being dependent on technological advances. The rights of individuals and the search for personal fulfillment also take on added importance. Belief in these rights leads to a strong emphasis on social equality and democracy. We will examine the characteristics of postindustrialism more thoroughly in Chapter 13.

Contrasting Societies. Sociologists have long been interested in how the social structures of preindustrial and industrial societies differ. In 1893, for instance, Emile Durkheim introduced the concepts of mechanical and organic solidarity to describe the types of social relationships found in preindustrial and industrial societies. According to Durkheim, preindustrial societies are held together by **mechanical solidarity**—the close-knit social relationships that result when a small group of people share the same values and perform the same tasks.

As the division of labor within societies becomes more complex, mechanical solidarity gives way to the organic solidarity that is characteristic of industrial societies. **Organic solidarity** is the impersonal social relationships that arise with increased job specialization. This increased specialization means that individuals no longer can provide for all of their own needs. Thus they become dependent on others for aspects of their survival. As a result, many societal relationships are based on need rather than on shared values.

The German sociologist Ferdinand Tönnies (TURN-yeas) (1855–1936) also was interested in the ways in which simple and complex societies differ. Tönnies was able to distinguish two ideal types of societies based on the structure of social relationships and the degree of shared values among societal members. He called these two types of societies *Gemeinschaft* (ga-MINE-shoft), which is the German word for "community," and *Gesellschaft* (ga-ZELL-shoft), which is the German word for "society."

Gemeinschaft refers to societies in which most members know one another. Relationships in such societies are close and activities center on the family and the community. In a *Gemeinschaft,* people share a strong sense of group solidarity. A preindustrial society and a rural village in a more complex society are examples of a *Gemeinschaft.*

In a *Gesellschaft,* on the other hand, most social relationships are based on need rather than on emotion. Thus relationships in a *Gesellschaft* are impersonal and often temporary. Traditional values generally are weak in such societies, and individual goals are more important than group goals. A modern urban society such as the United States is an example of a *Gesellschaft.*

SECTION 2 REVIEW

DEFINE dyad, triad, small group, social network

1. **Identifying Ideas** **(a)** What is a group? **(b)** Describe three of the most common features that are used to distinguish among groups.

2. **Organizing Ideas** What are the main characteristics of the five types of groups discussed in this section?

3. **Summarizing Ideas** List the characteristics of hunting and gathering, pastoral, horticultural, agricultural, industrial, and postindustrial societies.

4. **Understanding Ideas** **(a)** Describe what is meant by mechanical solidarity and organic solidarity. **(b)** What characteristics define a society as being either *Gemeinschaft* or *Gesellschaft?*

3 TYPES OF SOCIAL INTERACTION

Interaction can take many forms. Some forms of interaction help to stabilize the social structure. Other forms help to promote change. Among the most common forms of social interaction are exchange, competition, conflict, cooperation, and accommodation. These five types of interaction take place in societies throughout the world.

Exchange

Almost all daily interaction involves exchange. Whenever individuals, groups, or societies interact in an effort to receive a reward or a return for their actions, an **exchange** has taken place. Dating, friendship, family life, and politics all involve

Individuals in relationships do not always communicate well. According to exchange theory, if these people find that the costs of their relationship outweigh its rewards, they are likely to bring the relationship to an end. Exchange theorists believe that most social interactions are based on attempts to maximize rewards and reduce costs. Rewards and costs may be emotional as well as material.

exchanges. **Reciprocity**—the idea that if you do something for someone, they owe you something in return—is at the basis of exchange. Rewards can be both material and nonmaterial.

The importance of exchange in daily interactions has led to the emergence of **exchange theory.** Exchange theorists believe that people are motivated by self-interests in their interactions with other people. In other words, people do things for rewards. Behavior that is rewarded tends to be repeated. When the costs of an interaction outweigh the rewards, however, individuals are likely to end the relationship. According to exchange theorists, most of social life can be explained as the attempt to maximize rewards while minimizing costs.

Competition

You apply for a job at a local store to work after school and on weekends. There are many applicants, but there is only one job opening. You are in competition. **Competition** occurs when two or more persons or groups oppose each other to achieve a goal that only one can attain.

Competition is a common feature of Western societies. It is, for example, the cornerstone of the capitalist economic system and the democratic form of government. Advancement in business, school, and sports is achieved through competition. As long as it follows accepted rules of conduct, competition is viewed by most sociologists as a positive means of motivating people to perform society's needed roles. On the negative side, however, competition also can lead to psychological stress, a lack of cooperation in social relationships, inequality, and even conflict.

Conflict

The main emphasis in competition is on achieving the goal. With conflict, on the other hand, the emphasis is on defeating the opponent. **Conflict** is the deliberate attempt to control by force, oppose, harm, or resist the will of another person or persons. Unlike competition, conflict has few rules of conduct and even these often are ignored. Conflict may range from the deliberate snubbing of a classmate to the killing of an enemy.

For Better or For Worse®

by Lynn Johnston

Sociologist Georg Simmel identified four sources of conflict: wars, conflict within groups, legal disputes, and clashes over ideology, such as religion or politics. Sometimes conflicts begin as competition. Rival business organizations may first engage in intense competition for customers. As the competition increases, the emphasis shifts from attracting customers to harming the other business. One business, for example, may sell merchandise below cost to try to force the other business into bankruptcy.

Although we tend to think of conflict as negative, some sociologists have pointed out that conflict serves some useful purposes. For instance, conflict reinforces group boundaries and strengthens group loyalty by focusing attention on an outside threat. This also draws attention away from internal problems. Conflict also can lead to social change by bringing problems to the forefront and forcing opposing sides to seek solutions.

Cooperation

The members of an athletic team work together to win the game. The pep club, school band, and student body also work together to help the team win. If, in the end, the team takes a trophy, it will be shared by the entire school. Similarly, the employees of a corporation work together to increase sales for the organization. If their efforts are successful, everyone benefits. In each case, the people involved are cooperating to achieve a desired goal. **Cooperation** occurs when two or more persons or groups work together to achieve a goal that will benefit many people.

Cooperation is the social process that gets things done. No group can complete its tasks or achieve its goals without cooperation from its members. Cooperation often is used along with other forms of interaction. Competition, for example, may be used along with cooperation to motivate members to work harder for the group. Individuals who go out for a team sport, for instance, often compete with one another to make the varsity team.

Accommodation

In many of our interactions we neither cooperate nor engage in conflict. We simply accommodate each other—we give a little and we take a little. **Accommodation** is a state of balance between cooperation and conflict. One way to remember this type of interaction is by thinking about a motel accommodation. The owner of the motel is accommodating us by letting us stay for the night in exchange for $60. If the owner were cooperating with us, we would be able to stay for free. On the other hand, if the owner refused to let us stay under any condition, we would be in a conflict situation.

Accommodation can take a number of different forms. One of these forms is *compromise*. A compromise occurs when two parties both give up

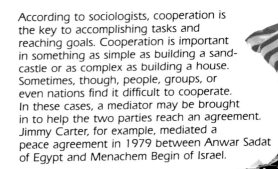

According to sociologists, cooperation is the key to accomplishing tasks and reaching goals. Cooperation is important in something as simple as building a sandcastle or as complex as building a house. Sometimes, though, people, groups, or even nations find it difficult to cooperate. In these cases, a mediator may be brought in to help the two parties reach an agreement. Jimmy Carter, for example, mediated a peace agreement in 1979 between Anwar Sadat of Egypt and Menachem Begin of Israel.

something to come to a mutual agreement. Say, for example, that you and a friend want to see different movies. To compromise, you might choose a third movie that you both would like. Another form of accommodation is the *truce*. A truce brings a halt to the conflict until a compromise can be reached. Sometimes, when two parties cannot agree on a compromise, they will use *mediation*. They will call in a third party who acts as adviser and counselor in helping the two parties reach an agreement. Or they may use *arbitration*. In arbitration, a third party makes a decision that is binding on both parties.

SECTION 3 REVIEW

DEFINE reciprocity, exchange theory

IDENTIFY Georg Simmel

1. **Summarizing Ideas** List and describe the five most common forms of social interaction.

2. **Comprehending Ideas** Describe the four forms of accommodation.

4 THE STRUCTURE OF FORMAL ORGANIZATIONS

Sociologists use a special term to designate a large, complex secondary group that has been established to achieve specific goals. Such a secondary group is called a **formal organization.** Formal organizations include a variety of groupings such as schools, businesses, government agencies, religious organizations, youth organizations, political organizations, volunteer associations, labor unions, and professional associations.

Many formal organizations have come to be structured in a form that is known as a bureaucracy. A **bureaucracy** is a ranked authority structure that operates according to specific rules and procedures. The term comes from the French word *bureau,* which referred to the cloth covering the desks of French government officials in the 1700s. Weber believed that bureaucracies arise in industrial societies because of an increasing tendency toward rationalization. **Rationalization** refers to the process by which every feature of human behavior becomes subject to calculation, measurement, and control.

Today we use the word bureaucracy to refer to any organization that has many departments or bureaus. If you have ever applied for a driver's license or been admitted to a large hospital, you have had to deal with a bureaucracy.

Weber's Model of Bureaucracies

The German sociologist Max Weber developed a model of bureaucracies that still is widely used by sociologists today. According to Weber's model, bureaucracies have the following characteristics:

- *A division of labor.* The work is divided among specialists in various positions. Each specialist is expected to perform specific duties.
- *A ranking of authority.* There are clear-cut lines of responsibility, with each individual responsible to a supervisor at a higher level.
- *Employment based on formal qualifications.* Specific qualifications are given for each job, and individuals are hired on the basis of tests, education, or previous experience.
- *Rules and regulations.* There are objective rules, regulations, and routine procedures that specify the exact responsibilities and authority of each person on the staff.
- *Specific lines of promotion and advancement.* It is assumed that employees expect a career with the organization. Thus there are clear-cut lines of promotion and advancement. Among the rewards for remaining with the organization are job security and seniority.

Organizational structure, specialization of roles, skilled workers, and officially stated rules and regulations make modern-day hospitals highly efficient bureaucracies.

Organization of One Public School System

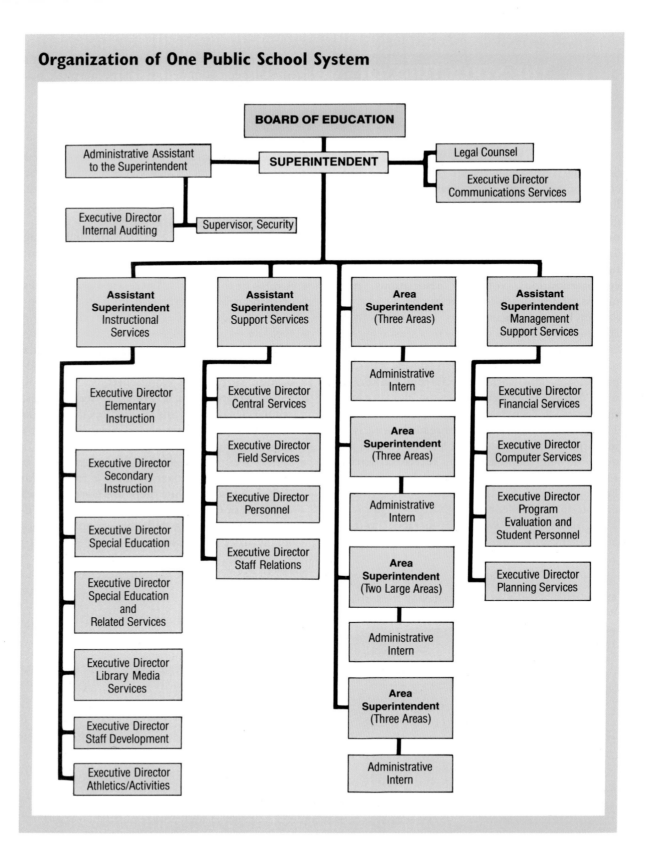

BOARD OF EDUCATION

Administrative Assistant to the Superintendent

SUPERINTENDENT

Legal Counsel

Executive Director Communications Services

Executive Director Internal Auditing

Supervisor, Security

Assistant Superintendent Instructional Services

Executive Director Elementary Instruction

Executive Director Secondary Instruction

Executive Director Special Education

Executive Director Special Education and Related Services

Executive Director Library Media Services

Executive Director Staff Development

Executive Director Athletics/Activities

Assistant Superintendent Support Services

Executive Director Central Services

Executive Director Field Services

Executive Director Personnel

Executive Director Staff Relations

Area Superintendent (Three Areas)

Administrative Intern

Area Superintendent (Three Areas)

Administrative Intern

Area Superintendent (Two Large Areas)

Administrative Intern

Area Superintendent (Three Areas)

Administrative Intern

Assistant Superintendent Management Support Services

Executive Director Financial Services

Executive Director Computer Services

Executive Director Program Evaluation and Student Personnel

Executive Director Planning Services

The chart on page 84 shows the bureaucratic organization of a large school system with approximately 85,000 students. Notice how the job titles represent specific duties.

Formal organizations have structures that fit Weber's model in varying degrees. Some organizations, such as certain governmental agencies, fit these characteristics very rigidly. Other organizations, such as voluntary associations, may be much less bureaucratic. A **voluntary association** is a nonprofit association formed to pursue some common interest. Membership in voluntary associations is by choice, and many of the workers tend to be unpaid volunteers. Examples of voluntary associations include amateur sports teams, professional associations, service clubs, and political interest groups.

Relationships in Formal Organizations

The formal and impersonal structure of an organization may have within it an informal structure based on strong primary relationships. For example, the director of sales in a large corporation may play golf every weekend with the director of purchasing. The treasurer and the director of public relations may have gone to the same college and may now attend religious services together. Thus there are primary relationships within the larger impersonal structure.

The importance of primary group relationships in formal organizations was first discovered during a now-classic research project at the Hawthorne plant of the Western Electric Company. The intended purpose of the study, conducted between 1927 and 1932, was to determine how various factors affected worker productivity.

As part of the research, the sociologists studied the interaction of a group of employees assigned the task of wiring complex telephone circuits. Three worker roles were involved—those of wirer, solderer, and inspector. The wirers connected the proper wires together. The solderers then soldered them. And the inspectors examined the completed circuits to make sure they met specifications. The company paid all workers according to the number of circuits, or units, they completed. Management assumed that each worker would try to complete as many units as possible in order to make more money.

In reality, however, this was not the case. An informal structure developed among the workers. Together they decided what the norms would be for a day's production. Those who produced more were called rate busters. Those who produced less were called chiselers. Workers who gave any information to a supervisor were called squealers. Through a system of negative sanctions, those who did not conform to the norms of the group were brought back into line. This informal structure operated independently of the formal structure of the organization and was far more important to the individual workers.

How Effective Are Bureaucracies?

Max Weber stated that the greatest advantage of bureaucracies is that they get things done with speed and efficiency. It has been suggested that bureaucracies are the best way to coordinate large numbers of people to achieve large-scale goals. Production volumes made possible by bureaucracies have offered us an untold amount of material goods at reasonable prices. It also has been suggested that bureaucracies create order by clearly defining job tasks and rewards. They also provide stability, since individuals come and go but the organization continues.

There are, however, some arguments against bureaucracies. One argument states that the purpose of bureaucracies becomes self-continuation, and the goals of individuals may be lost. Some government agencies, for example, continue to exist with very little change, regardless of the particular problems seen by their employees.

Another argument against bureaucracies is that individuals tend to develop bureaucratic personalities. The job becomes a ritual, and creativity is stifled. Rules often take the place of common sense. In his book, *The Peter Principle,* Laurence J. Peter states that in a bureaucracy employees often are promoted beyond their level of competence. Employees who were good at lower-level jobs sometimes are pushed up the bureaucratic ladder into positions for which they may have little ability.

A third complaint about bureaucracies is the "red tape" often involved in dealing with them. Individuals who work for a bureaucracy all play a

Text continues on page 88.

Why Things Seem to Go Wrong

Have you ever bought a new product or appliance only to have it break after you used it a few times? Have you ever been told to stand in the wrong line by a person who you thought understood your problem? Then, after an hour or so, did you find yourself once again waiting in a seemingly endless line to correct a situation that arose in the first place because of someone else's mistake?

Professor Laurence J. Peter describes incidents like these in his book *The Peter Principle*. To what does he attribute such occurrences? Quite simply, he notes:

In a hierarchy every employee tends to rise to his level of incompetence.

In other words, in all organizations in which members are arranged in order of rank, grade, or class, people are promoted into jobs that they are not truly qualified to perform.

Following are two examples of the Peter Principle at work.

CASE A: J.S. Minion

J.S. Minion was a maintenance supervisor in the public works department of Excelsior City. He was a favorite of the senior officials at City Hall. They all praised his constant friendliness.

"I like Minion," said the superintendent of works. "He has good judgment and is always pleasant and agreeable."

This behavior was appropriate for Minion's position. As supervisor, he was not supposed to make policy, so he had no need to disagree with his supervisors.

When the superintendent of works retired, Minion succeeded him. Minion continued to agree with everyone. He passed to his supervisor every suggestion that came from above. The resulting conflicts in policy, and the continual changing of plans, soon demoralized the department. Complaints poured in from the Mayor and other officials, from taxpayers, and from the maintenance-workers' union. Minion still says "Yes" to everyone, and carries messages briskly back and forth between his superiors and his subordinates. Though his title is superintendent, he actually does the work of a messenger. The maintenance department regularly goes above its budget, yet fails to fulfill its program of work. In short, Minion, a competent supervisor, became an incompetent superintendent of works.

CASE B: E. Tinker

E. Tinker was exceptionally hard-working and intelligent as an apprentice at G. Reece Auto Repair Inc. He soon rose to mechanic. In this job he showed outstanding ability in diagnosing obscure faults, and endless patience in correcting them. He was promoted to head of the repair shop.

But there his love of things mechanical and his perfectionism work against him. He accepts any repair job that looks interesting, no matter how busy the shop may be. "We'll work it in somehow," he says.

He will not let a job go until he is fully satisfied with it.

He meddles constantly. He is seldom at his desk. He is usually up to his elbows in a dismantled motor. Meanwhile the mechanic who should be doing the repair stands watching, and other workers sit around waiting to be assigned new tasks. As a result, the shop is always overcrowded with work.

Tinker cannot understand that most of his customers care little about perfection—they want their cars back on time! Tinker cannot understand that most of his workers are less interested in motors than in their paychecks. So Tinker cannot get along with his customers or with his subordinates. He was a competent mechanic, but is now an incompetent supervisor.

After analyzing hundreds of cases of occupational incompetence, Peter formulated his now-famous principle. He also noted that if there are enough ranks in the bureaucracy:

> In time, every post tends to be occupied by an employee who is incompetent to carry out its duties.

If this is the case, how, then, does any work get accomplished? If all of the employees in a bureaucratic organization eventually reach their level of incompetence, why does the structure not collapse? Peter answers that in most systems there are always some employees who have not yet been promoted beyond their capabilities. As a result:

> Work is accomplished by those employees who have not yet reached their level of incompetence.

Applying what you have learned in this article, answer the following questions:

1. Based on your experiences with different organizations, do you agree that in a bureaucracy every employee tends to rise to his or her level of incompetence? Why or why not?

2. Suppose you were working for a company for 10 years. You find out that a co-worker who has been with the company only 5 years has just been promoted. How would you feel? What role do you think seniority should play in promotion decisions? What role should ability play?

Although sociologists consider bureaucracies to be the most efficient type of organizational structure for modern industrial societies, individuals often find them frustrating. Bureaucratic red tape can lead to long lines and time consuming delays.

limited role in the operation of the overall structure. As a result, the knowledge or power of the workers very often is limited as well. This sometimes causes us to become entangled in red tape, or bureaucratic delay. Consequently, we spend a lot of time filling out forms, standing in seemingly endless lines, or being shuffled from one department to another before we accomplish our goals. Many of us know all too well how frustrating it can be to deal with a government agency or a large corporation.

A fourth criticism of bureaucracies involves their tendency to result in oligarchies. In an *oligarchy*, power is concentrated in the hands of a few people. When applied to bureaucracies, the concept refers to the tendency for power to become concentrated in the hands of a few people at the top of the bureaucracy. These people then use their power to promote their own interests over the interests of the organization. Sociologist Robert Michels called this tendency of organizations to become increasingly dominated by small groups of people the **iron law of oligarchy.**

Another interesting criticism of bureaucracies has become known as Parkinson's Law. This law states that "work expands to fill the time available for its completion." The following is an example of how Parkinson's Law works in a bureaucratic structure.

Assume that a civil servant is overworked. The person can solve the problem in one of three ways: (1) The person can resign. (2) The person can cut the work in half by sharing it with a new colleague. (3) The person can demand the assistance of two subordinates. Parkinson's Law says that the individual will always choose the third alternative. The first alternative is unacceptable because resigning will mean losing pension, medical, and other benefits. The second alternative is unacceptable because people who gain a new colleague then have a rival for promotion. If, however, people have two subordinates, then their job looks more important because they have control over two individuals. There must be *two* subordinates so that each is kept in line by fear of the other person's promotion.

Eventually one of the subordinates will complain about being overworked. Then that subordinate will need two subordinates. Naturally, if one subordinate gets two subordinates, the other subordinate must have two subordinates. Our civil servant soon has six subordinates. This should ensure a promotion. But now our civil servant is more overworked than ever before, because all six of the subordinates are sending work to be approved. The civil servant has to work overtime to get all the work done but concludes that late hours are a penalty of success.

DEFINE formal organization, rationalization, voluntary association, iron law of oligarchy

1. ***Understanding Ideas*** ***(a)*** What is a bureaucracy? ***(b)*** Describe Max Weber's model of bureaucracies.

2. ***Summarizing Ideas*** Describe the research that first established the importance of primary group relationships in formal organizations.

3. ***Organizing Ideas*** Describe the five criticisms of bureaucracies discussed in this section.

CHAPTER 4   SUMMARY

Social structure is the network of interrelated statuses and roles that guides human interaction. Social structure can be examined on the level of groups or on the societal level. When social structure is examined on the societal level, the emphasis often is on social institutions.

A status is a socially defined position in a group or in a society. Statuses can be either ascribed or achieved. The status that plays the greatest role in shaping a person's life and determining his or her social identity is called a master status.

Each status has attached to it one or more roles. A role is the behavior—the rights and obligations—expected of someone occupying a particular status. All roles have reciprocal roles. The socially determined behaviors expected of a person performing a role are called role expectations. A single status has many roles attached to it. Sociologists call these roles a role set. Contradictory expectations within and between role sets can lead to role conflict and role strain.

Human interaction takes place in groups. The most common types of groups are primary groups, secondary groups, reference groups, ingroups, outgroups, and social networks.

Societies also come in a variety of forms. Sociologists recognize three broad categories of societies: preindustrial, industrial, and postindustrial. Preindustrial societies can be further divided into hunting and gathering, pastoral, horticultural, and agricultural societies.

Social interaction can take many forms. The five most common forms of social interaction are exchange, competition, conflict, cooperation, and accommodation. Accommodation can be reached by means of a compromise, a truce, mediation, or arbitration.

Large, complex secondary groups that have been established to achieve specific goals are called formal organizations. Formal organizations differ in their degree of bureaucratic structure. A bureaucracy is a ranked authority structure that operates according to specific rules and procedures. The German sociologist Max Weber developed a model to help study the structure and function of bureaucracies.

READING ABOUT SOCIOLOGY: Analyzing Journal Articles

One of the principal ways in which social scientists share data is by publishing articles in professional journals. Among the leading journals in sociology are the *American Sociological Review* and *Sociological Quarterly.*

Journal articles are different in tone and style from articles in popular magazines. Journal articles tend to be much more technical than magazine articles. In addition, authors almost always support their arguments by referring to the work of other scholars. Thus journal articles generally contain footnotes or endnotes and references.

How to Analyze a Journal Article

To analyze a journal article, follow these steps.

1. **Identify the main idea.** Many articles begin with a summary, or abstract, of the information presented in the article. If there is no abstract, skim the article for a statement of purpose. Usually, the purpose is stated explicitly: "In this article, we will examine. . . ."

2. **Read the article carefully.** Read the article to identify the main ideas and supporting details. Also read the footnotes and endnotes.

3. **Separate fact from opinion.** Determine whether the ideas presented in the article are based on fact or on opinion. Facts are statements based on the observations or experiences of many people. Opinions are individually held beliefs, which may or may not be based on observation and experience. Although all social scientists hold beliefs about the nature of the social world (called assumptions), these beliefs should be based on fact.

4. **Search for bias or faulty reasoning.** Bias refers to the outlook or point of view of the author. People present biased views when they use facts selectively. Be alert to other explanations for the phenomena. Also be alert to faulty logic. Does the evidence presented by the author support the conclusion?

5. **Come to your own conclusion.** Evaluate the argument by drawing a conclusion of your own or by forming a generalization.

Applying the Skill

Read the excerpt from the article by anthropologist Napoleon A. Chagnon on pages 90–91. The article originally appeared in the February 26, 1988, issue of *Science*. In the original article, Chagnon included an abstract, section headings, charts and graphs, and many more notes and references. They have been omitted here due to space limitations.

In the article, Chagnon describes the characteristics of revenge killing in Yanomamö society. According to Chagnon, revenge killings most often result from fights over women. He suggests that the swift action characteristic of revenge raids serves to discourage future raids. Chagnon backs up his argument with direct observation of the Yanomamö and reinforces his conclusions by citing the works of other scholars.

Practicing the Skill

Select an article from a journal or popular magazine that contains articles of sociological interest. Following the guidelines presented above, prepare a brief written analysis of the article.

Life Histories, Blood Revenge, and Warfare in a Tribal Population

In this article I focus on revenge killing, using data collected among the Yanomamö Indians of southern Venezuela and adjacent portions of northern Brazil (9–11). . . . I am using the terms revenge and blood revenge here to mean a retaliatory killing in which the initial victim's close kinsmen conduct a revenge raid on the members of the current community of the initial killer (14). Al-

IMAGINATION

though Yanomamö raiders always hope to dispatch the original killer, almost any member of the attacked community is a suitable target. . . .

When conflicts emerge each individual must rely on his own skills and coercive abilities and the support of his close kin. Most fights begin over sexual issues: infidelity and suspicion of infidelity, attempts to seduce another man's wife, sexual jealousy, forcible appropriation of women from visiting groups, failure to give a promised girl in marriage, and (rarely) rape (9, 10, 17).

Yanomamö conflicts constitute a graded sequence of increasing seriousness and potential lethality: shouting matches, chest pounding duels, side slapping duels, club fights, fights with axes and machetes, and shooting with bows and arrows with the intent to kill (10). In all but the last case, fights are not intended to and generally do not lead to mortalities. Nevertheless, many fights lead to killings both within and between villages. If killing occurs within the village, the village fissions and the principals of the two new groups then begin raiding each other (17, 18). The most common explanation given for raids (warfare) is revenge (no yuwo) for a previous killing, and the most common explanation for the original cause of the fighting is "women" (suwä tä nowä ha) (9, 10, 17, 19).

At first glance, raids motivated by revenge seem counterproductive. Raiders may inflict deaths on their enemies, but by so doing make themselves and kin prime targets for retaliation. But ethnographic evidence suggests that revenge has an underlying rationality: swift retaliation in kind serves as a deterrent over the long run. War motivated by revenge seems to be a tit-for-tat strategy (20) in which the participants' score might best be measured in terms of minimizing losses rather than in terms of maximizing gains. . . .

REFERENCES AND NOTES. . . .

9. N. A. Chagnon, *Studying the Yanomamö* (Holt, Rinehart & Winston, New York, 1974).
10. _____, *Yanomamö: The Fierce People* (Holt, Rinehart & Winston, New York, 1983).
11. J. Lizot, *Tales of the Yanomamö* (Cambridge Univ. Press, Cambridge, 1985). . . .
14. Blood revenge in many other societies entails elaborate rules that specify who is obligated to avenge a death and, sometimes, the range of kinsmen (brother, cousin, and so forth) of the killer is an appropriate target for retaliation. Yanomamö revenge customs are not this specific. . . .
17. [N. A. Chagnon], thesis, University of Michigan, Ann Arbor (1966); in *War: The Anthropology of Armed Conflict and Aggression*, M. Fried, M. Harris, R. Murphy, Eds. (Natural History Press, New York, 1968), pp. 109–159.
18. The members of the villages reported here (and their recently deceased kin) have made approximately 200 garden-village sites in the region under consideration during approximately the last 50 years [see N. A. Chagnon, *Proceedings, Eighth International Conference of Anthropological and Ethnological Sciences* (Science Council of Japan, Tokyo, 1970), pp. 249–255 and (9) and (17) for further discussion of some of these settlement sites]. . . .
19. In 1986, a Ye'kwana Indian, totally unaware of the theoretical debates in anthropology about tribal warfare, described to me a conference in Caracas in which various anthropologists presented theories about customs and phenomena they had studied among Venezuelan native peoples. After one presentation on Yanomamö warfare he said he stood up and told the audience the following: "Even though I am Ye'kwana, I have also lived with the Yanomamö many years. I speak their language fluently and I know their warfare. While the last speaker used many words and elaborate arguments I do not understand, he missed the most fundamental fact about Yanomamö warfare. What he does not seem to understand is that their wars always start over women."
20. R. Axelrod and W. D. Hamilton, *Science* **211**, 1390 (1981); R. Axelrod, *The Evolution of Cooperation* (Basic Books, New York, 1984).

Reviewing Sociological Terms

On a separate sheet of paper, supply the term that correctly completes each sentence.

1. The network of interrelated statuses and roles that guides human interaction is called a _____ _____.

2. _____ _____ is the situation that occurs when a person has difficulty meeting the expectations of a single role.

3. A group with few enough members that everyone is able to interact face to face is called a _____ _____, while a two-person group is called a _____, and a three-person group is called a _____.

4. A _____ is a socially defined position in a group or in a society.

5. The situation that exists when fulfilling the expectations of one role makes it difficult to fulfill the expectations of another role is called _____ _____.

6. A _____ is a set of two or more people interacting on the basis of shared expectations and possessing some degree of common identity.

Thinking Critically about Sociology

1. *Extending Ideas*   Make a list of five sets of reciprocal roles not mentioned in the chapter.

2. *Seeing Relationships*   *(a)* How do the six types of societies discussed in the chapter differ in social structure?   *(b)* To what aspects of society do the concepts of mechanical solidarity, organic solidarity, *Gemeinschaft*, and *Gesellschaft* refer?

3. *Summarizing Ideas*   *(a)* What four requirements must be met for a group to exist?   *(b)* Compile a list of your current group memberships by type of group. Next compile from memory a similar list from elementary school. How have your group memberships changed as you have grown older?

4. *Comprehending Ideas*   *(a)* Describe the types of social interaction discussed in the chapter.   *(b)* Provide one example of each type of interaction, including the four forms of accommodation.

5. *Drawing Conclusions*   *(a)* Select a formal organization with which you are familiar and see how closely it meets the five characteristics of bureaucracies described by Max Weber.   *(b)* Which, if any, of the five criticisms of bureaucracies outlined in the chapter apply to your organization?

Exercising Sociological Skills

1. *Using Sociological Imagination*   Reread the Applying Sociology feature on pages 86–87. How might you structure a bureaucracy so that employees would not be pushed into positions for which they have little ability?

2. *Organizing Information*   Reread the Case Study feature on page 75. Describe the types of social networks formed by the elderly and the functions these networks serve.

3. *Analyzing Journal Articles*   Conduct library research to find a journal article dealing with a topic covered in this chapter. Analyze the article following the guidelines presented in the Developing Sociological Imagination feature on pages 90–91. If you cannot locate a journal, select an article from a popular magazine.

Extending Sociological Imagination

1. Select a group, such as a branch of the military or a religious order. What methods do members of this group use to separate themselves from members of outgroups? Be specific.

2. Collect 10 magazine pictures showing achieved statuses and 10 pictures showing ascribed statuses. Use the pictures to create a photo essay showing how the two types of statuses differ.

Working the Cultural Network

A bureaucratic structure is among the most obvious characteristics of a large corporation. According to organization consultants Terrence Deal and Allan Kennedy, however, it may not be the most important feature. More important to the health of a corporation may be the values, rites, rituals, and heroes that make up the organization's corporate culture. This corporate culture is transmitted to members of the corporation through the cultural network—the informal system of communication that exists in most corporations. Deal and Kennedy argue that it is within the cultural network that most work gets done in large corporations.

In the following excerpt from *Corporate Cultures: The Rites and Rituals of Corporate Life*, Deal and Kennedy explore the role that cultural networks play in daily business operations. While reading the excerpt, consider the positive and negative effects of such networks.

Everyone in a strong culture has a job—but he also has another job. This "other job" won't get stamped on a business card, but that doesn't matter. In many ways this work is far more important than budgets, memos, policies, and five-year plans. Spies, storytellers, priests, whisperers, cabals—these people form the *hidden hierarchy* which looks considerably different from the organization chart. In the hidden hierarchy, a lowly junior employee doubles as a highly influential spy. Or an "unproductive" senior manager gets the best office in the building, precisely because he does little but tell good stories—an ability that makes him tremendously valuable to the corporation as an interpreter of events. As consultants, we've found that these "other jobs" are critical to the effective management of any successful organization. They make up what we call the cultural network.

This network is actually the primary means of communication within the organization; it ties together all parts of the company without respect to positions or titles. The network is important because it not only transmits information but also interprets the significance of the information for employees. The official announcement from the CEO may be that the vice-president resigned to pursue other interests. But half a day after the announcement goes out, the network has circulated the unofficial "truth": the vice-president missed his sales budget for the third year in a row—performance that is not tolerated in this company.

We have found that many "modern" managers only deal with the tip of the iceberg as far as communications are concerned. They send a flurry of memos, letters, reports, and policy statements, hold pre-meetings, meetings, and management sessions where they use flip charts, decision trees, and statistical analysis to accomplish . . . well, sometimes they don't accomplish much. We think that 90 percent of what goes on in an organization has nothing to do with formal events. The real business goes on in the cultural network. Even in the context of a highly controlled meeting, there is a lot of informal communication going on—bonding rituals, glances, innuendos, and so forth. The real process of making decisions, of gathering support, of developing opinions, happens before the meeting—or after.

In a strong culture, the network is powerful because it can reinforce the basic beliefs of the organization, enhance the symbolic value of heroes by passing on stories of their deeds and accomplishments, set a new climate for change, and provide a tight structure of influence for the CEO. Top managers need to recognize and tap into this cultural network to accomplish their goals. Especially in large corporations, working the network can be the *only* way to get a job done.

Source Review

1. What is a cultural network and what function does it serve?

2. According to the authors, where and when is the real business conducted in a corporation?

3. What gives the cultural network its power?

ACROSS SPACE AND TIME

Language and Culture

One of the most influential social science ideas of the twentieth century has been the Sapir–Whorf hypothesis. Named after Edward Sapir and his student, Benjamin Whorf, this hypothesis states that language shapes the way we think and the way we perceive reality. Prior to the twentieth century, it was generally assumed that all languages reflect reality in the same basic way and that terms and concepts can be easily and accurately translated from one language to the next. Sapir and Whorf, however, came to the conclusion that different languages reflect the same phenomenon in different ways. They also concluded that language tends to structure reality rather than mirror it.

Whorf first noticed the way that words influence thought when he worked as an insurance inspector. While visiting sites where fires had occurred, Whorf observed that factory workers were very careful around drums of gasoline that were labeled "full." When these same drums carried the label "empty," however, the workers were likely to throw matches and cigarettes into them. The workers were associating the word "full" with gasoline, and so were cautious about the danger of explosion and fire. On the other hand, they were associating the word "empty" with an absence of gasoline. Thus the workers believed that the drums were safe. In reality, however, an empty gasoline drum is more dangerous than a full one because it contains gasoline vapors, which are extremely explosive. The language of the factory workers shaped the way they thought about the drums.

Whorf concluded from his observations that people in a society are conditioned by their language to notice some features of the real world and to ignore other features. For example, the Arabic language contains over 6,000 terms relating to camels. Camels are very important to Arabic culture. Thus the Arabic people must have a language rich enough to convey all of the varied characteristics of camels and to describe all of ways in which camels can be used. The absence from the English language of a significant number of words to describe camels reflects the fact that camels are relatively unimportant in American culture.

According to the Sapir–Whorf hypothesis, when the language of a society has no word to describe an object, that object has no significance for the people in that society. On the other hand, when the language of a society contains many terms to describe an object, that object has great significance for the people in that society. When many words are provided to describe a single object or condition, the people of the society are forced to think about the object or condition in a complex way.

The continuous presence of snow has great significance for the lives of the Eskimo people. This significance is reflected in their language. The Eskimo language contains over 20 terms describing different types and conditions of snow. For example, the Eskimos use different words to describe falling snow, hardpacked snow, and drifting snow. The variety of terms used by Eskimos to describe snow sensitizes them to their environment and allows them to think about it in a complex way.

The ancient Aztecs, on the other hand, had only one word to describe frost, ice, and snow. Presumably, the Aztecs thought of these phenomena in the same way. The English language also shows a lack of preoccupation with snow. Although Americans can construct phrases relating to the various conditions of snow, our vocabulary contains only two specific terms to describe snow: "snow" and "slush." Hence, English-speaking Americans cannot think about snow with the same degree of complexity afforded to the Eskimo people. Language paints the picture of reality, but what is considered reality may vary from language to language.

UNIT 1 REVIEW

Reviewing Sociological Ideas

1. **(a)** What is sociology? **(b)** What factors led to the rise of sociology as a distinct field of study? **(c)** What does it mean to have a sociological imagination?

2. **(a)** What is *Verstehen?* **(b)** What theoretical perspective in sociology would be most likely to employ *Verstehen* as a research method? **(c)** How do you suppose Emile Durkheim would have reacted to the use of *Verstehen* in sociological research? Why?

3. **(a)** What are mechanical and organic solidarity? **(b)** To what do *Gemeinschaft* and *Gesellschaft* refer?

4. **(a)** What is culture? **(b)** List and define the five components of culture. **(c)** Describe the three levels of culture that sociologists study.

5. **(a)** What are the basic values that form the foundation for American culture? **(b)** What new value is emerging?

6. **(a)** What is society? **(b)** What are the two major components of social structure and how do they affect human interaction?

7. **(a)** What is a formal organization? **(b)** What is a voluntary association? **(c)** What is a bureaucracy? **(d)** What is the iron law of oligarchy?

Synthesizing Sociological Ideas

1. **Applying Ideas** **(a)** Describe the basic characteristics of each of the three main theoretical perspectives in sociology. **(b)** If sociologists from each perspective were asked to study the adolescent subculture, how might the focus of their research differ?

2. **Drawing Conclusions** **(a)** What is the relationship between values and social norms? **(b)** What methods does society use to enforce social norms?

3. **Understanding Ideas** **(a)** What is a group? **(b)** What four requirements must be met for a group to exist?

4. **Summarizing Ideas** **(a)** Describe the six sources of social change discussed in your textbook. **(b)** Discuss the three important factors that produce resistance to social change.

5. **Analyzing Ideas** **(a)** What is a role set? **(b)** How does the existence of role sets lead to role conflict and role strain? **(c)** How does role conflict differ from role strain?

6. **Seeing Relationships** **(a)** Why are some cultural features common to all cultures and what are these common features called? **(b)** What factors account for variations among and within cultures? **(c)** What problem arises from cultural diversity and how do some sociologists attempt to deal with the problem when conducting social research?

7. **Contrasting Ideas** **(a)** What are the five most common types of groups? **(b)** Indicate how each type of group differs in relation to the length of time the group remains together, how the group is organized, and the group's size.

8. **Expressing a Viewpoint** **(a)** List the five characteristics of bureaucracies outlined in Weber's model. **(b)** Defend or refute the notion that these characteristics make bureaucracies an effective way to achieve large-scale goals.

Applying Sociological Imagination

1. Prepare a scrapbook of magazine photographs that show various aspects of daily life in the six types of societies discussed in Chapter 4. Divide the scrapbook into six sections, one for each type of society. Travel magazines and *National Geographic* are good sources for photographs of preindustrial societies.

2. Design a set of school rules that provides the best possible social control with the least loss of individual freedom.

3. Interview someone who works in a large bureaucracy. Ask this person to describe the types of informal structures that exist within the bureaucracy.

Among the most important of the life conditions to which all human beings must adjust is the presence of other people, who become involved in socialization as agents of instruction, as models to be imitated, and as sources of reinforcement.

TAMOTSU SHIBUTANI

THE INDIVIDUAL IN SOCIETY

Socializing the Individual

 Personality Development

Nature Versus Nurture
Isolation in Childhood

 The Social Self

Locke: The *Tabula Rasa*
Cooley: The Looking-Glass Self
Mead: Role-Taking

 Agents of Socialization

The Family
The Peer Group
The School
The Mass Media
Other Agents

Chapter Focus

Chapter 5 explores how people become functioning members of society. The chapter opens with a discussion of personality development and the effects of isolation on social behavior. Next, three theories describing how we develop a sense of self are presented. The chapter closes with a look at the major socialization agents in American society.

As you study the chapter, look for the answers to the following questions:

1. What is personality, and what four main factors affect the development of personality?
2. What effect does isolation in childhood have on development?
3. How does our sense of self emerge, and what theories have been put forth to explain the process of socialization?
4. What are the most important agents of socialization in the United States?

KEY TERMS

The following terms, while not the only terms emphasized in the chapter, are basic to your understanding of sociology. Determine the meaning of each term, either by using the Glossary or by watching for context clues as you read the chapter.

personality	socialization	significant others
heredity	looking-glass self	I
instinct	role-taking	me

INTRODUCTION

In some respects, we are all alike. We all have physical bodies that operate in somewhat the same way. We all eat and sleep. Each of us is born, ages, and eventually dies.

In other respects, we are only like some people. We speak a language shared by many but by no means all people. We wear clothes similar to those of many people, yet different from those of others. We hold beliefs that are accepted by some people but not by others. We create and use cultural artifacts that fit easily into our own society but might seem alien in other societies.

In still other ways, we are unique. No one else has our exact personality. No one else has our particular personal history.

It is the task of sociologists to look at the factors that bring about the similarities and differences among people. In this chapter, we will examine the process of personality development. We will learn how the factors that shape individual personality make each of us unique. We then will examine how various social forces attempt to mold us into functioning members of society in spite of our individual differences.

1 PERSONALITY DEVELOPMENT

Many of us think of personality in terms of social skills or social appeal. We use it to describe specific characteristics of individuals and as an explanation for people's achievements or failures. A woman's skill as a salesperson may be attributed to her "assertive" personality. Or a man's popularity may be credited to his "humorous" personality. A person's lack of friends, on the other hand, may be blamed on a "selfish" personality. When sociologists and psychologists use the term, however, they are referring to more than an individual's most striking characteristics. To social scientists, **personality** is the sum total of behaviors, attitudes, beliefs, and values that are characteristic of an individual.

Our personality traits determine how we adjust to our environment and how we react in specific situations. As we mentioned, no two individuals' personalities are exactly alike. All individuals have their own way of interacting with other people and with their social environment.

People's personalities continue to develop throughout their lifetimes. Specific traits change at different rates and to different degrees. Some personality traits seem to remain basically constant throughout a person's life. Other traits undergo dramatic changes. Personality development tends to be more obvious during childhood, when people are experiencing rapid physical, emotional, and intellectual growth. Once people reach adulthood, personality traits tend to change at a slower rate. Thus most adults appear to maintain stable personalities over time.

Nature Versus Nurture

Until fairly recently, a heated debate in the social sciences centered on whether it is **heredity**—the transmission of genetic characteristics from parents to children—or environment that gives rise to personality and social behavior. This debate was framed in terms of nature (heredity, or inherited genetic characteristics) versus nurture (environment and social learning).

Those who supported the nature viewpoint held that much of human behavior is instinctual in origin. An **instinct** is an unchanging, biologically inherited behavior pattern. We normally think of animal behavior in terms of instincts. Birds, for instance, possess the instinct to build certain types of nests and to migrate at particular times of the year. Nature supporters extended this notion of the biological basis of behavior to humans. They claimed that everything from laughing, motherhood, warfare, religion, and capitalism to the creation of society itself could be explained in terms of various instinctual drives. At the height of the debate in the early twentieth century, more than 14,000 human instincts had been suggested by social scientists.

Nurture supporters, on the other hand, attributed human behavior and personality to environmental factors and social learning. The American psychologist John B. Watson, for instance, claimed that he could take a dozen healthy infants and train them to become anything he wanted—doctors, lawyers, artists, beggars, or thieves—regardless of their abilities or ancestry.

Even though identical twins share the same genetic makeup, environmental factors contribute a great deal to their personalities and social behavior.

Most contemporary social scientists reject the nature versus nurture debate. Only sociobiologists still place a strong emphasis on the genetic basis of human behavior. Edward O. Wilson, a leading sociobiologist, defines **sociobiology** as the systematic study of the biological basis of all social behavior. According to sociobiologists, such varied cultural characteristics and behavioral traits as religion, cooperation, competition, slavery, territoriality, and envy are rooted in the genetic makeup of humans. In other words, sociobiologists believe that most of human social life is determined by biological factors.

Few social scientists, however, accept the explanation of human behavior put forth by sociobiologists. Instead, they believe that personality and social behavior result from a blending of hereditary and environmental influences, with environmental factors having the most influence. Among the principal factors they see influencing personality and behavior are birth order, parents, the cultural environment, and heredity.

Birth Order. Our personalities are influenced by whether we have brothers, sisters, both, or neither. Children with brothers and sisters have a different view of the world than do children who have no brothers or sisters. The order in which we are born into the family also influences our personalities. Individuals born first or last in a family have a different perspective than individuals born in the middle. Research has indicated, for example, that first-born children are more likely to be achievement-oriented, cooperative, and cautious than are later-born children. Later-born children, on the other hand, tend to be better in social relationships and to be more affectionate, friendly, and creative.

Parental Characteristics. Personality development in children also is influenced by the characteristics of the parents. The age of parents, for example, can have a bearing on development. Parents who are in their early 20s when their children are born are likely to relate differently to their offspring than parents who are in their middle-to-late 30s.

Other differences between sets of parents also are likely to affect personality development. Some

Personality and social development in children can be affected by factors such as home environment.

parental characteristics that can influence a child's personality are level of education, religious orientation, economic status, cultural heritage, and occupational background.

The Cultural Environment.

Culture has a strong influence on personality development. On a broad level, the cultural environment determines the basic types of personalities that will be found in a society. Each culture gives rise to a series of personality traits that are typical of members of that society. In the United States, for example, competitiveness, assertiveness, and individualism are common personality traits.

The Ik (pronounced "eek") of northern Uganda provide a powerful example of the effects of cultural environment on personality development. Prior to World War II, the Ik were hunters and gatherers who lived in a mountainous region of northern Uganda. Ik villagers were like one large family. Ik children viewed every adult in the village as a parent and all other children as brothers and sisters. After World War II, however, the Ugandan government turned much of the Ik tribal land into a national park. The government then resettled the Ik on barren land. Faced with insufficient food sources and with the total upheaval of their way of life, the Ik's social structure soon collapsed. In frustration, the people turned on each other.

Today, Ik children generally are thrown out of their homes at the age of three. They survive by forming age bands—groups of children of the same general age. These bands, which serve as protection against older children, are short-lived. By the time a child reaches the age of 12 or 13, he or she has formed and broken several protective alliances and has decided that in most instances it is better to act alone. Parents do not help their children, and adult children do not assist their aged parents. Only the strongest and most clever Ik survive.

How we experience our culture also influences our personalities. For instance, our experiences may differ depending on whether we are born male or female. Boys and girls are treated differently almost from the moment of birth. In some hospital maternity wards, the girl babies are wrapped in pink blankets, while the boy babies are wrapped in blue blankets. As they grow, male and female children often are nudged in different directions. Areas of difference include fields of interest, clothing, types of activities, speech, habits, and ideas. All of these cultural differences in attitudes, expectations, and behavior affect the personalities of males and females.

Regardless of whether we are male or female, subcultural differences also affect personality development. Growing up in an Italian American family provides an experience different from that found in a Polish American family. Both of these differ from the experience of growing up in an Anglo American family or in one in which there is not a clear ethnic pattern. Similarly, the region of the country or the type of neighborhood in which we are raised also affects personality.

Heredity.

It appears that our culture affects all areas of our personalities. What role, then, do biological factors play in personality development? Social scientists seek answers to this question by focusing on the effects of heredity.

Everyone has certain characteristics that are present at birth. These hereditary characteristics include physical traits such as one's body build or hair, eye, and skin color. Hereditary characteristics also include certain aptitudes. An **aptitude** is a capacity to learn a particular skill or acquire a particular body of knowledge. A natural talent for music or art, for instance, would be considered an aptitude. Most social scientists, however, do not limit aptitudes to inherited capabilities. Instead, they believe that some aptitudes can be learned as well as inherited. Nevertheless, many aptitudes result from inherited qualities or from a combination of heredity and environment.

In addition to inheriting genetic characteristics, we also inherit certain basic needs and capacities. Like all animals, for example, human beings have biological drives. The hunger drive makes us want to eat. But drives do not determine our specific behavior. The hunger drive does not tell us when to eat or what to eat or how to eat. We learn these things from interaction with other human beings within our culture. Heredity provides us with certain biological needs. Our culture determines how we meet these needs.

Heredity also plays an important role in shaping human personalities by setting limits on individuals. If you have little aptitude for music, you probably will not be a great musician. If your biological inheritance endowed you with a five-foot-tall frame, you are not likely to become a professional basketball player. On the other hand, you may not become one even if you are seven feet tall. The point is that inherited characteristics place limits on what is possible. But inherited characteristics do not determine what an individual will do. Nor do they alone determine what kind of personality an individual will have.

Isolation in Childhood

Remarkably, several recorded instances exist in which children have been raised without the influence of a cultural environment. In a few cases, children were found living with animals. In other instances, the children were isolated in their homes by parents or family members so that no one in the outside world would know of their existence. The result in each of these cases was that the child had few human characteristics other than appearance. These children had acquired no reasoning ability, no manners, no ability even to control their bodily functions or to move about like human beings. The evidence provided by these children points strongly to the conclusion that our personality—in fact our humanity—comes from our cultural environment.

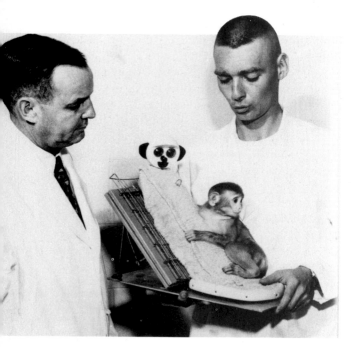

Research conducted in the 1950s and 1960s by Dr. Harry Harlow (left) found that even baby monkeys need love in order to thrive.

Three of the most famous examples of child isolation are the cases of Anna, Isabelle, and Genie. We also have learned a great deal about the connection between environment and human development from studies of children living in institutions such as hospitals and orphanages.

Anna. One of the earliest cases of child isolation investigated by a sociologist is that of Anna. Anna was born to an unmarried woman, a fact that enraged her mother's father. At first forbidden to bring the child into the house, Anna's mother attempted to place her in a children's home. When this proved too expensive, Anna was moved to a series of foster homes. Finally, at the age of six months, the child was returned to her mother. Because of the grandfather's hostility, Anna was confined to an attic room where she was given only a minimum of care. She was fed only enough milk to keep her alive and received almost no human contact. She was not spoken to, held, bathed, or loved.

Anna finally was discovered by a social worker in 1938. At six years of age, Anna was little more than a skeleton. She could not walk, talk, or feed herself. Her face was expressionless, and she showed no interest in other people. Over time, though, Anna made some progress. She learned, for instance, to walk, feed herself, brush her teeth, and follow simple directions. When she died at the age of 10, however, Anna had just begun to show the first signs of using language and had only reached the ability level of a toddler.

Isabelle. The story of Isabelle has a somewhat happier ending. Isabelle, whose mother also was unmarried, was found at about the same time as Anna. The child's grandfather kept her and her deaf-mute mother confined to a dark room. Although deprived of a normal cultural environment, Isabelle did have the advantage of her mother's company. But because she and her mother communicated only through gestures, Isabelle did not learn to speak. When she was found at the age of six-and-a-half years, she crawled around on her hands and knees making grunting, animal-like sounds. She ate with her hands and behaved in many ways like a six-month-old infant.

Isabelle was at first thought to be mentally retarded and mute. After several months of intensive training, however, she began to speak. Eventually she developed a considerable vocabulary. After about two years of training, Isabelle reached a level of social and mental development consistent with her age group. Kingsley Davis, the sociologist who studied both Anna and Isabelle, concluded that Isabelle's constant contact with her mother and her training by specialists allowed her to overcome her early social deprivation.

Genie. Sometimes it is impossible to reverse the effects of prolonged isolation, even with the help of specialists. This was true in the case of Genie, who was discovered in 1970 at 13 years of age. Genie had been confined to a small bedroom from the age of 20 months by her father, a man who hated children. Genie spent her days tied to an infant's potty chair and her nights wrapped in a sleeping bag enclosed in a mesh-covered crib. Her world was almost totally silent, and she was beaten when she made noise. Whenever Genie's father interacted with her, he acted like a wild dog, barking, growling, and baring his teeth. Consequently, Genie did not learn to talk.

The room in which Genie spent all of her time was bare except for the potty chair, the crib, two partially covered windows, a bare light bulb, and a closet. Sometimes two plastic raincoats hung outside the closet and Genie was allowed to play with them. Her only other toys consisted of things such as empty spools of thread and an empty cottage cheese container.

When Genie was found, she could not stand straight and had the social and psychological skills of a one-year-old child. Even after eight years of training, Genie had not progressed past the level

Text continues on page 108.

The "Wild Child of France" was found living in the woods in the 1700s, unable to speak. This photo was taken from a film based on his life.

APPLYING SOCIOLOGY

Are You a Product of Your Environment?

As we discussed in this chapter, the cultural environment helps to determine the kind of person you become. It influences the types of people you meet, the places you visit, and the things you come in contact with. But did you ever stop to think just how much your environment influences what you experience and learn? Let us conduct a simple experiment that might shed some light on this question.

In this project, you will be taking a brief test (actually a questionnaire). It will be similar to many tests you have taken in school. It will be different, however, in one important way. We will discuss this difference after you have answered all the questions.

First, number a blank sheet of notebook paper from 1 through 6. Next, read each statement carefully and select the answer that best completes the sentence. Then, place the letter of this answer next to the appropriate number on your paper. Remember, this is a test, so do not look up any answers. (You also will not be graded!)

1. Dalai Lama best describes
   a. an artist.
   b. a spiritual leader.
   c. an animal.
   d. an Eastern religion.

2. If someone gave you some Lapsang Souchong, you would
   a. spread it on bread.
   b. take it for an upset stomach.
   c. drink it.
   d. chew it.

3. Lhasa is
   a. a fashion designer.
   b. a type of dog.
   c. a capital city.
   d. a church.

4. The leader of a mountain-climbing expedition suggests that you use Sherpas on your next climb. The leader wants you to
   a. take vitamins.
   b. buy new equipment.
   c. round up animals to help carry the load.
   d. recruit members of a mountain people.

5. Yak butter is an important part of people's diet in
   a. India.
   b. Russia.
   c. Tibet.
   d. Alaska.

6. People in parts of Asia worship Choma-lungma. Choma-lungma is
   a. a holy man.
   b. a mountain system.
   c. a body of water.
   d. a type of plant.

Well, how do you think you did? We will go over the answers and you can check your score. The answer to question 1 is b. The Dalai Lama is the spiritual leader of the people of Tibet. Tibet is a region southwest of China.

Since Lapsang Souchong is a type of tea, the correct answer to question 2 is c. Lapsang Souchong is a favorite beverage of the people of Tibet. The answer to question 3 is also c. Lhasa is the capital city of Tibet.

In question 4, the correct choice is d. Sherpas are a mountain people that migrated from Tibet several hundred years ago. They now live in the mountains of nearby Nepal.

As you might have guessed by now, the correct answer to question 5 is c. Because Tibet is very mountainous, the climate is quite severe. The yak is one of the few animals that can survive in this harsh setting. Consequently, the Tibetans rely on the yak for food, clothing, and shelter. Yak butter forms a major part of the Tibetan diet.

In question 6, the correct answer is b. Chomalungma is the name of a mountain system that includes Mount Everest. Mount Everest is the highest mountain in the world and lies partly in Tibet.

How many questions did you answer correctly? Chances are that most of you did not know the answers to some of these questions? Why not?

As we mentioned earlier, this test differs in one important way from many other tests that you have taken. It is about Tibetan culture. Therefore, in order to know the correct answers, you would have to know about life in Tibet. If you had grown up in Tibet, the answers would seem very obvious to you.

Let us relate this test to American culture to see what we mean. Suppose, for example, that question 1 asked you to complete the following sentence about George Washington instead of the Dalai Lama:

1. George Washington was
  a. an artist.
  b. the first President of the United States.
  c. a poet.
  d. a student leader.

It is likely that you would know that the correct choice is b.

Similarly, what if question 5 asked you to name the country in which peanut butter is a popular food? As before, you would probably know the answer. You would say that peanut butter is eaten by many people in the United States.

In each case, you would not have to think very hard before the answer came to you. You would almost take it for granted that *everybody* knows that George Washington was our first President and that peanut butter is a popular food in the United States.

Of course, you know this information because you live in the United States. These facts are part of the American cultural environment. If you lived in Tibet, however, George Washington would seem as "foreign" as the Dalai Lama seems to you now.

From these examples, you can see the role that environment plays in socialization. If you had grown up in an environment other than the United States, your life would be different from what it is today.

of a four-year-old child. She eventually was placed in an institution. A description of Genie's behavior during her training can be found in the Interpreting Primary Sources feature on page 119.

Institutionalization. Even children raised in institutions such as orphanages or hospitals may show some of the characteristics of isolated children. In 1945, psychologist Rene Spitz studied the effects of institutionalization on a group of infants living in an orphanage. Even though they were given proper food and medical care, more than a third of the children died within a two-year period. They seemed simply to have wasted away from a lack of cuddling and love. The nurses, although well-trained and efficient, had little time for such things. Of the 61 children who survived, fewer than 25 percent could walk by themselves,

dress themselves, or use a spoon, even though they ranged in age from two to four years. And only one child could speak in complete sentences.

The cases of Anna, Isabelle, Genie, and the institutionalized infants illustrate how important human interaction is for social and psychological development. Recent research continues to support these earlier findings. Infants and young children who lack a caring environment generally develop their mental, physical, and emotional skills at a much slower pace.

SECTION 1 REVIEW

DEFINE personality, instinct, sociobiology, aptitude

IDENTIFY John B. Watson, Edward O. Wilson, the Ik, Kingsley Davis, Rene Spitz

1. ***Summarizing Ideas*** **(a)** What is heredity? **(b)** Briefly summarize the nature versus nurture debate.

2. ***Understanding Ideas*** List and describe the four principal factors that most contemporary social scientists see as influencing personality development and social behavior.

3. ***Drawing Conclusions*** What factors might have led to the different levels of success in teaching Anna, Isabelle, and Genie to function normally in society?

4. ***Seeing Relationships*** According to research by Rene Spitz, what effect does the lack of close human contact have on institutionalized children?

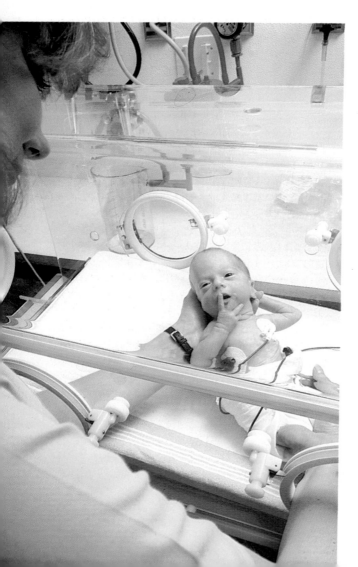

Knowing the importance of human touch for development, doctors and nurses devote much time to holding and cuddling hospitalized babies.

2 THE SOCIAL SELF

At birth, human beings cannot talk, walk, feed themselves, or even protect themselves from harm. They know nothing about the norms of society. Then, through interaction with their social and cultural environments, individuals are transformed into participating members of society. This interactive process through which individuals learn the basic skills, values, beliefs, and behavior patterns of the society is called **socialization.**

A number of theories exist to explain how we become socialized and develop a sense of self. Our **self** is our conscious awareness of possessing a distinct identity that separates us from other members of society. We will consider three of these theories—those of Locke, Cooley, and Mead.

Locke: The *Tabula Rasa*

The English philosopher John Locke (1632–1704) insisted that each newly born individual is a *tabula rasa,* or clean slate, on which can be written just about anything. Locke claimed that each of us is born without a personality. We acquire our personality as a result of our social experiences. Locke believed that human beings can be molded into any type of character. He further believed that, given a newborn infant, he could shape the

individual into whatever type of person he wanted. More than two centuries later, the psychologist John B. Watson was to make a similar claim.

Few people today would take such an extreme view. Nevertheless, many of our basic assumptions about socialization are related to Locke's views. Most sociologists think of socialization as a process by which we absorb those aspects of our culture with which we come into contact. Through the socialization process, we develop our sense of being a distinct member of society.

Cooley: The Looking-Glass Self

Charles Horton Cooley (1864–1929) was an American social psychologist and one of the founders of the interactionist perspective in sociology. In addition to developing the notion of the primary group, Cooley is most noted for his theory explaining how individuals develop a sense of self. Central to his theory is the concept of the looking-glass self. The **looking-glass self** refers to the interactive process by which we develop an image of ourselves based on how we imagine we appear to others. Other people act as a mirror, reflecting back the image we project through their reactions to our behavior.

According to Cooley, the development of the looking-glass self is a three-step process. First, we imagine how we appear to others. Second, based on their reactions to us, we attempt to determine whether others view us as we view ourselves. And

Calvin and Hobbes

by Bill Watterson

The earliest influences on the self-image of a child come from interaction within the family setting. According to Cooley, parents who treat their children as capable contribute to the children's sense of self-worth.

finally, we use our perceptions of how others judge us to develop feelings about ourselves.

The process of identity development begins very early in childhood. According to Cooley, a newborn baby has no sense of person or place. The entire world appears as one mass. Then, various members of the child's primary group—parents, brothers, sisters, other family members, and friends—interact with the growing infant. They pick up the child. They talk to him or her. They reward or punish the child's behavior. In short, they provide the child with a mirror that reflects his or her image. From this interactive process, the child develops a sense of self.

This theory puts a great deal of responsibility on parents and other primary group members who have contact with children. Parents who think little of a child's ability, and let their feelings be known, will likely give rise to feelings of inferiority in the child. On the other hand, parents who treat their children as capable and competent are likely to produce capable and competent children.

Cooley was quick to note that while this process starts early in childhood, it continues throughout our lives. We continually refine our self-images as we alter our interpretations of the way we think others view us.

Mead: Role-Taking

The American sociologist George Herbert Mead (1863–1931), another founder of the interactionist perspective, added to Cooley's theory of socialization and the emergence of the self. According to Mead, seeing ourselves as others see us is only the beginning. Eventually we come not only to see ourselves as others see us, but actually to take or pretend to take the role of others. This act of **role-taking** forms the basis of the socialization process by allowing us to anticipate what others expect of us. We thus learn to see ourselves through the eyes of others.

According to Mead, we first internalize the expectations of those closest to us—our parents, brothers and sisters, relatives, and other specific people who have a direct influence on our socialization. Although Mead did not use the term, sociologists now refer to the people closest to us as **significant others.** As we grow older, however, the expectations and attitudes of society take on added importance in guiding our behavior and reinforcing our sense of self. Mead called the internalized attitudes, expectations, and viewpoints of society the **generalized other.** We come to internalize the generalized other through the process of role-taking.

Children are not automatically capable of role-taking. They must develop the necessary skills through social interaction. Mead visualized role-taking as a three-step process involving imitation, play, and games.

Under about three years of age, children lack a sense of self. Consequently, they only can imitate the actions of others. Young children most often imitate the gestures and actions of family members and others in their immediate environment. Such mimicking is not role-taking, but rather preparation for learning role expectations.

At about the age of three, children begin to play and act out the roles of specific people. They may dress up in their parents' clothes, play house, or pretend to be doctors and nurses. For the first time, the children are attempting to see the world through someone else's eyes.

By the time children reach school age, they begin to take part in organized games. Organized games require children not only to take on roles of their own but also to anticipate the actions and

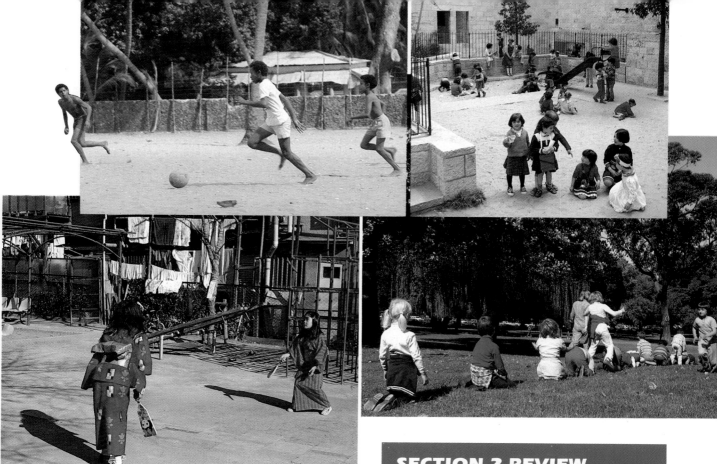

Children everywhere participate in games that help to further the socialization process.

expectations of others. Because it requires internalizing the generalized other, the game stage of role-taking most closely resembles real life.

Through role-taking, individuals develop a sense of self. According to Mead, the self consists of two related parts—the "I" and the "me." The **I** is the unsocialized, spontaneous, self-interested component of our personality and self-identity. The **me,** on the other hand, is that part of our identity that is aware of the expectations and attitudes of society—our socialized self.

As children, the I component of our personality is stronger than the me component. Through the process of socialization, however, the me gains power over the I, bringing our actions in line with the expectations of society. Nonetheless, the me never totally dominates the I, and both aspects of our personality are needed if we are to be well-rounded individuals.

SECTION 2 REVIEW

DEFINE socialization, self, significant others, generalized other

IDENTIFY John Locke, Charles Horton Cooley, George Herbert Mead

1. **Summarizing Ideas** Describe John Locke's theory of the socialization process.

2. **Organizing Ideas** **(a)** What is the looking-glass self? **(b)** List and describe the three steps involved in the development of the looking-glass self.

3. **Identifying Ideas** **(a)** What is role-taking? **(b)** What three stages do children go through in developing the skills needed for role-taking?

4. **Comprehending Ideas** According to Mead, what are the two components of the self and how are they related?

3 AGENTS OF SOCIALIZATION

The views of Locke, Cooley, and Mead are theoretical explanations of the socialization process. We still need to consider some specific forces and situations that shape socialization experiences. In sociological terms, the specific individuals, groups, and institutions that provide the situations in which socialization can occur are called **agents of socialization.** In the United States, the primary agents of socialization include the family, peer groups, the school, and the mass media.

The Family

The family is the most important agent of socialization in almost every society. The importance of the family rests primarily in its role as the principal socializer of young children. It is within the family that most children first learn how to behave in socially acceptable ways, to develop close emotional ties, and to internalize the values and norms of society.

Experiences within the family help determine the type of person an individual becomes. The cases of Anna, Isabelle, and Genie discussed in the first section of this chapter provide extreme examples of the negative consequences sometimes brought by harsh family environments. But even in stable families, variations in family composition, beliefs, behaviors, and circumstances produce a society of individuals who share in the patterns of the larger culture but who retain unique personalities and behavioral traits.

Socialization in a family setting can be both deliberate and unconscious. A father may teach his children about the importance of telling the truth or being considerate to others. A mother may instruct her children in how to spend and save money. These are deliberate, or intended, socialization activities.

There also are unconscious, or unintended, socialization activities. Many times these activities have an even greater effect on children than do deliberate attempts at socialization. Suppose, for example, a father carefully explains to his child about the importance of being polite. Then a situation occurs in which the father is impolite himself. Is the child likely to follow what the father says or what he actually does? Unintended socialization is very common. For every instance in which parents deliberately try to influence a child in one direction, there are numerous instances in which they send out unintended messages that push the child in another direction.

The Peer Group

The family provides many, if not most, of the socialization experiences of early childhood. Infants and very young children are particularly likely to spend almost all of their time in a family setting. As children grow older, however, they increasingly are influenced by forces outside of the family. In particular, they begin to relate more and more to their peer groups. A **peer group** is a primary group composed of individuals of roughly equal age and social characteristics.

To have friends and be accepted in society, it is important for us to be accepted by our peers. To win their acceptance, we behave according to their standards. Our personality thus is shaped by our peer group as we try to be the kind of person we think the group wants us to be.

Peer group socialization is somewhat unique. Socialization in the family and in the school tends to be more structured. The emphasis is on acquiring the skills that will enable an individual to fit into the larger society. In the case of peer groups, on the other hand, the focus is on group interests and acquiring the skills needed to fit into a subculture. Socialization also tends to be much more unstructured in a peer group setting.

Because the focus within peer groups is on the subculture, group goals sometimes are at odds with the goals of the larger society. Parents in particular become alarmed if they believe that the norms and values of the group are becoming more important to their children than family norms and values.

The School

For most young people, the school occupies large amounts of time and attention—anywhere from 13 to 20 or more years. Thus the school plays a

As children grow into teenagers, the peer group takes on added importance.

major role in socializing individuals. Much of this socialization process is deliberate. Class activities are planned for the deliberate purpose of teaching reading, writing, arithmetic, and other skills. Extracurricular activities, such as school dances, clubs, and athletic events, are intended to train the student for life in the larger society. Schools also attempt to transmit cultural values, such as patriotism, responsibility, and good citizenship.

A large amount of unintentional socialization also occurs within the school. Teachers may become models for students in such unintended areas as manners of speech or styles of dress. In addition, every school contains many peer groups that influence the habits of their members.

The Mass Media

While the family, the peer group, and the school probably are the most important agents of socialization, there are other agents as well. One of the most influential of these is the mass media. The **mass media** includes newspapers, magazines, books, television, radio, films, and other forms of communication that reach large audiences with no personal contact between the individuals sending the information and those receiving it.

Of the various forms of mass media, television probably has the most influence on the socialization of children. There is at least one television set in 98 percent of the homes in the United States. More importantly, research shows that tel-

evision sets are turned on in American homes for an average of seven hours a day.

The effects of television on children is a topic of ongoing debate. On the negative side, research has indicated that most children spend more time watching television than they spend in school. By age 18, these children will have witnessed countless fictional acts of murder, rape, robbery, and other forms of crime and violence. This is alarming in view of the fact that many studies have found a relationship between violence on television and aggression among viewers, particularly children.

Another long-standing criticism of television is that it presents an image of society that reflects white middle-class values. The life experiences of many racial, religious, and economic groups often are either ignored or portrayed in a negative light.

On the positive side, television expands our world. It can be a powerful educational tool. For example, television brings far-off places into our homes, makes world events immediate, and introduces us to subjects we might never experience on our own.

Other Agents

Religion is another important agent of socialization, particularly in the area of values transmission. Fully 65 percent of the population of the

In all of its varied forms, religion is an influential agent of socialization.

The Function of Fairy Tales

Parents and teachers have many tools at their disposal to assist in the socialization of young children. One of the most effective tools is literature. Of the various forms of literature written for children, the fairy tale has enjoyed the longest run of popularity. What is it about fairy tales that makes them such an enduring agent of socialization? Child psychologist Bruno Bettelheim has explored this question in his book *The Uses of Enchantment: The Meaning and Importance of Fairy Tales.*

According to Bettelheim, the value and appeal of fairy tales rests in the fact that they help children master the problems of growing up. Fairy tales do this by stimulating children's imagination and by allowing them to deal subconsciously with their fears.

In modern society, we stress the optimistic side of life. Humans are portrayed as being basically good. A successful life is seen as one that is easy and free from worry. These views of the world can be confusing for children. Children know that they are not always good and that life is not always easy. The message of fairy tales is that evil and virtue, good and bad exist in everything. Fairy tales also teach children that difficulties in life are unavoidable and must be met head on. Children see the fairy tale hero face the images of good and evil and find a way for good to triumph through cleverness or bravery.

The socialization lessons contained in fairy tales are indirect, however. According to Bettelheim, children do not identify with the "good" or "bad" act. Rather, they identify with the hero, who happens to be good. The hero serves as a role model for the young child. Children do not ask "Do I want to be good?" Instead they ask "Who do I want to be like?" This distinction is important because it enables children to accept socially sanctioned behavior before they are old enough to grasp the moral issues involved.

The structure of the fairy tale is ideally suited to the way young children think. Children cannot understand the complexities of the adult world. They see things in black and white rather than in shades of gray. Situations and people are right or wrong, good or bad. Fairy tales mimic this simplified view of the world. Fundamental issues are presented in an either/or format that children can easily grasp. The witch is bad and ugly, the princess is kind and beautiful, and the prince is strong and brave. Good always triumphs over evil.

More important than the structure of fairy tales is the subject matter. Love, fear, death, isolation, and abandonment are prominent themes. Rather than being frightening, these themes allow young children to deal with fears that they might not be able to express in words.

Fairy tales have the added advantage of taking on new meanings as a child grows. In the case of *Cinderella,* for example, very young children can understand the message of good Cinderella winning out over her bad stepsisters. Older children also might grasp the notion of sibling rivalry contained in the story. Similarly, young children can see in *Rapunzel* the story of a young girl escaping her evil, jealous mother. Older children also might recognize the conflict that is common between adolescents and parents as teenagers attempt to gain independence from their parents.

In short, the important function of fairy tales rests not in telling a literal story or providing simple moral truths. Instead, it rests in allowing children to grasp the contradictions that exist in human nature and social life. Fairy tales do this in a way that is particularly suited to the developmental skills of growing children. By capturing children's imaginations and allowing them to explore their unspoken fears, fairy tales help to mold social behavior.

United States claims membership in an organized church or synagogue. Other agents of socialization include organizations such as the Little League, Camp Fire Boys and Girls, and 4-H clubs. In addition, for those who are employed, jobs add another assist in the socialization process.

One rather unique agent of socialization is the total institution. A **total institution** is a setting in which people are isolated from the rest of society for a set period of time and are subject to the control of officials of varied ranks. Prisons, military boot camp, monasteries, and psychiatric hospitals are examples of total institutions.

Socialization in a total institution differs from the process found in many other settings. Total institutions primarily are concerned with resocializing their members. **Resocialization** involves a break with past experiences and the learning of new values and norms. In the case of most total institutions, resocialization is directed toward forcibly changing an individual's personality and social behavior. This is accomplished by means such

as altering the individual's style of dress, hairstyle, speech, and freedom of movement. Once the individual's sense of self has been shaken, it is easier for those in power to convince the individual to conform to new patterns of behavior.

SECTION 3 REVIEW

DEFINE agents of socialization, resocialization

1. **Summarizing Ideas** List and describe the main agents of socialization in American society.

2. **Contrasting Ideas** In what ways are total institutions different from other agents of socialization?

CHAPTER 5 SUMMARY

Personality is the set of behaviors, attitudes, beliefs, and values that are characteristic of an individual. Until relatively recently, the origin of personality was a hotly debated topic. The debate was presented in terms of nature versus nurture. The nature supporters claimed that human behavior is instinctual in origin. The nurture supporters, on the other hand, attributed personality development to the environment and social learning. Only sociobiologists still place strong emphasis on the genetic basis of personality and human behavior. Today, most social scientists view personality as the result of a combination of factors such as birth order, parental characteristics, the cultural environment, and heredity. The harmful effects that isolation produces in children illustrates how important environmental factors are in social and psychological development.

The interactive process through which individuals learn the basic skills, values, beliefs, and be-

havior patterns of society is called socialization. Several theories have been proposed to explain how individuals develop into functioning members of society. Three such theories are those of John Locke, Charles Horton Cooley, and George Herbert Mead. Locke viewed the newborn infant as a *tabula rasa*—a blank slate—on which social experiences could write any history. Cooley labeled the interactive process by which we develop an identity the looking-glass self. At the basis of the looking-glass self is the idea that we develop a self-image based on how we imagine we appear to others. Mead added the notion of role-taking—taking or pretending to take the role of the other—to the theories of socialization.

The individuals, groups, and institutions that provide the situations in which socialization can occur are called agents of socialization. The primary agents of socialization include the family, peer groups, the school, and the mass media.

DEVELOPING SOCIOLOGICAL

READING ABOUT SOCIOLOGY: Comparing Sociological Perspectives

A sociological perspective is a way of viewing the social world. Not all sociologists view the social world in exactly the same way. One reason for differences in sociological perspectives is that there are several theoretical orientations in sociology. Different theoretical orientations often give rise to different interpretations of the same phenomena. Thus it is important to be able to compare sociological perspectives. Comparing sociological perspectives involves analyzing the similarities and differences between arguments.

How to Compare Sociological Perspectives

To compare two or more sociological perspectives, follow these steps.

1. **Determine the nature of the source.** Note whether the reading is from a primary or secondary source.

2. **Read each source carefully.** Identify the main idea as well as all the supporting details contained in each source. As you read, note the similarities and differences between the sources. Identify any theoretical bias in either account.

Applying the Skill

Read Excerpts A and B. Following the guidelines listed above, compare the two sources. The chart on page 117 is an effective way of organizing information for comparison. You will note from the chart that Lionel Tiger and Robin Fox believe that human behavior is determined primarily by genetic characteristics (the position of the sociobiology perspective). Albert Bandura, on the other hand, believes that social learning—socialization—plays the key role in determining human behavior.

Excerpt A: From *The Imperial Animal*

The human organism is "wired" in a certain way so that it can process and emit information about certain facts of social life such as language and rules about sex, and that, furthermore, it can process this information only at certain times and only in certain ways. The wiring is geared to the life cycle so that at any one moment in a population of *Homo sapiens* there will be individuals with a certain "store" of behavior giving out information at another stage to others who are wired to treat this information in a particular way. The outcome of the interaction of these individuals will be certain "typical" relationships.

There is nothing specific in the genetic code about initiation ceremonies for young males. . . . But neither are male initiation ceremonies pure cultural inventions—results of the free activity of intellect. They occur because we are biologically wired the way we are. We can predict how older and younger males in a community will relate to one another because of the way their wiring allows them to be programmed and to program them in turn. In postadolescent males the genetic message is one of sinister and often undirected rebelliousness; this threatening information is received by older males, whose steadier hormonal systems go into a reaction and insist on containment. So all societies find ways of taming and using the young men and of forcing them to identify with the system.

Lionel Tiger and Robin Fox

Excerpt B: From *Social Learning Theory*

In the social learning view, people are neither driven by inner forces nor buffeted by environmental stimuli. Rather, psychological functioning is explained in terms of continuous reciprocal interaction of personal and environmental determi-

	Sociobiology Perspective	Social Learning Perspective
Main Thesis	Behavior is primarily determined by genetic factors.	Most behavior is learned through observation.
Supporting Evidence	All societies find ways of taming young men and forcing them to identify with the system.	Societies do not teach important skills by trial and error.
Conclusions	Biological wiring is geared to the life cycle and allows us to predict typical relationships, such as those between younger and older men.	Psychological functioning is explained in terms of continuous reciprocal interaction of personal and environmental determinants.
Assumptions	The human organism is "wired" in a certain way to process and emit information at certain times and in certain ways.	The capacity to learn through observation enables people to acquire large, integrated patterns of behavior quickly.

nants. Within this approach, symbolic, vicarious, and self-regulatory processes assume a prominent role.

Psychological theories have traditionally assumed that learning can occur only by performing responses and experiencing their effects. In actuality, virtually all learning phenomena resulting from direct experience occur on a vicarious basis by observing other people's behavior and its consequences for them. The capacity to learn by observation enables people to acquire large, integrated patterns of behavior without having to form them gradually by tedious trial and error.

The abbreviation of the acquisitional process through observational learning is vital for both development and survival. Because mistakes can produce costly, or even fatal consequences, the prospects for survival would be slim indeed if one could learn only by suffering the consequences of trial and error. For this reason, one does not teach children to swim, adolescents to drive automobiles, and novice medical students to perform surgery by having them discover the appropriate behavior through the consequences of their successes and failures. The more costly and hazardous the possible mistakes, the heavier is the reliance on observational learning from competent examples. Apart from the question of survival, it is difficult to imagine a social transmission process in which the language, lifestyles, and institutional practices of a culture are taught to each new member by selective reinforcement of fortuitous behaviors, without the benefit of models who exemplify the cultural patterns.

Albert Bandura

Practicing the Skill

Locate two commentaries on a sociological issue, each written from a different perspective. Then on a separate sheet of paper, construct a chart similar to the one shown on this page. Write a brief statement comparing the views of the two perspectives.

Reviewing Sociological Terms

On a separate sheet of paper, supply the term that correctly completes each sentence.

1. _____ is the interactive process through which individuals learn the basic skills, values, beliefs, and behavior patterns of society.

2. An unchanging, biologically inherited behavior pattern is called an _____.

3. _____ is the transmission of genetic characteristics from parents to children.

4. _____ involves a break with past experiences and the learning of new values and norms.

5. The capacity to learn a particular skill or acquire a particular body of knowledge is referred to as _____.

6. _____ is the set of behaviors, attitudes, beliefs, and values that are characteristic of an individual.

Thinking Critically about Sociology

1. **Comparing Ideas** *(a)* What is the self? *(b)* Compare the theories of Locke, Cooley, and Mead on the emergence of the self.

2. **Drawing Conclusions** *(a)* Describe the views held by early twentieth-century nature advocates and contemporary sociobiologists concerning personality and social behavior. *(b)* How are these views similar?

3. **Analyzing Ideas** *(a)* How does the cultural environment influence personality development? *(b)* What effect did a change in environmental conditions have on the Ik of northern Uganda?

4. **Using Sociological Imagination** *(a)* To what are sociologists referring when they speak of agents of socialization? *(b)* In what ways might the mass media, particularly television, reinforce and counteract the effects of the other agents of socialization?

5. **Interpreting Ideas** What does research on children reared in isolation indicate about the effects of the cultural environment on social and psychological development?

6. **Summarizing Ideas** According to contemporary sociologists, how does heredity affect personality development?

7. **Understanding Ideas** *(a)* According to Cooley, how does a sense of self develop in early childhood? *(b)* Does this process end with childhood? Explain.

Exercising Sociological Skills

1. **Investigating Ideas** The Applying Sociology feature on pages 106–107 examines the role of the environment in socialization. Research daily life in Tibet. Then, compile a list of the ways in which the nation's cultural and physical environments have affected socialization.

2. **Identifying Ideas** Reread the Case Study feature on page 114. *(a)* How do fairy tales affect the psychological development of children? *(b)* How do they accomplish this?

3. **Comparing Sociological Perspectives** Reread the discussion of the nature versus nurture debate in the first section of this chapter. Construct a chart, similar to the one on page 117, that compares the two perspectives.

Extending Sociological Imagination

1. Review the research findings on the effects of birth order on personality development. Next, watch a television program that centers on a family with several children. How do the characteristics of the television children compare to the birth order traits predicted in the scientific research?

2. Collect magazine pictures showing children engaged in each of the three steps of the role-taking process described by Mead.

INTERPRETING PRIMARY SOURCES
Genie

Isolation in childhood has a significant effect on an individual's social and psychological development. The longer the period of isolation and the harsher the treatment received during the isolation, the greater the difficulty in reversing the negative effects. A case in point is that of Genie, whose father kept her confined to her room for most of her first 13 years of life.

In the following excerpt, Susan Curtiss, a social scientist who studied Genie's development, describes the young girl's behavior following her discovery. The excerpt is taken from Curtiss's book *Genie: A Psycholinguistic Study of a Modern-Day "Wild Child."*

While reading the excerpt, consider the effects of long-term isolation on the socialization process. Also consider the role that socialization plays for society in maintaining orderly patterns of social interaction.

Genie was pitiful. Hardly ever having worn clothing, she did not react to temperature, heat or cold. Never having eaten solid food, Genie did not know how to chew, and had great difficulty in swallowing. Having been strapped down and left sitting on a potty chair, she could not stand erect, could not straighten her arms or legs, could not run, hop, jump, or climb; in fact, she could only walk with difficulty, shuffling her feet, swaying from side to side. Hardly ever having seen more than a space of 10 feet in front of her (the distance from her potty chair to the door), she had become nearsighted exactly to that distance. Having been beaten for making noise, she had learned to suppress almost all vocalization save a whimper. Suffering from malnutrition, she weighed only 59 pounds and stood only 54 inches tall. . . . Genie was unsocialized, primitive, hardly human.

Surprisingly, however, Genie was alert and curious. She maintained good eye contact and avidly explored her new surroundings. She was intensely eager for human contact and attention. In the face of her hunger for contact with her new world, her almost total silence had an eerie quality. Except for a high-pitched whimpering and a few words she is reported to have imitated when she was first admitted to the hospital, she was a silent child who did not vocalize in any way, who did not even sob when she cried. . . .

It was her lack of socialization that was most difficult to deal with, especially in public. Genie had a special fondness for certain things—anything made of plastic, certain foods, certain articles of clothing or accessories. If anyone she encountered in the street or in a store or other public place had something she liked, she was uncontrollably drawn to him or her, and without obeying any rules of psychological distance or social mores, she would go right up to the person and put her hands on the desired item. It was bad enough when she went up to someone else's shopping cart to reach in to take something out; but when the object of attention was an article of clothing, and Genie would simply attach herself to the person wearing that clothing and refuse to let go, the situations were extremely trying.

Even when Genie did not attach herself in quite such an embarrassing manner, she still went right up to strangers, stood directly in front of them, without any accepted distance between them, and peered into their faces with her face directly in front of theirs, pointing (without looking) at whatever possession of theirs held her interest. Other times, she very simply walked up to them and linked her arms through theirs or put her arms around them and was ready to walk on. All of this behavior, although charming and even endearing in the abstract, was quite embarrassing.

Source Review

1. What antisocial behaviors did Genie exhibit?

2. Why do you think Genie's behavior made people feel uncomfortable?

3. How does proper socialization simplify social interaction?

The Adolescent in Society

1 Adolescence in Our Society

The Concept of Adolescence
Characteristics of Adolescence

2 Teenagers and Dating

The Emergence of Dating
Why Date?
Dating Patterns

3 Problems of Adolescence

Teenage Sexual Behavior
Teenage Drug Use
Teenage Suicide

Chapter Focus

Chapter 6 explores adolescence, the period of the life cycle that falls between childhood and adulthood. The chapter opens with a discussion of the concept of adolescence and the factors that gave rise to its development in the United States. The characteristics of adolescence also are examined. Next we turn to a discussion of adolescent dating relationships. The chapter closes with a discussion of some of the serious social problems faced by teenagers today.

As you study the chapter, look for the answers to the following questions:

1. What factors led to the development of adolescence as a distinct stage of the life cycle in the United States?
2. What are the five general characteristics of adolescence?
3. What factors led to the development of dating, and what functions does dating fulfill?
4. What are some of the social problems facing contemporary teenagers?

KEY TERMS

The following terms, while not the only terms emphasized in the chapter, are basic to your understanding of sociology. Determine the meaning of each term, either by using the Glossary or by watching for context clues as you read the chapter.

adolescence
puberty

anticipatory socialization
homogamy

drug
social integration

"THERE'S THIS CUTE GUY IN MY HISTORY CLASS, AND I THINK HE KIND OF LIKES ME. I KNOW I REALLY LIKE HIM. UNFORTUNATELY HIS GIRLFRIEND LIKES HIM, TOO. WHAT DO I DO?"

A: Nothing, unless you want to get into one of the stickiest situations known to humankind. Solid relationships require trust and respect. That means everyone tells the truth and respects the feelings of others. Breaking apart a relationship requires lying, sneaking around, and manipulation. Sound exciting? It is—at first. Unfortunately relationships that start this way seldom work out, and in the end you just might hate yourself.

That said, it is possible for you to be a friend to this guy while you wait for the right—and I do mean right—time. Let him know that you like him and would like him even more if it made sense to do so. But don't cross that line. Unless they get married, you'll get your shot—not as the "other woman" but as one half of a couple ready, willing, and able to give each other a fresh start.

SEVENTEEN

Dealing with and catering to the special problems and interests of adolescents is an important feature of American society. On the positive side, there are magazines, movies, television shows, music, and clothes aimed at the adolescent market. The magazine *Seventeen,* for instance, has a paid circulation of more than 1,850,000 copies. The appeal of television programs such as "The Wonder Years," "Fresh Prince," and "Beverly Hills 90210" comes primarily from people's fascination with the experiences of adolescence. On the negative side, the growing number of teenagers in trouble has led to numerous services, agencies, and source materials designed to provide help.

Because adolescence is so much a part of American culture, it may surprise you to learn that it is not a universal phenomenon. In many parts of the world, the concept of adolescence simply does not exist. As a distinct stage of the life cycle, adolescence is the creation of modern industrial society. In this chapter, we will explore what it means to be an adolescent in American society.

1 ADOLESCENCE IN OUR SOCIETY

Adolescence is a unique stage in a person's life. The adolescent is caught between two worlds—no longer a child and not yet an adult in the eyes of society. **Adolescence** can be defined as the period between the normal onset of puberty and the beginning of adulthood. **Puberty** is the physical maturing that makes an individual capable of sexual reproduction. Unlike adolescence, puberty occurs in all human societies.

In American society, adolescence generally is considered to include the ages between 13 and 21. The beginning and end dates of adolescence are somewhat blurred, however, since puberty and acceptance into the adult world occur at different times for different people.

The Concept of Adolescence

As we have said, adolescence is not universal. In some preindustrial societies, such as the Ndembu of northern Zambia, young people go directly from childhood to adulthood once they have performed the necessary puberty rites. *Puberty rites* are formal ceremonies that mark the entrance of young people into adulthood. Puberty rites differ

Child labor was common throughout the 1800s. In 1831, for example, about 40 percent of all workers in the cotton textile mills of Rhode Island were children under the age of 12. The Fair Labor Standards Act, which went into effect in 1938, brought an end to child labor in most major industries. The act outlaws the employment of children under the age of 16 in industries that engage in interstate commerce.

from society to society. Common puberty rites include demonstrations of strength or endurance, ritual filing of the teeth, and tattooing or scarring of the skin.

At the age of 13 or 14, young people who successfully complete these puberty rites can marry, set up households, and become accepted members of adult society. For these people, adolescence is an unknown concept.

Adolescence as a life stage also is a relatively recent phenomenon. In the United States, this stage did not exist prior to the Civil War. Before this time, young people were treated simply as small adults. It has only been in the past 40 or 50 years that the adolescent experience has become an acknowledged stage of development in the United States and other industrialized nations.

Three factors have been particularly important in the development of adolescence as a distinct stage of the life cycle. The first factor is education. Young people are required to spend many years in school. State laws make education mandatory up to about the age of 16. Young people who attend college usually are in their early 20s when they graduate. For those people who pursue graduate degrees, educational requirements will lengthen the time spent in school even further. Educational pursuits tend to extend the period of adolescence because many people who are in school are dependent on others for their financial support. Also, many people in school do not take on the roles of adulthood—provider, parent, spouse, and so on.

The second factor that distinguishes young people as a separate group is the exclusion of youth from the labor force. In most states, child labor laws prevent people from entering the labor force until age 16. However, since most young people lack the training to compete for all but the most routine jobs, adolescents usually work only part time while continuing to go to school.

The third factor in the rise of adolescence as a distinct stage of the life cycle is the development of the juvenile justice system. By distinguishing between juvenile and adult offenders, our society has in effect created a separate legal status for young people.

Characteristics of Adolescence

The experiences of adolescence are not, of course, the same for everyone. There are, however, five characteristics that generally apply to all adolescents. These characteristics include biological growth and development, an undefined status, increased decision making, increased pressures, and the search for self.

Biological Growth and Development. Puberty is the one aspect of adolescence that is found in every society. Puberty is universal because it is biological rather than cultural in origin. Biological development is controlled by the brain and the endocrine system, which consists of glands that produce various hormones.

During early adolescence, individuals often experience spurts in height and weight, changes in body proportions, the development of primary and secondary sexual characteristics, and, for many, complexion problems. According to the U.S. Food and Drug Administration, about 80 percent of teenagers develop some form of acne. These various biological changes sometimes cause anxiety or embarrassment to the adolescent, particularly when the individual is physically way ahead or way behind others of the same age.

Undefined Status. Our society's expectations for children are quite clear. The expectations for adults also are known. For the adolescent, however, expectations often are vague. Some adults treat adolescents like children, and others treat them like adults. It is difficult for adolescents to determine their status. For instance, many states in the nation allow young people to get married with parental consent at age 16. They must be 18, however, before they can legally cast their vote.

Adult society seems to have conflicting attitudes toward adolescents. On the one hand, American society is considered to be youth-oriented. It has adopted some of the values and styles of dress that are popular among teenagers. On the other hand, adults often are critical of the way adolescents dress, the music they listen to, and the way they behave.

Increased Decision Making. Young children have most of their decisions made for them by adults. But when children reach adolescence, they must make many of their own decisions. What courses should be taken in school? What sports should be entered? What school clubs should be joined? Should a college education be considered? What career would be best? There seems to be no end to the decisions that must be made. Some of these decisions are of little long-term importance. Other decisions, such as choosing a career, will have far-reaching consequences.

Increased Pressure. Adolescents are faced with pressure from many sources. Parents, for instance, generally make rules stating what time their adolescent children must be home, who they can see, and where they can go. Yet parents also want their children to be sociable. Thus young

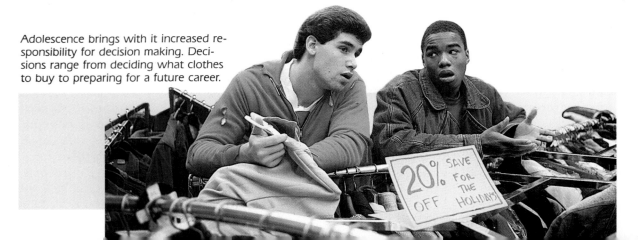

Adolescence brings with it increased responsibility for decision making. Decisions range from deciding what clothes to buy to preparing for a future career.

The Blurring of Adolescence

In recent years, a striking change has taken place in the images and roles of children and adults in industrialized nations. Children have tended to become more adult-like, while adults have taken on more of the characteristics of children. It is becoming increasingly difficult to tell where one stage ends and the next begins. This blurring of differences has occurred most notably in the areas of dress, behavior, language, and education.

Until relatively recently, one of the best indicators of age and role differences was clothing. Young people dressed in jeans and T-shirts. Suits, designer clothes, and other sophisticated fashions were left to the adults. Today, dressed in their jeans, sneakers, and cartoon-character T-shirts, many adults look like big kids. Children, on the other hand, look like miniature adults in their three-piece suits and designer dresses. And people of all ages—from infants to grandparents—wear designer jeans.

Many child and adult behaviors are becoming similar as well. For instance, the gestures, ways of sitting, and general posture of both groups are remarkably alike. Adults and children also play many of the same sports and even share an interest in certain toys. Video and computer games, for example, are popular with all ages. And unfortunately, many adults and children also share some of the same difficulties. In the past two decades, problems such as alcoholism and suicide have become much more common among young people.

Language also has spread across the generation gap. Adults have adopted many of the slang expressions and special vocabularies commonly used by adolescents. And even more significant, topics once discussed only by adults are now discussed freely and openly by children and adolescents alike.

Even education, which once was thought of as an institution designed to serve children, has been affected by the blurring of roles among adolescence and adulthood. There are growing numbers of adults who are returning to school in middle age. Some are taking continuing education classes, others are taking courses so that they can change careers.

The entertainment industry also has helped to narrow the gap between generations. On television and in the movies, children often are seen outsmarting adults. The movie *Home Alone* provides one such example. In some cases, such as in the movie *E.T.*, children even are shown as being more mature, sensitive, and intelligent than adults.

Television has played a major role in the creation of adult-like children. Prior to the electronic age, children received much of their social information from the books they read. Children read children's books, which contained information appropriate to a child's level of understanding. Adult information was contained in adult books, which children did not read. Today, children have access to adult information through television. Children are exposed to adult situations and adult views of life. Many social scientists hold that the removal of the barriers between child information and adult information has thrust children prematurely into the adult world.

Teenagers may be the biggest losers in this merging of adolescence and adulthood. Many childhood specialists fear that the shortening or blurring of adolescence may force young people to grow up too quickly. Social scientists argue that by rushing through adolescence, people are missing many of the special features that the period has to offer. For instance, the adult-like child is denied the opportunity to experiment with ideas and to try on new roles without being judged by adult standards. According to David Elkind, a child psychologist, one of the results of hurrying through childhood is increased stress during adolescence and young adulthood.

people are under pressure to strike a balance between parental wishes and peer pressure. Adolescents also have pressures placed on them in school. They are pressured to attend classes, complete assignments, pass tests, and participate in school clubs and activities.

Perhaps the greatest pressures come from peers. Teenagers want to be accepted by their peers and to become a part of the "in" group. If their friends have cars, most teenagers will feel some pressure to have cars of their own. Teenagers also are pressured to go along ith the latest fads and fashions. Billions of dollars are spent annually designing and marketing clothes, cosmetics, sports equipment, magazines, movies, tapes, and compact discs to teenage consumers. In most cases, the advertisements for these products make heavy use of peer pressure.

In addition, adolescents face pressure to establish relationships. Acceptance and popularity are central concerns. How can a meaningful relationship be established? What should be done to maintain it? What does it take to be popular? These questions are common during adolescence.

Many adolescents also face job pressures. The first pressure is finding a part-time or summer job. Then there is the pressure of having enough time for a job, schoolwork, a family life, and social activities. Adolescents are apt to find themselves in situations in which their various roles of son or daughter, employee, student, athlete, club member, and friend conflict with one another.

The Search for Self. Adolescents are mature enough to think about themselves and what they want out of life. They can sort through their values and decide what things really are most important to them. They can establish personal norms that will guide their behavior. They can set priorities for their lives. These abilities are important because when people know who they are, what they want out of life, and which values and norms will serve them best, they are in a better position to make the most of adulthood.

Participation in Extracurricular Activities by Categories of 10th Graders, 1990 (in percents)

Extracurricular Activity	White	African American	Hispanic American	Asian American	Native American
Baseball/softball	16.0	13.7	15.7	13.9	19.8
Basketball	18.2	30.9	16.6	22.8	21.8
Football	14.7	22.6	16.0	16.2	14.5
Swim team	4.1	2.8	3.3	5.2	3.7
Cheerleading	5.3	9.9	5.2	3.8	14.6
School band	21.7	22.3	14.1	20.1	19.5
School play	11.0	12.1	9.3	13.0	9.8
Student government	7.3	7.4	5.9	9.8	8.6
Honor society	7.3	8.1	7.5	13.9	7.7
Yearbook/newspaper	8.5	10.5	7.3	12.7	13.1
Service clubs	11.7	10.4	9.9	18.1	9.2
Academic clubs	31.1	25.1	26.7	35.9	31.2

Source: *Digest of Education Statistics, 1992*, p. 136.

Dating, volunteer work, and part-time jobs are important forms of anticipatory socialization for teenagers.

One aspect of finding yourself is preparing for future roles. Thus anticipatory socialization is an important part of adolescent development. The term **anticipatory socialization** refers to learning the rights, obligations, and expectations of a role in preparation for assuming that role at a future date. Playing house as a child is a form of anticipatory socialization for adult family roles. During adolescence, however, anticipatory socialization becomes much more important because the time for taking on adult roles is much closer at hand. A part-time job, club membership, and dating are three common forms of anticipatory socialization during adolescence.

These five characteristics are quite general. Individual experiences may differ somewhat. No one lives only in an adolescent subculture. Place of residence, economic status, and family composition, for instance, can affect life during adolescence. Similarly, race, religion, and cultural heritage can make a difference in the kinds of adolescent experiences a person has.

SECTION 1 REVIEW

DEFINE adolescence, puberty, anticipatory socialization

1. **Summarizing Ideas** What factors in our society have led to the development of a separate stage of life called adolescence?

2. **Understanding Ideas** What are the five general characteristics of adolescence?

3. **Using Sociological Imagination** How might such factors as where you live, the economic status of your family, your cultural background, or your family structure affect your experiences as an adolescent?

2 TEENAGERS AND DATING

Dating is a social behavior that is familiar to the vast majority of Americans, especially teenagers. Like adolescence, however, dating is not a universal phenomenon. In some societies, marriages are arranged by parents or by go-betweens who negotiate a formal contract between families. In some cases, the future spouses do not even see each other until their wedding day. Dating, as a form of social interaction, is most commonly found in societies that allow individuals to choose their own marriage partners.

Because dating is so familiar to us, it might seem as though it has been around forever. Dating actually is a relatively recent phenomenon. It did not emerge as a form of social interaction between the sexes until just after World War I. And, it is only in the past 60 years that sociologists have taken an interest in dating as a topic of study.

Prior to World War I, couples did not "date" in the modern sense of the word. Rather, a woman was "courted" by a man. Courtship during this time was expected to lead to marriage and usually was conducted under supervision.

Prior to the rise of dating in the United States, interaction between young unmarried men and women was restricted to courtship. Courtship differs from dating in that courtship's express purpose is eventual marriage. Dating, on the other hand, may eventually lead to marriage, but not necessarily so. Its main purpose is recreation and amusement, at least in the casual stages.

Because dating is the means through which individuals eventually do select their marriage mates in modern society, it might be helpful to view the process as a continuum. The continuum begins with casual dating, progresses to steady dating, and then moves to engagement and eventually to marriage. As individuals move along the continuum, the degree of commitment given to the relationship increases. Under our modern relationship system, however, the interaction is allowed to stop at any point along the continuum, and stages may be bypassed. This relationship system is a very flexible one.

The courtship system that existed prior to dating was not this flexible. To understand courtship in modern terms, we may place it somewhere between steady dating and engagement on the continuum. Courtship was not casual. To court a woman, a young man was expected first to meet her parents and ask their permission. It also was expected that the man's intentions would be honorable and, above all, marriage-minded.

Courtship usually was conducted in the parlor of the woman's home under close supervision or in a social situation among a group of people. Rarely was a couple left alone. If the relationship continued for any length of time, marriage was the expected outcome. Roles were very strictly defined during this time. And, while young people did have fun together, the main purpose of their interaction was to find a mate. It was from this base that modern-day dating emerged.

The Emergence of Dating

A number of factors led to the emergence of casual dating between unmarried men and women in the twentieth century. Among the most important of these factors are those associated with the rise of industrialization.

Prior to the Industrial Revolution, the economy of the United States was based primarily on agriculture. The timing of marriage was determined by the age at which a man acquired the property necessary to support a family. This generally meant that marriage was delayed until a young man's father was willing to transfer a portion of the family land to the son for his own use. Because family property was involved, parents tended to exercise considerable control over the marriage choices of their children.

The Industrial Revolution, however, encouraged people to move away from the land and into the cities. Young adults now were less dependent on their parents for economic security. They could seek employment away from the family farm and establish their own households independent of their parents' assistance. This economic freedom reduced parental control over courtship and set the stage for the development of dating.

Urban life coupled with child labor laws also helped to bring about the development of dating. No longer required to work in the fields and prohibited by law from working in factories, young people had increased free time on their hands. Because urban parents worked outside of the home, much of this free time was spent away from the direct supervision of adults.

Free public secondary education also helped to pave the way for dating. By the beginning of the twentieth century, the majority of secondary school students were enrolled in public schools. Unlike many private schools, public schools were coeducational. This meant that young men and women spent a good portion of their day with one another.

The trend toward dating accelerated after World War I. This partially was due to the fact that telephones and automobiles became more common. Telephones made it easier to arrange social engagements and automobiles gave young people added freedom of movement. The 1920s also was a period of increased social and political equality for women. More women entered the work force and took on active roles in the community. As a result, the interaction between single adult men and women increased. Under these changed social conditions, unchaperoned dating was a much more practical form of interaction than was the formal courtship system of earlier times.

One of the earliest sociological analyses of American dating patterns was offered by Willard

Waller. Based on an analysis of students at Pennsylvania State University during the late 1920s and early 1930s, Waller concluded that casual dating was a form of recreation that had little to do with mate selection. Status attainment and excitement were at the center of the dating process. Partners were selected on the basis of status characteristics, such as good looks, nice clothes, and popularity. According to Waller, this contrasted sharply with what occurred in the courtship, or mate-selection process. In mate selection, a person's character (based on factors such as dependability and honesty) was of primary importance.

Waller found that dating on the Pennsylvania State campus was almost totally limited to members of sororities and fraternities. Individuals dated people of similar social rank—members of the "best" fraternities dated members of the "best" sororities. Women ranked potential dates according to such status characteristics as fraternity membership, looks, money, clothes, cars, and dancing ability. The object was to be seen with

Sociologist Willard Waller was among the first social scientists to study American dating patterns. In the late 1920s and early 1930s, Waller examined dating practices at Pennsylvania State University.

the "right" people. To be seen with a person of lower status could damage one's own social standing on campus.

Research since the 1930s has not supported Waller's conclusion that casual dating is a process separate from mate selection. While status attainment and recreation certainly are major factors that attract people in casual dating, character and personality factors also are important. Research has indicated that there are similarities between the qualities that an individual looks for in a casual date and what he or she looks for in a marriage partner. Furthermore, research has shown that status attainment is important both in casual dating and in mate selection and that it is a function of homogamy. **Homogamy** is the tendency for individuals to marry people who have social characteristics similar to their own.

Why Date?

As already mentioned, the ultimate function of the dating process is mate selection. There are, however, at least four additional functions served by dating. First, dating is a form of recreation. Dating allows young people to get together simply to have fun. This is particularly true in the case of casual dating. Second, dating is a mechanism for socialization. It teaches individuals about members of the opposite sex and how to behave in social situations. It also helps individuals learn appropriate role behavior and define their self-concepts. Third, dating fulfills certain basic psychological needs such as conversation, companionship, and understanding. Fourth, dating helps individuals attain status. In a system in which individuals choose their own marriage partners, people are judged in part by whom they date. Dating a person who is valued by others as a potential date can raise one's own status.

All of these functions are not necessarily present at each stage of the dating continuum, or if present, they may not carry the same weight. In the case of casual dating, for instance, recreation and status attainment may be, as Waller suggested, the most important functions. As the level of commitment in a relationship increases, however, the functions of socialization and psychological fulfillment may be of primary concern.

Although it often leads to marriage, dating also serves many other important functions.

Dating Patterns

Dating patterns, like dating relationships, can be viewed as a continuum. At the far left are traditional dating patterns. These patterns are most closely associated with dating behavior prior to the 1960s. At the far right of the continuum are the informal patterns that are characteristic of contemporary society.

Traditional Dating Patterns. Although traditional dating patterns still can be found in some areas of the United States, particularly in small towns, they are most characteristic of dating during the 1940s and 1950s. Under the traditional dating system, responsibility for arranging a date fell to the male. He was expected to contact his intended dating partner, suggest a time and place

Text continues on page 134.

APPLYING SOCIOLOGY

Themes in Popular Songs

Music is a basic part of adolescence. Many adolescents consider it very important to own the latest tapes and compact discs. They also spend many hours listening to their favorite songs on the radio. What themes are stressed in these popular songs? How do these themes relate to the lives of adolescents? A little research in the form of content analysis can help us answer these questions.

Before focusing on the questions, however, re-read the sections in the chapter on the characteristics of adolescence and on the dating relationship. Based on the information, compile a list of issues that are important in adolescence. The list might include

A. the effects of or problems with physical maturity. *

B. the effects of or ways of dealing with the undefined status of adolescents in modern society.

C. the problems associated with or benefits of increased decision-making power during adolescence.

D. the increased pressures of adolescence.

E. the problems involved in establishing meaningful relationships.

F. the search for self-identity during adolescence.

G. the forms of anticipatory socialization common in adolescence.

H. the learning of correct ways to behave in social situations.

I. the importance of establishing friendships with members of the opposite sex.

J. the need to be flexible in a relationship.

K. the expectations and commitments involved in relationships.

Now you are ready to tackle the questions. First, you will need to obtain a list of the top 40 or 50 songs currently on the charts. Music stores and radio stations that play popular music have such a list. Next, listen to as many of the songs as you can. (It might be easier to use songbooks or other sources of printed lyrics when available.) As you examine each song, jot down information that will enable you to answer the following questions:

1. What is the name of the song?

2. What is the main theme of the song?

3. Are there any secondary themes?

4. What are the key words or phrases in the song that give a clue to the main theme or secondary themes?

After you have gathered this information for a sufficient number of songs, compare the song themes with the issues raised in the chapter. How do they compare? Which song theme appears most often in the popular songs? Why do you think this is so?

You might also conduct a similar study of the books that are most popular with adolescents. Such a study would give you additional insight into why adolescence is such a unique period of development.

To help you tabulate your findings, it might be helpful to construct a chart similar to the one on page 133. The letters refer to the issues in the list you compiled and the numbers refer to the songs or books. Each song or book can have an entry in as many lettered categories as applicable. Each time a song or book deals with an issue, place a mark in the appropriate square of the chart. Once you have analyzed all of the material, count the number of marks in each square to get an idea of which themes appear to be most common in popular songs or books.

for the date, select the activity, and pay for any expenses that arose.

Dating behavior was quite ritualized. Both parties knew what was expected of them because the rules of conduct were well defined by the group to which they belonged. Pressure to conform to expected behavior was strong. Behavior that was not in line with group expectations met with sharp resistance. In most cases, there was an established weekly timetable for setting up a date. If Wednesday was the designated day for arranging Saturday night dates, attempts made later in the week often met with rejection. Because everyone was expected to hold to the timetable, accepting a date late in the week was an admission on a young woman's part that she was not a young man's first choice. Dating was so expected and so tied to social status that individuals who did not have dates on prime dating nights often hid in their rooms in shame.

Dates, particularly in the early stages of a relationship, tended to revolve around set activities such as going to movies or to sporting events. This lessened the strain of getting to know one

Sociologists have found that today's teenagers are more likely to participate in friendship-based groups than they are to go steady.

another. Attention could be focused on the activity rather than on the individual if interaction between the dating partners became awkward.

If a couple continued to date casually over a period of time, the relationship often developed into one of steady dating. Steady dating carried with it a formal set of expectations and commitments. As a visible symbol of commitment, the young man often gave the young woman his class ring, identification bracelet, or letterman's jacket. Because of the level of commitment involved, steady dating was a form of anticipatory socialization for marriage. Nevertheless, it was not necessarily expected to lead to marriage. Individuals commonly had several "steadies" before settling on a marriage partner.

Contemporary Dating Patterns. Studies have found that dating since the 1960s has not followed such formal patterns. Today's youth tend to be more spontaneous in their interaction with one another. Dates often are not prearranged. Instead, a couple will break away from a group activity on the spur of the moment. Both males and females now actively initiate dates. Similarly, it is acceptable for either partner to pay for the date or for each person to pay his or her own way.

This tendency toward flexibility points out some important differences between traditional dating patterns and contemporary patterns. Under the traditional dating system, interaction was formal and the relationship centered on the couple. In order to obtain a date, the male had to have a good "line"—some method of selling himself to his intended date. Today, however, relationships tend to be based on friendship, and the group, rather than the couple, is the most important focus of interaction. Consequently, it is less often necessary to use a line to create a false favorable first impression.

One interesting contradiction to contemporary dating patterns can be found among the Amish of Lancaster County, Pennsylvania. The Amish have lived in the United States for hundreds of years but choose to have little to do with society outside of their own community. They devote themselves to intensive farming and live without electricity, telephones, automobiles, appliances, or any other mark of the modern world.

The dating activities that today's high school students take almost for granted practically are unknown to Amish youth. Amish communities have no movie theaters, beaches, football stadiums, or cars. Yet practically all Amish youth date, court, and eventually marry.

The best opportunity for Amish youth to get together is at the Sunday evening "singings." At these singings, the young people of the community gather around a long table to sing hymns and talk. Along with the singings, cornhusking, weddings, and picnics provide occasions for fun and relaxation.

Dating actually begins at around age 16 for Amish boys, when their fathers customarily buy them a "courting buggy." Girls usually begin dating at around age 14. The Amish only marry other Amish. Thus the young people are quite limited in whom they can date and marry. This sometimes is a problem because most Amish communities only number around 200 people. And, since the boys are limited in their transportation, they only can go as far as a horse and buggy can carry them in an evening. Hence, most Amish youth court with marriage in mind, and apparently they are quite successful in their choices. No divorces have yet been reported among the Amish.

SECTION 2 REVIEW

DEFINE homogamy

1. *Seeing Relationships* **(a)** What are the characteristics of courtship, and how does it differ from dating? **(b)** What factors led to the development of casual dating?

2. *Comprehending Ideas* What are the five functions served by dating?

3. *Comparing Ideas* How do traditional dating patterns differ from the patterns common today?

3 PROBLEMS OF ADOLESCENCE

Adolescence is a turbulent and often perplexing time of life. The characteristics of adolescence that mark it as a distinct stage in the life cycle give rise to pressures and problems generally not found in childhood. Caught between the relative safety of childhood and the supposed independence of adulthood, teenagers face important developmental tasks—carving out an identity, planning for the future, becoming more independent, and developing close relationships. Most teenagers accomplish these tasks with a minimum of trauma. Others, however, do not. For these teenagers, life at times seems overwhelming.

The 1980s and the 1990s have seen an explosion in scientific research on the adolescent stage of development. Much of this research has focused on the problems faced by today's teenagers. Some of the more serious issues concerning adolescents that currently are being addressed by social scientists are teenage sexual behavior, teenage drug abuse, and teenage suicide.

Teenage Sexual Behavior

Like so many other social phenomena, the norms governing sexual behavior vary widely from society to society and even within a single society over time. Some small preindustrial societies, such as the Mangaians of Polynesia, permit adolescents to engage in sexual behavior before marriage. In some of these societies, such as the Trobriand Islanders and the Illa-speaking peoples of central Africa, sexual experimentation even is encouraged. Such experimentation is viewed as preparation for marriage and as a way of determining whether a young girl is able to become pregnant.

In Western nations, on the other hand, traditional sexual values include strict norms against premarital sexuality. Traditional sexual values in the United States are an outgrowth of Puritan and Victorian views of sexual morality. According to these views, sexual activity should be confined to marriage.

Until the 1960s, traditional sexual values had the support of the vast majority of Americans—at least in principle, if not always in practice. In the 1960s and 1970s, however, the development of the birth control pill, a large youth counterculture, and the feminist movement encouraged an end to the sexual double standard and led to the development of what has been called the "sexual revolution."

During the so-called sexual revolution, the norms governing sexual behavior began to change. For many people, human sexuality became a topic that was openly discussed and explored. As a consequence, sexuality is today a familiar feature of American culture. Sexual references, for instance, are common in the programs and commercials seen by the 98 percent of American households that own television sets. Similarly, varying degrees

FOX TROT   by Bill Amend

© 1988 *Universal Press Syndicate*, reprinted with permission. All rights reserved.

of physical intimacy are found in almost every film that does not carry a G rating. In addition, advertisers have for years been using the lure of sexuality to sell their products.

One of the unanticipated consequences of the changing norms concerning sexuality has been a dramatic increase in adolescent sexual behavior. This has led social scientists to devote considerable time to measuring the rate of teenage sexual activity and analyzing the factors that influence teenage sexuality.

The Rate of Teenage Sexual Activity.

Survey data from the Centers for Disease Control and Prevention indicate that 29 percent of unmarried American females between the ages of 15 and 19 were sexually active in 1970. By 1990, the rate of sexual activity had increased to 48 percent for the same category of teenagers. Teenage childbearing has shown a similar pattern. In 1970, there were 22 births per 1,000 unmarried teenage females. By 1989, this figure had risen to 41 births per 1,000 unmarried females.

The birth rate among American teenagers is five times higher than it is among teenagers of other industrialized nations such as France, Denmark, and Japan. According to social scientists, this is not because American teenagers are more sexually active. Rather, it is because teenagers in the United States use birth control less effectively and with less regularity than teenagers in many other industrialized countries.

The Centers for Disease Control and Prevention reports that its national health objectives for the year 2000 include efforts toward increasing the proportion of American teenagers who abstain from sexual activity. For those teenagers unwilling to abstain, program efforts will encourage the use of effective methods of birth control.

Influences on Early Sexual Activity.

Social scientists have developed a number of explanations concerning the reasons why some adolescents engage in sexual activity. Most often, these explanations focus on social and economic factors or on subcultural factors.

Among the social and economic factors found to influence early sexual activity are family income level, parents' marital status, and religious participation. In general, teenagers from higher-income,

Many programs around the country are urging young people to abstain from sexual activity until they are married.

two-parent families tend to have lower rates of sexual activity than teenagers from low-income, one-parent families. Similarly, teenagers who actively practice their religion tend to hold less permissive attitudes and are less experienced sexually than nonreligious teenagers.

Explanations that focus on subcultural factors suggest that teenage sexual activity is influenced by subgroup norms concerning sexual behavior. Generally, teenagers whose friends engage in premarital sexuality are more likely to be sexually active than are those whose friends are not sexually active. Early sexual behavior also is associated with other risk-taking behaviors such as drug use and delinquency.

The Consequences of Early Sexual Activity.

Sexuality, like all human activity, has consequences. For teenagers, these consequences often are negative. Social scientists who study teenage sexuality tend to focus on the social and health factors associated with early sexual activity.

Research has indicated that only about one-third of American teenage women who engage in premarital sex use birth control methods on a regular basis. Thus it is not surprising that each year more than 10 percent of teenage women become pregnant.

Teenage pregnancy has been found to have a number of negative consequences. Chief among these are the following:

- Babies born to teenage mothers have lower birth weights and are more likely to die within the first year of life than are babies born to women over the age of 20.
- Death during childbirth is more common for teenage mothers than it is for women over the age of 20.
- Teenagers who become mothers and fathers are less likely to finish high school and college than are teenagers who do not become parents. This is particularly true for teenage mothers.
- Due in large part to lower levels of education, individuals who become parents during adolescence have lower lifetime earnings than do people who delay parenthood until later in life.
- Children of teenage parents are more likely to experience learning difficulties than are children of older parents.
- Children of teenage parents have an increased risk of becoming teenage parents themselves.

Even when pregnancy does not occur, early sexual activity can have a negative health impact by exposing teenagers to sexually transmitted diseases such as syphilis, gonorrhea, chlamydia, and acquired immune deficiency syndrome (AIDS). More than half of the people in the United States suffering from sexually transmitted diseases are under the age of 25. In 1991, for example, people aged 15–24 accounted for 34 percent of syphilis cases and over 61 percent of gonorrhea cases. Chlamydia also is widespread among the young.

AIDS is a fatal disease caused by a virus that attacks an individual's immune system, leaving the person vulnerable to a host of deadly infections. This fatal disease is becoming an increasingly serious threat among the teenage population. High rates of sexual activity combined with low rates of effective condom use put teenagers at risk of contracting the disease through sexual contact with infected partners.

Studies have shown that teenagers tend to believe that AIDS is something that cannot happen to them. According to a 1992 congressional report, however, HIV, the virus that is believed to cause AIDS, is spreading rapidly throughout the nation's adolescent population. More significantly,

AIDS now is the sixth leading cause of death among young people aged 15 to 24.

Teenage Drug Use

A **drug** is any substance that changes mood, behavior, or consciousness. Drugs exist in many forms, including alcohol, cigarettes, marijuana, cocaine, and heroin. Drug use has a long history. The Greeks smoked opium over 4,000 years ago, and hallucinogens commonly were used by the Aztecs. Even in the United States, the use of heroin and cocaine for nonmedical purposes was not outlawed until 1914, with the passage of the Harrison Narcotics Act. In fact, during the latter half of the 1800s, cocaine could be found as an ingredient in a wide variety of products, including Coca-Cola, cough medicines, and nasal sprays.

In recent years, however, the public has become increasingly alarmed over the social consequences of drug abuse. This alarm primarily is a result of concern over the dramatic increase in drug-related crime during the 1980s and 1990s.

Even more frightening than the muggings, robberies, and burglaries committed by addicts in search of drug money has been the growth in violence associated with drug trafficking. In 1985, for example, there were 508 drug-related murders in the United States. By 1991, that figure had climbed to more than 1,300 murders. This violence has resulted in large part from turf wars between rival gangs engaged in drug trafficking. In 1987, drug-related shootouts between gang members resulted in 387 deaths in Los Angeles. Over half of the people killed during that year were innocent bystanders. In 1990, Los Angeles gang members were responsible for 690 deaths.

Crack cocaine is the principle cause of the dramatic increase in gang violence. Crack, or "rock" as it also is known, is a highly addictive, smokable form of cocaine. While much of the crack trade is controlled by Jamaican gangs, called "posses," the foot soldiers tend to be children and teenagers. Children as young as 9 or 10 are hired as lookouts, eventually becoming runners and then drug dealers themselves.

Since crack first became common in the United States, drug-related juvenile arrests have skyrocketed. In Detroit, for example, arrests of juveniles for drug abuse violations have increased from 258

Trends in Drug Use Among High School Seniors

Drug	Percentage of Seniors Ever Having Used Drug												
	1979	1980	1981	1982	1983	1984	1985	1986	1987	1988	1989	1990	1991
Marijuana/hashish	60.4	60.3	59.5	58.7	57.0	54.9	54.2	50.9	50.2	47.2	43.7	40.7	36.7
Inhalants	18.2	17.3	17.2	17.7	18.2	18.0	18.1	20.1	18.6	17.5	18.6	18.5	18.0
Hallucinogens	17.7	15.6	15.3	14.3	13.6	12.3	12.1	11.9	10.6	9.2	9.9	9.7	10.0
Cocaine	15.4	15.7	16.5	16.0	16.2	16.1	17.3	16.9	15.2	12.1	10.3	9.4	7.8
Heroin	1.1	1.1	1.1	1.2	1.2	1.3	1.2	1.1	1.2	1.1	1.3	1.3	0.9
Other opiates	10.1	9.8	10.1	9.6	9.4	9.7	10.2	9.0	9.2	8.6	8.3	8.3	6.6
Stimulants	—	—	—	27.9	26.9	27.9	26.2	23.4	21.6	19.8	19.1	17.5	15.4
Sedatives	14.6	14.9	16.0	15.2	14.4	13.3	11.8	10.4	8.7	7.8	7.4	7.5	6.7
Tranquilizers	16.3	15.2	14.7	14.0	13.3	12.4	11.9	10.9	10.9	9.4	7.6	7.2	7.2
Alcohol	93.0	93.2	92.6	92.8	92.6	92.6	92.2	91.3	92.2	92.0	90.7	89.5	88.0
Cigarettes	74.0	71.0	71.0	70.1	70.6	69.7	68.8	67.6	67.2	66.4	65.7	64.4	63.1

Source: Based on information from the 1991 Monitoring the Future survey by Lloyd D. Johnston, Jerald G. Bachman, and Patrick M. O'Malley of the Institute for Social Research, University of Michigan.

in 1981 to 1,416 in 1987. The increases have been even more dramatic in New York City (from 349 in 1980 to 5,468 in 1990), Los Angeles (41 in 1980 to 2,423 in 1990), and Washington, D.C. (315 in 1980 to 1,068 in 1990).

The Rate of Teenage Drug Use. Since 1975, the University of Michigan's Institute for Social Research has been conducting an annual nationwide survey of high school seniors in an effort to measure drug use among teenagers. The table on this page shows changes in the rates of use for various drugs from 1979 through 1991.

As the table shows, usage patterns vary by type of drug. Although marijuana use has been in steady decline since 1979, it still is the most widely used illegal drug among high school seniors. Cocaine use has been in decline since 1985, but the use of hallucinogens such as LSD actually has increased slightly. In the case of cigarette smoking, the overall trend is downward, but reductions in recent years have been small despite repeated health warnings about the negative effects of smoking. Significantly, the surveys indicate that nearly 20 percent of high school seniors smoke on a daily basis.

Alcohol use among teenagers also has seen a slight decline in recent years, but it remains a widespread problem. Eighty-eight percent of the high school seniors surveyed in 1991 reported having used alcohol at some point, and 54 percent reported having had a drink as recently as a month before the survey was taken. In addition, 30 percent of the seniors surveyed said that they had had five or more drinks on a single occasion within two weeks of the survey. These findings are particularly significant considering the fact that it is illegal for virtually all high school students to purchase alcohol.

Although the downward trend in drug use is encouraging, two factors should be kept in mind when analyzing the data. First, even with the recent declines, the United States has the highest rate of drug use among adolescents of any industrialized nation. Second, the University of Michigan survey does not measure drug use among the approximately 15 to 20 percent of teenagers who do not graduate from high school. Research has indicated that high school dropouts have much higher rates of drug use than do high school graduates. This is especially true in the case of cigarette smoking and the use of cocaine and heroin. Thus it is likely that the survey underestimates the scope of the teenage drug problem.

Influences on Teenage Drug Use. Why do teenagers use drugs? Social scientists have found a number of factors to be associated with the regular use of drugs by teenagers. Chief among these factors are

- having friends who regularly engage in drug use;
- having social and academic adjustment problems; and
- living in a hostile and rejecting family setting.

Teenage Attitudes Toward Drug Use.

In addition to measuring the rate of drug use, the University of Michigan surveys have monitored changes in the attitudes of teenagers toward drug use. At the peak of marijuana use in 1979, only 42 percent of the seniors surveyed believed that regular marijuana use was harmful to one's health. By 1991, that figure had increased to about 80 percent. Similarly, in the late 1970s, approximately 69 percent of the seniors surveyed thought that regular cocaine use was harmful. By 1991, over 92 percent of those surveyed reported that regular cocaine use was harmful to one's health.

The view that cigarette smoking is harmful also has gained supporters over the years of the survey. In 1975, slightly more than 51 percent of the seniors believed that smoking one or more packs of cigarettes a day was harmful to one's health. By 1991, that figure had increased to around 70 percent. Attitudes toward the health dangers presented by alcohol, however, have remained quite low over the course of the University of Michigan surveys—less than 10 percent.

In recent years, the disapproval ratings for regular use of marijuana and cigarettes have increased. In 1977, for instance, slightly over 65 percent of the seniors surveyed disapproved of regular marijuana use. By 1991, more than 91 percent of those surveyed disapproved. The increase in the disapproval rate has been much smaller, however, in the case of cigarette smoking. In 1975, over 67 percent of the seniors responding to the University of Michigan survey disapproved of smoking one or more packs of cigarettes a day. By 1991, that figure had increased to only around 73 percent.

Negative attitudes toward regular use of drugs such as LSD, cocaine, heroin, amphetamines, and barbiturates have remained fairly constant over the course of the surveys. Depending on the drug, disapproval ratings have ranged from 90 percent to 98 percent. Daily use of alcohol also has received around a 90 percent negative response through the years of the survey.

Teenage Suicide

The rate of suicide among young people in the United States has nearly tripled in the past three decades. Each year, nearly half a million people between the ages of 15 and 24 attempt suicide. Approximately 5,000 of these attempts result in death. As the chart on page 141 shows, the suicide rate for young people currently exceeds the rate for the general population. Suicide is third only to accidents and homicides as the leading cause of death among people aged 15 to 24.

Social scientists who study suicide note that the actual number of suicides and attempted suicides probably is higher than official statistics indicate. Many attempted and completed suicides are reported as accidents. Researchers argue that suicide rates among the young would be much higher if single-car accidents, drug overdoses, and self-poisonings were taken into consideration.

In 1991, the Gallup Organization questioned young people aged 13 to 19 on the topic of suicide. Six percent of the respondents reported that they had tried to commit suicide. Another 15 percent said that they had come very close to trying. While these findings are startling, it is important to keep in mind that suicide is a much more serious problem among the elderly. The rate of suicide for people aged 75 to 84 is almost twice as high as it is among the young.

The Sociological View of Suicide.

When most people think of the causes and consequences of suicide, they think in terms of individuals. They see suicide as a personal act that results from psychological factors, such as depression or frustration. Sociologists acknowledge that suicide is an act committed by individuals, but they are more interested in the social factors that affect suicide rates. According to the sociological view of suicide, variations in suicide rates can be understood by studying the structure of society.

Emile Durkheim's classic 1897 study of the social causes of suicide still is the most comprehensive sociological analysis of suicide to date. Durkheim was interested in why some societies or groups within a society have higher rates of sui-

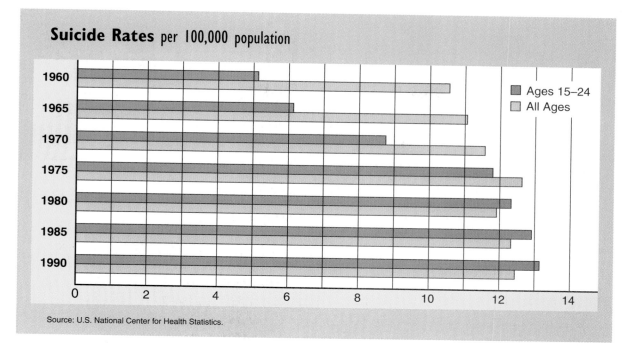

Suicide Rates per 100,000 population

Legend:
- Ages 15–24
- All Ages

Years shown: 1960, 1965, 1970, 1975, 1980, 1985, 1990

Scale: 0, 2, 4, 6, 8, 10, 12, 14

Source: U.S. National Center for Health Statistics.

cide than do others. According to Durkheim, variations in suicide rates can be explained by the level of social integration in a group or society. **Social integration** is the degree of attachment people have to social groups or to society as a whole. Durkheim predicted that groups or societies with particularly high or particularly low levels of social integration will have high rates of suicide.

According to Durkheim, high levels of social integration can lead to increased rates of suicide because group members place the needs of the group above their own personal needs. In traditional Eskimo society, for instance, the elderly walked off into the snow to die once they became a burden on the group. Strong community bonds made the elderly value the welfare of the group over their own welfare.

Even in Durkheim's time, suicides resulting from low levels of social integration were much more common than those resulting from high levels of integration. Low levels of integration occur in periods of social disorganization. This disorganization can result from many factors. Some common factors are rapid social change, increased geographic mobility, war or natural disasters, and sudden changes in economic conditions.

Suicide rates increase during periods of social disorganization because the norms that govern behavior weaken or become less clear. In addition, the social bonds that give individuals a sense of group solidarity—family ties and religion, for instance—tend to weaken during periods of social disorganization. Deprived of clear behavioral guidelines and adequate social support, some people turn to suicide as a last resort. Contemporary sociologists are most interested in the form of suicide caused by low levels of social integration, since this is the form most commonly found in modern industrialized societies.

Predictors of Teenage Suicide.   As teenagers move from the role of child to that of adult, they are faced with new freedoms as well as new restrictions. Many of the norms that governed proper behavior during childhood no longer apply. Yet many adult behaviors still are considered inappropriate. At the same time, friends and the larger society have more and more influence over teenagers' beliefs and actions. As the control of the family lessens, teenagers begin to take increasing responsibility for their own actions.

Most teenagers adapt to these changing expectations. For some, however, the confusion and self-doubt common in adolescence often are blown out of proportion. Because teenagers tend to focus so much on the present, often they do

The increase in teenage suicide has led most communities to institute a variety of programs designed to help troubled teens. Among the most common programs are suicide hotlines and group counseling.

not realize that most problems can be solved with time and patience. In some cases, social isolation and self-doubt lead to frustrations that may push adolescents toward suicidal behavior.

Suicide cuts across all social categories. There are cases of teenage suicide among both sexes, every economic level, and all races, religions, and nationalities. Nevertheless, certain social factors appear to affect the rates of teenage suicide. According to Brad L. Neiger and Rodney W. Hopkins, the following social factors are important.

- *Alcohol or drug use.* The risk of suicide increases along with an adolescent's use of alcohol and drugs. Social scientists offer three explanations for this fact. First, teenagers who are heavy users of alcohol and drugs typically have low levels of self-control and are easily frustrated. Second, teenagers under the influence of drugs or alcohol are more likely to act on impulse. Third, teenagers often use drugs and alcohol as the method by which to commit suicide.

- *Triggering events.* In most teenage suicides, a specific event or the anticipation of a specific event triggers the suicide attempt. Common events include fear of punishment, loss of or rejection by an important person, unwanted pregnancy, family crises, poor school performance, and fights with friends or parents.

- *Age.* The risk of suicide increases with age. Although children under the age of 13 do commit suicide, rates are much higher for older teenagers and young adults.

- *Sex.* Females are three times more likely than males to attempt suicide. Males, however, are much more likely to succeed. This is due in large part to the fact that teenage males often choose guns and other weapons as the means by which to commit suicide.

- *Population density.* Recent studies indicate that underpopulated areas have higher rates of teenage suicide than do heavily populated areas. Researchers believe that this may be due to the fact that social isolation is more likely in underpopulated areas. In addition, teenagers in underpopulated areas generally have access to fewer social services.

- *Family relations.* As Durkheim noted, the weakening of social bonds increases the likelihood of suicide. Thus it is not surprising that suicide rates are higher for teenagers from families in which violence, intense marital conflict, or the recent loss of a parent through divorce or death is evident. In addition, suicide is more common in those families in which parents show hostility or rejection toward their children.

- *Cluster effect.* A teenage suicide sometimes results in other suicide attempts among adolescents in a community. This is particularly true when a popular member of the community takes his or her life. In some instances, a well-publicized suicide can trigger "copycat" attempts in other communities as well. Mental health officials suggest that the cluster effect occurs because the news of a suicide acts as a fuse, igniting self-destructive behavior in already unstable adolescents.

As this list of factors indicates, teenage suicide rates are influenced by the same sociological factors that affect rates of suicide in the adult population. Chief among these factors are social isolation and the weakening of social bonds.

Most communities have programs and services geared toward helping teenagers over the rough spots common in adolescence. Perhaps what is most important for teenagers to learn is that they are not alone with their problems. Thus, teenagers suffering from feelings of isolation or frustration should be encouraged to seek help and guidance.

SECTION 3 REVIEW

DEFINE drug, social integration

1. ***Analyzing Ideas*** **(a)** How has the sexual behavior of American teenagers changed over the past few decades? **(b)** According to social scientists, what are some of the causes and consequences of early sexual activity?

2. ***Comprehending Ideas*** **(a)** How have rates of drug use among teenagers in the United States changed since 1979? **(b)** How have teenage attitudes toward drug use changed over the same time period?

3. ***Seeing Relationships*** What is the sociological view of suicide and how does it apply to the characteristics of teenage suicide?

CHAPTER 6   SUMMARY

Adolescence is the period in a person's life between puberty and adulthood. While puberty is a universal phenomenon, adolescence is a creation of modern industrial society.

There are five general characteristics of adolescence. First, adolescence is a time of biological growth and development. Second, the status of adolescents is undefined. Third, adolescence is a period of increased decision making. Fourth, adolescence is a time of great pressure from a variety of sources, most notably parents, school, and peers. And finally, adolescence is a time of finding oneself.

Dating plays a central role in adolescent life in modern society. This has not always been the case, however. Prior to the Industrial Revolution, courtship was the primary form of social interaction between unmarried members of the opposite

sex. Dating differs from courtship in that courtship's intended purpose is eventual marriage. Although dating is the means through which marriage partners are selected in modern society, eventual marriage is only one function of dating. Dating also serves as a form of recreation, a mechanism for socialization, a source of psychological fulfillment, and a means of status attainment.

The characteristics of adolescence that mark it as a distinct stage in the life cycle give rise to pressures and problems generally not found in childhood. In recent years, social scientists have devoted considerable time to the examination of the problems faced by today's teenagers. Among the topics being examined are the influences on and consequences of early sexual activity, the effects of drug and alcohol use, and the factors contributing to the increase in teenage suicide.

DEVELOPING SOCIOLOGICAL

INTERPRETING THE VISUAL RECORD: Interpreting Tables

Sociological data often are presented in the form of statistical tables. A statistical table presents numerical data in a single-column or multicolumn format. Single-column tables are used to present findings on a single set of data, such as the number of high school students who have cars of their own. Most statistical tables, however, are multicolumn. A multicolumn format is used to compare sets of data, such as the changes in labor force participation rates for male and female adolescents over a span of several years.

How to Interpret a Table

To interpret a table, follow these steps.

1. **Define the table's purpose.** The purpose of the table can be determined by reading the table's title and subtitle.

2. **Study the table's parts.** Read the table labels. Tables generally have two sets of labels: the labels at the head of each column and the labels along the left-hand side of the table. Be sure that you understand what the labels mean.

3. **Analyze the information.** First, determine what units of measurement are being used. The unit of measurement should be indicated in the table title or in the column headings. Usual units of measurement include hundreds, thousands, percentages, rates per 1,000 (such as 4 in every 1,000), or rates per 100,000. Second, note the time periods under consideration and the categories of data being presented. Also note the relationships among the data, such as any similarities, differences, and trends.

Labor Force Participation Rates for Adolescents, 1975–2005*

Sex and Age	Participation Rate (in percents)						
	1975	1980	1985	1990	1995	2000	2005
Male							
16–17 years	48.6	50.1	45.1	43.7	47.4	47.3	47.9
18–19 years	70.6	71.3	68.9	67.0	70.7	68.0	68.0
Female							
16–17 years	40.2	43.6	42.1	41.9	48.3	45.3	45.4
18–19 years	58.1	61.9	61.7	60.5	66.3	62.9	63.2

* The rates for 1995, 2000, and 2005 are projections.
Sources: *Statistical Abstract of the United States, 1988*, p. 366; *Statistical Abstract of the United States, 1992*, p. 381.

IMAGINATION

4. Put the data to use. Formulate conclusions based on the data.

Applying the Skill

Study the table on page 144, using the steps outlined above. The table shows labor force participation rates for adolescent males and females. Note that the figures are for five-year intervals beginning in 1975 and ending in 2005. The asterisk indicates that the figures for 1995, 2000, and 2005 are projections, or predictions of future events. The column headings list the years, and the labels along the left-hand side list two age intervals for men and two age intervals for women. Note that the figures are given in percents for five-year intervals. A comparison of the numbers indicates that participation rates are higher for males than for females. Rates also are higher for the older age category within each group. It can be concluded from the table that labor force participation increases with age and is slightly higher for males than for females.

Practicing the Skill

Study the table below. Then, on a separate sheet of paper, answer the following questions:

1. What is the purpose of the table?

2. What do the column headings and the left-hand labels indicate about the data?

3. What units of measurement are being used?

4. What relationships exist among the data?

5. What conclusions can be drawn from the data?

Unemployment Rate among Categories of Adolescents, Aged 16–19

| Year | Unemployment Rate (in percents) | | | | |
	Male	Female	White	African American	Hispanic American
1986	19.0	17.6	15.6	39.3	24.7
1987	17.8	15.9	14.4	34.7	22.3
1988	16.0	14.4	13.1	32.4	22.0
1989	15.9	14.0	12.7	32.4	19.4
1990	16.3	14.7	13.4	31.1	19.5
1991	19.8	17.4	16.4	36.3	22.9
1992	21.5	18.5	17.1	39.8	27.5

Source: U.S. Bureau of Labor Statistics.

Reviewing Sociological Terms

On a separate sheet of paper, supply the term that correctly completes each sentence.

1. _____ is the physical maturing that makes an individual capable of sexual reproduction.

2. The tendency for individuals to marry people who have social characteristics similar to their own is called _____.

3. _____ _____ is the learning of the rights, obligations, and expectations of a role in preparation for assuming that role at a future date.

4. _____ is the period between the normal onset of puberty and the beginning of adulthood.

5. The degree of attachment that people have to social groups or to society as a whole is called _____ _____.

Thinking Critically about Sociology

1. **Applying Ideas** Watch several television programs that focus on the daily life of one or more adolescents. **(a)** How many of the five general characteristics of adolescence appear to affect the teenagers on the programs? **(b)** Describe how the adults and teenagers on the programs deal with the consequences of the five characteristics of adolescence.

2. **Analyzing Ideas** **(a)** According to Willard Waller, how did casual dating patterns on the Pennsylvania State University campus during the late 1920s and early 1930s differ from courtship? **(b)** What conclusions have more recent researchers drawn concerning the relationship between casual dating and mate selection?

3. **Seeing Relationships** What role did the Industrial Revolution play in the rise of dating in the United States?

4. **Organizing Ideas** Prepare a structured overview of this chapter's discussion of teenage sexual behavior.

5. **Understanding Ideas** **(a)** What is the relationship continuum? **(b)** How do the functions of dating differ depending on what stage of the continuum is under consideration?

6. **Interpreting Graphics** Examine the table on participation in extracurricular activities on page 126. **(a)** Which activity has the highest rate of student participation? **(b)** Which group of students has the highest rate of participation in the school band?

7. **Using Sociological Imagination** **(a)** List the characteristics of traditional and contemporary dating patterns. **(b)** Next, create two fictional descriptions of a Saturday night date, one based on traditional patterns and one based on contemporary patterns.

Exercising Sociological Skills

1. **Conducting Research** Select five short stories that have adolescents as main characters. Conduct a content analysis of the short stories using the procedures outlined in the Applying Sociology feature on pages 132–133.

2. **Summarizing Ideas** Reread the Case Study feature on page 125. What factors have led to the blurring of adolescence?

3. **Interpreting a Table** Reread the Developing Sociological Imagination feature on pages 144–145. Use the steps outlined in the feature to write a brief description of the trends presented in the table on page 139.

Extending Sociological Imagination

1. Prepare a brief report on the social factors that affect teenage suicide rates.

2. Research the laws relating to juveniles in your state. How do these laws result in different treatment for juveniles and adults in the court and prison systems?

INTERPRETING PRIMARY SOURCES
Teenagers and Eating Disorders

Among the problems faced by some of today's teenagers are the eating disorders bulimia nervosa and anorexia nervosa. In this excerpt from the article "Eating Disorders Require Medical Attention," which appeared in the March 1992 issue of *FDA Consumer*, Dixie Farley discusses why bulimia nervosa and anorexia nervosa are a threat to good health. While reading the excerpt, consider what factors might influence teenagers to develop eating disorders. Also consider why such disorders are harmful.

For reasons that are unclear, some people—mainly young women—develop potentially life-threatening eating disorders called bulimia nervosa and anorexia nervosa. People with bulimia, known as bulimics, indulge in bingeing (episodes of eating large amounts of food) and purging (getting rid of the food by vomiting or using laxatives). People with anorexia, whom doctors sometimes call anorectics, severely limit their food intake. . . . Studies indicate that by their first year of college, 4.5 to 18 percent of women and 0.4 percent of men have a history of bulimia and that as many as 1 in 100 females between the ages of 12 and 18 have anorexia. . . .

As to the causes of bulimia and anorexia, there are many theories. One is that some young women feel abnormally pressured to be as thin as the "ideal" portrayed by magazines, movies and television. Another is that defects in key chemical messengers in the brain may contribute to the disorders' development or persistence. . . .

While normal food intake for a teenager is 2,000 to 3,000 calories in a day, bulimic binges average about 3,400 calories in 1 1/4 hours. . . . Some bulimics consume up to 20,000 calories in binges lasting as long as eight hours. . . . To lose the weight gained during a binge, bulimics begin purging by vomiting . . . or by using laxatives . . . , diuretics . . . , or enemas.

Extreme purging rapidly upsets the body's balance of sodium, potassium, and other chemicals. This can cause fatigue, seizures, irregular heartbeat, and thinner bones. Repeated vomiting can damage the stomach and esophagus . . . , make the gums recede, and erode tooth enamel. (Some patients need all their teeth pulled prematurely.) Other effects include various skin rashes, broken blood vessels in the face, and irregular menstrual cycles. . . .

Anorectics may exercise excessively. . . . Obsessed with weight loss and fear of becoming fat, anorectics see normal folds of flesh as "fat" that must be eliminated. When the normal fat is lost, sitting or lying down brings discomfort not rest, making sleeping difficult. As the disorder continues, victims may become isolated and withdraw from friends and family.

The body responds to starvation by slowing or stopping certain bodily processes. Blood pressure falls, breathing rate slows, menstruation ceases . . . , and activities of the thyroid gland (which regulates growth) diminishes. Skin becomes dry, and hair and nails become brittle. Lightheadedness, cold intolerance, constipation, and joint swelling are other symptoms. Reduced fat causes the body temperature to fall. Soft hair called lanugo forms on the body for warmth. Body chemicals may get so imbalanced that heart failure occurs.

If you think a friend or family member has bulimia or anorexia, point out in a caring, nonjudgmental way the behavior you have observed and encourage the person to get medical help. If you think you have bulimia or anorexia, remember that you are not alone and that this is a health problem that requires professional help. As a first step, talk to your parents, family doctor, religious counselor, or school counselor or nurse.

Source Review

1. What are the reasons why some people develop eating disorders?

2. According to the author, what are some of the physical problems caused by bulimia nervosa and anorexia nervosa?

The Adult in Society

 Early and Middle Adulthood

Levinson: Adult Male Development
Frieze: Adult Female Development

 The World of Work

The Labor Force
Job Satisfaction
Jobs in the 1990s

 The Later Years

Change Continues
New Opportunities

Chapter Focus

Chapter 7 explores the social characteristics of adulthood. The chapter opens
with a discussion of male and female development during the adult years,
with an emphasis on how the process differs for men and women. Next the
world of work is explored. The chapter closes with a look at the characteristics of late adulthood.

As you study the chapter, look for the answers to the following questions:

1. What is Levinson's theory of adult male development?
2. What is Frieze's theory of adult female development?
3. How are the nature of work and the composition of the labor force
   changing in the United States?
4. What are the characteristics of life during late adulthood?

KEY TERMS

The following terms, while not the only terms emphasized in the chapter, are
basic to your understanding of sociology. Determine the meaning of each
term, either by using the Glossary or by watching for context clues as you
read the chapter.

life structure	late adulthood	young-old
early adulthood	labor force	middle-old
middle adulthood	unemployment	old-old

Socialization does not end with childhood and adolescence. It continues throughout the life span. At every age, we are faced with new experiences and new demands that affect how we view ourselves and society. Our first paid job, marriage, our first child, a place of our own, various triumphs and disappointments, retirement, and our approaching death in old age add new dimensions to our sense of self and our relationships with others.

Sociologists and social psychologists are interested in the ways in which people adapt to the changing roles and statuses that accompany each stage of adult development. Topics of special importance in the area of adult development include the world of work and the transition to retirement.

In this chapter, we will examine the developmental process that occurs during early and middle adulthood. Because this process differs somewhat for men and women, we will examine male and female development separately. We also will look at the world of work, since it is work that occupies much of adulthood. We will close the chapter with an examination of later life.

1 EARLY AND MIDDLE ADULTHOOD

As we mentioned, the life patterns of adult males and females in American society are somewhat different. For instance, although almost 67 percent of women with children under the age of 18 work at least part-time, their work histories tend not to parallel those of men. For many women, a typical pattern is to enter the labor force, take time out to have children, and then go back to work once the children are partially grown. Men, on the other hand, generally remain in the labor force for most of adulthood.

The split employment pattern of women may be changing as more women choose to combine full-time careers with parenting. Nevertheless, the traditional pattern still is prevalent enough to warrant viewing male and female adult development as two separate processes. Consequently, we will look at two theories of adult development. We will look first at Daniel Levinson's theory of adult male development. We then will look at Irene Frieze's theory of adult female development.

Levinson: Adult Male Development

Psychologist Daniel Levinson and his colleagues at Yale University undertook an intensive, long-term study to determine the developmental stages through which males pass during adulthood. The research team, which included psychologists, sociologists, and psychiatrists, conducted in-depth interviews with 40 men between the ages of 35 and 45. Levinson and his colleagues selected participants for the study from four broad occupational categories. Ten of the men were business executives, 10 were hourly workers, 10 were biology professors, and 10 were writers of varying degrees of fame.

The researchers interviewed each subject for 10 to 20 hours over a period of time to determine how each had experienced personal development as an adult. The interviews focused on issues such as education, work, leisure, politics, and relationships with family and friends. From these interviews, Levinson and his colleagues determined each man's life structure. A **life structure** is the combination of statuses, roles, activities, goals, values, beliefs, and life circumstances that characterize an individual. Through the analysis of these life structures, the research team was able to distinguish patterns that appear to be characteristic of all men.

After analyzing the patterns, Levinson and his colleagues concluded that there are three basic eras of adulthood: **early adulthood** (ages 17 through 39), **middle adulthood** (ages 40 through 59), and **late adulthood** (age 60 and over). The diagram on page 152 shows how each era of adulthood is divided into several periods. Each era begins with a transitional period, which is followed by alternating stable and transitional periods. Transitional periods last from four to five years and stable periods are from six to eight years in length. Levinson places the greatest stress on the first five periods of adulthood: the early adult transition, entering the adult world, the age 30 transition, the settling down period, and the mid-life transition.

The Early Adult Transition. Early adulthood begins with the early adult transition period (ages 17 through 22). This period represents the bridge between adolescence and adulthood. According to Levinson, the most important task of the period is leaving home, both physically and psychologically. The process begins when young adults go away to college or take full-time employment and move out of the house. The break with parents, however, is not abrupt or total. College students, for instance, often receive financial support from their parents. Other young adults achieve economic independence when they enter the work world but continue to live at home in what amounts to a boarder status.

Entering the Adult World. The next stage in early adulthood is called entering the adult world (ages 23 through 27). The chief tasks of this period involve two slightly contradictory objectives. On the one hand, the individual is expected to explore a variety of relationships and career opportunities. This means that he must avoid strong commitments that would make it difficult for him to take advantage of new opportunities. On the other hand, the young adult is expected to become a responsible member of society and form a stable life structure.

This period also is characterized by the development of a dream of adult accomplishment. The dream almost always is phrased in terms of occu-

An individual's life structure changes over the developmental cycle. For the majority of young men, the most important developmental task is acquiring the basic skills needed in their chosen professions.

pational goals. For many, the dreams are very specific, such as becoming a Nobel Prize winner, a great athlete, or a famous writer. Although these dreams often prove to be unrealistic, they do provide the young person with a sense of direction and purpose.

Levinson's Developmental Stages of Adulthood

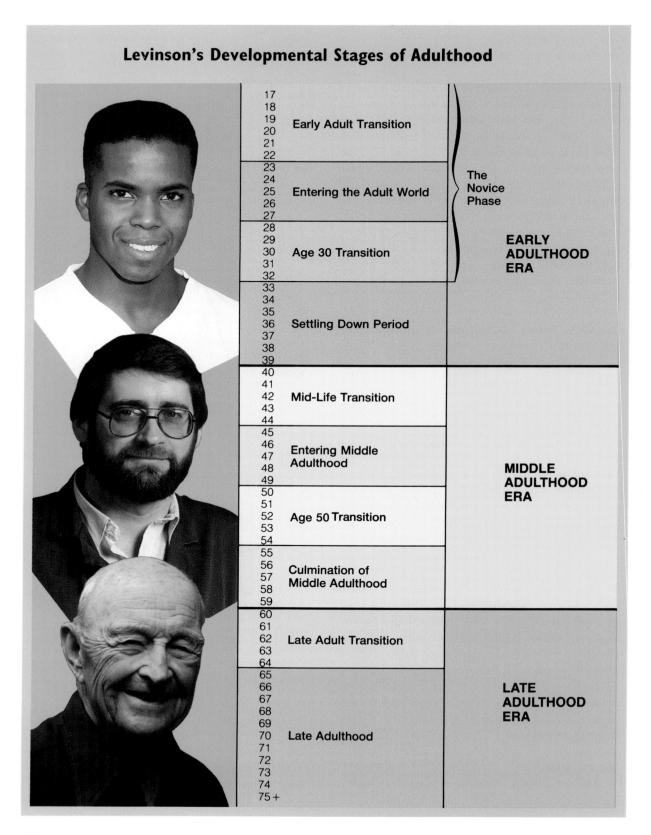

Age	Stage	Phase	Era
17–22	Early Adult Transition		
23–27	Entering the Adult World	The Novice Phase	EARLY ADULTHOOD ERA
28–32	Age 30 Transition		
33–39	Settling Down Period		
40–44	Mid-Life Transition		
45–49	Entering Middle Adulthood		MIDDLE ADULTHOOD ERA
50–54	Age 50 Transition		
55–59	Culmination of Middle Adulthood		
60–64	Late Adult Transition		
65–75+	Late Adulthood		LATE ADULTHOOD ERA

The Age 30 Transition. For many people, the age 30 transition (ages 28 through 32) is a difficult period. It is a time for taking stock of the choices that have been made up to this point. Divorces and career changes are common during this period as individuals reevaluate their current commitments. Levinson considers the age 30 transition to be crucial to future development because it often is characterized by shifts in direction. Sound choices provide a firm foundation for future development. Bad choices can have far-reaching consequences.

Levinson and his colleagues refer to the first three periods of the early adulthood era as the **novice phase.** It is during the novice phase that most people get married. In Levinson's sample, 50 percent of the subjects married between 17 and 22 years of age, 30 percent between 23 and 27 years of age, and 20 percent between the ages of 28 and 32. People in this older group were best prepared for marriage, although many viewed marriage as the last chance to "normalize" their lives. Actually, the researchers found that regardless of their ages, the men were never fully prepared for marriage.

The Settling Down Period. The last stage of early adulthood is the settling down period (ages 33 through 39). The major task of this period is what Levinson calls "making it" in the adult world. Individuals try to establish themselves in society, most usually by advancing in their chosen occupations. During this period, individuals form true commitments to things such as work, family, leisure, friendship, community, or whatever is most important in their lives. They also work to fulfill the dreams established in the previous period.

Near the end of the settling down period, men come to realize how much they are relying on others for role models and guidance. Feeling constrained by these influences, they begin a conscious effort to establish their own identities. Levinson refers to this process as Becoming One's Own Man (BOOM).

The first step in the process often involves separating oneself from a mentor. A **mentor** is someone who fosters an individual's development by believing in the person, sharing the person's dreams, and helping the person achieve these dreams. Usually the mentor is an older, experienced person in the world of work. The mentor functions as a role model and helps the individual get started in adult life. Although the break with a mentor often is painful, it is important because it allows individuals to stop viewing themselves as "apprentice adults."

The Mid-Life Transition. The first stage in the middle adulthood era is the mid-life transition (ages 40 through 44). This period serves as a bridge between early and middle adulthood. The mid-life transition, like the age 30 transition, is characterized by self-examination. Individuals once again question their life structures. They also take stock of their likelihood of achieving the dreams they formed during the second period of

According to Levinson and his colleagues, the settling down period is the time when men develop strong commitments to whatever is important in their lives. For most men, this means getting ahead in the business world.

early adulthood. In most instances, they come to realize that their earlier dreams are beyond fulfillment. The majority of people are able to reformulate their dreams along more realistic lines. Escaping from the power of unattainable dreams is one of the major tasks of the mid-life transition.

For 80 percent of the subjects in Levinson's study, the mid-life transition was a period of moderate to severe crisis. These men experienced both internal conflict and conflict with those around them. The possibility of death became more real to them. One of the ways in which many of the men worked through the crisis was by becoming a mentor. For those who successfully completed the transition, middle adulthood proved to be a fulfilling and creative period.

Support for Levinson's theory can be found in the fact that all of the subjects in the study went through the various periods in order and at relatively the same age. The research findings also indicate that the degree of difficulty an individual experiences in a period depends on his success in mastering the previous period.

Frieze: Adult Female Development

Although Levinson and his colleagues believe that their research findings are equally valid for women, the claim is much debated. The work of Irene Frieze lends support to the argument that adult women go through a slightly different developmental process. Frieze's research led her to suggest three phases in adult female development: leaving the family, entering the adult world, and entering the adult world again.

Phase I: Leaving the Family. As in the case of men, women's entry into the adult world begins with leaving home, making a psychological break from parents, and developing a life plan. For many women, however, the emphasis is less on a career than on marriage. Even when women plan to combine marriage with a career, marriage often is considered the more important step. In these instances, the specifics of the life plan are likely to be determined by marriage. This is particularly true in relationships in which the husband's career plans take priority. This emphasis on marriage over career is one factor that distinguishes female development from male development during adulthood.

Phase II: Entering the Adult World. Age at first marriage in the United States is the highest it has been since the turn of the century—an average of 24.1 years for women and 26.3 years for men. Nevertheless, most women still marry and become mothers during their 20s. Although many women find marriage and a career to be a workable combination, dual roles tend to put an added strain on women. Consequently, only 56 percent of new mothers who were in the labor force return to work before their children reach one year of age. According to Frieze, women's job advance-

For Better or For Worse®

by Lynn Johnston

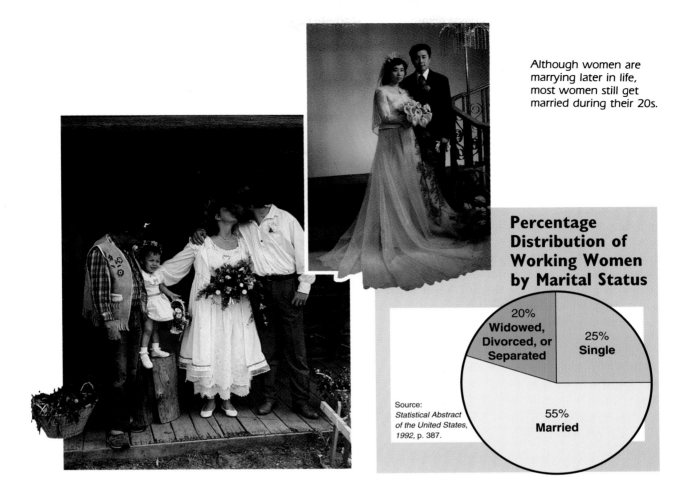

Although women are marrying later in life, most women still get married during their 20s.

Percentage Distribution of Working Women by Marital Status

Source: *Statistical Abstract of the United States, 1992,* p. 387.

- 20% Widowed, Divorced, or Separated
- 25% Single
- 55% Married

ment possibilities become limited when they remain out of the labor force while their children are young. This break in employment is another factor that distinguishes female development from male development during adulthood.

Phase III: Entering the Adult World Again.
Once their children reach school age, many mothers who left the labor force once again seek employment. According to Frieze, these women, most of whom are in their early 30s, find themselves in a situation similar to that of men in their 20s. Fewer obligations at home make it possible for them to actively pursue their career goals. Frieze notes that it is somewhat ironic that these women develop a commitment to their careers at a time when their husbands are beginning to have serious doubts about their own careers.

It is too early to tell whether the developmental phases suggested by Irene Frieze will hold as more women delay marriage and parenting. For now, however, the available evidence suggests that the developmental patterns of working-age men and women differ in several significant respects.

SECTION 1 REVIEW

DEFINE life structure, novice phase, mentor

IDENTIFY Daniel Levinson, Becoming One's Own Man, Irene Frieze

1. **Understanding Ideas** **(a)** What are the three eras of adulthood? **(b)** Describe the characteristics of the first five periods in Levinson's theory of adult male development.

2. **Summarizing Ideas** Describe the three phases in Frieze's theory of adult female development.

2 THE WORLD OF WORK

Work is an important aspect of adult life. If you begin working at age 18 and retire at 65, you will have spent 47 years in the labor force. Even if you go to college and perhaps graduate school or spend a number of years at home raising children, most of you still will be in the labor force for many years. What will the time spent in the labor force be like? An examination of the characteristics of the labor force, the degree of job satisfaction among workers, and the outlook for jobs in the future can help us answer this question.

The Labor Force

By definition, the **labor force** consists of all individuals 16 and older who are employed in paid positions or who are seeking paid employment. People who are not paid for their services, such as homemakers or retired people, are not considered to be part of the labor force. In 1992, approximately 66 percent of the United States population over the age of 16 was in the labor force. Who are the workers in America and what types of jobs do they hold?

In recent years, women have entered the professions in record numbers. Today over half of the professional jobs in the United States are held by women.

Composition. The composition of the American labor force is changing. One of the biggest changes involves the number of working women. In 1960, women made up 33 percent of the labor force. Today, they make up over 45 percent. Projections indicate that between now and 2005, women will account for approximately two-thirds of the growth in the labor force. Women now hold slightly more than half of the professional jobs in the United States. A **profession** is a high-status occupation that requires specialized skills obtained through formal education. Professional-level work includes occupations such as engineer, lawyer, teacher, dentist, and writer.

Another factor in the labor-force composition that is changing is the rise of minority workers as a percentage of the total labor force. This is particularly true of Hispanic Americans, who now are the fastest growing population group among American workers. Currently, Hispanic Americans make up less than 8 percent of the nation's labor force. This figure is expected to increase to more than 11 percent by the year 2005.

In addition, American workers now are better educated. In 1940, most workers had barely more than an eighth-grade education. Today, approximately 87 percent of labor-force workers aged 25 to 64 have graduated from high school, and almost half have some college education.

Unemployment. One way to gain an understanding of the employment patterns among the various groups and categories of people in society is to look at unemployment. **Unemployment** is the situation that occurs when people do not have jobs but are actively seeking employment. The **unemployment rate**—the percentage of the civilian labor force that is unemployed but actively seeking employment—varies by factors such as age, sex, race, and cultural background.

It is impossible to employ every adult member of society. There always are some people who are in the process of seeking employment. Other people cannot or do not want to work. Consequently, society sets a level of unemployment that is considered acceptable. In the United States, that level hovers around 5 percent. Thus the American economy is considered to have achieved "full employment" when approximately 95 percent of the labor force is employed. The graph on page 157

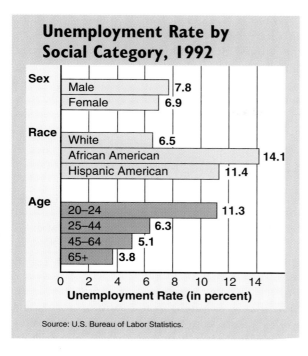

Unemployment Rate by Social Category, 1992

Sex
- Male **7.8**
- Female **6.9**

Race
- White **6.5**
- African American **14.1**
- Hispanic American **11.4**

Age
- 20–24 **11.3**
- 25–44 **6.3**
- 45–64 **5.1**
- 65+ **3.8**

Unemployment Rate (in percent)

Source: U.S. Bureau of Labor Statistics.

Occupations. What types of jobs are held by American workers? The chart at the bottom of this page gives a breakdown of the United States labor force by occupational category. Following are some examples of the types of jobs that fall into each category listed in the table:

- *Executive, administrative, and managerial:* business executives, office managers, sales managers, credit managers, personnel managers, public relations supervisors, and store managers.
- *Professional specialty:* doctors, lawyers, dentists, pharmacists, librarians, nurses, engineers, artists, veterinarians, psychiatrists, social workers, teachers, and accountants.
- *Technical occupations:* laboratory technicians, dental hygienists, medical assistants, licensed practical nurses, and X-ray technicians.
- *Sales workers:* manufacturers' representatives, retail salespeople, insurance salespeople, and real estate agents.
- *Administrative support occupations:* business machine operators, bookkeepers, office clerks, secretaries, receptionists, cashiers, telephone operators, postal workers, and bank workers.

shows the unemployment rate for various groups in American society.

Distribution of Employed Persons by Occupational Category

Occupational Category	Percent of Total	Male/Female Distribution within Category	
		□ Male	▨ Female
Managerial and professional specialty	26.5	53.7	46.3
Technical, sales, and administrative support	30.9	35.3	64.7
Service occupations	13.7	40.2	59.8
Precision production, craft, and repair	11.3	91.4	8.6
Operators, fabricators, and laborers	14.7	74.8	25.2
Farming, forestry, and fishing	2.9	83.9	16.1

Source: *Statistical Abstract of the United States, 1992,* pp. 392–394.

- *Service occupations:* private household workers—maids, cooks, butlers, and nursemaids; protective service workers—police officers and fire fighters; other service workers—waiters, waitresses, cooks, dental and nursing assistants, janitors, hairdressers, airline attendants, and child-care workers.
- *Precision production, craft, and repairworkers:* mechanics, television repairers, shoemakers, dressmakers, tailors, printers, carpenters, plumbers, electricians, concrete workers, and skilled precision production workers.
- *Operators, fabricators, and laborers:* riveters, packagers, assemblers, welders, truck and bus drivers, heavy equipment operators, freight handlers, warehouse workers, and laborers.
- *Farming, forestry, and fishing:* farm owners and operators, farm laborers, lumberjacks, fishers, hunters, and trappers.

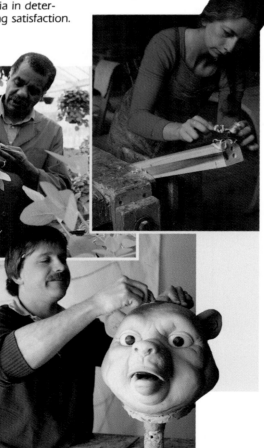

Job satisfaction is not always tied to salary. Having independence and work that is interesting often are the most important criteria in determining satisfaction.

As in the case of labor-force composition, there also have been changes in the nature of work in the United States. One of the most important changes has been the shift from a manufacturing economy to one based on the provision of services and the processing of information. As can be seen in the table, almost 70 percent of the occupations in the United States now fall into this category.

Job Satisfaction

Opinion polls and social science research indicate that the vast majority of workers in the United States are satisfied with their jobs. In general, 80 to 90 percent of all workers report satisfaction with their jobs. The level of satisfaction does vary, however, by type of job and the age of workers. Professionals and businesspeople, for instance, are more likely to report being satisfied with their work than are people in other occupational categories. Similarly, older workers are more likely than younger workers to express satisfaction with their jobs.

What factors produce job satisfaction? A recent Gallup poll indicates that the following are among the most important factors in determining job satisfaction:

- Having health insurance and other benefits.
- Having interesting work.
- Having job security.
- Having the opportunity to learn new skills.
- Being able to work independently.
- Having a job that helps other people.

Job satisfaction is not as dependent on the size of the paycheck as it has been in the past. With the increase in job layoffs and unemployment in recent years, workers have become more concerned with job security, job benefits, and working conditions than with the amount of money they receive for their work.

The fact that people generally are satisfied with their jobs does not mean that they are likely to remain in the same career for their entire working lives. Statistics indicate that the average worker will change careers from three to five times in a lifetime. Changing careers means that workers go into a new field for which their previous experience does not qualify them. Of course, people change jobs within occupational categories much

Projected Growth in Employment Opportunities in Selected Occupations, 1990 to the Year 2005

Occupation	Percentage Increase	Occupation	Percentage Increase
Registered nurses	44	Computer programmers	56
Truck drivers	26	Home health aides	92
Waiters and waitresses	26	Lawyers	35
Receptionists and information clerks	47	Marketing, advertising, and public relations	47
Teachers, secondary school	34	Physicians	34
Computer systems analysts	79	Automotive mechanics	22
Child care workers	49	Medical secretaries	68
Accountants and auditors	34	Electricians	29

Source: *Statistical Abstract of the United States, 1992*, p. 395.

more often than they change careers. Research suggests that the average worker under 35 looks for a new job about once every one-and-a-half years, while the average worker over 35 does so every three years.

Jobs in the 1990s

The types of jobs in which the majority of Americans are engaged have changed since the turn of the century. In 1900, nearly 40 percent of the labor force worked in farming. Of the remaining workers, slightly more than 40 percent were employed in nonfarm jobs that required physical labor. Machinery operators, construction workers, repair people, and other people who engage in manual labor would fall into this 40 percent. Only slightly more than 20 percent of the labor force worked in jobs that were based more on mental effort and interaction with people than on physical labor. Professionals, executives and managers, office workers, and salespeople would fall into this category.

Today, the situation is dramatically different. Farming now accounts for less than 3 percent of the jobs in the United States. The percentage of the labor force engaged in nonfarm physical labor also has declined, although not as significantly. Less than 30 percent of the labor force now is employed in such jobs.

Considerable growth, on the other hand, has occurred in those occupations that require little physical labor—the professions, office work, sales, and most service jobs. More than 70 percent of the people in the labor force are employed in

these areas. Much of this increase can be attributed to the growth of bureaucracies and the professions. Nearly 40 percent of the labor force is employed in managerial, professional, and administrative support positions. The table on this page lists some of the occupations that are expected to experience substantial growth in employment opportunities between now and the beginning of the twenty-first century.

SECTION 2 REVIEW

DEFINE labor force, profession, unemployment, unemployment rate

1. ***Examining Ideas*** How has the composition of the labor force changed in recent years?

2. ***Organizing Ideas*** What types of jobs fall under each of the nine categories of occupations listed in the chapter?

3. ***Summarizing Ideas*** What factors are among the most important in determining job satisfaction?

4. ***Seeing Relationships*** *(a)* How have the types of jobs held by the majority of Americans changed since the 1900s? *(b)* What jobs are projected to grow in employment opportunities between now and the year 2005?

APPLYING SOCIOLOGY

Exploring the World of Work

What do most people think about their jobs? Do they find them interesting and rewarding? Or would they seek satisfaction in another job if the opportunity presented itself?

Author Studs Terkel sought the answers to such questions by interviewing hundreds of people for his book *Working*. What did Terkel find out? Were people happy with their jobs?

A select few did express enthusiasm. For example, a Chicago stockbroker said:

> Without the stock market, the companies wouldn't be able to invest their capital and grow. This is my life and I count myself very fortunate to be in this work. It's fulfilling.

Others voiced pride in their jobs. A waitress notes:

> When I put the plate down, you don't hear a sound. When I pick up a glass, I want it to be just right. When someone says, "How come you're just a waitress?" I say, "Don't you think you deserve being served by me?"

For many, though, their jobs brought only bitterness and boredom. An auditor for an accounting firm complains:

> Many people in our firm don't plan on sticking around. The pressure. The constant rush to get things done. Since I've been here, two people have had nervous breakdowns. I have three bosses on any job, but I don't know who's my boss next week.

A Chicago steelworker also laments:

> It's hard to take pride in a bridge you're never gonna cross, in a door you're never gonna open. You're mass-producing things and you never see the end result of it. . . . I worked for a trucker one time. And I got this tiny satisfaction when I loaded a truck. At least I could see the truck depart loaded.

And a receptionist expresses similar sentiments:

> Until recently I'd cry in the morning. I didn't want to get up. I'd dread Fridays because Monday was always looming over me. Another five days ahead of me. There never seemed to be any end to it. Why am I doing this?

Yet, despite their misgivings, most people would rather be working than be unemployed. As a director of a bakery cooperative said:

> Work is an essential part of being alive. Your work is your identity. It tells you who you are.

Studs Terkel conducted interviews with hundreds of people while gathering information for his book. To gain an appreciation of the ways in which sociologists use interviews to gather data, conduct your own brief study of attitudes toward working. The following guidelines will help you plan your research and analyze your data.

1. Prepare a list of questions that will enable you to obtain the information you need. You might formulate questions that ask about any pleasant aspects of the job, things that cause job dissatisfaction, and what the ideal job would be like.

2. Think about whether you should speak with people you know very well or with people you hardly know at all. What advantages and disadvantages are there to each approach?

3. Look for certain patterns in people's responses. For example, do executives seem more content with their working lives than do factory workers? Or as another example, does satisfaction with work seem to be affected by the number of years spent in the labor force?

Using the guidelines that you have set up, interview several people to discover what they think about their jobs. (You may want to refer back to the discussion of survey methods and case studies in the Chapter 1 Applying Sociology feature.) Try to find out which aspects bring satisfaction, which aspects people would change if they could, and whether people would choose the same job again if given the choice.

Next, take some time to interpret your findings. Which people seem most content? Which people express the most dissatisfaction? Do any people *say* they are happy but *seem* dissatisfied? What gives you this impression?

Then, prepare a report on your findings. Include any conclusions you wish to draw. For example, can you group certain jobs in terms of overall job satisfaction? What seems to be the most common complaint expressed by people?

You might want to share your study with your classmates to see how their results compare with yours. Do there seem to be any patterns within a certain job category? Do all secretaries think that their work is appreciated? Do all executives feel overworked? Perhaps, as a class project, you can compile your interviews and prepare a "book" similar to the one written by Studs Terkel.

3 THE LATER YEARS

Improved health care has enabled more and more people around the world to live longer than ever before. People aged 65 and older are the fastest-growing segment of the world's population. In the United States, people aged 65 and older made up just over 11 percent of the population in 1980. This figure rose to almost 13 percent in 1991. Estimates indicate that by the year 2030, 21 percent of the population will be aged 65 and older.

What is the period of late adulthood like? To answer this question, we must turn to the field of gerontology. **Gerontology** is the scientific study of the processes and phenomena of aging. Because this is a sociology textbook, we are most interested in the study of the nonphysical aspects of the aging process. This subfield of gerontology is called **social gerontology.** In this section, we will look at what gerontologists have discovered about the characteristics of late adulthood.

Change Continues

As you have learned, people now are living longer. Thus it has become impossible to view the late adulthood era as a single period of development. Life at age 65 is very different from life at 85. In recognition of this fact, gerontologists place individuals aged 65 and older into three groups: the **young-old** (ages 65 through 74), the **middle-old** (ages 75 through 84), and the **old-old** (ages 85 and older).

The topics of interest to gerontologists differ depending on which age group is being studied. Among the young-old, for example, adjustment to retirement is one of the most important developmental issues. When the middle-old and the old-old are considered, issues surrounding mental and physical decline and death take on added importance. This shift in emphasis is due to the fact that the young-old generally are in good health and are capable of caring for themselves. Eventually, however, the body begins to wear out. For most of the elderly, physical and mental functioning declines as death approaches, although the level of decline varies widely. Thus health and

It is misleading to think of individuals over the age of 65 as a single group with common life experiences. Each stage of late adulthood brings with it new experiences and new challenges.

Most retired people adjust relatively quickly to the loss of the work role. The process is made easier when individuals have interests that are not related to their former occupations.

death issues become major areas of concern for the middle-old and the old-old. Let us look briefly at each of these issues.

Adjustment to Retirement. We tend to identify individuals with their jobs. When two people meet for the first time, sooner or later the question of what each does for a living is likely to arise. In light of the importance we place on an individual's role in the labor force, it is reasonable to assume that most people have difficulty adjusting to retirement. But is this actually the case?

For some people, the loss of the work role is a great shock. Research indicates, however, that role loss affects a much smaller number of retired people than generally is assumed. Among the current research findings on adjustment to retirement are the following.

- Few people suffer from feelings of uselessness and role loss following retirement. Most people adjust to not working within the first three months of retirement.
- Those who have difficulty adjusting to the loss of the work role often are people who believe they did not achieve their work-related goals or who have few nonwork-related interests and skills.
- Satisfaction with retirement is associated with financial security and good health.
- Retirement does not cause a sudden decline in psychological health.
- Those forced to retire are less satisfied with retirement than are those who retire voluntarily. (Mandatory retirement in the United States was raised in 1978 from age 65 to age 70 and then was abolished for most jobs in 1986.)

Adapting Patterns in Later Adulthood Used by Different Personality Types

Personality Type	Adapting Patterns

INTEGRATED PERSONALITIES: mature, flexible, happy people with rich inner lives who are open to new things and not afraid of their emotions.

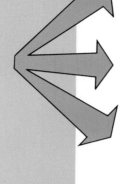

The **reorganizers** substitute new activities for lost ones. They give time to community or church affairs and keep active.

The **focused** select only one or two areas of activity and concentrate on them.

The **disengaged** abandon their commitments and are content to do so. They take a "rocking chair" approach to old age.

ARMORED PERSONALITIES: striving ambitious people who keep a tight control over their anxieties and impulses.

The **holders** are threatened by aging and find satisfaction by holding on to the patterns used in middle age.

The **constrictors** reduce their number of social interactions and close themselves off to experience. They are moderately satisfied with this low level of activity.

PASSIVE-DEPENDENT PERSONALITIES: passive people who are dependent on others.

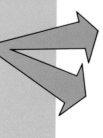

The **succorance-seeking** get along with medium activity and medium satisfaction as long as they have someone on which to lean.

The **apathetic** are kept from doing anything by long-standing patterns of passivity and apathy.

UNINTEGRATED PERSONALITIES: people with disorganized patterns of aging.

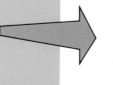

The **disorganized** exhibit low levels of activity and satisfaction. They can neither control their emotions nor think clearly.

Another factor related to retirement adjustment is the occupation of the worker. Professionals and executives seem to adapt most easily to retirement. This might be because they are accustomed to organizing their daily routines and are able to make good use of their time in retirement. They also are more likely to have established contacts with community and professional organizations and to continue participating in them. In addition, professionals and executives are more likely to have adequate retirement incomes.

Adjustment to retirement also is affected by the personality of the individual and the patterns he or she followed earlier in life. The Kansas City Study of Adult Life found that individuals use eight different adapting patterns to respond to retirement and old age. Which patterns they use depends on their personality type. These eight adapting patterns and four personality types are shown in the chart on page 164.

Individuals with *integrated personalities*—flexible, happy people who are open to new ideas—fare best. Whether they become involved in new activities or are content just to watch things happen, they tend to find a high level of satisfaction in retirement.

Individuals with *armored personalities*—controlled, striving, ambitious people—find adjustment more difficult. They either try to repeat the patterns of middle age or else close themselves off from the rest of the world.

People with *passive-dependent personalities*—people who have always been dependent on others—continue to be dependent in old age. They basically are satisfied with retirement as long as they have someone else on whom to depend.

Adapting to old age is most difficult for those with *unintegrated personalities*—people who have been disorganized throughout their lives. In old age, these people cannot think clearly or control their emotions.

Physical and Mental Functioning. As an individual ages, body cells begin to die. As a result, muscles and tissues shrink. The skin develops wrinkles. The entire body slowly loses weight. The weakened muscles lessen the individual's strength and endurance. The nervous system functions more slowly and less accurately. Hair gradually turns to gray or white as the cells in the roots produce less and less pigment. All the organs and functions of the body slow down. As a result, elderly individuals do everything more slowly than they did when they were younger.

Although people tend to slow down as they age, most remain mentally alert. For some people, however, aging is accompanied by mental decline. The most common cause of such decline is an organic mental disorder called Alzheimer's disease. **Alzheimer's disease** is an organic condition that results in the progressive destruction of brain cells. One of the early symptoms of Alzheimer's disease is the inability to remember current events, even though memories from the past can be recalled quite clearly. As the disease progresses, the individual suffering from Alzheimer's disease begins to forget how to do simple tasks. The person may be unable to perform his or her work duties or drive a car. As the memory loss continues, the person often becomes hostile and disoriented. Eventually, eyesight, speech, and muscle coordination begin to fail. In the final stages of the disease, the person often regresses to a childlike state and no longer is able to control his or her bodily functions.

People who are open to new experiences tend to adjust more readily to retirement.

Alzheimer's disease is a problem only for a small percentage of the elderly. Most older individuals remain mentally alert.

cultures. Second, young people tend to have more formal education than the elderly. With new testing techniques and revised test items more in line with the culture of the elderly, new results have been obtained that indicate little decline.

Also, instead of comparing older people with younger people, psychologists now are looking at changes in an individual's test scores over time. For example, a person's score at age 70 might be compared with his or her score at age 50. This approach reveals that intelligence may be more stable than had been previously realized. Healthy older people do not lose their ability to think abstractly or to make judgments. Number skills, inductive reasoning, and vocabulary continue to function until nearly the end of life.

We sometimes judge older persons as less competent because they tend to live in the past. Psychologists suggest that this is an important adaptive process for older adults as they seek to find their new identities in a rapidly changing world.

Of course, some of the elderly do have problems with mental decline, and problems becomes more common as individuals enter their 80s and 90s. Nevertheless, the percentage of elderly suffering from mental decline is small. The great majority of the elderly are independent and self-sufficient people who take care of themselves and lead quite active lives.

Dealing with Dependency and Death. For the middle-old and the old-old, the issues of dependency and death take on increasing significance. In this context, **dependency** is the shift from being an independent adult to being dependent on others for physical or financial assistance. Research has shown that becoming dependent is one of the greatest fears of old age.

Dependency changes an individual's status in society and necessitates new role behaviors. For instance, when an aged parent is forced to live with a grown child because of dependency, the parent–child relationship often becomes reversed. The child takes over the role of care giver and authority figure. The aged parent is expected to be grateful for the assistance and to follow the wishes of the child. This can be very difficult for a person who is accustomed to making his or her own decisions. Consequently, dependency often strains the parent–child relationship.

Fortunately, only about 5 to 10 percent of the elderly population suffers from mental impairment. Recent research has shown that most elderly retain their intellectual abilities throughout life. This finding runs counter to the earlier assumption that the loss of intellectual ability is an unavoidable part of the aging process. The earlier assumption was based on the results of intelligence tests given to people of different ages. Young people always did better on the tests. Researchers took this as an indication that intellectual ability declines with old age.

Psychologists now believe that two factors were influencing the test results. First, the items on the tests related mainly to the youth and young adult

The Role of Widow

One of the sad experiences of late adulthood often is the loss of a spouse. Approximately 14 percent of men aged 65 and older are widowers (the term for a male who has lost his wife). The percentage is much higher for women. Slightly less than half of all women over the age of 65 are widows (the female equivalent of a widower). This difference is due to the fact that women have a longer life expectancy than men. **Life expectancy** is the average number of years a person born in a particular year can be expected to live. The life expectancy of men is currently around 72 years, compared to slightly less than 79 years for women.

Little research has been done on the effects of widowhood on men. This is due primarily to the fact that relatively fewer men experience widowhood, and of those who do, most remarry. Researchers therefore have concentrated on the effects of widowhood on women. What little research that has been done on men indicates that the experiences of widowhood are different for men and women. The question of whether widowhood is more difficult for men or women is, however, still a matter of debate. Here we will concentrate on the findings concerning women.

Being a widow has emerged as a formal, although loosely defined, status. As with all statuses, the position carries with it certain expected role behaviors. For example, a woman is expected to keep the memory of her dead husband alive. Similarly, she is supposed to socialize with other widows and with her children, rather than with men.

Widowhood causes an identity crisis for many women, particularly those who have defined themselves primarily in terms of being a wife. Such women often continue to judge their own actions and life choices against the values of their dead husbands. In essence, these women continue to use the wife role as a guide to behavior long after they become widowed. This coping behavior is so well accepted in society that women who do not wish to retain the wife role must negotiate a new role with family, friends, and associates. Being defined as a person on the basis of something other than the wife role is a particularly important task to be accomplished prior to remarriage.

Widowed women often face economic problems. This is particularly true in the case of working-class women. The loss of employment income or the decrease in Social Security benefits that accompanies the death of a husband can push many working-class women into poverty. Less money means that it is more difficult for these women to enjoy activities outside of the home. This translates into increased levels of loneliness for many women.

Some categories of women are better able to adjust to widowhood than are others. Older widows, for instance, have fewer adjustment problems than do younger widows. In the case of older women, widowhood is seen as a "normal" occurrence. Consequently, society provides more social support systems to help older women cope with widowhood.

When the economic status of women is considered, middle-class women fare better than working-class women in long-term adjustment. More money and more outside interests help middle-class women adjust over the long run. When the emotional trauma of losing a spouse is considered, however, working-class women fare better than do middle-class women. This is due to the fact that working-class women are more likely to define themselves in terms of being mothers rather than in terms of being wives. Thus widowhood involves less role loss and necessitates fewer changes in identity for working-class women. These factors do not, however, translate into better long-term adjustment for these women. A lack of money and personal resources makes widowhood a much more difficult and trying time for the average working-class woman.

One of the greatest fears among older individuals is becoming physically or financially dependent on others.

Although the elderly do fear dependency, they do not appear to fear death. In fact, fear of death is much more common among the young. This is interesting when one considers that the likelihood of dying in the near future is much greater for the elderly. Researchers believe that several factors contribute to lower levels of fear of death among the elderly. First, the elderly are at the end of their lives. They see fewer prospects for the future, thus they feel they have less to lose. Second, many elderly, having lived longer than they expected, feel they are living on "borrowed time." Finally, facing the deaths of friends and family members who are close to them in age helps socialize the elderly into accepting their own death.

New Opportunities

Once they have retired, individuals have a chance to do many of the things they always wanted to do but for which they could not find the time. Many people use part of the time in late adulthood to travel. Others pursue an activity, such as crafts, golf, photography, or gardening, that they have been interested in for many years. Still others may become active in politics. They may, for instance, participate in such lobbying groups as the Gray Panthers or the American Association of Retired Persons. Some begin a second career, either for pay or as a volunteer. In recent years, part-time employment opportunities have increased for the elderly as businesses in the service sector (such as fast-food restaurants) have attempted to draw from this growing pool of potential workers.

Many programs provide opportunities for older people to get involved in the community. The RSVP (Retired Senior Volunteer Program) finds positions for people aged 60 and older in libraries, museums, and various social service agencies. Former managers and administrators may work with SCORE (Service Corps of Retired Executives). SCORE helps operators of small businesses solve business-related problems. In the Foster Grandparent Program, older adults spend 20 hours per week caring for youngsters in hospitals, correctional institutions, and day-care centers.

Research has shown that individuals who have planned ahead for retirement are in a better position to take advantage of the opportunities of this period in the life cycle. This preparation involves financial planning. It also involves broadening one's interests and perhaps developing some hobbies during middle adulthood. Similarly, it involves taking care of one's health. And, probably most important of all, it involves cultivating patterns of living that make the most of life in every growth period.

SECTION 3 REVIEW

DEFINE gerontology, social gerontology, Alzheimer's disease, dependency

1. **Understanding Ideas** **(a)** Gerontologists place the aged population into what three groups? **(b)** What ages are represented by each group?

2. **Summarizing Ideas** Describe the developmental issues that are important during late adulthood.

3. **Expressing Ideas** **(a)** Discuss the opportunities available during late adulthood. **(b)** How can an individual plan for an enjoyable retirement?

CHAPTER 7   SUMMARY

Socialization continues throughout adulthood. Daniel Levinson and his colleagues have explored the developmental process of adult males. On the basis of interviews with 40 men between the ages of 35 and 45, they have distinguished three eras in adult male development: early adulthood, middle adulthood, and late adulthood. Each of these eras is divided into a series of transitional periods and stable periods. The experiences of adulthood vary depending on the period under consideration, although the world of work has a bearing on each period.

Irene Frieze proposes a slightly different developmental sequence for women. According to Frieze, marriage and children play a major role in the adult life of women. She suggests a three-stage developmental process for women. Phase I consists of leaving the family. Phase II involves entering the adult world and centers on marriage and children. Phase III occurs when women reenter the adult world—the work world—once their children reach school age.

For both men and women, work plays a significant role during early and middle adulthood. Approximately 66 percent of the population of the United States age 16 and over is in the labor force. The composition of the labor force is changing. Some of these changes include increased participation by women and minorities and better educated workers.

Being unemployed is one of the most difficult experiences of adulthood. The unemployment rate varies by factors such as age, sex, and race. The types of jobs held by workers in the United States also are changing. The economy has shifted away from manufacturing and toward services and the processing of information.

As people live longer, the developmental issues of late adulthood take on added importance. Gerontologists have placed the elderly population into three categories: the young-old, the middle-old, and the old-old. Developmental issues vary depending on which stage of late adulthood is under consideration.

INTERPRETING THE VISUAL RECORD: Understanding Graphs

Many types of sociological data are presented in the form of graphs. Graphs are visual representations of information, especially statistical data. The three most important types of graphs are line graphs, bar graphs, and circle graphs.

Graph A

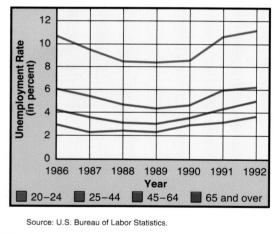

Unemployment Rates Among Adult Workers by Age Category, 1986–1992

☐ 20–24   ☐ 25–44   ☐ 45–64   ☐ 65 and over

Source: U.S. Bureau of Labor Statistics.

Graph B

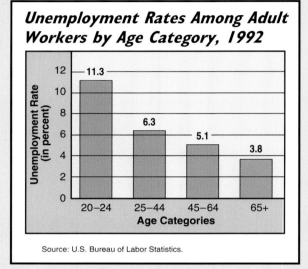

Unemployment Rates Among Adult Workers by Age Category, 1992

Source: U.S. Bureau of Labor Statistics.

Line graphs and bar graphs are useful in showing changes in quantities over time (see graph A) or in showing the distribution of cases (see graph B). These graphs have a horizontal axis and a vertical axis. In the case of line graphs, one axis generally lists numbers or percentages, while the other axis is marked off in periods of time. Time can be measured in days, months, years, or decades. Bar graphs can be used to indicate changes in quantities over time for a single case (such as the number of unemployed persons per year for a particular span of years). More often, however, they are used to indicate distributions among cases. In such instances, one axis is marked off in numbers or percentages, while the other lists categories of cases.

A circle graph shows percentages, or parts per hundred. Circle graphs also are called pie graphs or pie charts.

Graph C

Percentage Distribution of Population by Age Category

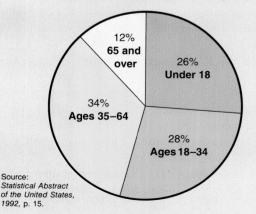

Source: Statistical Abstract of the United States, 1992, p. 15.

IMAGINATION

How to Understand a Graph

Follow these guidelines when using graphs.

1. Define the graph's purpose. Identify the type of graph shown. Read the title of the graph to determine the graph's purpose.

2. Study the graph's parts. Identify the information on the graph. For example, how does the graph show changes in quantities over time? Are the quantities measured in numbers or in percentages? What is the unit of time? If the graph shows the distribution of cases, what are the categories of cases? Are the changes measured in numbers or are they measured in percentages?

3. Analyze the information. In the case of line graphs and applicable bar graphs, note the changes in amounts over time. In the case of bar graphs that compare distributions of cases, note the relationships among the cases. For circle graphs, note the relationship of each part to the whole and rank the percentages.

4. Put the data to use. Formulate conclusions based on the data.

Applying the Skill

Study graphs A, B, and C using the steps above.

1. The title of graph A is Unemployment Rates among Adult Workers by Age Category, 1986–1992. It is a line graph. The unemployment rate in percents is listed along the vertical axis. The horizontal axis is marked off in one-year intervals. The graph charts the unemployment rate for four age categories over a seven-year period, with each age category represented by a different color. The unemployment rate is highest for the youngest age category and declines with age.

2. Graph B is a bar graph. The title of the graph is Unemployment Rates among Adult Workers by Age Category, 1992. The unemployment rate in percents is listed along the vertical axis.

The age categories are indicated on the horizontal axis. As was evident in graph A, the unemployment rate declines with age.

3. Graph C is a circle graph. The title of the graph is Percentage Distribution of Population by Age Category. The largest percentage of the population (34 percent) is 35–64 years of age, followed by 28 percent in the 18–34 category, 26 percent in the under 18 category, and 12 percent in the 65 and over category.

Practicing the Skill

Study graph D. Then on a separate sheet of paper, answer the following questions:

Graph D

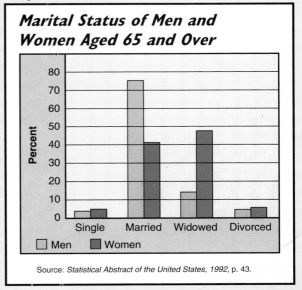

Marital Status of Men and Women Aged 65 and Over

Source: *Statistical Abstract of the United States, 1992*, p. 43.

1. Graph D is what type of graph?

2. What is the title of the graph?

3. How is the vertical axis marked? What categories are listed along the horizontal axis?

4. What conclusions can be drawn from the graph?

Reviewing Sociological Terms

On a separate sheet of paper, supply the term that correctly completes each sentence.

1. A _____ is a high-status occupation that requires specialized skills obtained through formal education.

2. The subfield of gerontology that studies the nonphysical aspects of aging is called _____ _____.

3. _____ _____ is the average number of years a person born at a particular period in time can expect to live.

4. The _____ _____ is the percentage of the civilian labor force that is unemployed but actively seeking employment.

Thinking Critically about Sociology

1. **Comparing Ideas** **(a)** How many times in a lifetime is the average worker likely to change careers versus change jobs? **(b)** What is the difference between changing jobs and changing careers?

2. **Understanding Tables** Examine the table on page 157, which gives a breakdown of the labor force by occupation. **(a)** Which categories of occupations represent the three largest sectors of the labor force? **(b)** Which categories represent the three smallest sectors?

3. **Contrasting Ideas** **(a)** What are the three phases in Irene Frieze's theory of adult female development? **(b)** According to Frieze, how does adult female development differ from the developmental sequences described by Levinson and his colleagues?

4. **Analyzing Ideas** **(a)** What biological changes occur in later life? **(b)** How have the views concerning intellectual ability in older adults changed in recent years and why have these views changed?

5. **Understanding Ideas** Describe the research findings on adjustment to retirement.

6. **Organizing Ideas** Reread the Developing Sociological Imagination feature on pages 40–41. Then develop a structured overview of Levinson's theory of adult male development, providing as much detail as possible.

7. **Seeing Relationships** **(a)** List the four personality types and the eight adapting patterns uncovered by the Kansas City Study of Adult Life. **(b)** How does adjustment to retirement and old age differ depending on the individual's personality type and the adapting pattern being employed?

8. **Synthesizing Information** Describe the ways in which the nature of work and the composition of the labor force are changing in the United States.

Exercising Sociological Skills

1. **Conducting Research** Reread the excerpts in the Applying Sociology feature on pages 160–161. **(a)** Make a list of the positive statements people made about work. Make a second list of the negative statements. **(b)** What do the lists indicate about the characteristics of an enjoyable job?

2. **Summarizing Ideas** Briefly summarize the characteristics of widowhood described in the Case Study on page 167.

3. **Using Graphs** Reread the Developing Sociological Imagination feature on pages 170–171. Use the steps outlined in the feature to write a description of the top graph on page 157.

Extending Sociological Imagination

Consult the *Statistical Abstract of the United States*. Locate the table that lists past and projected labor force participation rates by race, sex, and age. Draw a bar graph showing the participation rates (in percents) of blacks and whites for 1980, 1985, 1990, 1995, 2000, and 2005. Use graph D on page 171 as a model.

INTERPRETING PRIMARY SOURCES

Why Can't a Woman Be More Like a Man . . . ?

It sometimes seems that it is impossible to have it all. People must choose between families and careers. Traditionally, men have concentrated on careers, while women have devoted themselves to their families. In the following excerpt from *Passages: Predictable Crises of Adult Life,* Gail Sheehy explores how men and women describe their early adulthood years. While reading the excerpt, consider how men and women appear to differ in what they think is important in life.

For most of those in the twenties, a fantastic mystery story waits to be written over the next two decades. . . . Somehow, the source of our identity moves from outside to inside, and it is this psychological movement in sense of self that is the key to the mystery. It causes many men and women to switch from the opposite poles of their twenties to a different set of opposites by their forties.

This switch is strikingly revealed by the way in which men and women tell their life stories. The differences were particularly distinct in the way all of them spilled out the histories of the first half of their lives. The men talked about the actions they had initiated. The women talked about the people they had responded to.

That is, the men reconstructed their tracks according to the career line they had followed. They measured themselves at each step against the timetable approved for their particular occupational dream. Love patterns were filled in as adjuncts to their real love affair: courting the dream of success and seeking their identity through their work. The men talked about their wives and children largely in terms of how they helped or hindered the dream, but they rarely spoke, without prompting, about the needs or nourishing of the human beings closest to them. These human connections seldom converged with what a man saw as his main track of development until he had reached his forties.

Women, by contrast, spun out their stories around their attachments to, and detachments from, others: parents, lovers, husbands, children. The central thread running through their young lives was the state of these human connections. The pursuit of an individual dream was most often a stitch that was picked up, dropped, perhaps picked up again. It was what they did before they married, between babies, or after the divorce. Women whose lives incorporated a vital career line generally described that line as the either/or choice they had to make, the profession they doggedly pursued instead of marrying Peter or the exit route they took from Paul or the detour they made from family commitments and for which at some point they feared they would be charged a toll. Loaned time. It was rare to find a woman under 35, even a talented and successful one, who felt complete without a man.

Until very recently in our culture, most men and women spent a good part of their twenties and thirties living one of two illusions: that career success would make them immortal, or that a mate would complete them. (Even now, these illusions die very hard.) Men and women were on separate tracks. The career as an all-encompassing end to life turned out to be a flawed vision, an emotional cul-de-sac. But did attaching oneself to a man and children prove to be any less incomplete as life's ultimate fulfillment?

Each sex seemed to have half the loaf and was uncomfortable about the half they were missing. Did the missing halves even belong to the same loaf? Men had the credentials with which to barter for external advancement. Women had the perceptiveness to say: "What good is becoming president if you lose touch with your family and your feelings?"

The woman was jealous of the man's credentials. The man was disturbed by the woman's truth.

As men and women enter midlife, the tables begin to turn. Many men I interviewed found themselves wanting to learn how to be responsive. And a surge of initiating behavior showed up in most women.

Source Review

How do men and women differ in the ways in which they discuss their early adulthood years?

Deviance and Social Control

 1 **Deviance**

The Nature of Deviance
The Social Functions of Deviance
Explaining Deviance

2 **Crime**

Crime Statistics
Types of Crime
The Criminal Justice System

Chapter Focus

Chapter 8 explores deviance and crime in the United States. First, the basic aspects of deviance are considered, including the positive social functions served by low levels of deviance. Then, five influential theories of deviance are examined. Finally, the characteristics of crime and the criminal justice system are explored.

As you study the chapter, look for the answers to the following questions:

1. What is deviance and what are its social functions?
2. What theories have been proposed to explain deviance?
3. What are the principal types of crime in the United States?
4. What are the characteristics of the American criminal justice system?

KEY TERMS

The following terms, while not the only terms emphasized in the chapter, are basic to your understanding of sociology. Determine the meaning of each term, either by using the Glossary or by watching for context clues as you read the chapter.

deviance	anomie	white-collar crime
stigma	primary deviance	plea bargaining
differential association	crime	recidivism

INTRODUCTION

Deviance and crime are everyday events in modern society. Most communities have at least one "character"—someone known for his or her strange behavior. People living on the street, under bridges, and in abandoned buildings are increasingly common sights. Neighborhood Crime Watch signs are everywhere. Locks and dead bolts adorn almost every door in the United States. And, television programs and movies based on the activities of fictional criminals, private detectives, and lawyers are time-honored favorites. In this chapter, we will explore the nature of deviance and the types of crime that are characteristic of modern industrial society.

1 DEVIANCE

Read through the following list of five behaviors.

- Continuously talking to oneself in public
- Drag racing on a public street or highway
- Regularly using illegal drugs
- A man wearing women's clothing
- Attacking another person with a weapon

As we have said, most people internalize the majority of the norms in their society. But individuals do not internalize every norm. Even sanctions—the rewards and punishments used to enforce conformity to norms—cannot bring about complete social control. There always are some individuals who break the rules of the society or group. Behavior that violates significant social norms is called **deviance.** The five activities listed above are examples of deviant behavior in our society.

The Nature of Deviance

In any society, there are countless norms that govern behavior. Some norms deal with fairly insignificant behaviors, such as personal cleanliness or table manners. Other norms are vital to the smooth operation of society and the safety of its members. Norms governing the taking of another person's life or property, for instance, are essential in any society.

Although now more common, wearing a tattoo is considered deviant by many Americans.

Because there are so many norms existing in society, occasional violations are unavoidable. But not all norm violations are considered deviant acts. It is society that determines which acts are considered deviant. Moreover, an act that is considered deviant in one situation may be considered quite normal in another, even within the same society. As we mentioned in Chapter 2, for instance, it is generally illegal to kill someone. If, however, a member of the military or a police officer kills someone in the line of duty, the action is judged quite differently.

The consequences of actions also vary from society to society. Divorce, for example, is legal in the United States but impossible to obtain in the Republic of Ireland. Similarly, an act might be considered deviant in one historical period but not in another. For instance, throughout much of this century, it was illegal for stores to do business on Sunday. Today, however, it is quite common for shopping malls to be open on Sunday afternoons.

How does a person come to be considered a deviant? Suppose a person gets a ticket for driving his or her car too fast. The person would not be considered deviant on the basis of this one event. But if the person continued to get caught driving at high speeds and got the reputation of being a reckless driver, he or she might come to be considered a deviant. Repeating an offense, however, is not the only way a person comes to be labeled a deviant. People who commit acts that have serious negative consequences for society—such as murder, sexual assault, or robbery—are likely to be labeled as deviant on the basis of a single act.

The labeling of someone as deviant involves two components. To be considered deviant by society, an individual first must be detected committing a deviant act. A person will not be labeled as deviant unless his or her deviant behavior is in some way known to other people. Next, the individual must be stigmatized by society. A **stigma** is a mark of social disgrace that sets the deviant apart from the rest of society. Stigma has been used as a form of social control throughout history. The ancient Greeks, for instance, cut or burned signs into the bodies of criminals as warnings that these people were to be avoided. The chain gangs and the public punishments and executions that were common through much of history are other examples of outward signs of stigma.

The power of the outward sign as a form of social control still is understood today. Prison inmates in the United States, for example, wear special clothing and are assigned numbers as a visual sign of stigma. Some people have suggested that the cars of people convicted of driving under the influence of alcohol or other drugs be marked in some way, such as with a decal. The reasoning behind this suggestion is that the visual sign would serve both as a warning to others and as a form of public humiliation.

Although we often associate deviance with crime, crime is only one form of deviance. People who fail—for whatever reason—to uphold the norms and values of mainstream society often are labeled as deviant. The homeless, for example, are quickly stigmatized, regardless of the circumstances that led to their homelessness.

When sociologists speak of the stigma resulting from the label of deviant, they usually are not referring to outward signs. Rather, they are referring to the negative social reactions that result from being caught while committing a deviant act. According to sociologist Erving Goffman a person who is labeled as deviant has a "spoiled social identity." He or she no longer is seen as being normal or whole.

The Social Functions of Deviance

Although high levels of deviance are disruptive to society, low levels of deviance actually serve some positive functions. Deviance helps to unify the group, clarify norms, diffuse tension, identify problems, and provide jobs.

Unifying the Group.   As Emile Durkheim observed, deviance helps to unify a group. Much as war serves to unify a country, deviance serves to draw the line between conforming members of society and "outsiders"—the nonconforming members of society. This "us against them" attitude reinforces the sense of community and the belief in shared values. Deviance is so important to the maintenance of group unity that Durkheim suggested that it would have to be invented if it did not exist naturally.

Clarifying Norms.   Deviance also serves to define the boundaries of acceptable behavior. When rules are broken and the guilty parties are caught, members of society are reminded of the norms that guide social life. The punishment of norm violators serves as a warning to others that certain behaviors will not be tolerated by society. Some people, for example, believe that the death penalty discourages crime. This belief is based on the notion that people will not commit deviant acts if they are aware of how severe the consequences of these acts will be.

Diffusing Tension.   When people are unhappy with their lives or social conditions, they run the risk of striking out at society. Minor acts of deviance serve as a safety valve, allowing individuals to relieve tension without disrupting the basic fabric of society. Participating in unauthorized demonstrations, for example, allows people to express political or social discontent without destroying the social order.

Identifying Problems.   Deviance can help bring about social change by identifying problem areas. When a particular norm is violated by large numbers of people, it often is an indication that something in the organization of society needs to be changed. Once alerted to the problem, those individuals in authority can take steps to correct the situation.

Providing Jobs.   Deviance also provides legitimate jobs for a wide range of people. Judges, lawyers, police officers, prison personnel, parole officers, manufacturers of electronic security systems, crime reporters, and criminologists—the social scientists who study criminal behavior—have jobs that are based on the existence of deviance. In addition, there are many other jobs that are based in part on the existence of deviance.

THE FAR SIDE   By GARY LARSON

© 1985 Universal Press Syndicate

"A cat killer? Is that the face of a cat killer? Cat *chaser* maybe. But hey—who isn't?"

Cultural transmission theorists would agree that the people who defaced this building with graffiti did so because they associate with people who consider it acceptable to deface buildings.

Explaining Deviance

We can get a better understanding of deviance by considering various theoretical approaches to its study. Among the most influential theories used to explain deviance are cultural-transmission theory, structural-strain theory, control theory, conflict theory, and labeling theory.

Cultural-Transmission Theory.

One of the traditional theories used to explain deviant behavior is **cultural-transmission theory.** This theory views deviance as a learned behavior. According to the theory, deviant behavior is learned in much the same way that nondeviant behavior is learned—through interaction with others. In the case of deviant behavior, however, the interaction primarily is among individuals who are engaging in deviant acts. Thus the norms and values being transmitted are deviant. As a result, the individual is socialized into deviant behavior rather than into socially acceptable behavior.

At the center of cultural-transmission theory is the concept of **differential association.** This concept refers to the proportion of associations a person has with deviant versus nondeviant individuals. If the majority of a person's interactions are with deviant individuals, the person is likely to be socialized into patterns of deviant behavior. If, on the other hand, the person's associations primarily are with individuals who conform to expected patterns of behavior, the person also is likely to conform.

The concept of differential association first was proposed by American sociologist Edwin Sutherland. Sutherland based his ideas on the observation that certain neighborhoods seem to have consistently high rates of crime while others have

Text continues on page 182.

Observing Norms in Social Interaction

Have you ever thought about the number of norms you obey when carrying on an ordinary conversation or engaging in some common form of social interaction? Most of us probably have not given it much thought. Yet when talking to other people, we all follow certain guidelines. Among the most important of these guidelines are those concerning distance, hand gestures, eye contact, and facial expressions.

Social Distance

Suppose you and a friend decide to complete a homework assignment together. You sit down to begin work on the project. Where do you sit? Chances are you sit close enough to be able to work together, yet far enough away to be comfortable. But approximately what distance is considered socially acceptable?

To determine the answer to the above question, try the following experiment. The next time you and a friend sit down together—at lunch, at home, or in class—vary the distance between both of you. For example, skip a seat in the school cafeteria. Or, in contrast, sit so that your chairs almost are touching. Do this several times so that you have various measurements of the distance.

What is the reaction of the other person in each case? Based on this experiment, what can you conclude is an acceptable social distance?

Hand Gestures

Norms concerning hand gestures are equally important guidelines for conversation. Have you ever had discussions with people who "talked with their hands"? Did you find yourself losing track of the conversation in a frantic effort to follow every hand movement?

Or, have you ever had the misfortune of speaking with someone who emphasized every point by tapping your arm or who rested their hand on your shoulder while talking? What was your reaction to this individual?

In order to determine acceptable hand gestures, keep track of your hand gestures in any conversations you have today. In some conversations, do not use your hands at all. Keep your hands perfectly still at your side. At other times, use your hands to overemphasize every point you make either by touching the other person or by gesturing wildly. In still other conversations, use your hands only moderately.

How did the other person react to you each time? What purpose might hand gestures serve? What norms seem to guide the use of hand gestures in conversations?

Eye Contact

Eye contact is yet another aspect of interaction in which we are expected to follow certain norms. We are expected to keep our eyes on our teachers when they give their lessons. We usually get better results when we look directly at an interviewer during a job interview. We even are told by our parents to look at them when they speak to us.

How important is eye contact to you? Do you think people who avoid looking directly at you are less sincere or trustworthy? Do you think people who look you straight in the eye are more honest? How important do you think eye contact is to your friends?

To answer this last question, try not looking at your friends when you speak with them. Look at your shoes or at the ceiling or at another object in the room instead of looking directly at your friends while you are speaking. Or, if you are outside, look up at the sky. How do your friends react to you not looking at them while you are speaking with them? Do they carry on a normal conversation, or do they seem to be uncomfortable with your behavior?

Facial Expressions

Facial expressions form another part of our everyday interaction. How many times have people been able to "read your face"? How often do you suddenly realize that you are scowling?

Many times we are unaware of the appearance we are conveying to others. Sometimes, too, we intentionally try to put on a certain face. We smile to please a job interviewer. We try to look alert in class.

And, as with the other components of interaction, certain norms guide our facial expressions. We would not, for example, stick out our tongues at a police officer or at a judge! To try to determine what some of these norms are, observe your friends in conversation. What norms governing facial expressions do your friends appear to be following?

Also, deliberately use some unexpected facial expressions when speaking to a friend. You might wish to smile all the time or glare at your friend. What is the reaction of the other person? How do you feel when using these expressions? Why do you think you feel that way?

From these few experiments, we can see that social distance, hand gestures, eye contact, and facial expressions are important features of interaction. Because of their importance, we have established certain norms to help us use them properly. When we deviate from these norms, we generally receive negative reactions from others.

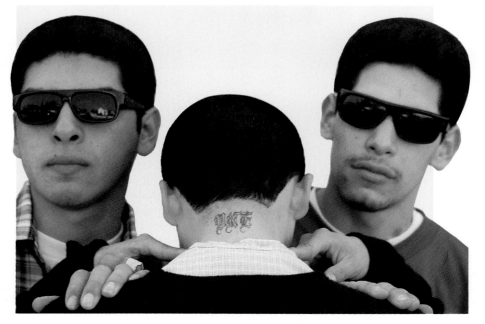

According to cultural-transmission theory, all people conform. Some people, however, conform to norms and values that are not acceptable to most members of society. These young gang members, for instance, strongly identify with the norms and values of the gang—so strongly that one member was willing to have the gang's initials tattooed on the back of his neck.

consistently low rates. Sutherland's work suggests that the learning of deviant behavior occurs in primary groups. People become deviant or conforming in the same way they learn how to speak English or Swedish—they have personal relationships with people who do these things. Thus cultural-transmission theory is an interactionist theory of deviance.

Cultural-transmission theory views all individuals as conformists. The difference between deviants and the rest of society lies in the norms to which each chooses to conform. The deviant individual conforms to norms that are not accepted by the larger community. The nondeviant, on the other hand, conforms to socially accepted norms.

Structural-Strain Theory. Another traditional theory of deviant behavior is **structural-strain theory,** which is a functionalist perspective on deviance. This theory, proposed by sociologist Robert K. Merton, views deviance as the natural outgrowth of the values, norms, and structure of society. According to Merton, American society places a high value on certain goals, such as economic success. Not everyone in society, however, has the legitimate means to achieve economic success. Individuals, for instance, may lack an ade-

quate education or they may be prevented from finding a job because of social conditions. Nevertheless, these people are expected to meet the goals of society and are judged on the basis of how well they do so.

Under the strain of incompatible goals and means, these individuals fall victim to anomie. **Anomie** is the situation that arises when the norms of society are unclear or are no longer applicable. Anomie leaves individuals without sufficient guidelines for behavior, thus causing confusion both for individuals and for society. The concept originally was proposed by Emile Durkheim to explain high rates of suicide in nations undergoing industrialization.

Merton suggests that individuals respond to the culturally approved goals and the legitimate means of achieving these goals in one of five ways—through either conformity, innovation, ritualism, retreatism, or rebellion. Whenever possible, individuals conform. When faced with anomie, however, people sometimes turn to deviance. The last four responses—or modes of adaptation, as Merton calls them—represent deviant behavior. The chart on page 183 lists Merton's five modes of adaptation. Following is a description of each mode of adaptation.

Merton's Structural Strain Theory of Deviance

	Mode of Adaptation	Cultural Goals	Cultural Norms
	Conformity	Accept	Accept
Deviant Responses	Innovation	Accept	Reject
Deviant Responses	Ritualism	Reject	Accept
Deviant Responses	Retreatism	Reject	Reject
Deviant Responses	Rebellion	Reject and Replace	Reject and Replace

Source: Adapted from Robert K. Merton, *Social Theory and Social Structure* (New York: Free Press, 1968), p. 194.

- *Conformity.* Most individuals in society accept both the cultural goals and the culturally approved means for achieving these goals. Some of these people are successful in reaching these goals. Others employ legitimate means but fail to achieve the goals. In either case, however, the people do not employ acts of deviance in their attempts.
- *Innovation.* Some members of society accept the cultural goals but do not accept the approved means for reaching these goals. They want to be successful in acquiring wealth, but find the goal too difficult or impossible to attain by acceptable means. Therefore they innovate.

When people reject both the accepted goals of society and the legitimate means for achieving these goals, they shut themselves off from most of society.

They devise new means for achieving the goals—ways that violate accepted norms. Thus they become deviants. Many criminals and some business people fit into this category.

- *Ritualism.* Other members of society also find it impossible to achieve cultural goals by acceptable means. Instead of violating the norms for achievement, however, they give up the goals while continuing to observe the expected rules of behavior. A worker, for example, may pass up opportunities for promotion rather than face possible failure. Or, a bureaucrat may make a ritual of upholding the rules and procedures of the organization while abandoning personal goals. The ritual of upholding the norms becomes an end in itself.

- *Retreatism.* Some individuals reject both the cultural goals and the socially acceptable means of attaining them. Examples of retreatists include drug addicts, beggars, and hermits.

- *Rebellion.* Not all individuals who reject the cultural goals and the socially acceptable means to attain them retreat. Some people rebel. Rebels want to substitute a new set of goals and means for the currently approved set. Members of any revolutionary movement fall into this category of deviant adaptation.

The four categories of deviant behavior—innovation, ritualism, retreatism, and rebellion—are not considered equally deviant. Innovators (such as criminals) and rebels attract the most attention. Many retreatists also pose serious problems. The ritualist, however, generally is not regarded as a serious threat to society.

Control Theory. Also influenced by the work of Emile Durkheim, **control theory**—like structural-strain theory—turns to the social structure for an explanation of deviant behavior. The focus, however, is somewhat different. Control theorists see deviance as a natural occurrence and conformity as the result of social control. Building on Durkheim's study of suicide, control theorists suggest that individuals who have weak ties to the community are likely to commit deviant acts. Those individuals who are integrated into the community are likely to conform. Communities in which most members have strong social bonds will have lower rates of deviance because community members will be able to exert stronger social control over those who deviate.

According to Travis Hirschi, a leading control theorist, people develop social bonds through attachment to others, belief in the moral codes of society, commitment to traditional societal values and goals, and involvement in nondeviant activities. People with strong community ties are likely to conform because they have too much to lose if they do not. On the other hand, people who lack attachments, moral beliefs, commitment, and involvement have less to lose when they engage in deviant acts.

Conflict Theory. Sociologists who apply conflict theory to the study of deviance believe that competition and social inequality lead to deviance. Conflict theorists see social life as a struggle between those with power—the upper classes—and those without power—the working and lower classes. People with power commit deviant acts in an effort to maintain their power. People without power, on the other hand, commit deviant acts for one of two reasons: either to obtain economic rewards or because they have low self-esteem and feelings of powerlessness.

According to conflict theorists, those people who are in power label as deviant any behavior that threatens their power base. They then establish ideologies—belief systems—that explain deviance as a problem found primarily among the lower classes. Thus law enforcement efforts most often are directed toward the types of crimes committed by the working and lower classes. As a result, these groups have higher rates of arrest and conviction. In the view of conflict theorists, people without power do not necessarily commit more crimes than do other people. Rather, they commit the types of crimes that are most likely to be detected and punished.

Labeling Theory. Instead of focusing on why people perform deviant acts, **labeling theory** focuses on how individuals come to be labeled as deviant. Like cultural-transmission theory, labeling theory grew out of the interactionist perspective. Some current labeling theorists, however, borrow ideas from the conflict perspective.

Labeling theory is heavily influenced by the work of sociologists Edwin Lemert and Howard

American Youth Gangs

Youth gangs have a long history in the United States. The first recorded youth gang was the Forty Thieves, founded around 1825 in New York's Lower Manhattan. By the 1920s and 1930s, gangs were viewed as one of the major social problems of the day. In fact, the first book published on the study of gangs, written in 1927 by criminologist Frederick M. Thrasher, described 1,313 gangs in Chicago alone. In today's world of escalating crime rates, news of gang involvement in drugs and violence adds to a rising climate of fear and mistrust.

One reason that youth gangs have generated rising concern in the 1990s is the fact that their numbers have increased dramatically in recent years. According to sociologist Malcolm W. Klein, only 23 American cities had serious gang problems in 1961. Today, however, youth gangs operate in more than 187 cities throughout the United States. Practically every state in the nation has some form of gang problem. Moreover, it is false to assume that gangs are a problem only in the inner cities of major urban areas. Suburban cities with populations as small as 5,000 have reported the existence of gangs.

Not only has the number of youth gangs increased in recent years, but the level of violence associated with them has increased as well. Many of today's youth gangs, whose members usually range in age from 13 to 19, are armed with illegal firearms such as AK-47 and Uzi assault weapons. Most often, these weapons are used in battles between rival gangs engaged in turf wars. Many victims of gang shootings, however, are innocent bystanders who are caught in the cross-fire of drive-by shootings or street violence. In Los Angeles, for example, only half of that county's 1,675 recent victims of gang violence were themselves members of gangs.

The involvement of gangs in the illegal drug trade also has generated increasing concern in recent years. The ready availability and low cost of crack cocaine in particular has enabled some youth gangs to develop highly sophisticated drug-trafficking operations. The money they make from the illegal drug trade often is what gangs use to purchase illegal firearms.

Central to the problem of youth gangs is the question of why some young people choose to join them. According to Léon Bing, author of a book of interviews with Los Angeles gang members, gangs often offer the only escape to young people from neighborhoods struggling with poverty, broken families, and limited economic opportunities. But poverty alone cannot explain the rise in gang membership, because gangs increasingly are found in middle-class areas. According to sociologist Jack Katz, the elaborate subculture of the gang, which includes the wearing of certain colors or articles of clothing, may be attractive to some young people who feel the need to rebel. Others appear to be willing to risk death, drug dependence, or imprisonment for the companionship and protection provided by fellow gang members. Also, some young people join gangs because they or their family members have been threatened by gang members with violence or death if they do not join.

Members of youth gangs who want to leave their gang often find that there are few ways out. Some who want to leave are forced to undergo a ceremony that consists of being beaten by fellow gang members for a specified amount of time. Often this leaves the individual with broken bones, lost teeth, cigarette burns, and bruises. Sometimes it results in death.

The destruction left in the wake of youth gangs has led to the development of many programs across the nation designed to keep young people from joining gangs. Some of these programs provide remedial education, skills training, and jobs. Others provide crisis intervention, social services, and counseling for young people and their families.

During the 1950s, Senator Joseph McCarthy leveled unsupported charges of Communist activity against many innocent people. It took years for some of these people to escape the label of deviant.

Becker. Lemert and Becker note that all people commit deviant acts at some time in their lives. These acts range from the minor to the serious. Yet not everyone comes to be considered deviant. The theorists suggest that this is because deviance is of two types: primary and secondary. **Primary deviance** is nonconformity that goes undetected by those in authority. The occasional deviant act and acts that are well concealed fall into this category. Individuals who commit acts of primary deviance do not consider themselves to be deviant and neither does society. **Secondary deviance,** on the other hand, results in the individual being labeled as deviant and accepting the label as true.

Once an individual is labeled as deviant and accepts that label, his or her life changes. People come to judge all or most of the individual's actions in light of the deviant label. Being a deviant becomes the individual's master status. In many instances, the label of deviant restricts an individual's options in the larger society and forces the individual into a deviant life-style.

SECTION 1 REVIEW

DEFINE deviance, differential association, primary deviance, secondary deviance

1. ***Comprehending Ideas*** What is meant by the statement that not all norm violations are considered deviant acts?

2. ***Comparing Ideas*** *(a)* What do sociologists mean by stigma? *(b)* How has stigma been used through history and how is it used now?

3. ***Organizing Ideas*** List and describe the five functions of deviance.

4. ***Summarizing Ideas*** Briefly describe the five theories of deviance discussed in this section.

2 CRIME

Crime affects everyone in the United States. Some people are victims. Some people are criminals. Some people are both. The majority of Americans, however, are affected by crime as bystanders. We are exposed to crime every day through newspapers, radio, television, and movies. As a result of our experiences and exposure through the mass media, most of us consider crime to be a serious social problem.

A **crime** is any act that is labeled as such by those in authority, is prohibited by law, and is punishable by the government. For example, a person who robs a bank—an act that is labeled "criminal," is prohibited by law, and is punishable by the government—has committed a crime. On the other hand, a champion swimmer who stands by and watches a friend drown instead of attempting to rescue the person has not necessarily committed a crime. The swimmer may have violated a moral code, but not necessarily a law.

The table on this page shows a breakdown of arrests by sex, race, and age. Note that males are much more likely than females to be arrested. In terms of race, over two-thirds of all people arrested are white. African Americans, however, who make up approximately 12 percent of the population, account for over one-fourth of the arrests. The percentages for age are particularly dramatic. Almost half of all arrests involve people under the age of 25. Moreover, almost 80 percent of all arrests can be accounted for if people under the age of 35 are grouped together.

Crime Statistics

One source for crime statistics is the *Uniform Crime Report,* published annually by the Federal Bureau of Investigation (FBI). The FBI uses data provided by local police departments to compile nationwide statistics. These statistics, however, have several serious problems that must be kept in mind. Social scientist Donald Black has uncovered the following characteristics about the filing of formal crime reports.

Persons Arrested, by Sex, Race, and Age

Characteristic	Percentage of Total
Sex	
Male	81
Female	19
Race	
White	69
African American	29
Other	2
Age	
Under 18	18
18–24	29
25–34	31
35–44	15
45–54	5
55 and over	2

Source: U.S. Bureau of Justice Statistics.

■ Not all of the complaints that citizens make to the police find their way into the official statistics. The responding officer decides whether or not to file a formal report. Officers are more likely to file a report in the case of serious offenses.

Not all crimes that are reported to the police are given the same official consideration.

- Individuals are less likely to report a crime if family or friends are involved.
- The police are more likely to file formal reports on serious crimes when the injured parties are from the higher social classes.
- Whether an officer files a formal complaint is influenced by the attitude of the individual making the complaint. An officer is more likely to file a formal complaint when the person making the complaint shows courtesy and respect toward the officer.

In addition, certain types of crime—such as sexual assault—are more likely to go unreported by the victims. Statistics also can be affected by changes in the way the statistics are reported or by incorrect reporting.

Types of Crime

The chart on page 189 shows how the Federal Bureau of Investigation (FBI) classifies crimes. The graph on this page shows the percentage of total arrests that fall into each category. For purposes of discussion, however, we can group crimes into five categories: violent crimes, crimes against property, victimless crimes, white-collar crime, and organized crime.

Violent Crime. Although violent crimes—murder, forcible rape, robbery, and aggravated assault—make up a very small percentage of all crimes, the statistics nonetheless are quite alarming. It is estimated that in the United States, an

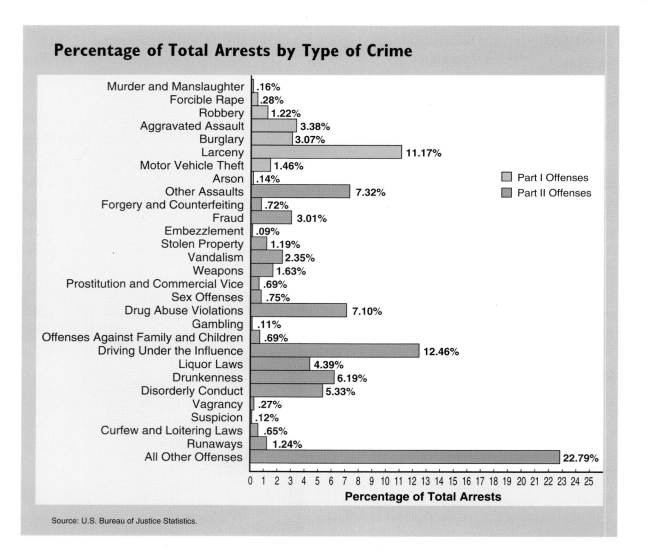

Percentage of Total Arrests by Type of Crime

Type of Crime	Percentage
Murder and Manslaughter	.16%
Forcible Rape	.28%
Robbery	1.22%
Aggravated Assault	3.38%
Burglary	3.07%
Larceny	11.17%
Motor Vehicle Theft	1.46%
Arson	.14%
Other Assaults	7.32%
Forgery and Counterfeiting	.72%
Fraud	3.01%
Embezzlement	.09%
Stolen Property	1.19%
Vandalism	2.35%
Weapons	1.63%
Prostitution and Commercial Vice	.69%
Sex Offenses	.75%
Drug Abuse Violations	7.10%
Gambling	.11%
Offenses Against Family and Children	.69%
Driving Under the Influence	12.46%
Liquor Laws	4.39%
Drunkenness	6.19%
Disorderly Conduct	5.33%
Vagrancy	.27%
Suspicion	.12%
Curfew and Loitering Laws	.65%
Runaways	1.24%
All Other Offenses	22.79%

Part I Offenses
Part II Offenses

Percentage of Total Arrests

Source: U.S. Bureau of Justice Statistics.

Types of Crimes

The Federal Bureau of Investigation (FBI) classifies crime into 29 categories:

Part I Offenses (More Serious)

1. **Murder and Nonnegligent Manslaughter–** The willful killing of one human being by another.
2. **Forcible Rape–**Sexual violation of a person by force and against the person's will.
3. **Robbery–**Taking anything of value from a person by using force or threat of force.
4. **Aggravated Assault–**An unlawful attack by one person on another for the purpose of causing great bodily injury.
5. **Burglary (breaking and entering)–**An attempt at or unlawful entry of a structure to commit a felony or theft.
6. **Larceny (theft, except auto)–**The unlawful taking or stealing of property or articles without the use of force, violence, or fraud. Examples include shoplifting, pocket picking, and purse snatching.
7. **Motor Vehicle Theft–**The unlawful stealing or driving away and abandoning of a motor vehicle.
8. **Arson–**Willful or spiteful burning, including attempts at such acts.

Part II Offenses (Less Serious)

9. **Other Assaults–**Attacks of a less serious nature than aggravated assault.
10. **Forgery and Counterfeiting–**Attempting to or making, altering, or possessing anything false that is intentionally made to appear true in order to deceive.
11. **Fraud–**Deceitful obtaining of money or property by false pretenses.
12. **Embezzlement–**Misappropriation or misapplication of money or property entrusted to the individual's care, custody, or control.
13. **Stolen Property–**Attempting to or buying, receiving, and possessing stolen property.
14. **Vandalism–**Willful or vicious destruction, injury, disfigurement, or defacement of property.
15. **Weapons–**All violations of regulations relating to manufacturing, carrying, possessing, or using firearms.
16. **Prostitution and Commercialized Vice–**Sex offenses of a commercialized nature.
17. **Sex Offenses–**Charges such as statutory rape (in which the girl consents but is under age) and offenses against common decency, morals, and chastity, or attempts at these offenses.
18. **Drug Abuse Violations–**The unlawful possession, sale, or use of narcotics.
19. **Gambling–**Promoting, permitting, or engaging in gambling.
20. **Offenses Against Family and Children–**Nonsupport, neglect, desertion, or abuse of family and children.
21. **Driving Under the Influence–**Driving or operating any motor vehicle while under the influence of liquor or narcotics.
22. **Liquor Laws–**Violations of state or local liquor laws.
23. **Drunkenness–**Intoxication.
24. **Disorderly Conduct–**Breach of the peace.
25. **Vagrancy–**Includes vagabondage, begging, and loitering.
26. **Suspicion–**Arrests for no specific offense, followed by release without placing charges.
27. **Curfew and Loitering Laws (Juveniles)–**Violations of local curfew and loitering laws, where such laws exist.
28. **Runaways (Juveniles)–**Limited to juveniles taken into custody under local statutes as runaways.
29. **All Other Offenses–**All violations of state and local laws except traffic laws and those listed here.

Generally the more serious crimes (Part I Offenses) carry a harsher sentence–a year or more in prison. These crimes are called *felonies*. They include murder, rape, robbery, auto theft, and larceny where the theft is major. *Misdemeanors* are less serious crimes with a penalty of a year or less in prison. The dividing line between felonies and misdemeanors, however, varies somewhat from state to state.

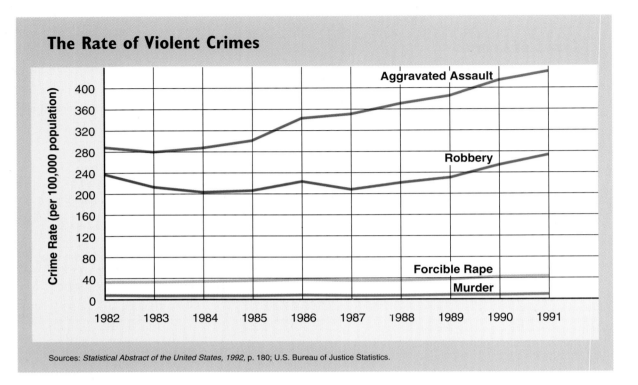

The Rate of Violent Crimes

Crime Rate (per 100,000 population)

400
360
320
280
240
200
160
120
80
40
0

Aggravated Assault

Robbery

Forcible Rape

Murder

1982 1983 1984 1985 1986 1987 1988 1989 1990 1991

Sources: *Statistical Abstract of the United States, 1992*, p. 180; U.S. Bureau of Justice Statistics.

aggravated assault occurs every 29 seconds, a robbery every 46 seconds, a forcible rape every 5 minutes, and a murder every 21 minutes. The crime rates for murder and forcible rape have remained relatively constant over the past 10 years. The rate for robbery has experienced periods of increase and periods of decline over the years, but the rate for aggravated assault has shown a steady increase. The graph on this page shows variations in the rate of violent crimes.

The victims of violence more often are African Americans. In the case of murder, for instance, African American males are much more likely to be victims. African American males have a victimization rate that is about 5 times that of African American females, over 7 times that of white males, and about 22 times that of white females.

The majority of murders are committed with guns and knives. Guns are used in about 64 percent of all murders, with handguns being the weapon of choice in about 49 percent of the cases. Another 17 percent of murders are committed with knives. The rate of handgun use in homicides is higher in the United States than it is in any other industrialized nation in the world.

Crime Against Property. Crimes against property—burglary, larceny (theft other than auto), motor vehicle theft, and arson—are much more common than crimes of violence. All property crimes involve either stealing someone else's property or intentionally causing damage to it. It is estimated that a property crime is committed every 2 seconds in the United States. The graph on page 191 shows the crime rates for larceny and burglary in recent years. Note that the rates have had periods of increase and periods of decline over the years.

Sociologists generally tie variations in the crime rate to changes in the population. As we have already noted, a large percentage of crimes are committed by people under the age of 25. As the size of this segment of the population changes, the crime rate varies in the same direction—the smaller the population, the lower the crime rate, for instance. In the 1980s and 1990s, however, increases in the crime rate appear to be at least partially the result of illegal drug use. Expensive drug habits often are financed through crime. In addition, many serious crimes are committed while under the influence of drugs.

Victimless Crime. Crimes such as prostitution, gambling, illegal drug use, and vagrancy are classified as victimless crimes. Crimes such as these are called victimless crimes because supposedly they harm no one but the person committing the act. This classification may be somewhat misleading in the case of some of these crimes, however. While others may not suffer directly, the consequences for society of such crimes as drug abuse can be significant.

White-Collar Crime. A crime that is committed by an individual or individuals of high social status in the course of their professional lives is called **white-collar crime.** Employees of corporations, politicians, and corporations themselves sometimes engage in white-collar crime. Misrepresentation, fraud, tax evasion, embezzlement, price fixing, toxic pollution, stock manipulation, and political corruption are examples of white-collar crime. Traditionally, white-collar crime has been played down by the public and the press even though it is a serious social problem. In recent years, however, crimes such as the insider-trading scandals on Wall Street, political corruption, corporate crimes, and computer crimes have received a great deal of attention.

By trading on insider information—information that is not available to the general public—investor Ivan Boesky (left) was able to make millions illegally in the stock market. His arrest set in motion an investigation of illegal activities on Wall Street that has had far-reaching consequences.

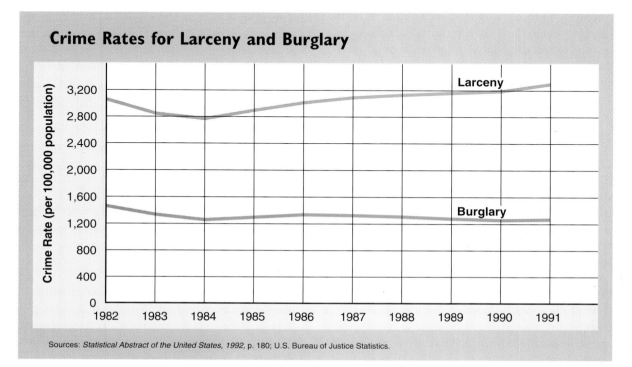

Crime Rates for Larceny and Burglary

Larceny

Burglary

Crime Rate (per 100,000 population)

3,200
2,800
2,400
2,000
1,600
1,200
800
400
0

1982 1983 1984 1985 1986 1987 1988 1989 1990 1991

Sources: *Statistical Abstract of the United States, 1992,* p. 180; U.S. Bureau of Justice Statistics.

It may seem odd that a corporation can be charged with a white-collar crime when it actually is people within the corporation who commit the offense. Corporations can be charged with offenses because under the laws of incorporation, they are considered "legal persons." Once incorporated, a business becomes subject to the same laws as any other person in the United States.

White-collar crime costs society billions of dollars each year. The costs of such crime, however, are not just financial. When political and corporate leaders engage in activities that fall outside the law, they also abuse the trust and confidence of the American people.

Organized Crime. Whereas some criminals engage in crime on an individual basis, other criminals are part of organized crime syndicates. A **crime syndicate** is a large-scale organization of professional criminals that controls some vice or business through violence or the threat of violence. These organizations pursue crime as a big business.

Such syndicates operate in all areas of business, many of them legal. They may carry out their operations through some legitimate organization, which serves as a front for criminal activities. This lets the syndicate reinvest its money through legal channels. Through methods such as loansharking (lending money at very high interest rates), drug trafficking, illegal gambling, unfair labor practices, the hijacking of merchandise, and cheating on income tax returns, organized crime syndicates make large profits.

The Criminal Justice System

Once a crime has been committed and reported, it falls under the jurisdiction of the criminal justice system. The most important components of the criminal justice system are the police, the courts, and corrections. A special category of the criminal justice system in the United States is the juvenile justice system.

Police. The police hold the most immediate control over who is arrested for a criminal act. It might seem reasonable to assume that the police arrest everyone who is accused of committing a crime. In reality, however, the police have considerable power to decide who actually is arrested. This power is referred to as *discretionary power.* The size of the United States population, the number of criminal offenses, and the number of full-time police officers make it necessary for the police to employ discretionary powers in their arrest decisions.

Research has indicated that several factors enter into a police officer's decision concerning whether to arrest a suspected criminal. First, the seriousness of the offense is considered. Less serious offenses are more likely to be ignored. Second, the wishes of the victim are taken into consideration. If the offense is serious or if the suspect is a male, victims generally press for an arrest. Third, the attitude of the suspect is considered. An uncooperative suspect is more likely to be arrested than is one who is polite or apologetic. Fourth, if bystanders are present, the police are more likely to make an arrest. Through an arrest, the police reinforce the point that they are in control of the situation. Finally, research has found that, in situations in which discretion may be used, police are more likely to arrest African Americans than they are to arrest whites.

Courts. Once a person is arrested, the responsibility shifts to the courts. We tend to think of the court's role as a twofold process. First, the court determines the guilt or innocence of the accused person by means of a trial. Second, if the person is found guilty, the court assigns some form of punishment. In reality, though, the vast majority of all criminal cases are settled through plea bargaining before the case goes to trial.

Plea bargaining is the process of legal negotiation that allows an accused person to plead guilty to a lesser charge in return for a lighter sentence. Research has shown that individuals who plea bargain get a lighter sentence than do individuals who plead innocent but are found guilty by the courts. Plea bargaining allows courts to reduce their caseloads in those instances in which the facts of the case are not in dispute.

Corrections. People who are found guilty of crimes must be punished. The sanctions—such as imprisonment, parole, and probation—that are used to punish criminals are called **corrections.** Corrections serve four basic functions.

Even though most criminal cases do not go to trial, individuals who are charged with crimes in the United States have the right to be judged by a jury of their peers.

- *Retribution.* The punishing of a criminal serves as an act of revenge for the victim and society.
- *Deterrence.* Corrections are intended to discourage offenders from committing future crimes and make the rest of society think twice about breaking laws.
- *Rehabilitation.* During the nineteenth century, prisons emerged as places in which to reform criminals so that they could return to society as law-abiding citizens.
- *Social protection.* By limiting the freedom of offenders, society prevents them from committing additional crimes. In the case of the death penalty, the threat of future criminal activity is eliminated completely.

The effectiveness of corrections is a topic of heated debate. One indication that corrections are not always effective is the rate of recidivism among convicted criminals. **Recidivism** is the term for repeated criminal behavior. Almost half of all convicted criminals eventually are arrested for another offense.

Courts can assign punishments ranging from fines to probation to imprisonment. The majority of convictions are punished through fines and probation. In the case of serious crimes, however—particularly murder and robbery—prison sentences are common. As can be seen in the graph on this page, the size of the prison population has increased dramatically in recent years.

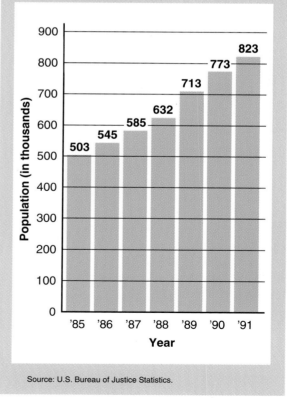

The United States Prison Population

Population (in thousands)

Year	Population
'85	503
'86	545
'87	585
'88	632
'89	713
'90	773
'91	823

Source: U.S. Bureau of Justice Statistics.

Chapter 8   Deviance and Social Control   **193**

Juvenile Justice System. The third largest category of criminals in the United States consists of juvenile offenders—offenders who are under 18 years of age. Until recently, juveniles charged with crimes had few rights and were not covered by the same legal safeguards that are provided for adult offenders. Laws that cover adult offenders refer to well-defined offenses, carry specific punishments, and apply equally to all offenders. The laws for juvenile offenses were much less specific. They contained vague provisions about, for example, "incorrigible, ungovernable" children who associate with "immoral or vicious persons." A juvenile offender could, and sometimes did, remain in custody for a longer period of time than an adult convicted of the same offense.

The reasoning behind separate regulations for juveniles was that juvenile offenders, because of their age, could not be expected to be as respon-sible as adults. Thus it was thought that they needed a special, more considerate kind of treatment. Sometimes, however, the result was that juveniles were denied equal protection under the law. Consequently, they were not granted the special care and attention intended by the juvenile court system.

To guard against such abuses, the courts now must guarantee juvenile defendants the same legal rights and privileges as adult defendants. At the same time, however, juvenile delinquents still are regarded as special kinds of offenders. Juvenile courts try, in principle at least, to provide many more services for offenders than does the adult criminal court system. Yet in some areas of the nation, particularly in large cities, tougher juvenile laws are being established. For instance, in some places, juveniles can be tried as adults for certain serious offenses.

In recent years, many states have instituted programs designed to keep first-time offenders out of the juvenile justice system. In these states, only those youths who are repeat offenders or who have been convicted of serious crimes generally find themselves confined to juvenile correction facilities.

Some juveniles who are arrested for serious crimes are tried in adult courts and receive the same punishments as adult offenders.

CHAPTER 8   SUMMARY

Society determines what is considered deviant. To be labeled as deviant, an individual must be detected committing a deviant act and then be stigmatized by society.

High levels of deviance are disruptive. Low levels, however, can serve positive social functions. Deviance can help to unify the group, clarify norms, diffuse tension, identify problems, and provide jobs.

Several theories have been devised to explain deviant behavior. Each takes a slightly different perspective. Among the major theories of deviance are cultural-transmission theory, structural-strain theory, control theory, conflict theory, and labeling theory.

A special category of deviance is crime. One source of crime statistics is the *Uniform Crime Report,* published annually by the Federal Bureau of Investigation (FBI). These statistics are not

completely accurate, however, because of various factors that affect police decisions concerning the filing of formal reports.

Crimes can be grouped into five categories: violent crime, crime against property, victimless crime, white-collar crime, and organized crime. Although violent crimes are a small percentage of all crimes, they produce the most fear in members of society.

Once a crime is committed and reported, it falls under the jurisdiction of the criminal justice system. The main components of the criminal justice system are the police, the courts, and corrections. Corrections serve four basic functions: retribution, deterrence, rehabilitation, and social protection. A special category of the criminal justice system in the United States is the juvenile justice system. This system serves individuals who are under the age of 18.

THINKING ABOUT SOCIOLOGY: Interpreting Statistics

You were introduced to the skills of reading statistical tables in Chapter 6, pages 144–145, and reading graphs in Chapter 7, pages 170–171. Sociology students often are required to interpret the statistics presented in tables and graphs and to use the information to form generalizations.

How to Interpret Statistics

To interpret statistics, follow these steps.

1. Identify the type of data. Note the table or graph's title, as well as all headings, subheadings, and labels.

2. Examine the components. Note the specific statistics given under each heading or subheading in the table or segment of the graph. Note whether any information about the statistics is given in the title (such as indicating that the figures are percentages) or in the footnotes. Check the source of the data and how current it is.

3. Identify relationships among the data. Note trends in the data. Determine similarities and differences as well as any cause-and-effect relationships.

4. Read footnotes. Pay attention to asterisks or other symbols that refer to footnotes.

5. Generalize from the data. Make a general statement from the information. The generalization must be based on facts, but cannot go beyond the facts at hand. When the tables and graphs are part of a text discussion on a subject, you can begin to formulate a generalization by looking for key words and phrases in the accompanying text.

Applying the Skill

Study the table on page 197. The title indicates that the subject of the table is the characteristics of prisoners under sentence of death for the years 1985–1991. The table is divided into years, and percentages are given for a variety of characteristics for each year. The table is based on information from the 1992 edition of the *Statistical Abstract of the United States* and from the U.S. Bureau of Justice Statistics.

Notice that the percentage distribution of characteristics within a particular year remain relatively constant over the span of years. For instance, the percentage of those people sentenced to death who are white was 57 percent in 1985, 56 percent in 1986, 57 percent in 1987, 58 percent in 1988, 1989, and 1990, and 59 percent in 1991. Also note that the percentage of death-row prisoners under the age of 25 has declined steadily since 1985.

Several generalizations can be made from these data. First, the nonwhite death-row population is overrepresented (ranging from 41 percent to 44 percent) in relation to its share of the general population (approximately 20 percent). Second, the largest percentage of the prison population under sentence of death is over the age of 25. And finally, the majority of people held in death row have less than a college education. What *cannot* be determined from the data are the reasons for these distributions.

Practicing the Skill

Study the graph on page 197. Then on a separate sheet of paper, answer the following questions:

1. What is the title and source of the graph?

2. In what form are the data given?

3. Which type of area experienced the highest rate of violent crime?

4. Within each category (type of area), which type of crime had the highest rate?

5. What generalizations can you make?

Characteristics of Prisoners Under Sentence of Death, 1985–1991 (in percents)

Characteristic	1985	1986	1987	1988	1989	1990	1991
Race							
White	57	56	57	58	58	58	59
Nonwhite	43	44	43	42	42	42	41
Age							
Under 20	1	1	1	1	1	1	1
20–24	13	12	11	9	8	7	7
25–34	51	49	49	49	48	47	44
35–54	33	36	37	39	41	42	45
55 and over	2	2	2	2	2	3	3
Education*							
7 years or less	11	10	10	9	9	9	8
8 years	12	11	10	10	9	9	8
9–11 years	36	37	37	36	37	37	37
12 years	32	33	33	35	35	35	36
More than 12 years	9	9	10	10	10	10	11

* Prisoners for whom information on education was available.
Sources: *Statistical Abstract of the United States, 1992*, p. 199; U.S. Bureau of Justice Statistics.

Violent Crime Rates (per 100,000 population) by Type of Area

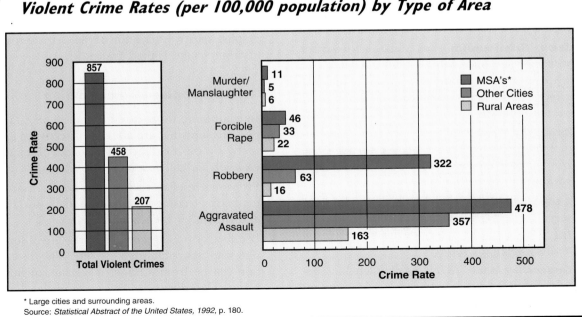

* Large cities and surrounding areas.
Source: *Statistical Abstract of the United States, 1992*, p. 180.

Reviewing Sociological Terms

On a separate sheet of paper, supply the term that correctly completes each sentence.

1. _____ is the term used for repeated criminal behavior.

2. A large-scale organization of professional criminals that controls some vice or business through violence or the threat of violence is called a _____ _____.

3. The process of legal negotiation that allows an accused person to plead guilty to a lesser charge in return for a lighter sentence is called _____ _____.

4. A _____ is any act that is labeled as such by those in authority, is prohibited by law, and is punishable by the government.

5. Behavior that violates significant social norms is called _____.

Thinking Critically about Sociology

1. **Comparing Ideas** *(a)* In what ways are structural-strain theory and control theory similar? *(b)* In what ways are they different?

2. **Seeing Relationships** *(a)* What factors affect whether the police will file a formal complaint when a crime is reported? *(b)* What factors affect whether a police officer will arrest a suspected criminal?

3. **Analyzing Viewpoints** *(a)* According to conflict theory, what causes people in power to commit deviant acts? *(b)* What causes people without power to commit deviant acts?

4. **Analyzing Ideas** *(a)* How does deviance serve to unify the group and clarify norms? *(b)* Why are minor acts of deviance considered a safety valve for society?

5. **Contrasting Ideas** *(a)* How does labeling theory differ from other theories of deviance? *(b)* How does primary deviance differ from secondary deviance?

6. **Comprehending Ideas** *(a)* What is anomie? *(b)* When people fall victim to anomie, what modes of adaptation can they take and what do these modes involve?

7. **Summarizing Ideas** List and describe the four basic functions of corrections.

8. **Expressing Ideas** Describe the role that differential association plays in cultural-transmission theory.

Exercising Sociological Skills

1. **Observing Norms** Reread the Applying Sociology feature on pages 180–181. List some of the norms that apply to conversations and describe possible reactions to violating these norms.

2. **Understanding Ideas** According to the Case Study on page 185, why do some young people join gangs?

3. **Interpreting Statistics** Reread the Developing Sociological Imagination feature on pages 196–197. Then examine the table on page 187 and the graphs on pages 188, 190, and 191. From the statistics presented in the table and graphs, write a description of the characteristics of crime in the United States.

Extending Sociological Imagination

1. In addition to those listed in the chapter, identify five jobs that are affected directly or indirectly by the existence of deviance. Describe each job and tell how it is affected by deviance.

2. Prepare a brief research paper on the modern methods of crime detection used by the Federal Bureau of Investigation (FBI).

3. Locate a written description of the life of someone who has committed a crime. The description can be from a book, magazine, or newspaper. Describe how being stigmatized as a criminal has affected the person's daily life and future goals.

INTERPRETING PRIMARY SOURCES
Crime and American Business

Individual citizens are not the only victims of crime. Each day in the United States, businesses large and small fall victim to a wide range of crimes.

In this excerpt from the article "Crime and the Bottom Line," which appeared in the April 13, 1992, issue of *U.S. News & World Report,* Terri Thompson, David Hage, and Robert F. Black discuss how crimes against American companies cost business billions of dollars annually. While reading the excerpt, consider why the American consumer is the ultimate victim of such crimes. Also consider why employee crime may be more widespread than we think.

U.S. banks have spent more than $650 million on security systems for cash machines, yet ATM [Automated Teller Machine] patrons are still robbed once every 88 minutes and large banks still lose an average of $41,741 a year to ATM fraud. . . .

Theft at ATMs, however, is small change compared with the walloping bill American business pays for crime in all its forms. *U.S. News* estimates—conservatively—that crime against business cost companies $128 billion last year in direct losses, litigation expenses and security outlays. That is eight times the cost of crimes committed against individuals and households, or, put another way, about 69 percent of after-tax corporate profits in America. Even worse for the balance sheet, the cost of crime has doubled since 1980.

Virtually the entire cost of crime against companies is passed on to consumers in the form of higher prices, which results in a "crime tax" of $1,376 for every American household. . . . At 2.3 percent of gross domestic product, the cost of crime is also a drag on the nation's economy, because a dollar spent on security guards is a dollar not spent on research or product quality. "You've got to build the price of security into the price of your product," says Lester Thurow of the Massachusetts Institute of Technology. "It means our goods are going to cost more than Japanese goods, even if we produce them more efficiently." . . .

Across the country, business was victimized by $11.6 billion worth of burglaries and robberies last year and spent $36.3 billion of guards, locks and surveillance cameras. These outlays are growing at two to three times the rate of inflation as companies scramble to protect customers and employees against crime and themselves against litigation. . . .

The biggest crooks sometimes occupy corner offices. Embezzlement and kickbacks cost business $27.2 billion last year, and some experts believe the figure is many times higher because most companies are too embarrassed to report internal wrongdoing or simply never see it. And the cost is rising fast: Federal embezzlement cases multiplied by 40 percent during the 1980s, far more swiftly than traditional forgery and burglary prosecutions. . . .

Unfortunately, some of the sophisticated technology now being used to combat crime against business is too expensive for many companies. Infrared cameras, for example, which convert heat radiation from people and objects to video images and are therefore ideal for spotting crimes in the dark, start at about $30,000 each.

The growing rate of crime committed against companies will almost certainly lead to increasingly high costs for business in the coming decade. As a result, already burdened bottom lines will be robbed of precious profits. And that is the last thing American companies need as they struggle through the slow-growth 1990s.

Source Review

1. According to the author, how does business pay for the high cost of crime against American companies?

2. Why is it impossible to know how much employee crime costs business each year?

Controlling Family Size in China

The size of the population in China reached one billion in 1982. This staggering figure roughly equals the estimated population of the entire planet in the year 1850. The rapidly growing population has presented the Chinese government with major economic and social problems. In recent years, the government has been attempting to modernize the Chinese economy and raise the standard of living of the Chinese people. The government realizes that if it is to achieve these goals, it must halt the rapid growth of the Chinese population. Thus in 1979, the Chinese government embarked on an ambitious program to limit the size of families.

The goal of the government program is to convince a substantial number of young couples to sign a pledge promising to have no more than one child. An intensive resocialization campaign is underway to change the thinking of a society traditionally used to having large families. In China's urban areas today, billboards and pamphlets proclaim the superiority of the one-child family. Chinese citizens are encouraged to take advantage of the free birth control counseling, family-planning clinics, and birth control devices that are widely available.

Peer pressure, educational programs, and a number of strong economic incentives have been initiated to achieve the goal of the one-child-per-family program. Couples who sign the pledge promising to bear only one child are awarded an "only child glory certificate." This certificate entitles couples to receive special monthly payments and food rations, free health care and schooling for their child, better access to housing and jobs, assistance in providing for their child's higher education, and higher pensions for those who work for the state. Couples who sign the pledge and later have a second child must repay all of the benefits they already have received.

By 1984, 34 million couples had signed the pledge promising to bear only one child. Despite this fact, it remains questionable whether China will be able to achieve its goal of population control. The great majority of China's mainland population lives in the countryside, where it is the custom to have large families. Parents in the countryside desire large families because sons are needed for farming. In addition, the move to encourage people to use effective birth control is made more difficult by the fact that a large proportion of the Chinese population cannot read and is suspicious of new ideas.

Despite efforts to change tradition, sons still are preferred over daughters in China. This leads the government to fear that couples will continue to have children until they bear a son or that they will fail to report the birth of daughters. Of even greater concern is the possibility that some parents who want to ensure that their only living child is a son are resorting to female infanticide, or murder of female babies.

Failure of the family-planning program would be a serious blow to China's modernization efforts. Success nevertheless presents at least one long-range concern. If the program is successful, it may become necessary for couples to support their four aged parents and single child at the same time. The Chinese people have a tradition of caring for their aged parents, and few social programs exist in the rural areas to help the elderly. Couples who do not have brothers and sisters to help them care for their aging parents may find themselves burdened beyond their means.

Societies are slow to change, and the effort to alter family life in China is meeting with resistance. Current projections already show that China's population will be higher than the goal set by the government for the year 2000. Moreover, the Chinese government has received sharp criticism from countries around the world on political, ethical, and religious grounds. Nevertheless, China's leaders are determined to continue their efforts long into the twenty-first century.

UNIT 2 REVIEW

Reviewing Sociological Ideas

1. **(a)** How does the personality differ from the self? **(b)** Describe the explanations given by Locke, Cooley, and Mead for the development of the self.

2. **(a)** What is an instinct? **(b)** According to sociobiologists, what role do genetics play in human behavior? **(c)** To what do most contemporary sociologists attribute human behavior?

3. **(a)** What are puberty and adolescence? **(b)** Why is puberty a universal phenomenon? **(c)** Describe the characteristics of adolescence.

4. **(a)** What is the difference between dating and courtship? **(b)** Describe the factors contributing to the development of dating in the United States.

5. **(a)** What is unemployment? **(b)** What level of unemployment is considered acceptable in the United States?

6. **(a)** What is Alzheimer's disease and how common is it among the elderly? **(b)** Describe the progression of Alzheimer's disease.

7. **(a)** What are primary deviance and secondary deviance? **(b)** How does being labeled a deviant affect a person's life?

Synthesizing Sociological Ideas

1. **Comprehending Ideas** **(a)** What is a total institution? **(b)** How do total institutions go about the resocialization of new members?

2. **Seeing Relationships** **(a)** How is personality influenced by birth order? **(b)** What do studies of children raised in isolation tell us about human interaction and personality development?

3. **Summarizing Ideas** **(a)** Summarize the discussion from your textbook on the primary agents of socialization. **(b)** Explain why the family is considered the most important agent of socialization.

4. **Organizing Ideas** **(a)** How has the rate of teenage drug use changed over the years? **(b)** What are the consequences of teenage sexual activity? **(c)** What are the predictors of teenage suicide?

5. **Comparing Ideas** **(a)** Describe the phases outlined in Levinson's theory of adult male development. **(b)** How do the phases of adult male development differ from the phases of adult female development?

6. **Explaining Ideas** Discuss the personality types and patterns of adapting to retirement and old age found by the Kansas City Study of Adult Life.

7. **Identifying Ideas** **(a)** What is white-collar crime? **(b)** What are the costs to society of white-collar crime? **(c)** What is a crime syndicate? **(d)** Through what criminal activities do crime syndicates make their money?

8. **Using Evidence** **(a)** Provide evidence to show that deviance has positive consequences for society. **(b)** Explain the functions served by punishment in society.

Applying Sociological Imagination

1. Watch several television programs that focus on families with children. Pay special attention to the birth order of the children to find out if there are identifiable patterns of behavior for first-born, middle-born, and last-born children. Design a chart showing the behaviors typical of each birth-order position.

2. Prepare a brief research paper on adolescence in Russia. Compare and contrast the problems common to Russian youth with the problems common to American youth.

3. Prepare as long a list as you can of jobs that have disappeared from the American scene.

4. Interview someone who works for the police department. Ask this person to describe how the tools and techniques of crime reporting have changed over the years.

Today, serious expressions of discontent with the prevailing modes of distributing goods and services mark the entire world. The discontent is, of course, eloquent testimony to its presence.

MELVIN M. TUMIN

SOCIAL INEQUALITY

CHAPTER 2

Social Stratification

 Systems of Stratification

Types of Stratification Systems
The Dimensions of Social Stratification
Explaining Stratification

2 **The American Class System**

Determining Social Class
Social Classes in the United States
Social Mobility

 Poverty

Defining Poverty in the
United States
The American Poor
The Effects of Poverty
Government Responses to
Poverty

Chapter Focus

Chapter 9 explores the topic of social stratification. The chapter opens with a discussion of caste systems and class systems—the two basic types of stratification systems. Several theories of stratification also are examined. Attention then is turned toward an analysis of social class and poverty in the United States.

As you study the chapter, look for the answers to the following questions:

1. What are the characteristics of caste systems and class systems?
2. What are the major theories that have been proposed to explain the existence of social stratification?
3. What are the characteristics of the American class system?
4. Who are the poor in America, and what steps have been taken by the federal government to lessen the effects of poverty?

KEY TERMS

The following terms, while not the only terms emphasized in the chapter, are basic to your understanding of sociology. Determine the meaning of each term, either by using the Glossary or by watching for context clues as you read the chapter.

social stratification	wealth	poverty level
caste system	power	life chances
endogamy	prestige	transfer payments

All societies distinguish between their members on the basis of certain characteristics. The characteristics that are used to distinguish between people and the degree to which the distinctions are made vary from society to society. Until quite recently in South Africa, for example, class distinctions based on race were part of the constitution and were reinforced by a rigid system of laws and customs. In Great Britain and the United States, on the other hand, people are considered equal under the law. Nevertheless, class distinctions are a recognized feature of the social structure in both of these nations.

Social inequality exists even in those nations that claim to be without a class structure. The former Soviet Union, for example, denied that it made class distinctions. In reality, however, access to scarce resources and social rewards in this former Communist nation were affected by such factors as party ranking and national origin.

In this chapter, we will examine social inequality. We will look first at the general characteristics of social stratification and at some of the theories that have been proposed to explain it. We will then examine the American class system and the problem of poverty in the United States.

1 SYSTEMS OF STRATIFICATION

Social stratification is the ranking of individuals or categories of people on the basis of unequal access to scarce resources and social rewards. Thus by definition, social stratification implies **social inequality**—the unequal sharing of social rewards and resources. In a bureaucracy, for example, positions are ranked according to degree of authority. As workers move up the bureaucratic ladder, their salaries and prestige levels increase. Those workers at the top of the ladder enjoy far greater social and monetary rewards than the workers below them. This also is the case on a societal level.

Access to social rewards can be based on any characteristic or set of characteristics a society chooses to employ. The characteristics vary from society to society and between historical periods. Among the most common characteristics are such ascribed statuses as ancestry, race, age, physical appearance, and whether one is male or female. Achieved statuses—such as educational attainment and occupation—also can be used to determine access to rewards. Other factors that play a part in determining access include talent and effort. We will learn how some of these factors are related to social stratification in the United States in Section 2 of this chapter.

Types of Stratification Systems

Access to rewards also varies depending on the degree to which the stratification system is open or closed. In a closed system, movement between the status levels, or strata, is impossible. A person is assigned a status at birth and remains at that level throughout life. In an open system, on the other hand, movement between strata *is* possible. The ease of movement depends on the degree of openness in the system.

The two basic types of stratification systems—caste systems and class systems—can be placed along a continuum from closed (far left) to open (far right). Caste systems fall at the far left of the continuum. In a caste system, a person's status is assigned at birth and, in all but rare cases, the individual remains in that status throughout life. Class systems, on the other hand, range along the continuum from slightly open to very open, depending on the society under consideration.

Caste Systems. In a **caste system,** scarce resources and rewards are distributed on the basis of ascribed statuses. A newborn child's lifelong status—or caste—is determined by the status of his or her parents. While effort and talent may affect an individual's position within a caste, they cannot help the person move to a higher status.

The way in which statuses are assigned makes it necessary for a caste system to have elaborate norms governing interaction between members of different castes. Marriage between members of different castes, for example, would make it difficult to assign a status to children. Which parent's status would be used? To avoid this problem, caste systems traditionally have forbidden the practice of **exogamy,** marriage outside of one's own social category. Instead, caste systems generally have practiced endogamy. **Endogamy** is marriage within one's own social category.

Caste systems once were a very common form of social organization. The most extreme example of a caste system is nineteenth-century India, where individuals by law were assigned to one of four castes: the Brahmans, the Kshatriyas, the Vaishyas, and the Sudras. These castes in turn were subdivided into thousands of subcastes based on specific occupations. Below these four castes was a class of outcastes, or untouchables. The untouchables were shunned by the other castes because of their lowly status, and were given only the most undesirable tasks to perform.

In the 1950s, India's legislature abolished the caste system as the legal basis for determining access to public facilities, legal protection, and economic resources. Endogamy also was removed as a requirement for a true marriage. In the urban areas, where the mixing of castes is unavoidable, distinctions between the castes now are blurring. In the rural areas, however, the caste system still plays an important role in organizing daily life. Nevertheless, some observers believe that the forces of industrialization slowly are moving India away from a caste system toward a system based on economic classes.

Under the caste system of India, the untouchables and the Brahmans held their vastly different social positions throughout life.

Class Systems. In a **class system,** the distribution of scarce resources and rewards is determined on the basis of achieved statuses. The basing of social class on achieved statuses means that individuals have some control over their place in the stratification system. Given talent, effort, and opportunity, individuals can move up the social-class ladder. The reverse also is true—circumstances can reduce an individual's standing in the stratification system.

Social class has been defined in various ways by sociologists. Sociologists who base their work on the theories of Karl Marx define social class in terms of who owns the means of production. The **means of production** are the tools, buildings, and materials needed to produce goods and services. In this view of social class, society is divided into two basic groups—those who own the means of production and those who own only their labor.

In a capitalist society, the owners of the means of production are called the **bourgeoisie** (boor-ZHWAH-zee), while the workers who sell their labor in exchange for wages are called the **proletariat.** According to Marx, social inequality exists in a capitalist system because the members of the bourgeoisie reap all of the profits even though the work is done by the proletariat.

Marx was writing in the 1800s during the height of the Industrial Revolution. Working and living conditions were horrible for much of the proletariat. And the social divisions between owners and workers were clearly drawn and striking. The same cannot be said of modern industrial society.

Growth in the professions, the managerial classes, the number of self-employed, and the rise of the service industry have altered the nature of work. In addition, large corporations have changed the relationship between ownership and control. In a corporation, ownership rests with the stockholders, who literally may number in the

thousands. Daily control of the company is in the hands of middle and upper management—individuals who are themselves employees. Consequently, most American sociologists find the Marxist definition of social class to be too narrow.

We will define a **social class** as a grouping of people with similar levels of wealth, power, and prestige. This definition builds on the work of Max Weber. Weber believed that society is stratified on the basis of economic class (wealth), social status as expressed by life-style (prestige), and party (political power). While the economic factor plays the most significant role in determining one's place in the stratification system, prestige and power also affect one's standing. For instance, the English lord who must open his family castle to tourists in order to make ends meet still may hold a position of power in the community. On the other hand, the wealthy individual who made his or her money through illegal means may be shunned by the established upper class.

Corporations have put ownership in the hands of the many. Stockholders, who often number in the thousands, must receive regular reports of their company's progress.

Many sociologists today define social class in relation to wealth, prestige, and power. To make it possible to rank individuals on these three dimensions, sociologists often calculate people's socioeconomic status. **Socioeconomic status,** or **SES,** is a rating that combines social factors such as educational level, occupational prestige, and place of residence with the economic factor of income. These combined factors then are used to determine an individual's relative position in the stratification system.

The Dimensions of Social Stratification

Theoretically, anything of value can be used as a social reward. Some rewards are more valued than others, however. As we already have mentioned, the three most common rewards on which social stratification is determined are wealth, power, and prestige.

Wealth. Wealth is the most obvious dimension of social stratification. An individual's **wealth** is made up of his or her *assets*—the value of everything the person owns—and *income*—money earned through salaries and wages. In the United States, wealth is concentrated overwhelmingly in the hands of a minority of the population. As can be seen from the graph on this page, the richest one-fifth (20 percent) of the population controls approximately 76 percent of the nation's assets.

Income also is distributed unequally in the United States, although not as strikingly as in the case of assets. Approximately 46 percent of our total national income is earned by the top one-fifth of income earners in the population. Sociologist Paul Blumberg estimates that top corporate executives make 100 times as much money as the lowest paid production workers. This fact recently has led to efforts to cap the amount of income that can be earned by corporate executives.

Power. People with considerable wealth usually possess considerable power. But the reverse of this also can be true—wealth can be a by-product of power. **Power** is the ability to control the behavior of others, with or without their consent. Power can be based on force, the possession of a special skill or type of knowledge, a particular social status, personal characteristics, or custom and tradition.

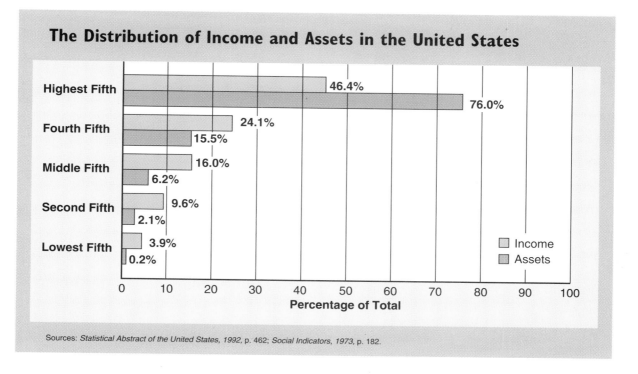

The Distribution of Income and Assets in the United States

	Income	Assets
Highest Fifth	46.4%	76.0%
Fourth Fifth	24.1%	15.5%
Middle Fifth	16.0%	6.2%
Second Fifth	9.6%	2.1%
Lowest Fifth	3.9%	0.2%

Percentage of Total

Sources: *Statistical Abstract of the United States, 1992,* p. 462; *Social Indicators, 1973,* p. 182.

Prestige. Just as individuals can be ranked on the amounts of wealth and power they possess, they also can be ranked according to prestige. **Prestige** is the respect, honor, recognition, or courtesy an individual receives from other members of society. Prestige can be based on any characteristics a society or group considers important. Income, occupation, education, family background, area of residence, possessions, mannerisms, and club memberships are among some of the most common determinants of prestige.

In the United States, occupation tends to be the most important determinant of prestige. When asked to rate occupations according to levels of prestige, Americans consistently place jobs that require higher levels of education and those that require mental rather than physical labor at the top of the list. The table on this page shows the

Polo is an expensive sport to pursue and so it tends to be played only by the wealthy. Because access to the sport is limited, polo is considered a prestigious pastime.

Prestige Ratings for Selected Occupations in the United States

Occupation	Rating	Occupation	Rating	Occupation	Rating
Physician	82	Statistician	55	Barber	38
College professor	78	Social worker	52	Jeweler	37
Judge	76	Funeral director	52	Watchmaker	37
Lawyer	76	Computer specialist	51	Bricklayer	36
Physicist	74	Stock broker	51	Flight attendant	36
Dentist	74	Reporter	51	Meter reader	36
Banker	72	Office manager	50	Mechanic	35
Aeronautical engineer	71	Bank teller	50	Baker	34
Architect	71	Electrician	49	Shoe repairer	33
Psychologist	71	Machinist	48	Bulldozer operator	33
Airline pilot	70	Police officer	48	Bus driver	32
Chemist	69	Insurance agent	47	Truck driver	32
Minister	69	Musician	46	Cashier	32
Civil engineer	68	Secretary	46	Sales clerk	29
Biologist	68	Foreman	45	Meat cutter	29
Geologist	67	Real estate agent	44	Housekeeper	25
Sociologist	66	Fireman	44	Longshoreman	24
Political scientist	66	Postal clerk	43	Gas station attendant	22
Mathematician	65	Advertising agent	42	Cab driver	22
High school teacher	63	Mail carrier	42	Elevator operator	21
Registered nurse	62	Railroad conductor	41	Bartender	20
Pharmacist	61	Typist	41	Waiter	20
Veterinarian	60	Plumber	41	Farm laborer	18
Elementary school teacher	60	Farmer	41	Maid/servant	18
		Telephone operator	40	Garbage collector	17
Accountant	57	Carpenter	40	Janitor	17
Librarian	55	Welder	40	Shoe shiner	9
		Dancer	38		

Source: James A. Davis and Tom W. Smith, *General Social Survey Cumulative File, 1972–1982.* Ann Arbor, Mich.: Inter-University Consortium for Political and Social Research, 1983.

prestige ratings for selected occupations. The ratings—which are based on a scale ranging from a low of 1 to a high of 100—have remained fairly constant over the past 40 years. Higher prestige jobs generally produce higher incomes. The Applying Sociology feature on pages 212–213 examines the relationship between occupational prestige and salaries.

Explaining Stratification

The causes and consequences of social inequality are a subject of theoretical debate in sociology. Two major theoretical approaches have been used to explain stratification: functionalist theory and conflict theory.

Functionalist Theory. Functionalists view stratification as a necessary feature of the social structure. The functionalist explanation of stratification, which first was proposed by Kingsley Davis and Wilbert Moore in the 1940s, assumes that certain roles in society must be performed if the system is to be maintained. Society ensures that these roles will be fulfilled by providing higher rewards for their performance. The more important the role and the more skill needed to perform the role, the higher the reward. Functionalists claim that without varying rewards, many jobs would not be filled and society could not function smoothly. Why, for instance, would someone take the time and expense to become a physician if the reward for being a garbage collector was the same?

Conflict Theory. Conflict theorists, on the other hand, see competition over scarce resources as the cause of social inequality. Conflict theorists who base their work on Marxist theory say that stratification comes from class exploitation. The owners of the means of production control the working class in order to raise their own profits and maintain their power in society.

Many American conflict theorists take a less class-based view of inequality. According to these theorists, various groups within society compete with one another for scarce resources. Once a group gains power, it is able to shape public policy and public opinion to its own advantage, thereby maintaining its position of power.

Evaluation. Neither functionalist theory nor conflict theory fully explains stratification. Functionalist theory ignores the fact that those people at the top of the stratification system often exploit those people at lower levels. It also fails to consider that everyone in society does not have equal access to the resources necessary for occupational success. Finally, it cannot explain why some positions—such as those in the sports or entertainment fields—appear to have limited social value yet are highly rewarded.

Conflict theory also takes a one-sided approach to stratification. One of its major shortcomings is that it fails to recognize that unequal rewards are based partially on differences in talent, skill, and desire. Not everyone is suited for every position in the social structure. Consequently, society must have some way to urge the proper individuals into positions that are vital to the smooth operation of society. One way to do this is through the offer of different rewards.

SECTION 1 REVIEW

DEFINE social stratification, social inequality, endogamy, means of production, bourgeoisie, proletariat, socioeconomic status (SES)

1. **Interpreting Ideas** **(a)** Describe the Marxist view of social class. **(b)** How does the Marxist definition of social class differ from the definition presented in the textbook?

2. **Summarizing Ideas** **(a)** Briefly describe the characteristics of a caste system. **(b)** What are the characteristics of a class system?

3. **Comprehending Ideas** List and describe the three dimensions of social stratification discussed in the section.

4. **Comparing Ideas** **(a)** How does functionalist theory explain the existence of social stratification? **(b)** How does conflict theory explain the existence of stratification?

Occupational Prestige and Salaries

Prestige can be assigned on the basis of any characteristic that a group or society considers important. In the military, for example, an individual's combat record is a source of prestige. In a society that is highly religious, an individual's dedication to his or her religion often determines prestige. Prestige also can be based on an individual's family background. In Great Britain, for example, being part of the aristocracy brings prestige. In industrial societies, however, occupation generally is the most common source of prestige. Consequently, sociologists periodically conduct research to determine the prestige rankings of various occupations.

Two of the largest studies of occupational prestige were conducted by the National Opinion Research Center (NORC) of the University of Chicago. The first of these two studies was carried out in 1947. Researchers asked a sample of Americans to rank 90 occupations as either "excellent," "good," "average," "somewhat below average," or "poor." Based on these rankings, the NORC researchers developed a scale of occupational prestige that enabled them to assign a prestige score to each occupation. The scores ranged from a low of 1 to a high of 100.

The highest prestige scores given went to those occupations that require a high level of training or skill and involve taking responsibility for the care of other people. At the head of the list were Supreme Court Justice, physician, state governor, member of the federal cabinet, diplomat in the Foreign Service, mayor of a large city, college professor, and scientist. At the bottom of the list were garbage collector, street sweeper, and shoe shiner.

The NORC conducted the second study in 1963 to determine if the rankings had changed over the years. The similarities in rankings between the two studies were striking. With the exception of slight gains in some scientific occupations and slight drops in some white-collar oc-

cupations, the scores were almost identical. Studies conducted by other researchers in the 1970s and 1980s have found similar results. Although the actual scores have changed somewhat, the relative order of occupational prestige in the United States has remained basically the same.

It is interesting to note that consistency in occupational prestige rankings is not limited to the United States. In the 1960s, NORC researchers examined prestige rankings in 24 industrialized nations around the world. The rankings were very similar to those found in the United States. Even more interesting are the findings of a 1970s study by Donald Treiman that compared occupational prestige rankings in 60 industrialized and industrializing nations. Treiman found that rankings were similar even in those nations that were just beginning to industrialize.

While the research on occupational prestige is interesting, prestige is only one dimension of social stratification. Wealth and power also are important dimensions. Let us use our sociological imagination to examine the connection between occupational prestige and wealth. Because we are talking about occupations, we will use salaries as an indicator of wealth.

The table on page 210 lists the current prestige ratings for selected occupations in the United States. The ratings for 29 of the occupations have been reproduced in the table on page 213. The average annual salaries for these occupations also are listed. The annual salaries are based on information presented in the eighth edition of the *Encyclopedia of Careers and Vocational Guidance*. Note that the figures represent *average* salaries. [For information on statistical terms, see pages 485–492 of the Appendix.]

Now, look at the table on page 213. Keep in mind that we wish to determine whether prestige and salary are related. The questions listed below the table should be of some assistance in this endeavor.

Prestige Ratings and Average Annual Salaries for Selected Occupations

Occupation	Prestige Rating	Annual Salary
Physician	82	$106,300
College professor	78	$ 37,000
Dentist	74	$ 59,000
Airline pilot	70	$ 80,000
Minister	69	$ 20,000
High school teacher	63	$ 26,100
Registered nurse	62	$ 27,800
Veterinarian	60	$ 43,000
Funeral director	52	$ 17,000
Stockbroker	51	$ 76,000
Bank teller	50	$ 12,960
Electrician	49	$ 33,700
Machinist	48	$ 27,450
Real estate agent	44	$ 22,800
Mail carrier	42	$ 29,430
Typist	41	$ 18,180
Plumber	41	$ 28,900
Farmer	41	$ 19,700
Carpenter	40	$ 35,500
Bricklayer	36	$ 34,000
Mechanic	35	$ 27,450
Baker	34	$ 11,260
Bus driver	32	$ 29,000
Cashier	32	$ 10,500
Meat cutter	29	$ 27,450
Longshoreman	24	$ 30,000
Bartender	20	$ 12,720
Waiter	20	$ 11,300
Janitor	17	$ 13,100

1. Do the salaries of most occupations seem to correspond to the level of prestige?

2. Which occupations have a low prestige rating but a high salary?

3. Which occupations have a high prestige rating but a low salary?

4. Which occupations seem to have the greatest difference between prestige and income? Do these jobs share any common characteristics? Explain.

On the basis of your answers to these questions, what can you conclude about the relationship between prestige and salary? Do the two necessarily go together? What other factors besides salary might influence an occupation's prestige level? What factors other than prestige might affect an occupation's salary level?

2 THE AMERICAN CLASS SYSTEM

By definition, social inequality exists in all class systems. What form the inequality takes varies from society to society. The fewer the number of ascribed characteristics used to determine access to rewards, the more open the system for all members of society.

In this section, we will look at the social class system in the United States. The United States has a fairly open system. The law forbids discrimination based on ascribed characteristics such as race, religion, ancestry, or whether one is male or female. In principle, therefore, all Americans have equal access to the resources needed for social advancement. This does not mean, however, that the United States has a narrow range of social classes. It also does not mean that rates of social mobility are equal for every segment of American society. To see why this is so, let us look at the characteristics of social class in the United States and the patterns of social mobility.

Determining Social Class

Sociologists do not agree on the number of class divisions there are in the United States. Some researchers identify three social classes: upper class, middle class, and lower class. Other researchers divide these three broad classes into six groupings: upper-upper class, lower-upper class, upper-middle class, lower-middle class, upper-lower class, and lower-lower class. Research has shown that individuals who fall into the upper-lower class resent the lower-class label. Consequently, many sociologists have adopted a five-category classification system: upper class, upper-middle class, lower-middle class, working class, and lower class. We will use this classification system in our examination of the American class system.

Sociologists rely on three basic techniques to rank individuals according to social class. The first technique used is the reputational method. In the **reputational method,** individuals in the community are asked to rank other community members based on what they know of their characters and life-styles. This method is suitable only when studying small communities in which everyone tends to know one another. The findings from these studies cannot be used to make conclusions about other communities.

The second technique is the subjective method. In the **subjective method,** individuals are asked to determine their own social rank. When the choices are limited to upper, middle, and lower class, most people tend to say that they are middle class. Researchers have found that people do not like to place themselves in the upper or lower classes. This problem can be partially eliminated by including upper-middle class and working class in the list of choices.

The third classification technique is the objective method. In the **objective method,** sociologists define social class in terms of factors such as income, occupation, and education. While the statistical basis of this method makes it the least biased determination of class, it is not without its shortcomings. The major problem with this technique rests with the selection and measurement of social factors. Each factor or combination of factors produces a slightly different picture of social class membership.

Social Classes in the United States

Regardless of the method used to identify class membership, sociologists generally agree on the basic characteristics of the American social class system. They also tend to agree on the relative distribution of the population within the system. Sociologists estimate that between 1 and 3 percent of the population of the United States belongs to the upper class. Another 10 to 15 percent of Americans are part of the upper-middle class, while the lower-middle class holds between 30 and 35 percent of the population. The largest percentage of Americans—40 to 45 percent—fall into the working-class category, and the remaining 20 to 25 percent are members of the lower class.

One major difference between the classes is, of course, income. But classes also differ in terms of factors such as life-style and beliefs. A brief look at the general characteristics of each class will help us understand how social class affects life patterns.

The great wealth held by members of the American upper-upper class comes mainly from inheritance.

The Upper Class. A sizable proportion of the nation's wealth is in the hands of the upper class. The upper class can be divided into two groups: the upper-upper class and the lower-upper class.

People in the upper-upper class represent the "old money" of society—people such as the Rockefellers, Vanderbilts, and Kennedys. The term *old money* refers to the fact that these families have been wealthy for generations. The great bulk of their wealth comes from inheritance. The family name and the accomplishments of previous generations are as important in determining social rank as the size of the family fortune. Members of this class are born into an atmosphere of wealth and power. They attend the most prestigious

schools, know the most famous people, and are seen in the most exclusive places.

The lower-upper class consists of the newly rich—the "new money" of society. Members of the lower-upper class generally have acquired wealth through their own efforts rather than through inheritance. New money is not as prestigious as old money because it is not backed by a long family heritage. It does, however, purchase most of the privileges of upper-class membership: expensive houses, luxurious cars, and fine art collections, for example. In fact, members of the upper-upper class tend to look down on the lower-upper class for their "conspicuous consumption." *Conspicuous consumption* is a term first used in 1899 by economist Thorstein Veblen to describe the purchase of goods for the status they bring rather than for their usefulness.

Not surprisingly, upper-class membership carries with it great power and influence. Top positions in government and private enterprise often are filled by members from both segments of the upper class. In addition, the upper class often devotes considerable time, money, and energy to helping the less fortunate in society. Members of this class tend to hold traditional views and to be politically conservative.

The Upper-Middle Class.

Members of the upper-middle class primarily are high-income business and professional people and their immediate families. Most have college educations, and many have advanced degrees. Their money buys them large houses and cars, yearly vacations, college educations for their children, and many added luxuries. Class membership, however, is based on income rather than on assets. Consequently, those in the upper-middle class tend to be career oriented. Class members also tend to be politically and socially active, but their power and influence rest on the community level rather than on the national level.

The Lower-Middle Class.

Most individuals in the lower-middle class also hold what have traditionally been considered *white-collar jobs*—jobs that do not involve manual labor. Their jobs, however, tend to require less education and provide a lower income than do the jobs held by the upper-middle class. Lower-middle-class jobs are in areas such as nursing, middle management, and sales. Owners of small businesses also belong to the lower-middle class. Members of this class live a comfortable life but must work hard to keep what they have achieved. They tend also to hold traditional values and to be politically conservative.

The Working Class.

The largest segment of the American population can be considered working class. Many people in this social class hold jobs that require manual labor. Factory workers, tradespeople, unskilled workers, and some service personnel, for instance, fall into this category. Such jobs traditionally have been labeled *blue-collar-jobs*. Some of these jobs pay as much or more than many of the positions held by the lower-middle class. These jobs do not, however, carry as much prestige. Other working-class people hold clerical, low-level sales, and various service jobs that do not require manual labor. These types of jobs sometimes are referred to as *pink-collar jobs* because traditionally they have been held by women. Members of the working class tend to have few financial reserves. Consequently, unexpected crises—such as medical emergencies or the loss of a job—can push working-class individuals into the lower class.

Although often high paying, many working-class jobs require manual labor.

The Lower Class. The lower class consists of people in the lowest-paying jobs, the unemployed, some of the elderly, the homeless, the unskilled, and those on public assistance. Some members of the lower class once belonged to the working or middle classes, but circumstances forced them into poverty. Others were born into poverty. In either case, these individuals survive from day to day. And because of a lack of education and opportunity, future prospects often are bleak. We will look more closely at the conditions of the lower class in the last section of this chapter.

Social Mobility

The United States has an open class system. By open, we mean that **social mobility**—the movement between or within social classes or strata—is an important feature of the system. Among the types of social mobility studied by sociologists are vertical mobility, horizontal mobility, and intergenerational mobility.

Vertical mobility refers to movement between social classes or strata. This type of mobility can be either upward or downward, depending on whether an individual moves to a higher or lower position in the stratification system. The monetary and social rewards of being promoted from a secretarial to a management position, for example, may move an individual from the working class to the middle class. **Horizontal mobility,** on the other hand, refers to movement within a social class or stratum. When an individual moves from one job to another job of equal social ranking, the individual is experiencing horizontal mobility. An accountant, for example, who moves from one firm to another firm experiences horizontal mobility.

Intergenerational mobility—status differences between generations in the same family—can be considered a special form of vertical mobility. When sociologists examine patterns of vertical mobility, they generally focus on changes during adulthood. In the case of intergenerational mobility, the focus is on differences between people's class of origin (their parents' social class) and their current position in the stratification system. The son or daughter of an automobile mechanic, for instance, who becomes a doctor experiences intergenerational mobility.

People in the United States believe that all Americans are free to reach their own particular level of achievement. Americans believe that those people with enough ability and motivation will rise to the top. Others will rise or fall to various levels, based on their efforts and abilities. In principle, this is true. The reality, however, is somewhat different. Research indicates that even though the majority of Americans achieve a higher occupational status than their parents, most remain within the same social class. When individuals do experience vertical mobility, they rarely move more than one social class above or below their class of origin.

Structural Causes of Upward Mobility. While luck and effort often play major roles in a person's movement up the social-class ladder, sociologists are more interested in the structural factors that influence patterns of social mobility. Among the structural factors that affect upward mobility are advances in technology, changes in merchandising patterns, and increases in the general level of education in the population.

When technologies change, the jobs available to workers also change. Although this can result in downward mobility for individuals caught in the shift, it often means upward mobility for the next generation of workers.

Advances in farming technology, for example, have made it possible to grow more food with fewer people. Consequently, the percentage of the work force engaged in agriculture has declined from 40 percent in 1900 to less than 3 percent today. Similarly, mechanization has drastically reduced the need for unskilled labor. The result has been intergenerational upward mobility as the sons and daughters of farmers and laborers have sought employment in higher status occupations. The same process now appears to be at work in the manufacturing sector of the economy. The millions of factory jobs that have disappeared over the past two decades are forcing a portion of new workers into higher-status jobs, primarily in the service industry.

Social mobility also has been affected by changes in merchandising patterns in the United States. Among recent changes have been an explosion in the credit industry, a greater emphasis on insurance, increased transactions in real estate,

Shifts in the economy and a lack of affordable housing have resulted in an enormous increase in the number of homeless families.

and an extraordinary growth in personal services. These changes have created a larger white-collar work force. In 1940, approximately 47 percent of all workers held white-collar jobs. Today, over 70 percent of the labor force is engaged in traditional white-collar and service-industry jobs.

Another structural factor that has promoted upward mobility is an increase in the general level of education among members of society. In 1940, more than 75 percent of the population aged 25 and older had not completed high school. Today, that figure is approximately 22 percent. A college education also has become more common. In 1940, less than 5 percent of the population aged 25 and older had graduated from college. Today, over 21 percent of people aged 25 or older have a college education. Research has shown that upward mobility increases with level of education.

Structural Causes of Downward Mobility.

Although upward mobility is more common, there always are some people who move down the social-class ladder. Personal factors such as illness, divorce, widowhood, and retirement can, of course, produce downward mobility. Once again, however, sociologists are more interested in structural factors.

Among the primary structural causes of downward mobility are changes in the economy. As

already mentioned, shifts in consumer tastes or breakthroughs in technology can alter the demand for labor. Individuals suddenly can find themselves without jobs and with skills that no longer are marketable. If these workers are unable to find new jobs that produce comparable incomes, they may experience downward mobility. Cutbacks in the automobile, steel, and oil industries, for instance, have resulted in downward mobility for many people. For younger workers, the drop in social status often is temporary. For older workers, however, the negative consequences can last a long time.

Shifts in the economy also can affect intergenerational mobility. In times of economic growth and low unemployment, individuals just entering the job market have less difficulty finding desirable employment. In times of economic recession, however, good jobs are not as plentiful. As a result, even highly qualified recent college graduates sometimes cannot find jobs in their chosen fields.

SECTION 2 REVIEW

DEFINE social mobility

1. **Summarizing Ideas** List and describe the three basic techniques sociologists use to rank individuals according to social class.

2. **Understanding Ideas** (a) Approximately what percentage of the United States population falls into each of the five social classes discussed in the section? (b) Describe the general characteristics of the five classes.

3. **Contrasting Ideas** How do vertical mobility, horizontal mobility, and intergenerational mobility differ from one another?

4. **Seeing Relationships** (a) What factors can affect upward social mobility? (b) What factors can affect downward social mobility?

3 POVERTY

The United States is one of the richest nations in the world. Not everyone in American society, however, shares equally in this prosperity. More than 35 million people—approximately 14 percent of the population—live below the poverty level. Many millions more are what can be considered the working poor. Their incomes are too low to meet their basic needs, yet they make too much money to qualify for public assistance. For all of these people, daily life often is a struggle.

Who we classify as poor depends on how we define poverty. In general, **poverty** can be defined as a standard of living that is below the minimum level considered decent and reasonable by society. As the definition indicates, poverty is a relative measure. What is considered poverty in one society might be considered an adequate standard of living in another society. Many of the poor in the United States, for example, live more comfortable lives than the majority of people in some industrializing nations. This does not mean, however, that there are no poor people in the United States. It simply means that the United States enjoys a particularly high standard of living.

What does it mean to be poor in the United States? In this section, we will examine this question. We will look at the characteristics of poverty in the United States and the effects that poverty has on the lives of the poor. We also will examine some of the ways in which the government responds to the problem of poverty.

Defining Poverty in the United States

The federal government defines poverty in relation to the minimum annual income needed by a family to survive. This minimum income is called the **poverty level.** Families with income levels below this amount are considered by the government to be poor.

The poverty level is determined by calculating the cost of providing an adequate diet, based on the U.S. Department of Agriculture's minimum nutritional standards, and then multiplying that

Poverty Level by Family Size

Family Size	Poverty Level (in dollars)
1 person	6,932
Under 65 years	7,086
Over 65 years	6,532
2 persons	8,865
Householder under 65	9,165
Householder over 65	8,241
3 persons	10,860
4 persons	13,924
5 persons	16,456
6 persons	18,587
7 persons	21,058
8 persons	23,605
9 persons or more	27,942

Source: U.S. Bureau of the Census.

figure by three. We multiply the figure by three because research has indicated that the poor spend a third of their income on food. Each year, the government recalculates the poverty level to take into account increases in the cost of living. The poverty level most often quoted is for a family of four. Actually, the government establishes a series of poverty levels that takes into account the number of people in the family. The table on this page lists the poverty levels for various family sizes.

The American Poor

Not every person in society runs an equal risk of being poor. Some segments of society are more likely than others to be poor. Among the characteristics that affect poverty are age, sex, race, and ethnicity, or cultural background.

Age. The largest percentage of people living below the poverty level are children. Of the poor, over 40 percent are under the age of 18. Not all children have an equal likelihood of being poor.

Percentage of the Population Below the Poverty Level by Selected Characteristics

Characteristic	All Races	White	African American	Hispanic American
Total population	14.2	11.3	32.7	28.7
Under 18 years old	21.8	16.8	45.9	40.4
18–24 years old	16.9	14.0	31.9	27.6
25–44 years old	11.2	9.1	24.4	22.7
45–64 years old	8.9	7.4	21.6	18.2
65 years old and over	12.4	10.3	33.8	20.8

Source: U.S. Bureau of the Census.

The consequences of poverty affect every aspect of life for the poor. For children, poverty means an increased likelihood of hunger, disease, and danger.

The level of poverty among African American and Hispanic children is more than 2.5 times greater than the level among white children. The table on this page gives the poverty rates for selected categories of people, including children.

Sex. Women make up one of the fastest growing segments of the poor population. More than 60 percent of the poor over the age of 18 are women. Also, more than one-half of all poor families are headed by women. As in the case of children, not all female-headed households are at equal risk. Around 50 percent of African American and Hispanic female-headed households are poor. This compares to a rate of less than 30 percent for families headed by white females.

Race and Ethnicity. As is obvious from the previously mentioned statistics, poverty varies by race and cultural background. Regardless of age or sex, African Americans and Hispanic Americans in the United States are more likely than whites to live in poverty. The poverty rate for whites averages 3 percentage points lower than the rate for the overall population of the nation. African Americans and Hispanics, on the other hand, have poverty rates that are more than twice that of the United States as a whole.

The Rural Poor

For most Americans, poverty statistics bring to mind images of the inner-city poor. We picture single mothers and their children living in dark and dingy tenements, often without private bathrooms or cooking facilities. We see images of crime-infested city streets controlled by drug dealers and street gangs who terrorize honest people. Or perhaps we picture families who are trapped generation after generation in government-financed housing projects. For others of us, images of the homeless come to mind—adults and children sleeping in parks, under bridges, or on the street, shut out from the mainstream of American life.

All of these images of poverty in the United States are true. Urban poverty, however, is only part of a larger story. Hidden away from the view of most Americans is another large group of the poor—the almost 9 million Americans who live in the rural areas of the United States. In recent years, the level of poverty in rural areas has exceeded the level found in big cities. More than 16 percent of rural Americans are considered poor by government standards. The rate is even higher among children. The U.S. Bureau of the Census estimates that nearly one out of every four rural children lives in poverty. African Americans also are hard hit—approximately 39 percent of rural African Americans have incomes that fall below the poverty level.

The rural poor face special problems. Unlike the poor in large cities, the rural poor seldom have easy access to government services. Social welfare offices, public health clinics, job-training programs, and federally funded day-care centers are rare in the small towns and sparsely populated areas that are home to the rural poor. Consequently, the rural poor receive only a small percentage of local, state, and federal welfare funds even though they make up nearly one-fourth of America's poor.

The rural poor are at particular risk in terms of health care. Rural hospitals are closing at a rapid rate, and registered nurses are in shorter supply in the remaining rural hospitals than they are in urban hospitals. In addition, the ratio of physicians to residents in small communities is less than one-third the national average. There are hundreds of rural communities in the United States that do not have any primary-care physicians at all.

Moreover, the already difficult employment situation of the rural poor is being threatened by changes in the economy. Many of the industries that traditionally supported the rural economy, such as farming, mining, timber, and manufacturing, suffered declines during the 1980s and 1990s. Many low-level rural jobs are being lost to automation and the movement of American jobs to countries that use cheap labor.

The situation of the urban poor is difficult to ignore. Urban poverty is visible. The social conditions it spawns—crime, drug abuse, violence—spill over into the larger community. Rural poverty, though, is less visible and easier to ignore. Interstate highways and airplane travel have done much to hide rural poverty. City dwellers can go about their daily lives, even crisscross the country, without ever coming into contact with the rural poor. From a distance, the shacks of the rural poor, nestled in the mountains of the Carolinas or tucked between fields of wheat in Kansas, look quaint.

The invisibility of the rural poor intensifies their problems and lessens their chances for a brighter future. They have no effective lobby to speak for them. Even concern over the plight of the family farmer has little obvious effect—less than 10 percent of rural residents live on farms. Yet, if the cycle of poverty is to be broken, steps will have to be taken to meet the special needs of the rural poor.

The Effects of Poverty

Millions of American adults and children live in poverty. The lives of these poverty-stricken people differ from the lives of the wealthier members of society. Two major ways in which their lives differ are in terms of life chances and patterns of behavior.

Life Chances. When sociologists speak of **life chances,** they are referring to the likelihood individuals have of sharing in the opportunities and benefits of society. Life chances include factors such as health, length of life, housing, and education. Research has shown that life chances vary by social class. The lower their social class, the less opportunity individuals have to share in the benefits of society.

Among the most important life chances are health and length of life. The poor are at a serious disadvantage in both of these areas. Rates of heart disease, diabetes, cancer, arthritis, anemia, pneumonia, tuberculosis, and influenza, for instance, are highest among the poor. In light of this fact, it is not surprising that the poor have a shorter life expectancy than do other members of society. **Life expectancy** refers to the average number of years a person born in a particular year can be expected to live. The differences in life expectancy are particularly dramatic in the case of infants. *Infant mortality*—the death of children during the first year of life—is twice as high among the poor as it is among the general population.

Two reasons for decreased health and a shorter life expectancy among the poor are inadequate nutrition and less access to medical care. The poor have less money to spend on food and often are less knowledgeable about what constitutes good nutrition. A lack of money also limits the amount of health care the poor receive. Consequently, diseases generally are not treated in their early stages. Health and life expectancy also are negatively affected by environmental factors. For instance, the working poor often hold jobs that involve considerable health risks.

The poor also are at a disadvantage in the area of housing. Housing is a major expense for all Americans. In the case of the poor, a large percentage of their incomes must go toward housing. This amount of money, however, often is not large enough to secure safe and comfortable living quarters. As a result, poor children are more likely to suffer from environmental hazards such as lead-paint poisoning and fires resulting from improper wiring or gas and oil heater malfunctions.

Money also affects the educational opportunities available to the poor. School funding is based in part on local property taxes. This means that schools in low-income areas often are inadequately funded because of low tax revenues. In addition, dropout rates are higher in poor communities. Finally, for most of the poor, college is financially out of reach. Limitations in education are particularly serious because of the positive effect increased education has on future life chances.

Calvin and Hobbes

by Bill Watterson

Calvin and Hobbes © 1986 *Universal Press Syndicate*. Reprinted with permission. All rights reserved.

One aspect of President Lyndon Johnson's War on Poverty was the development of VISTA (Volunteers in Service to America). VISTA volunteers work to help poor Americans in rural and urban areas improve their lives. The program continues to this day.

Patterns of Behavior. Certain behaviors also vary depending on social class. Divorce rates, for example, are higher among low-income families than among other segments of the population. The poor also are more likely to be arrested and convicted for crimes than are individuals from the higher social classes. This is due partially to the fact that the poor commit the types of crimes on which the police tend to focus—murder, assault, robbery, burglary, and auto theft.

Government Responses to Poverty

In the 1960s, President Lyndon B. Johnson instituted the War on Poverty. Since then, the United States government has taken an active role in attempting to reduce social inequality in America. The results have been mixed.

There still are more than 35 million people in the United States who live in poverty, and the poverty rate is higher now than it was in the 1970s. Nevertheless, there have been improvements. In 1960, for example, poverty among the elderly was almost three times as high as it was among the general population. Today, the poverty rate for the elderly is lower than the rate for the nation as a whole. This is due primarily to increases in Social Security benefits and the introduction of Medicare, the government-sponsored health insurance program for retired people.

The two principal ways in which the government attempts to reduce social inequality are through transfer payments and government subsidies. **Transfer payments** are designed to enable the government to redistribute money among various segments of society. The government

Transfer payments such as Social Security help the elderly survive following retirement.

takes a percentage of the money collected through taxes and gives it to groups that are in need of public assistance—primarily the poor, the unemployed, the elderly, and the disabled. Examples of transfer payments are Supplemental Security Income, Social Security, and Aid to Families with Dependent Children (AFDC).

Aid to Families with Dependent Children provides cash payments to parents whose incomes are below an established "needs standard." To qualify, children in the home must be under the age of 18. Since 1990, states have been required to provide a job opportunities and basic skills (JOBS) program designed to help recipients become self-supporting. AFDC is one of the government's largest assistance programs for the poor. In 1991, for example, over 4 million AFDC recipients received a total of around $20 billion, with an average family payment of $388 a month.

The second way in which the government assists the poor is through subsidies. Subsidies transfer goods and services rather than cash to the poor. Food stamps, Head Start, and subsidies for housing and school breakfasts and lunches fall under this category of assistance.

More than one-fourth of America's poor do not receive any form of government assistance. There are many reasons for this. Some of the poor cannot qualify for help because they have assets such as a car or savings. In the case of AFDC, two-parent families can qualify only when the primary breadwinner is unemployed.

Participation in government assistance programs also is affected by the availability of resources. In some areas of the United States, for instance, families have had their names on waiting lists for public housing for years. In addition, many government agencies do not have sufficient personnel to process all of the claims and requests for assistance that they receive. And finally, many poor people do not request assistance. Some people are unaware that they are eligible for government assistance. Other people either are intimidated by the process or believe that the effort is not worth the small amount of benefits they would receive.

If not for the government-sponsored school lunch program, many children would go hungry during the day.

SECTION 3 REVIEW

DEFINE poverty, poverty level, life chances, life expectancy, transfer payments

1. **Interpreting Ideas** What is the poverty level and how is it determined?

2. **Analyzing Ideas** How do age, sex, race, and ethnicity affect the likelihood of being poor in America?

3. **Summarizing Ideas** How do the life chances and behavioral characteristics of the poor differ from those of the wealthier members of society?

4. **Comprehending Ideas** What are the two principal ways in which the federal government attempts to reduce social inequality in the United States?

CHAPTER 9   SUMMARY

Stratification by definition implies social inequality—the unequal sharing of social rewards and resources. Access to social rewards can be based on either achieved or ascribed statuses.

Stratification systems can be closed or open. A caste system is a closed system. A class system, on the other hand, is an open system.

In a caste system, scarce resources and rewards are distributed on the basis of ascribed statuses. In a class system, scarce resources and rewards are distributed on the basis of achieved statuses. Sociologists define social class in a variety of ways. Here we define it as a grouping of people with similar levels of wealth, power, and prestige.

Sociologists use three basic techniques to rank individuals according to social class—the reputational method, the subjective method, and the objective method. Using these methods, the population of the United States can be divided into the upper class, the upper-middle class, the lower-middle class, the working class, and the lower class.

Because the United States has an open class system, social mobility is possible. Among the types of social mobility studied by sociologists are vertical mobility, horizontal mobility, and intergenerational mobility.

Poverty is a serious problem in the United States. Poverty can be defined as a standard of living that is below the minimum level that is considered decent and reasonable by society. Not every person runs an equal risk of being poor. Poverty varies by characteristics such as age, sex, race, and ethnicity. For example, children, women, African Americans, and Hispanics are at a higher risk of being poor. Two principal ways in which the United States government has attempted to lessen social inequality are through transfer payments and subsidies. Many poor people, however, do not receive any form of government assistance.

DEVELOPING SOCIOLOGICAL

THINKING ABOUT SOCIOLOGY: Determining Cause and Effect

Identifying and understanding the causal connections between events is a central theme in sociological research. Sociologists study cause and effect by examining the relationships among variables. A causal relationship exists when a change in one variable produces a change in another variable. Sociologists, like other scientists, use special terms to identify cause-and-effect variables. The cause—the variable that produces the change in the second variable—is called the *independent variable*. The effect—the variable that is altered by the presence of the independent variable—is called the *dependent variable*. A more in-depth discussion of independent and dependent variables is presented in the Appendix beginning on page 486.

Social life is not simple. All actions have consequences. Causal relationships therefore seldom are limited to a single cause and effect. Instead, a dependent variable may itself become an independent variable. The result is a type of causal chain of events in which a cause produces an effect, which in turn produces a change in another variable:

Cause → Effect/Cause → Effect

For example, changes in consumer demand can lead to factories being closed down. The closing of factories, in turn, produces unemployment. As a result of unemployment, some people are unable to meet their rent and mortgage obligations and therefore are evicted from their homes. If these people are unable to obtain new housing, the result may be an increase in the number of homeless. The following diagrams provide visual representations of two segments in this causal chain:

Cause Unemployment	→	Effect/Cause Evictions	→	Effect Homelessness

Cause Decreased consumer demand	→	Effect/Cause Factory closings	→	Effect Unemployment

How to Determine Cause and Effect

When sociologists report their research findings in professional journals and books, they generally state causal relationships in exact terms. At times, however, information may be presented in narrative form, such as when sociological information is used in the popular press. You may wish to compile sociological findings from a variety of sources and draw your own conclusions. To recognize cause-and-effect relationships, follow these guidelines.

1. **Look for cause–effect clues.** One of the best ways to spot causal relationships is to look for cause–effect clues as you read. Some of the clues are shown below.

Cause Clues	Effect Clues
leads to	upshot
brings about	outcome
spurs	outgrowth
induces	aftermath
provokes	as a consequence
instigates	results from
gives rise to	arises from
produces	proceeds from
inspires	dependent on
because	results in
as a result of	originates from
at the root of	
the origin of	
the source of	
the reason why	

Remember, however, that the link between cause and effect is not always stated using the above clues. Sometimes cause and effect must be drawn from the general discussion.

2. Check for basic connections. Next, arrange the independent and dependent variables into causal pairs. List each pair separately. Remember that a dependent variable in one pair can be an independent variable in another pair.

3. Check for complex connections. Examine the causal pairs to determine if they can be joined into a causal chain like the ones listed on page 226. In addition to a variable serving as both a cause and an effect, a single independent variable can be a part of more than one causal relationship.

Applying the Skill

The excerpt on this page is from an article by Eileen Quigley entitled "The Homeless," which was published in the April 7, 1992, issue of *CQ Researcher*. Using the guidelines above and on page 226, determine what causal relationships are discussed in the excerpt. Once you have determined the causal relationships, construct a diagram similar to the one shown on page 226.

Following is one set of causal relationships that you might uncover in the excerpt:

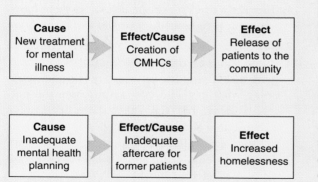

Cause	Effect/Cause	Effect
New treatment for mental illness	Creation of CMHCs	Release of patients to the community

Cause	Effect/Cause	Effect
Inadequate mental health planning	Inadequate aftercare for former patients	Increased homelessness

In February 1963, President John F. Kennedy called on Congress to take a "bold new approach" toward the seriously mentally ill, a challenge that would have profound implications for the homeless problem. Kennedy urged the creation of Community Mental Health Centers (CMHCs) to replace existing mental institutions.

Encouraged by the salutary [beneficial] effects that new psychotropic drugs had on psychotic mental patients, the nation embarked on a plan to release them to their communities and the new CMHCs.

From the outset, however, there was evidence that many recently released patients were not receiving the aftercare they needed to remain functional. Provisions often hadn't been made to forge a working relationship between the mental institutions and the CMHCs, and many of the mentally ill fell through the cracks.

The population of the country's mental institutions was 505,000 in 1963; today it is roughly a quarter of that, and many deinstitutionalized people are living on the streets. As Dr. E. Fuller Torrey noted, "[r]ather than deinstitutionalization, which implied that alternative community facilities would be provided, what took place was simply depopulation of the state hospitals. It was as if a policy of resettlement had been agreed upon but only eviction took place." . . .

When the Urban Institute, a public policy research organization in Washington, D.C., undertook a study of homeless people in 1987, it found that slightly more than half the adults had been institutionalized for mental problems, drug dependency, or criminal actions.

Practicing the Skill

Turn to the Interpreting Primary Sources feature on page 229. Read the excerpt and determine what basic and complex causal relationships are discussed. List the relationships that you have uncovered from your reading.

CHAPTER 9 REVIEW

Reviewing Sociological Terms

On a separate sheet of paper, supply the term that correctly completes each sentence.

1. _____ _____ is the unequal sharing of social rewards and resources.

2. A grouping of people who have similar levels of wealth, power, and prestige is called a _____ _____.

3. Marriage within one's own social category is called _____.

4. _____ _____ is the ranking of individuals or categories of people on the basis of differential access to scarce resources and social rewards.

5. _____ is a standard of living that is below the minimum level considered decent and reasonable by society.

Thinking Critically about Sociology

1. **Comprehending Ideas** **(a)** List some of the social factors that determine a person's socioeconomic status. **(b)** What does a person's socioeconomic status tell sociologists about that individual?

2. **Analyzing Ideas** **(a)** What do sociologists mean when they use the term life chances? **(b)** What factors contribute to lower life expectancy and higher infant mortality rates among the poor?

3. **Evaluating Ideas** What are the limitations of each of the three techniques used by sociologists to rank individuals according to social class?

4. **Seeing Relationships** **(a)** How has the caste system in India changed since the nineteenth century? **(b)** What factors have brought about these changes?

5. **Interpreting Tables** According to the table on page 219, what are the poverty levels for various family sizes in the United States?

6. **Drawing Conclusions** What are some of the reasons why not all poor people receive public assistance in the United States?

7. **Applying Ideas** Provide an example of each of the three types of social mobility discussed in the chapter.

8. **Organizing Ideas** Construct a chart listing the general characteristics of each of the five social classes discussed in the chapter.

Exercising Sociological Skills

1. **Determining Prestige** Reread the Applying Sociology feature on pages 212–213. Which of the jobs listed in the chart tend to be unionized? What effect does unionization appear to have on salary levels?

2. **Summarizing Ideas** According to the Case Study on page 221, what are some of the problems faced by the rural poor?

3. **Determining Cause and Effect** Reread the Developing Sociological Imagination feature on pages 226–227. Select a magazine or newspaper article that discusses the closing of a factory in a community. What are some of the basic and complex causal relationships presented in the article.

Extending Sociological Imagination

1. Prepare a brief report on one or more nongovernment programs designed to assist the poor.

2. **(a)** Plan a week's worth of meals typical of those eaten by the average family of four. Prepare a shopping list for these meals and determine what it would cost to purchase the necessary items. **(b)** Call the welfare department in your area and ask how much money a family of four on welfare is expected to spend for food per week. Compare this figure to the cost of preparing your meals.

INTERPRETING PRIMARY SOURCES

Homelessness in America

Not since the Great Depression has the United States been faced with such large numbers of homeless people. Over the past two decades, the release of psychiatric patients to the community and the loss of industrial jobs to factory closings have contributed to the problem. The most often-cited cause of homelessness, though, is the lack of affordable housing.

In this excerpt from "American Nightmare: Homelessness," which appeared in the March/April 1991 issue of *Challenge*, Peter Dreier and Richard Appelbaum explore the problem of homelessness in America. While reading the excerpt, consider how changing government policies affected the housing industry, and what communities are doing to help ease the problem of homelessness.

The spectacle of homeless Americans living literally in the shadow of luxury condos and yuppie boutiques symbolized the paradox of the decade [the 1980s]: It was a period of both outrageous greed and outrageous suffering. The media gave us "lifestyles of the rich and famous," but they also offered cover stories about homeless families. . . .

All this pertains directly to housing. While America was witnessing a growing disparity of incomes, the affluent began viewing a house less as a home than as an investment, as valuable for its tax benefits as for its Victorian details. Young baby boom generation professionals moved into urban neighborhoods, especially those close to the downtown core, where they found work in the growing service sector. Housing that had been abandoned or devalued decades earlier became more attractive to so-called "yuppies." As the affluent and the poor began to compete for scarce inner-city housing, prices skyrocketed. Low-rent apartments were converted to high-priced con-

dominiums. Rooming houses, the last refuge of the poor, were torn down or turned into upscale apartments. Businesses catering to the poor and working class families were replaced by high priced shops and restaurants.

The housing market failed to expand significantly the overall number of apartments, because it simply wasn't profitable to build housing for the poor. The situation was made worse when the Reagan Administration removed the two props that once served to entice some private investors into providing low-rent housing—subsidies which bring housing costs and poor peoples' incomes into line, and tax shelters which indirectly produce the same result. . . .

If there was one silver lining during the 1980's housing crisis, it was the emergence of locally based efforts to address community housing needs. A combination of community organizations, municipal governments, unions, and business groups developed a wide range of innovative local programs and strategies to cope with the impact of federal housing cutbacks, and the changes in local housing markets. . . .

These groups . . . fix up abandoned buildings and construct new homes for the poor. They apply pressure on local governments to protect tenants against unfair evictions. They lobby for stricter enforcement of health and safety codes. . . . They persuade banks to open up branches in minority neighborhoods and increase available mortgage loans for low-income consumers. They publish reports to dramatize the plight of the homeless, to highlight the widening gap between incomes and housing prices. . . .

But these have been primarily defensive efforts—brushfire battles to keep things from getting worse. Only the federal government has the resources needed to address housing issues and the problem of homelessness in a significant way.

Source Review

1. What discouraged private investors from providing low-rent housing?

2. How are communities around the nation battling homelessness?

Racial and Ethnic Relations

 1 Race, Ethnicity, and the Social Structure

Race
Ethnicity
Minority Groups

 2 Patterns of Intergroup Relations

Discrimination and Prejudice
Sources of Discrimination and Prejudice
Patterns of Minority Group Treatment

 3 Minority Groups in the United States

African Americans
Hispanic Americans
Asian Americans
Native Americans
White Ethnics

Chapter Focus

Chapter 10 explores racial and ethnic relations. The chapter begins with a discussion of the concepts of race, ethnicity, and minority groups. Sources of discrimination and prejudice and patterns of minority group treatment are then examined. The chapter closes with a discussion of minority group experiences in the United States.

As you study the chapter, look for the answers to the following questions:

1. What five characteristics distinguish minority groups from other groups in society?
2. What are three of the main sources of discrimination and prejudice?
3. What are the five most common patterns of minority group treatment?
4. Under what conditions do minority groups in the United States live?

KEY TERMS

The following terms, while not the only terms emphasized in the chapter, are basic to your understanding of sociology. Determine the meaning of each term, either by using the Glossary or by watching for context clues as you read the chapter.

race	prejudice	subjugation
ethnicity	stereotype	slavery
discrimination	cultural pluralism	genocide

Until quite recently in South Africa, economic, social, and political power rested in the hands of the nation's approximately 6 million white citizens. Although whites make up less than 15 percent of the population, they controlled the lives of South Africa's more than 34 million blacks, Indians, and people of mixed races. Through the system known as apartheid (uh-PAHR-tayt), or racial separation, the white government limited the access of these racial groups to housing, employment, education, health care, legal protection, and public facilities. Personal freedoms, such as the right to free speech, the right to travel, and the right to public assembly, also were affected by race. Although South Africa currently is dismantling the system of apartheid in favor of power sharing by the races, the process is slow and plagued by violence.

1 RACE, ETHNICITY, AND THE SOCIAL STRUCTURE

Although South Africa is an extreme case, it is not unique in its reliance on race as a determinant of social standing. Most societies base access to social rewards and resources, at least in part, on race and ethnicity. In this section, we will explore the issues of race and ethnicity.

Race

Since ancient times, people in the Western world have attempted to group human beings into racial categories on the basis of physical characteristics such as skin color, hair texture, and body structure. These attempts have produced a number of classification systems, ranging in size from 2 to 200 racial categories.

One of the best-known classification systems sorts people into three racial groups—Caucasoids, Mongoloids, and Negroids. According to this system, Caucasoids, or whites, are characterized by fair skin and straight or wavy hair. Mongoloids, or orientals, are identified by yellowish or brownish skin and by distinctive folds on the eyelids. And Negroids, or blacks, are distinguished by dark skin and woolly hair. In reality, however, people who are recognized as belonging to each of these racial categories exhibit a wide range of skin colors and hair textures.

In some instances, a group's characteristics cut across racial categories, making classification extremely difficult. How, for example, should the people of southern India, with their white facial features, black skin color, and straight hair, be classified? Or, how should the Ainu people of Japan, who have oriental features and almost white skin, be categorized? To which category do the Bushman of Africa, with their yellowish skin and oriental eyes, belong? And what racial group should be chosen for the Australian aborigines, who have dark skin and blond woolly hair?

As these examples indicate, it is not easy to classify people into clear-cut categories. Contributing to the difficulty is the fact that people often possess the traits of more than one race. This is because there are no biologically "pure" races. Over time, marriage between members of various races has produced wide variations within racial groups. For this reason, race as a biological classification is of little use to sociologists.

Most sociologists look at race from a social perspective. In sociological terms, a **race** is a category of people who share inherited physical character-

One well-known racial classification system sorts individuals into Caucasoid (left), Negroid (center), and Mongoloid (right) groups. Within each of these groups, however, identifying features such as hair texture and skin color can vary a great deal.

istics and who are perceived by others as being a distinct group. For the sociologist, the important issue is not that a person has a specific color of skin or a nose of a particular shape or hair of a certain texture. Rather, what is important is how people react to these physical characteristics and how these reactions affect individuals in society.

Ethnicity

American society, like many societies, includes people of different cultural backgrounds. The set of cultural characteristics that distinguishes one group from another group is called **ethnicity.** Individuals who share a common cultural background and a common sense of identity are known as an **ethnic group.** Ethnicity generally is based on such cultural characteristics as national origin, religion, language, customs, and values.

If an ethnic group is to survive over time, its cultural beliefs and practices must be passed from generation to generation. Some ethnic groups in the United States have been more successful than others in keeping their heritage alive. Asian Americans and Hispanic Americans, for instance,

tend to have strong ethnic roots. Many Irish Americans and German Americans, on the other hand, no longer feel deep ties to their ancestral homes. Consequently, they share few cultural characteristics with people in Ireland or Germany.

In some cases, ethnic identity cuts across racial or national boundaries. Jewish people worldwide, for instance, are thought to form an ethnic group. Their ethnic group status is based on their religious and cultural heritage. Even Jewish people who no longer firmly hold to the religious beliefs of Judaism are linked by factors such as a common history, and family values.

Ethnicity and race refer to two separate sets of characteristics—one based on cultural considerations, the other on physical considerations. Nevertheless, some ethnic groups also are racially distinct. African Americans, for example, are a racially distinct category in the United States. Many African Americans also share a common ethnic heritage that includes particular foods, types of music, forms of speech, and various cultural traits. Similarly, Japanese Americans, Chinese Americans, and Native Americans can be classified both ethnically and racially.

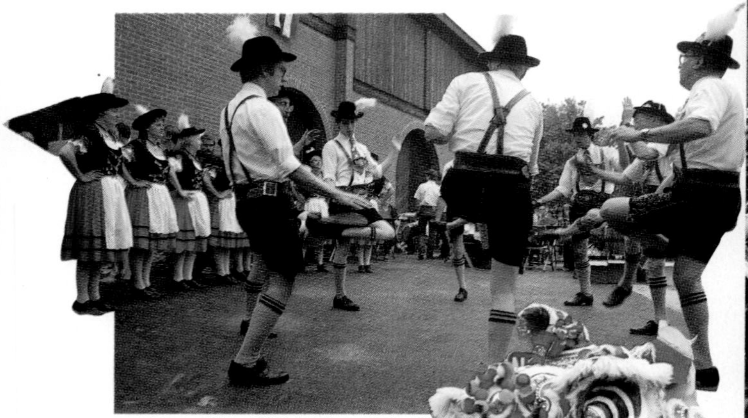

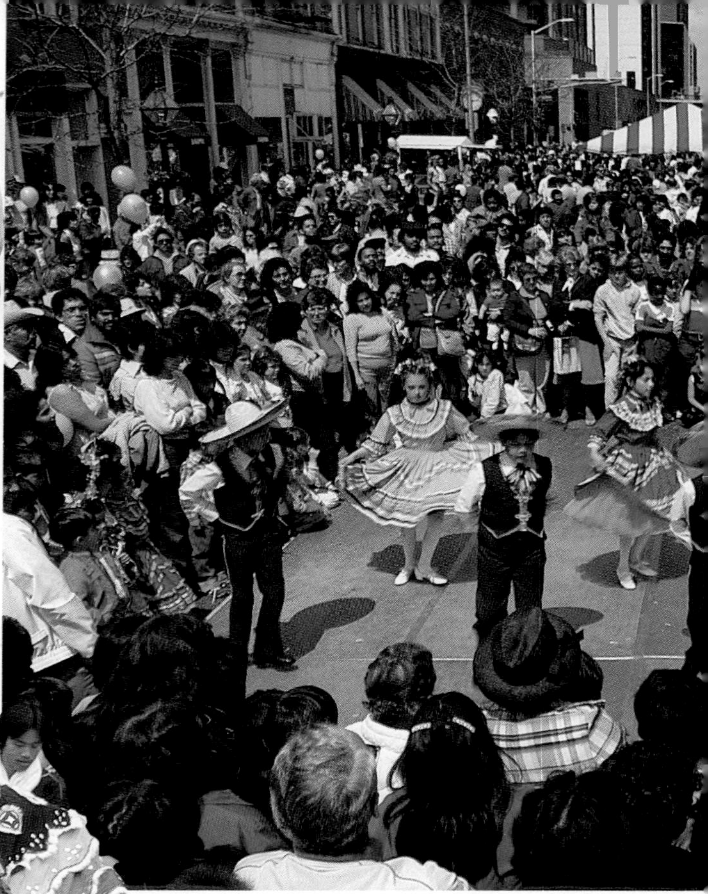

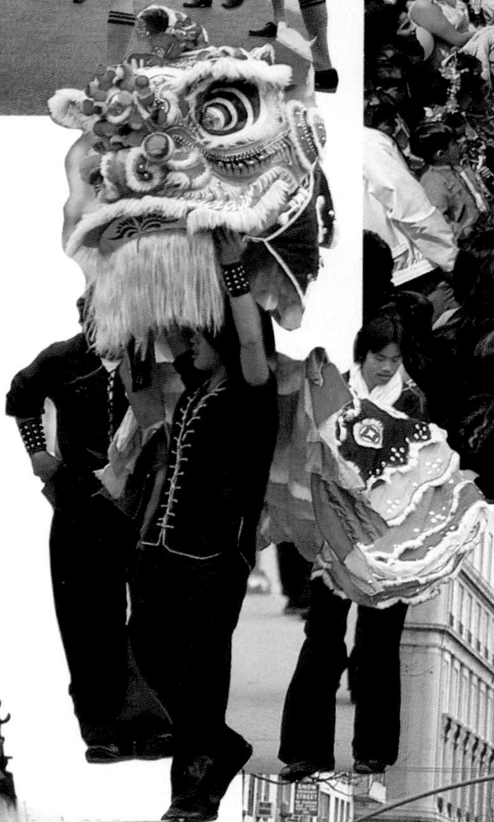

In recent years, minority groups in the United States have been encouraged to acknowledge the contributions that their cultural backgrounds make to a richer and fuller American life. Festivals and parades are two of the ways in which minority groups show pride in their cultural heritages.

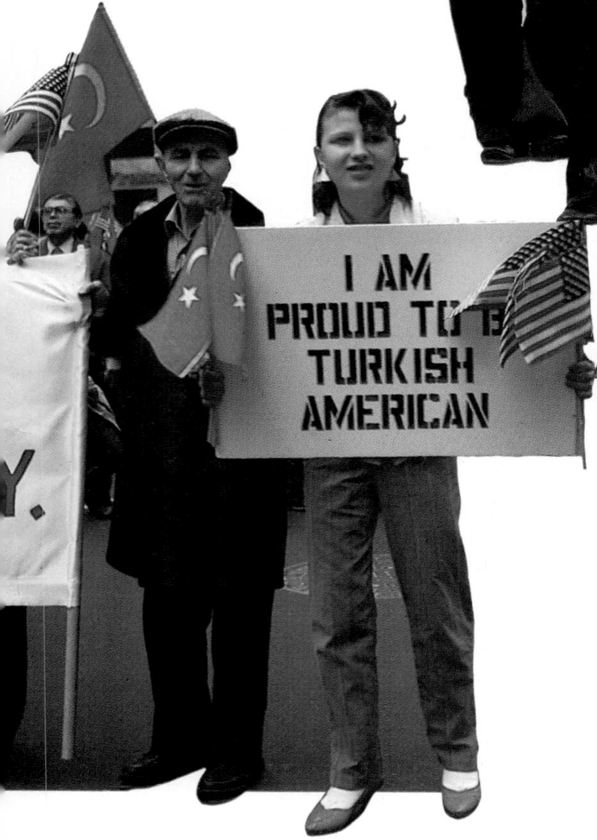

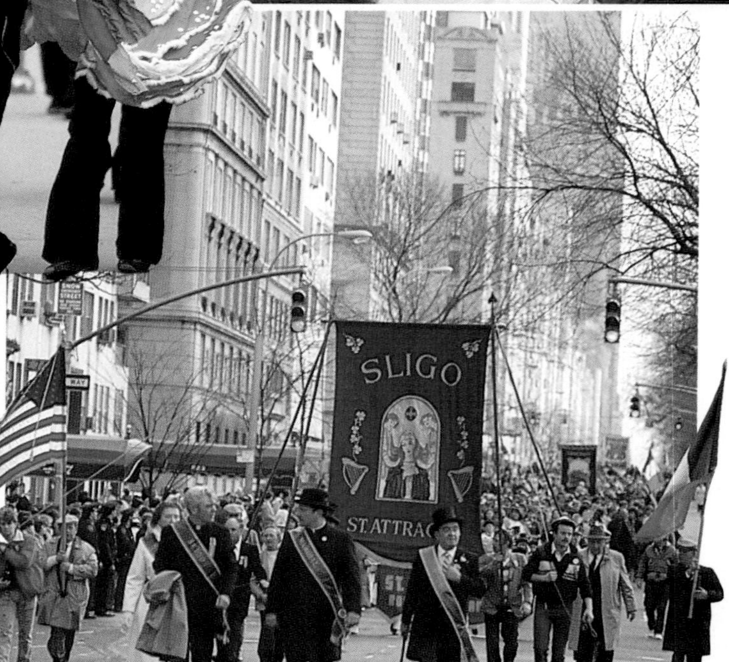

I AM
PROUD TO BE
TURKISH
AMERICAN

SLIGO
ST. ATTRAC

- The group possesses identifiable physical or cultural characteristics that differ from those of the dominant group.
- Group members are the victims of unequal treatment at the hands of the dominant group.
- Membership in the group is an ascribed status.
- Group members share a strong bond and a sense of group loyalty.
- Members tend to practice endogamy—marriage within the group.

To be considered a minority group, a group must exhibit all of the above characteristics. Exhibiting only one or two of the characteristics is not enough. For instance, blue eyes are an identifiable physical characteristic and having blue eyes is an ascribed status. Blue-eyed people, however, do not face ill-treatment because of their eye color. Consequently, they are not considered a minority group. Haitians in the United States or aborigines in Australia, on the other hand, are treated differently because of their racial and ethnic backgrounds. They therefore are considered to be minority groups.

Minority Groups

No particular skin color, physical feature, or ethnic background is by nature superior or inferior. The value placed on specific characteristics is determined by those who hold power in society—in other words, by the dominant group. By establishing the values and norms of society, dominant group members consciously and unconsciously create a social structure that operates in their favor. Their positions of power allow them to enjoy certain privileges, such as better housing, better schools, and higher incomes.

The resources and rewards found in society are limited. Consequently, the privileged position of the dominant group often is gained at the expense of the life chances of minority groups within the society. A **minority group** is a category of people who share physical characteristics or cultural practices that result in the group being denied equal treatment. Sociologists generally list five characteristics that distinguish minority groups from other groups in society.

SECTION 1 REVIEW

DEFINE race, ethnic group

1. **Summarizing Ideas** **(a)** Into what three racial categories does one of the best-known classification systems attempt to place people? **(b)** What are the supposed characteristics of each racial group?

2. **Interpreting Ideas** **(a)** What is ethnicity? **(b)** On what types of characteristics is ethnicity based?

3. **Comprehending Ideas** **(a)** What is a minority group? **(b)** According to sociologists, what five characteristics distinguish minority groups from other groups in society?

2 PATTERNS OF INTERGROUP RELATIONS

As we noted in the previous section, no particular skin color, physical feature, or ethnic background is by nature superior or inferior. Minority status exists because of the attitudes and actions of the dominant members of a society. Consequently, a wide range of interaction patterns are possible between groups within a society. In this section, we will explore the various ways in which a society can respond to the existence of minority groups.

Discrimination and Prejudice

Discrimination and prejudice are common features of the minority group experience. Although the words often are used interchangeably, discrimination and prejudice refer to two related but separate phenomena. **Discrimination** is the denial of equal treatment to individuals based on their group membership. By definition, therefore, discrimination involves *behaviors*. **Prejudice,** on the other hand, is an unsupported generalization about a category of people. Prejudice thus refers to *attitudes*. Often in daily conversation, we speak of being prejudiced *for* or *against* someone or something. Sociologists, however, generally focus on negative forms of prejudice.

Discrimination. Discrimination can be found either on the individual level or on the societal level. Discriminatory acts by individuals range from name calling and rudeness to acts of violence. In their most extreme forms, such acts can lead to physical harm or even death. For instance, during the first half of this century, more than 3,000 African Americans were lynched by white mobs in the United States. In the majority of cases, those lynched were guilty of such "crimes" as attempting to vote, using the same public facilities as whites, or simply being too successful.

Societal discrimination can appear in one of two forms: legal discrimination or institutionalized discrimination. **Legal discrimination** is discrimination that is upheld by law. **Institutionalized discrimination,** on the other hand, is discrimination that is an outgrowth of the structure of society.

Apartheid in South Africa is an example of legal discrimination. South Africa had an elaborate system of laws that defined the political, economic, and legal rights of whites and nonwhites within the country. Many other nations, at one time or another, have had systems of legal discrimination.

Until the passage of legislation such as the Civil Rights Act of 1964, the United States had a history of legal discrimination. Women, for instance, did not gain the right to vote until 1920, with the passage of the Nineteenth Amendment. And until as late as 1940, many states did not allow women to enter into legal contracts. African Americans

© GARFIELD   Reprinted by permission of UFS, Inc.

faced even more widespread legal discrimination. For example, the "Jim Crow" laws passed in southern states during the late 1800s required African Americans and whites to use separate public facilities and to attend separate schools. This doctrine of separate but equal facilities was upheld as constitutional by the Supreme Court in the 1896 case of *Plessy* v. *Ferguson*. It was not until 1954, in *Brown* v. *Board of Education of Topeka,* that the Supreme Court reversed its earlier decision.

Although legal discrimination is very serious, it may be less damaging than institutionalized discrimination. Because legal discrimination is based on laws, this type of discrimination can be corrected simply by changing the offending laws. Institutionalized discrimination, however, is an outgrowth of traditional patterns of discrimination and so is more resistant to change.

Over time, unequal access to the resources and rewards of society push some minority group members into less powerful positions in society. Once this occurs, it is not necessary to discriminate openly or consciously against these individuals in order to maintain a system of inequality. Discrimination becomes a part of the social structure, and thus self-perpetuating. This can occur even when the society takes legal steps to end discriminatory practices.

Take what can happen, for example, when minority groups are denied access to employment and housing over long periods of time. Economically disadvantaged and barred from certain neighborhoods, group members often become concentrated in low-income communities. If schools in these communities are poorly funded, minority group members may not acquire the skills needed to compete effectively in the labor market. Thus even when housing and employment restrictions are lifted, group members cannot qualify for higher-paying jobs. And without higher-paying jobs, they are unable to move to wealthier neighborhoods where their children might have better opportunities for advancement. The cycle of inequality therefore is maintained even in the absence of intentional discrimination.

Prejudice. Prejudice also can have grave consequences for society. If people are told often enough and long enough that they or others are socially, mentally, or physically inferior, they come

Sociologists view the Ku Klux Klan's belief in white supremacy as an extreme form of prejudice.

to believe it. It does not matter whether the accusations are true. In the early 1900s, the American sociologist W.I. Thomas recognized this fact when he stated his famous theorem: *If people define situations as real, they are real in their consequences.* In other words, individuals see reality based on what they *believe* to be true, not necessarily on what *is* true.

According to Robert K. Merton, a false definition of a situation can become a self-fulfilling prophecy. A **self-fulfilling prophecy** is a prediction that results in behavior that makes the prediction come true. If, for instance, members of a minority group are considered incapable of understanding technical information, they will not be given technical training. As a result, they will lack the skills needed to gain employment in highly technical occupations. This lack of employment in technical fields will then be taken as proof of the group's inability to understand technical information.

Thurgood Marshall (1908–1993) was a tireless champion of equal rights for all Americans. In 1954, for example (top, center), he argued and won *Brown v. Board of Education*, the Supreme Court case that outlawed school segregation. As the first African American to sit on the Supreme Court, Marshall (bottom) served the cause of justice from 1967 until his retirement in 1991.

For the dominant members of society, prejudice serves as a justification for discriminatory actions. Once individuals come to believe negative claims made against minority group members, they do not have to feel guilty about open acts of discrim-

ination. Prejudicial beliefs that serve as justifications for open discrimination often take the form of racism. **Racism** is the belief that one's own race or ethnic group is naturally superior to other races or ethnic groups. Racism causes people to view social inequality as an outgrowth of the naturally occurring qualities of minority groups rather than as a function of the social structure. Throughout history, racism has been used as a justification for the worst forms of discrimination.

While prejudice and discrimination are related phenomena, they do not always go hand-in-hand. According to Robert K. Merton, individuals can combine discriminatory behavior and prejudicial attitudes in four possible ways:

- The *active bigot* is prejudiced and openly discriminatory.
- The *timid bigot* is prejudiced but is afraid to discriminate because of societal pressures.
- The *fair-weather liberal* is not prejudiced but discriminates anyway because of societal pressure.
- The *all-weather liberal* is not prejudiced and does not discriminate.

The chart on page 239 presents a visual representation of these combinations.

Sources of Discrimination and Prejudice

Discrimination and prejudice arise from a number of sources. Among the sources recognized by sociologists are stereotyping, scapegoating, and the social environment.

Stereotyping. Prejudice and discrimination usually involve stereotypes. A **stereotype** is an oversimplified, exaggerated, or unfavorable generalization about a category of people. In stereotyping, an individual forms an image of a particular group and then applies that image to all members of the group. All African Americans, for example, might be viewed as lazy or as natural athletes. Or all Irish people might be seen as hot-tempered or as superstitious. If specific individuals in the group are found to differ from the stereotyped image, they become exceptions to the rule, rather than proof that the stereotype is wrong.

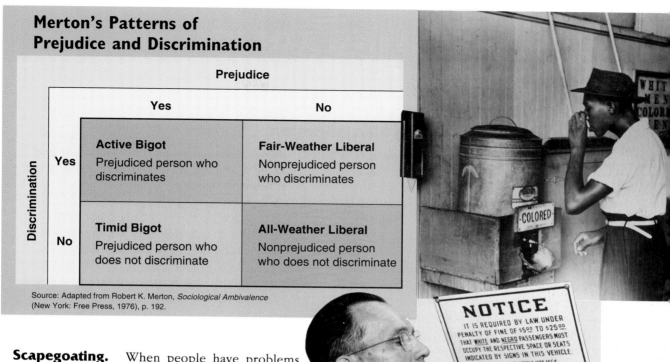

Merton's Patterns of Prejudice and Discrimination

		Prejudice	
		Yes	**No**
Discrimination	**Yes**	**Active Bigot** Prejudiced person who discriminates	**Fair-Weather Liberal** Nonprejudiced person who discriminates
	No	**Timid Bigot** Prejudiced person who does not discriminate	**All-Weather Liberal** Nonprejudiced person who does not discriminate

Source: Adapted from Robert K. Merton, *Sociological Ambivalence* (New York: Free Press, 1976), p. 192.

Scapegoating. When people have problems they cannot solve or when they are threatened but cannot fight back, they sometimes turn their frustration and aggression toward innocent groups. The practice of placing the blame for one's troubles on an innocent individual or group is called **scapegoating.**

Minority groups often are convenient targets of scapegoating because they lack power in society. Unemployed workers, for example, often blame immigrants and American-born minority groups for taking away their jobs and thereby causing their economic problems. By attacking less powerful groups, the unemployed workers gain a sense of superiority at a time when they are feeling basically powerless.

The Social Environment. Sociologists have found that certain social environments are more likely to produce prejudiced people than are other environments. A society in which groups interact closely on a basis of relative equality tends to exhibit low levels of prejudice. On the other hand, when there are vast differences between the degrees of power held by various groups in a society, prejudice often is widespread. Such is the case in Guatemala, where the native Indians have long been dominated by the more powerful Ladinos.

Until the Civil Rights Act of 1964, many states in this nation had laws that discriminated against African Americans. Today, everyone is entitled to seek legal protection against discrimination.

Prejudice and discrimination also increase when there is intense competition for scarce resources in a society. During the second half of the nineteenth century, for instance, large numbers of Chinese workers immigrated to the West Coast of the United States. In the beginning, they were welcomed as an inexpensive source of labor. When jobs became scarce, however, white workers began to view the Chinese as economic competitors. The whites reacted to this competition with open violence and eventually with legislation that restricted Chinese immigration.

Text continues on page 242.

A Study on Prejudice and Discrimination

What does it feel like to face discrimination? In a unique experiment, third-grade teacher Jane Elliot decided to let her students learn firsthand. Her story is described in *A Class Divided* by William Peters.

Elliot assigned her 28 students to one of two groups, depending on eye color. In the first group were 17 blue-eyed youngsters. The remaining 11 students were placed in the brown-eyed group. Each group represented the minority group for a day. During the first day of the experiment, the blue-eyed students were the objects of discrimination. Following is Peters's account of the first day's activities:

> "Today," Elliot told the class, "the blue-eyed people will be on the bottom and the brown-eyed people on the top." At their puzzled looks, she went on. "What I mean is that brown-eyed people are better than blue-eyed people. They are cleaner than blue-eyed people. They are more civilized than blue-eyed people. And they are smarter than blue-eyed people."
>
> When they still looked puzzled, Elliot nodded shortly. "It's true. It really is."
>
> Now the brown-eyed children began to look at each other in wonder. They sat up straighter in their chairs, waiting to hear more. The blue-eyed children frowned, stirred uneasily, not understanding. One blue-eyed boy slumped way down in his chair. "What color are your eyes?" Elliot asked him.
>
> "Blue," the boy said, straightening up.
>
> "Is that the way we've been taught to sit in class?"
>
> "No," the boy said.
>
> "Do blue-eyed people remember what they've been taught?" Elliot asked the class. There was a chorus of "No's" from the brown-eyed children as they began to see how it would work. The blue-eyed boy now sat bolt upright, his hands folded neatly in the exact center of his desk. A brown-eyed boy near him, one of his close friends in the room, gave him a withering disdainful look. It began that quickly.

Elliot made up the list of rules that both groups would have to follow. Brown-eyed children would be given five extra minutes of recess. They could go to lunch first and could go back for seconds. In addition, they could use the drinking fountain in the room. In contrast, the blue-eyed children would get a shorter recess period, would have to wait to go to lunch, and would have to use paper cups.

With the rules in place, Elliot took every opportunity to praise the brown-eyed students and to criticize those with blue eyes. For example, when a brown-eyed student missed a word while reading, she helped him. When a blue-eyed child did likewise, she nodded in disapproval and asked a brown-eyed student to read the passage correctly.

Similarly, when a blue-eyed boy curled a page of his book, Elliot held up the book and asked, "Do blue-eyed people take care of the things they are given?" The brown-eyed students shouted with glee, "No!"

How did the students react to the experiment? Elliot notes:

> By the lunch hour, there was no need to think before identifying a child as blue or brown eyed. I could tell simply by looking at them. The brown-eyed children were happy, alert, having the time of their lives. And they were doing far better work than they had ever done before. The blue-eyed children were miserable. Their posture, their expressions, their entire attitudes were those of defeat. Their classroom work regressed sharply from that of the day before. Inside of an hour or so, they looked and acted as though they were, in fact, inferior. It was shocking.

But even more frightening was the way the brown-eyed children turned on their friends of the day before, the way they accepted almost immediately as true what had been described as an exercise. For there was no question, after an hour or so, that they actually believed they were superior. The fact that we were going to change roles on Monday was forgotten. Everything was forgotten in the face of the undeniable proof that the blue-eyed children were inferior to them. It was as though someone had pointed out to them something they simply had not noticed before. Weren't the blue-eyed children making more mistakes than they were? Of course. Wasn't the teacher finding fault almost exclusively with the blue-eyed children? Of course. Wasn't it clear that she liked the brown-eyed children better? Of course. What better proof did you need?

On the second day of the experiment, the roles were reversed. The blue-eyed students were now told that they were superior, and the brown-eyed students were discriminated against. What happened this time? Elliot replies:

I had not expected that the brown-eyed children, knowing full well after their experience on Friday that it was all an exercise and that it would last only a day, would react as intensely as the others had to the experience of discrimination. But they did. Within minutes, they had become nervous, depressed, resentful. The only real difference that day was that the blue-eyed children, now on top, were noticeably less vicious in their treatment of the underlings than the latter had been to them.

In light of what you have read in the chapter about discrimination and prejudice, how would you answer the following questions?

1. If these children had to face discrimination every day, how might their self-images be affected? What other harmful effects might discrimination have?

2. Cite some examples from the experiment of how discrimination can lead to stereotyping. How might it lead to racism?

3. Why do you think the dominant group believed it actually was superior? Have any similar situations developed in history? What are they?

Patterns of Minority Group Treatment

Official policies toward minority groups within a society can range from total acceptance to total rejection. The most common patterns of minority treatment include assimilation, cultural pluralism, legal protection, population transfer, subjugation, and extermination.

Assimilation. Many racial and ethnic minorities today are attempting to hold on to some of their unique cultural features. Official policies, however, have not always favored such attempts. At one time in the United States, for instance, it was hoped that the various groups that make up American society could be blended into a single people with a common culture. This hope forms the basis of the image of America as a "melting pot." The blending of culturally distinct groups into a single group with a common culture and identity is called **assimilation.**

In most societies, some assimilation occurs voluntarily. Over time, the various groups within the society exchange many cultural traits as a natural outcome of daily interaction. Forced assimilation, however, rarely is accomplished without conflict.

In the 1980s, for example, the Bulgarian government waged a five-year-long campaign to forcibly assimilate the country's large Turkish minority. Thousands of Turks reportedly were killed or tortured in conflicts over assimilation policies that prohibited them from practicing their own religion, language, and ethnicity. The Turks responded to these actions with a series of terrorist bombings.

Cultural Pluralism. Another solution to ethnic and racial diversity is to allow each group within society to keep its unique cultural identity. Such a policy is called **cultural pluralism.** One example of a nation that practices cultural pluralism is Switzerland. This nation officially recognizes four languages—French, German, Italian, and Romansh—one language for each of its four major ethnic areas. Cultural pluralism also is evident in the United States. The belief of the American people in the rights of the individual has led to a basic tolerance of cultural differences.

Legal Protection. Many nations have taken legal steps to ensure that the rights of minority groups are protected. The Civil Rights Act of

One indication of cultural pluralism in the United States is the wide variety of food enjoyed by Americans.

1964 is an example of such legislation in the United States. Great Britain adopted similar legislation in 1965 with the passage of the Race Relations Act.

Affirmative action programs in the United States are another example of legal efforts designed to achieve equal rights. Affirmative action programs are designed to ease past imbalances in the educational and employment opportunities given to racial minorities and to women. Affirmative action policies require that government agencies and organizations receiving federal funds or government contracts set timetables and guidelines to hire or admit qualified racial minorities and women.

Population Transfer.

In some situations, the dominant group in a society solves the problem of minority relations by transferring the minority population to a new territory. In some cases, this transfer involves moving people to new locations within the country. Examples of internal transfers in the United States include the resettlement of Native Americans on reservations during the 1800s and the confinement of many Japanese Americans to relocation camps during World War II. (For a discussion of Japanese American relocation during World War II, see the Across Space and Time feature on page 288.)

Population transfers also can include expelling the group from the country. In the 1750s, for example, the Arcadians, a French-speaking minority, were expelled from Nova Scotia. A more recent example is the forceful removal of the Asian population from Uganda in 1972.

In some cases, the nation itself is divided to solve group conflicts. In 1947, for example, Pakistan was created out of portions of India to help ease tensions between Hindus and Muslims. More recently, on January 1, 1993, conflict-plagued Czechoslovakia was split into two separate nations: the Czech Republic and Slovakia.

Subjugation.

Rather than expel a minority group from the country, some nations resort to **subjugation**—the maintaining of control over a group through force. The most extreme form of subjugation is slavery. **Slavery** is the ownership of one group of people by another group. Examples of slavery can be found throughout history.

In the absence of slavery, subjugation often leads to segregation. **Segregation** is the physical separation of a minority group from the dominant group. Under a system of segregation, the minority group is forbidden to live in the same areas as the dominant group and cannot use the same public facilities. Segregation can be based on laws or on informal norms. Segregation based on laws is called **de jure segregation.** When segregation is based on informal norms, it is called **de facto segregation.**

History contains many examples of segregation. In the Middle Ages, for instance, Jews in Europe were forced to live in walled-off communities called *ghettos*. In the United States, segregation was practiced openly and legally until the 1960s. As a result of earlier segregation policies and housing restrictions, many American minority groups still tend to be concentrated into specific areas within cities.

The most extreme contemporary example of de jure segregation is South Africa's system of apartheid. Apartheid, which literally means "apart-ness," called for the legal segregation of all groups within the country. Political and economic power rested in the hands of the white minority and was rigidly maintained through force. International opposition to apartheid helped to bring about the current dismantling of the system.

Extermination.

The most extreme response to the existence of minority groups within a nation is extermination. When the goal of extermination is the intentional destruction of the entire targeted population, it is referred to as **genocide.** Genocide has been attempted many times, and sometimes achieved, throughout history.

Anti-Semitism, or hatred of the Jews, has led to several attempts at Jewish extermination. For example, after the assassination of the Russian czar in 1881, Jews in Russia became the target of severe persecution. Huge numbers of Jews were massacred. The official government policy was to force one-third of the Jewish population to leave the country, to convert another one-third to Orthodox Christianity, and to kill the remaining one-third. An even more shocking example of genocide, however, is the mass extermination of approximately six million Jews by Adolf Hitler's Nazi regime during World War II. In addition to

During World War II, Hitler's Nazi party exterminated millions of people. Special ovens were used to burn the bodies, and the ashes then were used as fertilizer.

the Jews, 400,000 Gypsies and at least two million Russian civilians were exterminated by Adolf Hitler's Nazi forces.

Other examples include the British extermination of the Tasmanians and the South African extermination of the Hottentots during the nineteenth century. More recent examples include the massacre of more than one million Armenians by Turks and the killing of thousands of Pakistanis by Indians during the first half of this century. More recently, ethnic Serbs in Bosnia-Herzogovina have waged a brutal campaign of "ethnic cleansing" aimed at eliminating Muslims and other non-Serbs from land they formerly shared.

SECTION 2 REVIEW

DEFINE discrimination, prejudice, racism, slavery, de jure segregation, de facto segregation

IDENTIFY active bigot, timid bigot, fair-weather liberal, all-weather liberal

1. **Contrasting Ideas** **(a)** How does legal discrimination differ from institutionalized discrimination? **(b)** List several examples of each type of discrimination.

2. **Seeing Relationships** **(a)** What is W.I. Thomas's famous theorem and how does it relate to the effects of prejudice? **(b)** How can a false definition of a situation become a self-fulfilling prophecy?

3. **Summarizing Ideas** Discuss the three sources of discrimination and prejudice described in this section.

4. **Comprehending Ideas** Describe the six most common patterns of minority group treatment.

3 MINORITY GROUPS IN THE UNITED STATES

In 1944, the Swedish sociologist Gunnar Myrdal examined the issue of race relations in the United States. He came to the conclusion that the American people faced a great psychological and cultural conflict. He referred to this conflict as "an American dilemma."

The dilemma that Myrdal uncovered was the gap between what Americans claim to believe and how they actually behave. While Americans express the ideals of equality, freedom, dignity of the individual, and inalienable rights, they have not always lived up to these ideals. The segregation of African Americans, the establishment of Indian reservations, and the internment of Japanese Americans during World War II are but a few examples of the denial of these ideals.

The conflict between ideals and actions has been part of the American experience since the arrival of white settlers on the North American continent in the 1500s. When the original English colonists came to this land, they brought with them the cultural values of English society. As these colonists established dominance in this new land, their values became the standards for the entire society.

These early settlers also provided the image of what many people think of as the typical American—white, of Anglo-Saxon (northern European) descent, and Protestant. This white Anglo-Saxon Protestant (WASP) image hardly does justice to the nation's great multicultural reality. The image has, however, been the yardstick against which other groups within the United States have been judged.

For the most part, minority groups have prospered in relation to how closely they adapt to the WASP image. Those who can more easily adapt are accepted into mainstream American society relatively quickly. For example, northern and western European immigrants from heavily Protestant nations such as Sweden, the Netherlands, and Germany generally gained dominant status within a generation. Other groups—such as African Americans, Hispanic Americans, Native

Americans, Asian Americans, and white ethnics—have had more difficulty in gaining acceptance. In this section, we will explore the current conditions under which various minority groups live in the United States.

Current Immigration to the United States

Country of Birth	Total Immigrants
Mexico	946,167
Philippines	63,596
Soviet Union*	56,980
Vietnam	55,307
Haiti	47,527
El Salvador	47,351
India	45,064
Dominican Republic	41,405
China, mainland	33,025
Korea	26,518
Guatemala	25,527
Jamaica	23,828
Pakistan	20,355
Colombia	19,702
Iran	19,569
Poland	19,199
Nicaragua	17,842
Peru	16,237
United Kingdom	13,903
Canada	13,504
Other	274,561
Total immigrants	**1,827,167**

* Republics of the former Soviet Union.
Source: *1991 Statistical Yearbook of the Immigration and Naturalization Service*, 1992.

African Americans

Comprising slightly over 12 percent of the population, African Americans are the largest minority group in the United States. With the possible exception of Native Americans, no other American minority group has suffered such a long history of prejudice and discrimination. First brought to this country as slaves in the early 1600s, African Americans only recently have gained an economic and political foothold in American society.

Race Relations in Great Britain

Great Britain, like most nations, is concerned with race relations. This concern, however, is a relatively recent one. It only has been in the past 40 years or so that large numbers of nonwhites have immigrated to the country. The majority of these new immigrants to Great Britain are blacks from the Caribbean and Asians from India and Pakistan.

In some neighborhoods, black and Asian immigrants have met with acceptance. In other neighborhoods, open hostility has been the norm. In an effort to understand why acceptance patterns vary, British sociologist Roger Hewitt studied race relations in two South London neighborhoods. Hewitt found that in one neighborhood, which he called Area A, race relations were hostile and tense. In the other neighborhood—Area B— whites and nonwhites lived in relative peace and harmony.

Hewitt concluded that there were two major factors that eased race relations in Area B. The first factor was the neighborhood's high density of blacks and Asians. The size of the immigrant population allowed strong social networks to develop through minority businesses, churches, and social organizations. These networks helped minority group members maintain their cultural identities.

The existence of a strong and highly visible minority community also made white adolescent contact with nonwhite cultures inevitable. When asked why they got along so well with other races, white adolescents replied that it was because they had grown up in a multiracial environment. Thus they were accustomed to interracial contacts. These contacts helped to reduce prejudice.

The second factor that promoted good race relations in Area B was the absence of peer pressure against nonwhite friendships. In fact, whites who held racist attitudes and did not associate with nonwhites were disliked.

In area A, on the other hand, racist youth groups often verbally and physically threatened white youths who became too friendly with nonwhites. According to Hewitt, these racist youth groups slowed the development of positive interracial relationships.

The skinheads were the most visible racist youth group in Area A. The skinhead movement—so named because many group members shave their heads—started in Great Britain in the late 1960s. After disappearing for a while, the movement reappeared in the late 1970s, this time with a political agenda that was anti-black and anti-Asian.

As in Area B, there were underlying factors that influenced race relations in Area A. Skinheads thrived in part because of the area's economic conditions. Adolescent unemployment in the area was almost 12 percent. Research has shown that open conflict and scapegoating—two central features of race relations in Area A—are common responses to economic competition.

The black and Asian populations of Area A became the target of white youths' anger over unemployment. The skinheads interviewed by Hewitt accused the government of ignoring the economic problems of whites while providing economic aid to immigrants. According to the skinheads, the immigrants—particularly the Asian immigrants—used government welfare to start businesses. Immigrants therefore were seen as becoming prosperous at the expense of whites.

The skinheads were particularly effective in keeping positive race relations from developing in Area A because of their secondary group nature. Membership in the group was based not on friendship but on a commitment to racism. To qualify for membership, a person needed only to support the group's racist beliefs. Over time, therefore, the number of skinheads grew and they became better able to influence the actions of others.

The civil rights movement of the 1950s and 1960s resulted in significant gains for African Americans. For instance, the percentage of the population completing high school now is almost identical for African Americans and whites. Also promising is the fact that over 16 percent of employed African Americans now hold managerial or professional jobs (as compared to slightly less than 28 percent of employed whites). This is a considerable increase over the past two decades. In fact, it is estimated that approximately one-third of African Americans now can be considered middle class. Possibly most important, since the passage of the Voting Rights Act in 1965, the number of elected African American officials has jumped from 200 to almost 7,500.

Other statistics, however, are not as promising:

- The percentage of African Americans completing four or more years of college is only slightly more than half that of whites.
- African American family income averages about 58 percent of white family income.
- The percentage of African American families living below the poverty level is over three times that of white families.
- Approximately 46 percent of African American children live below the poverty level.
- The unemployment rate among African Americans is approximately 2.2 times higher than the unemployment rate among whites.
- Approximately 28 percent of employed African American women over the age of 25 work in service occupations, compared to approximately 15 percent of employed white women.

Although these statistics represent a serious social problem, solutions are being sought. The process is being aided by the active role that African Americans are taking in the political process. Following the 1992 presidential election, for instance, African Americans Ronald Brown, Mike Espy, Hazel O'Leary, and Jesse Brown accepted appointments to Cabinet positions in President Bill Clinton's administration.

Hispanic Americans

The 1990 census of the population found that there were 22.4 million Hispanic Americans living in the United States. This represents a 53 percent increase in the size of the Hispanic population since 1980. During the same time period, the size of the general population grew only by about 10 percent. The Hispanic population is growing so fast that experts predict that Hispanic Americans may soon replace African Americans as the nation's largest minority group.

Until the 1960s, the Hispanic American population in the United States consisted primarily of people of Mexican, Puerto Rican, and Cuban ancestry. In the 1960s, however, immigrants from Central and South American nations such as El Salvador, Nicaragua, Guatemala, Colombia, and Ecuador and Caribbean nations such as the Dominican Republic began to swell the number of Hispanics living in the United States. The graph on this page shows a percentage breakdown of the Hispanic American population by area of origin.

Many of the immigrants who began arriving in the United States in the 1960s entered through legal means. Others arrived illegally, searching for political freedom and economic opportunities. Estimates of the number of illegal Hispanic immigrants in the United States range from a low of about 2 or 3 million to a high of about 5 million.

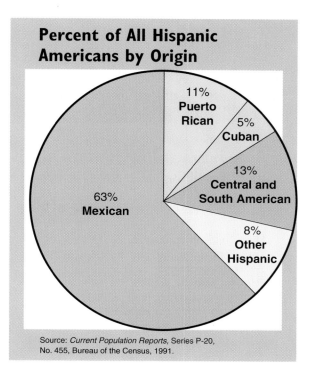

Percent of All Hispanic Americans by Origin

11% **Puerto Rican**

5% **Cuban**

13% **Central and South American**

8% **Other Hispanic**

63% **Mexican**

Source: *Current Population Reports,* Series P-20, No. 455, Bureau of the Census, 1991.

Selected Characteristics of Hispanic Americans and Non-Hispanic Americans

Characteristic	Hispanic American Origin					Non-Hispanic American
	Mexican	Puerto Rican	Cuban	Central and South American	Other Hispanic	
Average age in years	24.3	26.7	39.3	27.9	31.0	33.8
Percent completed high school	43.6	58.0	61.0	60.4	71.1	80.5
Average family income	$27,069	$23,131	$33,504	$30,697	$32,472	$38,069
Percent unemployed	10.7	10.3	6.4	10.3	6.9	6.9
Percent of families below poverty level	25.0	37.5	13.8	22.2	19.4	9.5
Percent female-headed households	15.6	33.7	15.3	21.5	19.5	11.4

Source: *Current Population Reports,* Series P-20, No. 455, Bureau of the Census, 1991.

Occupational Distribution of Hispanic Americans and Non-Hispanic Americans

Occupation	Hispanic Americans		Non-Hispanic Americans	
	Male	Female	Male	Female
Managerial and professional	11.4	15.8	27.6	28.0
Technical, sales, and administrative support	15.1	39.8	21.0	44.3
Service occupations	17.1	26.2	9.8	17.0
Farming, forestry, and fishing	8.6	1.2	3.7	0.9
Precision production, craft, and repair	18.7	3.0	18.8	2.1
Operators, fabricators, and laborers	29.1	14.0	19.1	7.6

Source: *Current Population Reports,* Series P-20, No. 455, Bureau of the Census, 1991.

The number of illegal immigrants included in Bureau of the Census figures is unknown. It is likely, however, that many illegal immigrants in the United States go unreported.

In recent years, Hispanic Americans have gained increasing political power and currently hold over 4,200 elected and appointed offices. In 1992, newly elected President Bill Clinton appointed two Hispanic Americans, Henry Cisneros and Federico Pena, to his Cabinet. Hispanic Americans also control large voting blocks in nine states, including California, New York, Texas, Illinois, and Florida.

Although Hispanic Americans are making gains, they still lag behind non-Hispanic Americans in areas such as education and employment. For instance, the poverty rate among Hispanics is almost three times as high as the rate among non-Hispanics. It is somewhat misleading, however, to make generalizations about Hispanic Americans. With the exception of a shared language and a shared religion (the majority are Roman Catholic), Hispanic Americans are a diverse people. The tables on page 248 indicate how different Hispanic American groups vary on selected social characteristics and how Hispanics compare with non-Hispanics on occupational distribution.

Asian Americans

Like Hispanic Americans, Asian Americans come from a variety of ancestral and national backgrounds. In the 1990 census, Asian Americans reported ethnic ties to 25 different Asian groups. The six largest groups of Asian Americans are of Chinese, Filipino, Japanese, Asian Indian, Korean, and Vietnamese ancestry. The growth of these six groups as a percentage of the United States population can be seen in the table below. The table also shows the growth of the total Asian American population from 1980 to 1990.

Representing roughly 3 percent of the total United States population, Asian Americans are the nation's third largest ethnic group. The 1980 census placed the size of the Asian American population at approximately 3.5 million. By 1990, that figure had doubled to over 7 million. Based on current growth rates, experts project that Asian Americans will make up 10 percent of the United States population by the year 2040.

The relatively small size of the Asian American population and its current high growth rate are a reflection of changes in the United States immigration policies over the years. The first wave of Asian immigration began in the 1850s when Chinese workers were brought to the West Coast to work in the gold mines and to help build the railroad. When the economy slowed and whites were forced to compete with Chinese workers for jobs, physical violence and discrimination against the Chinese became widespread. In response to the threat of economic competition, Congress passed the Chinese Exclusion Act in 1882. This act, which barred Chinese men from bringing their wives and children into the country and outlawed the holding of certain types of jobs, ended

Growth in Selected Asian American Groups: 1980 to 1990

1980 Census			1990 Census				Number Change 1980–1990	Percent Change 1980–1990
Group	Number	Percent of Population	Group	Number	Percent of Population	Group		
Chinese	806,040	0.4	Chinese	1,645,472	0.7	Chinese	839,432	104.1
Filipino	774,652	0.3	Filipino	1,406,770	0.6	Filipino	632,118	81.1
Japanese	700,974	0.3	Japanese	847,562	0.3	Japanese	146,588	20.9
Asian Indian	361,531	0.2	Asian Indian	815,447	0.3	Asian Indian	453,916	125.6
Korean	354,593	0.2	Korean	798,849	0.3	Korean	444,256	125.3
Vietnamese	261,729	0.1	Vietnamese	614,547	0.2	Vietnamese	352,818	134.8
Total Asian Americans	3,500,439	1.5	Total Asian Americans	7,273,662	2.9	Total Asian Americans	3,773,223	107.9

Source: *The Universal Almanac, 1993*, p. 284.

For much of the first part of the twentieth century, Asian immigrants to the United States faced open hostility and discrimination. Several laws over the years even restricted the number of Asians who could immigrate to the United States. Today, Asian Americans, such as Senator Daniel Inouye from Hawaii, are an economically secure and highly respected minority group.

Chinese immigration. It was not until 1940, when labor once again was in short supply, that the ban on Chinese immigration was lifted.

The second wave of Asian immigration began in 1890 when Japanese workers came to Hawaii and California in search of work. The majority of these early immigrants were employed as agricultural laborers. As in the case of Chinese workers, however, labor competition soon resulted in discrimination. In 1905, the *San Francisco Chronicle,* with the support of local labor unions, launched an anti-Japanese movement. A series of anti-Japanese laws were passed in California over the next two decades. Then, in 1924, the National Origins Act was passed by Congress. This act, which set

Asian immigration quotas at nearly zero, virtually stopped the flow of Asians into the United States.

Filipinos were the only Asians excluded from the National Origins Act. The annexation of the Philippines as an American possession in 1898 meant that Filipinos could freely enter the United States. They soon replaced the Chinese as the largest Asian American group. Then, in 1934, the Tydings–McDuffie Act limited Filipino immigration to 50 people per year, causing the number of Filipinos in the country to decline.

The third wave of Asian immigration was ushered in with the passage of the McCarran–Walter Act of 1952. This act allowed Asians to enter the United States on the basis of national quotas and eligibility for citizenship. Immigration policy was further liberalized in 1965, causing a jump in Asian immigration. Between 1971 and 1989, people from Asia accounted for 40 percent of all immigrants entering the United States. This last wave of immigrants largely have come from the Philippines, China, Korea, India, and Vietnam. New immigration policies passed in the early 1990s are expected to increase the number of Asian immigrants coming to the United States.

Much has been written about the commitment to education exhibited by Asian Americans. For example, Asian American students consistently achieve high scores on both the verbal and mathematical sections of the Scholastic Aptitude Test.

Moreover, 1991 figures show that 39 percent of the Asian American population over the age of 24 have 4 or more years of college. This compares to a figure of 22 percent for white adults. Asian Americans have used education as a vehicle for moving up the economic ladder.

The success of Asian Americans in achieving economic security and social acceptance has led them to be called a model minority. Many Asian Americans resent this label because it hides the fact that the group has faced severe hardships in its quest for acceptance. The road to economic success has been littered with anti-Asian laws, open violence and discrimination, and the internment of 120,000 Japanese Americans during World War II.

The label also serves to blur differences among the various national groups that make up the Asian American population in the United States. Although the group as a whole tends to hold high status jobs and be better educated than the general population, not all Asian American groups are equally successful. Recent immigrants from Southeast Asia, for example, often face language barriers. They therefore tend to be concentrated in low-paying service jobs. In general, when compared with the Asian American population as a whole, recent immigrants to the United States have lower incomes and a higher percentage are classified as poor. Given the Asian American emphasis on educational achievement, though, it is doubtful that this pattern will continue from generation to generation.

Native Americans

Estimates indicate that when the first Europeans set foot on the shores of what is now the United States, the native population numbered in the millions. These people, the ancestors of contemporary Native Americans, or American Indians, were divided into hundreds of tribes, each with its own rich history and culture. By the end of the nineteenth century, however, disease, warfare, and the destruction of traditional ways of life had reduced the Native American population to only a quarter of a million people. Although their numbers have climbed once again over the million mark—1.9 million according to the 1990 census—as a group, Native Americans are the nation's most poverty-stricken minority. The statistics speak for themselves.

- Approximately 15 percent of Native American males aged 16 and over are unemployed. The unemployment figure for Native American females is around 13 percent.
- Almost 31 percent of all Native Americans live below the poverty level. On reservations, the number of people living in poverty may be even higher.
- The suicide rate is nearly twice as high among Native Americans as it is among the general population. Also, alcohol abuse causes one in three Native American deaths.
- Only around 65 percent of Native Americans aged 25 and over have graduated from high school, and less than 10 percent have graduated from college.

Native American poverty is the result of a history of changing governmental policies toward American Indians. During the early years of contact, the government took Indian land by force and through treaties. Then, in the late nineteenth century, a new policy was adopted. Native Americans were made wards of the United States government and most of them were moved to reservations.

The government also created policies aimed at assimilating Native Americans into white society. The men were encouraged to become farmers, even though most traditionally were hunters or herders. Tribal property was redistributed to male heads of households, thus disrupting the communal nature typical of Native American societies. Children were separated from their parents and sent to boarding schools. Native Americans who lived away from the reservations and adopted the ways of white society were rewarded with United States citizenship. Most American Indians, however, did not gain citizenship until 1924, when Congress awarded citizenship to all Native Americans living in the United States.

Today, Native Americans, both individually and collectively, are celebrating their past and looking toward the future. Legislation passed in 1989 established a museum of American Indian history and culture as part of the Smithsonian Institution in Washington, D.C. Ben Nighthorse Campbell,

American artist Robert Lidneux painted this picture, entitled *Trail of Tears,* to depict the forced march of 16,000 Cherokee to Oklahoma during the winter of 1838. Around 4,000 Cherokee died during the march. Native American artists today are working to record the experiences of their people.

the only Native American in Congress, was active in helping to pass laws to protect Native American gravesites. Other Native Americans are centering their efforts on business development and the restoration of tribal lands.

White Ethnics

Not all white European immigrants were quickly accepted into mainstream society. During the nineteenth and early twentieth centuries, immigrants from the predominantly Catholic countries of Ireland, Italy, France, Poland, and Greece entered the United States in great numbers. These immigrants—who are referred to collectively as **white ethnics**—often faced open discrimination at the hands of the American-born white Protestant majority.

The discrimination faced by white ethnics was based on cultural and economic concerns. Unlike earlier European immigrants, white ethnics came to the United States with little money and few skills. They often spoke little or no English and most of them were Catholic. Opposition by the American-born white majority was vocal and often violent. Anti-Catholic riots were common and lynchings occurred in several states. Many job announcements carried a notice stating that "only Americans need apply." When work could be found, it generally was in the lowest-paying and least prestigious jobs.

Many white ethnics responded to discrimination by assimilating rapidly into mainstream society. Some adopted American-sounding names and required their children to speak English at home as well as in public. Other white ethnics chose the opposite response. They banded together in ethnic neighborhoods in an attempt to hold on to their ancestral identities.

Today, many white ethnics have been accepted into mainstream society. Other white ethnics, however, still are struggling against prejudice and economic discrimination. White ethnics often are stereotyped as politically conservative, racially bigoted, and poorly educated. In reality, though, half of all white ethnics have attended college (about the same percentage as white non-ethnics), many are middle class, and some are politically moderate or liberal.

SECTION 3 REVIEW

IDENTIFY Chinese Exclusion Act, Tydings–McDuffie Act, McCarren–Walter Act

1. **Summarizing Ideas** What are some of the gains that have been made by African Americans, and what problems still remain?

2. **Comparing Ideas** Provide examples of how the various Hispanic American groups differ on social characteristics.

3. **Analyzing Viewpoints** Why have Asian Americans been called a model minority, and why do they resent the label?

4. **Comprehending Ideas** How have governmental policies added to the problems of Native Americans?

5. **Interpreting Ideas** Why did the experiences of white ethnics differ from those of other European immigrants?

CHAPTER 10   SUMMARY

In sociological terms, a race is a category of people who share inherited physical characteristics and who are perceived as being a distinct group. Ethnicity, on the other hand, refers to the cultural characteristics that distinguish one group from another. The people who share a common cultural background and a common sense of identity are called an ethnic group. When an ethnic or racial group possesses physical characteristics or cultural practices that result in the group being denied equal treatment in society, the group is classified as a minority group.

Minority group members face the related problems of discrimination and prejudice. Discrimination is the denial of equal treatment to individuals based on their group membership. Prejudice, on the other hand, is an unsupported generaliza-tion about a category of people. The most common sources of discrimination and prejudice recognized by sociologists are stereotyping, scapegoating, and the social environment.

Treatment of minority groups can range from total acceptance to total rejection. The most common patterns of acceptance include assimilation, cultural pluralism, and legal protection. Population transfer, subjugation, and extermination are the most common patterns of rejection.

Not all groups in the United States have been equally successful in carving out a secure place in society. Among the racial and ethnic groups that have faced the most difficulty in gaining acceptance are African Americans, Hispanic Americans, Asian Americans, Native Americans, and white ethnics.

DEVELOPING SOCIOLOGICAL

THINKING ABOUT SOCIOLOGY: Identifying Assumptions

Actions and beliefs are heavily influenced by assumptions. An assumption is a statement that is taken for granted as being true. Following is an assumption: *Certain social environments tend to encourage prejudice.* The statement is assumed to be true and often is used as the basis for arguments about race and ethnic relations.

Science could not proceed if scientists did not hold assumptions about phenomena. For assumptions to be valid, however, they must be consistent with existing knowledge and with the conclusion they are meant to support. While these assumptions sometimes are stated outright, they most often are implied. Thus sociology students must be able to identify and evaluate the basic assumptions that underlie an argument.

How to Identify an Assumption
To identify an assumption, follow these guidelines.

1. Identify the conclusion. As you read or listen to the argument, look for clues that point to a concluding statement. Some examples are *in summary, thus,* and *however.*

2. Identify which statements are assumptions. Make a list of the statements about the phenomenon. Determine which statements of fact are not supported by direct evidence. Label these statements as assumptions.

3. Evaluate the assumptions. Examine the assumptions. Determine whether the assumptions appear consistent with the conclusion and with the existing body of knowledge.

Applying the Skill
Read the following excerpt on the Eastern Cherokee by William Hodge. The excerpt originally appeared in Hodge's book *The First Americans: Then and Now.* The conclusion of the excerpt is that the Eastern Cherokee people will continue to survive even though they largely have been denied access to the benefits of society.

In the excerpt, Hodge makes a number of assumptions about non-Indian white culture. Among these assumptions are that (1) the white dominant culture expects the Eastern Cherokee to abandon their Indian heritage, (2) the white dominant culture resists the efforts of minority group members to join mainstream society, (3) some members of the white dominant culture profit from the minority status of the Eastern Cherokee, and (4) the white dominant culture will do little to improve the status of the Eastern Cherokee in the future. These assumptions appear to be consistent with the conclusion.

> Today the Eastern Cherokee Reservation or Qualla Boundary is located in western North Carolina, 50 miles west of Asheville. The largest town, Cherokee, stands at the junction of U.S. Highways 441 and 19. The 43,554 acres of the Qualla Boundary consist of about 80 percent of forested mountain slopes, the rest being bottom land and river valleys. The five main centers of population in the Qualla Boundary are each centered around a section of bottom land. They are Big Cove, Wolfstown, Painttown, Cherokee Village, and Birdtown. . . .
>
> The Eastern Cherokees have established crucial economic, social, and religious ties with the greater American society. The creation and maintenance of such a linkage have been slow and painful processes. The net result of such ties has been fully satisfactory to neither Indians nor non-Indians.
>
> Wage labor and various forms of part-time relief supply a marginal kind of financial support. Formal education, though providing the essentials of learning, prepares most Cherokees for little more than unskilled and semiskilled labor. Enrolled Indian students do come to realize that most Whites would prefer that they abandon their heritage and conform, for the most part, to middle-class expec-

tations. Available facilities, however, constitute neither the means nor the motivation for such a transition.

Most contemporary Cherokees take a serious interest in institutionalized Christianity. Their churches are Baptist or Methodist with a fundamentalist orientation. Many of the clergymen are lay Cherokees who work at a second job to support themselves. Churches are an important focus of social life, and the doctrines preached there endorse many traditional Cherokee beliefs. The fundamentalist, literal translation of Scripture, however, often provides inappropriate answers to the complex problems of Indian survival in a White world.

The physical and mental health of a significant portion of the Cherokees is poor. Alcohol abuse is frequent and often leads to criminal behavior. There are high incidences of respiratory diseases and diabetes as well as many hypertensive, endocrine, nutritional, and metabolic disorders. The accident rate is high.

Reservation life, particularly those crucial activities associated with the family and household, is turbulent and often chaotic. The behavior of children and adults frequently reflects this instability. Listlessness, apathy, and lack of initiative are evident at both the individual and community levels. Violent acts are frequent. Although a Cherokee may be given a number of options with regard to behavioral models such as part-time professional or tourist Indian, the traditional Cherokee conservative backwoodsman, or the successful, middle-class Indian, he is never allowed to forget the fact that by the standards of the world outside the reservation he remains an Indian and hence a subordinate, powerless member of a larger complex society that has little place for him.

The Eastern Cherokees have finally become the kind of Indians that their White contemporaries will allow them to be. More than 250 years of White contact have resulted in their assumption of a subordinate, underclass status for the vast majority of people. Logistical insufficiency produced a series of military defeats by more powerful forces. The resulting political impotence during the first half of the nineteenth century made it impos-

sible for the Cherokees to achieve an economic and social equality with the larger society that surrounded them. The amount and kind of cultural change that accompanied these developments have been extensive. Although much of the Cherokee language and syllabary, the ideas and practices associated with traditional medicine, and a mature adaptable sense of ethnicity have persisted, early eighteenth-century political, economic, and social institutions have long ceased to exist. . . .

The people called Cherokee, however, have shown a remarkable vitality in the face of formidable odds, largely because they have been able to survive on resources that the dominant society has not cared enough about to take away from them, particularly areas of land that had little or no obvious commercial use. Even these places, to a great extent, are shared with non-Indians who are successful and prominent entrepreneurs in the tourist industry. The Eastern Cherokees appear keen to accept use and ownership of only a very few places, which serve as residential or dormitary communities. An ethnicity that centers around an erratic submission to American influences will probably persist for the foreseeable future as long as a number of supporting circumstances continue. The tourist industry firmly rooted in the existence of the Great Smoky Mountain National Park should provide various segments of the Cherokee population with a marginal kind of income sufficent for survival and yet inadequate to produce healthy economic growth. Limited welfare programs stemming from federal and local sources will also continue to perpetuate their existence. Economic resources to a large extent will be changed to social resources, which nourish a supporting network of kinsmen, friends, and neighbors. The factors of common occupational positions, residential stability and concentration, plus a dependence on common institutions and services will function to maintain a Cherokee people in North Carolina.

Practicing the Skill

Reread the essay to identify and evaluate the assumptions made about Native American culture.

Reviewing Sociological Terms

On a separate sheet of paper, supply the term that correctly completes each sentence.

1. _____ is the maintaining of control over a group through force.

2. The set of cultural characteristics that distinguishes one group from another group is referred to as _____.

3. Individuals who share a common cultural background and a common sense of identity are called an _____ _____.

4. _____ is the blending of culturally distinct groups into a single group with a common culture and identity.

5. _____ is the intentional extermination of an entire population.

6. The ownership of one group by another group is called _____.

7. _____ _____ is the policy that allows each group within society to keep its unique cultural identity.

Thinking Critically about Sociology

1. **Seeing Relationships**   What is scapegoating and what functions does it serve?

2. **Organizing Ideas**   According to Robert K. Merton, what are the four ways in which an individual can combine discriminatory behavior and prejudicial attitudes?

3. **Using Sociological Imagination**   **(a)** What is a self-fulfilling prophecy?   **(b)** Provide an example not listed in your textbook of how prejudice can become a self-fulfilling prophecy.

4. **Synthesizing Ideas**   How can unequal access to social rewards and resources lead to institutionalized discrimination?

5. **Interpreting Ideas**   **(a)** Why is it difficult to classify people racially?   **(b)** How do sociologists approach the concept of race?

6. **Comprehending Ideas**   **(a)** What is segregation?   **(b)** Describe the two principal types of segregation.

7. **Analyzing Ideas**   What function does prejudice serve for members of the dominant group in a society?

Exercising Sociological Skills

1. **Expressing Viewpoints**   Reread the Applying Sociology feature on pages 240–241. Does the children's behavior provide any insights into how events such as the massacre of Jews by Hitler's German forces can occur? Explain.

2. **Summarizing Ideas**   According to the Case Study on page 246, what factors led to differing race relations in the two South London neighborhoods studied by Hewitt?

3. **Recognizing Stereotypes**   Reread the Developing Sociological Imagination feature on pages 254–255. Select a television program that depicts the lives of racial or ethnic characters.   **(a)** What stereotypes are being supported by the program?   **(b)** What stereotypes are being broken?

Extending Sociological Imagination

1. Select any three of the six patterns of minority group treatment discussed in the chapter and write a brief description of how each pattern has been used by an actual society. The examples you use may be either contemporary or historical.

2. Describe the ways in which African Americans, Hispanic Americans, Asian Americans, Native Americans, and white ethnics exhibit the five characteristics of minority groups listed on page 235. Draw your examples from the information presented in the chapter and from outside research.

INTERPRETING PRIMARY SOURCES
Tracking Hate Crimes

Crimes motivated by prejudice appear to be on the rise in the United States. Concern over these "hate crimes," as they are called, led Congress to pass a law requiring the Federal Bureau of Investigation (FBI) to compile annual statistics on the number of such crimes occurring nationwide. Although this task has proved to be difficult, early findings are providing some insight into the nature of hate crimes.

In the following excerpt from the article "Hate Crimes," which appeared in the January 8, 1993, issue of *CQ Researcher*, Kenneth Jost discusses the recent effort to track such crimes. As you read the excerpt, consider why it might be difficult to collect hate crime data. Also consider what factors might motivate these crimes.

Under the Hate Crimes Statistics Act of 1990, the FBI was directed to publish annual reports on the number of crimes committed each year that "manifest [clearly show] prejudice based on race, religion, affectional or sexual orientation or ethnicity." But the FBI's first report, released Jan. 4, contains figures from only a sixth of all law enforcement agencies around the country.

For the year 1991, just 2,771 out of more than 16,000 law enforcement agencies around the country furnished hate crime data to the FBI. The agencies reported a total of 4,558 hate crime incidents in 1991. Participation in the program was limited because law enforcement agencies were not required to provide the data and many said that they had no money to pay for a new data collection effort. . . .

The FBI report listed racial bias as the motivation in 62 percent of the incidents covered. Blacks were the most frequent target—36 percent of the total number—but anti-white offenses accounted for 19 percent of the total. Religious bias was the motivation for 19 percent of the incidents. Anti-Jewish offenses

were the largest component of that category: 17 percent of the total. Ethnic and sexual orientation bias each accounted for 10 percent of the total.

The offenders were known in just 57 percent of the incidents reported. Whites were listed as the offenders in nearly two-thirds of those cases, blacks as the offenders in about one-third. The most common offense listed was intimidation (34 percent), closely followed by vandalism or other property damage (27 percent). The FBI data listed 773 cases of aggravated assault and 12 murders. . . .

Experts cite several factors to explain the apparent increase in hate crimes. [Dr. Howard] Ehrlich points to increased immigration in the 1980s as a major reason. More than 8 million people entered the country during the decade—making it the second-largest period of in-migration in the nation's history.

Economic problems are also cited as a factor, especially for some of the anti-Asian incidents. "Quite often, minorities may be looked at as people holding jobs that other people might have lost," Pat Sullivan of the Arapahoe County Sheriff's Department in Colorado told the Senate subcommittee in August.

Affirmative action programs are often blamed for leading to resentment in the workplace and on college campuses. Civil rights groups say those tensions were [heightened] by the conservative political climate in the 1980s. . . .

Despite the lack of solid statistics, law enforcement experts say the federal law and the FBI's work in implementing it have helped sensitize police around the country to the hate crime problem. "As police departments reach out to the victims, victims come forward," says Jack McDevitt, director of the Center for Applied Social Research at Northeastern University in Boston.

Source Review

1. Besides lack of funding, why might it be difficult to collect data on hate crimes?

2. Why do hate crimes appear to be on the rise in the United States?

Gender, Age, and Health

 Gender

The Roles of Men and Women
The Politics of Gender
Gender Inequality in the United States

 Age

The Aging World
The Politics of Aging
Age Inequality in the United States

3 **Health**

Health Care in the United States
The Politics of Health
Health and Social Status

Chapter Focus

Chapter 11 focuses on social inequality based on gender, age, and health. The chapter begins with a discussion of gender inequality. Attention then is turned to the elderly in America. The chapter closes with a discussion of health and health care in the United States, with special emphasis on the needs of Americans with disabilities and the victims of AIDS.

As you study the chapter, look for the answers to the following questions:

1. How do gender roles affect the life chances of men and women in society?
2. What effect is the aging of the population having on society and on the life chances of the elderly?
3. What is the state of health care in the United States?
4. What are some of the special health-care concerns of various segments of society?

KEY TERMS

The following terms, while not the only terms emphasized in the chapter, are basic to your understanding of sociology. Determine the meaning of each term, either by using the Glossary or by watching for context clues as you read the chapter.

gender
gender roles
Equal Rights Amendment

sexism
ageism
baby-boom generation

Medicare
acquired immune
    deficiency syndrome

INTRODUCTION

Race and ethnicity are not the only factors that affect a person's standing in society. An individual's position in the social structure also is influenced by whether he or she is male or female, young or old, able-bodied or disabled. In general, to be female, old, or disabled is to be in a position of lesser power in society. The degree of that power difference varies from society to society, but it exists to some degree in all societies.

Consider the following statistics from the United States:

- Only 8 percent of America's engineers and approximately 20 percent of the nation's doctors, lawyers, and judges are female.

- Only 60 percent of the medical bills of the elderly are covered by Medicare and Medicaid.
- More than 14 percent of Americans are not covered by health insurance.
- Although most Americans with disabilities want to work, only 42 percent of working-age men with disabilities and 20 percent of working-age women with disabilities are employed.

In this chapter, we will explore the social factors that have given rise to these statistics. We also will examine some of the steps that have been taken in the United States to lessen social inequality based on gender, age, and health.

1 GENDER

If you were asked to prepare a list of the ways in which males and females differ, some of the items on your list would be based on biological characteristics. It is an undeniable fact that males and females differ on physical traits such as average height and weight, amount of body hair, and muscle to fat ratio.

Most of the items on your list, however, probably would refer to differences in **gender**—the behavioral and psychological traits considered appropriate for males and females. Unlike biological traits, which are the same in all societies, gender traits are socially created and thus may vary from culture to culture.

We learn gender differences early in life. Many of the lessons are indirect, as journalist Susan Brownmiller points out in the following excerpt from her book *Femininity:*

> We had a game in our house called "setting the table" and I was Mother's helper. Forks to the left of the plate, knives and spoons to the right. Placing the cutlery neatly, as I recall, was one of my first duties, and the event was alive with meaning. When a knife or a fork dropped to the floor, that meant a man was unexpectedly coming to dinner. A falling spoon announced the surprise arrival of a female guest. No matter that these visitors never arrived on cue, I had learned a rule of gender identification. Men were straight-edged, sharply pronged and formidable, women were softly curved and held the food in a rounded well. It made perfect sense, like the division of pink and blue that I saw in babies, an orderly way of viewing the world.

No matter how indirect the lessons, the consequences of gender differentiation are far-reaching. It is gender, not biology, that determines the majority of the roles males and females play in society. And, equally as important, it is primarily beliefs about gender that determine the distribution of power between the sexes. In this section, we will examine the social significance of gender.

The Roles of Men and Women

When we speak of a man being masculine or a woman being feminine, we mean that the person exhibits behaviors and attitudes considered appropriate for his or her sex. All societies have norms governing how males and females should act. The specific behaviors and attitudes that a society establishes for men and women are called **gender roles.**

Gender roles result from the division of labor. In all societies, individuals and groups specialize to some degree in the performance of economic activities. The purpose of this specialization is to increase efficiency. In most societies, men and women do different kinds of work. In a division of labor based on sex, women generally are assigned child-care and domestic duties, while men are assigned the tasks of providing for the economic support and physical safety of the family.

Although this Fulani male's makeup and clothes seem unusual by American standards, they are perfectly acceptable in his society.

Cross-Cultural Variations. While the majority of preindustrial societies—and to a lesser extent, most industrial societies—follow a division of labor similar to the one mentioned above, there are exceptions. In a few societies, such as the Tchambuli, one of the three New Guinea societies studied by Margaret Mead in the 1930s, men care for the children. Women, on the other hand, provide food for the family. Even in societies in which men are the principal breadwinners, gender-based duties can vary widely. For instance, in most preindustrial societies, basket making, weaving, and the manufacture of clothing are considered women's work. In some societies, however, these tasks fall to men.

Even more variation exists in the psychological characteristics considered appropriate for men and women. For example, in her study of the Arapesh, Mundugumor, and Tchambuli societies of New Guinea, Margaret Mead found that appropriate gender traits varied from society to society. Arapesh men, like Arapesh women, were expected to be passive and emotionally warm,

traits considered feminine in most cultures. The traditionally masculine trait of aggressiveness, on the other hand, was the norm among men and women alike among the Mundugumor.

Among the Tchambuli, gender roles were reversed. The women were bossy and efficient, while the men were gossipy and artistic. In addition, the men wore cosmetics and curled their hair, while the women wore few adornments. Other researchers have noted similar practices of wearing cosmetics and acting in a feminine manner among the men of the Fulani of northern Africa.

Most sociologists take cross-cultural variations as evidence that gender roles are socially created rather than biologically based. They argue that if gender roles were based primarily on biology, few variations in gender behavior would exist within or between cultures.

Gender Role Socialization. Individuals learn appropriate gender role behavior through socialization. As we mentioned in Chapter 5, socialization is the interactive process through which individuals learn the basic skills, values, beliefs, and behavior patterns of their society. In virtually all societies, gender socialization begins at birth and continues throughout life.

In the United States, for example, a baby's gender often is reinforced at birth through the selection of sex-specific clothes, toys, and nursery furnishings. Traditionally, girl babies are dressed in pink and boy babies are dressed in blue. Infant girls are given dolls, while infant boys are given stuffed animals. And, nursery furnishings tend toward delicate pastels and frills for girl babies, while boys' nurseries often are done in strong primary colors and clean lines.

Although these gender variations are less pronounced today than they were 10 or 20 years ago,

Circumstances affect expectations for gender behavior. Pat Schroeder was criticized for crying when she withdrew from the 1988 presidential primary, even though crying traditionally has been acceptable for women. And, while crying traditionally has been unacceptable for men, few people would question the appropriateness of this man's tears as he stands before the Vietnam Memorial.

it is in the treatment of girls that change is most evident. Girls' clothes now come in a wide range of colors, fabrics, and styles. And, most people no longer discourage girls from playing with traditionally male toys, such as model cars, trucks, and airplanes. Boys, on the other hand, rarely are dressed in pink or in clothing that has ribbons, lace, or other frills on it. Moreover, few boys are encouraged to play with dolls or other traditionally feminine toys.

Even more important than the physical trappings of masculinity and femininity are the different expectations that people tend to hold for girls and boys. Most of us are familiar with the following nursery rhyme:

> What are little boys made of?
> What are little boys made of?
>   Frogs and snails,
>   And puppy-dogs' tails,
> That's what little boys are made of.
>
> What are little girls made of?
> What are little girls made of?
>   Sugar and spice
>   And all that is nice,
> That's what little girls are made of.

Although the nursery rhyme is from the 1800s, the underlying attitude toward proper gender behavior still is evident today. For the most part, little boys are expected to be adventuresome, aggressive, and physically active, while little girls are expected to be polite, gentle, and passive. Parents and teachers often express concern over a boy who is too gentle or too passive. Little girls who are thought to be too aggressive or too adventuresome tend to bring forth similar concerns from adults.

Differing gender expectations extend to school and career pursuits. Males are expected to be good at math and science and to be mechanically inclined. Females are expected to excel in reading and the social sciences and to be creative. The woman who chooses to marry and raise children rather than pursue a career is acting within the bounds of expected behavior. The man who chooses the same course is viewed by many as being something less than a man. The same is true for men who appear too emotional, too nonaggressive, or too disinterested in women.

Women in the Military

Until quite recently, service in the defense of the United States was a male domain. Prior to the 1940s, women's participation in the military mainly was limited to nursing, clerical work, and laundry duties. After World War II broke out, however, personnel needs led to the establishment of the Women's Army Auxiliary Corps (WAAC) in 1942. This action paved the way for separate women's corps in all branches of the service. Although the Army Air Corps allowed women to work alongside men in a number of roles, most military women in the 1940s were segregated in separate auxiliaries.

Women were not integrated into the military until the Women's Armed Services Integration Act was passed in 1948. This act, however, limited the proportion of women in the military to 2 percent and barred women from achieving high service ranks. Women also could be discharged upon marriage or pregnancy. For the next two decades, women made up only slightly more than 1 percent of the military and generally were confined to health care and clerical work.

During the 1960s, the expanding role of women in the labor force and the personnel needs of the Vietnam War led the Department of Defense to reassess women's role in the military. In 1967, the government lifted the 2 percent cap on female enlistment and opened all but the top officer ranks to women. Still, women's participation in the military did not increase significantly until an all-volunteer force was created in 1973, following the end of the draft. A 1975 law permitting women to attend West Point and other service academies contributed to the increase in female recruits. By 1980, the proportion of women in the military had risen to 8 percent.

Today, the over 200,000 women on active military duty make up 11 percent of the nation's armed forces. Another 1.5 million American women are veterans. These servicewomen played important combat-support roles in the United States invasion of Grenada in 1984, the raid on Libya in 1986, and the Panama invasion in 1989. The first major test of women in prolonged combat, however, was in 1991 during the Persian Gulf War. More than 40,000 women participated in this action, called Operation Desert Storm, designed to drive invading Iraqi troops from Kuwait.

Servicewomen performed many nontraditional duties during their time in the Persian Gulf. Navy women, for example, piloted helicopters and reconnaissance aircraft. Army women piloted aircraft and set up traffic routes for the invading forces. Air Force women flew and were crew members of transports, tankers, and reconnaissance planes. Marine Corps women fulfilled vital support duties for ground units. By war's end, two American women had been taken prisoner and 13 more had lost their lives.

The contribution of women to the American victory in the Persian Gulf fueled a heated debate concerning the assignment of women to combat roles. Supporters of the combat role for women argued that the exclusion of women from positions that bring them into direct combat stifles their career advancement. Indeed, a recent report by the General Accounting Office (GAO) found that the combat-exclusion policy blocked most women from reaching the military's highest ranks. For example, in 1992, only 11 women held the rank of general or admiral, out of a total 1,021 slots.

Opponents of the combat role for women argued that women in combat would undermine national security. Critics charged that servicemen would be hampered in their duties by trying to protect servicewomen. Opponents also charged that women do not have the strength or endurance to perform effectively in combat.

The debate was settled in 1993 when the long-standing ban on combat roles for women was lifted. This action toppled the final barrier to women's full participation in the military.

Much gender socialization takes place within the family, with parents, brothers and sisters, and other relatives serving as role models. Through the family's conscious and unconscious actions, children quickly learn what gender behaviors are expected of them. These gender expectations are reinforced by schools, peer groups, and the media. During adulthood, peer groups and the media take on increasingly important roles in the gender socialization process.

Gender Roles and Social Inequality. For many social scientists, interest in gender roles goes beyond socialization. These social scientists are most interested in the inequality between men and women that arises from a division of labor based on sex. Anthropologist Ernestine Friedl is one of the social scientists who has explored the effects of a sex-based division of labor on the social status of women.

According to Friedl, power in society is based on control of the distribution of scarce resources. Individuals who are in a position to exchange goods and services with nonfamily members have higher statuses than do individuals who are not in such a position. In the majority of societies, the distribution of resources to nonfamily members is the responsibility of men. Women's contributions tend to center on the family. Friedl argues that the degree to which men control the distribution of scarce resources determines the level of inequality between the sexes in a society.

To support her argument, Friedl presents evidence from hunting and gathering societies. Although hunting and gathering societies are rare today, all people lived in such societies until approximately 10,000 years ago. In hunting and gathering societies, individuals survive by hunting wild animals, fishing, and gathering wild fruits and vegetables. Because of their simple social structure and low level of technology, hunting and gathering societies are the most egalitarian of all societies. Nevertheless, some differences in power between males and females do exist.

According to Friedl, men gain power in hunting and gathering societies through the division of labor. In most hunting and gathering societies, women collect fruits, vegetables, and insects, while men hunt. Even though women often provide the bulk of the food, hunting tends to carry more prestige because of the ways in which food is distributed within the group. The food gathered by women generally is reserved for their families. Meat, on the other hand, is almost always shared with the larger group. Through the distribution of meat, men establish a system of mutual obligations with nonfamily members. In other words, men who provide meat are owed meat by others. These obligations, in turn, provide men with a source of power within the group.

Friedl argues that gender inequality becomes more pronounced as the proportion of meat supplied by men increases. Men and women are most equal in those hunting and gathering societies in which food collection is either a group effort, as it was among the Washo Indians of what is now Southern California, or a totally independent effort, as it is today among the Hadza of Tanzania. In Washo society, everyone shared equally in the food collected by the group. As a result, no one was in a position to gain power through the distribution of meat. In Hadza society, on the other hand, no one can gain power through the distribution of meat because everyone is responsible for collecting his or her own food.

At the opposite extreme is Eskimo society. The inequality between men and women is greater among traditional Eskimos than among any other group of hunters and gatherers. Friedl argues that this inequality is a function of the society's division of labor, which confines Eskimo women's contributions only to domestic chores. Meat provides the bulk of the Eskimo diet. The provision of meat for the family and for distribution to nonfamily members is the sole responsibility of men. Women's duties are confined to the preparation of food and to the care of the home and children. Thus Eskimo women have no power base.

Friedl contends that the same dynamics are at work in industrial societies. Those individuals who control the distribution of scarce resources to nonfamily members hold the power in society. In industrial societies, as in less technologically advanced societies, those in power most often are men. Friedl argues that gender inequality will continue to be a problem in industrial societies as long as women's economic contributions center on the family.

Friedl notes that homemakers are particularly vulnerable because they are financially dependent

Although women are making progress, men still control most corporate boardrooms.

on their husbands. Working women, however, also are at a disadvantage. Although working women may have more power within the family, they are still less powerful than men on the societal level.

According to Friedl, the problem faced by working women is twofold. First, women's incomes generally go toward the maintenance of the family. Until women invest a portion of their incomes in stocks, bonds, and other money-producing enterprises, they will not gain power in society. Thus Friedl argues that like men, women need to create mutual obligations through economic exchanges with nonfamily members. Second, the majority of working women hold lower-status jobs. Until a sufficient number of women move into the ranks of professionals, managers, and politicians, they will have little influence over the distribution of goods and services and thus have little social power relative to men.

The Politics of Gender

Families in industrial societies generally are small and most people live well into their 70s. As a result, women spend much of adulthood free from the responsibilities of child care. In addition, few jobs in industrial societies require such strength that women cannot perform them. This has led many sociologists to suggest that it no longer is efficient for women to confine their work activities to the home. Yet many traditional gender roles continue to exist in industrial societies.

One explanation for the persistence of gender roles in industrial societies is offered by conflict theorists. Sociologists arguing from a conflict perspective claim that gender roles simply are a reflection of male dominance. Through their control over the economic and political spheres of society, men have been able to establish laws and customs that protect their dominant position. In so doing, men have blocked women's access to power.

Conflict theorists, as well as many political activists, often cite the failure of the **Equal Rights Amendment (ERA)** as an example of the extent of male dominance in the United States. In 1972, Congress approved the ERA, which states that "equality of rights under the law shall not be denied or abridged by the United States or any State on account of sex." To become part of the Constitution, it was necessary for 38 states to ratify the amendment. The amendment was defeated,

Text continues on page 268.

APPLYING SOCIOLOGY

The Goals of Men and Women

Are women more apt than men to fear success? In a study conducted in the late 1960s, psychologist Matina Horner attempted to answer this question. Horner asked 90 female and 88 male college students to tell a story based on the following sentence: "After first-term finals, John/Anne finds himself/herself at the top of his/her medical school class." The males were asked to tell stories about John, the females were to write about Anne. Following are excerpts from Horner's study:

Consider Phil, a bright young college sophomore. He has always done well in school. He is in the honors program and has wanted to be a doctor as long as he can remember. We ask him to tell us a story based on this clue: *"After the first-term finals, John finds himself at the top of his medical-school class."* Phil writes:

"John is a conscientious young man who worked hard. He is pleased with himself. John has always wanted to go into medicine and is very dedicated . . . John continues working hard and eventually graduates at the top of his class."

Now consider Monica, another honors student. She too has always done well, and she too has visions of a flourishing career. We give her the same clue, but with "Anne" as the successful student: *"After first-term finals, Anne finds herself at the top of her medical-school class."* Instead of identifying with Anne's triumph, Monica tells a strange tale:

"Anne starts proclaiming her surprise and joy. Her fellow classmates are so disgusted with her behavior that they jump on her in a body and beat her. She is maimed for life."

These two responses were not unique. Over 65 percent of the females told stores in which Anne became lonely, expressed guilt over success,

or avoided success. In contrast, fewer than 10 percent of the males told similar stories about John. Most expressed delight at John's success and predicted a grand future for him. As Horner reports:

The differences between male and female stories were enormous. Two of the stories are particularly revealing examples of this male-female contrast. The women insisted that Anne give up her career for marriage:

"Anne has a boyfriend, Carl, in the same class and they are quite serious . . . She wants him to be scholastically higher than she is. Anne will deliberately lower her academic standing the next term, while she does all she subtly can to help Carl. His grades come up and Anne soon drops out of medical school. They marry and he goes on in school while she raises their family."

But of course the males would ask John to do no such thing:

"John has worked very hard and his long hours of study have paid off . . . He is thinking about his girl, Cheri, whom he will marry at the end of med. school. He realizes he can give her all the things she desires after he becomes established. He will go on in med. school and be successful in the long run."

Horner concluded that women are driven to avoid success because of the way they are socialized. As children, boys are encouraged to succeed, but girls are taught to focus on the home and family. According to Horner, women who succeed in traditional male roles are portrayed as being unfeminine and unmarriageable. As a result, women come to associate success with negative consequences. Therefore, when placed in competitive situations, women tend to strive toward failure.

When analyzing Horner's findings, it is important to keep in mind that the study was conducted in the 1960s. Much progress toward gender equality has taken place since then. More recent studies have indicated that women now suffer less fear of success. And, some research even has shown that more college men than college women fear success. Researchers believe these changes come from shifts in what is considered appropriate gender role behavior for men and women.

In an effort to determine the gender-based attitudes toward success held by your generation, conduct a study similar to Horner's study. Ask six people (three males and three females) to complete the following sentences. Use "Tom" for the sentences given to males and "Sue" for those given to females. Make sure that your subjects do not put their names on their responses.

1. Tom/Sue is getting ready to enter high school and is trying to decide whether to take an academic, vocational, or commercial program of study. Tom/Sue should _____ .

2. Tom/Sue is at the top of his/her class and is deciding what to do after graduating from college. Tom/Sue should _____ .

3. Tom/Sue was offered an excellent job in another city. In order to take the job, he/she would have to move. Tom/Sue should

_____ .

4. Tom/Sue has been working for several years and is ready for a change. Tom/Sue should

_____ .

Now, analyze your findings. What types of responses did the males give for Tom? What kinds of answers did the females give for Sue? How did your two sets of responses differ?

Next, combine your data with those of your classmates. Total up the number of males who had Tom avoid success. Do the same for the females who had Sue avoid success. What can you conclude about the tendency of males and females among your generation to avoid success?

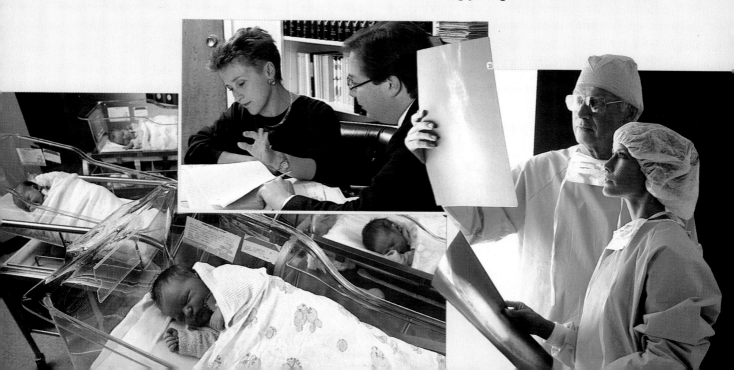

when it won ratification only in 35 state legislatures. The main opposition did not come from the public—opinion polls have shown that two-thirds of adult Americans support the ERA. Rather, the strongest opposition came from male legislators and from STOP ERA, an organization headed by Phyllis Schlafly. People who oppose the Equal Rights Amendment tend to view it as a threat to traditional family values.

Passage of the ERA, however, would not automatically solve the problem of gender inequality in the United States. This is because women, like members of most minority groups, face institutionalized discrimination. While laws can be changed with a stroke of a pen, it takes generations to erase discriminatory social customs.

Sexism—the belief that one sex is by nature superior to the other—is at the heart of gender-based discrimination. The long history of male economic and political dominance has led many people in society to adopt the view that men possess natural qualities that make them superior to women. This view, in turn, has been used as a justification for continued male dominance.

As with racism, sexism becomes a self-fulfilling prophecy. People who believe that women are emotionally, intellectually, or physically incapable of occupying positions of power make choices based on this belief. Men who see women as inferior often oppose the entrance of women into powerful positions in business, politics, and the professions. And, women who accept this stereotype do not attempt to pursue careers in traditionally male fields. Consequently, the number of women in powerful positions remains too small to provide women with a power base that could lead to increased access for all women.

Gender Inequality in the United States

Progress toward gender equality is being made in almost every area of American social life. Equality, however, is far from achieved. Some of the most important areas in which women are at a disadvantage relative to men are in educational attainment, the work force, and the political arena.

Education.   Prior to 1980, women were underrepresented among the ranks of college students.

Phyllis Schlafly of STOP ERA has been a vocal opponent of the Equal Rights Amendment.

Since that time, however, women have outnumbered men on college campuses. Yet women still are much less likely to pursue professional and doctoral degrees. The college majors of men and women also differ. More men pursue degrees in science, engineering, business, and other fields that allow entrance into high-paying careers. Women, on the other hand, tend to concentrate in the social sciences, humanities, and other majors that lead to lower-paying careers.

The World of Work.   While the majority of adult women are employed at least part-time in the labor force, they are heavily concentrated in low-status, low-paying jobs. As a result, the median income of female full-time workers is approximately $21,000 a year, compared to a median income of around $29,000 for male full-time workers. On average, female workers earn approximately 72 cents for every dollar earned by

During World War II, women filled many industrial positions normally held by men. Following the war, however, most women moved back into traditional areas of employment.

male workers. Even when we examine the incomes of men and women working in the same occupations, women consistently earn less money.

The Political Arena. Even though women make up over 50 percent of the voting-age population, men dominate the political arena. In 1993, for example, only 6 percent of U.S. senators, 11 percent of U.S. representatives, and 6 percent of state governors were women. Although these figures represent large increases over previous years, women still are underrepresented in government. More promising perhaps is President Bill Clinton's appointment of three women—Hazel O'Leary, Janet Reno, and Donna Shalala—to Cabinet posts in his administration.

SECTION 1 REVIEW

DEFINE gender, gender roles, sexism

IDENTIFY Equal Rights Amendment (ERA)

1. **Comprehending Ideas** *(a)* How do gender roles arise? *(b)* Describe some of the gender-role variations found in societies around the world. *(c)* Why do most sociologists take these variations as evidence that gender roles are socially created?

2. **Contrasting Ideas** How do gender expectations differ for males and females in the United States?

3. **Analyzing Ideas** *(a)* According to Ernestine Friedl, how is power in society determined and what effect does this have on equality between the sexes? *(b)* What evidence does Friedl present to support her argument?

4. **Interpreting Ideas** According to conflict theorists, why do gender roles persist in industrial societies?

5. **Summarizing Ideas** Provide examples of how women in the United States are at a disadvantage relative to men in the areas of education, employment, and politics.

2 AGE

Different societies place different value on age. In preindustrial societies, the social standing of individuals tends to increase with age. The older members of society are viewed as sources of knowledge and as the enforcers of social customs. In industrial societies, on the other hand, middle-age people hold the greatest social power. Fewer meaningful roles exist for the elderly. Employment opportunities, for instance, decline with age. The closer one approaches retirement age, the more difficult it is to find reemployment in the event of a job loss. And, job retraining programs seldom are geared toward older workers. This is extremely important in light of the fact that employment is one of the major indicators of social status in industrial societies.

Ageism—the belief that one age category is by nature superior to another age category—is at the heart of age-based role loss. Although ageism can apply to any age group, in industrial societies it most often is directed toward the elderly. One way in which ageism can be seen is in the stereotypes used to portray them. The elderly often are portrayed as unproductive, cranky, and physically or mentally impaired. In reality, however, the vast majority of people aged 65 and older are self-sufficient and active members of society.

In American society, ageism is reinforced by the media. In television commercials, for instance, elderly people seldom are used to sell household products, cosmetics, clothing, or automobiles. Instead, the elderly endorse products such as over-the-counter medications, health-related devices, denture preparations, or insurance and burial plans. Moreover, the presentation of the elderly by the news media most often focuses on the negative aspects of aging, such as poor health, poverty, and loneliness.

Daily life in most preindustrial societies is guided by social customs. Because they are seen as enforcers of these customs, the elderly generally are held in high regard.

Efforts now are being made to change the image Americans have of the elderly. In the United States, television programs, movies, and children's books that present older adults as positive role models are beginning to appear. Nevertheless, much age discrimination still exists—a fact that is particularly significant in light of current world population trends.

The Aging World

The world's population is aging. Today there are approximately 332 million people aged 65 and older worldwide. It is estimated that by the year 2000, this number will have grown to more than 426 million. In 1991, 27 nations had elderly populations of over 2 million. The five nations with

The 10 Oldest and 10 Youngest Nations of the World

Rank	Nation	Population Median Age	Percentage of Population Under Age 15	Percentage of Population Aged 65 and Over
Oldest Nations				
1	Sweden	39.3	16.5	18.3
2	Germany	38.2	17.0	14.0
3	Switzerland	38.1	16.4	15.3
4	Japan	37.2	18.5	11.7
5	Denmark	37.2	17.0	15.5
6	Luxembourg	37.1	17.1	13.4
7	Bulgaria	36.7	20.0	13.0
8	Hungary	36.5	19.9	13.4
9	Finland	36.3	19.3	13.2
10	Italy	36.3	17.3	14.2
Youngest Nations				
1	Kenya	14.2	52.1	2.8
2	Cote D'Ivoire	15.3	49.4	2.2
3	Zambia	15.4	59.1	2.3
4	Tanzania	15.4	49.1	2.3
5	Rwanda	15.5	48.9	2.4
6	Nigeria	15.7	48.4	2.4
7	Botswana	15.7	48.5	2.4
8	Uganda	15.7	48.5	2.5
9	Syria	15.9	48.1	2.6
10	Jordan	16.0	47.9	2.5

Source: Timothy O'Donnell, Amanda Lambert, Maureen Gorelick, and Beth Browning, *World Quality of Life Indicators*. Santa Barbara, Cal.: ABC-CLIO, 1991.

the highest number of people aged 65 and older were China (67,967,000), India (32,780,000), the United States (32,045,000), Japan (15,253,000), and Germany (12,010,000). Projections indicate that by the year 2020, these figures will have climbed to over 179 million for China, 88 million for India, 52 million for the United States, 33 million for Japan, and 18 million for Germany. The chart on this page shows selected characteristics for nations with the oldest and the youngest populations.

Population trends in the United States reflect what is happening worldwide. In 1990, approximately 12 percent of the population in the United States was aged 65 or older. This figure is expected to reach 14 percent by the year 2010 and to exceed 17 percent by the year 2020. Moreover, by the year 2030, one in every five Americans will be 65 years of age or older. Sociologists refer to this phenomenon as the "graying of America." The chart on page 272 presents selected statistics on the graying of America.

There basically are two reasons for the graying of America. First, advances in health care and better living conditions have resulted in more people surviving to old age. Second, variations in birth rates have changed the age structure of the United States. Birth rates in the United States rose sharply from 1946 through 1964, as family life resumed following World War II. The approximately 76 million children born during this period are known as the **baby-boom generation.**

The Graying of America

Characteristic	1970	1990	2010
Population			
Aged 65–84 (in millions)	18.7	28.2	33.1
85 and over (in millions)	1.4	3.1	6.3
65+ as percent of population	10%	12%	14%
Life Expectancy			
Total	70.8	75.4	77.9
Male	67.1	72.0	74.4
Female	74.7	78.8	81.3
White	71.7	76.0	78.3
African American	64.1	70.3	75.0

Sources: *Statistical Abstract of the United States, 1992*, p. 76; *The Universal Almanac*, 1993, p. 285.

Following 1964, however, the birth rate in the United States began to drop and has remained relatively low ever since. This increase and then decline in the birth rate means that the baby-boom generation is the largest segment of the American population. Today the baby boomers are in their early 30s to late 40s. By the year 2030, all of the baby boomers will have reached 65 years of age, thereby swelling the ranks of the elderly.

The Politics of Aging

The changing age structure of the United States has thrust the elderly into the center of American politics, both as a political force and as a topic of debate. The image of the elderly has been transformed from one of an underprivileged and forgotten segment of society to one of a powerful and effective voting bloc. Exactly how organized a voting bloc the elderly represent is unclear. What is clear, however, is that few politicians today are willing to run the risk of ignoring the needs of the elderly.

Groups such as the American Association of Retired Persons, the National Council of Senior Citizens, the National Council on Aging, the Na-

tional Caucus on the Black Aged, and the Gray Panthers have been effective in bringing the special needs of the elderly to national attention. The most successful of these organizations has been the American Association of Retired Persons (AARP). With 32 million members, the AARP is the largest special-interest group in the United States. In addition to its political lobbying efforts, the AARP operates a credit union and the largest group health-insurance plan in the United States. The organization also offers travel and prescription drug discounts, publishes *Modern Maturity*, the third highest circulation magazine in the nation, produces a weekly television series, and operates a wire service that provides newspapers with information on issues of the elderly.

Some of the strongest lobbying support for the elderly, however, has come from groups that are not based on age, such as labor unions and political organizations. Social scientists suggest that broad cross-generational support arises in part from the desire of middle-aged children to share with the government the burden of caring for elderly parents. Regardless of the reason for support, the influence of the elderly on the political process has grown in recent years. It is likely that this influence will continue to grow as the ranks of the elderly swell with the aging of the baby boomers.

Nevertheless, legislation aimed at helping the elderly is not without its opponents. Some people are beginning to express fears that the Social Security system is not up to the task of caring for future generations of elderly. The Social Security system is funded by workers. Current workers pay for the benefits received by current retirees. Declining birth rates and longer life expectancies mean that there are fewer workers available to support growing numbers of retirees. In 1945, there were 35 workers for every person receiving Social Security benefits. By 1985, this ratio had declined to three workers for every one retiree. The problem will become even more pronounced when the 76 million baby boomers reach retirement age.

Longer life expectancies present another problem for the Social Security system. Because of increasing life expectancies, the fastest growth in the elderly population is among the old-old—individuals aged 85 and older. In each decade since

Protection of Social Security benefits and the establishment of a long-term health care program are major concerns of today's elderly Americans. The elderly use strong lobbying techniques to make their concerns known to legislators.

1940, the number of old-old has risen by 50 percent. In 1970, for example, there were approximately 1.4 million Americans aged 85 or older. By 1990, the number had reached 3.1 million. Projections show that the old-old will make up about 15 percent of the elderly population by the year 2010. The old-old are the elders most likely to be in poor health. This will present an added strain on government transfer programs, particularly **Medicare**—the government-sponsored insurance plan for the elderly and the disabled. These issues have stirred much heated debate in recent years concerning the taxing of Social Security benefits and proposals to freeze cost of living adjustments for beneficiaries.

Age Inequality in the United States

Many critics of the Social Security system claim that government transfer payments have made the elderly in the United States financially secure at the expense of younger generations. Critics base this claim on the fact that poverty among Americans aged 65 and older has dropped from 35 percent in 1960 to slightly more than 12 percent currently. On the surface, these statistics paint a bright picture. In comparison, the poverty rate is approximately 14 percent for the general population and about 22 percent for children under the age of 18. In reality, however, the 12 percent figure masks a great deal of variation in living

The fact that elderly women are much more likely than elderly men to live alone contributes to their higher rates of poverty.

men. Among elderly African American women, the figure is about 39 percent. Poverty levels also are higher among the old-old.

Even these statistics mask the seriousness of the situation. The poverty level for a single person aged 65 or older is just under $7,000 a year. Social Security benefits and other government transfer payments have managed to pull most elderly individuals above this level, but often by only a few hundred dollars. Thus many elderly people—particularly women—are living their lives in near-poverty conditions.

conditions among the different segments of the elderly population in the United States.

Although the overall poverty rate among older Americans is below the national average, some segments of the elderly population have been less fortunate. For instance, almost 34 percent of elderly African Americans live in poverty. For elderly Hispanic Americans, the figure is around 21 percent. Poverty among elderly whites, on the other hand, is approximately 10 percent. Women are harder hit by poverty than are men. About 16 percent of women aged 65 and older are poor, compared to approximately 8 percent of elderly

SECTION 2 REVIEW

DEFINE ageism, baby-boom generation, Medicare

IDENTIFY American Association of Retired Persons (AARP)

1. **Understanding Ideas** **(a)** What is one of the ways in which ageism is evidenced in industrial societies? **(b)** How is ageism reinforced in American society?

2. **Identifying Trends** **(a)** Summarize the population trends that are occurring in the United States and the world. **(b)** What two factors are leading to the graying of America?

3. **Interpreting Ideas** Why are some people expressing fears about the future of the Social Security system in the United States?

4. **Analyzing Ideas** **(a)** Why do some critics of the Social Security system claim that government transfer payments have made America's elderly financially secure? **(b)** Why does this view lack support when particular groups within the elderly population are examined?

3 HEALTH

In a 1991 nationwide Gallup poll, the majority of respondents expressed the view that medical costs in the United States are excessive and the quality of health care is low. In fact, health care in the United States has become such a major concern that in 1993, President Bill Clinton called for a complete overhaul of the nation's health-care system. To understand why such an undertaking is necessary, we must examine the state of health care in the United States.

Health Care in the United States

Two major issues are at the center of concern over health care in the United States. The first issue involves the cost of health care. The second issue involves access to such care.

The Cost of Health Care. The United States spends more money on health care than any other nation in the world. In 1992, health-care expenditures in the United States reached $838 billion, an increase of 12 percent over the previous year. Everything from the cost of a stay in the hospital to health-insurance premiums has increased dramatically in recent years. In 1980, for example, Americans paid approximately $73 billion in health-insurance premiums. By 1990, this figure had increased to almost $217 billion. Similarly, Medicare payments increased from $37 billion in 1980 to over $111 billion in 1990. Group insurance plans also have been hard hit. In 1991, for example, American companies paid an average of $3,605 per worker for health benefits, an increase of 12 percent over 1990.

Many factors are contributing to the rise in health-care costs. At the top of the list is hospital care, which accounts for nearly 40 percent of all medical expenditures. In recent years, hospitals have been attempting to contain costs through shorter hospital stays and increased treatment on

Long-term health care is one of the most serious financial burdens faced by the elderly and their families. The average cost of nursing-home care in the United States is approximately $30,000 a year, an amount well beyond the means of many families. Medicaid funds paid for over 45 percent of the total $53.1 billion spent on nursing-home care in 1990.

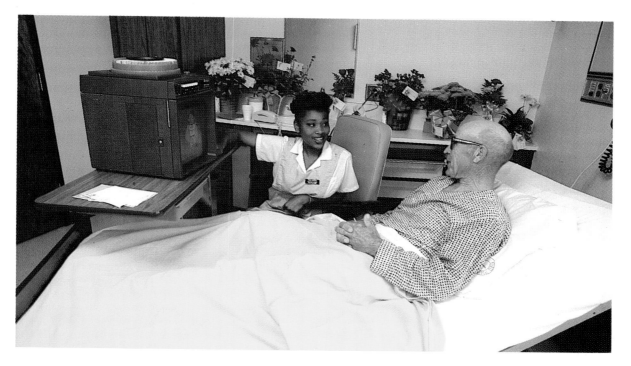

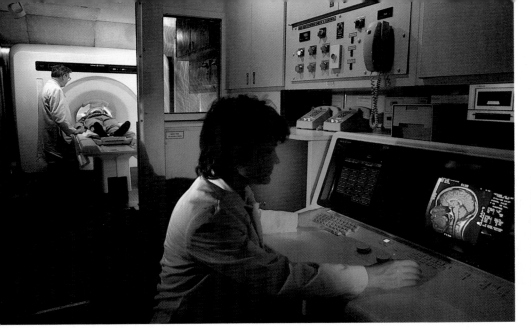

The use of such sophisticated diagnostic tests as magnetic resonance imaging and computerized axial tomography (CAT scans) has helped to increase the costs of medical care in the United States.

an outpatient basis. Even with these efforts, however, hospital care cost the nation $256 billion in 1990.

Another reason for the rise in health-care costs in the United States is the nation's rapidly expanding elderly population. The elderly account for a larger proportion of government health-care expenditures than any other segment of society. Health-care costs also have risen due to increased numbers of crime, drug, and accident victims who require medical services.

Health-care costs also have been affected by advances in medical technology. Doctors now have at their disposal more than 1,000 diagnostic tests, ranging from simple blood tests to high-technology techniques. Some of these tests, such as magnetic resonance imaging (MRI) and computerized axial tomography (CAT) scanning, are very expensive to administer. Nevertheless, many doctors rely heavily on such testing in their efforts to provide the best health care possible.

Fears of malpractice lawsuits also are playing a part in the increased use of expensive diagnostic techniques. Doctors—particularly those in high-risk specialty areas—often order batteries of tests simply as a precaution against possible lawsuits. As a result, many of the diagnostic tests involved in "defensive medicine," as it is called, are unnecessary. Estimates indicate that defensive medicine may cost Americans as much as $100 billion a year.

Escalating medical costs affect all sectors of society. Nearly half of the nation's annual medical expenditures are paid for by the government. Rising medical costs mean a bigger chunk out of the federal budget. For businesses, higher medical costs mean that they must either accept lower profits or raise prices. When businesses raise prices, they run the risk of becoming less competitive. American consumers, however, may be the biggest losers. Approximately 25 percent of annual health-care expenditures come directly out of the pockets of consumers. The burden of these expenditures is evident in the fact that nearly half of all personal bankruptcies in the United States are brought on by devastating medical bills.

Access to Health Care. In 1980, a government task force predicted that by the year 2000, there would be a surplus of 150,000 physicians in the United States. This is not particularly surprising given the fact that the United States has more physicians per capita than any other industrialized nation in the world. What is surprising, however, is that access to health care is a problem for many Americans in spite of this growing surplus. One of the major factors affecting access to health care is the distribution of physicians, both geographically and within the medical profession.

Geographically, physicians tend to concentrate in more wealthy urban and suburban areas. In such areas, a ratio of one physician for every 500 people is the norm. In poor inner-city and rural areas, on the other hand, the ratio is closer to one physician for every 4,000 people.

Professionally, physicians tend to concentrate in specialty fields such as cardiology, internal medicine, obstetrics, and psychiatry. It is among specialists, not general practitioners, that surpluses are developing. Of the approximately 615,000 government and private physicians in the United States, only about 70,000 are in general practice. Consequently, even people in relatively wealthy areas often have difficulty securing the services of a general practitioner. This is partially due to the fact that general practitioners earn less money than do specialists. For example, the average yearly income for obstetricians is $221,800. General practitioners, on the other hand, earn about $111,500 a year.

The Politics of Health

An aging population and rising medical costs have made health an important political issue in the United States. Among the issues that have been debated in recent years are the need for a national health-care system, the rights of people with disabilities, and the treatment of AIDS.

National Health Care. The United States is one of the few industrialized nations in which health care is not financed by the government. In many industrialized nations, the government actually owns and operates the health-care system. Medical care is provided free or nearly free of charge to all citizens, regardless of their level of income. In Great Britain, for example, all citizens have access to the National Health Service (NHS). Hospitals in the NHS system are controlled and funded by the government, and NHS physicians are government employees. People in Great Britain also are free to seek health care from private physicians and from private hospitals.

The government, however, will not assist people with the costs for such services.

In other industrialized nations, health care is financed by the government through national health insurance. Under such a system, the government pays for health services, but physicians are not government employees. Canada, for example, operates a national health-insurance system. Participation in Canada's system is voluntary, both for physicians and for patients. A recent Gallup poll found Canadians to be very satisfied with health care in their nation.

Although most Americans oppose government control of the health-care system, they do favor some form of national health insurance. Nevertheless, national health-insurance legislation has been consistently defeated in Congress for decades. Many sociologists point to strong lobbying efforts by the American Medical Association (AMA) as the single most important reason for failure of the legislation. The AMA strongly opposes government intervention in private health care. At the same time, private health insurance has become so costly that more than 36 million Americans currently are uninsured.

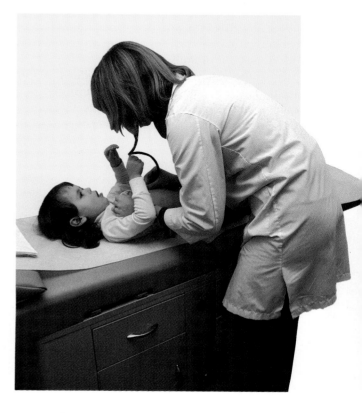

The National Health Service (NHS), which was established in Great Britain in 1948, was the first national health-care program in the West. Although the NHS provides health service to the entire British population, citizens are free to seek private medical care.

Americans with Disabilities. There are 43 million people with disabilities in the United States. Counted among the nation's disabled population are people with physical disabilities, serious health impairments, mental retardation, mental illness, and visual, hearing, or speech impairments. The table on page 279 shows the distribution of the major disabling conditions.

In addition to dealing with their health problems, Americans with disabilities have had to deal with the social consequences of having a disability. Among the most significant of these consequences is the difficulty in finding meaningful employment. Although the majority of Americans with disabilities would like to work, most are unemployed. As a result, the poverty rate among disabled adults is almost three times the rate among able-bodied adults.

Disability-rights activists have struggled for decades to bring about legislation aimed at helping people with disabilities gain meaningful employment, independence, and the civil rights afforded to other groups in society. And, over the years, progress has been made. For instance, the Education for All Handicapped Children Act of 1975 guaranteed children with disabilities a public education geared toward their needs and abilities. In 1988, the Fair Housing Act Amendments added persons with disabilities as a group protected from discrimination in housing.

It is the Americans with Disabilities Act of 1990, though, that will provide the most sweeping changes in the lives of disabled people. Containing various provisions that go into effect over a period of several years, the ADA addresses four main areas: employment, public services, public accommodation, and telecommunications.

In employment, the ADA makes it illegal to discriminate against people with disabilities in regard to job application procedures, hiring, advancement, and employee compensation. In addition, the ADA requires companies to provide job training and aids such as readers or interpreters, if these steps will improve job opportunities and not bring undue hardship to the company.

The ADA also makes it illegal to deny Americans with disabilities the benefit of public services, programs, or activities, including transportation facilities. This provision means that all new public buses and trains must be made accessible to disabled citizens.

The ADA also requires changes in public accommodations. Hotels, restaurants, theaters, and other businesses that serve the public must install ramps, widen doorways, and make other changes to provide access to people with disabilities.

Advanced technologies such as voice-activated computers allow people with even severe disabilities to participate in the labor force. For such technologies to be of use, however, disabled people must have regular access to public transportation.

Percentage Distribution of Major Disabling Conditions

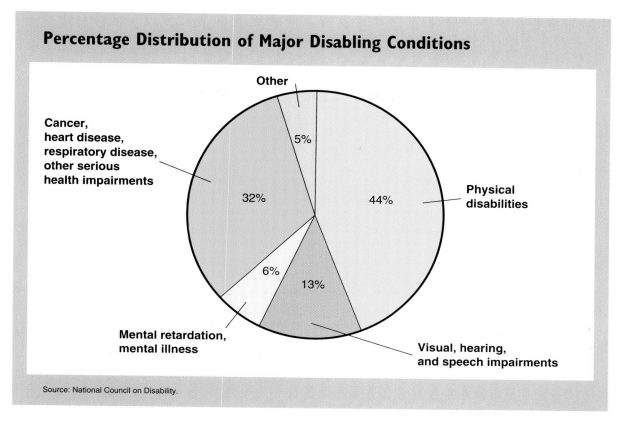

Other — 5%

Cancer, heart disease, respiratory disease, other serious health impairments — 32%

Physical disabilities — 44%

Mental retardation, mental illness — 6%

Visual, hearing, and speech impairments — 13%

Source: National Council on Disability.

The ADA's telecommunications provision requires that interstate and intrastate telecommunication services be made available to all hearing-impaired and speech-impaired individuals. These services must be available 24 hours a day.

Although the ADA is certain to improve the quality of life for disabled Americans, it is not without controversy. Critics charge that the changes required by the law are vague and confusing, making compliance difficult. Critics also worry that the costs involved in making these changes will force some businesses to close or to pass their costs on to consumers. Despite these criticisms, the Americans with Disabilities Act is a milestone in the long struggle to achieve equal rights for all Americans.

The Victims of AIDS. When the first few cases of a strange new ailment were reported in the United States in 1981, no one imagined the potential impact on society. In just a decade, however, the ailment has developed into the most serious public-health crisis of modern times.

Acquired immune deficiency syndrome (AIDS) is a fatal disease believed to be caused by a virus that attacks a person's immune system, leaving the person vulnerable to a host of deadly infections. The number of AIDS victims has grown from a few hundred in 1981 to over 240,000 in 1992. And it is estimated that another 1 million to 2 million Americans are infected with HIV, the virus believed to cause AIDS. Although these people do not have AIDS, they are at high risk of developing it.

Original estimates suggested that from 20 percent to 30 percent of those testing positive for HIV would develop the disease within five years. Researchers now believe, however, that virtually all people who test positive for HIV eventually will develop AIDS if a cure is not found. This has led researchers to predict that by 1996, there will be at least 1 million confirmed cases of AIDS in the United States. Moreover, by the year 2000, maternal deaths from AIDS will orphan an estimated 80,000 American children and adolescents.

AIDS, which is transmitted through sexual contact, contaminated blood and tissue, and the use of contaminated needles, does not threaten every segment of society equally. The groups at highest risk of acquiring AIDS are homosexual or bisexual men, intravenous drug abusers, persons receiving blood transfusions, the sexual partners of high-risk persons, and the babies of high-risk mothers. There is no evidence that AIDS is transmitted through casual contact. The table on this page shows the distribution of AIDS sufferers by risk group.

As the table indicates, homosexual and bisexual males account for the largest percentage of AIDS

Percentage Distribution of AIDS Cases by Transmission Category

Category	White	African American	Hispanic American	Other/ Unknown	Total
Adults/Adolescents					
Homosexual/bisexual male	75	35	40	70	58
Intravenous drug abuser (IVDA)	9	39	40	7	23
Homosexual male and IVDA	7	6	6	5	6
Hemophilia/coagulation disorder	1	0	0	2	1
Heterosexual cases	3	13	7	4	6
Transfusion, blood/components	3	1	1	5	2
Other/undetermined	3	6	5	7	4
Percent of all adult/adolescent cases	53	29	17	1	100
Children					
Hemophilia/coagulation disorder	15	1	3	13	5
Mother with/at risk of AIDS	64	94	88	64	86
Transfusion, blood/components	19	3	7	23	7
Undetermined	2	2	2	—	2
Percent of all child cases	21	54	24	1	100
Total (percent of all cases)	52	30	17	1	100

Source: Adapted from *HIV/AIDS Surveillance Report*, Centers for Disease Control, October 1992, p. 9.

The Names Project Quilt was begun in 1985 to preserve the memory of those Americans who have lost their lives to AIDS. The 6-by-3-foot panels that make up the quilt contain the names of AIDS victims and are contributed by the victims' friends and family members. Shown here in Washington, D.C., in 1992, the quilt now includes over 20,000 panels and covers an area of 15 acres.

sufferers (58 percent). The next largest category is that of intravenous drug abusers (nearly 30 percent). The number of new AIDS cases among homosexual and bisexual men has dropped in recent years, however, while the number of new cases among intravenous drug abusers has increased dramatically. An increase in AIDS cases also has been seen among the heterosexual population. In fact, AIDS is spreading faster among heterosexuals than among any other group, although these cases still make up only a small percentage of all reported cases.

Many AIDS activists claim that the United States government has not responded adequately to the AIDS crisis. Regardless of the truth in critics' claims, the government is taking steps to combat this deadly disease. In 1992, for example, the federal government allocated $1.8 billion to the Public Health Service for HIV/AIDS. The

bulk of this money goes to the National Institutes of Health for research purposes. Other recipients of HIV/AIDS funding are the Food and Drug Administration, Health and Human Services, the Indian Health Service, and the Centers for Disease Control and Prevention.

In addition to providing funds for HIV/AIDS research, the government has sponsored educational programs to teach people about the risk of AIDS. In 1988, for example, the government mailed an eight-page booklet, *Understanding AIDS,* to 114 million American households to provide individuals with basic information on the disease. The National AIDS Information Clearinghouse, a service of the Centers for Disease Control, provides free educational publications, posters, and videotapes that deal with AIDS. In addition, an AIDS Hotline is available to answer questions from the public about HIV and AIDS.

Thousands of new health-care professionals will be needed by the year 2000 to care for the growing number of AIDS victims.

Schools and the media also have joined in the effort to teach people about the disease.

Although education may be the best means of stemming the spread of AIDS, it does not solve the policy problems that surround those people who already have the disease. Two of the most important public-policy debates center on the relationship between public health and individual rights and the question of who should bear the costs of AIDS treatment.

The issue of individual rights is at the core of the controversy over the legal rights of AIDS victims. Under the provisions of the 1990 Americans with Disabilities Act, people with AIDS receive the same protections afforded other disabled Americans. AIDS activists and many government officials argue that the inclusion of AIDS victims in the ADA was necessary to protect victims against discrimination. Without such protection, the fear of losing their jobs or homes would stop people from seeking voluntary AIDS tests. Opponents of the ADA's inclusion of AIDS victims argue that the law provides special rights for homosexuals and other high-risk groups while putting the general public at risk.

The financing of AIDS treatment is no less controversial. In 1988, the cost of caring for an AIDS patient through the course of the disease was $57,000. By 1992, that figure had climbed dramatically to $102,000. The Public Health Service estimates that total AIDS-related health-care costs ranged from $5 billion to $13 billion in 1992. Currently, **Medicaid**—the state and federally funded health-insurance program for people with little or no money—picks up about 45 percent of AIDS health-care costs. The remaining costs are paid by insurance companies and by the AIDS patients themselves.

It is the response of insurance companies that raises the most protest from AIDS activists. Insurance companies now do firmly stand by their obligation to pay the insurance claims of those people who are already insured. Most insurance companies argue, however, that they should not be required to unknowingly take on new policyholders who are at high risk of acquiring AIDS. These companies argue that insuring potential or actual AIDS victims runs up the cost of health insurance for all policyholders. Thus many commercial insurance companies screen new applicants for AIDS, either by asking them AIDS-related questions or by requiring blood tests.

Access to insurance is particularly important in the case of AIDS patients because the disease eventually robs people of the ability to work. As a result, many AIDS victims find themselves without employer-sponsored health insurance at the very time they need it most. If they are unable to obtain private health insurance, these people cannot meet their health-care expenses. When this occurs, the government must assume the costs of medical care. In recognition of this fact, several states have taken legal action to prevent insurance companies from screening for AIDS.

Health and Social Status

In the United States, as in most nations, health is directly related to social status. Because of crowded and unsanitary living conditions, inadequate diets, and the absence of regular medical care, the poor are much more likely than wealthier segments of society to experience serious health problems. The following statistics give some idea of the seriousness of the problem.

- Children born to poor families are 50 percent more likely to die within the first year of life than children born to wealthier families.
- People with family incomes under $10,000 a year are absent from school or work almost three times as many days as people with annual family incomes of $35,000 or more.
- Tuberculosis (TB), once a leading cause of death in the United States, has begun to reappear in poor urban neighborhoods. Complicating the situation are new strains of TB that are resistant to drug therapy.
- Only 28 percent of people with family incomes under $14,000 characterize their health as excellent, compared to 52 percent of people with family incomes over $50,000 a year.

The poor also suffer disproportionately from diseases such as influenza, pneumonia, tuberculosis, hypertension, alcoholism, and heart disease. Thus it is not surprising that the poor have a much lower life expectancy than the wealthier segments of society.

SECTION 3 REVIEW

DEFINE   acquired immune deficiency syndrome (AIDS), Medicaid

IDENTIFY   National Health Service

1. **Summarizing Ideas**   Describe the two major issues that are at the center of concern over health care in the United States.

2. **Composing Essays**   Write essays on each of the following topics: **(a)** the need for a national health-care system, **(b)** the provisions of the Americans with Disabilities Act, and **(c)** policy issues surrounding AIDS and AIDS victims.

3. **Seeing Relationships**   In what way is health related to social status in the United States? Provide examples.

CHAPTER 11   SUMMARY

The specific behaviors and attitudes that a society establishes for men and women are called gender roles. Gender roles result from the division of labor that assigns different tasks to men and women. Individuals learn proper gender behavior through the socialization process.

Many social scientists are interested in studying gender inequality. One such social scientist is anthropologist Ernestine Friedl. Friedl claims that power in society is based on who controls the distribution of scarce resources. Since men control the distribution of scarce resources, they hold the greatest degree of power.

Conflict theorists are in basic agreement with Friedl's position. According to conflict theorists, gender roles in industrial society are a reflection of male dominance. Through the control of economic and political structures, men have established laws and customs that protect their dominant position by blocking women's access to power. Sexism—the belief that one sex is by na-

ture superior to the other—is at the heart of gender-based discrimination.

The elderly in industrial societies also suffer from discrimination in the form of ageism. Ageism is the belief that one age category is by nature superior to another age category. Although Social Security benefits and other government transfer payments have reduced the level of poverty among the elderly, some segments of the elderly population still suffer from high rates of poverty.

In addition to gender and age, health also plays a role in determining equality within industrial societies. As health-care costs climb and access to medical care declines in rural and inner-city areas, Americans increasingly are expressing concern over the state of the nation's health care. Consequently, health has become an important political issue. Among the topics discussed in recent years are the need for a national health-care system, the rights of disabled Americans, and policy issues involving the treatment of AIDS.

THINKING ABOUT SOCIOLOGY: Analyzing Sociological Viewpoints

A Better Life—Not a Longer One

What do we owe each other as we grow old? I think we would be justified in saying that beyond a certain age we will simply not provide expensive, life-extending care. We will always relieve your pain and suffering, but we will not give you organ transplantations, we will not give you access to open-heart surgery, or even possibly access to an intensive-care unit. We will really say: "Look, we have already done justice to you in our society by getting you this far. And we cannot be asked to indefinitely extend your life."

We've got a whole range of social problems that we are not adequately addressing—inadequacies in our public-school system, in our transportation system, in our urban ghettos, for example. So we need to stand back and ask, "What's really good for our society?"

The provision of health care for the elderly is a kind of endless frontier. Because the body always decays, there will always be more things to do. . . . We can't afford indefinitely to go on our present course. Despite well over a decade now of efforts at cost containment, the medicare program is increasing at an inflationary rate of approximately 18 percent a year. One of the major reasons is the constant development of new technologies. Physicians are trained to use technologies, and always when in doubt to extend life as vigorously as possible. There are some projections that would show us in the next 20 to 30 years hitting close to 45 percent of the gross national product going into health care for the elderly. I think as a practical matter the elderly have to recognize that if younger age groups begin seeing them as a group that is just intent upon gobbling up as much money as it can for its own welfare, they're bound to resent it.

Daniel Callahan

In the above excerpt from "A Better Life—Not a Longer One," which originally appeared in the February 22, 1988, issue of *U.S. News & World Report,* social philosopher Daniel Callahan explores the question of whether steps should be taken to extend the lives of the elderly in the case of serious illness. He concludes that the answer is no. He bases his response on the belief that people have the right to expect only so much from the government, given the limited resources available.

Not all sociologists would agree with Callahan. In the second excerpt, "Spare the Old, Save the Young," which appeared in the June 11, 1988, issue of *The Nation,* sociologist Amitai Etzioni presents a very different view. Which view one favors depends on a number of factors, including the attitudes one holds toward the elderly and toward the proper role of the government. The student of sociology must be able to analyze sociological viewpoints by separating fact from opinion and by checking for bias.

How to Analyze Sociological Viewpoints
To analyze sociological viewpoints, follow these steps.

1. **Read the material carefully.** Note the author's main ideas. Identify supporting details that back up the main ideas.

2. **Ask yourself questions.** Determine what people or issues are involved. If dealing with a situation or event, note whether the author explains how, where, or why the situation or event occurred.

3. **Weigh the evidence.** Distinguish between fact and opinion in the viewpoint. In sociology, a fact is a statement about a phenomenon that is based on the observations or experiences of a large number of people. Opinions are individually held beliefs. They may or may not be based on observation and experience. While sociological viewpoints include beliefs

about the nature of the social world, they must be backed up by facts if they are to be considered valid.

4. Search for bias or faulty reasoning. Bias refers to the general outlook or point of view of the writer or speaker. People present biased views when they use facts selectively. Be alert to the possibility of other viewpoints. Also be alert to faulty logic. Does the evidence support the author's conclusion?

5. Come to your own conclusion. Evaluate the argument by drawing a conclusion of your own or by forming a generalization.

Applying the Skill

In the excerpt on page 284, Daniel Callahan holds a particular bias concerning the rights of the elderly and the consequences of prolonging their lives. Callahan's argument assumes that extending health care to the elderly robs not only the younger generations but also future generations of a chance at a satisfactory life.

In addition to a bias against the elderly, Callahan fails to consider whether the government could take alternate actions that would provide for the needs of the younger generations while caring for the elderly. Before accepting Callahan's argument, one must carefully consider the biases contained in the argument and possible alternative courses of action.

Spare the Old, Save the Young

In order to free up economic resources for the young, [social philosopher Daniel] Callahan offers the older generation a deal: Trade quantity for quality; the elderly should not be given life-*extending* services but better years while alive. Instead of relentless attempts to push death to an older age, Callahan would stop all development of life-extending technologies and prohibit the use of ones at hand for those who outlive their "natural" life span, say, the age of 75. At the same

time, the old would be granted more palliative medicines (e.g., pain killers) and more nursing-home and home-health care, to make their natural years more comfortable. . . .

It is instructive to look at the list of technologies he would withhold: mechanical ventilation, artificial resuscitation, antibiotics and artificial nutrition and hydration. Note that while several of these are used to maintain brain-dead bodies, they are also used for individuals who are temporarily incapacitated but able to recover fully; indeed, they are used to save young lives, say, after a car accident. But there is no way to stop the development of such new technologies and the improvement of existing ones without depriving the young of benefit as well. . . .

The advocates of changing the intergenerational allocation of resources favor rationing health care for the elderly but nothing else. This is a major intellectual weakness in their argument. There are other major targets to consider within health care, as well as other areas, which seem, at least by some criteria, much more inviting than terminating care to those above a certain age. Within the medical sector, for example, why not stop all interventions for which there is no hard evidence that they are beneficial? Say, public financing of psychotherapy and coronary bypass operations? Why not take the $2 billion or so from plastic surgery dedicated to face lifts, reducing the behinds and the like? Or require that all burials be done by low-cost cremations rather than using high cost coffins? . . . If we cannot stop people from blowing $25 billion per year on cigarettes and convince them to use the money to serve the young, shouldn't we at least cut out public subsidies to tobacco growers before we save funds by denying antibiotics to old people?

Amitai Etzioni

Practicing the Skill

Read the above excerpt and then write an evaluation of Etzioni's position using the steps outlined under the heading "How to Analyze Sociological Viewpoints."

Reviewing Sociological Terms

On a separate sheet of paper, supply the term that correctly completes each sentence.

1. _____ is the belief that one sex is by nature superior to the other.

2. _____ is the government-sponsored insurance plan for the elderly and the disabled.

3. Individuals born between 1946 and 1964 are known as the _____ _____ _____.

4. _____ _____ are the specific behaviors and attitudes that a society establishes for men and women.

5. _____ is the belief that one age category is by nature superior to another age category.

Thinking Critically about Sociology

1. *Comparing Ideas*   According to Ernestine Friedl, in what ways are the forces that determine the distribution of power between the sexes the same in industrial societies as they are in hunting and gathering societies?

2. *Interpreting Ideas*   How will the provisions of the Americans with Disabilities Act (ADA) help disabled Americans find and keep meaningful employment?

3. *Applying Ideas*   Observe at least 10 television commercials that use one or more elderly characters. What images of the elderly are reflected in these commercials?

4. *Seeing Relationships*   *(a)* What factors are contributing to the rise in health-care costs in the United States? *(b)* How do rising health-care costs affect all segments of society?

5. *Understanding Ideas*   *(a)* What is AIDS, how is it transmitted, and what groups are at highest risk of acquiring the disease? *(b)* What steps are being taken by the government to halt the spread of AIDS? *(c)* In what way have individual versus group rights become an issue in the debate over AIDS?

6. *Solving Problems*   What can American teenagers do to help stop discrimination against women, the elderly, disabled Americans, and the victims of AIDS?

7. *Drawing Conclusions*   Why are poor people more likely than wealthier people to experience serious health problems?

8. *Analyzing Ideas*   Why would passage of the Equal Rights Amendment not automatically solve the problems of gender inequality?

Exercising Sociological Skills

1. *Evaluating Ideas*   Reread the Applying Sociology feature on pages 266–267. Next, examine the statistics on male and female employment presented in the chart on page 157. Do these statistics tend to support or disprove the findings of Horner's study? Explain.

2. *Summarizing Ideas*   Reread the Case Study on page 263. Then write a brief summary of women's experiences in the armed services.

3. *Analyzing Viewpoints*   Conduct library research to locate two articles that present opposing viewpoints on the issue of homosexuals in the military. Using the skills presented in the Developing Sociological Imagination feature on pages 284–285, analyze the viewpoints presented in the articles.

Extending Sociological Imagination

1. Choose a television program that has a female lead and a male lead. Compile lists of the gender behaviors exhibited by each of the two lead characters, one list for each character. If you were from another country, what conclusions concerning proper gender behavior might you draw from analyzing the lists?

2. Write an imaginative essay describing what your life will be like when you retire.

3. Prepare a brief report on new technologies that have been developed to help disabled people.

INTERPRETING PRIMARY SOURCES

American Business: Confronting the Americans with Disabilities Act

The Americans with Disabilities Act (ADA) was passed by Congress in order to help disabled citizens achieve full participation in American society. Many businesses, however, are unsure about what the new law requires them to do and how they can best comply.

In the following excerpt from the article "Away with Barriers," which appeared in the July 20, 1992, issue of *U.S. News & World Report*, Mary Lord examines some of the questions business owners have about the ADA and how businesses can easily and economically comply with the law. While reading the excerpt, consider why a commonsense approach to meeting the requirements of the ADA will help American businesses keep down their costs.

> While few employers quarrel with the ADA's aim of integrating some 43 million disabled Americans into the workplace, many are uncertain about their precise obligations in achieving it. Can companies be sued if they fail to install elevators or undertake other costly renovations? What if reassigning a disabled employee violates union seniority rules? . . .
>
> ADA experts argue that employers actually have great flexibility because of the statute's ambiguities. "I tell businesses they've got to use common sense," says Liz Savage, a sight-impaired attorney and training director for the Disability Rights Education and Defense Fund in Washington, D.C. "If I sued every hotel that didn't have a large-print phone list in the room, I'd be spending all my time in litigation. Life is tough enough."
>
> Contrary to their worst fears, business owners find that compliance can prove cheap and easy. . . . Instead of splurging on Braille menus, which fewer than 20 percent of all sight-impaired Americans can read, restaurants can have a waiter read the menu aloud. Cup dispensers provide an inexpensive alternative to lowering drinking fountains for wheelchair-bound employees, while simply insulating exposed hot-water pipes under bathroom sinks allows paraplegics to wash up without scalding their legs. Indeed, according to a survey by the Job Accommodation Network, one of several federally funded ADA clearinghouses, 31 percent of all modifications cost nothing and two thirds can be done for under $500. . . .
>
> For all the brouhaha over physical modifications, it is the psychological adjustments required under the ADA—from application procedures to employment practices—that could prove the bigger legal challenge. For instance, simply giving a telephone number to call in a want ad may discriminate against individuals with hearing or speech impairments; ADA experts advise giving applicants the option to write for interviews. Du Pont, considered one of the country's most sensitive employers, changed its rules to allow new hires to use any photo identification instead of a driver's license, since that would exclude people with sight impairments, cerebral palsy or a host of other disabilities. . . .
>
> Business owners may have a thorny time trying to determine whether a job applicant's health can keep him from performing essential tasks. The ADA forbids employers from asking about a job applicant's disabilities—even if they are germane [relevant] to the job. Thus, a warehouse operator would be on safer legal ground to inquire if a prospective stevedore can lift 100 pounds rather than quizzing him on back problems. Companies also cannot refuse to hire an individual for fear his disability, or a family member's, will boost the cost of the firm's health insurance. However, an employer need not bolster that individual's benefits package or make special allowances for someone caring for a sick spouse. Ultimately, the courts will have to settle many of the compliance questions now troubling employers.

Source Review

1. What do survey results show regarding the costs of the modifications required by the ADA?

2. How can employers ensure that they do not discriminate against disabled job applicants?

ACROSS SPACE AND TIME

The World War II Internment of Japanese Americans

On December 7, 1941, the Japanese bombed Pearl Harbor, signaling the entrance of the United States into World War II. At the time, there were more than 284,000 Japanese Americans and resident aliens of Japanese ancestry living on the United States mainland and in Hawaii. Following the bombing, these people became the unfortunate victims of a wave of racial prejudice.

In an attempt to quiet racial fears in California, President Franklin D. Roosevelt signed Executive Order 9066 on February 19, 1942. The order authorized the forced removal of almost 120,000 Japanese Americans from the West Coast to internment camps located in the interior of the United States. Although it was a startling example of hostility toward Japanese Americans, the order actually followed decades of strained race relations.

Originally recruited as a source of cheap agricultural labor in California, the Japanese immigrants prospered and soon owned and controlled large areas of land. California growers resented this competition and sought ways to stop the growth of Japanese farms. In 1913, the California State legislature passed the Alien Land Law, which restricted land ownership by foreigners. Other legislative acts enacted over the years restricted Japanese immigration and denied the *Issei* (EE say), or immigrant generation, citizenship in the United States.

Barred from the land, many Issei moved to the cities, where they established small businesses such as restaurants, laundries, barbershops, and dry goods stores. Whites became increasingly hostile toward the success of the Japanese businesses and attempted to halt their growth through the use of boycotts. The Japanese were highly organized, however, and countered these attempts with their own boycotts of white-owned businesses.

Although they faced continuing prejudice and discrimination, the Japanese immigrants worked hard to make homes for themselves and their families in their new land. Japanese children born in the United States, called the *Nisei* (NEE say), or second-generation Japanese Americans, were automatically granted the right to citizenship. As it became increasingly difficult for the *Issei* to own land, many of the *Issei* placed their land holdings in their children's names. The success of the Japanese Americans in the United States fueled the hostilities felt by whites fearful of the loss of jobs to foreigners.

When World War II broke out, the nation's hostility toward Japanese Americans turned to hysteria. In many communities, Americans of Japanese ancestry were faced with curfews and arrests. The fear among many whites was that the Japanese Americans would place their loyalties with Japan during the war and, in so doing, pose a threat to the safety of the United States. This unfounded fear branded all Japanese Americans as potential spies and traitors.

The signing of Executive Order 9066 by President Roosevelt in 1942 was fueled by the fear of a nation. More than two-thirds of the 120,000 Japanese Americans uprooted from the West Coast were second- and third-generation United States citizens. Branded as disloyal without trial or due process of law, the Japanese Americans were rounded up and moved to 10 internment camps located in barren parts of the country. These people were stripped of all legal rights and lost millions of dollars worth of income and property. Most spent an average of two-and-a-half years behind barbed wire.

Life in the camps was harsh. Dormitory-style living disrupted authority patterns and the privacy of family life. Food and medical care often were in short supply. The humiliation of internment is felt even today by many survivors and their children. In recent years, however, the United States government has begun to issue apologies and payments to the people whose lives were shaken by the wartime internment program.

UNIT 3 REVIEW

Reviewing Sociological Ideas

1. **(a)** What is social stratification? **(b)** How do open and closed systems of stratification differ?

2. **(a)** What is exogamy? **(b)** What is endogamy? **(c)** How do these practices relate to the marriage norms found in caste systems?

3. **(a)** What is social mobility? **(b)** Describe the structural causes of downward social mobility.

4. **(a)** What is ethnicity? **(b)** How does an ethnic group differ from a race? **(c)** What are the supposed characteristics of each of the three racial groups in the best-known racial classification system?

5. **(a)** What is discrimination and what two forms can it take? **(b)** What is prejudice and what function does it serve for the dominant group in society? **(c)** Describe three of the sources of prejudice and discrimination recognized by sociologists.

6. **(a)** What are gender roles? **(b)** How do gender roles come about in society?

7. **(a)** What is ageism? **(b)** How is the American Association of Retired Persons helping the elderly in the United States?

Synthesizing Sociological Ideas

1. **Analyzing Information** **(a)** What is poverty? **(b)** Present evidence to show that the poor are at a serious disadvantage in terms of life chances.

2. **Seeing Relationships** **(a)** How does the commonly accepted definition of social class differ from the Marxist definition of social class? **(b)** What social and economic conditions gave rise to the Marxist definition of class and how have changes in these conditions affected the current definition of social class used by sociologists? **(c)** What three techniques do sociologists use to rank people according to social class?

3. **Understanding Ideas** **(a)** Describe horizontal and vertical mobility. **(b)** Why is intergenerational mobility considered a special form of vertical mobility?

4. **Summarizing Ideas** **(a)** What is a minority group? **(b)** Briefly describe the social characteristics of the five principal minority groups in the United States.

5. **Debating Ideas** **(a)** What is sexism? **(b)** Provide evidence for or against the view that American women face gender inequality.

6. **Expressing Ideas** List and describe the six common patterns of minority group treatment.

7. **Using Evidence** **(a)** How are longer life expectancies contributing to the problems of the Social Security system and Medicare? **(b)** Provide information to show that Social Security has not made all groups of the elderly financially secure.

8. **Outlining Ideas** Prepare an outline detailing the major issues of concern in the debate over health care in the United States.

9. **Comprehending Ideas** **(a)** Define acquired immune deficiency syndrome. **(b)** How is AIDS transmitted? **(c)** What steps are being taken to stem the spread of AIDS?

Applying Sociological Imagination

1. According to Robert K. Merton, individuals can combine discriminatory and prejudicial attitudes in four ways. Write a short story in which the main character adopts one of the four attitudinal combinations in response to new next-door neighbors.

2. Conduct library research and prepare a research report on one of the following topics: **(a)** the struggle of disabled citizens to achieve equal rights in the United States; **(b)** changes in the treatment of the mentally retarded over the past 100 years.

The great institutions are the outcome of that
organization which human thought naturally takes on
when it is directed for age after age upon a particular
subject, and so gradually crystallizes in definite forms—
enduring sentiments, beliefs, customs, and symbols.

CHARLES HORTON COOLEY

SOCIAL INSTITUTIONS

The Family

The Family in Cross-Cultural Perspective

Family Systems
Marriage and Kinship Patterns
The Functions of the Family

The American Family

Courtship and Marriage
Family Disruption
Trends in American Family Life

Chapter Focus

Chapter 12 explores the family as a social institution. The chapter opens with a discussion of the basic characteristics of the family from a cross-cultural perspective. Attention then is turned to the American family. First, the American family life cycle is examined. Next, the issues of divorce and family violence are explored. The chapter closes with a discussion of current trends in American family life.

As you study the chapter, look for the answers to the following questions:

1. How do norms influence the ways in which marriage patterns around the world are organized?
2. Which basic societal needs does the family institution satisfy?
3. In what ways can family life be disruptive for family members?
4. What are some of the trends in American family life currently being examined by sociologists?

KEY TERMS

The following terms, while not the only terms emphasized in the chapter, are basic to your understanding of sociology. Determine the meaning of each term, either by using the Glossary or by watching for context clues as you read the chapter.

nuclear family	marriage	bilateral descent
extended family	monogamy	homogamy
kinship	polygamy	voluntary childlessness

INTRODUCTION

If a society is to survive over time, certain basic needs must be met. For instance, new members must be added to the population to replace those members who have died or moved away. People must be clothed, sheltered, and fed. Goods and services must be produced and made available to those who need and desire them. The young must be educated and socialized into society. The elderly and the sick must receive care. Order must be maintained and power must be distributed among the members of society. Societies satisfy these needs through social institutions.

As we noted in Chapter 4, a **social institution** is a system of statuses, roles, values, and norms that is organized to satisfy one or more of the basic societal needs. Sociologists traditionally have recognized five major social institutions: family, economy, politics, education, and religion. In recent years, sociologists have noted the development of several new social institutions in industrialized societies. Two of these emerging social institutions are science and sport. We will examine each of these seven social institutions in this unit, beginning with the family.

1 THE FAMILY IN CROSS-CULTURAL PERSPECTIVE

Over the past few decades, we have seen the traditional family—with the father as the sole bread-winner and the mother as the stay-at-home caretaker of the children—become the exception rather than the rule in the United States. Working women, divorce, one-parent families, and stepfamilies now are common features of American family life.

The following statistics tell the story of the changing nature of the family in the United States:

- Approximately 58 percent of all married women are employed in the labor force. In 1950, only 25 percent of married women worked outside the home.
- The United States has the highest divorce rate of any nation in the world. In 1992 alone, nearly 1,200,000 marriages in the United States ended in divorce.

- Over 16 million children—fully 25 percent of all children under the age of 18—live with one parent. Another 16 percent of today's children live in stepfamilies.

These statistics, and others like them, have led some people to predict the eventual collapse of the American family. Few social scientists, however, would agree that the future is that bleak. Undeniably, the family is undergoing a transition in the United States, as it is in other industrialized nations. In the course of that transition, many traditional American values are being severely tested. In the final analysis, though, the family as an institution is likely to survive. The fact that the family can exist in its varied forms points to its strength as an enduring social institution.

This belief in the ultimate survival of the American family rests on the fact that the family is a universal phenomenon. In all societies, no matter how small, the family serves as the basic social unit. The form that the family takes, however, varies from society to society and even within a single society over time. The American family, as we perceive it in its traditional form, is only one possible form the family may take. In this section, we will explore the variety of ways in which family life is organized around the world.

Family Systems

A **family** is a group of people who are related by marriage, blood, or adoption and who live together and share economic resources. When we think of families, we generally think of the nuclear family. A **nuclear family** consists of one or both parents and their children. The nuclear family is the family form most recognizable to Americans.

During his or her lifetime, a person normally is a member of two different, overlapping nuclear families. An individual's **family of orientation** is the nuclear family into which the person is born. This family is composed of the individual and his or her siblings (brothers and sisters) and parents. When an individual marries, a new family is formed. This nuclear family—called the **family of procreation**—consists of the individual, his or her spouse, and their children.

In many societies, the nuclear family is embedded in a larger family group. In these societies, the preferred family unit is the extended family. An **extended family** consists of three or more generations of a family sharing the same residence. An example of such a system is the Chinese family, which typically includes grandparents, parents, and their children all living under the same roof.

Nuclear families and extended families often are part of a much larger kinship system. **Kinship** refers to a network of people who are related by marriage, birth, or adoption. Kinship systems can be quite large. In fact, there are 191 possible categories of relatives in some kinship systems. In such systems, relatives can be grouped into three categories—primary, secondary, and tertiary—depending on their relationship to an individual.

An individual's closest relatives are called *primary relatives*. These are the members of an individual's families of orientation and procreation. The seven possible categories of primary relatives include mother, father, sister, brother, spouse, daughter, and son. An individual's next closest relatives are called *secondary relatives*. Secondary relatives are the primary relatives of an individual's primary relatives. Secondary relatives consist of 33 additional categories of people, including grandparents, grandchildren, in-laws, aunts, uncles, nephews, and nieces. When the primary relatives of an individual's secondary relatives are considered, another 151 categories of people are added to the kinship system. Individuals at this level are called *tertiary relatives*. Tertiary relatives

While the nuclear family tends to emphasize flexibility in role performance, behavior in the extended family is strongly tied to age and gender.

would include great-grandparents, great-grandchildren, great-aunts, great-uncles, and cousins. These 191 categories can translate literally into hundreds of relatives, since each category can be occupied by several people.

Marriage and Kinship Patterns

Some form of family organization exists in all societies. The exact nature of the family, however, varies from society to society and even within societies. Family organization is determined by how a society or group within a society answers four basic questions: (1) How many marriage partners may a person have? (2) Who will live with whom? (3) How will family membership be determined? (4) Who will make the decisions in the family?

Before examining the ways in which societies around the world answer these questions, it would be helpful to distinguish what is meant by marriage. The term **marriage** is reserved not for the married couple itself, but for the set of norms that specifies the ways in which family structure should be organized. This set of norms influences the way in which a society answers the questions of family organization.

Marriage Partners. There is no universal norm concerning the number of marriage partners an individual may have. In most industrialized nations, an individual is allowed to marry only one person at a time. The marriage of one man to one woman is called **monogamy.** Monogamy is the marital system most familiar to Americans. In the majority of preindustrial societies around the world, however, individuals are permitted to have multiple marriage partners. Marriage with multiple partners is called **polygamy.**

Polygamy can take either of two forms. The most common form of polygamy is polygyny. In **polygyny,** a man is permitted to marry more than one woman at a time. The practice of polygyny in preindustrial societies appears to be profitable when there are large areas of land available for cultivation. Men who have two or more wives gain additional workers for the land and produce more children. These factors add to the men's prestige and economic wealth.

A much rarer form of polygamy is polyandry. In **polyandry,** a woman is permitted to marry more than one man at a time. Polyandry, which is found primarily in a few societies in South Asia, appears to arise in response to extreme societal poverty and a shortage of women. The Toda of India, for example, practiced female infanticide—the killing of female babies. As a result, there were not enough women to provide monogamous partners for all of the men in the society. The Toda solved this shortage through polyandry. When a woman married a man, she became a wife to all of his brothers. This practice also served to keep the birthrate down, which is important in a poverty-stricken society that cannot afford to support a large population.

Although polygamy is the preferred marital system in the majority of preindustrial societies around the world, most people in polygamous societies take only one spouse. There are two reasons for this. First, it is very expensive to take more than one marriage partner. In all polygamous societies, individuals are expected to marry only

Because only the wealthiest men in polygamous societies can afford to support more than one wife, men with multiple wives tend to have high status.

the number of spouses that they can support. Few people can support two or more spouses and their children. Polygamy thus tends to be limited to the wealthy few in a society and serves to increase their status and prestige.

Second, most societies tend to produce roughly equal numbers of men and women. If a substantial number of people in a society took multiple spouses, there simply would not be enough eligible partners to enable everyone to marry. This situation would prove to be very disruptive to the functioning of the society.

Residential Patterns. Once individuals are married, they must decide where to live. Rules of residence vary from society to society. In some societies, the newly married couple is expected to live with or near the husband's parents. This residential pattern is called **patrilocality** (*patri* meaning "father," *locality* meaning "location"). Patrilocality is the rule of residence found most commonly around the world. In some societies, the couple is expected to live with or near the wife's parents. This pattern is called **matrilocality** (*matri* meaning "mother"). One residential pattern, called **bilocality** (*bi* meaning "two"), allows the newly married couple to choose whether they will live near the husband's parents or near the wife's parents. Patrilocal, matrilocal, and bilocal rules of residence encourage the development of extended family living.

In most industrial societies, however, the newly married couple is free to set up their residence apart from both sets of parents. This residential pattern is called **neolocality** (*neo* meaning "new"). Neolocal residence is most commonly associated with nuclear family living.

Descent Patterns. In some societies, people trace their kinship through the father's side of the family. In other societies, kinship is traced through the mother's side of the family. In still other societies, kinship is traced through both parents.

Societies that trace kinship through the father's family follow the rule of **patrilineal descent.** Patrilineal descent is common in preindustrial societies in which men produce the most valued resources. In a patrilineal society, property is passed from father to son. The pattern called **matrilineal descent**—the tracing of kinship

Although the Navaho are a matrilineal society, men tend to hold the power.

through the mother's family—is much less common around the world. In matrilineal descent, property is passed from mother to daughter.

Most industrial societies practice bilateral descent. In **bilateral descent,** kinship is traced through both parents and property can be inherited from either side of the family. This form of descent is the one most familiar to us, since it is the pattern practiced in the United States.

Rules for descent are important for the smooth operation of society because they establish who is eligible to inherit property from whom. The need to maintain lines of descent can, however, lead to some interesting practices. In a few patrilineal societies, for instance, a father can declare one of his daughters to be a "son" if he does not have male heirs. This "son" takes a bride, who then bears children by various men. These children are considered members of the "son's" kinship group.

The "marriage" between the two women is in name only, however. The women never live together. In fact, the "son" may already be married to a man from another village. The only purpose of the marriage is to produce children who will qualify as legitimate members of the "husband's" kinship group, thereby ensuring that the kinship group will continue.

Authority Patterns. In theory, there are three possible patterns of authority in families. A family system may be a **patriarchal system,** in which

In recent years, the United States and other industrialized nations around the world have been moving toward a more egalitarian system of family authority. As more and more women work outside of the home, their husbands increasingly are sharing in household and child-care responsibilities.

case the father holds most of the authority. It may be a **matriarchal system,** in which case the mother holds most of the authority. Or it may be an **egalitarian system,** meaning that authority is shared by both the mother and the father.

The vast majority of societies around the world are patriarchal. In fact, no true matriarchal societies currently exist, and it is likely that none have existed historically. Even in societies that practice matrilineal descent, true authority rests with the mother's brothers. And although many industrialized societies, such as the United States, are moving toward more egalitarian authority patterns, patriarchal authority still is the cultural norm.

The Functions of the Family

Sociologists who follow the functionalist perspective have long been interested in how families satisfy certain basic needs of society. Among the most important functions performed by the family are the regulation of sexual activity, reproduction, socialization, and the provision of economic and emotional security.

Regulation of Sexual Activity. All societies regulate the sexual activities of their members to some degree. At the very least, they enforce some type of incest taboo. An **incest taboo** is a norm forbidding sexual relations or marriage between certain relatives. The incest taboo is found universally, but which relatives are included in this taboo varies from society to society.

In the United States, for instance, a person cannot marry his or her parents, siblings, grandparents, aunts, uncles, nieces, or nephews. Twenty-one states, however, allow marriages between first cousins. Marriages between first cousins also are allowed among the patrilineal Yanomamö of Venezuela and Brazil. These marriages, however, are restricted to cross cousins—the children of an individual's paternal aunt or maternal uncle. Marriages between parallel cousins—the children of an individual's maternal aunt or paternal uncle—are considered incestuous.

The labeling of biologically related individuals as nonrelatives is common in patrilineal and matrilineal societies because ancestry is traced only through one side of the family. Among the Lakher of Southeast Asia, for example, individuals can marry their maternal half-siblings but not their paternal half-siblings. Because the Lakher are a patrilineal group, they do not consider their maternal half-siblings to be relatives.

Reproduction. As mentioned earlier, societies must replace members who die or move away. In every society, the family is the approved social unit for the performance of this function. Consequently, societies establish norms governing childbearing and child rearing. These norms determine such things as who is eligible to marry and to bear children, the number of children that is considered appropriate, and the rights and responsibilities of parents.

Socialization. Children must be taught the ways of the society into which they are born. The family is the first agent of socialization that most children encounter. It is within the family that most children first learn about the values and norms of society. Parents, siblings, and other relatives also tend to serve as the earliest role models for children.

Economic and Emotional Security. The family acts as the basic economic unit in society. In all societies, there is a division of labor based on sex. By this we mean that some tasks in the

It is within the family setting that children first learn how to interact with other people.

family will fall to males and some tasks will fall to females. All societies also have a division of labor based on age. Tasks are divided within the family depending on the ages of the family members. Through this division of labor, the family ensures that its members are fed, clothed, and housed.

Although all societies have a division of labor within the family, specific roles vary from society to society. For example, in some societies that rely

The Granger Collection, New York

Families in preindustrial America largely were self-contained, self-sufficient units. The economic, religious, and educational functions now shared by the family with other institutions once were fulfilled solely within the family setting.

on horticulture—simple gardening—for food production, plants are tended by the men. In other such societies, this task is assigned to women. The division of labor also varies among industrialized nations. In Russia, for instance, most physicians and sanitation workers are women. In the United States, on the other hand, these jobs more often are held by men.

In addition to economic support, the family also provides emotional support for its members. As the basic and most intimate primary group in society, the family is expected to guide the individual's psychological development and to provide family members with a loving and caring environment. In practice, of course, not all families provide such an environment.

In industrialized societies, many of the traditional functions of the family have been taken over in part by other social institutions. For example, the educational system plays a major role in socializing young people in modern societies. Similarly, the government fulfills many of the economic functions that would be the task of families

in traditional societies. We will examine the functions of these other social institutions in the remaining chapters of this unit.

SECTION 1 REVIEW

DEFINE social institution, family, nuclear family, family of orientation, family of procreation, extended family, kinship

1. ***Summarizing Ideas*** Describe how family structure can vary in terms of *(a)* number of marital partners, *(b)* residential patterns, *(c)* descent patterns, and *(d)* authority patterns.

2. ***Comprehending Ideas*** List and describe the basic functions of the family.

2 THE AMERICAN FAMILY

Many adult Americans have images of family life colored by television programs of the 1950s and 1960s. The families depicted on television programs such as "Father Knows Best" and "Leave It to Beaver" were strong and child-centered. Duties within the family were rigidly defined—the father was breadwinner and the mother was homemaker. The most serious problems faced by the children on these programs was how to spend their allowances or how to deal with having two dates on the same night.

These images no longer represent the reality of family life in the 1990s. Today, the vast majority of children live in families in which both parents work or in which only one parent is present. While allowance and dating still are important factors in the lives of young people, drugs, physical abuse, premarital sex, and run-ins with the law have been added to the list of youthful concerns. In this section, we will examine contemporary marriage and family life in the United States.

Courtship and Marriage

Although the majority of families would not be considered traditional if we took "Father Knows Best" as our model, most people in the United States do marry. It is estimated that approximately 95 percent of all adults marry at least once during their lifetimes. This gives the United States one of the highest marriage rates of any industrialized nation. In the early 1990s, approximately 64 percent of American males and 59 percent of American females over 18 years of age were married at any one time. It is important to note, however, that marriage rates are declining slightly among younger Americans. Sociologists estimate that more than 10 percent of today's younger Americans will remain single.

Selecting a Mate. In the United States, at least, romantic love generally is the basis of marriage. People marry because they are emotionally and physically attracted to one another. But love is neither blind nor random. Americans overwhelmingly tend to marry individuals who have social characteristics similar to their own. Marriage between individuals with similar social characteristics is called **homogamy.** Homogamy is based on such characteristics as age, socioeconomic status, religion, and race.

People in the United States overwhelmingly tend to marry within their own religious, ethnic, or racial group.

In general, Americans tend to marry individuals who are close to them in age, with the husband being slightly older than the wife. Americans also tend to marry within their own socioeconomic class. When differences between a couple do exist, it is most often the woman who is of a lower socioeconomic standing.

In the case of religion, marriages between individuals from different Protestant denominations are relatively common. It is much less common, however, for Protestants to marry non-Protestants. The same is true for Catholics and Jews. Most people marry within their faith. When individuals from different religious backgrounds do marry, one of the partners sometimes adopts the other partner's religion.

Homogamy is even stronger when it comes to race. Only about 2 percent of all marriages involve individuals from different races. This partly is due to the fact that until the Supreme Court struck down such legislation in 1967, interracial marriages were illegal in 20 states. Since the Supreme Court decision, the number of interracial marriages in the United States has doubled.

Although homogamy still is the rule in the United States, an increasing number of marriages are heterogamous. **Heterogamy** is marriage between individuals who have different social characteristics. This increase in heterogamy is a function of changing social conditions. Individuals in the United States choose their own marriage partners. As contact between people of differing social backgrounds increases, the likelihood of heterogamous marriages also increases. Some of the factors that have contributed to heterogamy are higher college enrollments, more geographical mobility, and the increased participation of women in the work force.

Marital Satisfaction. At the beginning of this section, we said that the vast majority of Americans marry at least once in their lifetimes. But are most American marriages happy? One way in which sociologists attempt to answer this question is to ask couples to rate how happy they are with their own marriages. Until recently, research indicated that most Americans rate their marriages either as pretty happy or as very happy. New research by Norval Glenn and Charles Weaver, however, has begun to cast a doubt on the degree to which marital status affects an individual's level of happiness. Glenn and Weaver found that the level of happiness reported by married individuals, particularly women, has declined since the early-to-mid-1980s. At the same time, happiness among single people, particularly males and young adults, has increased.

Glenn and Weaver suggest several possible reasons for the reported decline in marital happiness. First, society has become more tolerant of close physical and emotional relationships outside the realm of marriage. Second, as it has become easier to obtain a divorce, the emotional and financial security provided by marriage has declined. Finally, Americans have become increasingly individualistic and therefore less committed to social groups, including the family.

Among marriages that are happy, several common characteristics emerge. Some of these characteristics of happy marriages are

- having parents who are successfully married;
- having known each other for at least two years;
- getting married at an older age;
- holding traditional values;
- having had an engagement that was relatively free from conflict;
- being of the same race and religion;
- having a college education;
- having parental approval of the marriage.

Marital happiness also is affected by the presence of children. Research has shown that childless couples and couples with grown children report higher levels of satisfaction than do couples with children under the age of 18. In addition, men appear to be more satisfied with married life than are women.

Family Disruption

Not all experiences within the family are positive. Consider the following statistics:

- Approximately 25 percent of the murders committed in the United States each year involve family members.
- Approximately 28 percent of the women murdered each year are killed by their husbands or boyfriends.

Alcoholism and the Family

More people in the United States are addicted to alcohol than to any other substance. Government reports estimate that there are 9 million alcoholics currently in this country. An additional 6 million people are considered to be problem drinkers. The statistics concerning alcohol use in this country are alarming. For example, the United States has one of the highest per capita rates of alcohol consumption in the world. Alcohol is a factor in nearly half of the murders, suicides, and accidents that occur each year. At least 100,000 human lives are lost annually to alcohol.

The disease of alcoholism exacts a very high price on its sufferers, both physically and emotionally. But there are other victims of alcoholism who suffer in silence—the family members of alcoholics. Researchers have only just begun to uncover the lifelong effects of alcoholism on the family. This is significant in view of the fact that one family in four in the United States is affected by alcoholism. Seven million children under the age of 18 currently are growing up with an alcoholic parent.

Children of alcoholic parents must deal everyday with a family life filled with disruption and distrust. They are warned not to talk to outsiders about their parents' problems. Few children bring friends home because of fear and embarrassment. Meals are served haphazardly, if at all. Trips in the car with parents who are drunk may be filled with terror. The children sometimes blame themselves and believe that in some way they are causing their parents to drink.

Many people believe that the effects of growing up in an alcoholic home end when the children leave home. In reality, however, millions of children from alcoholic families become alcoholics themselves. Research has found that sons of alcoholic fathers are four times more likely to become alcoholics than are sons of nonalcoholic fathers. Similarly, daughters of alcoholic mothers are three times more likely to become alcoholics than are daughters of nonalcoholic mothers.

It once was thought that children of alcoholic parents tended to become alcoholics themselves due to the stress of growing up in homes where the parents drank. Recent studies have shown, however, that children of alcoholics may inherit a greater susceptibility to alcoholism than do other people. Studies conducted in Sweden have shown that when sons of alcoholics are adopted and raised by other families, they are just as likely to become alcoholics as are sons raised by their biological parents.

Not all children of alcoholics become alcoholics too, of course. But a great many suffer from other problems in adulthood. Many have trouble trusting other people and establishing healthy relationships. Some turn to illegal drugs and crime. Others spend their entire adult lives trying to understand why so much of their childhood was consumed by helplessness and terror.

The realization that alcoholism is an illness affecting entire families has led to an enormous growth in the number of organizations designed to provide counseling and support. Programs such as Alcoholics Anonymous, Al-Anon, Alateen, and The Children of Alcoholics are helping growing numbers of people to gain insight into the problems of alcoholism and to put aside the years of pain.

For additional information on alcoholism, contact the following organizations.

National Council on Alcoholism
12 West 21st Street
New York, N.Y. 10010

National Clearinghouse for Alcohol and
Drug Information
P.O. Box 2345
Rockville, Md. 20852

- Based on their research, sociologists Murray Straus and Richard Gelles estimate that 1.6 million wives are seriously abused by their husbands each year. Other surveys indicate that as many as 7 million couples are involved in at least one physically violent encounter each year.
- It is estimated that 1.5 million children are severely assaulted by adults each year. Most researchers agree that the actual incidence of violence against children is much higher.
- According to official statistics, child abuse resulted in the deaths of almost 1,200 children in 1990. Experts estimate, however, that the true figure was closer to 5,000. Many abuse-related deaths are attributed to other causes.
- Approximately half of all recent marriages will eventually end in divorce, making the United States the nation with the highest divorce rate.

Family Violence. Until relatively recently, family violence was considered a fairly rare phenomenon. The violence that did exist was thought to be confined to families in the lower social classes. Sociologists now know that family violence is a serious problem among all social classes and racial and ethnic groups.

One of the reasons that family violence was at first considered a problem of the lower classes was the way in which statistics were collected. Most early research was based on police and hospital reports. Because the police and hospitals were more likely to be involved in cases of domestic violence involving lower-income families, these families were represented more often in the statistics. Cases of violence among middle- and upper-income families generally went undetected.

The widespread nature of family violence was confirmed in a 1975 national study conducted by Murray Straus, Richard Gelles, and Suzanne Steinmetz. The researchers found that nearly one-third of the people they interviewed had experienced some form of family violence in the course of their marriages. Moreover, almost two-thirds of the people interviewed reported hitting their children, usually more than once. The study also revealed that wives were nearly as likely to commit violent acts within the family as were husbands. The acts committed by wives, however, were more often committed in self-defense and were less violent in nature.

Numerous studies have found that parents who abuse their children suffered abuse at the hands of their own parents.

Straus and Gelles repeated this study in 1985 and found that the rate of family violence had lessened somewhat. Cases of spouse abuse were down by 28 percent, while cases of child abuse were down by 47 percent. Straus and Gelles believe these drops came from a change in public attitudes. Many of the actions that were considered acceptable 15 or 20 years ago now are defined as abusive and thus socially unacceptable. Furthermore, in recent years, numerous private and government agencies have been established to treat the problem of family violence. For example, in 1975, there existed only a few shelters for abused wives. Today there are more than 1,200 such shelters around the country.

It is important to note that the 1985 findings of Straus and Gelles contradict official statistics on family violence. According to figures gathered by various government and private agencies, family violence—particularly child abuse—is on the increase. In response to this fact, Straus and Gelles suggest that the government and agency statistics represent higher rates of reporting, not actual increases in violent acts. Regardless, most experts agree that figures on family violence underestimate its actual occurrence in society.

Divorce. Between 1965 and 1980, the divorce rate in the United States more than doubled—from 2.5 divorces per 1,000 population in 1965 to 5.2 divorces per 1,000 population in 1980. In the mid-1980s, the divorce rate began to decline slightly and now appears to have leveled off at its present rate of 4.7.

Although most industrialized nations have experienced rising divorce rates, the United States has the highest divorce rate in the world. The statistic most often cited by the media is that one out of every two marriages eventually will end in divorce. This figure, though, is somewhat misleading. It is true that sociologists estimate that around half of all women in their 30s will eventually end a marriage in divorce. This does not mean, however, that 50 percent of all marriages end in divorce. It simply means that, based on current divorce rates among women in their 30s, it is likely that half of all *recently* married women will experience a divorce.

The rate of divorce varies among different segments of the population. For instance, couples who marry during their teenage years have a greater likelihood of divorce than couples who marry after the age of 20. Education also influences the rate of divorce. Couples with college educations are less likely to divorce than couples who have not attended college.

Divorce also varies by race and ethnicity. African American women are more likely than white women to be separated or divorced. Hispanic American women, on the other hand, are slightly less likely than white women to experience divorce. The higher rate of divorce among African American women is partially explained by the fact that a higher percentage of African American women are young and poor when they marry.

Divorce affects not only adults but also children. Each year, more than 1 million children under the age of 18 witness the breakup of their parents' marriage. Current estimates indicate that half of all American children—at least one-third of all white children and two-thirds of all African American children—will experience the divorce of their parents.

Text continues on page 308.

Many couples who are thinking about getting a divorce find that talking to a marital counselor helps them work through their problems together.

The Changing American Family

In the face of all the changes that are sweeping our society, the family, too, is changing. It is taking many forms that were uncommon in the past. Of course, the traditional American family—a wage-earner husband, a homemaker wife, and their two children—still can be found. However, such families are now a minority in our society.

What are some of the new forms that the American family is taking? What are some of the problems confronting these families? The following case studies will provide some answers to these questions.

Case Study A

Marie and Tom Arnow are the parents of two children aged 10 and 12. They both also are business executives. Despite the rigors of their jobs and the challenges of rearing children, they successfully have combined their careers with a warm family life.

Up until six years ago, Marie was a traditional homemaker. She was content to stay home and take care of her house and family. She thought it was important for a mother always to be available to her preschool-age children.

Then the situation began to change. Economic conditions made it difficult for the family to live comfortably on one income. Although Tom was earning a good salary, the cost of basic necessities seemed to be rising in leaps and bounds. The family no longer could afford some of the luxuries it had come to take for granted.

Marie also was becoming restless. The children were in school part of the day now, and she had time on her hands. She decided to return to the advertising company where she had worked before the children were born. After several promotions, she became a senior account executive.

Both partners have adjusted well to Marie's job. Both share household and child-rearing responsibilities. Tom takes the children to school in

the morning, and Marie picks them up after work. The children, too, seem content. Because many of their friends' mothers also work, they do not feel deprived. They also enjoy many of the luxuries that the two incomes make possible, such as tickets to baseball games and vacation trips.

Case Study B

Every morning John Stevens gets up, fixes breakfast for his family, and makes sure the children get to school on time. He then does the dishes, makes the beds, and cleans the house.

While John is tending to his household duties, his wife, Allison, is working as a biologist at a nearby university. Her job is very demanding, and she often works long hours. Yet Allison is happy with her work. Her family, too, is supportive, especially since her salary provides most of the family's income.

When John and Allison chose to have children eight years ago, they decided that most of the responsibility for child care would rest with John. At that time, John was unhappy with his job and was eager to be an active participant in child rearing. Allison, on the other hand, had just started a well-paying and interesting job at the university. Although she looked forward to motherhood, she also wanted to be able to advance in her career. They thought their solution would be the best for all concerned.

Both John and Allison are content with their roles. John does not mind being called a "house-husband" and has learned to accept the puzzled looks he gets from people when he takes the children to the playground. Allison also likes her present situation. She believes that she is getting the best of both worlds.

Case Study C

Allen Stone had been married for 10 years. On graduation from college, he married the woman he had been dating steadily since high school. Things were ideal for the first nine years. Allen had a good job as a computer programmer. His wife had a part-time job as a secretary and enjoyed taking care of their son.

Over time, however, the marriage began to falter. Both partners saw no hope for improvement and decided on a divorce. Allen was awarded sole custody of their seven-year-old son.

At first Allen found the situation trying at best. He found it almost impossible to be both mother and father to an active child. His work began to suffer as well. After staying up almost half the night catching up on his work, taking care of the house, and doing various chores, Allen found it difficult to concentrate on his job.

He also felt burdened by well-meaning friends and relatives. Always giving advice or offering to help out, these people were placing a severe strain on Allen.

Then things started falling into place. Allen and his son developed household routines, sharing in the cooking, cleaning, and shopping. Allen also has found time to share in the child's school activities. He has joined the PTA. In addition, both father and son now realize that their situation is not unique.

In these three case studies, we can see some of the new forms that the American family is taking. We also can see some of the problems facing families today. What problems did these three families have to overcome? How successful were they in doing so? Do you think they are typical of other families in similar situations? What other obstacles still might lie ahead?

Based on what you have learned about American family patterns, write an imaginary case study describing what you think the family of the future will be like.

Sociologists suggest several reasons for the high divorce rate. First, the laws governing the divorce process have become less complicated, and the cost of obtaining a divorce has decreased. For instance, most states now have some form of no-fault divorce law. In no-fault divorces, neither party has to state a specific reason for seeking the divorce. Second, the increase in the number of dual-earner families and the growth of day-care facilities have decreased the economic dependence of women. It now is financially possible for more women to remove themselves from unhappy marriages. Third, society in general has become more tolerant of divorce. Divorce no longer carries the social stigma it did 20 or 30 years ago. Finally, people now may expect more of marriage and be less accepting of marital problems. If these problems become too severe, divorce often is seen as an acceptable alternative to staying in an unsatisfactory marriage.

Trends in American Family Life

The high rate of divorce is not the only trend evident in American family life. Among the other trends that are of particular interest to sociologists are delayed marriage, delayed childbearing, dual-earner families, one-parent families, and remarriage.

Delayed Marriage. In 1890, the median age at first marriage was 22.0 years of age for women and 26.1 years for men. By 1960, the median age at first marriage had dropped to 20.3 years for women and 22.8 years for men. In recent years, however, this trend toward earlier marriages has reversed itself.

In 1992, for instance, the median age at first marriage was 24.4 years for women and 26.5 years for men. The 1992 median ages at marriage for both men and women are the highest they have ever been since the Bureau of the Census first began recording this information in 1890. (See the table on this page.)

Some sociologists view this tendency toward later marriage as an indication that singlehood has once again become an acceptable alternative to marriage. Relatively common in the early part of the century, singlehood lost ground in the marriage-minded years following World War II. By

1970, only 6.2 percent of American women aged 30 to 34 had never been married. This was down from 16.6 percent in 1900. Then in the 1970s and 1980s, the marriage rate began to slow. By 1992, the proportion of women aged 30 to 34 who had never been married had increased to 19 percent.

Sociologists believe that young people today are delaying marriage in order to finish their educations and launch their careers. This is particularly true of women. Sociologists also note that the increase in singlehood may be partially the result of more couples living together outside of marriage. Sociologists refer to this practice as *cohabitation*. In 1992, there were more than 3 million cohabiting couples in the United States. This is up from 450,000 couples in 1960. Although most individuals who cohabit eventually marry someone (although not necessarily their current partners), the practice tends to delay marriage.

Median Ages at Marriage in the United States

Year	Men	Women
1992	26.5	24.4
1991	26.3	24.1
1990	26.1	23.9
1989	26.2	23.8
1988	25.9	23.6
1987	25.8	23.6
1986	25.7	23.1
1980	24.7	22.0
1970	23.2	20.8
1960	22.8	20.3
1950	22.8	20.3
1940	24.3	21.5
1930	24.3	21.3
1920	24.6	21.2
1910	25.1	21.6
1900	25.9	21.9
1890	26.1	22.0

Source: U.S. Bureau of the Census, *Current Population Reports*, Series P-20, No. 450 and No. 461.

cathy®

by Cathy Guisewite

Panel 1: SAY HI TO AUNT CATHY, ZENITH. / "AUNT CATHY, AUNT CATHY"... THIS IS WHAT YOU'RE DOOMING YOURSELF TO.

Panel 2: A LIFETIME OF OTHER PEOPLE'S CHILDREN CALLING YOU "AUNT CATHY," BUT NO ONE TO CALL YOUR OWN. YOUR FATHER AND I THINK IT'S JUST PATHETIC.

Panel 3: SAY HI TO AUNT GRANDMA, ZENITH. / AUNT GRAND-MA?? AM I YOUR AUNT GRANDMA??

Panel 4: YOU TRICKED ME. / COME ON IN HERE, UNCLE GRANDPA!!

Delayed Childbearing.   Another trend in American family life that sociologists have noted in recent years is the fact that married couples are tending to delay childbearing. In the 1960s, for example, the average length of time between marriage and the birth of the first child was 15 months. By the 1970s, that interval had increased to 27 months. Today, it is not at all uncommon for women to have their first child after the age of 30. In fact, women aged 30 to 34 accounted for 21 percent of all births in 1990. An additional 8 percent of the births in 1990 were to women aged 35 to 39.

The reasons for delaying childbearing are similar to the reasons for delaying marriage. Studies have found that married women who delay childbearing tend to have higher levels of education and to be involved in their careers. These women usually wait to have children until they are well established in their chosen fields. They also tend to be more concerned with financial security and personal freedom than are women who do not delay childbearing.

There also has been an increase in recent years in the number of married couples who never have children. Some couples who at first plan just to delay parenting find later that they have waited

Increasing numbers of women today are deciding to postpone childbearing until their careers are launched.

too long. Other married couples, however, consciously choose never to have children. Sociologists call this conscious choice to remain childless **voluntary childlessness**. The number of voluntarily childless couples has skyrocketed in recent years. Between the years 1968 and 1985, for example, the number of young couples who chose never to have children increased 75 percent. During that same time period, the number of young couples with children increased only 8 percent.

Studies have found that married couples who choose to remain childless have high levels of education and income, are nonreligious, have egalitarian attitudes, and share household maintenance tasks. Voluntarily childless couples also tend to use more effective methods of birth control than do couples who plan to have children. Compared to women who have or who want to have children, women who plan to remain childless believe that the disadvantages of having children outweigh the advantages.

Dual-Earner Marriages. Another trend in American family life is an increase in the number of dual-earner marriages. This is due, of course, to the increased numbers of married women entering the labor force. The percentage of married women who work outside the home has been increasing steadily for over 50 years. In 1940, for example, only 15 percent of married women were

Studies have found that the daughters of women who work outside the home expect to have careers of their own when they are adults.

employed outside the home. This figure rose to 20 percent by the end of World War II, and, by 1960, 31 percent of married women were in the labor force. Today, approximately 58 percent of all married women work outside the home at least part time.

Married women work for the same basic reason that married men work—economic necessity. Few families today can survive on a single salary. Also, in the past few years, more and more women have been entering colleges and universities, a factor that enables them to pursue more attractive positions in the labor market. Another reason for the increase of married women in the labor force is the fact that the stigma once attached to working wives and mothers has been lessening in recent years as more and more women work outside of the home.

The labor market itself has been a factor in the increase of dual-earner families. Since World War II, there has been a tremendous rise in the number of available jobs in service and other industries that traditionally employ large numbers of women. Also, many women are entering nontraditional occupations at a rate never before seen in the United States. For example, women today make up 20 percent of the doctors, 34 percent of the computer scientists, and 41 percent of the college and university teachers in this country.

Women's participation in the labor force is influenced by the ages of their children. In 1991, for example, only about 60 percent of women with children under the age of 6 were employed outside the home, compared to about 74 percent of women with children aged 6 to 17. Women with newborn children in the home tend to leave the labor force for a period of time. The Family and Medical Leave Act of 1993, however, is designed to help parents care for their newborn children without having to drop out of the labor force. Under the new law, workers who meet certain conditions may take up to 12 weeks of unpaid leave to care for a new baby in the home.

Some people have expressed concern that the increased participation of married women in the labor force may have negative consequences on their children. Research, however, has failed to establish any meaningful positive or negative effects of maternal employment on sons. Daughters of working women, on the other hand, do seem

Parents who are raising their children alone face responsibilities usually shared by couples in two-parent families.

to be affected by their mothers' employment. Daughters of working women make fewer differentiations between men's work and women's work, see women as being less restricted to the home, and are more favorable toward women's employment. They also are more likely than the daughters of nonworking women to expect to work themselves when they get married and have children.

One-Parent Families.   Another trend in American family life that has gained the attention of social scientists in recent years is the increase in one-parent families. One-parent families are formed through separation, divorce, death, adoption by unmarried individuals, or births to unwed mothers.

Most one-parent families in the United States are the result of divorce. The mother is the single parent and the head of the household in almost 9 out of every 10 one-parent families. One-parent families account for about 26 percent of the families in the United States with children under the age of 18. Estimates indicate that approximately 61 percent of today's young children will spend some time living in a one-parent family.

The figure of 26 percent refers to all families with children under 18. This figure, however, varies by race. Approximately 20 percent of white families with children under the age of 18 are headed by one parent. In comparison, 30 percent of all Hispanic American families and 58 percent of all African American families with children under 18 are headed by one parent.

Although all families naturally experience problems, single parents are subject to a special set of stresses and strains. Sociologist Robert S. Weiss has identified three such problems common to the single-parent experience. Weiss calls one source of stress found among single parents *responsibility overload.* In two-parent households, husbands and wives share the responsibility of making plans and decisions. Single parents, on the other hand, must make their plans and decisions alone. They also are alone in ensuring the care and well-being of their families.

Weiss calls a second source of stress among single parents *task overload.* Single parents must handle all of the tasks usually distributed between two people. Single parents must maintain their homes, care for their children, and perform satisfactorily in their jobs. Single parents spend so much time handling the tasks that must be completed on a daily basis that often they have little or no time for themselves.

A third source of stress identified by Weiss is called *emotional overload.* Single parents often must cope with the emotional needs of their children by themselves. Coping with their children's emotional needs, in addition to maintaining a home and holding a job, very often means that the emotional needs and wants of single parents must go unfulfilled.

A more pressing problem, particularly among single mothers, concerns money. Around 45 percent of female-headed households have incomes below the poverty line, and this figure is expected to increase. Divorced women who are single parents are at a serious financial disadvantage. Many did not work while their children were young and, upon divorce, find that they must take low-paying, low-status jobs to support their families. Studies have found that female heads of household are subject to ongoing stress because of low incomes and low levels of social support.

The financial situations of many single mothers are complicated by the fact that only about half of the fathers who are ordered by the courts to make child-support payments pay the full amount. Moreover, one-fourth of the fathers who are ordered to pay support for their children pay nothing. Although the Internal Revenue Service now has the authority to withhold tax refunds from people who do not make their child-support payments, this action has done little to help the majority of women who need help. As a result, a growing number of single mothers and their children are living under poverty conditions.

Remarriage. Another trend in American family life that is of interest to sociologists is an increase in the rate of remarriage. In more than 40 percent of the marriages occurring today, one or both of the partners have been previously married. Research shows that the majority of the people who get divorced remarry within five years. Apparently most divorced Americans continue to support the institution of marriage.

The high rates of divorce and remarriage in the United States have led to a large increase in the number of stepfamilies. Stepfamilies, also called *blended families,* arise when one or both of the marriage partners bring children from their previous marriages into their new marriage. Approximately one out of every six American children under the age of 18 now lives in a stepfamily situation. Estimates indicate that by the year 2000, around 25 percent of all children will have a stepparent.

Becoming part of a stepfamily involves a period of adjustment for all members of the new family. For the marital partners, this period of adjustment includes taking on the parenting roles formerly held by biological parents. This process sometimes is a source of conflict in the family. Children may resent stepparents who appear to be trying

Remarriage often means that children from previous marriages are blended into one family.

to take the place of a biological mother or father. Similarly, stepparents may resent not being treated with the love and respect usually given to parents. It is important for stepparents and stepchildren alike to remember that they are undergoing an important transition in their lives and to continue to communicate with each other throughout the period of adjustment. Studies have shown that it takes approximately four years for children to accept a stepparent in the same way that they accept a biological mother or father.

Learning to accept new stepparents is not the only adjustment children in a stepfamily have to make. For example, they may find themselves with four sets of grandparents where once there were only two. They also may have to adjust to having new stepbrothers or stepsisters living in the home with them. This adjustment often involves learning how to share a parent's affections with their new siblings.

Adjusting to life in a stepfamily takes patience, understanding, and a willingness to work together. The reward can be a strong family unit.

SECTION 2 REVIEW

DEFINE homogamy, heterogamy

1. **Expressing Ideas** Summarize the research findings concerning marital satisfaction in the United States.

2. **Understanding Ideas** **(a)** Why was it assumed in the past that family violence was confined to the lower classes? **(b)** Why has the rate of family violence appeared to lessen in recent years?

3. **Organizing Ideas** How do divorce rates vary among segments of the population in the United States?

4. **Summarizing Ideas** List and describe the five trends in American family life discussed in this section.

CHAPTER 12 SUMMARY

The family as a social institution is a universal phenomenon. The family system varies however, from society to society and even within a single society over time. The term marriage refers to the set of norms that specifies the ways in which family structure should be organized. Among the most important norms are those governing number of spouses, residence, kinship, and authority patterns within the family.

In all societies, the family system performs certain functions. It regulates sexual activity, produces new members for the society, socializes children, and provides economic and emotional security. In industrialized societies, many of the traditional functions of the family have been taken over in part by other social institutions.

The great majority of Americans marry. Nevertheless, marital happiness appears to be on the decline. One reason for this is that society has become more tolerant of close relationships outside of marriage. Also, the ease with which divorces may be obtained has lessened the financial and emotional security provided by marriage. Another explanation lies in the fact that Americans have become increasingly less committed to social groups, including the family.

The family may be disrupted through violence or divorce. Family violence has been shown to occur among all social classes and races. The United States has the highest divorce rate in the world. The incidence of divorce is affected by factors such as age at marriage, level of education, race, and ethnicity.

Sociologists have noted a number of trends in American family life. These trends include delayed marriage, delayed childbearing, and increases in the number of dual-earner families, one-parent families, and remarriages.

READING ABOUT SOCIOLOGY: Understanding Census Data

How has marital status in the United States changed since the year 1920? Sociologists answer this question by examining statistical reports. Particularly useful are data collected and recorded by the Bureau of the Census.

The Bureau of the Census was established by Congress as a permanent office in 1902 and is authorized to collect, tabulate, and publish statistical information about the people and the economy of the United States. All information collected by the Bureau is kept strictly confidential and is used solely for statistical purposes.

Among the useful publications of the Bureau is a two-volume set entitled *The Historical Statistics of the United States.* These volumes include statistics on topics such as population, employment, marriage, education, and poverty. The statistics in the two volumes are organized into charts and tables. By analyzing and comparing data, sociologists are able to note trends and to draw conclusions about social, economic, and political changes over time.

You, too, can use these volumes in your study of sociology. When using the *Historical Statistics,* consult the index to locate the tables appropriate to your inquiry. Often, the needed statistics appear on separate tables. Follow the guidelines for reading statistical tables presented in Chapter 6, pages 144–145, and for interpreting statistics, presented in Chapter 8 on pages 196–197. Concentrate on finding relationships between the numbers in the tables. Look for patterns of change. Then draw conclusions based on your analysis of the statistics.

Applying the Skill

The chart on this page was adapted from tables presented in *The Historical Statistics of the United States.* It contains the kinds of data that sociologists use to determine how marital status in the United States has changed over the years.

Study the chart at the bottom of this page, which covers the period from 1960 to 1990 and which gives statistics on the marital status of

Marital Status of the Population, by Sex: 1960–1990 (in percents)*

| Year | Male** | | | | | Female** | | | | |
	Total	Single	Married	Widowed	Divorced	Total	Single	Married	Widowed	Divorced
1990	100.0	25.8	64.3	2.7	7.2	100.0	18.9	59.7	12.1	9.3
1980	100.0	23.8	68.4	2.6	5.2	100.0	17.1	63.0	12.8	7.1
1970	100.0	18.9	75.3	3.3	2.5	100.0	13.7	68.5	13.9	3.9
1960	99.9	17.3	76.6	3.7	2.3	100.0	11.9	71.7	13.3	3.1

Some percentages may not add to 100 due to rounding error.
Marital status figures are given for the population aged 18 and older.
Varying methods of statistical calculation may result in slightly different figures.

Sources: *Historical Statistics of the United States.* Figures for 1980 and 1990 from *Statistical Abstract of the United States, 1992,* p. 44.

males and females at 10-year intervals. These statistics provide some interesting information on the ways in which marital status has been changing over the years. For example, notice that the percentages of males and females who are divorced have been rising steadily since 1960. Notice also that since 1960, the percentages of males and females who are single have been on the increase. The increase in the percentage of people who are single can be at least partially explained by the growing tendency among individuals to delay the time of marriage.

Some interesting information also is gained by comparing marital status for males and females. Notice that for every time interval, females are far more likely than males to be widowed. This finding can be partially explained by the fact that females tend to live longer than do males. Also, widowed males are more likely than widowed females to remarry, since they have a much higher number of potential partners from which to choose. You can see from the chart that at each time interval, males are more likely to be married than are females. The statistics in the other columns reveal further relationships among data about marital status in the United States.

Practicing the Skill

On this page is another chart adapted from tables in *The Historical Statistics of the United States*. Study the chart, keeping in mind the information you gathered from the chart on the previous page. Then on a separate sheet of paper, answer the following questions:

1. (a) What is the subject of the chart on this page? **(b)** How does the subject examined in this chart differ from the chart on page 314?

2. (a) According to the chart on this page, what can you say about the statistics concerning divorce in the United States from 1920 to 1950? **(b)** How does this compare to the statistics on divorce for the years 1960 to 1990? **(c)** In general, are males or females more likely to be divorced?

3. (a) According to the chart on this page, what can you say about the statistics concerning singlehood in the United States from 1920 to 1950? **(b)** How does this compare to the statistics on singlehood for the years 1960 to 1990? **(c)** In general, are males or females more likely to be single?

Marital Status of the Population, by Sex: 1920–1950 (in percents)*

| Year | Male** | | | | | Female** | | | | |
	Total	Single	Married	Widowed	Divorced	Total	Single	Married	Widowed	Divorced
1950	100.0	20.2	73.2	4.5	2.1	100.0	14.1	70.6	12.7	2.6
1940	100.0	27.8	66.1	4.7	1.4	100.0	20.3	65.4	12.5	1.8
1930	100.0	28.5	65.3	5.0	1.2	100.0	20.4	66.1	12.0	1.5
1920	100.0	29.8	64.3	5.2	0.7	99.9	21.4	65.6	12.1	0.8

Some percentages may not add to 100 due to rounding error.
Marital status figures are given for the population aged 18 and older.
Varying methods of statistical calculation may result in slightly different figures.

Source: *Historical Statistics of the United States.*

Reviewing Sociological Terms

On a separate sheet of paper, supply the term that correctly completes each sentence.

1. _____ is the term used for the set of norms that specifies the ways in which family structure should be organized.

2. A group of people who are related by marriage, blood, or adoption and who live together and share economic resources is called a _____.

3. _____ refers to a form of polygamy in which a woman is permitted to marry more than one man at a time.

4. The residential pattern known as _____ allows a newly married couple to set up their residence apart from both sets of parents.

5. The _____ _____ is a norm that forbids sexual relations or marriage between certain relatives.

6. The authority pattern in which the father holds most of the authority is called the _____ _____.

Thinking Critically about Sociology

1. **Analyzing Information** *(a)* Why have some people predicted the eventual collapse of the American family? *(b)* Why is it likely that the family as an institution will survive?

2. **Comprehending Ideas** How can a person be a member of two nuclear families at the same time?

3. **Drawing Conclusions** *(a)* How common are matriarchal authority systems? *(b)* Who tends to hold the authority in family systems that practice matrilineal descent?

4. **Interpreting Tables** According to the table on page 308, what years showed the youngest median ages at marriage for men and women?

5. **Summarizing Ideas** What factors appear to be related to increases in heterogamy?

6. **Seeing Relationships** *(a)* Why has the rate of divorce been on the increase in recent years? *(b)* How does the likelihood of divorce vary by race?

7. **Making Comparisons** How do voluntarily childless couples differ from couples who want to have children?

8. **Expressing Ideas** *(a)* Why is the poverty rate so high among female-headed households? *(b)* What kinds of adjustments must people in a stepfamily make?

Exercising Sociological Skills

1. **Determining Cause and Effect** Reread the Applying Sociology feature on pages 306–307. *(a)* What factors caused the home life of the family in Case Study A to change? *(b)* What were the effects of divorce on the man in Case Study C?

2. **Synthesizing Information** According to the Case Study on page 303, what happens to the children of alcoholic parents in adulthood?

3. **Examining Census Data** Reread the Developing Sociological Imagination feature on pages 314–315. *(a)* In what year did the percentage of widowed females reach 12 percent? *(b)* In what year did the percentage of widowed males reach 5.2 percent?

Extending Sociological Imagination

1. Prepare a brief research paper describing what family life was like in Colonial America.

2. Watch several weekly television programs, some of which contain one-parent families and some of which contain two-parent families. Make a list of the problems encountered by the families on these programs and the methods the families use to solve their problems. How do the problems and solutions of one-parent families and two-parent families on these programs differ?

INTERPRETING PRIMARY SOURCES

Help for Working Parents

Most sociologists agree that the dual-earner family has become a permanent fixture of the American landscape. Attending to the needs of both work and family, however, can be quite stressful. In this excerpt from the article "Work, Family and Stress," which appeared in the August 14, 1992, issue of *CQ Researcher*, Charles S. Clark discusses the time demands placed on working parents and the policies being instituted by some companies to help workers meet their family obligations. While reading the excerpt, consider why the number of dual-earner families is likely to increase and how companies are changing to accommodate them.

In the collective memory of modern Americans squeezed for time are vivid black-and-white images from the television world of the 1950s: genial fathers strolling home to be greeted by neatly dressed children and serene well-coiffed housewives named June Cleaver or Harriet Nelson. Such images stand in stark contrast to the reality of life in today's two-career families.

"Increasingly, family schedules are intricate applications of time-motion principles, with everything engineered to the minute and with every piece designed to fall in the right place at the right time," writes Barbara Dafoe Whitehead, a social historian at the New York City–based Institute for American Values, a research organization concentrating on family issues. . . .

To most men and women, however, returning to the idyllic days of June Cleaver is hardly an option. . . . Currently, about 58 percent of U.S. households with children have two breadwinners, compared with only 18.6 percent in 1960, according to the Bureau of Labor Statistics. Women's participation in the work force is expected to grow in coming decades as the economy experiences a shortage of skilled workers.

As for the traditional nuclear family—an employed husband, homemaker wife and children—it's now found in only 15 percent of U.S. households, according to the Census Bureau. . . .

For both economic and personal career reasons, many women see the stay-at-home option as a luxury they can't afford, even temporarily. "Many women say they want to quit because the degree of stress has become unmanageable," observes Barbara Geiger-Green, administrator of the Association of Part-Time Professionals in Falls Church, Va. "But they want to remain viable in the work force. Most want a little piece of both actions."

Notwithstanding the recent shift in attitudes away from work and toward the family, the decades-old influx of women into the work world shows few signs of abating in the long run. In 1991, the American Council of Education's survey of 211,000 college freshmen at 410 campuses showed the number of females who were planning to become full-time homemakers at only half of 1 percent. . . .

The solution to the time famine that attracts support across the political spectrum is the movement to make the workplace "family friendly." The smorgasbord of benefits that many companies have begun to offer includes varying combinations of on-site child care, financial aid or referral services for child care, job sharing, voluntary part-time work with benefits, maternity leave, leave for adoptive parents or employees with elderly relatives who are sick, flexitime, telecommuting [working at home via computers] and flexible combinations of benefits, known as "cafeteria" plans. . . .

A recent survey of 1,000 major firms by Hewitt Associates found that 66 percent are providing some form of help with child care, 36 percent help with elder care, 53 percent offer flexible scheduling and 51 percent offer parental leave.

Source Review

1. Why is the number of two-career families likely to increase in the future?

2. What are some of the things that companies are doing to help working parents?

The Economy and Politics

1 **The Economic Institution**

The Nature of Economic Systems
Economic Models
Postindustrial America

2 **The Political Institution**

The Legitimacy of Power
Types of Government
The American Political System

Chapter Focus

Chapter 13 focuses on economic and political institutions. The chapter begins with a discussion of the characteristics of economic systems. Special attention is paid to the economic models of capitalism and socialism and to the characteristics of postindustrial America. The chapter then turns to a discussion of politics, focusing on the exercise of power, types of government, and the American political system.

As you study the chapter, look for the answers to the following questions:

1. How do preindustrial, industrial, and postindustrial systems differ in terms of what sector of the economy is emphasized?
2. What are the characteristics of pure capitalism and pure socialism, and what factors affect how closely the American economy follows the capitalist model?
3. How does the exercise of power vary by type of government?
4. What are the characteristics of the American political system?

KEY TERMS

The following terms, while not the only terms emphasized in the chapter, are basic to your understanding of sociology. Determine the meaning of each term, either by using the Glossary or by watching for context clues as you read the chapter.

economic institution	oligopoly	authority
capitalism	power	democracy
socialism	political institution	authoritarianism

When the world was populated by small bands of people, the family was the main authority in society. The family institution coordinated all economic activities and established the rules of society. Today, in a world where events in one nation can dramatically affect events in other nations and where powerful nations compete with one another for influence, ultimate power no longer rests with the family institution.

In place of the family, various other institutions that attempt to coordinate the activities of millions of people have gained prominence. The economy and politics are two of the most important of these institutions. The economic and political institutions ensure that the economic activities of individuals are controlled and that order is maintained in society.

The forms that economic and political institutions take vary widely from society to society. In some societies, these institutions are influenced by a belief in human freedom. In other societies, these same institutions greatly limit personal freedom. In this chapter, we will examine the basic characteristics of economic and political institutions and explore the rich variety that is found around the world.

1 THE ECONOMIC INSTITUTION

In every society, certain needs must be met if the health and happiness of societal members are to be maintained. Some of these needs—such as the need for food and shelter—are basic to survival. Other needs—such as the need for health care, clothing, education, and entertainment—add to the quality of life. To satisfy these needs, every society develops a system of roles and norms that governs the production, distribution, and consumption of goods and services. This system is called the **economic institution.**

The need for economic institutions is rooted in the problem of scarcity. People's needs always are greater than the resources available to satisfy them. Consequently, societies must decide how best to use their limited resources to satisfy the most needs. Societies do this by answering three basic questions: (1) What goods and services should be produced? (2) How should these goods and services be produced? (3) For whom should these goods and services be produced?

How a society answers these three basic questions is determined in large part by the society's available factors of production and its level of technology. **Factors of production** are the resources that can be used to produce and distribute goods and services. The factors of production include natural resources (such as land, water, minerals, plants, animals, and the sun and wind), human resources (labor), and capital resources (money and the tools, machinery, buildings, and structures used in the production and distribution processes). A society's available factors of production and its technological ability to manipulate those resources shape the nature of its economic system.

The Nature of Economic Systems

All economic systems contain three basic sectors: the primary sector, the secondary sector, and the tertiary sector. The **primary sector** deals with

the extraction of raw materials from the environment. Examples of activities in the primary sector include fishing, hunting, mining, and farming. The **secondary sector,** on the other hand, concentrates on the use of raw materials to manufacture goods. Activities in the secondary sector can range from turning a log into a primitive canoe to manufacturing a rocket that can travel deep into space. In the **tertiary sector,** the emphasis shifts to the provision of services. The shaman who mediates between individuals and the supernatural world in a preindustrial society is a member of the tertiary sector, just as is a doctor or religious leader in an industrial or postindustrial society.

The degree to which any one of these sectors is emphasized over the others depends on a society's available resources and its level of technology. In technologically advanced societies, for instance, the majority of workers are engaged in providing services, a tertiary-sector activity. In addition, the division of labor becomes more specialized. The evolutionary nature of economic development becomes evident when one examines the characteristics of preindustrial, industrial, and postindustrial economic systems.

In no society is economic activity limited to a single sector. Even in preindustrial societies, where most economic activity is concentrated in the primary sector, some activities take place in the secondary and tertiary sectors. Similarly, in the United States, workers are employed in every sector of the economy, even though the emphasis in the economy is on the tertiary sector.

Preindustrial Economic Systems. Because human labor and animal power provide the main sources of energy in preindustrial societies, technology remains at a relatively low level. One of the major consequences of this low level of technology is a relatively inefficient system of food production. As a result, the majority of the population must engage in the production of food, a primary-sector activity.

Although labor in all preindustrial societies is heavily concentrated in the primary sector, the degree of concentration varies by type of society. As we learned in Chapter 4, there are four types of preindustrial societies: hunting and gathering, pastoral, horticultural, and agricultural. As the mode of subsistence progresses from a hunting and gathering base to an agricultural base, the complexity of the economic system increases.

In the simplest preindustrial societies, particularly low levels of technology mean that providing sufficient food to feed the population demands the efforts of the entire population. Consequently, the secondary and tertiary sectors are very small and never command the full-time attention of societal members. Even essential secondary-sector activities, such as the production of clothes, tools, and household goods, are carried out along with food production.

As societies increase their level of food production, full-time participation in the secondary and tertiary sectors becomes more widespread. Higher productivity allows more people to transfer their labor from the primary sector to the secondary and tertiary sectors without affecting food supplies. Nevertheless, the number of people holding secondary and tertiary positions still is smaller than the number of people engaged in food production.

Industrial Economic Systems. In industrial societies, the main emphasis in the economy shifts from the primary sector to the secondary sector. This shift is brought about by the introduction of

In 1776, economist Adam Smith suggested that specialization could greatly increase productivity. Today, specialization and new technologies make it possible for American automobile manufacturers to produce millions of vehicles each year.

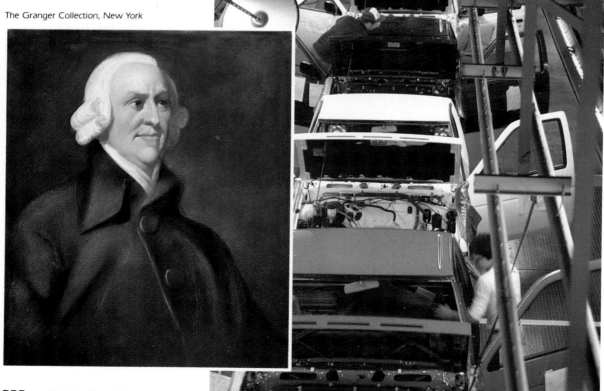

The Granger Collection, New York

machines and the development of new sources of energy. These advances in technology have numerous consequences for society. One of the most fundamental consequences is an increase in agricultural productivity. Higher agricultural productivity means that industrial societies can support larger populations. Higher productivity also means that fewer workers are needed in the primary sector. Consequently, the labor pool for the secondary and tertiary sectors swells.

Technological advances also change the nature of work. Jobs become specialized. Job specialization first was suggested by the Scottish economist Adam Smith in his book *The Wealth of Nations,* published in 1776. Smith argued that production could be greatly increased by dividing the manufacturing process into a series of tasks and assigning each task to a different individual. He used the now-famous example of a pin factory to illustrate his point.

According to Smith, one worker could manufacture about 20 pins a day. Ten workers thus could produce 200 pins. If, however, the process were divided into a series of tasks (such as wire cutting and point sharpening), with each task being assigned to a different person, the 10 workers could produce 48,000 pins a day. Production would increase because each person would become more efficient at completing his or her task, thereby cutting the time it took to make each pin.

In addition to increasing productivity, job specialization increases the variety of jobs found in the secondary and tertiary sectors. The variety of jobs increases because people no longer create the goods and services they need for their own daily lives. Instead, people perform their jobs in return for wages. They then use these wages to buy goods and services created by other workers.

Postindustrial Societies. In postindustrial societies, the tertiary sector becomes the most important area of the economy. Several factors lead to this shift. First, as technological innovations such as automation lead to more efficient production techniques, the number of jobs available in the secondary sector begins to decline. Second, the emphasis on all forms of knowledge and on the collection and distribution of information creates a great demand for administrative, managerial, professional, technical, and service personnel. And finally, the higher standard of living characteristic of advanced industrial societies increases the demand for services. We will examine the characteristics of postindustrialism more fully in our discussion of postindustrial America later in this section.

Economic Models

Industrial and postindustrial societies are categorized by the type of economic model they follow. Sociologists recognize two basic economic models: capitalism and socialism. The differences between the two models hinge on who owns the factors of production in society and on how economic activity is regulated. In **capitalism,** the factors of production are owned by individuals rather than by the government. Economic activity is regulated by the forces of profit and competition. In **socialism,** on the other hand, the factors of production are owned by the government, which regulates all economic activity.

It is important to keep in mind that capitalism and socialism are ideal types—that is, they are descriptions of the essential characteristics of the systems in their purest forms. In reality, no society follows a pure capitalist or pure socialist model, although some societies lean heavily toward one or the other. The United States and Canada, for example, follow the capitalist model. The People's Republic of China and Cuba, on the other hand, follow the socialist model. Between these extremes are a host of nations that combine the elements of capitalism and socialism to various degrees. Great Britain, France, and Sweden, for instance, fall in the middle of the spectrum. In these nations, the government controls many essential services and industries, such as health care, energy production, and the manufacture of industrial goods. A wide range of businesses, however, are owned by individuals.

Capitalism. In a pure capitalist system, the economy is regulated by self-interest and market competition. Self-interest regulates the economy by guiding the actions of consumers and producers. Self-interest leads consumers to try to purchase the goods and services they desire at the lowest prices possible. Producers, on the other hand, are guided by self-interest to undertake only those business ventures that have the potential to make a profit.

Market competition regulates the economy by influencing the answers to the three economic questions of what to produce, how to produce, and for whom to produce. Businesses that produce goods or services wanted by consumers at prices consumers are willing to pay will be successful. Businesses that cannot do this soon will fail. For competition to be effective in regulating the market, however, it must operate with limited government interference.

Rather than being regulated by the government, prices in a pure capitalist system are set by the laws of supply and demand. The **law of supply** states that producers will supply more products when they can charge higher prices and fewer products when they must charge lower prices. The **law of demand** states that the demand for a product increases as the price of the product decreases. On the other hand, the demand for a product decreases as the price increases.

As market regulators, the forces of supply and demand work something like this: Suppose that the various electronics manufacturers are selling car stereos at prices ranging from a low of $90 to a high of $1,000. If consumers are unwilling to pay more than $700 for a car stereo, regardless of quality, those manufacturers selling the stereos for more than $700 will have to lower their prices. If these manufacturers cannot lower their prices and still make a profit, they will be forced out of business. If, on the other hand, consumers demand more car stereos than are being produced at any particular price, manufacturers will be able to raise their prices somewhat without negatively affecting demand.

Economist Adam Smith called this interplay between the forces of supply and demand the "invisible hand." According to Smith, if government interference is kept to a bare minimum and if competition is not restricted, the invisible hand of market forces will keep the economy in balance. This pure form of capitalism is sometimes referred to as *laissez-faire* (lay-say-FAIR) capitalism. *Laissez-faire* is French for "to let people do as they choose."

In practice, all capitalist systems have government regulations that protect the consumer and ensure fair business competition. These regulations, however, do not prevent individuals from setting up and running their own businesses with limited government interference. This commitment to limited government control of business operations has resulted in the labeling of capitalist economies as *free enterprise systems*.

Socialism. In a pure socialist system, economic activity is controlled by social need, rather than by self-interest, and by the government in the form of central planning, rather than by market forces. Thus the three basic questions of what to produce, how to produce, and for whom to produce are answered quite differently under pure socialism than they are under pure capitalism.

In a capitalist system, when the demand for products decreases, suppliers often reduce prices to attract buyers. Once demand increases, however, the sale signs are likely to disappear.

Most factories in the former Soviet Union are outdated. As a result, production levels fall far short of those possible in the technologically advanced factories of the West.

What to produce is determined by the needs of society. If a good or service is needed by the members of society, it is provided, regardless of whether it can be produced profitably. Need is not determined by consumer demand, however. Instead, need is determined by economic planners in the central government.

How to produce products also is determined by central planners. These central planners decide which factories will produce which goods and at what supply level. Rather than a range of similar products from which to choose, government planners provide consumers with basically one variety of each good. Thus market competition is not a factor in regulating supply and demand in a pure socialist economy.

For whom to produce is determined by need rather than by the ability to pay. It is for this reason that the means of production are owned by the government in a socialist system. Supporters of the socialist system claim that equal access to goods and services cannot be guaranteed if the means of production are owned by individuals.

The principles guiding socialism are social equality and economic fairness. In the pure so-

cialist model, socialism's ultimate goal is communism. **Communism** is a political and economic system in which property is communally owned. In such a system, social classes cease to exist and the role of the government declines as individuals learn to work together peacefully and willingly for the good of all.

According to Karl Marx and other early socialists, the sharp class divisions and social inequality that were characteristic of early capitalism would eventually lead the working class (the proletariat) to overthrow the capitalist class (the bourgeoisie). After the revolution, a dictatorship of the proletariat would be established to assist in the transformation to communism.

The goal of communism never has been achieved in practice. A major problem is the fact that nations that adopt a strong socialist model for their economies also adopt totalitarian forms of government. We will talk more about totalitarianism in the next section of this chapter. For now, it is sufficient to say that those in power in totalitarian governments hold complete authority over the lives of societal members. Public opposition to government policies rarely is allowed and most personal freedoms are greatly restricted. Before it began its move toward democracy in the early 1990s, the former Soviet Union was an example of such a society.

In the Western world, we refer to societies that combine socialism with a totalitarian government as communist, and it is generally the Communist party that is in power in such societies. Yet such systems are far from the communist ideal outlined by Karl Marx and the early socialists. In defense of this fact, modern socialist states argue that they have not yet achieved a communist system. Instead, they see themselves as being at an intermediate stage on the road to communism.

Many critics of socialism argue that socialist societies actually are stalled on the road to communism. And, according to these critics, the reason is very simple—the communism envisioned by Karl Marx is unworkable in the modern world. As proof, they point to the fact that the social conditions that were supposed to bring about the rise of communism no longer exist.

When Karl Marx and his colleague Friedrich Engels wrote *The Communist Manifesto* in 1848, living conditions for the working class were extremely harsh and class divisions were distinctly drawn. Today, workers in many capitalist nations enjoy very high standards of living. In contrast, severe social and economic problems plague socialist nations such as Cuba. The former Soviet Union is finding it very difficult to remedy the problems left in the wake of its socialist past. Critics of socialism point to the failings of socialist systems as evidence of the natural superiority of the free enterprise system.

Postindustrial America

Although the United States is one of the best examples of a free enterprise system, it does differ from the pure capitalist model. Among the factors that account for this difference are: (1) the rise of corporate capitalism, (2) the globalization of the economy, (3) the expanding role of government in regulating the economy, and (4) the changing nature of work in postindustrial America.

The Rise of Corporate Capitalism.
In Adam Smith's time, economic activities were controlled by the efforts of individual capitalists. By

the late 1800s, however, corporations had replaced individual capitalists as the moving force behind the economy. A **corporation** is a business organization that is owned by stockholders and is treated by law as if it were an individual person. Because it has the same legal rights as a person, a corporation can enter into contracts, negotiate bank loans, issue stocks and bonds, and buy and sell goods and services.

The rise of corporate capitalism has changed the relationship between business ownership and control. Like the owners of most small businesses and privately held companies today, early capitalists managed the day-to-day affairs of the businesses they owned. The same is not true in the case of modern corporations. Few corporate stockholders participate in daily business operations. And, in many cases, stockholders are not even individuals. Most American corporate stocks are owned by other corporations, Wall Street financial firms, foreign governments, and pension and mutual funds.

Corporations are the driving force behind the free enterprise system of the United States. Even though corporations account for only about 20 percent of all American businesses, they generate the overwhelming majority of all business sales each year.

Although corporations account for only about 20 percent of the businesses in the United States, they generate approximately 90 percent of business sales. Even more significant is the fact that the vast majority of these sales are produced by the nation's top 500 corporations.

One of the chief consequences of this shift of power from individual capitalists to corporations is the growth of oligopolies. An **oligopoly** exists when a few producers control an industry. The American automobile industry is one example of an oligopoly. The three companies that form the core of the American automobile industry—General Motors, Ford, and Chrysler—produced 64 percent of the cars sold in the United States in 1992. It is estimated that approximately 60 percent of all manufacturing in the United States is oligopolistic.

Critics of corporate capitalism argue that the concentration of wealth and power that occurs in oligopolistic markets weakens the self-regulatory features of the free enterprise system. Although price and quality still influence consumer decisions in such markets, oligopolies limit competition by reducing the number of producers vying for business. Less competition means a larger share of the market for each firm in the oligopoly.

Critics point out that oligopolies also limit competition by using pressure tactics in the political arena. Because such firms control large shares of the market, they often are able to push through legislation that increases their competitive edge. Currently, American automobile manufacturers, having suffered huge losses in sales to Japanese carmakers, are calling on the government to impose trade policies that are considered protectionist in

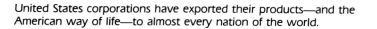
United States corporations have exported their products—and the American way of life—to almost every nation of the world.

nature. **Protectionism** is the use of trade barriers to protect domestic manufacturers from foreign competition. Common trade barriers include *quotas*—limits on the amount of goods that may be imported—and *tariffs*—surcharges on goods entering the country.

Supporters of protectionism argue that such policies safeguard American businesses from unfair foreign practices. As examples of such practices, supporters point both to the extremely low wages paid in some foreign nations and to the practice of *dumping,* the selling of goods below cost. Opponents of protectionism, on the other hand, argue that **free trade**—trade between nations that is unrestricted by trade barriers—is a cornerstone of free enterprise. According to these critics, in the absence of trade barriers, natural market forces will maintain economic efficiency by weeding out noncompetitive businesses.

The Globalization of the Economy.

The controversy over protectionism versus free trade is a result of profound changes in the nature of economic activity in the modern world. Today, the goods and services produced in one nation are bought and sold around the world. And many

companies not only sell their products in foreign markets but also produce them worldwide.

One of the major consequences of the globalization of markets is that nations become economically interdependent. As a result, the economic policies of one nation often affect the policies of other nations. And, even more important, economic conditions in one nation tend to trigger economic and political events in other nations.

At the center of the global economy are the world's major economic powers, called the "Group of Seven" (G-7): Canada, Great Britain, Germany, Italy, France, Japan, and the United States. The leaders of these nations meet annually to discuss issues relating to international economic policy.

The Expanding Role of Government.

Although the debate over foreign competition has brought the issue of government interference in economic affairs to the forefront, government's role in the economy has been expanding since the late 1800s. A growing population and the rise of corporate capitalism in the 1800s led the government to assume increased responsibility for the operation of the economy.

Principal among the economic functions that the government serves are

- *The regulation of economic activity.* Since the late 1800s, the government has passed a host of legislation aimed at promoting fair business competition, preventing the abuse of workers, and minimizing the negative side effects (such as pollution, traffic congestion, and soil erosion) of economic activities. In addition to legislation, the government has established federal agencies, such as the Office of Economic Opportunity and the Occupational Safety and Health Administration, to monitor business activities.

- *The protection of consumers.* Federal agencies such as the Food and Drug Administration, the Consumer Product Safety Commission, the Federal Trade Commission, and the Office of Consumer Affairs have been established to protect the rights and health of consumers.

- *The provision of public goods.* **Public goods** are goods and services that the government provides for everyone in society. Highways, public education, and national defense are examples of public goods. The government provides these goods because it would be impractical or impossible for private businesses to do so.

- *The promotion of economic well-being.* The government promotes economic well-being by redistributing tax revenues to individuals and businesses in need of assistance. Transfer payments are used to assist individuals, while businesses generally are assisted through subsidies.

The Changing Nature of Work.

One of the most significant consequences of the globalization of the economy has been America's continuing shift from an industrial base to a service base. This shift is due in part to advances in technology. Automation and increased efficiency have reduced the number of workers needed to meet demand. But even more important has been competition from the newly industrializing countries (NICs), particularly those in Latin America and Asia. Attracted by tax breaks and lower wage rates, many multinational corporations have set up shop in Mexico, Venezuela, South Korea, Taiwan, and other NICs.

The vacuum left by the loss of American manufacturing jobs has been filled in part by service jobs. Although some of these new jobs are in low-paying, low-skill fields, many require technical training and most require strong basic skills in reading, writing, and math. And, many of the manufacturing jobs that remain require analytical skills. Yet studies have indicated that as high as 20 percent of the American work force is functionally illiterate. Faced with growing competition from nations such as Japan, where only 1 percent of the work force is functionally illiterate, government and business leaders are calling for a strengthened commitment to quality education in the United States.

SECTION 1 REVIEW

DEFINE economic institution, factors of production, law of supply, law of demand, oligopoly, protectionism, free trade, public goods

1. *Comprehending Ideas* **(a)** Describe the characteristics of the primary sector, secondary sector, and tertiary sector.
   (b) How do preindustrial, industrial, and postindustrial economic systems differ in terms of which of these sectors is emphasized?

2. *Summarizing Ideas* **(a)** What are the characteristics of the pure capitalist model? **(b)** What are the characteristics of the pure socialist model?

3. *Seeing Relationships* Describe how the American free enterprise system has been affected by **(a)** the rise of corporate capitalism, **(b)** the globalization of the economy, **(c)** the expanding role of government, and **(d)** the changing nature of work.

2 THE POLITICAL INSTITUTION

No society can survive for long if each person in the society does exactly as he or she pleases. For society to run smoothly, people must act together for the common good. Thus all societies exercise some degree of power over societal members.

Power is the ability to control the behavior of others, with or without their consent. In very simple societies, power is held by the family. But in more complex societies, ultimate power falls to the **state**—the primary political authority in society. The power of the state is shaped by the **political institution**—the system of roles and norms that governs the distribution and exercise of power in society.

Functionalist sociologists analyze the political institution in terms of the functions of the state. Primary among these functions are the creation and enforcement of laws, the settling of conflicts between individuals, the provision of services, the establishment of economic and social policies, and the maintenance of relations with other nations. All of these functions center on the task of maintaining order in society.

Sociologists who adopt the conflict perspective, on the other hand, focus on how the political institution brings about social change. According to conflict theorists, different groups in society compete with one another for power. Although the political institution generally favors the wealthier segments of society, ongoing conflict causes the distribution of power to shift enough to result in varying degrees of social change.

The Legitimacy of Power

Regardless of their theoretical orientation, sociologists who study the political institution often focus on the legitimacy of power. **Legitimacy** refers to whether those in power are viewed as having the right to control, or govern, others. When power is exercised with the consent of the people being governed, it is considered legitimate. Power is considered illegitimate, on the other hand, when it is exercised against the will or without the approval of those being controlled.

Authority. Max Weber referred to legitimate power as **authority.** In his analysis of authority, Weber was particularly interested in how leaders come to be viewed as having the legitimate right to exercise power over others. According to Weber, the right to govern can be based on one of three types of authority: traditional authority, charismatic authority, or rational-legal authority.

Traditional authority is power that is legitimated by long-standing custom. In other words, people accept the exercise of power as legitimate because it has been considered legitimate in the

Some charismatic leaders, such as Iraq's Saddam Hussein, have such strong holds over their followers that their followers are willing to sacrifice their lives without question.

past. The claim to traditional authority usually is based on birthright, since it is passed down from generation to generation. Kings, queens, and tribal chieftains are examples of leaders who rely on traditional authority for their right to rule. Until the rise of the modern political state, traditional authority was the most common form of legitimate power.

Charismatic authority is power that is legitimated by the personal characteristics of the individual exercising the power. Charismatic leaders are able to exercise authority because their followers believe that such leaders possess special qualities that merit devotion and obedience. Charismatic leadership generally arises during periods of social unrest when people are searching for leaders who can offer them a better life. Examples of charismatic leaders include Buddha, Jesus, Adolf Hitler, Mahatma Gandhi, Mao Zedong, the Reverend Martin Luther King, Jr., the Ayatollah Khomeini, and Saddam Hussein. As is evident from the names mentioned on the list, charismatic leadership can have either positive or negative consequences for society.

Rational-legal authority is power that is legitimated by formal rules and regulations. In most instances, these rules and regulations are contained in a written constitution and set of laws that clearly outline the rights and obligations of those in power. Power rests not in the individual but in the office or position the individual holds. Thus the authority to govern is lost when an individual leaves or is removed from office. The president of the United States, for example, has the right to govern only while in office. Rational-legal authority is the most common form of authority in modern societies.

Coercion.   When those who govern lack legitimacy, control often takes the form of coercion. **Coercion** is power that is exercised through force or the threat of force. Examples of coercion include the use of armed troops to maintain order in a society. The use of troops is common in societies in which government leaders have come to power without the consent of most of the citizens. Coercion, however, is not limited to physical violence. Placing restrictions on the press or denying citizens the right to hold public meetings also are examples of coercion.

All political systems use force to some degree to maintain order. The threat of being sent to prison for breaking a law is a form of coercion. The difference between the force used in a legitimate political system versus the force used in an illegitimate system is a matter of degree. In a legitimate system, force is used as a last resort. In an illegitimate system, on the other hand, force or the threat of force is the principal method through which order is maintained.

Types of Government

Although the terms often are used interchangeably, the "state" is not the same thing as the "government." The combined political structures of a society, such as the presidency, Congress, and Supreme Court in the United States, form the state. The government, on the other hand, consists of the people who direct the power of the state. In the United States, for example, the federal government includes the president, the members of Congress, and the Supreme Court justices. The individuals who make up the government come and go. It is the state that gives a society's political system continuity by providing an underlying structure.

How power is exercised by the state varies by type of government. Sociologists recognize two basic types of government: democratic systems and authoritarian systems. As in the case of economic models, these systems are ideal types. Actual governments vary widely in their characteristics. All governments, however, can roughly be categorized as either democratic or authoritarian.

Democratic Systems.   In a **democracy,** power is exercised through the people. The central feature of a democracy is the right of the governed to participate in the political decision-making process. In practice, modern democratic systems are *representational democracies*—voters elect representatives who are entrusted with the task of making political decisions. If these elected officials do not perform to the liking of the electorate, they can be voted out of office.

For much of history, democracies were rare. It was much more common for states to establish

Text continues on page 334.

Economic Aid to Russia

The breakup of the Soviet Union in 1991 was an event of global importance, signaling the end of the Cold War and a significant move toward democracy throughout Eastern Europe. But the transition from communism to democracy and a free-market economy is proving difficult for the former Soviet republics. In the following excerpt from the article "Aid to Russia," which appeared in the March 12, 1993, issue of *CQ Researcher*, Rodman D. Griffin explores the current situation in Russia, the former Soviet Union's largest republic, and Russia's need for economic aid from the United States.

The same fear haunts Boris Nemtsov, the governor of Nizhniv Novgorod, Russia's third-biggest city, and President [Bill] Clinton: They worry that the world's largest nation may not survive the transition to a true democracy. Instead, they see the fledgling Russian Federation sliding back toward political and economic instability, becoming, in Nemtsov's words, "a monster armed with missiles."

Clinton sounded the alarm during the 1992 presidential campaign, warning that "no national security issue is more urgent" than preserving Russia's new democracy. . . .

"If we are willing to spend trillions of dollars to ensure communism's defeat in the Cold War," Clinton said, "surely we should be willing to invest a tiny fraction of that to support democracy's success where communism failed."

Although the amount Clinton is seeking is indeed tiny as foreign aid goes, the president's forcefulness suggested that he knows he faces a tough sell. In fact, according to a recent *Wall Street Journal*/NBC News poll, foreign issues and crises are the public's lowest-ranking priorities.

Reflecting political and economic realities at home, freshman Rep. Peter I. Blute, R-Mass., told the *Journal*: "We need assistance in Worcester and Fall River as much as they need it in Minsk and Kiev." Across the political aisle, Rep. Peter J. Visclosky, a five-term Indiana Democrat, put it just as bluntly: "My constituents believe charity begins at home."

Meanwhile, the bleak conditions in Russia prompt experts to sound an ominous and axiomatic warning: Desperate people do desperate things. In short, if the United States doesn't deliver major aid to Russia, these pessimists say, Clinton may face a crisis that not only dwarfs problems in Bosnia and Somalia but makes bygone Cold War hostilities seem like a lovers' spat: the emergence of an unstable, combative Russian state embroiled in territorial disputes and armed to the teeth with nuclear weapons.

The Economic Situation in Russia

With international aid in short supply, [Russian President Boris] Yeltsin is doing what he can. He has engineered several significant economic changes during the past 14 months. Price controls have been lifted on most consumer products. The ruble freely trades, more or less. And state-run auctions have transformed some 46,000 state-owned enterprises into privately owned businesses. Most experts say former President Mikhail S. Gorbachev logged fewer victories during his six years in the Kremlin.

Yet Yeltsin's bold moves have had a downside, too. While a few entrepreneurial types have become millionaires by taking advantage of the reforms, economists say up to half the 149.5 million population may have slipped below the poverty level. In addition, industrial production dropped 25 percent last year, twice the rate of decline during the Great Depression in the United States, and inflation soared to a staggering 2,200 percent. The resulting high prices virtually wiped out personal savings.

The hardships have relegated many members of Russia's solid middle class to a new class, the so-called "new poor." Moscow seamstress Nina Senatorova and her husband, Yuri, an engineer, are among those who have found the going tough. "Over the last year we have become paupers," 56-year-old Nina told *The Washington Post*. "We have forgotten the smell of roast chicken. Virtually all our money goes on food for the children."

The newly impoverished range from factory workers to engineers in defense factories; from once-privileged intellectuals to high-level members of the Communist Party. Few Russians could survive on the average monthly salary for workers of 7,000 rubles, roughly $12, without the generous state subsidies for housing and transportation.

Needy Russians received an estimated $3 billion in Western medicine and food last year. But that's small potatoes, experts say, compared with the vast amounts still needed—and the sweeping structural changes the vast region must undergo— if Russia is to withstand the shock of transition and become economically successful. . . .

Should the U.S. Provide Aid?

Given the size and number of [former Soviet] republics and the depth of their problems, many lawmakers on Capitol Hill feel the United States cannot afford to provide enough aid to make a difference. They point to the huge $100 billion annual tab for unifying Germany—and West Germany's economic system and government were already in place and able to embrace its communist neighbor. By comparison, experts say, transforming the former Soviet republics could cost a staggering $2 trillion.

Still other experts see another major money problem revolving around aid to the former Soviet republics. When the Soviet Union broke up, it owed some $80 billion to Western lenders. That money must still be repaid, but if international loans are made to the republics, they will, as one reporter put it, "simply amount to Western taxpayers bailing out Western banks for the bad loans they made to the Soviet Union in years past."

"A very large amount of the monies that will be disbursed under the IMF [International Monetary Fund] and World Bank loans is just going to go right back to Western Europe in debt service," Melanie Tammen, director of the Project on Global Economic Liberty at the Cato Institute, told *Insight*

magazine. "And this is startlingly similar to what happened in Latin America in the 1980s." Even so, Russia likely will be treated as a special case. "The West realizes that while communism is dead, stable democracies have yet to arise in that part of the world," says John Tedstrom, an economist who specializes in Russia at the Rand Corporation in Santa Monica, Calif. "We battled the Soviet monster for so long, the West feels some collective responsibility to help."

The danger, of course, is that without substantial assistance . . . , severe domestic problems could encourage the revival of authoritarianism.

Though that prospect seems remote to many, aid proponents argue that if the world turns its back on the former U.S.S.R.—with its huge army and lethal nuclear arsenal—it does so at its own peril. If nothing else, hard times in the republics would probably send hundreds of thousands of desperate refugees into Eastern Europe.

"There is legitimate concern that if reforms fail, there will be social unrest that would be dangerous for us—and the world," says Clifford G. Gaddy, a research associate at the Brookings Institution. "That's the ultimate motivation for support."

"Virtually everyone agrees we have to help," adds Stephen Cohen, director of Russian studies at Princeton University. "We said we would during the Cold War. More important, it is in our national security interest. After all, $3 billion in aid to Russia is 1 percent of our defense budget."

Of course, the 149.5 million people in the Russian Federation offer an alluring market for Western goods. Simply put, helping now could be a very good investment.

1. Describe the economic successes of Boris Yeltsin. What economic problems still remain?
2. According to the author, what do experts fear might happen if Russia does not receive sufficient economic aid?
3. Write a brief essay opposing or supporting United States aid to Russia.

Under the rules of Great Britain's constitutional monarchy, members of the House of Lords have limited power. Most legislative power is held by the members of the House of Commons, who are elected to office.

Democracies are becoming more common because the conditions that nourish the growth of democratic systems are found in increasing numbers of societies. Among the conditions needed for a democracy to thrive are the following:

- *Industrialization.* Although industrialization does not necessarily lead to democracy, most democratic societies are industrialized. According to sociologist Gerhard Lenski, one reason for this is that the literate, urban populations characteristic of advanced industrial societies generally expect to have a voice in the political process.

- *Access to information.* Democracy requires well-informed voters. Thus democracies are strongest in those societies in which the public and the media have open access to information.

- *Limits on power.* All governments exercise power. In democracies, however, clear limits are placed on the scope of government power. One way in which power is limited is by spreading the power base among many different groups. When power is divided among the branches of government and among nongovernmental organizations such as labor unions, businesses, and religious organizations, it cannot become concentrated in the hands of a few people.

- *Shared values.* Although the right to hold opposing views is a cornerstone of democracy, a shared set of basic values is essential. Without some agreement among voters on basic values, it would be difficult to reach the compromises necessary in a democratic system.

Democratic governments can be distinguished by the type of economic model they adopt. Many democracies have capitalist economies. The United States is an example of a democratic nation with a capitalist economy. Other democracies, such as many of those in Western Europe, have socialist economies. The combination of a democratic government and a socialist economy is called **democratic socialism.** Under democratic socialism, the government owns some of the factors of production, but individuals have basic human rights and maintain control over economic planning through the election of government officials. Sweden, Denmark, and Austria are examples of democratic socialist states.

monarchies. A **monarchy** is a type of government in which one person rules. The ruler—known as the *monarch*—comes to power through inheritance. Most of the few remaining monarchies have limited power. True political power primarily rests with elected officials. In many instances, the monarch is nothing more than the symbolic head of state. This type of monarchy is called a **constitutional monarchy.** Constitutional monarchies are considered to be democratic because the ultimate power rests with elected officials. Great Britain is an example of a constitutional monarchy.

Authoritarian Systems. In a government based on **authoritarianism,** power rests firmly with the state. Members of society have little or no say in the political decision-making process. And, in most cases, government leaders cannot be removed from office through legal means.

Authoritarian governments exist in a variety of forms. An **absolute monarchy** is an authoritarian system in which the hereditary ruler holds absolute power. Bahrain and Oman are two nations ruled by absolute monarchies. An authoritarian system in which power is in the hands of a single individual is called a **dictatorship.** Malawi, which has neither a prime minister nor a vice president, is ruled by Hastings K. Banda, named president for life in 1970. A **junta** is an authoritarian system in which political power has been seized from the previous government by force. Juntas are very common in Africa.

The most extreme form of authoritarianism is totalitarianism. Under **totalitarianism,** government leaders accept few limits on their authority. Because totalitarian governments allow little opposition to their policies, the lives of individuals in totalitarian states are rigidly controlled.

Although authoritarian governments have existed throughout history, totalitarianism is a twentieth-century development. This is due in large part to the fact that social control in a totalitarian state is dependent on closely monitoring the activities of societal members. Technological advances, such as computers and electronic surveillance equipment, have made it easier for totalitarian states worldwide to collect and store information about people.

Nazi Germany under Adolf Hitler, the Soviet Union under Joseph Stalin, and Cambodia under the Khmer Rouge probably present the most

Authoritarian governments, such as Chile under General Augusto Pinochet (top) and the Soviet Union prior to democratization (bottom), use shows of military strength as reminders of their ultimate authority. Note that the Chilean soldiers are using the goose step, a march characteristic of totalitarian societies.

striking examples of totalitarianism. The world, however, does not lack for current examples. Among the nations that are totalitarian or nearly totalitarian are North Korea, China, Cuba, Iraq, Libya, Myanmar, and Syria.

Of more interest to sociologists than which nations are totalitarian is the question of why individuals submit to totalitarian rule. The Interpreting Primary Sources feature on page 400 explores this topic in the case of Nazi Germany.

The American Political System

Since the time of Max Weber, sociologists have devoted considerable attention to the analysis of political systems. Among the topics of special interest to sociologists studying the American political system are (1) the role of political parties, (2) the effect of special interest groups on public policy, (3) variations in voter participation, and (4) the question of who actually rules America.

Political Parties.   A **political party** is an organization that seeks to gain power in the government through legitimate means. Political parties distinguish themselves from one another by adopting specific points of view on issues of interest to voters and by formulating programs for legislative action.

By supporting candidates from the party that most closely represents their views, voters directly influence government decision making. A party that cannot get enough of its candidates elected to office will not be able to put its programs into effect. Political parties thus form a bridge between the will of the people and government actions. These parties also provide a check on the concentration of power.

In the United States, voters can choose between candidates from the Democratic party or the Republican party. Although various other parties occasionally field candidates for local, state, and national office, nearly all elected officials since before the Civil War have been members of either the Democratic party or the Republican party. For this reason, the United States is considered to have a two-party system.

A two-party system is relatively rare in a democracy. Most democracies, such as many of those in Western Europe, have multiparty systems.

These parties generally hold clearly differentiated views on the major issues. Therefore, they tend to appeal to specific groups of voters.

Appealing to limited numbers of voters is workable in such multiparty systems because of the way in which legislative seats are assigned. If, for example, a party receives 10 percent of the popular vote on the national level, it will receive 10 percent of the seats in the national legislature. This system is called *proportional representation.* Proportional representation ensures that minority parties—and thus minority viewpoints—receive a voice in the government.

In the United States, on the other hand, candidates are elected to office on the basis of a *simple plurality*—whichever candidate receives the most votes wins. Critics argue that this winner-takes-all rule prevents citizens who hold minority views from having a say in the government, since minority-party candidates cannot hope to win a majority of votes.

Critics also argue that in addition to discouraging the formation of minority parties, the winner-takes-all rule also discourages sharp differences between the policy positions of the Republican and Democratic parties. According to this view, the two parties adopt positions that are only slightly different from one another for fear of alienating voters. Extremely conservative positions or extremely liberal positions would cost the parties too many votes.

In the 1992 presidential election, voter disenchantment with the policy positions of the two major party candidates was at least partially responsible for the unusually strong showing of a third-party candidate. In that year, independent Ross Perot vied with Democrat Bill Clinton and Republican George Bush for election to our nation's highest office. Although election results gave the presidency to Clinton, Perot's share of the popular vote was the highest of any third-party candidate since Theodore Roosevelt in 1912. The results of the 1992 presidential election can be seen in the chart on page 337.

Interest Groups.   In nations with proportional representation, legislators can be counted on to vote with their party. The same is not true in the United States. As is evident from the chart on page 337, Americans tend to vote their conscience

Results of the 1992 Presidential Election (in percents*)

The Voters	Percent of All Voters	Bill Clinton	George Bush	Ross Perot
Sex				
Male	46	41	38	21
Female	54	46	37	17
Race				
White	87	39	41	20
African American	9	82	11	7
Political Affiliation				
Democrat	38	78	10	13
Republican	34	10	72	17
Independent	27	38	32	30
Selected Voter Groups				
Democrats for Bush—1988	10	54	27	19
First-time voters	11	48	30	22
Working women	31	46	36	19
Military veterans	17	41	37	22
Single parents	8	50	29	21
Issues of Concern				
Economy/jobs	43	52	24	24
Budget deficit	21	36	26	38
Health care	19	67	19	14
Family values	15	23	65	11
Taxes	14	26	57	17
Abortion	13	37	55	8
Education	13	60	25	15
Foreign policy	8	9	86	5
Environment	6	73	14	13
Election Results				
Popular vote (percent)	100	43	38	19
Electoral vote (number)	525	357	168	0

* Some percentages may not add to 100 due to rounding error.
Source: Adapted from Election Day exit poll conducted by Voter Research & Surveys, an association of ABC News, CNN, CBS News, and NBC News.

CASE STUDY

The Mass Media and Presidential Politics

The mass media has changed the nature of American presidential politics. According to political scientist Doris A. Graber, politics in the age of television is characterized by a decline in the influence of political parties, an increase in the role played by the media in candidate selection, an attraction for candidates who "televise well," and an emphasis on made-for-media campaigning.

In the 1940s, when social scientists first began to examine the effects of the media on presidential campaigns, party affiliation was the most important factor that voters used to determine whether they would vote for a candidate. A candidate's personality and his or her stand on the issues ranked third and fourth on the list of factors of interest to voters. Today, personality has replaced political affiliation as the most important determinant of voter appeal.

One reason that party affiliation has dropped in importance is the ability of candidates to speak directly to the public. Prior to the use of television, voters relied on the party to inform them of the candidates' stands on the issues. Today, however, candidates can reach voters in their homes through television and radio advertising and through news coverage. Consequently, candidates no longer are dependent on their political parties to pass on their views.

As personality has come to play a stronger role in influencing voter opinions, the power of the media to influence which candidates are successful in their election bids also has increased. Early in the primaries, members of the media define which candidates have a chance of winning and which issues will be of importance in the campaign. The media's efforts are assisted by the use of public opinion polls. Candidates who perform better than early polls predict they will are perceived as winners and thus receive added news coverage. On the other hand, candidates who perform below expectations often are discounted early in the race and thus receive little media attention.

Negative or inadequate media coverage can be devastating for candidates. First, it is difficult for candidates who perform poorly in early polls to better their standings in future polls once they have been labeled as "losers." Second, candidates who do not make strong showings in the polls often cannot raise enough money to adequately finance their campaigns.

Because of the need to attract media support, the skill with which a person can play to the cameras is an important consideration in recruiting candidates to run for president. It often has been noted that Abraham Lincoln—with his rough facial features and lanky appearance—would have had considerable difficulty getting elected in the age of television. Image is so important that candidates often hire full-time media advisers and acting coaches to help them develop effective television personalities.

The importance of media coverage also has changed the way candidates campaign. Candidates now plan campaign appearances with media exposure in mind. Thus they tend to favor press conferences, talk show appearances, and trips to interesting places—events that will play well to wide audiences.

The 1992 presidential election campaign illustrates the enormous influence of the media on American politics. During the month before the election, third-party candidate Ross Perot spent almost $37 million to air eight campaign commercials—seven half-hour programs and one full-hour program. These commercials were watched in an estimated 13 million American households. Moreover, on election eve night, Perot spent an additional $3 million for air time on the three major television networks. Although Perot lost the election, such intense media exposure helped him to win almost 20 percent of the popular vote.

rather than the party line. This characteristic of the American political system has led to the rise of interest groups. An **interest group** is an organization that attempts to influence the political decision-making process.

Interest groups use a variety of techniques to raise political and public support for the issues of interest to their members. Contributing money to the political campaigns of candidates who might vote on special-interest issues is one of the most common pressure techniques used by interest groups. Much of the funds distributed by interest groups are collected by political action committees (PACs). In 1992, for example, PACs contributed over $179 million to congressional candidates. There currently are more than 4,100 PACs operating in the United States. Interest groups also apply pressure by collecting petitions, organizing letter-writing campaigns, filing lawsuits, and promising to have their members vote for sympathetic candidates.

Many large interest groups—such as the National Rifle Association (NRA), the National Education Association (NEA), and the National Organization for Women (NOW)—also launch expensive media campaigns to sway public opinion. In addition, most groups employ lobbyists to meet directly with government officials in order

One way that members of interest groups affect the political decision-making process is by presenting testimony at congressional committee hearings.

to win their support. Estimates indicate that more than 20,000 political lobbyists now work in Washington, D.C.

Political Participation. Public participation is at the heart of the democratic process. Yet the United States has one of the lowest rates of voter participation among the democratic nations of the world. More than 30 percent of voting-age Americans are not registered to vote. And, among registered voters, only around 55 percent voted in the 1992 presidential election. The percentage of registered voters who cast ballots in nonpresidential elections is even lower. Thus when candidates speak of winning landslide victories and of having the mandate of the people, they generally are basing their claims on having received the support of less than a third of the potential voters.

As can be seen in the chart on this page, voter participation varies among different groups of Americans. For example, whites and African Americans are much more likely to vote than are Hispanic Americans. Similarly, employed people are far more likely to vote than are people who are unemployed. Voter participation also varies by level of education—people with college educations have a higher voter participation rate than do people who have never attended college.

Age also is associated with voter participation. Traditionally, people aged 45 to 64 have had the highest voter participation rate. Each election year, however, the participation rate of people aged 65 and older has increased. In 1992, the rate for the elderly surpassed the rate for people aged 45 to 64. It is, however, too early to tell whether

Voter Participation by Selected Characteristics

Characteristic	Percentage Voting
Sex	
Male	60.2
Female	62.3
Race	
White	63.6
African American	54.0
Hispanic American	28.9
Age	
18–20 years old	38.5
21–24 years old	45.7
25–34 years old	53.2
35–44 years old	63.6
45–64 years old	70.0
65 and over	70.1
Education	
Less than eight years of school	35.1
High school graduate	57.5
College graduate	81.0
Region	
Northeast	61.2
Midwest	67.2
South	59.0
West	58.5
Employment status	
Unemployed	46.2
Employed	63.8

Source: U.S. Bureau of the Census, 1993.

Bloom County, © 1986 Washington Post Writers Group. Reprinted with permission.

this trend will continue. People under the age of 25 are the least likely to vote.

Who Rules America?   Low voter turnout, among other features of the American political system, has led sociologists to question who actually rules America. Sociologists who examine this question generally adopt one of two models: the power-elite model or the pluralist model.

The **power-elite model,** first presented by C. Wright Mills, states that political power is exercised by and for the privileged few in society. According to Mills, the top ranks in America's political, economic, and military organizations are controlled by people who are linked by ties of family, friendship, and social background.

The **pluralist model,** on the other hand, states that the political process is controlled by interest groups that compete with one another for power. Although supporters of this model view power as being distributed unequally in society, they argue that competition among the groups prevents power from becoming concentrated in the hands of a few people.

CHAPTER 13   SUMMARY

The economic institution is the system of roles and norms that governs the production, distribution, and consumption of goods and services in a society. All economic systems contain three basic sectors: the primary sector, which deals with the extraction of raw materials; the secondary sector, which deals with manufacturing; and the tertiary sector, which deals with the production of services. Which sector is emphasized depends on whether the society has a preindustrial, industrial, or postindustrial economy.

Industrial and postindustrial societies can be categorized by the type of economic model that they follow. Sociologists recognize two basic models: capitalism and socialism. The United States follows the capitalist economic model but does not mirror it. Four factors account for this: the rise of corporate capitalism, the globalization of the economy, the role of the government in the economy, and the changing nature of work in postindustrial society.

The political institution is the system of roles and norms that governs the distribution and exercise of power in society. Power can be legitimate or illegitimate. According to Max Weber, legitimate power, which is called authority, can take three forms: traditional authority, charismatic authority, or rational-legal authority.

How political authority is exercised varies by type of government. Sociologists recognize two basic types of government: democratic systems and authoritarian systems. In a democracy, power is exercised through the people. In an authoritarian system, power rests with the state. The American political system is a democracy. Political parties, interest groups, voter participation, and the question of who actually rules America are among the topics of particular interest to sociologists.

INTERPRETING THE VISUAL RECORD: Analyzing Editorial Cartoons

An editorial cartoon is a drawing that presents a point of view on an economic, political, or social issue or topic. Editorial cartoons have been used throughout United States history to influence public opinion. Some cartoons present a positive point of view. Most editorial cartoons, however, are critical of a policy, event, person, or group. Editorial cartoons typically are found in the editorial sections of newspapers and newsmagazines.

The two most important techniques that cartoonists use to express their message are caricature and symbolism. A *caricature* is a drawing that exaggerates or distorts physical features. *Symbolism* is the use of one thing to represent another idea, feeling, or object. Common symbols for the United States, for example, include the bald eagle and Uncle Sam. Cartoonists often include titles, captions, or other labels to get across their messages.

How to Analyze an Editorial Cartoon

To analyze an editorial cartoon, follow the steps in the next column.

1. **Identify the caricatures.** Identify the people or objects in the cartoon. Note whether the cartoon figures are exaggerated or distorted. Determine whether the cartoonist's point of view is positive or negative.

2. **Identify the symbols used.** Determine the meaning of each symbol. State how the symbols are connected to the message being communicated by the cartoonist. Decide how the symbols clarify the message.

3. **Read all labels.** Editorial cartoonists often use labels to identify people, objects, events, or ideas. Determine how the labels help express the cartoonist's point of view.

4. **Read the caption.** Many cartoons carry a caption in addition to other labels. If the cartoon has a caption, state the relationship of the caption to the editorial cartoon. Determine whether the viewpoint being expressed is that of the cartoonist, the cartoon figure, or other persons or institutions shown in the cartoon.

IMAGINATION

Applying the Skill

Study the editorial cartoon on page 342. The cartoon analyzes the advisability of giving top-level government employees huge raises at a time when the nation faces a budget deficit and a host of social problems. The government employees are symbolized by three large, well-dressed men. The budget deficit is symbolized by a shady looking man. The social problems facing the nation are symbolized by an elderly man, a homeless man, a poor woman, and a small child puzzling over the costs of an education. The government employees are recognizable by what they say. The other figures are labeled. The tone of the cartoon leads the reader to conclude that the cartoonist believes that the money would be better spent on social problems and on reducing the federal deficit.

Practicing the Skill

Study the editorial cartoon on this page. Then, on a separate sheet of paper, answer each of the following questions:

1. Who are the central figures in the editorial cartoon?

2. What symbol is being used to represent these central figures?

3. (a) Why is the drawing of Fidel Castro a caricature? (b) What symbol is used to represent Cuba's political system?

4. What social issue is being examined in the cartoon?

5. (a) What is the message of the cartoon? (b) What is the cartoonist's point of view?

Castrosaurus Habitat: Cuba

Deng Xiaoceratops Habitat: China

STILL WALKING THE EARTH

JEFF KOTERBA
Omaha World-Herald

© 1991 Jeff Koterba. Courtesy Omaha World Herald.

Reviewing Sociological Terms

On a separate sheet of paper, supply the term that correctly completes each sentence.

1. A _____ is a business organization that is owned by stockholders and is treated by law as if it were an individual person.

2. The _____ _____ is the system of roles and norms that governs the exercise of power in society.

3. The _____ _____ is the system of roles and norms that governs the production, distribution, and consumption of goods and services.

4. _____ is a political and economic system in which property is communally owned.

Thinking Critically about Sociology

1. ***Comprehending Ideas*** *(a)* What do the laws of supply and demand state? *(b)* How do the laws of supply and demand help regulate a capitalist economy?

2. ***Summarizing Ideas*** Describe the four major economic functions performed by the American government.

3. ***Developing a Structured Overview*** Review the rules on pages 40–41 for developing a structured overview. Then construct an overview of this chapter's discussion of preindustrial, industrial, and postindustrial economic systems.

4. ***Seeing Relationships*** *(a)* What is an oligopoly? *(b)* According to critics of corporate capitalism, how do oligopolies undermine the self-regulatory features of the free enterprise system?

5. ***Applying Ideas*** *(a)* What distinguishes legitimate power from illegitimate power? *(b)* Provide several specific examples of each of the three legitimate forms of power outlined by Max Weber. *(c)* Provide several specific examples of illegitimate power.

6. ***Understanding Ideas*** What effect do factors of production have on which sector of the economy a society emphasizes?

7. ***Analyzing Ideas*** *(a)* How has the globalization of the economy given rise to the controversy over protectionism versus free trade? *(b)* What effect has the globalization of the economy had on the nature of work in the United States?

8. ***Contrasting Ideas*** Describe the characteristics of the two basic types of government recognized by sociologists and explain how they differ in terms of the exercise of state power.

Exercising Sociological Skills

1. ***Analyzing Viewpoints*** Reread the Applying Sociology feature on pages 332–333. Then, using the skills presented in the Developing Sociological Imagination feature on pages 284–285, analyze the arguments for and against giving aid to Russia.

2. ***Interpreting Ideas*** According to the Case Study on page 338, how has the media affected presidential politics in America?

3. ***Analyzing Editorial Cartoons*** Select an editorial cartoon from a newspaper or newsmagazine. Then analyze the cartoon using the skills presented in the Developing Sociological Imagination feature on pages 342–343.

Extending Sociological Imagination

1. Prepare a brief report on one of the following topics: *(a)* multiparty versus two-party political systems; *(b)* the role of political action committees (PACs) in campaign financing; or *(c)* variations in voter participation rates by social characteristics.

2. Prepare a chart comparing the basic characteristics of the pure capitalist and pure socialist economic models.

INTERPRETING PRIMARY SOURCES
The Authoritarian Character

Psychoanalyst Erich Fromm originally published *Escape from Freedom,* his classic study on why people submit to totalitarianism, in 1941 during Adolf Hitler's reign of terror. The free world was shocked by the brutality of Hitler's Germany. The question of the day was how a civilized nation could act in such an inhumane manner. According to Fromm, the answer rests in people's desire to escape feelings of isolation and powerlessness. By submitting to the will of those more powerful or by dominating those less powerful, people achieve a sense of security. Fromm labeled the personality structure that gives rise to this response the "authoritarian character."

In the following excerpt from *Escape from Freedom,* Fromm—whose early training was in sociology—describes the authoritarian character using illustrations from Hitler's Germany. While reading the excerpt, consider how the authoritarian character leads people to submit to totalitarianism.

The feature common to all authoritarian thinking is the conviction that life is determined by forces outside of man's own self, his interest, his wishes. The only possible happiness lies in the submission to these forces. . . . The authoritarian character does not lack activity, courage, or belief. But these qualities for him mean something entirely different from what they mean for the person who does not long for submission. For the authoritarian character activity is rooted in a basic feeling of powerlessness which it tends to overcome. Activity in this sense means to act in the name of something higher than one's own self. . . . The authoritarian character wins his strength to act through his leaning on superior power. . . .

The courage of the authoritarian character is essentially a courage to suffer what fate or its personal representative or "leader" may have destined him for. To suffer without complaining is his highest virtue—not the courage of trying to end suffering or at least to diminish it. Not to change fate, but to submit to it, is the heroism of the authoritarian character.

He has belief in authority as long as it is strong and commanding. . . . For him the world is composed of people with power and those without it, of superior ones and inferior ones. . . . He experiences only domination or submission. Differences, whether of sex or race, to him are necessarily signs of superiority or inferiority. A difference which does not have this connotation is unthinkable to him. . . .

The essence of the authoritarian character has been described as the simultaneous presence of sadistic and masochistic drives. Sadism was understood as aiming at unrestricted power over another person more or less mixed with destructiveness; masochism as aiming at dissolving oneself in an overwhelmingly strong power and participating in its strength and glory. . . .

The *sadistic craving for power* finds manifold expressions in *Mein Kampf.* It is characteristic of Hitler's relationship to the German masses whom he despises and "loves" in the typically sadistic manner. . . . He speaks of the satisfaction the masses have in domination. "What they want is the victory of the stronger and the annihilation or the unconditional surrender of the weaker." . . .

[The] masochistic side of the Nazi ideology and practice is most obvious with respect to the masses. They are told again and again: the individual is nothing and does not count. The individual should accept this personal insignificance, dissolve himself in a higher power, and then feel proud in participating in the strength and glory of this higher power. Hitler expresses this idea clearly in his definition of idealism: "Idealism alone leads men to voluntary acknowledgment of the privilege of force and strength and thus makes them become a dust particle of that order which forms and shapes the entire universe."

Source Review

1. How does the authoritarian character lead individuals to submit to totalitarianism?

2. Why is Hitler's Germany a good example of the authoritarian character?

Education and Religion

1 The Sociology of Education

The Functionalist Perspective on Education
The Conflict Perspective on Education
Issues in American Education

2 The Sociology of Religion

The Functions of Religion
The Nature of Religion
Religion in American Society

Chapter Focus

Chapter 14 focuses on education and religion as social institutions. The chapter opens with a discussion of the functionalist and conflict perspectives on education. Attention then is paid to contemporary issues in American education. Finally, the chapter turns to a discussion of religion, focusing on the functions of religion, the nature of religion, and religion in American society.

As you study the chapter, look for the answers to the following questions:

1. How do the views of functionalist and conflict sociologists differ concerning education?
2. What are some of the current issues in American education?
3. Which basic societal needs are served by religion and how does the nature of religion vary around the world?
4. What are the distinctive features of religion in American society?

KEY TERMS

The following terms, while not the only terms emphasized in the chapter, are basic to your understanding of sociology. Determine the meaning of each term, either by using the Glossary or by watching for context clues as you read the chapter.

education
mandatory education
hidden curriculum

bilingual education
religion
sacred

profane
theism
denomination

INTRODUCTION

Education and religion, like all social institutions, arose in response to basic human needs. Providing children with the knowledge they need to inherit the world of their elders and the emotional strength they need to face that world are among the goals that bind groups of people together as social beings.

The form that education takes varies widely from society to society. The educational process may be as simple as a few tribal elders passing on their ancient lore to apprenticed youth or as complex as any bureaucracy found in modern society.

The institution of religion also is found in various forms, depending on how a society attempts to provide answers for life's mysterious questions. In some societies, people seek these answers through the worship of one all-powerful God. In other societies, these answers are sought in nature or through the worship of ancestors. No society exists without some form of religion. In this chapter, we will examine the basic characteristics of the educational and religious institutions and learn the varied ways in which they serve the needs of human groups.

1 THE SOCIOLOGY OF EDUCATION

Societal survival depends in large part on the socialization of new members into the ways of the society. The young must be taught the norms and values of the society and must learn the skills necessary to take over the work of adults. Societies must ensure that children, as well as immigrants, acquire the knowledge, skills, behavior patterns, and values necessary to become functioning members of their society. To accomplish these goals, every society develops a system of roles and norms that ensures the transmission of knowledge, values, and patterns of behavior from one generation to the next. This system of roles and norms is called **education.**

In some small preindustrial societies, education is largely informal and occurs mainly as socialization within the family. Family members teach children the norms and values of the society as well as certain basic skills. Mothers may teach young daughters the skills of cooking, pottery, and food gathering. Fathers may teach young sons the skills of hunting and fishing. Children learn the ways of society mainly by participating in adult activities.

As societies become more complex, the family comes to share the process of educating the young with more formally established organizations. Formal education, which involves instruction by specially trained teachers who follow officially recognized policies, is called **schooling.**

Because informal education typically occurs within the family setting, this form of socialization usually is of interest to family sociologists. Sociologists who study the educational institution typically look at the socialization that occurs outside the family setting in the form of schooling.

As with many topics in sociology, functionalist sociologists and conflict sociologists differ in their views on the educational institution. The functionalist perspective tends to focus on the ways in which education serves to integrate societal members and contribute to the smooth operation of society. The conflict perspective, on the other hand, tends to focus on the ways in which education serves to limit the access of individuals and groups to power. Neither perspective alone, however, gives a complete picture of the educational institution.

Although the methods used to teach young people differ worldwide, every society must pass on its culture to the next generation.

The Functionalist Perspective on Education

Sociologists who follow the functionalist perspective believe that the functions performed by education work to maintain the stability and smooth operation of society. Among the most important of these functions are the transmission of culture, social integration, the creation of knowledge, and occupational placement.

Transmission of Culture. For societies to survive over time, they must pass on the components of their culture to succeeding generations. After families, schools are perhaps the most important and obvious means through which children learn their societal norms, values, and beliefs. In addition to teaching classroom subjects such as history, geography, mathematics, and reading, schools also teach students patriotism, loyalty, and socially acceptable forms of behavior.

Patriotism is taught to schoolchildren throughout the course of their educations through songs, rituals, plays, and stories. In the United States, for example, young children are taught to salute the flag, recite the Pledge of Allegiance, and stand when the national anthem is played. Even though they may not know all of the words to the Pledge

of Allegiance, or even what these words mean, children learn very early that this is an important ritual accompanied by feelings of pride. This sense of pride in the nation is strengthened through the teaching of courses such as United States history and civics. American schools also emphasize the benefits of the free enterprise system, individualism, and democracy, values on which the United States is based.

All societies use the schools to socialize their young into support of their own social and political systems. Japanese education, for example, emphasizes conformity, cooperation, group loyalty, and respect for elders, traits highly valued in Japan. Before the former Soviet Union was democratized, schoolchildren there were taught the principles of the socialist system.

Socializing the young into accepting the superiority of their own political and social systems often is at least partly accomplished by teaching them to believe that other such systems are inferior. This serves to create a bond of unity and loyalty among societal members. Loyalty to one's nation then is reinforced by emphasizing the nation's accomplishments in history books, while very often downplaying or ignoring the less positive aspects of the nation's history.

Schools also help to teach socially acceptable forms of behavior. Children learn to be punctual, to obey rules, and to respect authority by encountering a series of rewards and punishments designed to encourage these behaviors. Teachers may award gold stars, certificates, and badges to students not only for good academic performance, but for good citizenship as well.

Because teachers and administrators are such visible authority figures, the school is a powerful agent of social control. But schools do not rely on the strength of sanctions alone to enforce acceptable behavior. Their ultimate goal is to produce citizens who have internalized cultural norms and so have learned to control their own behavior in the social world.

Social Integration. Functionalist sociologists also believe that education serves to produce a society of individuals who share a common unity. Modern societies very often contain a number of different religious, ethnic, and racial groups. This is particularly true in the United States, which each year admits large numbers of immigrants from all around the world. Schools are expected to provide a common set of cultural values and skills that will allow all members of society to take advantage of occupational, economic, and political opportunities.

This expectation formed the basis of the "melting pot" view of American society. Laws concerning **mandatory education,** or enforced schooling, largely came about during the early twentieth century when large numbers of immigrants were entering the United States. Then, schools were expected to "Americanize" students by eliminating all traces of their cultural backgrounds.

Today, many schools around the nation are teaching a multicultural curriculum designed to help students understand how their racial and ethnic heritages contribute to a richer American culture. At the same time, however, schools continue to foster social integration and a national unity by teaching a core set of skills and values common to the American way of life.

Creation of Knowledge. In addition to its function as a transmitter of existing knowledge, education also serves to generate new knowledge and new technology. Societies must be able to adapt to changing conditions and education provides the means with which individuals may develop new approaches and new solutions to problems. Schools stimulate intellectual inquiry and the critical thinking skills necessary to serve the needs of the future.

Because the acquisition of new knowledge and technology is important for societal growth and development, much of the research conducted in colleges and universities worldwide is funded by governmental agencies. In many societies, the funds for research also come from private corporations eager for new developments and inventions that can be used to increase profits.

Occupational Placement. Education also serves to screen and select the members of societies according to the work they will do as adults. In societies that do not assign adult positions on the basis of ascribed statuses, such as family background or wealth, some system must exist for identifying and training the people who will do the important work of society.

According to the functionalist perspective, schools in industrialized nations such as the United States very early identify students who show special talents and abilities and train them to occupy the important positions in society. Beginning in elementary school and continuing throughout their educational lives, children are tested and evaluated as to their achievements and abilities. These evaluations are used to steer some students toward college-bound courses, some toward vocational courses, and some toward low-level positions in the labor force.

The occupational selection function of education is particularly evident in Japanese society. In Japan, students are admitted into universities only if they pass the entrance examinations, regardless of their financial backgrounds. These examinations are particularly grueling, and most students spend their entire educational careers preparing for those few hours of test taking that literally will determine the course of their lives. Families hire tutors to supplement classroom instruction, and high school students spend much of their free time studying and working toward what Japanese society calls the "examination war."

These examinations are a national event each year in Japan, gaining wide media coverage. Fam-

Acceptance into one of Japan's competitive universities requires years of intense study.

ily, friends, and observers stand literally for hours in the early morning waiting for university officials to post the names of those students who have passed the examinations. The wisdom of the examination war has been questioned recently by Western observers concerned about the pressures students must face. Admission to a Japanese university, however, assures future employment in that society's most prestigious corporations.

The Conflict Perspective on Education

Sociologists who follow the functionalist perspective believe that the functions performed by education work to maintain the stability and smooth operation of society. Sociologists who follow the conflict perspective, however, view education in a different light. Conflict sociologists believe that the educational system serves to limit the access of individuals and groups to power and social rewards. These sociologists typically point to two factors as evidence that education helps to maintain inequality: social control and tracking. Additionally, conflict sociologists note that achieve-

ment in school tends to reflect existing inequalities in society tied to socioeconomic status.

Social Control. Although functionalist sociologists view the school as an agent of social control, they believe the purpose of this control is to produce citizens who share a common set of values. Conflict sociologists, on the other hand, believe that this control serves to produce citizens who largely accept the basic inequalities of the social system and who do not question the existing order. Conflict sociologists further believe that most individuals are unaware of this process.

Sociologists use the term **hidden curriculum** to describe the transmission by schools of cultural goals that are not openly acknowledged. The hidden curriculum involves teaching a conservative set of values that center around obedience to authority. According to conflict sociologists, this serves the dominant groups in society by helping them maintain their positions of power.

From the time of their earliest experiences in school, children are taught to be punctual, to stand in line, to be quiet, and to obey. Students who do

Text continues on page 354.

Education in the Land of Opportunity

Because of mandatory education laws, most of us take school for granted. We go to sleep each evening knowing what is in store for us the next day. We make plans based on our schedule of classes, our homework assignments, and our after-school activities.

Yet for many immigrants coming to the United States around the turn of the century, going to school was a momentous event. It was the road to opportunity and to a new life in a new land. These immigrants looked to education to help make them Americans.

What was school like in the eyes of these new members of our society? Author Mary Antin, a Russian immigrant, gives us a personal account of her first year at school.

> On our second day [in America] . . . a little girl from across the alley came and offered to conduct us to school. My father was out, but we had a few words of English by this time. We knew the word school. We understood. This child, who had never seen us till yesterday, who could not pronounce our names, who was not much better dressed than we, was able to offer us the freedom of the schools of Boston! No application made, no questions asked, no examinations, rulings, exclusions. . . . The doors stood open for every one of us. The smallest child could show us the way.

However, because the term was almost over, Mary had to wait until September before starting school. Then, at that long awaited time, her dream of getting an education became a reality:

> Father himself conducted us to school. He would not have delegated that mission to the President of the United States. He had awaited the day with impatience equal to mine, and the visions he saw as he hurried us over the sunflecked pavements transcended all my dreams. . . .
> [My father] took long strides in his eagerness, the rest of us running and hopping to keep up.

> At last [we] stood around the teacher's desk; and my father, in his impossible English, gave us over in her charge, with some broken word of his hopes for us that his swelling heart could no longer contain. . . .
> I think [the teacher] guessed what my father's best English could not convey. I think she divined that by the simple act of delivering our school certificates to her he took possession of America.

Although she was almost a teenager, Mary was placed in the first grade. But this did not prevent her from pursuing an education.

> I was not a bit too large for my little chair and desk in the baby class, but my mind, of course, was too mature by six or seven years for the work. So as soon as I could understand what the teacher said in class, I was advanced to the second grade. . . .
> There were about half a dozen of us beginners in English, in age from six to fifteen. [The teacher] made a special class of us, and aided us so skillfully and earnestly in our endeavors to "see-a-cat," and "hear-a-dog-bark," and "look-at-the-hen," that we turned over page after page of the ravishing history, eager to find out how the common world looked, smelled, and tasted in the strange speech. . . .

All along, Mary had the help and guidance of dedicated teachers. For this she was forever grateful.

> Whenever the teachers did anything special to help me over my private difficulties, my gratitude went out to them silently. It meant so much to me that they halted the lesson to give me a lift, that I . . . must love them for it. . . .
> Apostles all of an ideal, they go to their work in a spirit of love and inquiry, seeking not comfort, not position, not old-age pensions, but truth. . . .

From this reading, we can gather what being able to go to school meant to Mary Antin. To further understand the importance of education to the hundreds of thousands of people who immigrated to this country, answer the following questions:

1. What academic skill was most important to Mary's progress in school?

2. Why do you think school meant so much to Mary's father, even though he would not have the opportunity to get a formal education? How important is school today both to parents and to students?

3. What norms, values, and roles are present in the educational institution, as shown in these excerpts?

The Granger Collection, New York

THE NIGHT SCHOOL.

According to conflict sociologists, punishments and rewards given in school teach obedience to authority and produce adults who will not disrupt society.

not fall in line with these expectations often have difficulties in school, no matter how well they perform academically. Once students are identified and labeled as behavior problems, they often are watched closely by teachers and administrators. The goal of the schools in this regard is to eliminate the disruptive influences of people who will not conform. Conflict sociologists believe that the goal of the hidden curriculum is the creation of a cooperative adult work force who will accept things the way they are.

Tracking. Another way that the educational system maintains inequality, according to conflict sociologists, is through tracking. **Tracking** is the assignment of students to different types of educational programs. Common types of educational programs include general studies, vocational training, and college-bound programs.

Students are assigned to tracks on the basis of intelligence and aptitude test scores, classroom grades, and teacher evaluations. The goal of tracking is to allow students to progress at their own pace by grouping them with other students of similar abilities.

Functionalist sociologists view tracking as a means to ensure that people of differing abilities are trained to take over the wide variety of jobs that exist in society. Conflict sociologists, on the other hand, view tracking as a means through which the wealthy and powerful maintain their positions in society, while keeping down the disadvantaged and the poor.

Conflict sociologists argue that most typically it is members of the lower social classes and minority groups who are assigned to the lower, or lesser ability, tracks. These tracks are geared toward blue-collar or vocational jobs in which salaries and prestige are low. Middle-class students, on the other hand, are more likely to be assigned to college tracks, giving them access to prestigious, high-paying occupations.

Conflict theorists go on to point out that research suggests that methods of classroom instruction differ according to track. One study, for example, examined 900 high school classes in the United States. The study found that higher-track classes, which generally contain large numbers of higher-income students, encourage creative and independent thinking, self-direction, and an active participation in the educational process. Lower-track classes, which generally contain large numbers of lower-income and minority students, focus instead on classroom drill and memorization. Lower-track classes also tend to emphasize conforming behavior, cooperation, and getting along with other people.

Conflict sociologists believe that the type of instruction students receive in the different tracks works to mold their behavior to fit their future occupations. For example, students in the higher tracks learn creativity, independence, and self-motivation—traits desirable in managerial and professional jobs. Students in the lower tracks, on the other hand, learn to work under supervision, follow a routine, and obey instructions—traits typically called for in vocational-level jobs.

Although in theory students may switch tracks during their educational careers, this seldom occurs. One reason conflict sociologists give to explain why students rarely change tracks is the self-fulfilling prophecy, a prediction that leads to behavior that makes the prediction come true. Tracking creates a ranking system within the schools that can have a major impact on the self-concepts of the students. Students in the higher tracks come to think of themselves as bright and capable because they have been and continue to be treated as bright and capable people.

Students in the lower tracks, on the other hand, may come to think of themselves as inferior because their track is a highly visible and continuing testimony to their lesser abilities. Once students believe that they are intellectually inferior, they behave in such a way as to confirm that belief. Their teachers, family members, and peers come to expect less from them, and the students themselves may stop trying to achieve. Thus they fulfill the prophecy of their educational tracks.

Socioeconomic Status and Education. Americans have long believed that education is

the key to social mobility. And, indeed, there is a strong relationship between education and income. As is evident from the chart on page 356, income increases as education increases.

Although functionalist sociologists view education as a system that gives all people the chance to succeed according to their own abilities and talents, conflict sociologists do not agree. Rather, conflict sociologists believe that the opportunities for educational success and social mobility are distributed as unequally as wealth, power, and prestige. In this way, achievement in school reflects existing inequalities in society.

Educational achievement appears to be tied strongly to socioeconomic status. Middle- and upper-class students tend to stay in school longer and to do better while in school than students from the lower socioeconomic classes. Higher-status individuals also are more likely to attend college, to graduate from college, and to translate this experience into success in the work world. And, since socioeconomic status and race overlap to a great extent, minority groups tend to have less educational experience and, hence, less access to social mobility.

Conflict theorists believe that socioeconomic status affects the distribution of educational achievement in a number of ways. First, the expectations that families have for their children's achievement differ by socioeconomic class. Higher-status families tend to assume that their children will achieve educationally and so tend to motivate them more toward this end. Lower-status families, on the other hand, hope that their children will be successful, but they do not necessarily believe that education is the key to this success. They therefore may stress the value of getting a good job over higher education, even though education is tied to economic success.

Second, higher-status families are better able than are lower-status families to provide a home environment designed to enrich learning. For example, the homes of middle- and upper-class students are more likely to contain books and toys that stimulate thought and creativity. Higher-status children also are more likely to be exposed to cultural events that broaden their horizons and to values that emphasize long-term goal setting. Lower-status families, on the other hand, have less opportunity to provide their children with these

Average Income by Years of School Completed*

	Education Completed		Average Income
Male			
	Elementary:	8 years or less	$19,188
	High School:	1–3 years	$22,564
		4 years	$28,043
	College:	1–3 years	$34,188
		4 years	$44,554
		5 or more years	$55,831
Female			
	Elementary:	8 years or less	$13,322
	High School:	1–3 years	$15,381
		4 years	$18,954
	College:	1–3 years	$22,654
		4 years	$28,911
		5 or more years	$35,827

* For year-round full-time workers 25 years old and over.
Source: *Statistical Abstract of the United States, 1992*, p. 454.

Conflict sociologists argue that socio-economic status can affect the degree to which students are prepared to face the challenges of education.

things because their incomes often are barely enough to provide even the basic necessities of life.

Finally, the expense involved in keeping a child in school is high, particularly when that child's potential income is needed to help a family survive. Families with higher incomes are better able to bear the cost of keeping their children in school. Higher-status families also are better able to pay the expenses involved in putting their children through college. This then perpetuates the access of higher-status people to well-paying and prestigious jobs.

Issues in American Education

Americans always have had a great deal of faith in the institution of education. There is a strong belief in this nation that education not only can cure social ills, but also that it can uphold and encourage the ideals of democracy and free enterprise around the world.

Because Americans believe so strongly in the value of education, educational issues often have been the focus of public concern. In the early part of this century, the issues in American education revolved around mandatory education laws and the assimilation of a steady stream of immigrants. Several decades ago, Americans looked to education to produce a nation able to compete against the Soviet Union in the space race. Among the contemporary issues in education being discussed are educational reform, violence in the schools, and bilingual education.

Educational Reform. In 1983, the National Commission on Excellence in Education published a report entitled *A Nation at Risk*. This report detailed a sharp decline in the level of quality in American education, a decline that threatens the future of the United States as a world leader. The commission's report charged that the United States has fallen behind other industrialized nations in math, science, and literacy skills, and predicted that a continuation of this trend would hurt the United States in its efforts to compete in world markets. The report also stated that the skills of American youth are not keeping pace with our nation's own increasing technology.

In addition to addressing the deficits found in American schools, the commission made specific recommendations urging swift and considerable reforms in the nation's educational system. Among the recommendations made by the commission were a more demanding curriculum, an emphasis on achievement, and stricter requirements for graduation. The commission also urged more homework, more discipline in the schools, better attendance, and a longer school year.

In the years since the commission's report was published, many states and school districts have overhauled their educational systems and most have raised their requirements for graduation. Teacher salaries have increased and many states now require new teachers to pass strict competency exams.

Despite these reforms, however, many people believe that the United States still is a nation at

Calvin and Hobbes

by Bill Watterson

Adult Illiteracy in the United States

Living in the United States today are an estimated 25 million adults who cannot read or write. For these people, the fact of illiteracy is accompanied everyday by frustration, embarrassment, and sometimes even danger. The illiterate cannot order from restaurant menus, fill out job applications, understand the instructions on prescription medicine bottles, or help their children with their homework.

An additional 35 million people in the United States lack the reading, computational, and critical thinking skills necessary to meet the demands of an increasingly technological society. Researchers estimate that between 13 and 20 percent of the nation's 17-year-olds fit into this category. Among minority youth, the figure may be as high as 40 percent.

Many entry-level positions in service occupations currently are going unfilled because applicants lack the necessary reading, writing, and arithmetic skills. The New York Telephone Company, for example, recently tested over 22,000 applicants for operator and repair technician positions. Only 14 percent of the applicants passed the tests.

The toll that illiteracy takes on the individual is high. The toll that it takes on society may be even higher. Several years ago, for example, a Navy recruit damaged $250,000 worth of equipment because he could not read a repair manual. The Navy reports that about 30 percent of its new recruits are a danger to themselves and to others because they cannot read or follow simple instructions.

Today's prison inmate population in the United States has an estimated 60 to 80 percent illiteracy rate. Illiteracy also is associated with chronic unemployment, crime, and welfare. A recent report published by the Sunbelt Institute, a non-profit research organization, quotes statistics from the United States Labor Department show-ing that illiteracy costs the South $57 billion a year in lost tax revenue, lost productivity, crime, and welfare.

The rapid growth and spread of technology is increasing the level of skill required for employment in all sectors of the economy. Some experts believe that by the year 2000, jobs will be all but nonexistent for those people who do not have at least a twelfth-grade reading, writing, and computational level.

The growing need to compete in world markets is fast making the illiteracy problem in the United States a matter of considerable concern. Experts fear that the United States will lose the competitive edge it has long held in the global economy. To help combat the problem, a number of educational, governmental, and corporate organizations are spending millions of dollars on adult literacy programs around the nation. Unfortunately, only about 9 percent of the people who need help with their literacy skills currently are being reached.

Part of the problem lies in the widespread misconception that the United States is well on its way toward eliminating illiteracy within its borders. By international standards, only 5 percent of America's population is illiterate. The international standard for literacy, however, is only a fourth-grade reading level. This level once served the needs of America's work force, but that time is past. Studies show that about 70 percent of the reading material in a cross-section of jobs nationwide now are written for a ninth-grade comprehension level.

Adding to the problem of illiteracy is the fact that many people who cannot read and write feel too ashamed to seek help. The illiterate often construct elaborate strategies to keep other people from finding out their secret. Sometimes even their own children do not realize that the parent cannot read or write.

risk. For example, scores on the nationwide Scholastic Aptitude Test have not increased in the decade since the commission's report was first released. And, according to the National Assessment of Educational Progress, the reading proficiency scores of nine-year-old students also have not increased over the years. Moreover, American students continue to lag behind students in other industrialized nations in math and science.

To improve the quality of education in the United States, the federal government in 1993 unveiled a $420 million package of education legislation. This legislation calls for the creation of a National Education Goals Panel, consisting of educators and leaders from business, labor, state governments, and local governments. The panel will oversee the progress of American schools in meeting goals designed to make American students lead the world in math, science, and other core subjects by the year 2000. The legislation also calls for improved job training for those students who are not bound for college.

Violence in the Schools.

A Gallup poll conducted in 1991 found that 20 percent of Americans are concerned about the issue of discipline in the schools. As a matter of fact, polls conducted over the past two decades consistently have shown that the American people believe that lack of discipline is one of the chief problems affecting the nation's schools.

The problem of school discipline perhaps is most glaringly apparent in the high number of assaults, rapes, and robberies that occur in American schools. Teachers increasingly are the victims of this violence. In Detroit, for example, student assaults against teachers rose 900 percent between 1985 and 1990. In Cleveland, over 7,000 violent incidents against teachers were reported in 1991.

Although no nationwide statistics exist to indicate whether school violence is on the rise, most experts agree that violent episodes increasingly involve deadly weapons. According to the 1990 Youth Risk Behavior Survey, conducted by the Centers for Disease Control, 20 percent of high school students carry a weapon at least once a month for self-protection or for use in a fight. One out of 20 high school students in the United States carries a firearm at least once a month. Thus

it is not surprising that shootings and hostage situations in schools have occurred in at least 35 states around the nation. Furthermore, handgun homicides are now the second leading cause of death among high school students.

To discourage students from carrying weapons, growing numbers of schools are installing sophisticated security devices. For instance, one-fourth of the nation's large urban schools now use the hand-held or walk-through metal detectors most commonly seen at airports. In addition, about 245 of the nation's 15,000 school districts have their own police or security departments. In fact, New York City's school security force is the sixth-largest police force of any kind in the United States.

Some educators believe that the best approach to curbing violence in schools lies in educational programs that teach young people how to resolve their disputes peacefully. The philosophy behind such programs is that young people who learn cooperation, concern for others, and problem-solving skills will be less likely to resort to violence. Thousands of schools across the nation, including elementary schools, now offer some kind of violence-prevention program.

Bilingual Education.

One of the most controversial issues in American education centers around bilingual education. **Bilingual education** refers to a system in which non-English-speaking students are taught in their native languages until they can attend classes taught in English. Bilingual education was established in the United States a few years after a 1974 Supreme Court decision required schools to provide language programs for students with limited proficiency in English. Prior to the development of bilingual education, children who were new to the United States immediately were placed in regular classrooms, where they had to "sink or swim."

Supporters of bilingual education believe this system is the best way to ensure that non-native-speaking students can progress in school while they are becoming familiar with the English language. Opponents of bilingual education, on the other hand, believe that this system interferes with the assimilation of students into mainstream society. Critics argue that it may take four to five years under the bilingual program for students to

In order to protect students and teachers from violence, many schools around the nation have installed security devices such as metal detectors.

learn English, during which time they lose critical language development skills.

The debate over bilingual education undoubtedly will continue for some time to come. According to figures from the U.S. Department of Education, approximately 2 million students currently are classified as having limited English proficiency. The drive to continue bilingual education has been especially strong in California and Florida, states that contain large ethnic populations. A battle is being waged, however, by opposing forces who wish to have English declared the only officially recognized language of the United States. More than a third of the states around the nation already have instituted statutes making English their official language.

SECTION 1 REVIEW

DEFINE education, schooling, mandatory education, hidden curriculum

1. **Comparing Ideas** How do conflict and functionalist sociologists differ in their views concerning education?

2. **Summarizing Ideas** Describe the concerns involved in the issues of **(a)** educational reform, **(b)** violence in the schools, and **(c)** bilingual education.

2 THE SOCIOLOGY OF RELIGION

Throughout time and in all places, human beings have searched for answers to the ultimate questions of life and death. Societies have struggled with the needs to give meaning to human existence and to provide societal members with the motivation for survival. According to sociologist Emile Durkheim, societies universally have attempted to satisfy these needs by making a sharp distinction between the sacred and the profane.

The **sacred** is anything that is considered to be part of the supernatural world and that inspires awe, respect, and reverence. The **profane,** on the other hand, is anything considered to be part of the ordinary world and thus commonplace and familiar.

It is the sharp distinction between the sacred and the profane that is at the heart of all religions. **Religion** may be defined as a system of roles and norms organized around the sacred realm that binds people together in social groups. As with all basic institutions, religion is a universal phe-

nomenon. The form that religion takes, however, varies from society to society and even within a single society over time. Religion appears in many forms because different societies give sacred meaning to a wide variety of objects, events, and experiences. No one thing is considered to be sacred by everyone on earth.

According to sociologists, religion is a social creation. Things take on sacred meaning only when they are socially defined as such by a group of believers. Things that are sacred in one society may be profane in another society. In Hindu society, for example, the cow is revered as holy. To Christians, however, a cow is regarded as a source

While some religions consider the lighting of candles to be sacred, others find holiness in meditation. Still other religions give sacred meaning to the written word. To people outside of the particular religion, however, these things may seem ordinary.

of food. Similarly, many Christians believe that a wafer given in a religious ritual is a sacred symbol, but Hindus would regard this wafer simply as something to eat. Some societies worship their ancestors; other societies honor animals and trees. Anything can take on sacred meaning when it is socially defined as such, including a rock, a house, a book, or a stick.

Religion also is a social creation because it is a communal activity based on institutionalized beliefs and practices. The personal belief system of an individual does not form a religion. Because religion is a shared activity, it is influenced by the same social characteristics, such as technology, social class, and ethnicity, that influence the other basic institutions.

Religion focuses on the supernatural world, and thus belief in the truth of religion is based on faith rather than on science. Sociologists, therefore, are not concerned with the truth or falsity of any religion. Rather, sociologists focus on the social characteristics of religion and the consequences that religion has for society. One of the topics of interest to sociologists centers on the functions of religion.

The Functions of Religion

The fact that religion is a universal phenomenon suggests that it serves essential functions for individuals and for society as a whole. Among the most important of these functions are social cohesion, social control, and emotional support.

Social Cohesion. One of the most important functions of religion is that it adds to social cohesion, the strengthening of bonds among people. However, some societies that contain a variety of religions have been the sites of hostile and continuous conflict. Pakistan, for example, was created from portions of India in 1947 to ease tensions between Muslims and Hindus. More recently, the Middle East has been the scene of strife among Christians, Muslims, and Jews.

For individuals, participation in religious rituals and the sharing of beliefs create a sense of belonging that makes them feel less alone in the world. In his classic study of suicide, Emile Durkheim found that suicide rates were lowest among those people who had the strongest attachments

to religious groups. These attachments served to anchor people to society, providing them with support and purpose.

Social Control. Religion also serves as a powerful agent of social control, encouraging conformity to the norms of society. Norms and values surrounding important societal issues may not only be formalized in laws but also may be supported by religious doctrine. Belief by followers in the sacred quality of writings such as the Bible and the Koran gives a divine purpose to conformity. Religion also works to maintain the traditional social order by presenting this order as one commanded by God.

Some religions also provide formalized means through which individuals may rid themselves of guilt for straying from acceptable norms and values. Rituals such as confession and communion serve as emotional releases for individuals while contributing to the unity of the group. Religion thus works to maintain a strong control over behavior by providing a yardstick against which individuals may judge themselves and be judged by other people.

On the other hand, the emphasis of religion on conformity to the existing order may inhibit innovation, freedom of thought, and social reform. When a society gives sacred meaning to its norms and values, it may deny individuals the freedom to question or change unjust practices that support inequality. Obedience to religious doctrine may leave little room for ideas and beliefs contrary to that doctrine.

Emotional Support. A third function of religion is to provide emotional support for people during difficult times. Religion helps people endure disappointments, suffering, and deprivations by providing comfort and a belief that harsh circumstances have a special purpose. This belief motivates people to survive even when happiness appears out of reach and life seems hopeless.

Religion also provides answers to the ultimate questions of life and death, answers that cannot be provided by science and common sense. These answers lend strength and calm to people as they approach the unknown and the unexpected.

The emotional support lent by religion may, however, block social progress and social

Inside View of a Goal in the Inquisition, shewing the several methods of Torture and Cruelty, as exercised in presence of the Inquisitor, &c.

During the Inquisition of the 1200s, religious leaders had the power to torture disbelievers.

change. Religion often encourages people to accept their lives as they are because their future rewards will be that much greater in the spiritual life. If people receive too much support and encouragement to endure life as it is, they may never attempt to seek out the source of their troubles and make changes. Suffering may go unchallenged by individuals and groups who believe that their problems are trivial in the great scheme of things.

The Nature of Religion

Religion exists in varied forms around the world. All religions, however, contain certain basic elements. Among these elements are rituals, belief systems, and organizational structures.

Rituals. In terms of religion, a **ritual** may be defined as an established pattern of behavior through which a group of believers experiences the sacred. The variety of religious rituals found around the world is enormous, but some ritual behavior is a part of every religion.

Religious rituals often are used to mark changes in status, such as those surrounding birth, marriage, and death. Baptisms, weddings, and funeral ceremonies, for example, usually are conducted in sacred places by persons acknowledged as religious leaders.

Rituals also are used to unite believers and reinforce faith. Prayer meetings, worship services, and religious feasts, for instance, allow believers to express their devotion to the religion while contributing to the unity of the group.

Some rituals involve asking divine beings to intervene in human affairs, while other rituals focus on giving thanks to divine beings for benefits that have been received. These rituals generally include the sacred symbols of the faith. Clothing, herbs, chalices, crosses, books, and other religious symbols often are used only in special places on special days to emphasize their sacred character.

Belief Systems.   Religions found around the world vary considerably in the content of their belief systems. In general, belief systems can be organized into three basic types: animism, theism, and ethicalism.

Animism is a belief system in which spirits are active in influencing human life. Animals, plants, rivers, mountains, and even the wind are believed to contain spirits. Societies with animistic religions do not worship these spirits as gods, but rather see them as supernatural forces that can be manipulated to human advantage. Rituals such as fasting, dancing, and purification of the body often are used to bring about the good will of the spirits or to thank them for gifts.

One type of animism is called shamanism. In **shamanism,** the spirits communicate only with one person in the group, who is acknowledged to be a specialist. This person, called the shaman, is believed to communicate with the spirits either by speaking to them directly or by making his soul leave his body and enter the spirit world. Because followers believe the shaman can communicate

All religions are guided by a set of beliefs that define the relationship between human beings and the supernatural world. Although the content of these belief systems vary widely around the world, all such systems serve to provide individuals and groups with rules for living in society.

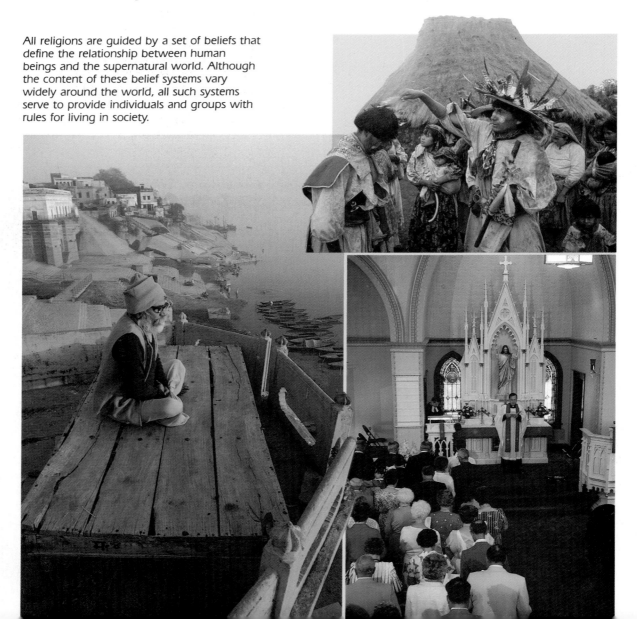

with spirits, they also believe he can heal the sick, predict the future, and see events happening over wide distances. Shamans, also called *witch doctors* and *medicine men*, can be found among small preindustrial societies in northern Asia and North and South America.

Another type of animism, called totemism, is most commonly found in Australia and some Pacific islands. With **totemism,** there is a belief in a kinship between humans and animals or natural objects. The animal or object, called a *totem*, is considered sacred and is thought to represent a family, clan, or its ancestors. Because of its supposed supernatural quality, the totem is treated with awe and respect, and no one is allowed to hurt, eat, kill, or even touch it. Totems are seen as helpful protectors who watch over the group.

A second belief system found around the world is theism. **Theism** is the belief in a god or gods. In theism, the god is considered a divine power worthy of worship who is thought to be interested in human existence. There are two subtypes of theism: monotheism and polytheism.

Monotheism may be defined as the belief in one god. Judaism, Christianity, and Islam are examples of monotheistic religions. Christianity, with more than a billion-and-a-half followers, is the world's largest religion. All monotheistic religions contain an organizational structure, sacred writings, worship rituals, and an organized priesthood or ministry.

Polytheism refers to the belief in a number of gods. The best-known polytheistic religion probably is Hinduism. Polytheistic religions usually center around one powerful god who has control over a number of lesser gods. The lesser gods are thought to have their own separate spheres of influence, controlling such things as harvests, childbirth, and earthquakes.

The third religious belief system, **ethicalism,** is the belief that moral principles have a sacred quality. Ethical religions are based on a set of principles, such as truth, honor, and tolerance, that serve as a guide to living a righteous life. Some examples of ethical religions, which are found mainly in Asia, are Buddhism, Confucianism, and Shintoism. Ethicalism involves meditation and purity of thought and action. The goal for followers of ethical religions is to reach their highest human potential.

Organizational Structures. The organizational structure of religion can be categorized into four types: ecclesia, denominations, sects, and cults. These categories are ideal types of organizational structures that apply mainly to religions found in the Western World.

An **ecclesia** is a type of religious organization in which all people in the society are members by virtue of their birth. Ecclesia are formally allied with the state and are structured, bureaucratic organizations. These structures usually are long-lived, with trained officials who use considerable power. Ecclesia do not tolerate religious differences among the population, often making membership a matter of law. Although there no longer are true ecclesia in the world, fundamentalist Islam in Iran resembles this type of organization.

A **denomination** is a well-established religious organization in which a substantial portion of the population are members. Examples of denominations include Presbyterians and Baptists. Like the ecclesia, denominations are formal, bureaucratic structures with trained officials. Denominations typically are tolerant, holding strongly to their own beliefs while acknowledging the rights of others to hold beliefs that differ. Denominations tend to be long-lived and to have middle- and upper-class memberships. Although many members are born into denominations, these organizations usually welcome converts.

A **sect** is a relatively small religious organization that typically has split off from a denomination because of doctrinal differences. Examples of sects include Assemblies of God, Jehovah's Witnesses, and Hassidic Jews. Sects tend to claim exclusive access to religious truth and generally are intolerant of other faiths. These organizations also tend to be hostile toward the existing power structure, seeing it as corrupt and worldly.

Members, who tend to be of lower socioeconomic status, are recruited by conversion and must show continuing and highly visible signs of their commitment to the faith. The clergy tend not to have had formal training, and worship ceremonies encourage emotion, spontaneity, and active participation by the entire congregation. Many sects are short-lived, but some, like the Methodists, become denominations over time.

A **cult** is a religious group founded on the revelations of a person believed to have special

Some cults meet tragic ends. On orders from their leader, Jim Jones, all members of the People's Temple committed suicide in 1978 by drinking Kool-Aid laced with cyanide.

knowledge. Cults typically are led by charismatic figures who are believed by their converts to have supernatural qualities. Cults generally reject the rest of society, including its institutions. People who join cults typically are disillusioned by traditional religion and by life in general.

In 1993, Branch Davidian cult leader David Koresh and his followers waged a 51-day standoff against federal agents at the cult's compound near Waco, Texas. The siege began when agents raided the compound to serve search warrants and an arrest warrant for Koresh on illegal weapons charges. Cult members opened fire on the agents, killing four of them. Despite Koresh's promise to surrender, he and his followers remained in their heavily armed compound. When federal agents attempted to end the siege by pumping tear gas into the compound, cult members set fire to the buildings. Koresh and dozens of his followers, including children, died in the blaze.

Religion in American Society

The United States has long been a haven for religious freedom. For centuries, numerous immigrant groups have looked to America to provide sanctuary from religious persecution. As a result, one feature of contemporary American religion is its great variety, which reflects the pluralism of American culture. The United States now is home to hundreds of different religious denominations, sects, and cults within its boundaries.

Religion in the United States also is characterized by the high value that Americans place on it. There is a general opinion in the United States that all people should hold to some religious beliefs. According to a recent poll taken by the Gallup Organization, over 90 percent of Americans believe in God or a Universal Spirit. The same organization found 84 percent of Americans reporting that they pray to God. Americans tend to use their religious beliefs to uphold other treasured American values, such as democracy, hard work, individualism, and charitableness.

Another feature of American religion is the separation of church and state, which is given formal sanction in the Constitution. For the protection of all religions in the United States, the government lacks the official power to either support or deny any religious beliefs. Hence, the United States, unlike Italy, has no national religion.

Sociologists who study religion in the United States generally focus on religious affiliation and religious participation. An additional topic that has gained the attention of sociologists in recent years is the rise of fundamentalist Christianity.

Religious Affiliation. Although over 90 percent of Americans express a religious preference, only about 70 percent are affiliated with some religious organization. This figure has remained relatively stable over the past few decades. Even though the United States contains a plurality of religions, most people claiming religious affiliation are members of mainstream denominations.

If we were to examine religious affiliation by looking at the major faiths—Protestantism, Roman Catholicism, and Judaism—we would find that Protestants are the most numerous in the United States. But breaking down the faiths into denominations yields different findings.

As can be seen in the table on this page, the Roman Catholic Church, with almost 59 million members, is the largest religious organization in the United States. Moreover, Roman Catholics tend to be a unified organization, unlike most of the other denominations. Methodists, for example, may claim affiliation in any of nine different denominational organizations, including the United Methodists, the Fundamental Methodists, and the Southern Methodists.

Studies have found a number of demographic differences among religious groups. Jews, Episcopalians, and Presbyterians, for example, tend to be better educated and to have higher incomes than other religious groups. In terms of region, Baptists and Methodists reside mainly in the South and Midwest. The largest proportions of Catholics, Jews, Episcopalians, and Presbyterians live in the Northeast. There even are political differences among the major faiths. Protestants traditionally have backed the Republican party, while Catholics and Jews tend to give their support to the Democrats.

Religious Participation. Although the majority of Americans express religious preferences, only about 41 percent of people attend religious services on a regular basis. The proportion of people who attend church or synagogue regularly has remained fairly stable over the past few decades. Women, African Americans, and older Americans are more likely to participate regularly in services. Among the major faiths, Catholics go to services more often than do Protestants or Jews.

Regular attendance at a church or synagogue, however, is a poor indicator of religious involvement. Sociologists generally find it difficult to measure **religiosity,** or the importance of religion in a person's life. At the heart of the problem is the fact that religious experience and commitment vary so much from person to person. Affiliation with a religious organization, and even participation in that religious organization, gives little information about religiosity because people attend services for a variety of reasons, including socializing and making business contacts. What sociologists generally do agree on is that religious

Religious Membership in the United States*

Group	Members	Group	Members
Roman Catholic	58,568,015	Jehovah's Witnesses	858,367
Baptist	30,872,761	Adventist	745,375
Methodist	12,418,110	Christian Methodist Episcopal	718,922
Lutheran	8,347,519	Church of the Nazarene	573,834
Muslim	8,000,000	Reformed	571,115
Churches of God	5,744,879	Salvation Army	445,566
Latter-Day Saints	4,459,231	Mennonite	364,739
Jewish	4,300,000	Polish National Catholic	282,411
Presbyterian	4,225,736	Christian & Missionary Alliance	279,207
Eastern Orthodox	4,205,453	Brethren (German Baptist)	200,794
Pentecostal	3,785,500	Evangelical Free Church	192,352
Episcopal	2,452,615	Unitarian Universalist	141,315
Churches of Christ	1,683,346	Friends	112,957
United Church of Christ	1,599,212	Wesleyan	110,561
Christian Churches & Churches of Christ	1,070,616	Baha'i	110,000
Disciples of Christ	1,039,692	Christian Congregation	109,919

* Groups of 100,000 or more.
Source: *The World Almanac and Book of Facts, 1993,* pp. 717–718.

participation has many dimensions and can be experienced in many ways.

Fundamentalist Christianity.

While participation in the mainstream denominations has been declining, membership in fundamentalist, or evangelical, Christian groups has been on the rise. A variety of fundamentalist Christian groups exist in the United States, but they all share similar features. They believe unquestioningly in the complete accuracy of the Bible, insist on a literal translation of Scripture, and view their beliefs as the one true religion. They also believe in personal salvation through conversion—the "born again" experience—and share a commitment to bring Jesus Christ into the lives of all nonbelievers.

Evangelical groups have been remarkably successful in their recruitment of new members. Currently, around 35 million Americans consider themselves to be born again or evangelical Christians. According to research by the Gallup organization, 87 percent of evangelical Christians consider religion to be an important part of their lives. Most members of fundamentalist faiths attend religious services on a regular basis.

In recent years, fundamentalist Christian ministers and followers have joined together to exert

In contrast to more reserved worship services characteristic of the mainstream religions, fundamentalist services tend to be expressive, spontaneous, and emotional. Members of fundamentalist groups are encouraged to give visible evidence of their devotion to their beliefs.

a powerful political influence in America. The 5 million Religious Right activists, as they are called, donate money to political causes, contact officials, attend political meetings, and campaign for politicians who share their beliefs. These beliefs generally include opposition to issues such as abortion, homosexuality, gun control, and sexual permissiveness, and support of issues such as prayer in schools, traditional family values, and community service for nonviolent criminal offenders.

Research has found that 39 percent of Religious Right activists are high school graduates and 19 percent are college graduates. Slightly more than half live in the South, and most tend to be Republicans. Although the strength of the Religious Right seems likely to grow, social analysts believe that its impact will be limited only to single issues rather than to an overall revision of the American political system.

SECTION 2 REVIEW

DEFINE   religion, animism, shamanism, totemism, theism, monotheism, polytheism, ethicalism

1. *Contrasting Ideas*   Distinguish between the sacred and the profane.

2. *Summarizing Ideas*   List and describe
   (a) the three functions of religion and
   (b) the four basic elements of religion.

3. *Composing an Essay*   Compose an essay on the effects of   *(a)* religious affiliation,   *(b)* religious participation, and *(c)* fundamentalist Christianity on religion in the United States.

CHAPTER 14   SUMMARY

Education is the system of roles and norms that ensures the transmission of knowledge, values, and patterns of behavior from one generation to the next. Sociologists who study education tend to focus on schooling.

According to functionalist sociologists, education serves to maintain the stability and smooth operation of society by transmitting culture, increasing social integration, creating knowledge, and channeling people into occupations. Conflict theorists, though, argue that education serves to maintain social inequality by teaching obedience to authority and by tracking students into different educational programs. In addition, conflict theorists believe that socioeconomic differences in academic achievement reflect the unequal distribution of power and resources in society.

Educational issues have long held the attention of the American public. Among the contemporary issues in education being discussed are educational reform, violence in the schools, and bilingual education.

According to Emile Durkheim, at the heart of all religions is a distinction between the sacred and the profane. Religion is the system of roles and norms organized around the sacred realm that binds people together in social groups. Religion is composed of three elements: rituals, belief systems, and organizational structures. Rituals vary widely throughout the world. Belief systems are categorized as animism, which appears as shamanism and totemism; theism, which appears as monotheism or polytheism; and ethicalism, which gives sacred meaning to moral principles. Ideal types of religious organizational structures include ecclesia, denominations, sects, and cults.

Religion in American society is characterized by a pluralism and by the value that Americans place on religious beliefs. For the protection of all religions, the United States Constitution guarantees the separation of church and state. While participation in mainstream religions has been decreasing in the United States, participation in fundamentalist Christianity has been on the rise.

DEVELOPING SOCIOLOGICAL

WRITING ABOUT SOCIOLOGY: Summarizing Sociological Information

Sociology provides us with important information about the social world and human relationships. In reading sociology, however, it is not important to memorize every word that you read. As the eye moves over the words, the mind automatically sorts information by identifying the main ideas being presented and the supplemental evidence used to support these main ideas. In effect, the mind summarizes the information.

A summary recaps the major points contained in a body of information. Minor points usually are excluded because the purpose of a summary is to highlight major ideas. See the Summary for Chapter 14 on page 369, for example. This summary highlights the major points concerning education and religion in just a few paragraphs.

Summarizing information is a useful tool in the writing of sociology. When you write an answer to an essay question for homework or on a test, you are using the skill of summarizing. You also summarize information when you collect notes to use for the writing of a research paper.

How to Summarize Information
To write a summary, follow these steps:

1. **Identify main ideas.** As you read information to be summarized, note the main ideas. Main ideas often are presented in a single sentence called the topic sentence. Sometimes a topic sentence combines two or more sentences. At other times, the main idea is implied and must be formulated from the sense of all the sentences in a paragraph.

3. **Use your own words.** Restate the main ideas in your own words. Using your own words helps you understand and remember the main ideas.

4. **Think in broad terms.** Write a list of the main ideas. Look for main ideas that are connected and that relate to a still broader topic.

Use the broader idea as the first sentence in your summary. Continue this process until all main ideas have been related to other, larger topics and your summary is complete.

Applying the Skill
In the following excerpt, key sentences have been underlined. First, read the entire excerpt as a whole. Then, reread only the underlined sentences.

In addition to its manifest, or recognized and intended, functions, <u>education also has latent, or unrecognized and unintended, functions.</u> One of the latent functions of education is its role as a provider of custodial care. <u>Schools free parents from many hours of child care and allow them to contribute their labor to the work force.</u> The importance of this function is growing as the numbers of single-parent and two-earner families in the United States continue to increase. Not only are students kept off the streets for many hours per day, but they also are under the supervision of authority figures who set standards for their behavior.

The custodial function of <u>education</u> is important for another reason—it <u>keeps young people out of the labor force.</u> Before the time of mandatory education, there was an enormous demand in the United States for a large pool of unskilled workers. Young children and adolescents helped fill this demand, and often worked long hours under harsh conditions. As industrialization and urbanization progressed, however, the need for unskilled labor declined and children began to attend school in large numbers. The demand for unskilled labor today is so low that <u>children would swell the ranks of the unemployed if mandatory education did not keep them out of competition for jobs.</u>

<u>Another latent function of education concerns its role in bringing together potential marriage partners.</u> High schools, colleges, and universities

provide a meeting ground for marriage-age people of somewhat similar backgrounds who otherwise would never meet if they went directly from their homes into the work force. <u>Through continuous daily contact, young people are given the opportunity to evaluate and choose traits they consider desirable in a spouse.</u>

The following paragraph is a summary of the excerpt above. In it the underlined sentences have been restated.

One of the unrecognized, or latent, functions of education is to provide custodians for children so that adults can work. This function also keeps children out of competition for jobs, which is important because children's lack of skills would increase the unemployment rate. Another latent function of education is that it provides a place where people can meet and evaluate potential future spouses.

Practicing the Skill

Read the following excerpt about the need for a well-educated work force. On a separate sheet of paper, list the topic sentences of each paragraph. Then, restate the sentences in your own words, formulating a written summary.

History is not kind to idlers. The time is long past when America's destiny was assured simply by an abundance of natural resources and inexhaustible human enthusiasm, and by our relative isolation from the malignant problems of older civilizations. We live among determined, well-educated, and strongly motivated competitors. We compete with them for international standing and markets, not only with products but also with the ideas of our laboratories and neighborhood workshops. America's position in the world may once have been reasonably secure with only a few exceptionally well-trained men and women. It is no longer.

The risk is not only that the Japanese make automobiles more efficiently than the Americans and have government subsidies for development and export. It is not just that the South Koreans recently built the world's most efficient steel mill, or that American machine tools, once the pride of the world, are being replaced by German products. It is also that these developments signify a redistribution of trained capability throughout the globe. Knowledge, learning, information, and skilled intelligence are the new raw materials of international commerce and are today spreading throughout the world as vigorously as miracle drugs, synthetic fertilizers, and blue jeans did earlier. If only to keep and improve on the slim competitive edge we still retain in world markets, we must dedicate ourselves to the reform of our educational system for the benefit of all—old and young alike, affluent and poor, majority and minority. Learning is the indispensible investment required for success in the "information age" we are entering.

Our concern, however, goes well beyond matters such as industry and commerce. It also includes the intellectual, moral, and spiritual strengths of our people which knit together the very fabric of our society. The people of the United States need to know that individuals in our society who do not possess the levels of skill, literacy, and training essential to this new era will be effectively disenfranchised, not simply from the material rewards that accompany competent performance, but also from the chance to participate fully in our national life. A high level of shared education is essential to a free, democratic society and to the fostering of a common culture, especially in a country that prides itself on pluralism and individual freedom. . . .

Part of what is at risk is the promise first made on this continent: All, regardless of race or class or economic status, are entitled to a fair chance and to the tools for developing their individual powers of mind and spirit to the utmost. This promise means that all children by virtue of their own efforts, competently guided, can hope to attain the mature and informed judgment needed to secure gainful employment and to manage their own lives, serving thereby not only their own interests but also the progress of society as well.

Reviewing Sociological Terms

On a separate sheet of paper, supply the term that correctly completes each sentence.

1. _____ is the term used for instruction by specially trained teachers who follow officially recognized policies.

2. _____ refers to the importance of religion in a person's life.

3. The term _____ refers to an established pattern of behavior through which a group of believers experience the sacred.

4. A religious organization in which all people in the society are members by virtue of their birth is called a(n) _____.

5. The assignment of students to different types of educational programs is called _____.

Thinking Critically about Sociology

1. **Analyzing Ideas** *(a)* What functions does religion serve for society? *(b)* How can the functions of religion block social change and social progress?

2. **Comparing Ideas** Compare the views of functionalist and conflict sociologists concerning the social control function of schools.

3. **Explaining Facts** *(a)* What are the characteristics of religion in American society? *(b)* What purpose is served in the United States by the separation of church and state?

4. **Interpreting Tables** According to the table on page 356, how do the incomes of males and females compare at each level of education?

5. **Comprehending Ideas** *(a)* How do schools foster the creation of new knowledge? *(b)* Why do corporations often fund research?

6. **Contrasting Ideas** *(a)* How do the religious belief systems of animism, theism, and ethicalism differ? *(b)* What are the subtypes of animism and theism?

7. **Seeing Relationships** *(a)* How does socioeconomic status affect achievement in school? *(b)* What is the relationship between tracking and socioeconomic status?

8. **Drawing Conclusions** Compare the percentage of people in the United States who claim a religious preference with the percentage who are formally affiliated with a religious organization. What can you conclude from this comparison?

Exercising Sociological Skills

1. **Extending Ideas** Reread the Applying Sociology feature presented on pages 352–353. *(a)* How did the schools help give immigrant students a common identity? *(b)* How might the schools have helped the immigrant parents as well?

2. **Understanding Ideas** According to the Case Study on page 358, why are illiteracy programs reaching so few of the people around the nation who need help?

3. **Summarizing Sociological Information** Reread the Developing Sociological Imagination feature presented on pages 370–371. Use the skills presented in this feature to summarize the three major contemporary issues in American education.

Extending Sociological Imagination

1. Prepare a brief report on one of the following topics: *(a)* the educational system in Japan; *(b)* mandatory education laws in your state; *(c)* the importance of religion to the African American community; or *(d)* membership trends in the major religious faiths over the past 50 years.

2. Prepare a chart comparing the four religious organization structures in terms of size, type of leadership, life span, and characteristics of followers.

INTERPRETING PRIMARY SOURCES
The Impact of Religious Lobbies

The impact of religion on the American political system is growing as more and more religious interest groups make their voices heard through lobbying organizations. In this excerpt from *Religion in American Politics*, contributor Allen D. Hertzke discusses the two major ideological lobbying camps and their combined influence on the American political system. As you read the excerpt, consider the differences between these two groups and how religious lobbying groups in general influence the American power structure.

From the abolitionist movement of the nineteenth century, to the crusade against alcohol, to the more recent civil rights struggle, religion-based movements in America have attempted to influence public policy often with dramatic results. What is striking about the contemporary era, however, is the extent to which religious engagement, across the theological and ideological spectrum, is institutionalized into national lobbying organizations. . . .

Religious groups, not surprisingly, are deeply involved (on all sides) in such highly charged issues as abortion, school prayer, the Equal Rights Amendment, and aid to parochial schools. But they will also be found embroiled in battles over a host of social welfare, military, and foreign policy issues. . . .

Anchored in [Washington] is the left-leaning "peace and justice" cluster, comprising the liberal mainline Protestants . . . , the peace churches (Mennonites, Friends, Brethren), the black churches, and some Catholic groups. . . . At the other end of the spectrum are those emphasizing traditional values—Christian fundamentalists . . . , some evangelical groups, and Catholic anti-abortion lobbies. . . .

Christian fundamentalists have been most successful in shaping the congressional agenda on issues that resonate with the cultural conservatism of their constituents, such as support for school prayer and opposition to abortion and pornography. Most of this influence comes from their ability to mobilize their sympathizers to flood Washington with letters and calls. . . .

When Christian Right leaders have moved beyond social issues to a conservative military and economic agenda, they have been far less successful, in part because they have not been able to generate the same intensity of member responses, but also because they find it strategic to concentrate on issues that are "hot buttons" for fund raising. . . .

For the "peace and justice" cluster the picture is similarly mixed. While these groups have been less successful at mobilization than the fundamentalists, they have access to information gained through church networks . . . that makes up for this deficiency. The mainline churches run a multitude of domestic social service agencies . . . and are also connected to international relief agencies, development programs, and members scattered across the globe. On the basis of these networks, church lobbyists routinely testify on the Hill about the effects of domestic and foreign policies, and key congressional committees find this information useful in countering statements made by the administration. . . .

History is filled with examples of disparities between leaders and members of organizations. . . . Thus the religious groups, by virtue of their pluralism, contact with citizens, and issue specialization, provide countervailing power in the pressure system. . . .

The impact of religious groups on national representation is . . . viewed in a positive light because tactical decisions, specialization, and the imperatives of constituency mobilization overcome, to an extent, the oligarchic effect of leadership. Neither interest group scholars nor those who study religion and politics have emphasized enough this strategic interplay between faith and politics in the American system.

Source Review

1. How do the two major ideological camps differ in their approaches to lobbying?

2. Why does the author believe that religious lobbies counterbalance oligarchic leadership?

Science and Sport

1 Science As a Social Institution

The Institutionalization of Science
The Norms of Scientific Research
The Realities of Scientific Research

2 Sport As a Social Institution

The Institutionalization of Sport
Sociological Perspectives on Sport
Issues in American Sport

Chapter Focus

Chapter 15 focuses on the institutions of science and sport. The chapter begins with a discussion of the rise of modern science and its current characteristics. Special attention is paid to how the norms that are supposed to govern scientific research differ from the realities of research. The chapter then turns to a discussion of sport, focusing on the characteristics of modern sport and issues in American sport.

As you study the chapter, look for the answers to the following questions:

1. What factors contributed to the institutionalization of science?
2. How do the norms of scientific research differ from the realities of scientific research?
3. What seven characteristics distinguish sport as an institution?
4. What are the sociological findings concerning racial discrimination in organized sports and the state of women's athletics?

KEY TERMS

The following terms, while not the only terms emphasized in the chapter, are basic to your understanding of sociology. Determine the meaning of each term, either by using the Glossary or by watching for context clues as you read the chapter.

science	norm of organized skepticism	paradigm
sociology of science	norm of communalism	sport
norm of universalism	norm of disinterestedness	stacking

Society is constantly changing. Consequently, the institutional structure of society also changes. Not only do old institutions take on new characteristics, but new institutions develop. Two institutions that have gained increasing importance over the past 150 years are science and sport.

Our lives are touched on a daily basis by the effects of science. Our health; our immediate environment; the way we learn, communicate, and travel; what goods and services we produce and how we produce them; and our vision of the future are influenced by science. So great is the influence of science on society that the level of scientific literacy of adults and children has become an issue of public debate.

Sport also invades our daily lives. Annually, people in the United States spend billions of dollars on sports-related equipment and activities. Many of us are obsessed with our bodies, our health, and our athletes. And, on television, sporting events are among the most popular form of programming. Sports are so popular with Americans that cable television is willing to provide 24-hour-a-day, 7-day-a-week coverage.

Given the vast influence of science and sport on modern society, it is not surprising that sociologists have turned their attention to the analysis of these institutions. In this chapter, we too will turn our attention to the analysis of the institutions of science and sport.

1 SCIENCE AS A SOCIAL INSTITUTION

Although **science**—the pursuit of knowledge through systematic methods—is a central feature of all industrialized nations, its status as an institution is relatively recent. For much of human history, explanations for natural phenomena were sought in the supernatural. Not until the seventeenth and eighteenth centuries did science come to replace other belief systems as the principal method by which to understand nature.

The question of how modern science took root can be examined from many angles. Historians of science, for example, tend to focus on the role of genius. From this perspective, the growth of science is seen as resulting from the creative energies of individuals.

Sociologists do not deny the role of genius in the development of scientific knowledge. Most sociologists are more interested, however, in how the structure of society and the organization of science itself affects scientific development. The sociological perspective that examines how scientific knowledge develops is the **sociology of science.** It is the sociology of science perspective that we will use to examine science as a social institution in this chapter.

The Institutionalization of Science

People of genius have existed since ancient times. Great thinkers in early Babylon, Egypt, Greece, India, and Mexico, for instance, developed elaborate systems of mathematics and astronomy in an attempt to understand the world around them. These early thinkers, however, were among the societal elites and often pursued such knowledge as a pastime.

The Birth of Science. Not until the fourth century B.C. did science emerge as a recognizable system. In Greece, great thinkers such as Plato and Aristotle explored the fields of mathematics, astronomy, the biological sciences, physics, and medicine. During the Hellenistic Age (roughly 323 to 30 B.C.), Greek culture spread to other nations. In Egypt, great libraries and centers of learning were established in large cities, providing employment for scholars and scientists. And, although the Romans themselves did not produce any notable scientists, Greek scientists living in the Roman Empire continued to make significant contributions.

Throughout most of this period, science was linked to the study of philosophy and religion. With the decline of the Roman Empire, however, the quest for systematic knowledge slowed. At the same time, the Church grew in power and influence. Over time, people turned away from science and toward philosophy and religion for explanations of the workings of the natural world.

Although scientific scholarship continued in isolated pockets after the fall of the Roman Empire, the topics of research and the interpretation of findings were strongly influenced by the Church. As a result, many lines of scientific inquiry were no longer pursued. And, most of the scientific research that continued was recast in terms that were supportive of Church beliefs. It took nearly a thousand years before science experienced a true rebirth in Europe.

The Rebirth of Science. Four main factors contributed to the rebirth of European science. The first factor was the Renaissance, which began in Italy in the 1300s. The Renaissance, with its emphasis on art and learning, was in part a by-product of trade with the East. The wealth produced by such trade provided merchants, bankers, and nobility with the leisure time to pursue art and learning. This led many of the wealthy to become patrons, often bringing scholars and artists into their homes to act as tutors.

The work of Renaissance scientists Nicholaus Copernicus *(above)* and Johannes Kepler *(left)* helped lay the foundation for the field of modern astronomy.

The second factor contributing to the rebirth of science was a growth in knowledge concerning mining and metallurgy. Eventually, the understanding of the properties of metals reached a level that allowed for the development of alloys that were strong enough to be used for molds in which to cast movable type. Once this obstacle was overcome, Johann Gutenburg succeeded in developing a practical printing press. By the end of the fifteenth century, every major city in Europe had a printing press. The availability of inexpensive books greatly facilitated the spread of scientific knowledge.

The third factor contributing to the rebirth of European science was the Age of Exploration, the period from approximately 1450 to 1650. During this period, the nations of Europe sailed the world in search of all-water routes to the East. Exploration increased the demand for science in two ways. First, advances in astronomy and mathematics were needed to assist navigation. Second, explorers brought back from the places they visited strange plants, animals, and diseases that sparked scientific curiosity.

The final factor contributing to the rebirth of science in Europe was the Protestant Reformation. Early Protestants rejected the idea that the power of religious salvation rested in the hands of priests. Instead, they argued that people could find salvation through their own efforts. This emphasis on individualism lessened public resistance to scientific inquiry. The Church no longer was seen as the final authority on all matters.

Science was given a further boost by seventeenth-century Calvinism. Calvinists believed that salvation could be achieved through good works. When the Calvinists included science among the good works that could lead to salvation, scientific activity gained respectability.

By the 1700s, these various factors combined to produce a revolution in scientific thought. This scientific revolution redefined the nature of the universe, the methods of scientific research, and the functions of science. In place of a world controlled by human and divine spirits, scientists envisioned a mechanistic universe that operated according to systematic properties and laws. In place of philosophical speculation, scientists employed observation, controlled experiments, and careful data collection. And, in place of the view of science as an intellectual exercise, scientists saw as the function of science the merging of scientific knowledge and technology.

The scientific revolution was part of a larger revolution in social thought. This revolution, called the Enlightenment, supported reason over

The Granger Collection, New York

Most scientific findings and theories are extensions or revisions of previous scientific knowledge. Sir Isaac Newton *(right)*, for instance, built on the work of Galileo Galilei *(above)* and Johannes Kepler to develop his theory of gravity.

The Granger Collection, New York

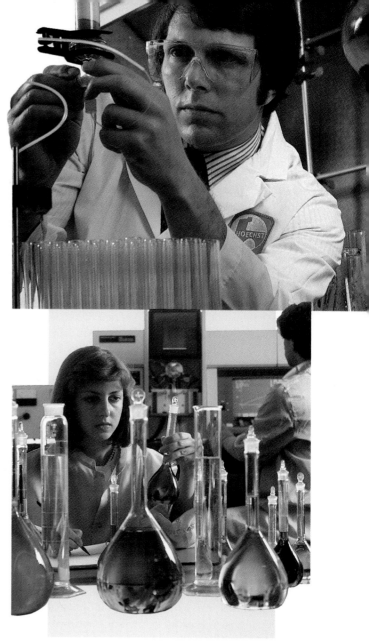

One of the many consequences of the institutionalization of science has been an increase in the level of specialization among present-day scientists.

religious dogma. The main weapons of the revolution were the scientific method and scientific facts. Democracy was the revolution's stated goal. One of the consequences of the Enlightenment—and of the French Revolution, which it helped spark—was a state-supported system of education. In addition to spreading scientific knowledge, the system provided new positions in teaching and research.

Modern Science. In spite of the Enlightenment and the French Revolution, science, for the most part, was of interest only to a small segment of society during the eighteenth century. Not until the nineteenth and twentieth centuries did science become a central force in society.

The transformation of science from an intellectual pastime to a social institution was brought about by industrialization. The central theme of industrialization was progress and science was seen as a tool of progress. In addition to pure research, scientists increasingly saw as their task the creation of new technologies that could improve the human condition.

By the early twentieth century, the modern organization of science was in place. A general interest in natural phenomena was replaced by a tendency toward specialization. The number of disciplines and subdisciplines in science multiplied, and most scientists narrowed their areas of interest to specific fields of research. This tendency toward specialization was reinforced by the university system, which encouraged students to concentrate their studies in a single area or sub-area of science.

Specialization also was reinforced by the professionalization of science. The last traces of private sponsorship gave way to employment in universities, research institutes, private industry, and the government. Increasingly, the availability of funding, the views of fellow scientists, the established goals of scientific organizations, and the needs of business and government replaced general curiosity as the springboard for scientific research and development.

The Norms of Scientific Research

As the previous discussion indicates, science is pursued within a social context. Thus existing values and norms influence the pursuit of scientific knowledge. According to Robert K. Merton—the person most credited with establishing the sociology of science as a distinct specialty—the modern scientific community is guided by four basic norms. These norms are universalism, organized skepticism, communalism, and disinterestedness.

Universalism.

The **norm of universalism** holds that scientific research should be judged solely on the basis of quality. A scientist's social class, race, gender, nationality, or religion should have no bearing on how his or her research findings are evaluated. The norm of universalism helps ensure that the pursuit of scientific research is open to everyone, regardless of their social characteristics.

Organized Skepticism.

According to the **norm of organized skepticism,** no scientific finding or theory is immune to questioning. Even after a theory or finding has gained wide acceptance, scientists should be willing to question its accuracy or applicability. This skepticism is built into the system as part of the scientific method, hence the label "organized." Furthermore, scientists are supposed to suspend judgment until sufficient facts have been collected. The norm of organized skepticism helps ensure that scientific knowledge does not stagnate and that facts and theories are not blindly accepted.

Communalism.

The belief that all scientific knowledge should be made available to everyone in the scientific community forms the basis of the **norm of communalism.** This norm also serves to reinforce the idea that findings belong to the entire community, not to individual scientists, despite the fact that scientific findings and phenomena sometimes are named for their discoverers. The sharing of scientific knowledge is important because science is additive—new discoveries generally build on existing knowledge. The norm of communalism helps ensure that scientists have access to existing knowledge.

Disinterestedness.

According to the **norm of disinterestedness,** scientists should seek truth, not personal gain. Thus research topics should be chosen without reference to possible awards, political or religious criteria, or currently popular views. Similarly, scientists should not alter their data in an effort to gain acceptance nor should they unfairly judge the work of others who hold positions contrary to their own.

The Realities of Scientific Research

Although scientists may in principle accept the norms of universalism, organized skepticism, communalism, and disinterestedness, the realities of scientific inquiry often fall far short of these ideals. Among the problems that can affect scientific research are fraud, the negative effects of competition, the Matthew effect, and conflicting views of reality.

Fraud.

The Piltdown hoax is a classic example of fraud in science. In 1912, a group of professional and amateur scientists announced the discovery of several skull fragments and the lower jaw of what appeared to be the "missing link" between apes and humans. The bones were found in a gravel pit near Piltdown Common in Sussex, England. The discovery came to be known as the Piltdown man.

Doubts over whether the Piltdown find was authentic surfaced immediately. Critics claimed that the skull fragments and jawbone did not appear to belong together. Most critics were quieted, however, by the announcement in 1917 that a second Piltdown man had been discovered several years earlier. Interest in the discovery faded until 1953, when Oxford scientist J. S. Weiner once again fueled public debate when he expressed doubts over whether the bones were authentic. Troubled by news that the location of the second Piltdown discovery was unknown, Weiner launched an investigation that eventually proved that the Piltdown finds were fraudulent.

Although outright fraud is relatively rare in science, it does occur. In the early 1980s, for instance, John Darsee, a Harvard Medical School researcher, falsified data that formed the basis for about 100 scientific articles on heart disease. The fraud was discovered by Darsee's laboratory chief, Robert Kloner. More recently, the attention of the scientific community focused on a bitter dispute between American scientist Robert Gallo and French scientist Luc Montagnier over which of the two had first isolated a possible AIDS virus. The controversy ended when it was discovered that the virus grown by Gallo was the genetic twin of a virus sent to him several years earlier by Montagnier. Gallo was discredited for his failure to acknowledge the source of his work.

In 1912, the Piltdown man was presented to the world as the ''missing link'' between apes and humans. It was not until 1953 that the bone and jaw fragments were proved to be fraudulent.

THE ILLUSTRATED LONDON NEWS,

No. 3845. VOL. CXLI   SATURDAY, DECEMBER 28, 1912.   SIXPENCE.

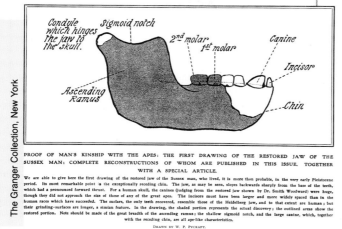

PROOF OF MAN'S KINSHIP WITH THE APES: THE FIRST DRAWING OF THE RESTORED JAW OF THE SUSSEX MAN: COMPLETE RECONSTRUCTIONS OF WHOM ARE PUBLISHED IN THIS ISSUE, TOGETHER WITH A SPECIAL ARTICLE.

We are able to give here the first drawing of the restored jaw of the Sussex man, who lived, it is more than probable, in the very early Pleistocene period. Its most remarkable point is the exceptionally receding chin. The jaw, as may be seen, slopes backwards sharply from the base of the teeth, which had a pronounced forward thrust. For a human skull, the canines (judging from the restored jaw shown by Dr. Smith Woodward) were huge, though they did not approach the size of those of any of the great apes. The incisors must have been larger and more widely spaced than in the human races which have succeeded. The molars, the only teeth recovered, resemble those of the Heidelberg jaw, and to that extent are human; but their grinding-surfaces are longer, a simian feature. In the drawing, the shaded portion represents the actual discovery; the outlined areas show the restored portion. Note should be made of the great breadth of the ascending ramus; the shallow sigmoid notch, and the large canine, which, together with the receding chin, are all ape-like characteristics.

DRAWN BY W. P. PYCRAFT.

The Granger Collection, New York

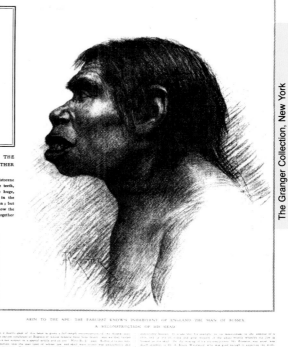

AKIN TO THE APE: THE EARLIEST KNOWN INHABITANT OF ENGLAND, THE MAN OF SUSSEX A RECONSTRUCTION OF HIS HEAD

The Granger Collection, New York

Competition.

Many scientists and sociologists of science argue that competition is one of the principal causes of norm violations among scientists. The fear of being "beaten to the punch" on an important discovery can cause scientists to refuse to share unpublished information with their colleagues. In some instances, this fear even can cause scientists to publish data that contain a few intentional inaccuracies designed to throw off the competition.

More often, competition results in scientists rushing their data into publication. Publishing data prematurely can result in misinformation, thereby slowing down scientific progress. The rush to publish stems from the fact that scientific achievement is measured in terms of peer recognition. To gain recognition, scientists must share their data with fellow scientists, either by publishing in professional journals or by presenting papers at conferences. The pressure to publish is particularly severe for scientists working in university or research settings—job security often is tied directly to the quantity of publications.

The Matthew Effect.

In a 1968 article, Robert K. Merton noted that honors and recognition tend to go to those scientists who have already achieved recognition. On the other hand, they tend to be withheld from scientists who have not yet made their mark. Merton named this phenomenon the **Matthew effect,** after Matthew 25:29 in the Bible: "For to every one who has will more be given, and he will have abundance; but from him who has not, even what he has will be taken away."

According to Merton, if two scientists make the same discovery independently at about the same time, most or all of the credit will go to the more famous of the two scientists. Similarly, if a group of scientists of varying degrees of fame work together on a project, most of the credit will go to the scientist with the greatest name recognition, regardless of how the work actually was divided.

Sociologists of science have noted that the consequences of the Matthew effect are mixed. On the one hand, the Matthew effect can hamper the careers of young scientists by preventing them from gaining recognition. On the other hand, because the views of famous scientists are more readily accepted than are the views of relative

Text continues on page 384.

APPLYING SOCIOLOGY

Reforming Science Education

In the following excerpt from an article published in the September 1992 issue of *Popular Science,* Arthur Fisher explores the crisis in science education in the United States and the steps being taken to remedy it.

In thousands of American school districts, the teaching of science has virtually disappeared from elementary education. By high school few students find science classes fun, according to a 20-year research project carried out by the National Assessment of Educational Progress (NAEP). "Especially considering the technological needs of today's society," a 1990 NAEP report states, "a disproportionately low percentage of these students possess an in-depth scientific knowledge." . . .

The result is a massive, impending shortage of American scientists, mathematicians, and engineers. Walter E. Massey, director of the National Science Foundation, describes the problem this way: "Of every 4,000 seventh-graders in school today, only six will ultimately receive a Ph.D. in science or engineering. Of these six, only one will be a female.

"By the year 2000, minority students will account for 40 percent of our elementary and secondary school population. Yet 4 percent of undergraduate science and engineering degrees are awarded to minorities."

A study last year by the Council of Chief State School Officers showed that less than half of American high school graduates have taken chemistry and Algebra II, both of which are considered crucial preparation for college work in math and science.

These are not merely intellectual or elitist concerns. What Lewis M. Branscomb has described as "a crisis become chronic" is a literal threat to America's national security and viability. Branscomb was the head of a task force on K-12 math and science education assembled by the Carnegie Commission on Science, Technology, and Government. Their report puts the case clearly:

"Inadequacies in precollege math and science education are a chronic and serious threat to our nation's future. The national interest is strongly bound up in the ability of Americans to compete technically. All young people, including the non-college-bound, the disadvantaged, and young women, must be given the opportunity to become competent in mathematics and science." . . .

The Need for a "Hands-On" Approach

Children begin to learn science from the moment they become aware of their environment. They are born with an imperative that says, "Make sense of what is going on." And they build models of the real world through constant and repeated operation and experience, models that help them understand what they have seen and heard and to predict what may happen next.

What this means is that the teaching—and learning—of science and math should rely on a "hands-on" approach, emphasizing experiment, discussion, cooperation, and participation. Yet only 33 percent of eleventh-graders have used an electrical meter, only 59 percent have ever written up the results of an experiment, and only 20 percent have ever gone on a science field trip.

"For years," says Milton Goldberg, a director of research for the Department of Education, "science and math educators have espoused hands-on learning. However, student experiments and hands-on assignments have [actually] declined in recent years. Students spend more time in lectures or reading about science in textbooks than actively participating in science. Time spent in laboratory work is declining." . . .

To combat this deadening, oppressive approach, scientists and mathematicians, federal agencies, universities, and businesses are collaborating to launch new programs that train teachers in hands-on science and math learning. . . . The scale of these local programs is dwarfed by the size of the problem overall; but they show what could be achieved nationally if enough will, expertise, and money were applied. Some of these programs specifically address the problems of school systems with large or predominantly minority populations. Not only are minorities the most educationally disadvantaged in science and math, but by the year 2000, more than half of those retiring from the work force will be white males, while 70 percent of those entering the work force will be minorities, women, and immigrants.

Parallel to the "minority gap" in math and science exists a gender gap. Today, women represent 45 percent of the total U.S. work force, but only 13 percent of the nation's scientists and engineers. In the fourth grade, girls and boys do about equally well in science and math. But girls lag as they move up through the grades. [Former] Education Secretary Lamar Alexander says that "cultural attitudes" convey the message of inherent inferiority in science and math to girls. . . .

Creating Standards for Reform

Behind all of [the] efforts to upgrade the achievements of U.S. students lies a nagging question. What exactly do we mean by science and math achievement and just what do we want high school graduates to know about these subjects? The answers to these questions must determine what is taught, and learned, in the classroom. Says Francie Alexander, a member of the National Assessment Governing Board: "If you don't even have agreement on what kids should know, what does it matter?"

Until recently, there has been little agreement and much debate, with a resulting hodgepodge of school curricula—the rules that specify what and how to teach and in what grade to teach it. Children in one locality may leave sixth grade knowing how frogs reproduce but not the difference between alternating and direct current, while somewhere else the opposite may prevail.

That chaotic situation is beginning to change. Teachers, professional scientists and mathematicians, and concerned citizens are coming together to forge what can best be called standards in science and math. Rather than specifying in numbing detail just what happens during the school year, a standard specifies what students should know and be able to do at various age levels, listing milestones, say, instead of accounting for every foot traveled. . . .

The project aims to build on past efforts by groups such as the National Science Teachers Association (NSTA), the American Association for the Advancement of Science (AAAS), and the American Chemical Society. The AAAS's Project 2061 (named for the next arrival of Halley's comet) is an attempt to define what science literacy is by setting out a general set of goals for twelfth-graders, including knowledge of key concepts and principles of science. It deemphasizes the amount of detailed information students need to memorize.

The NSTA's Program is called the Scope, Sequence, and Coordination Project. It focuses on grades 7–12, and aims to do away with the traditional "layer cake" approach, in which biology, chemistry, and physics are each taught in successive one-year courses, with no integration. The Scope, Sequence, and Coordination Project calls for spreading the teaching of all the traditional disciplines over six full years, with the connections among them emphasized.

If the various science constituencies are indeed successful in uniting on a set of goals for science education in this country, and if they can join the mathematics standards in stimulating the nation's 15,000 school districts to adopt them, then the lofty goal of "first in the world" for U.S. science and math students may yet be achieved.

1. According to the author, why should science education rely on a hands-on approach?

2. What reforms are being planned for the future of science education in the United States?

3. Write a brief essay opposing or supporting the notion that scientific literacy is important in an advanced industrial society.

unknowns, the Matthew effect can speed the rate at which new findings are incorporated into the existing body of scientific knowledge.

Conflicting Views of Reality. As sociologist W.I. Thomas noted a half century ago, if people define situations as real, they are real in their consequences. When, for instance, the bubonic plague wiped out nearly one-third of the population of Europe during the Middle Ages, many people attributed the epidemic to the wrath of God. In response, some people joined a funda-

mentalist sect called the Brotherhood of Flagellants. Members of the sect publicly whipped themselves in hopes of appeasing God. Other people blamed the Jews and took revenge by burning Jews alive. The fact that the epidemic actually was due to filthy living conditions and was spread by flea-infested rats had no bearing on the actions of individuals. These people had defined reality in a certain way and acted accordingly.

Contrary to the norm of organized skepticism, science—no less than any other social creation—is affected by views of reality. Thomas S. Kuhn,

People's views of reality affect how they interpret data. The giant bird that decorates the Nazca plain in Peru *(left)* and the Indian carvings that cover the ground near Needles, California *(below)*, are artifacts of ancient cultures. Their origins have long been a matter of speculation for scientists and nonscientists alike. Belief in the existence of life on other planets has led some people to argue that the carvings are the work of ancient astronauts from far-away galaxies.

a historian of science, has coined the term **paradigm** to describe the set of shared concepts, methods, and assumptions that make up the scientific reality at any point in time. Paradigms determine what topics are appropriate for scientific inquiry, what methods can be used to collect and analyze data, and what interpretations of data are considered acceptable.

As this nineteenth-century drawing implies, Charles Darwin's theory of evolution met with a certain degree of public opposition from the very beginning.

The Granger Collection, New York

During periods of what Kuhn calls "normal science," the scientific community shares a common paradigm. Eventually, however, it becomes impossible to explain all existing phenomena within the context of the established paradigm. As a result, a new paradigm emerges.

The transition to a new paradigm seldom is smooth. When the views of individual scientists run counter to the long-established paradigm, the new ideas often meet with violent resistance. In the 1600s, for example, Galileo proposed that the Earth was not the center of the universe, contrary to the accepted view of science and of the Church. So alien were Galileo's views that the Church forced him to give up his theories. It was only after several decades of controversy that Galileo's views finally gained acceptance.

The perceptions of the general public or of the government also can affect science. In the former Soviet Union, for instance, bureaucratic red tape, political ideology, isolationism, and a reluctance to employ Western technology greatly slowed Soviet scientific progress. In addition, basic research tools such as computers, photocopying machines, and international journals are in short supply at most of the former Soviet research institutes.

SECTION 1 REVIEW

DEFINE science, sociology of science, paradigm

IDENTIFY Piltdown man, Robert K. Merton, Thomas S. Kuhn

1. **Understanding Ideas** Describe the historical development of science as a social institution.

2. **Summarizing Ideas** List and describe the four basic norms of science.

3. **Seeing Relationships** **(a)** According to the textbook, what four problems can affect scientific research? **(b)** In what ways do these problems represent violations of the norms of science?

The first task in examining sport as a social institution is to define what is meant by sport. **Sport** refers to competitive games that are won or lost on the basis of physical skills and are played according to specific rules. By this definition, games such as dice or chess, which rely on chance or strategy, are not considered sport. Neither are such childhood games as tag, leapfrog, or hide-and-seek.

The central role played by sport in modern society hides the fact that sport as a social institution is a relatively recent phenomenon. In this section, we will examine what characteristics distinguish sport as a social institution. We also will examine the effect of sport on American society.

The Institutionalization of Sport

Archaeological evidence indicates that physical games have been a part of human culture from earliest times. It took the social changes brought on by the Enlightenment and the Industrial Revolution, however, to give rise to modern sport. The central themes of the Enlightenment and industrialization—democracy, achievement, competition, efficiency, and the desire for measurable progress—found expression in modern sport. Thus the rise of sport closely follows the rise of modern industrial society. It is not surprising, therefore, that modern sport first emerged in England and then spread to the United States, Western Europe, and the rest of the world.

According to sociologist Allen Guttmann, sport as a social institution is distinguished by the same seven characteristics that distinguish modern industrial society. These characteristics are secularization, equality, specialization, rationalization, bureaucratization, quantification, and the quest for records.

Secularization. For sport to be considered an institution, it must have roles, norms, and values that distinguish it from other institutions. For much of history, sport did not meet this criterion.

Instead, games of physical skill most often were undertaken as part of religious festivals.

Archaeological evidence indicates, for instance, that the soccer-like game played by the ancient Mayans was a life-or-death struggle in honor of the gods. Stone reliefs found at the Chichén Itzá site in Yucatán clearly show players being beheaded in sacrifice to the gods. Belief in the religious nature of the game is reinforced by the fact that all of the ball courts discovered to date have been located within temple complexes.

Even the ancient Greek Olympic games—the forerunners of modern sports—were carried out as part of a religious festival honoring Zeus. Other Greek athletic festivals also were religious. Those at Delphi and Nemea paid tribute to Apollo, while those at Corinth were held in honor of the god Poseidon.

As long as sport remained a part of the religious institution, its influence was relatively minor. To become an institution in its own right, sport had to move from the realm of the sacred to that of the profane. Sociologists refer to this process as **secularization.**

A slight move toward secularization was indicated by the ancient Greek practices of providing pensions for winning athletes and building athletic facilities for the general population. It was not until the eighteenth and nineteenth centuries, though, that sport became independent from religion. With industrialization came the overall secularization of society. This secularization led to a wider role for sport in society.

Equality. In most past societies, an individual's right to participate in sporting events was based on ascribed rather than achieved characteristics. In medieval times, for instance, only people of noble birth were allowed to compete in organized sporting events. Wealth and social status—not physical skill—determined eligibility. Similarly, in many hunting and gathering societies, participation in athletic events is tied to specific cultural practices. Adolescent boys, for example, may be expected to engage in tests of strength or athletic ability as part of puberty ceremonies. In this instance, age rather than ability is the criterion by which participants are selected.

This is not the case in modern sport—at least in principle. Two basic norms of modern sport are

(1) that competition is open to everyone and (2) that the same rules of competition apply to all contestants. Unfortunately, as the discussion under Issues in American Sport indicates, expectations do not always match reality.

Specialization. Although specialization was evident in the Olympic games of the ancient Greeks (some athletes specialized in running, others in wrestling, and still others in discus throwing), at no other time in history has sport specialization been as refined as it is today. A football player, for instance, not only specializes in football but generally concentrates on playing a single position within the sport. In addition to specialized players, a football team has owners, managers, coaches, trainers, scouts, doctors, and recruiters, each fulfilling a specific role.

According to sociologists, the high degree of specialization evident in modern sports results from the stress on achievement. The underlying assumption is that an individual who is allowed to concentrate on a single task will have a better chance of excelling in that task than will an individual who divides his or her talents among numerous sports.

Although some athletes compete in more than one sport, the degree of training and commitment demanded in modern athletics causes most athletes to specialize in a particular sport.

Rationalization.   According to Max Weber, rationalization is the hallmark of modern capitalist society. **Rationalization** refers to the processes by which every feature of human behavior becomes subject to calculation, measurement, and control. As an important part of modern society, it is not surprising that sport also has become highly rationalized. Every major sport is played according to established rules that are subject to periodic modification. Because these rules are recognized as "official" and thus are widely accepted, modern sports are played in basically the same way everywhere in the world. People playing basketball in China, for instance, play the game according to the same general rules as people playing the game in South Carolina.

Bureaucratization.   Bureaucratization goes hand-in-hand with rationalization. If a sport is to be played according to specific rules, there must be a formal organization charged with the task of developing and enforcing those rules and settling disputes. In addition to these tasks, sports organizations generally organize competitions—ranging from local contests to international competitions—and keep official records against which to measure future athletic feats.

The first athletic organizations appeared in Great Britain in the middle of the nineteenth century. Today, every major sport (and many minor ones) has a national or international organization that serves as the final governing authority for the sport.

Quantification.   Modern sport, like many other aspects of industrial society, centers on achievement. While it may have been enough for an athlete in ancient Greece to have won an individual sporting event, modern athletes want to know where they stand in relation to other athletes, both past and present. Thus quantification is an essential element in modern sports. Every year, the methods of measurement become more sophisticated. In recent years, for instance, the stopwatch has been replaced by the computer and by electronic sensors. As a result, in today's high-tech world, sports records are won and lost by milliseconds.

The Quest for Records.   A belief in the importance of achievement not only leads to quantification but also to the quest for records. Winning becomes the most important element in competition. The desire to win and the continuous

Ben Johnson became a hero when he won a gold medal in the 100-meter dash in the 1988 Summer Olympics. Victory soon turned to defeat, however, when he was disqualified for steroid use. Johnson's continued use of steroids recently led him to be banned from international competition for life.

need to set new records can have negative consequences. The quest for records can, for instance, blind athletes to the dangers of steroids. Steroids are drugs that supposedly increase muscle mass and strengthen an athlete, thereby improving his or her performance. An athlete determined to win at all costs often is willing to risk heart, kidney, and liver damage—three common side effects of steroid abuse—in exchange for the drug's supposed benefits. Health risks, including the possibility of death, become just another price to pay for the promise of a winning edge.

Sociological Perspectives on Sport

Sociologists examine the effect of sport on society from two basic perspectives: the functionalist perspective and the conflict perspective. Sociologists who adopt the functionalist perspective concentrate on the ways in which sport helps to maintain stability in society. Sociologists who adopt the conflict perspective, on the other hand, are more interested in how sport reflects and reinforces social inequality.

The Functionalist Perspective. According to functionalists, sport serves at least two very important positive functions for society. The first function is that of social integration. By providing a common interest for people of different racial, ethnic, and economic characteristics, sport serves

to unite members of society. The second function is the reinforcement of important social norms and values. Sport, with its emphasis on competition and winning, teaches people to value hard work, team spirit, and obedience to authority—traits that are important in a capitalist society.

The Conflict Perspective. Rather than concentrating on the positive functions of sport, conflict theorists focus on how sport serves to maintain social inequality. Some conflict theorists focus on the ways in which sport maintains social inequality through its ability to draw the attention of

Conflict theorists claim that sports such as hockey and football legitimate violence.

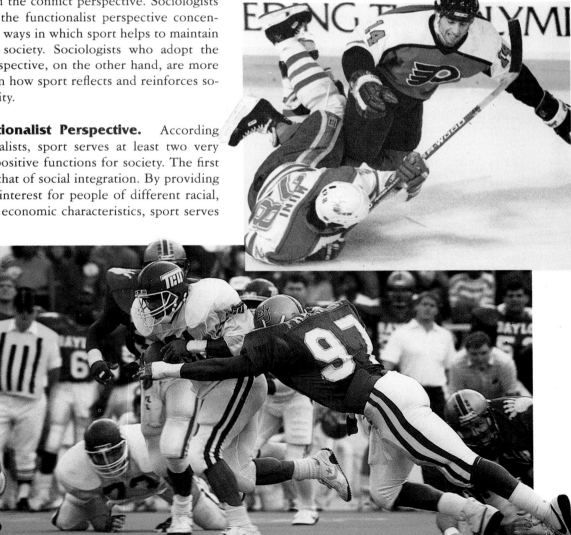

CASE STUDY

Sports and Television

Changes in technology often have a strong effect on social institutions. Nowhere is this more evident than in the case of television's influence on sports. In their book *Sports for Sale,* David A. Klatell and Norman Marcus examine the ways in which television has changed the nature of sports in America.

One of the most basic changes that television has produced in sports is the way in which Americans watch sporting events. According to Klatell and Marcus, the instant replays, the slow-motion and close-up camera shots, the in-depth interviews and commentaries, and the nonstop action characteristic of television coverage of sports have made sporting fans lose faith in their ability to interpret games unassisted. As proof of this lost faith, Klatell and Marcus note that it now is common for fans to bring their television sets to live games. And, in many stadia and sporting facilities, giant replay screens are provided so that spectators in the stands will not be at a disadvantage relative to their stay-at-home counterparts.

Television also has changed the way sports are played. Television timeouts are common in professional football, basketball, and hockey games. And, as often as not, it is the television producer rather than the coach who calls timeouts. Similarly, in professional football, the two-minute warning serves the needs of television advertisers, not coaches. Basketball also has bowed to the needs of television. The National Basketball Association, for instance, has banned the zone and instituted the 24-second clock to accommodate television coverage. In college basketball, the 45-second clock keeps the game moving for television audiences.

In tennis, yellow balls have replaced white balls to accommodate television coverage—the yellow looks better against blue skies. Even golf has adapted to the requirements of television.

Match scoring has been replaced by 72-hole tournament scoring to make televised coverage more exciting for home viewers. In baseball, night games have become the norm everywhere in the United States.

The distribution of professional teams also is affected by television. More often than not, teams and leagues are located in cities that have "television potential." In some cases, concerns over television coverage have lured teams away from cities with loyal fans to new cities with higher viewer appeal. Television also has been the driving force behind team expansion. More teams mean more television coverage.

Even the scheduling of games is influenced by the needs of television programming. Games in California often are delayed until 6 P.M. to accommodate viewers in the East. Similarly, football games scheduled to kick-off at 1 P.M. sometimes are delayed until 4 P.M. to enable television networks to attract larger audiences. Unfortunately, in many cases, the ticket-buyers do not learn of the scheduling changes until just days before the game.

Why does television have such a strong hold over sports? The answer is money. Currently, the money a team can earn from television rights and from advertisers far exceeds the money generated through ticket sales. Consequently, organized sports have become increasingly dependent on television for financial survival. According to Klatell and Marcus, this may have negative consequences for the future of sports. As competition among television networks and cable stations increases, the profits earned by the networks are declining. This, in turn, is affecting the fees paid to teams and leagues for the rights to televise sporting events. As a result, the ticket-buying fans of the future may well be faced with the necessity to shoulder more of the burden of financing organized sports.

people away from personal and social problems. According to the conflict perspective, sport serves to lessen people's unhappiness with their lot in life by providing a distraction. The bored worker, the poor inner-city dweller, and the unemployed adult or teenager can forget their troubles by watching or participating in sports. In addition, violent sports such as football, boxing, and hockey serve to legitimate violence, making it more acceptable in other areas of life. And finally, by reinforcing the idea that achievement comes through hard work, sport provides a justification for the unequal distribution of wealth. People who achieve wealth and power are seen as doing so through personal talent and effort, not through social advantage. Other conflict theorists take a less extreme position. They tend to focus on how organized sports mirror the inequality that already exists in society.

Issues in American Sport

Sport is a tremendously important part of American society. Commercial sports ventures generate more than $5 billion worth of business a year. Annual attendance at major league baseball games averages over 55 million people, while yearly attendance at professional football and basketball games tops 17 million and 18 million, respectively. Even more people attend college football and basketball games. And now, with the advent of sport stations on cable television, sport fans can enjoy sports 24 hours a day, 7 days a week in the comfort of their own homes.

Given America's love affair with sports, it is not surprising that social scientists have devoted considerable attention to analyzing how the institution of sport affects individuals in society. In this section, we will examine two areas of interest to sociologists of sport: racial discrimination in organized sports and women's athletics.

Racial Discrimination. Racial discrimination within organized sports has long been of interest to social scientists. Because of the widespread participation of African Americans in sports, researchers have focused on African American players when examining racial discrimination.

Studies on racial discrimination in sports tend to focus on one of two areas: (1) the practice of stacking or (2) salary differences between white and African American players. **Stacking** refers to the tendency to assign people to central or noncentral athletic positions on the basis of race or ethnicity. Sociologists label positions as central or noncentral on the basis of leadership responsibility. Central positions are those positions that require leadership responsibility and that afford players greater opportunity to affect the outcome of the game. Social scientists have found that African American players tend to occupy noncentral positions in college and professional team sports, while white players occupy central positions.

In football, for instance, whites are overrepresented in offense and special-team positions.

© 1986 Washington Post Writers Group. Reprinted with permission.

About 75 percent of the players in the National Basketball Association are African Americans. Yet, on average, African American players earn 20 percent less than their white teammates. Sociologists take this as evidence of racial discrimination in sports.

(noncentral). Similarly, African Americans still are underrepresented in the central roles of coaches, trainers, managers, owners, and referees, although some gains now are being made.

Sociological explanations for stacking often center on the perceptions of coaches concerning the strengths and weaknesses of African American players. Some conflict sociologists, for instance, argue that coaches perceive African Americans as lacking in the skills needed to carry out the decision-making duties associated with central positions. As a result, they seldom are given the chance to prove their abilities at leadership.

Social scientists also have found evidence of racial discrimination in the salaries of white and African American professional athletes. In the case of basketball, for instance, although many of the highest-paid players are African American, pay discrimination exists. According to research by economists Lawrence Kahn and Peter Sherer, African Americans in the National Basketball Association (NBA) earn 20 percent less than their white teammates, all things being equal, even though approximately 75 percent of NBA players are African American. Sociologists James Koch and C. Warren Vander Hill have found similar results in their analysis of salaries in the NBA.

According to Kahn and Sherer, higher pay for whites is a function of fan preference—white fans in many franchise areas tend to prefer teams with white players. Consequently, management is willing to pay higher salaries to attract white players. Kahn and Sherer base their conclusion on the fact that attendance at home games increases as the number of white players on a team increases.

Koch and Vander Hill offer three possible explanations for pay discrimination. (1) Team owners *assume* that fans prefer white players and take that assumption as justification for paying higher salaries to whites. (2) Some whites dislike playing basketball with African Americans. Thus management believes it must pay higher salaries to white players to compensate them for playing on predominantly African American teams. (3) Pay differences are a latent rather than a manifest function of discrimination. Because many African Americans come from economically disadvantaged backgrounds, they perceive any contract offer as adequate. As a result, they do not negotiate as aggressively as their white counterparts.

These positions include quarterback, center, and left and right guard, kicker, and punter—positions considered central by sociologists. African Americans, on the other hand, are concentrated in defensive positions—positions considered noncentral. The same tendency occurs in baseball. Whites are concentrated in the infield (central), while African Americans are concentrated in the outfield

Women's golf professional Nancy Lopez was the only female member of her high school golf team. She went on to become the eleventh member of the LPGA Hall of Fame.

Women's Athletics. Money also enters into the analysis of women's athletics. The gap between the earnings potential of female and male professional athletes has long been an area of concern for women athletes. Women's prize money in professional tennis, for instance, lags behind men's prize money by about 30 percent. The same holds true for women's professional golf. In 1991, for example, Corey Pavin—the top-earning male golfer—took home prize money totaling $979,430. Pat Bradley, the top-earning female golfer, on the other hand, had prize winnings totaling only $763,118.

The situation is no better in college athletics. Prior to the 1970s, funding for women's athletics was nonexistent or practically nonexistent at most coeducational colleges and universities. In fact, it has only been since 1973 that women have received college athletic scholarships. In 1973,

swimmer Lynn Genesko was awarded an athletic scholarship by the University of Miami, a private university in Florida. She thus became the first woman to qualify for a scholarship based on athletic ability. Even today, however, only one-fifth of the total funding for college sports is earmarked for women's athletics.

What progress has been made primarily is the result of Title IX of the Education Amendment Act of 1972. Title IX, which did not go into effect until 1975, bars discrimination on the basis of gender in any program—including athletics—at any educational institution receiving federal funds. As a result of the act, female participation in intercollegiate sports jumped from approximately 16,000 in 1972 to roughly one-third of all college athletes today. Similarly, female participation in high school sports rose from 294,000 to nearly 2 million in 1992.

Controversy over the act itself has slowed some of the hoped-for benefits for women's athletics. Always loosely enforced, the act received a major blow in the 1984 Supreme Court case of *Grove City College* v. *Bell*. In its ruling, the Supreme Court held that the antidiscrimination measure only applied to federally funded programs or activities within an institution, not to the institution as a whole. In other words, specific programs within an institution could lose federal funding if they were found to be discriminatory, but funding for nondiscriminatory programs within the institution would not be affected. Because few sports programs are federally funded, the ruling had the effect of eliminating the requirement for educational institutions to provide equal athletic facilities for women. Fortunately for women's sports, Congress passed legislation that overturned the Supreme Court decision in 1988.

Also of interest to many sociologists is the degree to which female participation in organized sports is considered socially acceptable. In 1961, sociologist James Coleman published a study on status systems in high schools. He found that athletic participation was the major determinant of social standing for males, while participation in school activities was the major determinant for females. Because few females participated in organized school sports in the early 1960s, Coleman did not include athletic participation as one of the possible status-determining roles for females.

In light of changing attitudes toward appropriate gender behavior for women, many recent studies have focused on whether athletic participation for female high school students is gaining acceptance. The findings have been mixed. Some studies have found that participation in sports increases a female's standing within the social stratification system of high school. Other studies have found that male and female students rate female athletic participation well down on the list of roles associated with high social standing.

In an attempt to determine whether these contradictory findings might be the result of lumping together all sports participation, Mary Jo Kane

Traditionally, women's participation in athletics has been limited to figure skating, golf, tennis, swimming, diving, and track. In recent years, however, women have become more active in sports generally considered to be the domain of men.

revised Coleman's study to distinguish between five sports: tennis, golf, volleyball, basketball, and softball. Based on the amount of body contact, the weight of sports equipment, and the degree of face-to-face competition, Kane classified basketball and softball as gender-inappropriate sports for women, and tennis, golf, and volleyball as gender-appropriate sports.

Kane found that male students preferred to date female athletes who participate in gender-appropriate sports. Similarly, when female students were asked to list which type of female athlete they would prefer to have as a friend, they too chose participants in gender-appropriate sports. In all cases, tennis was seen as the most-favorable sport for females. Kane concluded that male and female students still are operating under the influence of traditional gender-role stereotypes.

SECTION 2 REVIEW

DEFINE sport, stacking

1. **Summarizing Ideas** List and describe the seven characteristics that distinguish sport as a social institution.

2. **Contrasting Ideas** How does the view of sport presented by functionalist theorists differ from the view presented by conflict theorists?

3. **Composing an Essay** Summarize the two issues in American sport discussed in this section.

CHAPTER 15   SUMMARY

Science is the pursuit of knowledge through systematic methods. Science as a social institution is a relatively recent phenomenon. The process of institutionalization has taken centuries, however. Among the factors that led to the development of science as a social institution were the Renaissance, the growth in knowledge concerning mining and metallurgy, the Age of Exploration, the Protestant Reformation, and the Industrial Revolution. The sociological perspective that examines how scientific knowledge develops is called the sociology of science.

According to sociologist Robert K. Merton, the modern scientific community supposedly is guided by four norms. These norms are universalism, organized skepticism, communalism, and disinterestedness. In reality, however, scientists often fall far short of practicing these ideals. Among the problems that affect modern science are fraud, competition, the Matthew effect, and conflicting views of reality.

Sociologists use the term *sport* to refer to competitive games that are won or lost on the basis of physical skills and are played according to specific rules. Throughout history, people have played games. Sport as a social institution, however, is a relatively recent development. Modern sport is distinguished by seven characteristics: secularization, equality, specialization, rationalization, bureaucratization, quantification, and the quest for records.

Sociologists differ on how they view the effect of sport on society. Sociologists who adopt a functionalist perspective view sport as serving at least two important functions for society: social integration and the reinforcement of important social norms and values. Sociologists who adopt a conflict perspective, on the other hand, view sport as a mechanism to promote social inequality.

Social scientists have devoted considerable attention to the analysis of American sport. Two issues that have been of particular interest to sociologists are the continuing problem of racial discrimination in organized sports and social and social-psychological factors associated with women's professional and amateur athletics.

DEVELOPING SOCIOLOGICAL

THINKING ABOUT SOCIOLOGY: Determining Fallacies in Reasoning

Students of sociology often are called on to analyze and evaluate sociological statements and viewpoints. To do this, it is necessary to recognize fallacies in reasoning. A fallacy in reasoning is either an unsound or unsupported argument or an incorrect conclusion. Fallacies in reasoning fall into two broad categories: cause–effect fallacies and fallacies of proof.

Cause–Effect Fallacies

Some errors in reasoning result from mistakes in determining cause–effect relationships. The three most common cause–effect fallacies are as follows:

- **Single-Cause Fallacy.** The single-cause fallacy involves identifying only one cause for a major event. The statement "All human behavior is determined by biology" contains a single-cause fallacy. Many factors, some biological and others social, affect human behavior.

  The single-cause fallacy should not be confused with accurate statements about the main causes of sociological phenomena. A sociologist who writes about a "major cause" or the "main cause" of a sociological event or condition is ranking causes by importance. He or she is not attributing the phenomenon to a single *possible* cause.

- **Correlation-as-Cause Fallacy.** The correlation-as-cause fallacy involves identifying an event that occurs at the same time as another event as the cause of that event. The following statement illustrates the correlation-as-cause fallacy: "An American weather satellite crashed to the ground last week, resulting in six days of unseasonably cold weather." There is no scientific evidence to indicate that a weather satellite falling from orbit could affect the weather in any way. It is only a coincidence that the two events occurred at the same time.

- **Previous-Event-as-Cause Fallacy.** The previous-event-as-cause fallacy involves identifying an event that occurred prior to another event as the cause of the second event when, in fact, the two events are not directly related. The reasoning is that if Event A happened before Event B, it must have caused Event B. An example of this fallacy in reasoning is the statement: "The election of Richard Nixon to the presidency enabled Congress to pass the Education Amendment Act of 1972." In fact, many factors led to the passage of the act.

Fallacies of Proof

When a conclusion is incorrectly drawn from evidence, a fallacy of proof occurs. In the study of sociology, fallacies of proof often result when facts are misused or misinterpreted. The three most common fallacies of proof are as follows:

- **Insufficient-Evidence Fallacy.** The insufficient-evidence fallacy involves using insufficient data to prove a major point. Suppose, for example, a sociologist is trying to prove that college athletic programs for women are funded below the level of men's programs in the majority of industrialized nations. To prove this, the sociologist must collect data on funding for college sports from as many industrialized nations as possible. If the sociologist only collects data from the United States and Canada and considers the point proved, the sociologist has committed an insufficient-evidence fallacy.

- **Irrelevant-Evidence Fallacy.** The irrelevant-evidence fallacy involves using unrelated information to prove a major point. Continuing the example of the sociologist studying the funding of college athletic programs in industrialized nations, suppose the sociologist also collects data from industrializing nations. Any conclusions based on the evidence are in error because data from industrializing nations are irrelevant to the point.

■ **Majority-View Fallacy.** The majority-view fallacy involves arguing that something is true because "everyone" says it is true. The statement "Everyone knows that female athletes are less willing than are male athletes to make sacrifices for their sport" is a majority-view fallacy. Although this may be a widely held view, it is not supported by the facts.

How to Recognize Fallacies

To recognize fallacies in sociological reasoning, follow these guidelines:

1. Read the statement carefully. Identify the main idea and the conclusion.

2. Identify fallacies in reasoning. Ask how each conclusion was reached.

3. Evaluate the statement or argument. Determine the validity of the statement based on the reasoning and the evidence presented.

Applying the Skill

Read the following hypothetical statement. Then identify the fallacies in this statement.

> Upward social mobility is a perfect example of biological determinism. At the dawn of human existence, some people possessed a gene for upward mobility. Within 10 or so generations, that gene became concentrated in the upper class. This occurred because only those individuals who possessed the gene for social mobility were able to move up the social ladder, and only they were able to pass on the gene to future generations. Thus it is people's genetic makeup, not effort, luck, ability, or social conditions, that determines social stratification.

The main idea of the passage is that people are genetically predisposed to occupy certain social classes. According to the passage, effort, luck, ability, and social conditions have nothing to do with a person's chances of bettering his or her lot in life.

There are two fallacies of reasoning in the passage. The first fallacy is a single-cause fallacy. According to the statement, social stratification is caused solely by the genetic makeup of the population. In reality, however, effort, ability, luck, and social conditions work together to affect the stratification system in a society. The second fallacy is an insufficient-evidence fallacy. The passage does not provide any evidence that a gene for social mobility exists or has ever existed.

Practicing the Skill

Read the following passage, which is representative of the views of some sociobiologists and ethologists (animal behaviorists). Then on a separate sheet of paper, answer the questions below.

> Everyone knows that humans are inherently aggressive. Just look at our early ancestors. It was the natural instinct to kill with a weapon, not hunger, that led these early humans to take up hunting. Even fire—the great invention that separated our early ancestors from lower animals—was used as a weapon. Proof is found in the fact that the bones of our ancestors are resting among the ashes of prehistoric fires. What is the cause of innate human aggression, from verbal disputes to all-out war? Territoriality. Humans, like all animals, are genetically predisposed to carve out and defend their territory. Just look at the tendency of modern Americans to fence in their backyards!

1. (a) What is the main idea of the passage?
(b) What conclusion does the author draw?

2. Identify a single-cause fallacy in the passage and explain why it is a single-cause fallacy.

3. Identify a correlation-as-cause fallacy and explain why it is a correlation-as-cause fallacy.

4. Identify an insufficient-evidence fallacy and explain why it is an insufficient-evidence fallacy.

5. Identify a majority-view fallacy and explain why it is a majority-view fallacy.

Reviewing Sociological Terms

On a separate sheet of paper, supply the term that correctly completes each sentence.

1. The tendency to assign people to central or noncentral athletic positions on the basis of race or ethnicity is called _____.

2. _____ is the pursuit of knowledge through systematic methods.

3. A _____ is the set of shared concepts, methods, and assumptions that make up the scientific reality at any point in time.

4. The sociological perspective that examines how scientific knowledge develops is the _____ _____ _____.

5. _____ refers to competitive games that are won or lost on the basis of physical skill and are played according to specific rules.

Thinking Critically about Sociology

1. **Interpreting Ideas** What effect did the Enlightenment and the Industrial Revolution have on the development of modern science?

2. **Summarizing Ideas** Describe the characteristics of science during the time of the ancient Greeks and Romans.

3. **Extending Ideas** **(a)** Describe each of the seven characteristics of modern sport outlined by Allen Guttmann. **(b)** Explain how each characteristic can be seen as a natural outgrowth of industrial society.

4. **Seeing Relationships** What evidence have social scientists collected to support the view that racial and gender discrimination exists today in organized sports?

5. **Understanding Ideas** Describe how the Renaissance, the growth in knowledge concerning mining and metallurgy, the Age of Exploration, and the Protestant Reformation contributed to the rebirth of science in Europe.

6. **Expressing Viewpoints** Summarize the functionalist and conflict views of sport and then tell why you believe one or the other of the two views best describes the impact of sport on society.

7. **Analyzing Ideas** **(a)** How do conflicting views of reality influence the pursuit of science? **(b)** What is the Matthew effect and what are its consequences for science?

8. **Organizing Ideas** Prepare a chart describing each of the four norms of science. The first column in the chart should list each norm, the second column should list the characteristics of each norm, and the third column should list the purpose of each norm.

Exercising Sociological Skills

1. **Using Sociological Imagination** Reread the Applying Sociology feature on pages 382–383. What steps might be taken to improve the level of scientific literacy in the United States?

2. **Composing an Essay** Based on the information presented in the Case Study on page 390, write an essay describing the effects of television on American sports.

3. **Determining Fallacies in Reasoning** Reread the Developing Sociological Imagination feature on pages 396–397. Then, select an article of scientific interest from a supermarket tabloid. What, if any, fallacies in reasoning appear in the article.

Extending Sociological Imagination

1. Prepare a brief report on one of the following topics: **(a)** racial discrimination in sports broadcasting or team management; or **(b)** the history of women's participation in the Olympic games.

2. Research a famous hoax in science (such as the Piltdown man) and report your findings to the class.

The Hazards of Steroid Use

Americans are fascinated by athletes and athletic competition. The desire to achieve the size, strength, and speed of athletic heroes has led some Americans, particularly teenagers, to try to achieve these goals through artificial means—the use of steroids. Despite a growing body of evidence about the hazards of steroids, and despite the fact that nonmedical steroid distribution became a federal offense in 1991, steroid use continues to flourish.

In the following excerpt from the article "Pumped Up," which appeared in the June 1, 1992, issue of *U.S. News & World Report,* Joannie M. Schrof explores the phenomenon of steroid abuse among teenagers. While reading the excerpt, consider both the physical and psychological effects of steroid use.

It's a dangerous combination of culture and chemistry. Inspired by cinematic images of the Terminator and Rambo and the pumped-up paychecks of athletic heroes with stunning physiques and awesome strength, teenagers across America are pursuing dreams of brawn through a pharmacopeia of pills, powders, oils and serums that are readily available—but often damaging. Despite the warnings of such fallen stars as Lyle Alzado, the former football player who died two weeks ago of a rare brain cancer he attributed to steroid use, a *U.S. News* investigation has found a vast teenage subculture driven by an obsession with size and bodybuilding drugs. . . .

The risks are considerable. Steroids are derivatives of the male hormone testosterone, and although they have legitimate medical uses—treatment of some cancers, for example—young bodybuilders who use them to promote tissue growth and endure arduous workouts routinely flood their bodies with 100 times the testosterone they produce naturally. The massive doses, medical experts say, affect not only the muscles but also the sex organs and nervous system, including the brain. "Even a brief period of abuse could have lasting effects on a child whose body and brain chemistry are still developing," warns Neil Carolan, who directs chemical dependency programs at BryLin Hospitals in Buffalo and has counseled over 200 steroid users.

Male users—by far the majority—can suffer severe acne, early balding, yellowing of the skin and eyes, development of female-type breasts and shrinking of the [sex organs]. . . . In females, the voice deepens permanently, breasts shrink, periods become irregular, the [sex organ] swells and hair is lost from the head but grows on the face and body. Teen users also risk stunting their growth, since steroids can cause bone growth plates to seal. . . .

"Juicers" often enjoy a feeling of invincibility and euphoria. But along with the "pump" can come irritability and a sudden urge to fight. So common are these uncontrolled bursts of anger that they have a name in the steroid culture: "roid rages." The aggression can grow to pathological proportions; in a study by Harvard researchers, one eighth of steroid users suffered from "bodybuilder's psychosis," displaying such signs of mental illness as delusions and paranoia. So many steroid abusers are ending up behind bars for violent vandalism, assault and even murder that defense attorneys in several states now call on steroid experts to testify about the drugs' effects. . . .

Meanwhile, the ambience [environment] of gyms and health-food stores serves to cloak the use of performance-enhancing drugs in the veneer of a healthy lifestyle. Since all of the trappings of their world have to do with hard work, fitness and vitality, kids who use the substances see them as just another training aid. . . .

Ultimately, to reach children, educators will have to crack the secretive steroid subculture. So inviting is the underground world that, according to a recent study, 1 in 10 users takes steroids primarily out of desire to belong to the tightknit group.

Source Review

1. What are the physical effects of steroid use?

2. What are the psychological effects of steroid use?

The Abuse of Power: The Nazi Holocaust

During the years 1939 to 1945, the German government gave official sanction to the destruction of Europe's Jews. The Nazi party, under the leadership and direction of Adolf Hitler, led a reign of terror that haunts and horrifies many people to this day.

What was to become the Nazi Holocaust actually had its beginnings years earlier than 1939. Germany during the 1920s was reeling from the humiliating defeat it had suffered during World War I. A depression in 1929 further dampened the spirits of the German people, leaving them hungry for change.

Adolf Hitler, the hypnotic speaker and charismatic leader of the Nazi party, filled the German people with new hope, promising them that Germany once again would hold its head up high. Hitler blamed the problems of Germany on the Jews and the Communists, providing the population with scapegoats for their anger and frustration. Hitler also told the Germans that they, the "Aryans," were the master race meant to conquer the world and that all other groups of people were inferior.

Hitler's emotional speeches stirred the support of all segments of the population. In the German election of 1930, the Nazi party won many seats in the parliament, but not enough to form a government by themselves. Finally, in 1932, Hitler's party won two-thirds of the vote. President Paul von Hindenburg, conceding to pressure, appointed Hitler as chancellor.

Hitler then staged an elaborate scheme to achieve the popular support he needed to gain complete control. Under mysterious conditions, the parliament building was set ablaze, and the fire was blamed on a Communist uprising. In the chaos that followed the blaze, Hitler immediately was granted emergency powers to deal with the Communist threat. He seized this opportunity to make himself dictator and to bring the Nazi party to power.

Germany was transformed into a police state. Opposition parties and labor unions were disbanded, and the formation of new organizations opposing the Nazi program was outlawed. Newspapers and radio stations were taken over or closed down. The Gestapo, a secret-police force, entered the homes of citizens at will, beating and silencing those who opposed the Nazis.

Communists, Socialists, and liberals were rounded up by the Nazis and thrown into large prisons. These prisons were called concentration camps. Hitler's long-time hatred of the Jews erupted. He established policies designed to deprive the Jews of their civil rights. Other groups, such as Gypsies, homosexuals, Jehovah's Witnesses, and Seventh-Day Adventists, became victims of Nazi persecution as well. Anybody who opposed the Nazis was suspect. But the Jews became the main target of the Nazi venom. Over the next few years, persecution against the Jews escalated. The ideology of hatred against the Jews was formalized in 1935 by the passage of the Nuremberg Laws. These laws outlawed marriage between Germans and Jews and paved the way for Hitler to strip the Jews of their last remaining civil rights.

What followed was a carefully organized plan for the genocide of an entire group of people. Hitler referred to this plan as the "Final Solution" for the Jewish "problem." Millions of people were caught in a nightmare of terror and death that spread like a net throughout almost all of Europe. With the Holocaust, the moral, religious, and intellectual traditions of Western civilization were cast aside. In a nation that at the time was considered the most advanced in the world, mass murder became a civic duty. The principles of democracy failed, and national interests were placed above human rights. This grave abuse of power resulted in a catastrophic war and in the destruction of a Jewish life and tradition that had enriched European civilization for centuries.

UNIT 4 REVIEW

Reviewing Sociological Ideas

1. *(a)* What is a social institution? *(b)* Describe the seven social institutions discussed in this unit.

2. *(a)* Describe the characteristics of the three basic sectors found in all economic systems. *(b)* How do preindustrial, industrial, and postindustrial societies differ in terms of which sector is emphasized?

3. *(a)* What is authoritarianism? *(b)* In what forms can authoritarian governments exist?

4. Provide a definition for each of the following terms: *(a)* nuclear family, *(b)* family of orientation, *(c)* family of procreation, *(d)* extended family, and *(e)* kinship.

5. *(a)* What are the three functions of religion? *(b)* What are the four basic elements of religion?

6. *(a)* What is power? *(b)* What is the difference between legitimate and illegitimate power? *(c)* Describe the three forms of legitimate authority outlined by Max Weber.

7. *(a)* What is homogamy? *(b)* What is heterogamy?

8. *(a)* What is a democracy? *(b)* Describe the conditions needed for a democracy to thrive.

9. What seven characteristics distinguish sport as a social institution?

Synthesizing Sociological Ideas

1. *Drawing Conclusions* *(a)* What factors contributed to the institutionalization of science? *(b)* How do the norms of science differ from the realities of scientific research?

2. *Comprehending Ideas* Describe how the structure of the family can vary in relation to *(a)* the number of marriage partners, *(b)* residential patterns, *(c)* kinship patterns, and *(d)* authority patterns.

3. *Summarizing Ideas* List and describe the four functions of the family.

4. *Seeing Relationships* *(a)* According to functionalist sociologists, how does education serve to maintain the stability of society? *(b)* According to conflict theorists, how does education serve to maintain social inequality in society?

5. *Expressing Ideas* Describe the research findings on marital satisfaction in the United States.

6. *Comparing Ideas* How do the characteristics of the pure capitalist system differ from those of the pure socialist system?

7. *Organizing Ideas* Develop a structured overview of the discussion of the American political system presented in Chapter 13.

8. *Understanding Ideas* *(a)* What four factors have influenced the nature of the free enterprise system in the United States? *(b)* What effect have these factors had on economic activity in the United States?

9. *Presenting Evidence* Provide evidence to support the idea that racial and gender discrimination exists in organized sports.

Applying Sociological Imagination

1. Prepare a summary of the information presented in Chapter 12 on the following trends in American family life: *(a)* delayed marriage, *(b)* delayed childbearing, *(c)* dual-earner families, *(d)* one-parent families, and *(e)* remarriage.

2. Prepare a brief research paper on one of the following topics: *(a)* patterns of religious affiliation in the United States, *(b)* changes in the rates of religious participation among Americans over the past several decades, or *(c)* the political influence of Religious Right activists.

3. Conduct library research to select and summarize one magazine or journal article on each of the following topics: *(a)* educational reform, *(b)* violence in the schools, and *(c)* bilingual education.

UNIT 5

No social change occurs outside of the world context; and though the strengths and weaknesses of individual states and societies are largely determined by internal causes, it is the way these characteristics of societies interact with the world systems that determines the direction, intensity, and speed of further internal changes.

DANIEL CHIROT

THE CHANGING SOCIAL WORLD

Collective Behavior and Social Movements

Collective Behavior

Preconditions for Collective Behavior
Characteristics of Collectivities
Types of Collectivities
Explaining Collective Behavior

Social Movements

Types of Social Movements
Life Cycle of Social Movements
Explaining Social Movements

Chapter Focus

Chapter 16 focuses on collective behavior and social movements. The chapter begins with a discussion of the preconditions that lead to collective behavior. Special attention is paid to types of collectivities and to theories that have been developed to explain collective behavior. The chapter then turns to a discussion of social movements, focusing on types of social movements, the life cycle of social movements, and theories of social movements.

As you study the chapter, look for the answers to the following questions:

1. What preconditions are necessary for collective behavior to occur, and how do these preconditions build on each other?
2. How do the various types of collectivities differ, and what explanations for collective behavior have been proposed?
3. What types of social movements exist and how do they differ?
4. What stages are present in the life cycle of social movements, and how can the existence of social movements be explained?

KEY TERMS

The following terms, while not the only terms emphasized in the chapter, are basic to your understanding of sociology. Determine the meaning of each term, either by using the Glossary or by watching for context clues as you read the chapter.

collectivity	rumor	social movement
panic	urban legend	relative deprivation
fashion	public	resource mobilization

- In the year 1634, a frenzied passion for tulips swept over the Dutch in Holland. Tulips became so desirable and were bought at such a dizzying pace that one bulb soon became as expensive as a house. The Dutch were sure that the world would share their love for tulips, making the sellers wealthy beyond belief. This prediction was not to be, however, and thousands of people were bankrupted when the price of tulips plunged.

- In 1965, a California policeman made a routine arrest of an intoxicated driver in a poor section of Los Angeles known as Watts. Some people in the crowd that gathered began to hurl bottles and insults at the arresting officer. As the crowd grew, rumors began to fly that the arrest was racially motivated. The next day rioting broke out in Watts. When the riots ended four days later, 34 people were dead, over 1,000 people were injured, and 200 buildings had been burned to the ground.

- The 1963 publication of Betty Friedan's book *The Feminine Mystique* signaled the start of a social movement that would change the way people think of male and female roles. Since that time, millions of men and women in the United States have actively sought gender equality in all spheres of life.

1 COLLECTIVE BEHAVIOR

In general, social behavior is patterned and predictable. People expect others to act in accord with established norms and usually they do. In fact, without this predictability and cooperative spirit, social interaction would be impossible.

Sometimes, however, situations occur, such as those mentioned above, in which the norms of behavior are unclear. Often in these situations, it appears as though people are making up new norms as they go along. Sociologists refer to this action as **collective behavior**—the relatively spontaneous social behavior that occurs when people try to develop common solutions to unclear situations.

Social scientists generally have found collective behavior a difficult topic to study. For one thing, the range of material covered under collective behavior is enormous, including such varied phenomena as lynch mobs, fads, panics, and rumors. Each of these types of collective behavior takes a different form and has different consequences.

Collective behavior also is difficult to study because it is relatively short-lived, spontaneous, and emotional. This sometimes makes it difficult to understand how the behavior arises and to measure the reactions of people to the situations that spark the behavior. Adding to the problem is the fact that collective behavior usually involves large numbers of people who do not know each other. Because episodes of collective behavior are not enduring aspects of society, it is difficult to subject them to systematic, scientific study.

Although collective behavior has always been a fundamental fact of human existence, sociologists in the United States have been studying this type of behavior for only a couple of decades. The knowledge they have amassed in this amount of time, however, adds an important dimension to our overall understanding of society and the patterns of social life. In this section, we will examine preconditions for collective behavior, characteristics and types of collectivities, and theories of collective behavior.

Preconditions for Collective Behavior

According to sociologist Neil Smelser, there are six basic preconditions for collective behavior. These preconditions build on one another and guide the outcome of collective behavior. The six preconditions are structural conduciveness, structural strain, growth and spread of a generalized belief, precipitating factors, mobilization for action, and social control.

Structural Conduciveness. Structural conduciveness refers to the surrounding social structure that makes it possible for a particular type of collective behavior to occur. In 1991, for example, a passerby videotaped the apparent beating of African American motorist Rodney King by four white Los Angeles police officers. The acquittal of the police officers at their subsequent trial ignited three days of rioting in South Central Los Angeles that left 53 people dead and more than 2,000 injured. The swift and repeated nationwide broadcast of the videotape and the intense media coverage of the trial fueled the conditions for collective behavior.

Structural Strain. The second precondition for collective behavior is structural strain. Structural strain refers to social conditions that put strain on people and so encourage them to seek some collective means to relieve this strain. Structural strain can be produced by conditions such as poverty, overcrowding, discrimination, and conflict. These conditions were present in the predominantly African American South Central Los Angeles area at the time of the trial. Thus the residents of the area were experiencing structural strain.

Growth and Spread of a Generalized Belief. The growth of a generalized belief makes the structural strain personally meaningful for people as individuals begin to identify the problem, form opinions about it, and share ways of dealing with it. In the example of South Central Los Angeles, the residents shared a strong resentment of the police and hoped that the four officers would be found guilty of beating Rodney King. At the same time, many residents doubted that

The videotaped beating of African American Rodney King set off a chain of events that ended in three days of rioting in South Central Los Angeles.

the all-white jury would give a fair verdict in the case.

Precipitating Factors.   Precipitating factors, the fourth precondition for collective behavior, refer to some kind of triggering mechanism that sets off the behavior. These factors usually are quite dramatic and give confirming evidence to the generalized belief. The confirming evidence then adds to the structural strain felt by people. In the Rodney King beating trial, the news that the jury had found the white officers not guilty was a precipitating factor in the riot.

Mobilization for Action.   The first four preconditions in the sequence of collective behavior set the stage for people to act. When the Los Angeles residents realized that community leaders could do nothing to change the verdict, they mobilized to express their collective anger and frustration through looting and random acts of destruction. By the time community leaders organized to intervene in the situation, the rioting was out of control.

Social Control.   At this point in the sequence, collective behavior can be controlled if mechanisms exist to prevent or minimize the situation. In the case of the Los Angeles riot, the mayor of the city called in the National Guard and imposed a curfew on the residents. In addition, President George Bush sent in federal troops. These actions helped put an end to the riot.

Characteristics of Collectivities

Collective behavior occurs within a collectivity. A **collectivity** is a collection of people who have limited interaction with each other and who do not share clearly defined, conventional norms. Collectivities exist in many forms, but three factors generally distinguish all forms of collectivities from the social groups discussed in Chapter 4:

- *Limited interaction.* Members of social groups generally interact with each other directly, often for long periods of time. Interaction among members of collectivities, however, is limited and sometimes nonexistent.

- *Unclear norms.* The norms that guide behavior in social groups are clearly defined and widely understood. In collectivities, however, norms for behavior either are unclear or they are unconventional.
- *Limited unity.* The people who form social groups generally are united by an awareness that they are members of these groups. Members of collectivities, on the other hand, seldom share a sense of group unity.

Types of Collectivities

Collective behavior includes an enormous range of phenomena. Among the types of collectivities identified by sociologists are crowds, mobs, riots, panics, mass hysteria, fashions, fads, rumors, urban legends, and public opinion.

Crowds.   A **crowd** is a temporary collection of people who are in close enough proximity to interact. Sociologist Herbert Blumer has identified four types of crowds: casual crowds, conventional crowds, expressive crowds, and acting crowds.

A *casual crowd* is the least organized and most temporary type of crowd. The people in this type of crowd interact little, if at all. Examples of casual crowds include people waiting in line to buy movie tickets and people gathered at a beach.

Behavior in a *conventional crowd* is much more structured than is the behavior in a casual crowd. People may not interact with each other very much, but they act according to established rules of behavior. Usually they are gathered together for a common purpose, such as a funeral, a public lecture, or a baseball game.

An *expressive crowd* has no seeming goal or purpose. This type of crowd forms around activities that have an emotional character to them, such as a religious revival or a rock concert. Laughing, shouting, crying, and other behaviors that are common in expressive crowds would be considered inappropriate in many other social situations.

An *acting crowd* is a violent crowd. The emotions that typify an acting crowd are much more intense than those found in an expressive crowd. The emotions usually are hostile and destructive and generally focus on one particular target. An acting crowd often is formed by a dramatic event and results in the violation of established norms

The hostile emotions typical of acting crowds often lead to destructive behavior.

denly, the British fans stampeded toward the Italians, destroying a fence that separated the two groups. Hundreds of helpless spectators were trampled in the rush. More horrifying than this, 38 people were killed and another 400 were seriously injured.

Mobs and Riots. The most violent form of acting crowd is a mob. A **mob** is an emotionally charged collectivity whose members are united by a specific destructive or violent goal. This type of collectivity usually has leaders who urge the group toward the common action and who enforce conformity among the group's members. Although mobs generally are unstable and limited in duration, their actions represent a threat to social order and a challenge to official authority.

One example of mob behavior that was common in the southern and western United States during the early twentieth century is the lynch mob. Lynch mobs were formed by vigilante groups who, without due process of law, administered supposed justice to people they perceived as criminals or as undesirables. Most lynch mobs were composed of whites who attempted to maintain their domination over African Americans and other minority groups through violence. Anyone who opposed the violence became a scapegoat for the mob's hatred. More than 5,000 people in the United States, most of whom were African

In 1985, for example, the European Cup Finals competition between Italy and Great Britain drew 60,000 soccer fans to Brussels, Belgium. Before the game even started, British spectators began to jeer at the Italian fans. Emotions became increasingly heated until both sides eventually began throwing rocks and bottles at each other. Sud-

Americans and ethnics, were hanged by lynch mobs during the years 1880 to 1930.

Somewhat related to a mob is a riot. A **riot** is a collection of people who erupt in generalized destructive behavior, the purpose of which is social disorder. Riots are less unified and less focused than are mobs. People who participate in riots typically lack access to power and so vent their frustrations through destructive actions. A riot often begins when long-standing tensions are triggered by a single event. In 1989, for example, a policeman killed an African American youth in Liberty City, a section of Miami. In response, protestors rioted for several days, looting stores, setting cars on fire, and throwing bottles and rocks. Unlike mobs, which generally break up once the violent goal has been reached, riots end only when the participants exhaust themselves or when social control is regained by officials.

Panics. Some collectivities are formed not by violence, but by fear. One such collectivity is a panic. A **panic** is a spontaneous and uncoordinated group action to escape some perceived threat. Panics generally occur only when people believe that their means of escape are limited or soon to be closed off. The fear of being trapped often results in faulty communication about the threat, which fuels the fear and keeps people from forming logical escape plans.

In a panic, mutual cooperation breaks down and the norms that govern conventional behavior are lost. The panicked reactions of a group sometimes result in more damage than what is produced by the threat itself. In 1903, for example, a fire broke out in Chicago's Iroquois Theater. Although the fire was quickly put out and actually did little damage to the building, more than 600 people were killed in their panic to reach the exits. Most of these people were smothered or trampled to death in the stampede.

Panics are most likely to occur in situations that are outside the realm of everyday experience, such as fires, floods, and earthquakes. Few norms of behavior exist for such situations, and so the response sometimes is irrational and emotional. Sometimes a panic is avoided, however, when a leader emerges who can channel the behavior of the individuals involved and direct them toward logical action.

Mass Hysteria. Another form of collective behavior formed by fear is mass hysteria. **Mass hysteria** is an unfounded anxiety shared by people who are scattered over a wide geographic area. This anxiety involves irrational beliefs and behaviors that spread among the population, sometimes unwittingly fueled by the media. Episodes of mass hysteria usually are short-lived, vanishing as people come to realize that their anxieties have no basis in fact.

One incidence of mass hysteria that had dramatic consequences occurred in 1692 in Salem, Massachusetts. In this Puritan community lived a black slave named Tituba, who had been brought from the island of Barbados and who was said to be skilled in black magic. A group of young girls from the community met regularly with Tituba to listen to her tell exciting and fantastic stories. In time, however, two of the girls in the group began to have strange and unexplainable convulsions, rolling and twisting on the ground as if possessed. Soon, many of the girls in the community were behaving in this same way. Hysteria spread quickly among the villagers, who feared that the girls had been bewitched.

Seeking the source of the bewitchment, Salem's clergy forced the girls to name the people responsible. At first, the girls named only Tituba and two other women as witches. Later, however, few people were safe from their false accusations. The hysteria grew so fevered that people refused to help the accused for fear that they themselves would be branded as witches and thrown in jail. By the time the girls' accusations finally were called into question, the Salem witch trials had resulted in the conviction and execution of 20 innocent people.

Fashions and Fads. Not all types of collective behavior that are spread among the population involve fear. **Fashions,** for example, refer to enthusiastic attachments among large numbers of people for particular styles of appearance or behavior. Most fashions are related to clothing, but any cultural artifact that gains a substantial appreciation by a large number of people can be a fashion. Fashions typically are short-lived and are subject to continual change.

Fashions generally are the products of modern industrialized societies. Nearly everyone of the

This wedding picture from 1885 and the two magazine covers from 1913 and 1926 illustrate how quickly fashions change in modern industrial societies.

same sex and age in small preindustrial societies dresses alike, and the styles of clothing in these societies change little over the years. In industrialized societies, on the other hand, fashions tend to change rapidly and to build on previous fashions.

Fashions are prominent in industrialized societies for two reasons. First, change is associated with progress in such societies and so tends to be valued. In the United States, for example, the term "old-fashioned" generally carries a negative meaning, while the terms "new" and "improved" tend to bring approval. Second, industrialized societies typically emphasize social mobility. Thus they give people more opportunities to take on new social statuses and the artifacts that symbolize these statuses, such as automobiles, clothing, homes, adornments, and points of view.

Somewhat similar to a fashion is a fad. A **fad** is an unconventional thought or action that a large number of people are attached to for a very short period of time. Fads differ from fashions in that they are less predictable, less enduring, and less socially respectable. In fact, people who embrace fads tend to be seen as frivolous by the majority of the population. A fad that was popular among college students several decades ago, for instance,

involved swallowing live goldfish. The majority of the population considered this to be a revolting pastime.

Some more recent fads include inline skates, Trivial Pursuit, the "grunge" look, Teenage Mutant Ninja Turtle characters, tattoos, Barney dolls, and earrings on men. Fads tend to appeal primarily to young people, who participate in the fads mainly as a way of asserting their personal identities. Fads tend to die out when they become so widespread that they cease bringing special notice to the participants.

Rumors and Urban Legends. All collectivities rely on communication among the participants. Some forms of collective behavior, however, consist solely of communication. A **rumor,** for example, is an unverified piece of information that is spread rapidly from one person to another. Rumors, which may be true or false, tend to thrive when large numbers of people lack definite information about some subject of interest to them.

The content of a rumor is likely to change over time as it passes from person to person. Each person evaluates the truth of the rumor and, when transmitting it, tends to emphasize some aspects of the rumor and eliminate others. The changes that the rumor goes through as it is passed among people reflect each person's hopes, fears, and biases about the information. Rumors generally are difficult to control and some even may persist for years. Once a rumor begins, the number of people who are aware of it increases dramatically as each individual spreads the rumor to several others. Rumors typically end only when substantiated evidence is widely provided, but still there will be some people who doubt that the information is factual.

The Proctor and Gamble Company, well-known maker of products such as Crest toothpaste and Comet cleanser, was the victim of a rumor several years ago. For over a century, the company had used the symbol of a moon and stars as its product trademark. In 1982, however, an unproved rumor connected the Proctor and Gamble trademark with a Satanic cult. Even though the company flatly denied any connection between itself and Satan worship, and even though no evidence was forthcoming to prove the accusation, the company's reputation and sales began to suffer. Because they were unable to eliminate the rumor, the company decided in 1985 to remove the trademark from all of its products.

Sociologists and urban anthropologists recently have become interested in a form of collective communication known as urban legends. **Urban legends** are stories that are untrue but that seem realistic and teach a lesson. Like rumors, urban legends arise and spread because of unclear situations. These stories seem realistic because they usually are attributed to specific times and places and sometimes are said to have happened to someone distantly known by the teller. The stories quickly become a sort of urban folklore, the purpose of which is to clarify situations by teaching moral lessons.

One typical urban legend, called "The Boyfriend's Death," tells the story of a boy and his date who park their car off a particular highway by a Holiday Inn. After spending some time there, the girl tells the boy that she needs to go home. He tries to start the car, but it will not start. After telling the girl to lock herself in the car, the boy starts out on foot for the Holiday Inn, where he plans to call for help. Much time goes by, but the boy does not return. Eventually, the girl hears a

scratching noise on the roof of the car. Too afraid to investigate the continuous scratching sound, she stays in the car all night long. At daylight, some people come by and help the girl out of the car. She looks up to find that her boyfriend is hanging from the tree and that his shoes have been scraping the roof of the car. This is the origin of the road's name—"Hangman's Road."

This same story appears in many versions in many places, but the moral of the tale is that teenagers should not park in secluded places. This story also represents the uneasiness parents feel about the freedom given to teenagers by the automobile. Other unclear situations, such as hitchhiking, changing gender roles, and teenage sexuality, also tend to provoke the growth and spread of urban legends.

Public Opinion. Another form of collective behavior that depends mainly on communication is public opinion. Although it is common to refer to everyone in a society as *the* public, social scientists reserve the term **public** for a group of geographically scattered people who are interested in and divided by some issue. Societies therefore actually contain many publics, since there is a different public for each social issue. And, the public for each single issue, such as gun control, abortion, or school prayer, changes as people gain or lose interest in it. The interest that a public has in an issue takes the form of attitudes, or opinions, concerning the issue.

Public opinion, then, refers to the collection of differing attitudes that members of a public have about a particular issue. Public opinion is subject to rapid change because members of a public very often change their views on issues. Nevertheless, democratic, capitalist nations such as the United States pay an enormous amount of attention to public opinion. Public-opinion polls on behalf of individuals seeking elected offices have high visibility in the United States, and businesses use market research and analysis as tools to fill consumer demands and increase profits.

Public opinion has such an important place in American society that politicians, interest groups, and businesses spend billions of dollars each year to influence these opinions. The most effective means through which these individuals and groups attempt to sway public opinion is propaganda.

Propaganda is an organized and deliberate attempt to shape public opinion. Although this term usually is thought of in a negative way, propaganda does not necessarily contain only false information. Like rumors, propaganda may be true, partly true, or false. The intent of propaganda, however, is always the same: to shape the opinions of the public toward some specific conclusion.

A democratic nation such as the United States depends on citizens who can make wise and rational decisions both when they cast their votes and when they make their purchases. Thus it is important to be alert to the techniques used by propagandists to sway public opinion. Social scientists have identified six such techniques: testimonials, bandwagon, name calling, plain-folks appeal, glittering generalities, and card stacking.

The *testimonials* technique refers to the use of endorsements from famous people to sell products or secure votes. For example, advertisers often use sports heroes to promote sports equipment or clothing. Famous actors often are enlisted to make speeches for politicians. The goal is to persuade people to transfer their admiration for a celebrity to the products or candidates endorsed by the celebrity.

The *bandwagon* technique appeals to the public's desire to conform. For example, a politician or product may be promoted as the one already most popular with the public. This technique assumes that people want to be on the winning side of an election or own what appear to be highly desirable products.

The *name calling* technique refers to the use of negative labels or images in order to make competitors appear in an unfavorable light. For example, politicians may accuse their opponents of being reckless spenders or uncaring about the needs of the public. The aim of this technique is to persuade the public to associate the politician or product with the unfavorable label.

The *plain-folks appeal* attempts to sway public opinion by appealing to the average American. Thus a politician may be portrayed as a plain, hard-working American who just wants to do good things for the nation. Similarly, average Americans with whom everyone can identify may be shown endorsing a product or candidate.

The *glittering generalities* technique refers to the use of words that sound positive but have little real meaning. For example, to say that a politician believes in freedom, democracy, and the American way sounds positive, but actually provides little information about the politician's views on the issues.

Card stacking refers to the use of facts in such a way as to place politicians or products in a favorable light. For example, newspapers may give a great deal of attention to politicians they favor and little attention to those they do not. Similarly, advertisers may use statistics or survey results in such a way as to favor their products over their competitors.

Explaining Collective Behavior

A number of theories have been proposed over the past century to explain collective behavior. These theories have been most useful for explaining types of collective behavior in which people are in close proximity with each other, such as crowds, mobs, riots, and panics. Foremost among the theories of collective behavior are contagion theory and emergent-norm theory.

Contagion Theory. The first systematic theory of collective behavior was developed in 1896 by Gustave Le Bon. According to Le Bon's **contagion theory,** the hypnotic power of a crowd encourages people to give up their individuality to the stronger pull of the group. Individuals become anonymous, with no will power or sense of responsibility. The crowd in effect becomes a single organism operating under one collective mind. In this situation, conventional social norms lose their meaning and, as emotion sweeps through the crowd, behavior becomes unrestrained.

According to Le Bon, three factors give crowds power over individuals. First, because of the sheer numbers of people involved in a crowd, individuals gain an anonymity that makes them feel unconquerable. Second, the spread of emotion is so rapid and contagious that it overtakes the members of a crowd like an epidemic. Third, members of a crowd rapidly enter a state of suggestibility, during which time they are not conscious of their actions. This suggestibility makes them particularly open to the manipulations of charismatic leaders.

Text continues on page 416.

APPLYING SOCIOLOGY

Analyzing Television Commercials

How much attention do you pay to television commercials? Perhaps you leave the room, stretch your legs, or fix yourself a snack whenever a commercial appears. Yet, advertising is an important part of television broadcasting. Advertisements enable you to watch television free of charge because the advertisers pay the cost of programming. Advertisers spend billions of dollars each year attempting to persuade viewers that their products are the best and most desirable products available.

Advertising actually is a form of propaganda. Advertisers present the advantages of their products in order to gain a favorable image. What products are advertised on television most often? Are different products advertised at different times of the day? You can apply your sociological skills to answer these questions and gain a better understanding of how advertisers attempt to sway public opinion.

Because there are so many hours of programming each week, it probably would be best to do this project together as a class. Just follow these steps:

Choosing the Programs. Students should look at a local television guide and decide which programs they would like to watch. Then, each student should choose a block of time for which he or she will be responsible. The choices should be somewhat evenly divided between hours before 6 P.M. and hours after 6 P.M.

Making the Tally Sheet. Next, each student should make a tally sheet similar to the one that appears on page 415. Make sure to leave enough room to record your data.

Watching the Programs. Students now are ready to watch the selected programs and to record the data about the television commercials on their sheets. Be sure to record every advertisement that appears during the block of time for which you are responsible.

Combining the Data. After all students have completed their observations, one student should collect all of the data sheets, making sure all information has been recorded. That student should sort the tally sheets into two piles, one for commercials appearing before 6 P.M. and the other for those appearing after 6 P.M.

Organize the class into two groups and give one pile to each group. Students in each group should combine the figures from all data sheets onto a master sheet. They then will have the total number of food products that were advertised, the total number of automobiles and related products, and so on. The next step is to add up these figures to get the total number of advertisements that appeared.

Combining the Data for Both Groups. At this point, you have two sets of data, one for each group. To find out which products are advertised most frequently, *regardless of when the commercial appeared,* you will have to find out the total number of food products, automobile-related products, and so on. Add the total for each type of product from both master tally sheets. Then, add the two totals at the bottom of the pages to get the sum total of all advertisements. Now, in order to answer the questions posed at the beginning of this feature, consider the following questions:

1. What is the total number of advertisements that appeared? Which type of product was advertised most frequently?

2. Which products were advertised most often before 6 P.M.? Least often?

3. Which types of commercials appeared most frequently after 6 P.M.? Least frequently?

4. How can you explain the differences found in the answers to questions 2 and 3?

TYPE OF PRODUCTS ADVERTISED	TALLY MARKS	TOTAL
1. All foods and food products		
2. Automobiles and related products (gas, tires, oil, accessories, etc.)		
3. Alcoholic beverages (beer, wine, whiskey, etc.)		
4. Nonalcoholic beverages (soft drinks, coffee, tea, etc.)		
5. Clothing and accessories (jewelry, watches, purses, billfolds, etc.)		
6. All home products (building materials, carpets, furniture, appliances, tools, wax, soap, drain cleaners, etc.)		
7. Personal articles and patent medicines (hair sprays, deodorants, cosmetics, aspirin, cold remedies, soap, etc.)		
8. All products related to pets		
9. Personal services (banking, loans, insurance, investments, telephone, etc.)		
10. Leisure time and recreational activities (sporting goods, camping supplies, travel, records, games, movies, dining out, hotels, airlines, resorts, amusement parks, etc.)		
11. Public relations advertisements (those that do not push a product but tend to build the image of the company)		
12. Other advertisements (all those that do not fit into one of the categories above)		
BEFORE 6:00 P.M. ☐ **AFTER 6:00** P.M. ☐	**TOTAL**	

Groups such as the Ku Klux Klan tend to generate high emotions among the public. Without police escorts, Klan demonstrations might lead to a breakdown of social norms among members of the crowd, with violent results.

According to **emergent-norm theory,** the people in a crowd often are faced with a situation in which traditional norms of behavior do not apply. These people in effect find themselves with no clear standard for their behavior. Gradually through interaction, however, new norms emerge when one or more leaders initiate new behaviors. These new norms then provide a common motivation for group action where none existed before. When a film being shown in a movie theater breaks, for example, one person may start stamping his or her feet. Even though this behavior does nothing to help fix the film, the action spreads quickly among the people in the theater. Even if individuals inwardly disagree with the action being taken, they often feel obliged to conform to the group norms. Crowd behavior therefore appears to be unanimous, when in fact it often is not.

Contagion theory has been criticized by contemporary sociologists, however. Studies have shown no indication that a collective mind exists in crowds. Any number of motivations for behavior can be found among crowd participants. Also, behavior in crowds tends not to be as uniform as suggested by Le Bon. Still, contagion theory has been useful for explaining how behavior spreads among the members of a crowd, freeing them from the restraints of conventional social norms. This theory also is helpful in understanding how emotions work to encourage people toward collective action.

Emergent-Norm Theory. Most contemporary social scientists favor the emergent-norm theory of collective behavior, which was developed by sociologists Ralph Turner and Lewis Killian. Contrary to contagion theory, emergent-norm theory acknowledges that individuals in a crowd have different attitudes, behaviors, and motivations. Rather than attributing the unanimous nature of crowd behavior to a collective mind, Turner and Killian look instead to the social control function of social norms.

2 SOCIAL MOVEMENTS

The types of collectivities discussed in the previous section generally are short-lived and rarely do they have a serious impact on the whole of society. Social movements, on the other hand, are much more deliberate and long-lasting forms of collective behavior. A **social movement** may be defined as a long-term conscious effort to promote or prevent social change. Social movements may develop around any issue of public concern.

Three factors distinguish social movements from other forms of collective behavior: a long duration, a highly structured organization with formally recognized leaders, and a deliberate attempt to institute societal change. These factors combine to give social movements the potential to attract memberships that number in the millions. In this section, we will examine types of social movements, the life cycle of a social movement, and theories that have been developed to explain social movements.

Types of Social Movements

The goal of most social movements is to change society, but social movements differ in the amount of change they seek. Sociologists have identified four types of social movements according to the goals of the movement: resistance movements, reform movements, utopian movements, and revolutionary movements.

Resistance Movements. The main goal of **resistance movements** is a return to traditional ways of acting and thinking. Resistance movements attempt to reverse current social trends, to "turn back the clock." The members of resistance movements usually are suspicious of and hostile toward social change.

The Religious Right, for example, seeks a return to the traditional family and social values of the past. This group is particularly active in the anti-abortion movement. One of the major goals of the anti-abortion movement is the reversal of the 1973 Supreme Court decision in *Roe* v. *Wade*. This Supreme Court case declared all anti-abortion laws as unconstitutional, stating that pregnant women have a right to privacy guaranteed under the Fourteenth Amendment of the Constitution. According to the Court, the right to privacy legally entitles women to choose abortion during

The social movement for women's rights, which gained the vote for women in 1920, continues to seek equality between the sexes.

the first three months of pregnancy. The anti-abortion movement, however, disagrees with the legal right of women to end their pregnancies. Consequently, this increasingly vocal movement is seeking to reinstate former anti-abortion laws.

Reform Movements. The goal of **reform movements** is to improve some part of society through social change. Reform movements use legal channels in seeking change, because they generally support the existing social system as a whole. This type of movement typically focuses on a single issue. The women's movement and the gay rights movement, for example, both seek to eliminate discrimination. The aim of the environmental movement is to end environmental pollution. The members of these movements make effective use of political lobbyists, the media, and the courts in seeking reform.

One early reform movement that had significant results began in late nineteenth-century industrial America. Because she was concerned about slum conditions and the lives of the poor in Chicago's swelling urban center, Jane Addams founded Hull House. Among its many activities, Hull House provided hot lunches for factory workers and conducted classes in cooking and English. More importantly, Hull House served to instruct hundreds of people about the need for social reform. These people went on to found their own settlement houses and to become lobbyists and politicians. The reform movement begun by Jane Addams and those trained at Hull House resulted in the first playgrounds and public baths in Chicago, the first Illinois factory inspection law, the first juvenile justice court in the United States, and the beginnings of industrial medicine.

Utopian Movements. A general dissatisfaction with society leads to **utopian movements.** People involved in this type of social movement seek to remove themselves from society and create their own ideal society. The members of utopian movements believe that the number of their supporters will grow as people come to believe in the ideals represented by the movement. These utopian ideals, however, often are vaguely presented and vaguely understood. A modern example of a utopian social movement is the peace movement of the 1960s.

One nineteenth-century utopian movement was established in Oneida, New York, by John Humphrey Noyes, a charismatic religious leader. Members of the Oneida Community believed in the doctrine of *perfectionism,* which held that it was possible for people to live perfect and sinless lives on earth. Noyes and the Oneidans also believed in the sharing of wealth, group marriage, and the elimination of private property. Many of their practices proved too radical for their neighbors in surrounding communities, however, and the Oneidans came under attack. Noyes fled to Canada and, like most utopian movements that lose their charismatic leaders, the Oneidans were left with little leadership to hold the community together.

As is the case with most utopian movements, the Oneida Community was a relatively short-lived experiment. But of the many utopian movements seen in the United States, the Oneida Community was the most successful. One of the numerous and quite profitable projects begun by the Oneidans during their 30 years together was the manufacture of silverware. This endeavor gave the community a net worth of $600,000 at the time of its breakup. The Oneidans used this money to form a joint-stock company still known to millions of Americans today—Oneida, Ltd.

Revolutionary Movements. The main goal of **revolutionary movements** is a total and radical change of the existing social structure. Their ultimate aim is to overthrow the existing government and replace it with their own version of how a government should work. Revolutionary movements typically involve violent or illegal actions and sometimes can result in drastic and widespread social change. This type of movement usually arises when people see no chance for reform to occur. Examples of revolutionary movements include the Bolshevik Revolution in Russia and the American Revolution.

Fidel Castro's 1959 Cuban Revolution resulted in the total transformation of that society. Although Castro's drive toward socialism began with a small military group in the countryside, it was fueled by a large peasant class who lived under harsh conditions with no hope for change. The result was a military overthrow of the existing government and the formation of a new socialist government under the leadership of Fidel Castro.

CASE STUDY

Terrorism

In recent years, terrorism has become one of the most serious threats to the stability of the world. **Terrorism** may be defined as the use of threatened or actual violence in the pursuit of political goals. According to sociologist Paul Johnson, terrorism has three essential elements.

First, the individuals or groups who engage in terrorism believe that intimidation and violence are legitimate and necessary tools to achieve their aims. Guided by this belief, terrorist acts are deliberately and purposefully planned. As such, participants in terrorist group activities reject all of the standards of morality and channels of negotiation that normally guide other political and social actions.

Second, although terrorism runs counter to democratic political institutions, it is compatible with totalitarian governments. Because totalitarian political systems allow little opposition to their policies, the lives of individuals in totalitarian states are rigidly controlled. This control often is maintained through government-sanctioned intimidation and violence. The military forces in nations such as Cambodia and Guatemala use control tactics, torture, and even murder to keep the masses in line.

Third, the civil freedoms characteristic of democratic nations—such as freedom of movement—make these nations particularly open to acts of terrorism. The United States, for instance, often is the target of terrorist attacks—approximately one-third of all terrorist attacks around the world have been aimed at Americans.

The frequency and intensity of terrorist attacks have been escalating at an alarming rate over the past decade. Members of terrorist groups around the world have kidnapped hundreds of business leaders and political figures, hijacked airliners, bombed embassies, and assassinated world leaders. Even Pope John Paul II was the victim of an unsuccessful terrorist attack in the early 1980s.

Moreover, terrorist groups fund their efforts through illegal means such as forgery, counterfeiting, bank robbery, and ransom demands.

Why do some groups turn to terrorism when there are more peaceful and legal means available to help them achieve their aims? According to sociologist Ian Robertson, there are two reasons. First, terrorists are fanatics who believe nothing, including human life, is more important than their cause. As self-styled "freedom fighters," they excuse and justify any act, no matter how destructive, that will further their goals. Second, terrorists are people who lack the patience and power to bring change through peaceful means. They therefore seek to equalize the balance of power through the spread of fear and destruction.

The United States recently experienced the most destructive terrorist attack ever to occur in our nation's history. On February 26, 1993, a bomb explosion rocked the twin towers of the World Trade Center in Manhattan—the second tallest building in the world. The bomb blew out a crater 200 feet by 100 feet wide and five floors deep, visibly shaking the 110-story towers. Fires raged, windows exploded, and smoke quickly rose throughout the building. The massive destruction caused by the blast left six people dead and more than 1,000 people injured.

Following the blast, state and federal agencies quickly joined together to launch an investigation into its cause. Investigators soon learned that a rental van carrying explosives had detonated in the parking garage of the World Trade Center. A fragment from the vehicle led the FBI to arrest Mohammed Salameh, reported to be an Islamic fundamentalist. Since that time, several other people of Middle East origin have been arrested in connection with the bombing. The investigation of this terrorist action, however, is expected to continue for some time to come.

Life Cycle of Social Movements

Although social movements differ in the goals they hope to attain, successful movements appear to have certain characteristics in common. Many of these movements proceed through a series of stages that eventually lead to their acceptance by society. Sociologists Malcolm Spector and John Kitsuse have identified four stages in the life cycle of social movements: agitation, legitimation, bureaucratization, and institutionalization.

Agitation. Social movements typically emerge out of the perception that some problem exists. In this early stage of the life cycle, a small group of people attempt to stir up public awareness of the issue, often with the intention of gaining widespread support for a social movement. More often than not, potential social movements die out at this point, due either to lack of support or to lack of resources.

Legitimation. Those movements that find support for their concerns enter the legitimation stage of the life cycle. In this stage, the social movement becomes more respectable as it gains increasing acceptance among the population. The leaders of the movement, who previously were dismissed as cranks, now are seen as legitimate spokespersons of a just cause. Governmental or other authorities also begin to recognize the movement's concerns

as legitimate. At this point, the movement often attracts media attention, which in turn serves to bring the movement's goals to the attention of increasing numbers of people. Demonstrations and rallys add to the visibility of the movement.

Bureaucratization. As the organizational structure of the movement becomes more formal, it enters the third stage of the life cycle—bureaucratization. At this point, the movement has developed a ranked structure of authority, official policies, and efficient strategies for the future. The original goals of the movement sometimes get swept aside during this stage, as increasing amounts of time and energy are needed to handle the daily administrative requirements of the organization itself.

Institutionalization. In the final, or institutional, stage, the movement has become an established part of society. The excitement and idealism that once were generated among the movement's members now are lost or dulled. Organizational leadership is provided by administrators who oversee daily operations. Ironically, the movement has by this time become such an established part of society that it tends to resist any proposals for social change.

The life cycle of a social movement clearly can be seen in the American labor union movement, which had its beginnings in the late nineteenth century.

- *Agitation.* Low pay and harsh working conditions led many workers to seek support for unions that would protect employee interests.
- *Legitimation.* After many years of often violent confrontations between workers and management, and resistance from many segments of the population, labor unions finally received official governmental recognition.
- *Bureaucratization.* Over the years, labor unions have grown in size and number. Today, they are firmly established and powerful organizations.
- *Institutionalization.* Labor unions now are so well-established in society that they resist any attempts to change their operating procedures, even though some have been accused by their membership, the media, and officials of violent and often illegal activities.

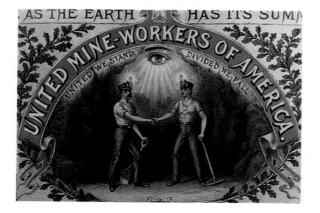

This *United Mine Workers'* emblem from 1890 stood as a symbol for the unity of workers seeking change through unionization.

Explaining Social Movements

A number of theories have been devised to explain the existence of social movements. Psychological explanations, for instance, were popular until about the 1960s. One such explanation was offered by Gustave Le Bon, who believed that only psychologically disturbed people would question the existing social order. As such, Le Bon viewed social movements as little more than irrational, mob-like collectivities. Similar psychological theories held that social movements are made up of people who have some kind of personality defect. According to these theories, people join movements as a way to hide from their personal problems and satisfy their psychological needs for purpose and meaning.

Sociologists, however, tend to reject the notion that people join social movements because something is wrong with them as individuals. Rather, sociologists look to problems in the social structure for explanations of social movements. Two sociological explanations that have been proposed for the existence of social movements are deprivation theory and resource-mobilization theory.

Deprivation Theory. From the perspective of **deprivation theory,** social movements arise when large numbers of people feel economically or socially deprived of what they think is necessary for their well-being. This deprivation can take one of two forms: absolute deprivation or relative deprivation. **Absolute deprivation** refers to a situation in which people lack one or more social rewards. **Relative deprivation,** on the other hand, refers to a situation in which people have a lesser portion of social rewards compared to other people or groups. According to this theory, some form of deprivation, either absolute or relative, makes people feel dissatisfied. Thus deprivation causes them to organize into a social movement to demand change.

Deprivation theory is similar to Karl Marx's explanation of revolution. Marx believed that capitalist economy, with its reliance on machines and assembly-line production, deprives and frustrates workers by keeping their access to wages and power at minimal levels. According to Marx, once workers realize that employers are mistreating them, the workers will band together and overthrow the capitalist system. Although Marx's prediction of a socialist revolution has not come to pass in the United States, labor unions designed to protect workers against deprivation now are a common feature of society.

Conflicts in the Middle East have deprived people of property and freedom. Deprivation is one of the factors that encourage the rise of social movements.

Deprivation alone will not lead to movements for social change. The ability to mobilize resources such as leadership, money, and media attention also is important.

Resource-Mobilization Theory. Few sociologists today agree that feelings of deprivation alone are sufficient to trigger social movements. Some form of deprivation, either absolute or relative, is common among groups in all societies. Yet not all situations of deprivation lead people to organize into social movements.

Most contemporary sociologists believe that social movements can occur only if people are successful in **resource mobilization,** the organization and effective use of resources. According to **resource-mobilization theory,** not even the most ill-treated group with the most just cause will be able to bring about change without resources. The resources necessary to generate a social movement include a body of supporters, financial resources, and access to the media.

The body of supporters must include talented people who have the time and skills necessary to work toward change. College students are partic-

ularly likely to support efforts for change since they have time and are well educated. College students, for example, were very active in the civil rights movement, organizing sit-ins and participating in demonstrations, marches, and voter registrations in the South. Leadership ability and organizational skills are crucial to the ongoing success of the movement. Leaders also must be personally attractive and well-spoken so that others will be encouraged to join the movement.

Social movements also must be able to mobilize financial resources. Money is needed to print leaflets and posters, travel to demonstrations and rallys, rent meeting places, and hire press agents and lawyers. Legal defense often is needed to protect the legal rights of demonstrators who are arrested and sometimes to bring court actions for change. Legal actions also are particularly helpful in bringing the concerns of the movement to the attention of the public.

PEANUTS, reprinted by permission of U.F.S. Inc.

Resource-mobilization theory also emphasizes that successful social movements need to gain access to the media. Wide media coverage is the surest way of bringing the movement to the attention of the most people possible. Media coverage, which in effect is free publicity, also serves to help movements reserve some of the finances they normally would spend on publicizing the movement.

While resource-mobilization theory helps explain how social movements get started and become successful, this theory has been criticized for minimizing the importance of deprivation and dissatisfaction. It seems logical to assume that both dissatisfaction and resource mobilization are necessary for the creation of social movements. People will not mobilize resources unless the perception arises that change is needed, and the move to make changes will not be successful unless the needed resources can be mobilized.

CHAPTER 16   SUMMARY

People in a society generally follow established norms. Thus behavior tends to be patterned and predictable. Sometimes, however, situations arise in which social norms are unclear or absent. The responses that people have to situations such as this fall under the umbrella of collective behavior. According to sociologist Neil Smelser, six preconditions lead to collective behavior: structural conduciveness, structural strain, growth and spread of a generalized belief, precipitating factors, mobilization for action, and social control.

Collective behavior takes place within collectivities. Three factors distinguish collectivities from social groups: limited interaction, unclear norms, and limited unity. There are many types of collectivities, the most common of which include crowds, mobs and riots, panics, mass hysteria, fashions and fads, rumors and urban legends, and public opinion.

A number of theories have been developed to explain collective behavior. Most contemporary sociologists favor the emergent-norm theory of collective behavior. According to this theory, new norms emerge in situations in which conventional norms are absent or lacking.

Social movements are forms of collective behavior that are intended either to promote or prevent social change. Social movements may develop around any issue. Four general types of social movements have been identified: resistance movements, reform movements, utopian movements, and revolutionary movements. Although social movements differ in their goals, all successful social movements appear to go through four stages: agitation, legitimation, bureaucratization, and institutionalization.

Contemporary sociologists look to the social environment for explanations of social movements. Deprivation theory holds that social movements arise when large numbers of people feel economically or socially deprived. Resource-mobilization theorists, however, believe that deprivation alone is insufficient to explain social movements. According to these theorists, social movements will not arise unless people can mobilize the necessary resources.

DEVELOPING SOCIOLOGICAL

WRITING ABOUT SOCIOLOGY: Investigating Oral History

To bring episodes of collective behavior alive, sociologists often seek out personal accounts of the event. They interview participants and eyewitnesses, then record the interview either in writing or with a tape recorder. Such interviews are called oral histories, and they add much to a sociologist's store of information. Such oral histories can be considered primary sources. For this reason, the time lapse between the event's occurrence and the interview may be an important consideration.

Students of sociology often are called on to conduct and interpret interviews. The process of conducting an interview requires planning and research. Only by applying the proper techniques of interviewing can useful information be gained from an oral history.

How to Prepare an Oral History

There are three parts to effective interviewing: preparation, interviewing, and post-interview analysis and reporting. To prepare an oral history, follow these guidelines.

1. **Identify the topic.** Determine what information is needed and from whom the information may be obtained.

2. **Research the topic.** Gather available information on the topic from which to base your questions.

3. **Schedule the interview.** Identify yourself and state clearly the purpose of the interview. Arrange a time when the interview can be conveniently scheduled.

4. **Prepare questions.** Devise questions that will draw forth the information you need. Group the questions into categories. Determine a direction for the interview so that one question leads logically to the next.

5. **Conduct the interview.** Explain again to your subject the purpose of the interview. Be an active listener, paying close attention to the responses and interacting when appropriate. Be sure to record the responses accurately. This can be done most easily through the use of a tape recorder. If you use a tape recorder, though, make sure that you receive permission from the subject before you begin.

6. **Write the oral history.** Accurately transcribe the information collected in the recorded interview.

7. **Analyze the interview.** Apply the skill you have developed to analyze the information gathered in the interview. Then, prepare a summary of the information.

Applying the Skill

Studs Terkel wrote an oral history of life in the United States, entitled *American Dreams: Lost and Found.* A number of people Terkel spoke to had participated in causes of various sorts. Read the following excerpt. Then, determine what questions Terkel might have asked.

> The first group to oppose a nuclear plant at Seabrook were the clam diggers. That's how we got our name. Clamshell Alliance. What a great name, getting away from all those politically yicky acronyms. It was catchy, it was fun to hear, it had an environmental vibe.
>
> We made a commitment to nonviolent civil disobedience to stop the plant, to occupy the site. Eighteen were arrrested. The majority of the Seabrook people were against the plant. One of the main anti-nuclear voices was the wife of the police chief.
>
> We called a second demonstration. The Seabrook police refused to make any arrests. The state police were called and arrested a hundred eighty people. They thought we were gonna be a bunch

of crazies. They found old, young, middle-aged, responsible, disciplined, respectable people. They used five busses to carry us away. The bus drivers were state police themselves. The chief ordered them to drive a mile away from the site so the demonstrators wouldn't see them. Two of the five bus drivers disobeyed. They drove up to the rally, parked the busses, and allowed everybody to cheer and wave and express their love. Then they drove away.

The state police locked 'em up for a night in the armory, all in one big room. There was a lot of dialogue between the demonstrators and the police.

Sam Lovejoy

Terkel asked Lovejoy questions such as "How did your anti-nuclear group get its name?" and "What was the official reaction to your anti-nuclear demonstrations?" Terkel, of course, asked many other questions to gather information for his oral history.

Practicing the Skill
Read the following excerpt from *American Dreams: Lost and Found*. Then, list the questions that Terkel most likely asked when recording the oral history. Next, list the questions that you would ask to obtain further information.

My father was a coal miner. He was killed in the mines, 1914. He was loadin' coal for fifteen cents a ton, and he was pushin' it on a wooden track about a hundred fifty feet. The coal operators didn't bury 'im and they didn't give my mother not one penny. Miners would get killed. Just almost every week, you'd see a man brought out. If he wasn't dead, he was crushed.

You could see the miners—I'd go sometimes at four o'clock in the morning—they had a little kerosene lamp that they put on their cap and it had a wick in it. Like fireflies, the mountains would be full of 'em agoin' to the mines. They'd go in there and maybe never come out. They didn't have

safety nor anything. It was a real hard life to lead, without a union. So in 1917, they got the union and miners together. They began to get better wages.

When they got the union—why, it was 1922—they come out on strike again. The guards and thugs started there after the miners, and the miners had to hide out in the woods. They'd get together and organize. They sent the National Guard in to put the men out, put their furniture out and everything.

Oh, my husband was a miner, too. He has black lung. He was organizin'. They would go from one mine to another to get the men to come out. The thugs'd come and ask him if he'd come back to work, and he said if they got a contract, he would. If they didn't, he wouldn't. And they started on him. They wanted to do away with him. So they arrested him and took him to Harlan jail. They took him out thar and they stopped. They thought if he'd try to run away, they'd shoot him. They wanted an excuse. So he wouldn't run. He just set there until they got ready to take him. They took him on to jail and kept him there with five more men on the concrete floor. One of the men went up there and tried to make bond for him, but they wouldn't let him. So the next day, they took him to Pineville jail.

And then he came home. But they still kept after him. John Henry Blair, he was with the coal operators. He was the high sheriff, and he would hire what he said was deputy sheriffs, but they were gun thugs, real gun thugs. They would search miners' houses, and if they had any guns, they'd take the guns. They'd take the miners off to jail.

So they come to our houses and they come in four or five carloads. They'd have two pistols, they'd have belts of cartridges, they'd have high-powered rifles. So they come up here, they searched our houses, and they looked in everything in our house. They looked in suitcases, under the mattress, in the stove, in the chest. In a few days, they'd come back and say: "Well, we're back."

Florence Reese

Chapter 16 Collective Behavior and Social Movements **425**

Reviewing Sociological Terms

On a separate sheet of paper, supply the term that correctly completes each sentence.

1. _____ is the term used for a spontaneous and uncoordinated group action to escape some perceived threat.

2. A _____ is a group of geographically scattered people who are interested in and divided by some issue.

3. A long-term conscious effort to promote or prevent social change is called a _____ _____.

4. The term _____ refers to the organized and deliberate attempt to shape public opinion.

5. _____ is the threatened or actual use of violence in the pursuit of political goals.

6. The organization and effective use of resources is called _____ _____.

Thinking Critically about Sociology

1. **Contrasting Ideas** How does relative deprivation differ from absolute deprivation?

2. **Using Sociological Imagination** *(a)* Describe the six basic preconditions for collective behavior. *(b)* Develop a hypothetical riot or mob situation in which these six preconditions are present.

3. **Analyzing Ideas** *(a)* How does resource-mobilization theory explain the rise of social movements? *(b)* What criticism has been leveled against resource-mobilization theory?

4. **Summarizing Information** *(a)* What is a crowd? *(b)* Prepare a chart listing the characteristics of each of the four types of crowds identified by Herbert Blumer. Provide examples of each type of crowd.

5. **Comparing Ideas** *(a)* According to deprivation theory, what factors give rise to social movements? *(b)* How is deprivation theory similar to Karl Marx's theory of revolution?

6. **Applying Ideas** Trace the four-stage life cycle of a social movement using an actual example from history. Choose an example other than labor unions.

7. **Comprehending Ideas** *(a)* What is collective behavior? *(b)* Why do sociologists have difficulty studying collective behavior?

8. **Understanding Ideas** What is a collectivity and what are its three major characteristics?

9. **Collecting Evidence** Collect two examples of actual occurrences of each of the following collectivities: *(a)* mass hysteria, *(b)* fads and fashions, *(c)* rumors, and *(d)* public opinion.

Exercising Sociological Skills

1. **Extending Ideas** Reread the Applying Sociology feature on pages 414–415. Follow the same steps outlined in the feature, but this time limit your analysis to magazine advertisements.

2. **Drawing Conclusions** According to the Case Study on page 419, why do terrorists resort to violence rather than using more peaceful channels for change?

3. **Analyzing Oral Histories** Reread the Developing Sociological Imagination feature on pages 424–425. Next, locate an oral history and analyze it following the steps outlined in the feature.

Extending Sociological Imagination

1. Prepare a brief report on one of the following topics: *(a)* the civil rights movement of the 1960s; *(b)* Joseph McCarthy and the Communist threat of the 1950s; *(c)* the American Revolution; or *(d)* the Shaker movement.

2. Start a collection of urban legends. Possible sources of urban legends are the features section of your local newspaper and magazine advice columns. For each legend you collect, try to identify the moral lesson being taught.

INTERPRETING PRIMARY SOURCES

The Martian Invasion

On Halloween night in 1938, actor Orson Welles narrated a radio dramatization of *The War of the Worlds*, a fictional account written by H. G. Wells about an invasion of Earth by Martians. The result was a mass hysteria that touched millions of people in the United States. In this excerpt from the article "Night of the Martians," which appeared in the October 1988 issue of *American History Illustrated*, Edward Oxford describes what that night was like. As you read the excerpt, think about why people panicked and the lessons to be learned from that panic.

It was not as though listeners hadn't been warned. Most simply didn't pay close attention to the program's opening signature (or tuned in a few seconds late and missed it all together): "The Columbia Broadcasting System and its affiliated stations present Orson Welles and the Mercury Theatre on the Air in *The War of the Worlds* by H.G. Wells. . . ."

Many in the radio audience failed to associate what they heard with prior newspaper listings of the drama. And, by the time a single station break came late in the hour with reminders that listeners were hearing a fictional story, many others were too agitated to comprehend that they had been deceived.

Skillfully choreographed by Welles and [John] Houseman, the program—a play simulating a montage of real-life dance band "remotes" and news bulletins—began with deliberate calm. Millions of listeners, conditioned by recent news reports of worldwide political turmoil—and by their inherent trust in the medium of radio—believed what they heard. . . .

A current of fear flowed outward across the nation. Real-life police switchboards, first in New Jersey, then, steadily, throughout the whole Northeast, began to light up: "What's happening?" "Who's attacking America?" "When will they be here?" "What can we do?" "Who are they—these Martians?" . . .

Thousands of telephone calls cascaded into radio stations, newspaper offices, power companies, fire houses, and military posts throughout the country. People wanted to know what to do . . . where to go . . . whether they were safer in the cellar or the attic.

Word spread in Atlanta that a "planet" had struck New Jersey. In Philadelphia, all the guests in one hotel checked out. Students at a college in North Carolina lined up at telephones to call their parents for the last time. When a caller reached the CBS switchboard, the puzzled operator, asked about the end of the world, said: "I'm sorry, we don't have that information." . . .

In a sprightly epilogue, Welles then explained away the whole unsettling broadcast as the Mercury Theatre's "way of 'dressing up in a sheet and saying Boo!' . . . We annihilated the world before your very ears, and utterly destroyed the CBS. You will be relieved, I hope, to learn that we didn't mean it. . . ."

He tried cheerily to dispel the darkness: "So goodbye everybody, and remember . . . the terrible lesson you learned tonight. . . . And if your doorbell rings and nobody's there, that was no Martian . . . it's Hallowe'en." . . .

The next morning headlines in major city newspapers reported the hoax: "Radio Listeners in Panic, Taking War Drama as Fact" (*New York Times*); "U.S. Terrorized By Radio's 'Men From Mars'" (*San Francisco Chronicle*); "Radio Drama Causes Panic" (*Philadelphia Inquirer*); "Listeners Weep and Pray, Prepare for End of World" (*New Orleans Times-Picayune*). . . .

In a column that turned the tide of public opinion in favor of Welles and company, Dorothy Thompson called the broadcast "the news story of the century—an event which made a greater contribution to an understanding of Hitlerism, Mussolinism, Stalinism, anti-Semitism, and all the other terrorism of our time than all the words about them that have been written by reasonable men."

Source Review

1. What factors led people to believe that the fictional Mars invasion was real?

2. How could America's reaction to the radio broadcast lead to an understanding of real-life terrorism?

CHAPTER 17

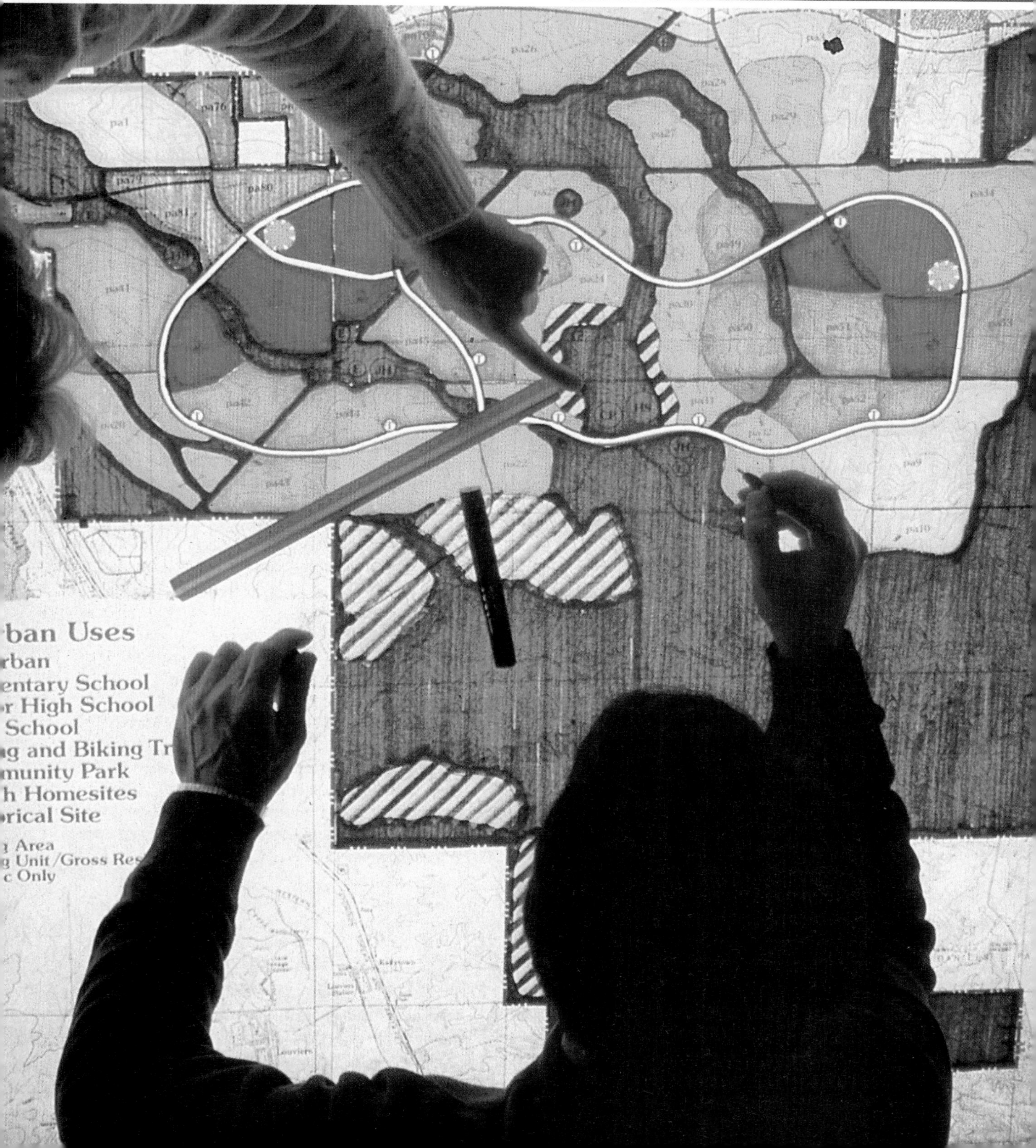
ban Uses
rban
entary School
r High School
School
g and Biking Tr
munity Park
h Homesites
rical Site
Area
g Unit/Gross Res
c Only

Population and Urbanization

Population Change

Measuring Population Change
Explaining Population Change
Controlling Population Growth

Urban Life

The Evolution of the City
Urban Ecology
Explaining City Life

Chapter Focus

Chapter 17 focuses on population and urbanization. The chapter begins with a discussion of the factors that affect population size. Special attention is paid to theories of population and to programs for controlling population growth. The chapter then turns to a discussion of urbanization, focusing on the evolution of cities, models of city structure, and theories of city life.

As you study the chapter, look for the answers to the following questions:

1. What factors affect the size and structure of populations, and how do sociologists measure these factors?
2. What theories have been proposed to explain population change, and what programs have been instituted to control population growth?
3. How did cities evolve, and why is urbanization such a recent event?
4. What models have been proposed to explain the structure of cities, and what theories have been put forth to explain city life?

KEY TERMS

The following terms, while not the only terms emphasized in the chapter, are basic to your understanding of sociology. Determine the meaning of each term, either by using the Glossary or by watching for context clues as you read the chapter.

demography	migration	city
fertility	doubling time	overurbanization
life expectancy	Malthusian theory	urban ecology

Until relatively recently in human history, the world was populated by small bands of people who lived and roamed in primary groups. Today, there are more than 5 billion people living in the world, and even more growth is expected in the near future. The growth of the population in recent years has had a tremendous impact on many aspects of our changing social world.

Nowhere is the impact of population growth felt more clearly than in the cities. The movement of large numbers of people from the countryside to the cities is a relatively recent phenomenon.

The effect on social life, however, has been tremendous. It is estimated that by the year 2000, nearly half of the world's population will be concentrated in urban areas.

These two major forces, population growth and urbanization, have changed the face of the world in a relatively short amount of time. Thus it is not surprising that sociologists have devoted considerable time to studying the ways in which population and urbanization have affected the social world and the nature of human interaction. These two forces are the focus of this chapter.

1 POPULATION CHANGE

Sociologists are interested in many aspects of human population. A **population** is the number of people living in an area at a particular time. The subarea of sociology devoted to the scientific study of human populations is **demography.** Demography is a subarea of sociology because most features of population and population change tend to be associated with social factors. Demographers, the sociologists who study human populations, tend to rely heavily on the collection and analysis of statistical data from large groups of people. One of the topics pursued by demographers concerns the measurement of population change.

Measuring Population Change

Three factors affect the growth or decline of a population in any given society: the birth rate, the death rate, and the rate of migration into or out of the society. These demographic factors determine the size of a population, the population's composition and distribution, and the ways in which the population changes over time.

Birth Rate. One factor that affects population is the number of children that are born into a society. The measure most often used by demographers to describe the births in a population is the birth rate. The **birth rate** refers to the annual number of live births per 1,000 members of a population. Demographers calculate the birth rate by dividing the number of live births in a particular year by the total population of the society for that year. This figure then is multiplied by 1,000. Mathematically, the formula is presented as

$$\text{Birth rate} = \frac{\text{Live births}}{\text{Total population}} \times 1,000$$

In the United States, for example, there were approximately 4.1 million live births in 1992 within a total population of about 253 million people. Dividing the number of live births by the total population and then multiplying that figure by 1,000 yields a birth rate of 16.2. This figure tells us that there were 16.2 live births for every 1,000 members of the United States population in 1992. The table on page 432 shows the 1992 birth rates for a number of selected nations around the world.

Demographers often refer to the birth rate as the *crude birth rate.* This measure is considered crude because it is based on the total population of a society, which includes males, children, and females who are past the age of childbearing. Thus it is somewhat misleading to compare the birth rates of various societies, because societies differ a great deal in the numbers of childbearing-age females they contain. Childbearing-age females are women who roughly are between the ages of 15 and 44. The crude birth rate also does not take into account the fact that, within a single society, various ethnic, racial, and religious groups may have different birth rates.

Nevertheless, the birth rate gives a relatively clear picture of the fertility of women in any given society. **Fertility** refers to the actual number of births occurring to women of childbearing age. Demographers usually distinguish between fertility and **fecundity,** the biological potential for reproduction. In the roughly 30 years between the onset and end of menstruation, women have the biological capacity to bear between 20 and 25 children. But, because of various social, economic, and health factors, women reproduce far below their biological potential. In all societies, in fact, these factors result in fertility that is much lower than fecundity.

Death Rate.   Another factor that affects population is **mortality,** or the number of deaths in a society. The measure most often used by demographers to describe the deaths in a population is the death rate. The **death rate** refers to the annual number of deaths per 1,000 members of a population. Demographers calculate the death rate in much the same way they calculate the birth rate. The number of deaths in a particular year is divided by the total population of the society for that year. This figure then is multiplied by 1,000. Mathematically, the formula is presented as

$$\text{Death rate} = \frac{\text{Deaths}}{\text{Total population}} \times 1,000$$

In the United States, for example, there were approximately 2.2 million deaths in 1992 within a total population of about 253 million people

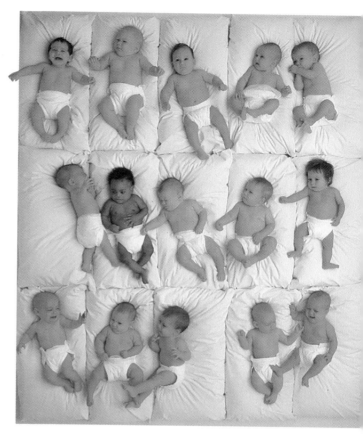

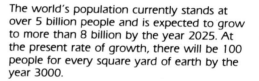

The world's population currently stands at over 5 billion people and is expected to grow to more than 8 billion by the year 2025. At the present rate of growth, there will be 100 people for every square yard of earth by the year 3000.

Dividing the number of deaths by the total population and then multiplying that figure by 1,000 yields a death rate of 8.7. This figure tells us that there were 8.7 deaths for every 1,000 members of the United States population in 1992. The table on page 432 shows the 1992 death rates for a number of selected nations.

The death rate often is called the *crude death rate* because it does not take into account the varying death rates found among subgroups in the population. Also, the death rate is crude because it is somewhat misleading to compare the rates of different nations. Because the death rate is a crude measure, demographers often examine infant mortality rates and life expectancies. These measures give a clearer picture of the health and life

Birth and Death Rates for Selected Nations

Nation	Birth Rate	Death Rate	Infant Mortality Rate	Life Expectancy (Male/Female)
Africa				
Ethiopia	47	20	139	46/48
Gambia	46	21	138	42/46
Kenya	45	9	62	59/63
Mauritius	21	7	20	65/72
South Africa	34	8	52	61/67
Tunisia	27	6	44	65/66
Zaire	46	14	83	50/54
Asia				
Afghanistan	48	22	172	41/42
Bangladesh	37	13	120	54/53
Cambodia	38	16	127	47/50
China	20	7	34	68/71
Israel	21	6	9	75/78
Japan	10	7	5	76/82
Singapore	19	5	7	72/77
Yemen	51	17	124	48/51
Europe				
France	13	9	7	73/81
Germany	11	11	7	72/78
Hungary	12	14	15	65/74
Italy	10	9	9	73/80
Sweden	11	11	6	75/80
Former USSR				
Armenia	24	7	35	69/75
Russia	14	11	30	64/75
Tajikistan	38	6	73	67/72
Latin America				
Argentina	21	8	26	66/73
Bolivia	36	10	89	58/64
Guatemala	39	7	61	60/65
Haiti	45	16	106	53/56
Puerto Rico	19	7	14	70/78
North America				
Canada	15	7	7	73/80
United States	16	9	9	72/79
Oceania				
Australia	15	7	8	73/80
Papua-New Guinea	34	11	99	53/55
Solomon Islands	41	5	32	60/61

Source: Adapted from *1992 World Population Data Sheet*, Population Reference Bureau, Inc.

situations of different nations. Infant mortality rates and life expectancies for selected nations can be seen in the table on page 432.

The **infant mortality rate** is the annual number of deaths among infants under one year of age per 1,000 live births in a population. Demographers calculate the infant mortality rate by dividing the number of deaths of infants under one year of age in a particular year by the number of live births in that same year. This figure then is multiplied by 1,000. The formula can be shown as

$$\text{Infant mortality rate} = \frac{\text{Deaths among infants}}{\text{Total live births}} \times 1,000$$

The infant mortality rate provides a general measure of the overall health and quality of life in a society or among various segments of a society. Infants are particularly open to disease and malnutrition. Thus the probability of surviving the first year of life is greater in those societies that are able to provide adequate medical attention and proper nutrition.

As can be seen in the table on page 432, more developed nations, such as Japan, Canada, and the United States, have relatively low rates of infant mortality. **More developed nations** are those nations that have high levels of per capita income, industrialization, and modernization. On the other hand, **less developed nations** are those nations that have low levels of per capita income, industrialization, and modernization. Less developed nations, such as Ethiopia, Gambia, and Afghanistan, tend to have relatively high rates of infant mortality. In Afghanistan, for example, 172 infants died in 1992 for every 1,000 children that were born that year.

Demographers also examine life expectancies when comparing the health and life situations of different nations. **Life expectancy** refers to the average number of years a person born in a particular year can be expected to live. This figure most often is expressed as the number of years a newborn child can be expected to live. Life expectancy is related to the rate of infant mortality in a nation.

As the table on page 432 shows, life expectancies in more developed nations are much higher than life expectancies in less developed nations. In Gambia, for example, where 138 infants died for every 1,000 born, life expectancy is only 42 years for males and 46 years for females. In Japan, where only 5 infants died for every 1,000 born, life expectancy is 76 years for males and 82 years for females. Within a single society, however, life expectancies can differ according to sex, race, religion, ethnicity, and other social factors.

Life expectancy must be distinguished from life span. **Life span** is the maximum length of life that is biologically possible. The life span of humans generally is held to be about 100 years. Although life expectancy in many nations around the world has increased dramatically during the twentieth century, life span has not. This is because the increases in life expectancy largely have come about through reductions in the infant mortality rates. It has proved far easier to combat the diseases of childhood than it has been to fight the aging process and the diseases common to old age. As a result, the life span of humans has remained practically unchanged for centuries.

Migration Rate. The third factor that affects population is migration. **Migration** is the movement of people from one specified area to another. Migration refers both to movement into a specified area and movement out of a specified area. Demographers examine both these factors when measuring migration.

The annual number of people who move into a specified area per 1,000 members of a population is called the *in-migration rate*. The *out-migration rate,* on the other hand, refers to the annual number of people who move out of a specified area per 1,000 members of a population. Both these processes are likely to be occurring in a specified area at the same time. Because of this, demographers calculate the **migration rate** as the annual difference between in-migration and out-migration. The effects of the migration rate ordinarily are not as significant as the effects of the birth rate and the death rate, since the movement of people does not add to the global population.

Migration occurs as a result of what demographers call push and pull factors. A *push factor* is something that encourages people to move out of a certain area, such as religious or political persecution, famine, racial discrimination, or overpopulation. A *pull factor,* on the other hand, is something that encourages people to move into a

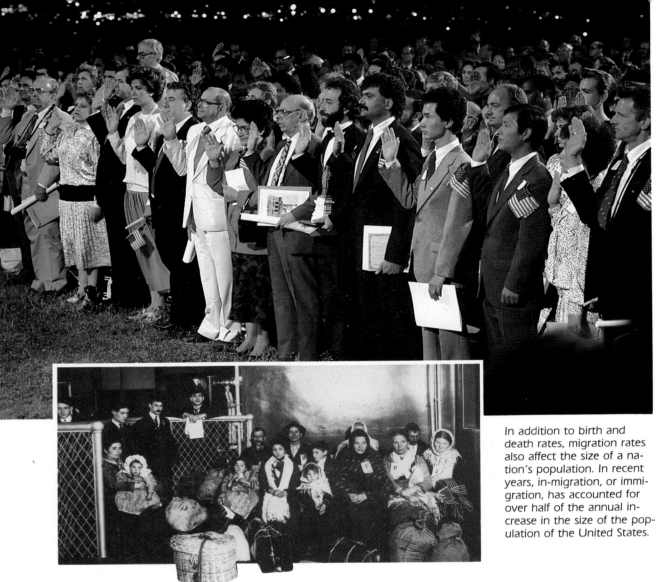

In addition to birth and death rates, migration rates also affect the size of a nation's population. In recent years, in-migration, or immigration, has accounted for over half of the annual increase in the size of the population of the United States.

certain area, such as religious and political freedom, occupational opportunities, and a high standard of living.

Growth Rate. The birth rate, death rate, and migration rate all affect the size of a nation's population. Birth and death rates, however, are of major importance and so demographers tend to focus on these factors when examining a population's growth rate. The **growth rate** of a population is the birth rate minus the death rate.

The growth rate of a nation indicates the rate at which the nation's population is increasing. The figure used to express the growth rate usually is given as a percent. The United States, for instance, had a birth rate in 1992 of 16.2 per 1,000

people and a death rate of 8.7 per 1,000 people. Subtracting the death rate from the birth rate and rounding up leaves 8. Thus in 1992, the United States had a growth rate of 0.8 percent, meaning that 8 people were added to the population for every 1,000 members. The growth rates for selected nations are shown on page 435.

The growth rates in more developed nations typically are much lower than the growth rates in less developed nations. This is because modern industrialized nations generally have low birth rates. Nations with lower levels of technology, on the other hand, typically have birth rates that far exceed their death rates. In Kenya in eastern Africa, for example, the birth rate in 1992 was 45, while the death rate was 19. Thus the growth rate

Growth Rates and Population Doubling Times for Selected Nations

Nation	Growth Rate	Doubling Time (in years)
Africa		
Ethiopia	2.8	25
Gambia	2.6	27
Kenya	3.7	19
Mauritius	1.5	48
South Africa	2.6	26
Tunisia	2.1	33
Zaire	3.1	22
Asia		
Afghanistan	2.6	27
Bangladesh	2.4	29
Cambodia	2.2	32
China	1.3	53
Israel	1.5	45
Japan	0.3	217
Singapore	1.4	51
Yemen	3.5	20
Europe		
France	0.4	169
Germany	-0.1*	(-)
Hungary	-0.2*	(-)
Italy	0.1	1,386
Sweden	0.3	210
Former USSR		
Armenia	1.8	40
Russia	0.2	301
Tajikistan	3.2	22
Latin America		
Argentina	1.2	56
Bolivia	2.7	26
Guatemala	3.1	22
Haiti	2.9	24
Puerto Rico	1.2	59
North America		
Canada	0.8	89
United States	0.8	89
Oceania		
Australia	0.8	83
Papua-New Guinea	2.3	31
Solomon Islands	3.6	20

*A negative number indicates that this nation has a death rate higher than its birth rate; thus the population is shrinking rather than growing.

Source: Adapted from *1992 World Population Data Sheet,* Population Reference Bureau, Inc.

in this less developed nation was 3.7 percent, meaning that 37 people were added to Kenya's population in 1992 for every 1,000 members.

Because growth rates are expressed as percents, a growth rate of 3.7 appears deceptively small. In reality, though, the long-term consequences of such a growth rate for population size are enormous. This is because the growth rate is related to a population's **doubling time,** the number of years necessary for a population to double in size, given its current rate of growth.

A population growth rate of only 1 percent will cause that population to double its size in about 70 years. A growth rate of 2 percent doubles the population in about 35 years, while it takes a population with a growth rate of 3 percent only 23 years to double in size. The United States population, for instance, has a growth rate of .8 percent and will double in size in 89 years, given its current rate of growth. Kenya, with its current growth rate of 3.7 percent, will double its population in only 19 years. The expected doubling times of selected nations, given the 1992 rate of growth, can be seen in the table on this page.

To illustrate the significance of doubling time, consider the fact that the population of the world doubled from half a billion to 1 billion between 1650 and 1850, a span of 200 years. The population doubled again from 1850 to 1930, reaching 2 billion in only 80 years. About 50 years later, in 1980, it doubled to 4 billion. Demographers estimate that at its current rate of growth, the population of the world will take only 40 years to reach the 8 billion mark.

Population Composition. In addition to changes in population size, demographers also study the composition, or structure, of populations. Age and sex are the factors most often used to show the composition of a population.

To study a nation's composition, demographers use a **population pyramid,** a graphic representation of the age and sex distribution of a population. These pyramids are two-sided graphs that show the percentages of males and females falling into each designated age group. The pyramid-like shape of the graph results from the fact that the chances of death increase with age.

Demographers gain a significant amount of information about a population from these graphs.

For example, the graphs indicate the percentage of elderly who must be supported, the percentage of childbearing-age women, and the percentage of people available for employment. Perhaps most important, population pyramids indicate a population's potential for growth. A nation with a large percentage of children has an enormous potential for growth. This is because these children soon will grow and have children of their own. A nation with a small percentage of children, on the other hand, will have fewer people entering their childbearing years and hence future population growth will be slow.

A population pyramid for the United States is shown on this page. The bulge in this pyramid, representing people aged 25 to 49, reflects the fact that the birth rate rose sharply from 1946 through 1964, as family life resumed following World War II. The pyramid also shows that this *baby boom* was followed by a *baby bust*—a sharp decline in the birth rate. Birth rates in the United States have remained relatively low ever since, making the baby-boom generation the largest percentage of the population. Because the United States has a relatively low birth rate, population growth likely will be slow.

The graph on page 437 presents population pyramids for Sweden and Mexico. Notice that the base of Sweden's pyramid indicates that the birth rate has been in relatively steady decline for a number of years and that children make up a very small percentage of the population. This means that Sweden is producing fewer young people who will grow up and have children themselves. Hence Sweden's future population growth will be slow, slower even than that of the United States.

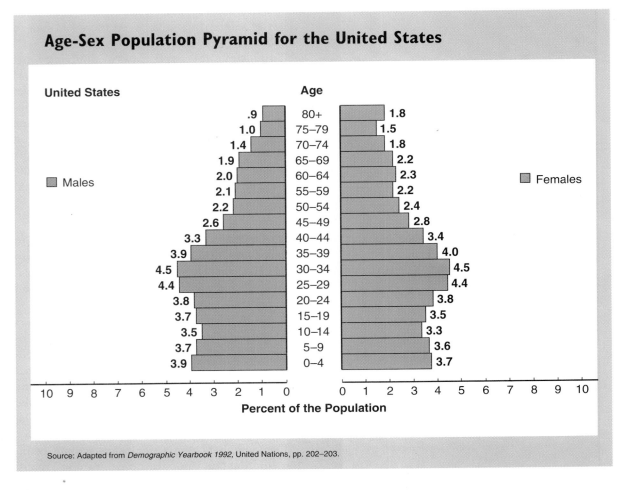

Age-Sex Population Pyramid for the United States

United States   Age

Males	Age	Females
.9	80+	1.8
1.0	75–79	1.5
1.4	70–74	1.8
1.9	65–69	2.2
2.0	60–64	2.3
2.1	55–59	2.2
2.2	50–54	2.4
2.6	45–49	2.8
3.3	40–44	3.4
3.9	35–39	4.0
4.5	30–34	4.5
4.4	25–29	4.4
3.8	20–24	3.8
3.7	15–19	3.5
3.5	10–14	3.3
3.7	5–9	3.6
3.9	0–4	3.7

Percent of the Population

Source: Adapted from *Demographic Yearbook 1992,* United Nations, pp. 202–203.

Age-Sex Population Pyramids for Sweden and Mexico

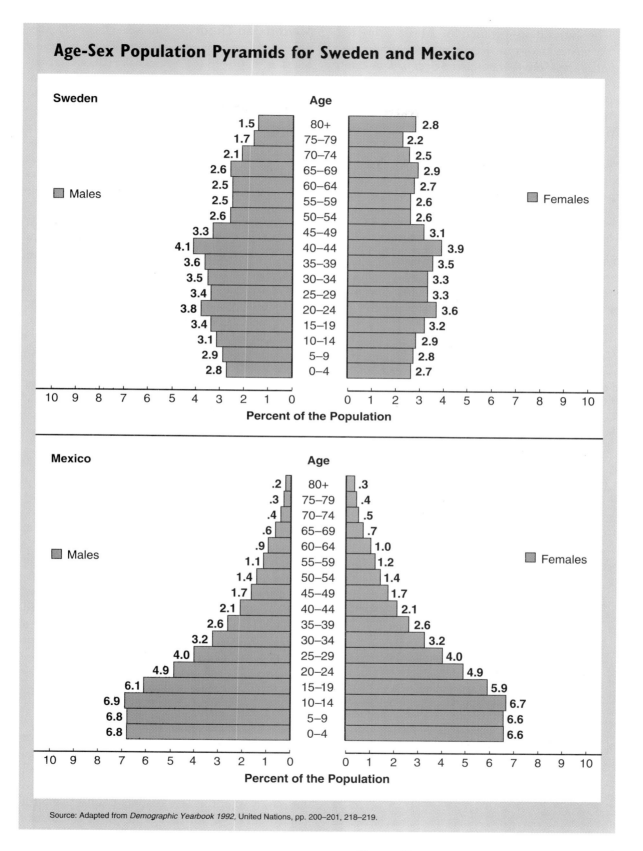

Sweden

Males	Age	Females
1.5	80+	2.8
1.7	75–79	2.2
2.1	70–74	2.5
2.6	65–69	2.9
2.5	60–64	2.7
2.5	55–59	2.6
2.6	50–54	2.6
3.3	45–49	3.1
4.1	40–44	3.9
3.6	35–39	3.5
3.5	30–34	3.3
3.4	25–29	3.3
3.8	20–24	3.6
3.4	15–19	3.2
3.1	10–14	2.9
2.9	5–9	2.8
2.8	0–4	2.7

Percent of the Population

Mexico

Males	Age	Females
.2	80+	.3
.3	75–79	.4
.4	70–74	.5
.6	65–69	.7
.9	60–64	1.0
1.1	55–59	1.2
1.4	50–54	1.4
1.7	45–49	1.7
2.1	40–44	2.1
2.6	35–39	2.6
3.2	30–34	3.2
4.0	25–29	4.0
4.9	20–24	4.9
6.1	15–19	5.9
6.9	10–14	6.7
6.8	5–9	6.6
6.8	0–4	6.6

Percent of the Population

Source: Adapted from *Demographic Yearbook 1992*, United Nations, pp. 200–201, 218–219.

The population pyramid of Mexico, on the other hand, stands in sharp contrast to the situations in the United States and Sweden. The graph of Mexico is almost a perfect pyramid shape. This indicates that large numbers of children are being born, but that few people in the population are living to old age. When today's children reach their childbearing years, the population of Mexico will explode unless the birth rate slows. Mexico's population pyramid is typical of many less developed nations around the world.

Explaining Population Change

A number of theories have been proposed over the years to explain population and population change. Among the theories most often discussed by demographers are Malthusian theory and demographic transition theory.

Thomas Malthus painted a very bleak picture of the long-term effects of population growth.

The Granger Collection, New York

Malthusian Theory. One early theory of population change was proposed by Thomas Robert Malthus (1766–1834), an English economist. Malthus outlined a rather gloomy picture of population change in his *Essay on the Principles of Population,* published in 1798.

Malthus argued that the already rapidly growing population of the eighteenth century would continue to grow at ever faster rates. He based this prediction on the fact that population grows through multiplication. In most instances, this multiplication progresses geometrically. A *geometric progression* is represented by the series of numbers 2, 4, 8, 16, 32, and 64. Following the progression to its logical conclusion, **Malthusian theory** predicted that the population soon would reach astronomical numbers.

According to Malthusian theory, the geometric progression of population has serious social consequences because food production progresses arithmetically. An *arithmetic progression* is represented by the series of numbers 2, 3, 4, 5, and 6. Food production is arithmetic because the amount of land available for cultivation is limited. Thus a rapidly growing population will eventually outpace food production, thereby resulting in worldwide starvation.

Malthus suggested that two factors could slow population growth. He called one factor *positive checks.* Positive checks include war, disease, and famine. The other factor he called *preventive checks.* Preventive checks include birth control, sexual self-control, and delayed marriage.

Malthus, however, did not think that people would use preventive checks to control the coming disaster. In addition to being an economist, Malthus also was a clergyman and as such rejected the use of artificial birth control. Furthermore, he thought that people would halt their sexual activity only when faced with actual famine conditions. Consequently, Malthus predicted that nature would use disease and famine to bring the population in line with the available food supply.

Malthus's predictions failed to foresee two important developments, however. First, he did not anticipate that advances in agricultural technology would allow farmers to produce vastly increased yields on their available land. Second, Malthus foresaw neither the development of effective birth control methods nor their widespread acceptance and use. Modern birth control methods have been particularly effective in reducing the birth rates in more developed nations since the 1960s.

Thus Malthus's predictions have not yet come to pass. Some demographers warn, however, that the Malthusian theory still is a possibility, particularly if nations continue to expand their populations while using up scarce resources.

Demographic Transition Theory. Although Malthusian theory has contributed much to our understanding of population change, demographers tend to favor demographic transition theory. **Demographic transition theory** holds that population patterns are tied to a society's level of technological development. According to the theory, which is based on population changes in Western Europe over the past 300 years, a society's population moves through three stages, as shown in the graph on this page.

In Stage 1, typical of preindustrial agricultural societies, both the birth rate and the death rate

are high. The birth rate is high in these societies because children are valued as sources of labor and because no effective means of birth control are used. The death rate is high because of the relatively low standard of living and the lack of medical technology to stem the spread of disease. The high birth rate and high death rate result in a fairly stable population, with little growth and little decline. This was the situation in Western Europe prior to industrialization. Modern-day examples of Stage 1 societies can be found in some areas of central Africa.

As societies enter the industrial phase, Stage 2, improved medical techniques, sanitation, and increased food production work to reduce the death rate. Children still are highly desired, however, and so the birth rate remains high. The high birth rate and low death rate combine to produce a rapid growth in the population. This is the situation today in many developing nations around the world, such as Kenya, Zambia, and Bangladesh.

Text continues on page 442.

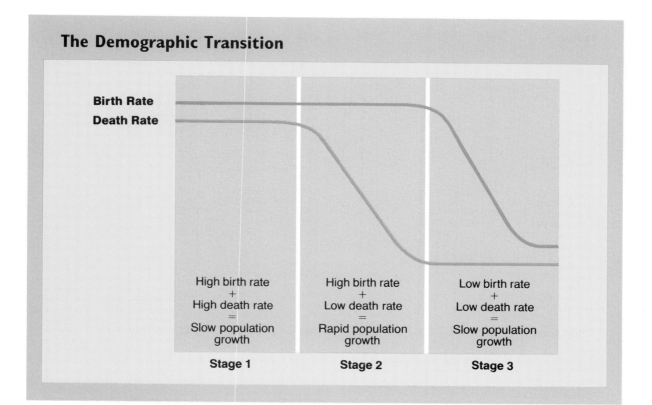

The Demographic Transition

	Stage 1	Stage 2	Stage 3
	High birth rate + High death rate = Slow population growth	High birth rate + Low death rate = Rapid population growth	Low birth rate + Low death rate = Slow population growth

APPLYING SOCIOLOGY

Adjusting to an Aging Population

As we noted in the chapter, birth rates in most more developed nations have fallen sharply since the mid-1960s. Consequently, as their existing populations age, the number of young people as a percentage of the total population continues to decrease in these societies. When this is coupled with longer life expectancies, the result is an aging population. The table on this page shows the projected growth in the aged populations of the more developed nations.

Population changes always have consequences for a society's social structure. The Organization for Economic Cooperation and Development (OECD) has analyzed some of the future social changes that its member nations are likely to face as their populations age. The OECD was formed in 1961 to encourage economic growth and stability among member nations and to promote world trade and assist developing nations in their efforts at industrialization. Members of the OECD include the United States, Canada, Japan, Australia, New Zealand, and the more developed nations of Europe. The OECD regularly publishes reports on a wide range of subjects of concern to member nations.

According to the OECD, among the social consequences of an aging population will be changes in the age composition of the work

Percentage of the Population Aged 65 and Over, 1980–2050*

Nation	1980	1990	2000	2010	2020	2030	2040	2050
Australia	9.6	11.1	11.7	12.6	15.4	18.2	19.7	19.4
Austria	15.5	14.6	14.9	17.5	19.4	22.8	23.9	21.7
Belgium	14.4	14.2	14.7	15.9	17.7	20.8	21.9	20.8
Canada	9.5	11.4	12.8	14.6	18.6	22.4	22.5	21.3
Denmark	14.4	15.3	14.9	16.7	20.1	22.6	24.7	23.2
Finland	12.0	13.1	14.4	16.8	21.7	23.8	23.1	22.7
France	14.0	13.8	15.3	16.3	19.5	21.8	22.7	22.3
Germany	15.5	15.5	17.1	20.4	21.7	25.8	27.6	24.5
Greece	13.1	12.3	15.0	16.8	17.8	19.5	21.0	21.1
Iceland	9.9	10.3	10.8	11.1	14.3	18.1	20.1	21.1
Ireland	10.7	11.3	11.1	11.1	12.6	14.7	16.9	18.9
Italy	13.5	13.8	15.3	17.3	19.4	21.9	24.2	22.6
Japan	9.1	11.4	15.2	18.6	20.9	20.0	22.7	22.3
Luxembourg	13.5	14.6	16.7	18.1	20.2	22.4	22.0	20.3
Netherlands	11.5	12.7	13.5	15.1	18.9	23.0	24.8	22.6
New Zealand	9.7	10.8	11.1	12.0	15.3	19.4	21.9	21.3
Norway	14.8	16.2	15.2	15.1	18.2	20.7	22.8	21.9
Portugal	10.2	11.8	13.5	14.1	15.6	18.2	20.4	20.6
Spain	10.9	12.7	14.4	15.5	17.0	19.6	22.7	22.9
Sweden	16.3	17.7	16.6	17.5	20.8	21.7	22.5	21.4
Switzerland	13.8	14.8	16.7	20.5	24.4	27.3	28.3	26.3
Turkey	4.7	4.0	5.0	5.5	7.0	8.9	10.2	11.5
United Kingdom	14.9	15.1	14.5	14.6	16.3	19.2	20.4	18.7
United States	11.3	12.2	12.2	12.8	16.2	19.5	19.8	19.3
OECD Average	**12.2**	**13.0**	**13.9**	**15.3**	**17.9**	**20.5**	**21.9**	**21.2**

*Figures for 1980 are actual; figures for 1990 through 2050 are projections.

Source: Organization for Economic Cooperation and Development.

force and shifts in the social spending priorities of governments. The graphs on this page present OECD projections of changes in these two areas.

Based on the graphs and on the table, answer the following questions and complete the following activities.

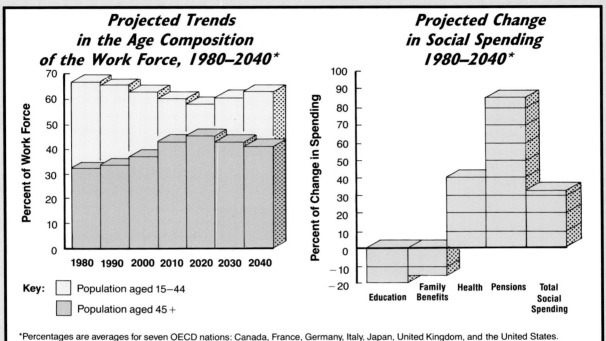

Projected Trends in the Age Composition of the Work Force, 1980–2040*

Percent of Work Force

1980 1990 2000 2010 2020 2030 2040

Key: ☐ Population aged 15–44
⬜ Population aged 45 +

Projected Change in Social Spending 1980–2040*

Percent of Change in Spending

Education Family Benefits Health Pensions Total Social Spending

*Percentages are averages for seven OECD nations: Canada, France, Germany, Italy, Japan, United Kingdom, and the United States.
Source: Organization for Economic Cooperation and Development.

1. *(a)* In which nations was more than 15 percent of the population aged 65 and over in 1980? *(b)* In which nations was less than 10 percent of the population aged 65 and over in 1980?

2. *(a)* By the year 2000, which nations are projected to have more than 15 percent of their population aged 65 and over? *(b)* Which nations are projected to have less than 10 percent of their population aged 65 and over by the year 2000?

3. *(a)* By the year 2050, which nations are projected to have more than 20 percent of their population aged 65 and over? *(b)* Which nations are projected to have less than 15 percent of their populations aged 65 and over by the year 2050?

4. *(a)* Calculate the percentage increase between 1980 and 2050 in the size of the population aged 65 and over for each of the OECD nations. *(b)* Which nations will have increases greater than 10 percent?

5. Write a brief description of the projected changes in the age composition of the work force based on the information presented in the graph on this page.

6. *(a)* In which two areas will social spending decrease between 1980 and the year 2040? *(b)* In which area will the greatest increase in social spending occur?

7. What does the information presented in the table and graphs indicate about the social consequences of an aging population?

Stage 3 societies have a fully developed industrial economy. The standard of living is relatively high during this stage and children no longer are needed as workers. During this stage, the birth rate falls due to the increased use of effective birth control methods and a relatively high standard of living. The death rate remains low during this stage. The low birth rate and low death rate produce a fairly stable population in which growth occurs very slowly.

Some stage 3 societies may even approach **zero population growth,** the point at which nearly equal birth rates and death rates produce a growth rate of zero. Only the most technologically advanced nations of the world, such as those found in North America, Europe, and Japan are in Stage 3 of the demographic transition. Some nations, such as Hungary and Germany, even have fallen below zero growth, with birth rates lower than their death rates. The populations in these nations thus are shrinking.

Some demographers believe that Stage 2 nations currently experiencing rapid growth in their populations will stabilize as they move to the industrially advanced systems typical in the West and Japan. Critics of the demographic transition theory, however, are less optimistic.

These critics believe it is unlikely that all nations will follow the stages of technological development found in Europe and North America over the past few centuries. As today's preindustrial nations begin to industrialize, the introduction of modern medicine causes their death rates to drop much more quickly than was the case in Western Europe. Modernization in these nations thus is continually hampered by the fact that more people are living longer and birth rates continue to be high. These factors hamper modernization because any economic gains brought about by industrialization must be used simply to maintain the same level of subsistence for a rapidly growing population.

Over the past decade, women from around the world have taken an active role in the debate over population growth.

UNITED NATIONS DECADE FOR WOMEN CONFERENCE NAIROBI, KENYA. 15ᵀᴴ-26ᵀᴴ JULY, 1985.

Controlling Population Growth

The world now contains more than 5 billion people. Although the growth rate currently is down to 1.7 percent from a high of 2 percent in the late 1960s, the population of the world continues to grow. Almost 95 percent of this growth is occurring in the less developed nations of Africa, Asia (except Japan), and Latin America, which now make up 77 percent of the world population.

Concerns over growth and the desire for economic development have led many nations, including most less developed nations, to adopt strategies aimed at controlling population. These strategies fall basically into two types—strategies to lower the birth rate through family planning and strategies to improve economic conditions.

Family Planning. One strategy that has been used to lower the birth rate in some nations is family planning. **Family planning** is the conscious decision by married couples to have only the number of children they want. The goal of family planning programs is to reduce the number of unplanned and unwanted pregnancies. Family planning involves the careful use of effective birth control techniques.

According to demographers, however, family planning strategies alone have been insufficient to reduce the birth rate in many nations. The main reason for this is that family planning allows parents to choose the number of children that they want. In many less developed nations around the world, children are considered economic and social assets and thus the norm is to have large families. Often the number of children parents choose to have is far greater than what will help to slow the population growth. And, although millions of people have turned to family planning in nations around the world, many do so only after they have already produced large families.

Some nations that have found family planning insufficient to reduce population growth have turned to antinatalism. **Antinatalism** involves official policies designed to discourage births. Antinatalism policies by nature are more forceful than voluntary family planning. Such policies involve resocializing the population to value small rather than large families. This resocialization usually includes rewards and punishments designed to encourage people to have fewer children.

China, for example, now is involved in an intensive campaign to reduce the number of births to one child per family. Birth control devices are freely available and couples are counseled as to their use. There is strong pressure from officials and peers alike to obey the norm. Those people who do not conform are faced with financial penalties and are treated as social deviants. Couples who do follow the official policies receive special

China accounts for approximately one-fifth of the world's population. Concern over the consequences of rapid population growth has led the Chinese government to adopt population-control policies.

The governments of most more developed nations believe that economic assistance can help less developed nations slow their population growth.

housing, employment, and financial benefits from the government. China's policy has brought a significant reduction in the birth rate, as have similar policies in Singapore and Hong Kong.

Economic Improvements. Some critics of family planning policies believe that economic development must proceed before people in less developed nations will limit their family size voluntarily. Supporters of economic development believe that better diets and higher levels of income and education will lead to lower birth rates.

While this appears to be true, most less developed nations do not have the resources to achieve the economic development necessary to raise living standards. Many demographers have found that economic assistance packages designed to help less developed nations improve living conditions have resulted in increased standards only for a very small portion of the population. As a result, the majority of the population remains in poverty and the birth rates remain high.

In light of this, some demographers suggest that less developed nations would be better served by redistributing resources more evenly among all members of society, thereby reducing poverty. According to this view, once they no longer want for the basic necessities of life, people will voluntarily limit the size of their families.

SECTION 1 REVIEW

DEFINE demography, fecundity, infant mortality rate, more developed nations, less developed nations, zero population growth

1. ***Summarizing Ideas*** *(a)* List and describe the three factors that affect population size. *(b)* What is the relationship between the growth rate and population doubling time?

2. ***Analyzing Ideas*** How does a population pyramid indicate a population's potential for growth?

3. ***Contrasting Ideas*** Contrast the ways in which Malthusian theory and demographic transition theory attempt to explain population change.

4. ***Understanding Ideas*** *(a)* Describe the two major strategies that have been instituted in recent years to control population growth. *(b)* What problems have been found to be associated with these strategies?

2 URBAN LIFE

Sociologists are interested not only in the ways that population changes affect the social world, but also in the social change that is produced by the movement of people across the globe. In fact, sociology developed initially from the efforts of early theorists to understand the changes accompanying industrialization and urbanization.

Urbanization refers to the concentration of the population in cities. A **city** is a permanent concentration of relatively large numbers of people who are engaged mainly in nonagricultural pursuits. Urbanization is a relatively recent phenomenon in the history of the world, but it has profoundly changed the way that most people live their lives.

The Evolution of the City

The first recognizable cities appeared about 6,000 years ago, but until very recently, only a small proportion of the population lived in urban areas. In fact, it is estimated that as late as 1850, only about 2 percent of the world's population lived in cities of more than 100,000 inhabitants. Today, about 43 percent of the world's people live in urban areas, and this figure is expected to reach 50 percent by the year 2000.

Why did it take so long for urbanization to come about? According to sociologists, the rise of cities appears to be tied to two important developments: the Agricultural Revolution and the Industrial Revolution.

The Agricultural Revolution, which involved the cultivation of grain, the domestication of animals, and the development of a basic agricultural technology, allowed people to produce a surplus of food for the first time. The production of surplus food freed large numbers of people from

Urban congestion has been a problem since the time of the Industrial Revolution.

agricultural pursuits and encouraged them instead to take up more specialized types of work. Specialized types of work, such as those involving crafts, trades, and merchandise, are most conveniently pursued where there are large, permanent concentrations of people. Thus, cities initially arose when people in specialized roles came together in centralized locations.

The further development and spread of cities had to wait for centuries, however, until the Industrial Revolution. The Industrial Revolution replaced hand tools with machines. It also replaced traditional human and animal sources of energy with new sources such as coal, water, and steam. These new sources of energy dramatically increased productivity and led to the rise of the factory as a system of production. These new factories, which generally were located in or near cities, required large pools of labor. Thus thousands of people left the countryside in search of employment opportunities in the cities.

The Industrial Revolution also produced more advanced technologies for the transportation and storage of food. This allowed cities to support ever-increasing numbers of people who could fill the labor demands generated by the new industrial development.

The Preindustrial City. Cities first arose about 6,000 years ago on the fertile banks of rivers such as the Nile in Egypt, the Tigris and Euphrates in the Middle East, the Indus in Pakistan, and the Yellow River in China. Similar urban settlements appeared centuries later in other parts of the world.

Compared with the cities of today, early urban settlements were very small. Most preindustrial cities contained between 5,000 and 10,000 people. Population size was limited by inefficient agricultural techniques that could not produce the surplus food needed to support more people. In addition, communication and transportation methods were primitive by modern standards—food had to be carried into the cities from farming areas either by animals or by humans. Transportation was made particularly difficult by the fact that roads practically were nonexistent.

Life in the early cities was very different from what we know today. There was almost a complete lack of sanitation, with the result that death rates in the cities were higher than the death rates in rural areas. Contributing to the high death rates were ineffective medical techniques, crowded conditions, and a lack of sewer facilities. Because of these conditions, epidemics could drastically

The bubonic plague wiped out nearly a third of the population of Europe during the Middle Ages. Although many people attributed the epidemic to the wrath of God, it actually was due to filthy living conditions and was spread by flea-infested rats.

reduce the population of a city in only a matter of weeks. In fact, the "Black Death," or bubonic plague, killed a third of Europe's population between the years 1348 and 1350.

In addition, life in preindustrial cities was built around kinship relations and the extended family. With rare exceptions, governments were organized either as monarchies or oligarchies. Because people traveled on foot, traders usually worked out of their homes, which they used as shops. There also was no designated "downtown" area. People who followed particular crafts or trades lived and worked in distinct sectors of the city, with each occupational grouping having its own quarter. People also were segregated into classes or castes, with the poor living on the outskirts of the city and the wealthy living in the center.

The Industrial City. The nature of life in the preindustrial cities changed little for almost 5,000 years. Then, the Industrial Revolution produced an explosive growth in both the size and number of cities.

Mechanization allowed farmers to produce an even greater surplus of food, which freed large numbers of people from agriculture. Workers no longer needed on the farms moved to the cities, where they filled the need for factory workers. Improved communication and transportation allowed these expanding cities to support ever-increasing numbers of people.

Compared with the preindustrial city, the industrial city was larger, contained more people, and offered more diversity. Commerce became the focal point of life in the city. Central business districts, including stores, offices, and banks, replaced the segregated workplaces common in preindustrial cities.

Social life in the industrial city also was transformed. People now left their homes to travel to work in impersonal offices or factories. The hold of the family over the individual lessened as many single people gained their independence in the city. According to sociologists, urbanization also contributed to the rise of a number of social problems, such as crime, overcrowding, and pollution from industrial wastes.

The rapid urbanization produced by the Industrial Revolution can be seen in the history of the United States. In 1790, for instance, only 5 per-cent of the American population lived in cities. By 1860, about a third of the population were urban dwellers, but urbanization was largely confined to the Northeast. Today, about 75 percent of Americans live in urban areas.

Urbanization in the developed nations has followed a generally ordered fashion and has resulted in relatively high rates of literacy, economic opportunities, and health care. While problems do exist in the cities of the modern world, urbanization and industrialization have led to a standard of living never before known in the world.

Urbanization in the less developed nations, however, has been less orderly and more rapid than has urbanization in the more developed nations. The population of Mexico City, for instance, rose from 5 million people in 1960 to more than 20 million today. This figure is expected to reach 30 million by the year 2000.

In many of the less developed nations, rapid urbanization is leading to what is called overurbanization. **Overurbanization** is the situation in which more people live in the city than the city can support in terms of jobs and facilities. As a result, people in these overurbanized cities do not have adequate housing, food, sewage disposal, or medical services. The crowded and unsanitary living conditions contribute to high rates of illness and death. In Calcutta, India's largest city, more than half a million people live on the streets. High rates of migration to urbanized areas combined with the high birth rates common in less developed nations have led to similar conditions in many areas of Latin America, Asia, and Africa.

Urban Ecology

During the 1920s and 1930s, sociologists interested in urban life developed an approach to the study of cities called urban ecology. The **urban ecology** approach examines the relationship between people and the urban environment. In essence, this approach argues that human behavior determines the overall layout of the urban environment, which in turn affects human behavior.

According to sociologists, urban areas do not develop in random patterns. Rather, different areas of a city tend to be used for different, set purposes. As a result, people, buildings, and activities in a city are distributed in certain patterns.

CASE STUDY

The American City

In 1820, almost 80 percent of the American population lived on farms. Today, over 75 percent of the people in the United States live in urban areas. What is more, the majority of Americans—two out of every three—live in urban areas with populations of 1 million people or more.

When sociologists speak of urban areas, they are referring to more than central cities. Following the lead of the Bureau of the Census, sociologists refer to any area with more than 2,500 residents as an urban area. This definition of an urban area does not recognize the boundaries between cities. Thus, an urban area generally includes a central city and its suburbs. A **suburb** is a politically independent community that is next to or near a city. When an urban area—either a city or a central city and its suburbs—has a total population of 50,000 or more, it is termed a **metropolitan statistical area (MSA)** by the Census Bureau. At present, there are more than 280 MSAs in the United States.

Urban areas sometimes include more than one city and its suburbs. When central cities and their suburbs run together, forming a series of metropolises, the area is called a **megalopolis.** The Census Bureau recognizes 23 megalopolises, or consolidated metropolitan statistical areas (CMSAs), as they also are called, in the United States. Among these megalopolises is the one that runs from Boston, Massachusetts, to Washington, D.C., which has a combined population of approximately 60 million.

According to the Census Bureau, over 100,000 Americans live in suburbs. It is the central cities, however, that hold the most interest for sociologists. As more members of the middle and upper classes flock to suburbs, low-income minority residents are making up an increasingly higher percentage of the population of most central cities. Many large cities—such as St. Louis, Detroit, Newark, Washington, D.C., and Baltimore—now are predominantly nonwhite.

One of the chief problems presented by the flight of the middle and upper classes from the central cities is the loss of tax revenues. City services, such as roads, schools, police and fire protection, sanitation, and public parks, are funded in large part through property taxes. When the majority of a city's middle- and upper-income residents move to the suburbs, the burden of providing for city services falls to the poorer members of the community.

Property taxes are based on property values. The poor tend to live in houses with low property values. Thus, the tax base declines when the poor are responsible for generating the bulk of tax revenues. A decline in tax revenues, in turn, generally leads to a decline in city services. Once city services begin to decline, many of the remaining members of the middle and upper classes move out of the city.

During the 1960s and 1970s, state and federal governments attempted to restore the central cities through urban renewal. **Urban renewal** programs were designed to provide adequate housing for low-income families and to rebuild the economies of the central cities. In many instances, renewal efforts resulted in single-family homes being bulldozed to make room for high-rise buildings designed to house the poor. These often poorly constructed buildings quickly became breeding grounds for crime and violence.

In response to the failure of previous urban renewal efforts, the federal government now is attempting to ease the housing problems in the central cities by increasing the availability of low-income, single-family housing. In addition, many cities are trying to increase tax revenues through regentrification. **Regentrification** is the upgrading of specific neighborhoods in an attempt to encourage the middle and upper classes to relocate to the cities. Critics of regentrification argue that the process further reduces the availability of adequate housing for the poor.

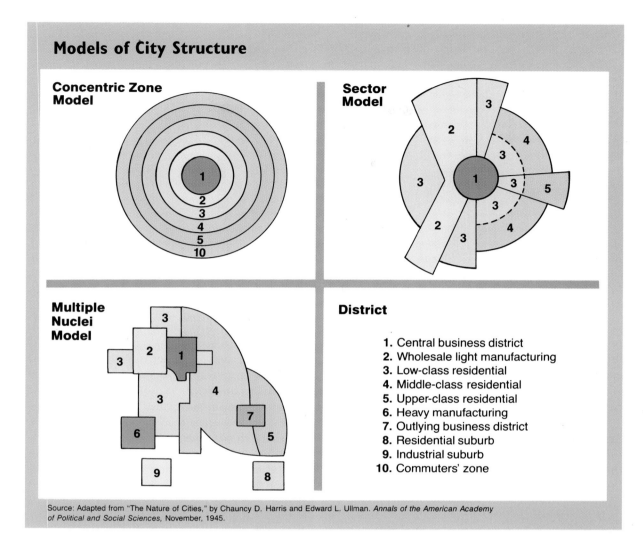

Models of City Structure

Concentric Zone Model

Sector Model

Multiple Nuclei Model

District

1. Central business district
2. Wholesale light manufacturing
3. Low-class residential
4. Middle-class residential
5. Upper-class residential
6. Heavy manufacturing
7. Outlying business district
8. Residential suburb
9. Industrial suburb
10. Commuters' zone

Source: Adapted from "The Nature of Cities," by Chauncy D. Harris and Edward L. Ullman. *Annals of the American Academy of Political and Social Sciences,* November, 1945.

Sociologists have developed three models to describe this pattern: the concentric zone model, the sector model, and the multiple-nuclei model. The graph on this page gives a visual representation of each of these three models.

Concentric Zone Model. In 1925, Ernest W. Burgess proposed the concentric zone model to describe urban structure. According to the **concentric zone model,** a typical industrial city spreads outward from the center, resulting in a series of circles within circles. Each of these circles, or zones, differs in terms of the way in which the land is used. At the center of the circles is the central business district, an area used for hotels,

banking, commerce, offices, and entertainment. Next to this zone is the wholesale light manufacturing zone, also called the *transition zone.* The transition zone is characterized by run-down buildings and high crime. The expansion of the first two zones outward results in higher rents and forces people to move farther away from the center of the city.

Beyond the second circle, according to Burgess, are a series of increasingly expensive residential areas. Farthest away from the center of the city is the commuters' zone, where the wealthy live in large, single-family houses away from the noise and bustle of the city. The people who live in this zone travel to their jobs in the city.

In 1960, approximately 60 million Americans lived in the suburbs. Today, more than 100 million Americans are suburbanites. Critics of surburban life argue that the suburbs lack the diversity that is characteristic of life in the city.

Not all sociologists agreed with Burgess's early portrayal of the industrial city. While it did describe some cities, such as Chicago during the early twentieth century, not all cities have concentric zones. The sector model was developed in response to this fact.

Sector Model. Homer Hoyt proposed the sector model in 1939 to expand on concentric zone theory and to describe a greater number of cities. Like Burgess, Hoyt believed that cities grow outward from the center and that the central business district is the core of the city. Unlike the concentric zone model, however, the **sector model** argues that growth occurs in wedge-shaped sectors that extend outward from the center to the edge of the city.

According to Hoyt, the way in which transportation is laid out in urban areas determines the repetition of certain patterns of land use along railroad lines, waterways, and highways. Thus land use tends to follow the transportation routes that radiate out from the center of the city. Warehouses, for example, tend to follow along a railroad that extends toward the edge of the city. The poor tend to live next to the transportation routes near factories. The rich, on the other hand, live near the fastest lines of transportation in attractive areas of the city. Hoyt argued that each type of land use, such as that used for residences or industry, extends in sectors until it reaches some kind of boundary.

While the sector model painted an accurate picture of some cities, such as San Francisco, it

tended to reflect the limited transportation routes available before the widespread use of the automobile. The influence of the automobile on urban ecology is reflected in the multiple-nuclei model of urban ecology.

Multiple-Nuclei Model.

The mutiple-nuclei model was proposed by Chauncy Harris and Edward Ullman in 1945. This model acknowledges the influence of the automobile and highways on the development of cities.

According to the **multiple-nuclei model,** urban areas have a number of specialized centers or "nuclei" devoted to different types of land use, such as retailing, residences, or light manufacturing. Rather than a single core as the center of development patterns, cities have a number of separate and distinct nuclei that influence the development of the area around them. Multiple nuclei are able to develop because of the widespread use of automobiles and highways that eliminate transportation problems.

These three models are ideal types of cities, and thus are not expected to be exact reflections of all American urban areas. In combination, however, the models generally do reflect the pattern of land use in cities. Urban areas do tend to grow outward in circles from the core, but there usually are sectors within this pattern. A number of distinct centers usually are present in the city as well.

Explaining City Life

A number of theories have been proposed over the years to explain the nature of life in the city. Among these theories are urban anomie theory, compositional theory, and subcultural theory.

Urban Anomie Theory.

According to sociologist Louis Wirth and his **urban anomie theory,** the city is an anonymous and unfriendly place that carries serious negative consequences for those who live there. Wirth argues that the size, density, and diversity of urban life discourage the formation of primary group relationships, especially those based on kinship ties and the neighborhood. Consequently, life in the city is characterized by associations only within impersonal secondary groups. The lack of primary group relationships results in anomie, or normlessness. According to Wirth, the anomie of the city leads to increased rates of mental illness, crime, and juvenile delinquency.

Why does city life produce anomie? According to Wirth, city dwellers come into contact with many people on a daily basis. Because most of these people are strangers, interaction tends to be short-lived, formal, and shallow. To keep themselves from having to become personally involved with everyone with whom they come into contact, city dwellers often take on an unfriendly, impersonal attitude. This attitude discourages interaction and communication, leading individuals to draw further away from each other. The result is a lack of involvement with others and thus a feeling of detachment.

According to urban anomie theory, the anonymous and impersonal nature of city life extends itself to situations that call for social involvement and responsibility. This is particularly true when officially designated agencies such as the police or fire fighters are highly visible. City dwellers, for instance, scarcely notice the person lying on the sidewalk or acknowledge the cries for help from victims of crime. City residents withdraw from social responsibility partly because they expect others to take on this responsibility.

The classic example of the withdrawal from social responsibility is the 1964 murder of Kitty Genovese. Returning home from work, Genovese was stabbed repeatedly by an assailant in front of her New York City apartment building. Although the attack lasted for an extended period of time, no one came to her aid. Police investigations later discovered that 38 people either had heard Genovese screaming or had actually witnessed the murder. Most of these people said that they did not intervene because they did not want to get involved.

A number of sociologists in recent years have criticized Wirth's portrayal of urban life for being too negative concerning the effects of the city on the individual. Compositional theory and subcultural theory have been proposed to present a more balanced view of life in the city.

Compositional Theory.

Rather than focusing on the city itself, **compositional theory** examines the ways in which the composition of a city's population influences life in the city. Factors

Cities generally exhibit a wide range of life-styles. Because of this diversity, most city-dwellers are able to form relationships with others who share similar interests.

that affect the composition of a city include age, race, ethnicity, income, and occupation. Compositional theory argues that the great diversity of people who live in the city leads to a greater variety of life-styles than is common in most small towns in the United States.

According to sociologist Herbert J. Gans, there are five identifiable life-styles that can be found among urban dwellers:

- *The cosmopolites.* The cosmopolites are the professionals or intellectuals of the city. They are attracted to life in the city because of its culture, entertainment, and excitement. They also tend to have the financial resources that allow them to take full advantage of the diverse attractions offered by city life.
- *The unmarried or childless.* These people work in the city and enjoy the attraction of cultural events and the company of urban friends. Some of these people move to the suburbs if they decide to have children, but others spend their entire lives in the city.
- *The ethnic villagers.* Ethnic villagers are those people who are attracted to the small ethnic areas typical of big cities, such as "Little Havana" or "Little Italy." Life among others of the same cultural heritage works to preserve traditions and provides a sense of unity for ethnic villagers.

- *The deprived.* The deprived are those city dwellers who live in disadvantaged or unfavorable circumstances because of poverty, mental or physical disability, race, or ethnicity. According to Gans, the deprived live in the city because it provides low-skilled jobs, relatively low rents, and public assistance programs.
- *The trapped.* The trapped stay in the city because they cannot afford to leave. Often these are elderly people who are living on fixed incomes and who remain in the same neighborhood for decades.

According to Gans, individuals who live in cities form communities with others who share the same life-style, neighborhood, or interests. Although the city may seem to be an unfriendly, anonymous place, it actually is a mosaic composed of a number of groups, each providing a sense of unity and community to its members. In essence, individuals are able to protect themselves from the anonymity of city life by forming primary groups with others who are like themselves.

Subcultural Theory. Claude Fischer employs **subcultural theory** to explain the nature of city life. According to Fischer, the characteristics of the city encourage rather than discourage the formation of primary group relationships. Because of the size and diversity of urban populations, it is possible for people to find others who share the same interests and life-styles. This leads to the development of many different subcultures within which close ties may form.

A person living in a small town who is interested in photography, for instance, might find only a handful of others with the same interest. In a city, on the other hand, there might be hundreds of people who are interested in photography. The sheer numbers of people who share this interest would encourage the development of a wide range of clubs, activities, and friendships geared around photography. This subculture continually would attract new people as group members met others who shared their interest.

According to subcultural theory, cities provide a place where people develop close ties with others based on their associations in a number of different groups. These groups can be formed on the basis of such diverse things as occupation, hobbies, friendships, ethnicity, or even stage in the life cycle. Subcultural theory argues that city dwellers, rather than being separated from others, are involved in a rich and diverse social life that includes close relationships with many friends, associates, neighbors, and relatives.

SECTION 2 REVIEW

DEFINE   urbanization, overurbanization

1. **Summarizing Ideas**   Summarize the evolution of cities, focusing on the differences between life in preindustrial cities and life in industrial cities.

2. **Comparing Ideas**   Compare the views of urban ecology presented by Burgess, Hoyt, and Harris and Ullman.

3. **Comprehending Ideas**   What are the characteristics of life in the city as explained by urban anomie theory, compositional theory, and subcultural theory?

CHAPTER 17   SUMMARY

Changes in population size result from three demographic processes: the birth rate, the death rate, and the migration rate. In addition to population size, demographers also are interested in the composition, or structure, of a population.

Several theories have been proposed to explain population growth. Thomas Malthus, for example, believed that the inability of people to control the birth rate would result in worldwide starvation because the food supply would not be able to keep up with population growth. Demographic transition theory, on the other hand, argues that population growth goes through a series of stages, each tied to a society's level of technology.

Nations concerned about rapid population growth have adopted strategies to control this growth. Some nations have encouraged the use of family planning. Other nations have sought to control population size through the introduction of economic improvements.

Urbanization is a relatively recent phenomenon and appears to be tied to two important developments: the Agricultural Revolution and the Industrial Revolution. The evolution of cities advanced very rapidly with the development of industrialization.

Urban ecology examines the relationship between people and the urban environment. Three major models of urban structure have been proposed: the concentric zone model, the sector model, and the multiple-nuclei model.

The nature of urban life has long interested sociologists. Urban anomie theory views the city as an unfriendly, anonymous place for people to live. Compositional theory argues that people are protected from the anonymous nature of city life by their primary group associations. Subcultural theory, on the other hand, views the city as a place that encourages rather than discourages the development of primary group relationships.

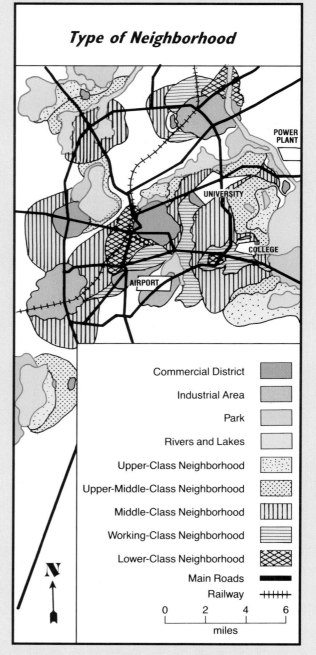
INTERPRETING THE VISUAL RECORD: Analyzing Sociological-Data Maps

A sociological-data map is a map that provides information on sociological topics such as land use, housing patterns, racial or ethnic distributions, income distributions, or crime rates. Any social characteristics or data that can vary geographically can be presented in the form of a sociological-data map. Sociological-data maps, like charts and graphs, are visual representations of sociological information.

How to Analyze Sociological-Data Maps

To effectively analyze sociological-data maps, follow these steps.

1. **Read the map's title.** The title states the sociological topic of the map.

2. **Study the map key, or legend.** The legend explains the map's symbols and color code.

3. **Note all labels.** The names of national or geographic features, key terms, or other information often are written on the map.

4. **Note relationships.** Study the data on the map. Record key data. Note variations or patterns in the distribution of the variable or variables under consideration.

5. **Use the map's information.** Formulate generalizations or draw conclusions from the data.

Applying the Skill

Population and urbanization data often are presented in map form. The sociological-data map on this page shows the distribution of neighborhoods by type in an urban area. Note the legend. Its color code indicates commercial areas (stores and offices), industrial areas, parks, and rivers and lakes. The legend also supplies the codes for types of neighborhoods: upper-class,

Type of Neighborhood

POWER PLANT

UNIVERSITY

to COLLEGE

AIRPORT

| Commercial District |
| Industrial Area |
| Park |
| Rivers and Lakes |
| Upper-Class Neighborhood |
| Upper-Middle-Class Neighborhood |
| Middle-Class Neighborhood |
| Working-Class Neighborhood |
| Lower-Class Neighborhood |
| Main Roads |
| Railway |

N

0   2   4   6
miles

upper-middle-class, middle-class, working-class, and lower-class. In addition, the symbols for main roads and the railway are listed, along with a scale for miles.

Several generalizations can be made from the data presented in the map. One generalization is that upper- and upper-middle-class neighborhoods are likely to be located in areas near parks, lakes, and rivers. The recreational opportunities located in these areas improve the standard of living for area residents. Another generalization is that middle- and working-class neighborhoods tend to be located near commercial and industrial areas.

Practicing the Skill

Study the sociological-data map on this page. On a separate sheet of paper, answer the following questions.

1. *(a)* What is the title of the map? *(b)* What does the map show?

2. What is represented by each of the colors on the map?

3. How are the age ranges of the houses indicated on the map?

4. *(a)* In what area(s) are the oldest and next-to-the-oldest houses found? *(b)* In what area(s) are the newest and next-to-the-newest houses found?

5. What generalizations can be made about the direction or directions in which the town has grown since it was first founded 100 years ago?

6. Compare the map with the map that shows types of neighborhoods. Both maps are of the same urban area. Based on the distribution of neighborhoods, which social classes are buying most of the new houses?

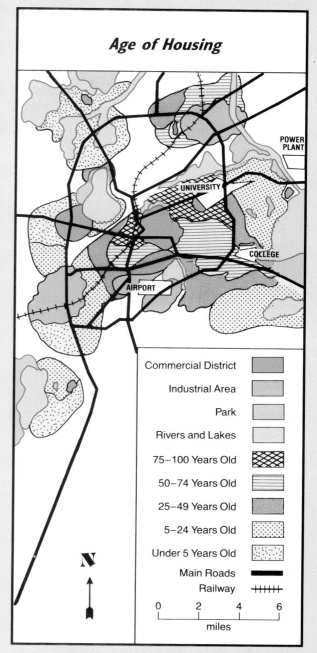

Age of Housing

POWER PLANT

UNIVERSITY

COLLEGE

AIRPORT

Commercial District	
Industrial Area	
Park	
Rivers and Lakes	
75–100 Years Old	
50–74 Years Old	
25–49 Years Old	
5–24 Years Old	
Under 5 Years Old	
Main Roads	
Railway	

0 2 4 6
miles

N

Reviewing Sociological Terms

On a separate sheet of paper, supply the term that correctly completes each sentence.

1. _____ is the term used for the number of deaths in a society.

2. A _____ is the number of people living in an area at a particular time.

3. The conscious decision by married couples to have only the number of children that they want is called _____ _____.

4. _____ results when more people live in a city than the city can support in terms of jobs and facilities.

5. The approach that examines the relationship between people and the urban environment is called _____ _____.

6. The movement of people from one specified area to another is called _____.

7. _____ _____ _____ is the point at which nearly equal birth rates and death rates produce a growth rate of zero.

Thinking Critically about Sociology

1. *Contrasting Ideas* Contrast the positions taken by urban anomie theory, compositional theory, and subcultural theory concerning the nature of urban life.

2. *Analyzing Ideas* *(a)* What are birth and death rates and why are they considered to be crude measures? *(b)* How are birth and death rates used to determine the population growth rate?

3. *Summarizing Information* Describe life in *(a)* the preindustrial city and *(b)* the industrial city. *(c)* What problems do today's less developed nations face due to urbanization?

4. *Comprehending Ideas* *(a)* What is migration and how is the migration rate measured? *(b)* What factors account for migration?

5. *Comparing Ideas* *(a)* Compare Malthusian theory and demographic transition theory in terms of their views of population change. *(b)* What problems have been found with each of these theories?

6. *Using Graphs* Turn to the population pyramid on page 436. What is the youngest age group within which the percentage of females is larger than the percentage of males?

7. *Understanding Ideas* Describe the three urban ecology models.

8. *Collecting Evidence* Collect two examples of actual nations not discussed in the chapter that are using the following population strategies: *(a)* family planning; *(b)* antinatalism; and *(c)* economic improvements.

Exercising Sociological Skills

1. *Using Tables* Reread the Applying Sociology feature on pages 440–441. According to the table, which nation will have the smallest percentage of elderly in the year 2000?

2. *Drawing Conclusions* According to the Case Study on page 448, what is regentrification and why has it been criticized?

3. *Analyzing Sociological-Data Maps* Locate a map in a magazine and analyze it using the skills presented in the Developing Sociological Imagination feature on pages 454–455.

Extending Sociological Imagination

1. Prepare a brief report on one of the following topics: *(a)* population changes in the United States over the past 50 years; *(b)* the rise of suburban living; or *(c)* urban crime.

2. Contact the urban planning office in your city. Speak to an urban planner about the decisions now being made in your city concerning transportation, housing, and commerce. Write a brief report on your findings.

INTERPRETING PRIMARY SOURCES
The Problems of Urbanization

Among the many problems associated with urban living are poverty, disease, and pollution. In the following excerpt from the article "Megacities," which appeared in the January 11, 1993, issue of *Time*, Eugene Linden explores how the growing trend toward urbanization is compounding these problems in some of the world's most populated cities. While reading the excerpt, consider the problems that heavily populated cities must cope with and why it is crucial that solutions be found.

Faster than ever before, the human world is becoming an urban world. Near the end of this decade, mankind will pass a demographic milestone: for the first time in history, more people will live in and around cities than in rural areas.

Explosive population growth and a torrent of migration from the countryside are creating cities that dwarf the great capitals of the past. By the turn of the century, there will be 21 "megacities" with populations of 10 million or more. Of these, 18 will be in developing countries, including some of the poorest nations in the world. Mexico City already has 20 million people and Calcutta [India] 12 million. According to the World Bank, some of Africa's cities are growing by 10% a year. . . .

Is the trend good or bad? Can the cities cope? No one knows for sure. Without question, urbanization has produced miseries so ghastly that they are difficult to comprehend. In Cairo [Egypt], children who elsewhere might be in kindergarten can be found digging through clots of ox dung, looking for undigested kernels of corn to eat. Young, homeless thieves in Papua New Guinea's Port Moresby may not know their last names or the names of the villages where they were born. In the inner cities of America, newspapers regularly report on newborn babies dropped into garbage bins by drug-addicted mothers. . . .

Large cities are breeding grounds for novel, antibiotic-resistant strains of old germs and for entirely new kinds of microbes. Not since the bubonic plague has the world encountered anything like the AIDS virus, which has infected at least 10 million people. No one knows exactly where AIDS originated, but it has become an epidemic in the cities of Africa, Europe, Asia, Latin America and the U.S. In addition to its own deadly impact, AIDS fosters the spread of other diseases. The tuberculosis germ, for example, attacks weakened AIDS victims and uses them as a beachhead for invading healthy populations.

The threat of disease is heightened by urban pollution. . . . Nowhere is pollution more palpable than in Mexico City. When the wind is still, the fumes of 3 million cars and 35,000 industrial sites become trapped by the high ring of mountains that surrounds the city. Last February a cloud of smog pushed ozone readings above 0.35 parts per million on some days, severe enough to harm even healthy people and four times the level considered safe. . . .

Even the best-managed cities have trouble coping with the crush of population growth. Tokyo is overwhelmed by its own trash—22,000 tons each day—despite massive recycling and incineration programs. . . . At the present discard rate, Tokyo will run out of dump sites by 1995. The city has been building artificial islands in Tokyo Bay to hold garbage, but cannot continue to do so without threatening both the fishing and shipping industries. . . .

The historical cycle of urban growth and collapse will be hard to break, but hope can be found in the stubborn self-reliance shown by people in some of the world's poorest cities. Like the cumbersome bumblebee that flies in the face of aerodynamic theory, the megacities will have to defy gravity and invent a sustainable future for themselves. Since the fate of the world is entwined with the fate of its cities, humanity has no other choice.

Source Review

1. How has urban growth affected Cairo, Port Moresby, Mexico City, and Tokyo?

2. Why is it important that we solve the problems of the megacities?

Social Change and Modernization

Explaining Social Change

Cyclical Theory
Evolutionary Theory
Equilibrium Theory
Conflict Theory

Modernization

The Process of Modernization
The Consequences of Modernization

Chapter Focus

Chapter 18 focuses on the process of social change and the effects of modernization on society. The chapter begins with a discussion of the theories of social change. Next, the process of modernization is explored. The chapter closes with a discussion of the effects of modernization on the social and natural environments.

As you study the chapter, look for the answers to the following questions:

1. What theories have social scientists offered to explain the process of social change?
2. How do modernization theory and world-system theory differ in their views on modernization in less developed nations?
3. What are some of the positive and negative consequences of modernization for social life and the natural environment?

KEY TERMS

The following terms, while not the only terms emphasized in the chapter, are basic to your understanding of sociology. Determine the meaning of each term, either by using the Glossary or by watching for context clues as you read the chapter.

social change
ideational culture
sensate culture

idealistic culture
principle of immanent change
modernization

core societies
peripheral societies
ecology

Sociology grew out of the social turmoil of the seventeenth and eighteenth centuries. Thus, it is not surprising that sociologists have devoted considerable attention to the study of social change. Sociologists define **social change** as alterations in various aspects of a society over time.

In the last section of Chapter 3, we examined some of the sources of social change. Although social change results from many factors, we limited our discussion to values and beliefs, technology, population, diffusion, the physical environment, and wars and conquests. We then closed the examination of social change in Chapter 3 with a discussion of the reasons why people sometimes resist change. The factors we examined were ethnocentrism, cultural lag, and vested interests.

In this chapter, we will build on the information presented in Chapter 3. First, we will examine the theories sociologists have developed to explain how and why societies change. We then will turn our attention to an analysis of the social changes that accompany modernization.

1 EXPLAINING SOCIAL CHANGE

Through the years, sociologists have suggested numerous theories to explain the process of social change. The most significant of these theories can be grouped into four broad categories: cyclical theory, evolutionary theory, equilibrium theory, and conflict theory.

Cyclical Theory

As we noted in Chapter 15, scientists are influenced by their views of reality. Social scientists are no less subject to this tendency than are other scientists. Thus it is not surprising that during periods of extreme social turmoil, cyclical theories of social change sometimes appear.

A **cyclical theory of social change** views change from a historical perspective. Societies are seen as rising and then falling or as continuously moving back and forth between stages of development. The appeal of cyclical theories during periods of extreme social upheaval rests in the fact that social events and conditions usually are considered to be beyond the control of human actions. Social change is seen as resulting from a natural tendency for societies to pass through stages of development.

In some cyclical theories, societies are seen as passing through stages of development that mirror the human life cycle. According to this view, societies are born, grow to maturity, decline in old age, and eventually die. From the ruins of dead societies emerge new societies that repeat the developmental process. Other cyclical theories hold that societies develop to a certain point and then reverse their development, only to reverse it again in the future. Among the most notable of cyclical theories are those developed by Oswald Spengler and Pitirim Sorokin.

Oswald Spengler. German historian Oswald Spengler was deeply troubled by World War I. The brutality of the war led Spengler to question whether social change always results in progress. In his two-volume book, *The Decline of the West,* Spengler suggested that societies do not continuously progress toward higher levels of complexity or achievement. Rather, each society develops to a certain level and then declines to the point of death. According to Spengler, Western civilization was in its final stages of life in the 1920s. As

The Chichén Itzá site in the Yucatán stands as evidence of ancient Mayan culture. Cyclical theorist Oswald Spengler would have viewed the disappearance of Mayan culture as part of the natural course of social change.

evidence of the West's approaching death, Spengler offered the events of World War I.

Pitirim Sorokin. The Russian-American sociologist Pitirim Sorokin presented a slightly different theory of social change. According to Sorokin's view, all societies fluctuate between two extreme forms of culture. At one extreme are ideational cultures. In an **ideational culture,** truth and knowledge are sought through faith or religion. At the other extreme are sensate cultures. In a **sensate culture,** people seek knowledge through science. Ideational cultures tend to be "otherworldly," while sensate cultures are practical and materialistic. During the period in which a society is shifting from one extreme to the other, its culture can be classified as idealistic. An **idealistic culture** contains both ideational characteristics and sensate characteristics.

According to Sorokin, external factors—such as war or contact with other societies—can hasten a society's shift from one form of culture to another. These external factors, however, do not *cause* the shift. Instead, Sorokin believed that the tendency toward change is present at a society's birth. Something in the society's structure causes it to swing back and forth between an ideational and a sensate culture. Sorokin referred to this natural tendency toward social change as the **principle of immanent change.**

Critics of cyclical theories point out that such theories tend to concentrate on describing what *is,* rather than attempting to explain *why* things happen. From a sociological perspective, the interesting point is not that societies have a life cycle. The real question of interest is *why* some societies decline or disappear, while others continue to grow and adapt to changing conditions.

Evolutionary Theory

In contrast to a cyclical theory of social change, an **evolutionary theory of social change** views change as a process that moves in one direction—toward increasing complexity. As members of society attempt to adapt to social and physical conditions in their environment, they push the society forward in development. Each new adaptation serves as the basis for future adaptations. Thus change is seen as an additive process.

When talking about evolutionary theory, it is important to distinguish between the views of early evolutionary theorists and those of modern social evolutionists. Although all evolutionary theories hold that societies develop toward increased complexity, views on how that development takes place have changed over the years.

Early Evolutionary Theories.

Evolutionary theorists of the nineteenth century believed that all societies progress through the same distinct stages of social development. Each stage of development was supposed to bring with it improved social conditions and increased societal complexity. Not surprisingly, these early theorists viewed Western civilization as the height of social development.

One of the earliest social evolutionists was Auguste Comte, who suggested a three-stage theory of development. According to Comte, in the first stage of development, people in society seek explanations for events by turning to the supernatural. In the next stage of development, answers are sought in religion or philosophy. Finally, in the highest stage of development, members of society turn to science for answers to the causes of events.

Later in the century, Herbert Spencer carried the idea of social evolution a step further. Influenced by the 1859 publication of Charles Darwin's *On the Origin of Species*, Spencer argued that societies, like living organisms, evolve from simple to complex. According to Spencer, this evolution is guided by the process of natural selection. Those societies whose members are able to adjust to changes in the social and natural environments progress to higher stages of development. Societies die out, on the other hand, when members cannot adapt. Spencer referred to this idea as "the survival of the fittest."

Evolutionary theories were popular during the late nineteenth and early twentieth centuries because they justified the social and political conditions in Europe and the United States. This was particularly true of Spencer's idea that only the strongest societies are meant to survive. This idea transformed the domination of the weak by the strong into a natural part of social development. Thus it was justifiable for Europe and the United States—the industrial giants of the world—to militarily and economically exploit weaker nations. It also meant that class differences within nations were a natural phenomenon. According to the evolutionary view, individuals who could and should rise to the top would naturally do so.

Critics of early evolutionary theory note that in addition to possessing an ideological bias, evolutionary theorists did not attempt to explain *why* social change takes place. Instead, they were satisfied with providing scattered data to support their idea that all of the world's societies were traveling along the path toward eventual industrialization. When social scientists began to collect extensive data from around the world, they soon discovered that social change is not an orderly process. By the early 1920s, evolutionary theory no longer was considered valid.

Modern Evolutionary Theories.

Evolutionary theory did not disappear for long. When it reappeared, however, it had abandoned many of the ideas that had caused earlier evolutionary theories to fall from favor. Modern evolutionary theorists do not claim that all societies pass through a single set of distinct stages of development on their way toward the ideal of Western society. Instead, they hold that societies have a *tendency* to become more complex over time. Change, however, can result from many sources and can take many paths. Modern social evolutionists also do not assume that change always produces progress or that progress means the same thing in all societies.

An equally important difference between modern and early evolutionary theory is that modern theorists attempt to explain *why* societies change. According to social scientist Gerhard Lenski, for instance, social evolution takes place because of changes in a society's economic base and its level of technology. New technologies and improvements in old technologies enable societies to change their subsistence patterns. As a society changes its form of subsistence, say from hunting and gathering to simple horticulture, all of the society's other social institutions are changed to some degree. Each new level of development provides the basis for future changes.

Critics of modern evolutionary theory agree that it has avoided many of the problems that plagued earlier evolutionary theories. Modern theories, however, still provide only limited explanatory power. They do not, for instance, attempt to explain events such as wars or short-term changes within individual societies.

Equilibrium Theory

As we have noted throughout the textbook, functionalist theory focuses on the ways in which societies maintain order. It is, however, impossible to ignore the fact that societies do change. In response to this fact, functionalist theorist Talcott Parsons offered the **equilibrium theory of social change.**

According to evolutionary theory, technological improvements have transformed the open-air markets of Medieval England into the modern shopping malls characteristic of post-industrial England.

Building on the functionalist idea that society is like a living organism, Parsons argued that a change in one part of the social system produces changes in all other parts of the system. This occurs because a social system, like a living organism, attempts to maintain stability. When stability is disrupted by change in one part of the system, the other parts of the system adjust to the degree needed to bring the system back into balance, or equilibrium. Although order has been restored, the new system is slightly different from the old system. Thus social change has taken place.

Parsons also was interested in how social equilibrium is maintained in the case of evolutionary change. According to Parsons, evolutionary change takes place through a two-step process of *differentiation* and *integration.* As a society becomes more complex, its social institutions become differentiated—that is, they become more numerous and more distinct. These new institutions, however, must work effectively with other parts of the system if social stability is to be maintained. To ensure that this integration take place, new values and norms are developed to resolve conflicts between new and existing institutions. Thus equilibrium is maintained even in the face of evolutionary change.

Critics of equilibrium theory note that it suffers from the same problems facing all functionalist theory. The emphasis on social order makes it difficult for equilibrium theory to explain widespread social change within or between societies.

Conflict Theory

According to the **conflict theory of social change,** most social change is the result of conflicts between groups with opposing interests. In most cases, conflicts arise from disputes over the legitimacy of authority or over access to power and wealth. Because conflict theorists view conflict as a natural condition in all societies, they see social change as inevitable. Thus they hold that societies are in a constant state of change or potential change.

Conflict theory is rooted in Karl Marx's theory of class conflict. Over the years, however, most conflict theorists have moved away from an emphasis on class conflict. Modern conflict theorists, such as Ralf Dahrendorf, take a much broader view of conflict, focusing instead on social conflict in general.

Karl Marx and Class Conflict. Karl Marx held that all of human history is the history of class conflict. By this he meant that all societies throughout history have been subject to conflicts between the people who have power and those who lack power. According to Marx, social change results from the efforts of the powerless to gain power. Most usually, these efforts involve the violent overthrow of those in power. Thus Marx saw violence as a necessary part of social change.

As we noted in Chapter 13, Marx was most interested in how this process would occur in industrial societies. Marx believed that the sharp class divisions and social inequality that were characteristic of early industrial societies eventually would lead the proletariat (the working class) to overthrow the bourgeoise (the owners of the means of production). After the revolution, a dictatorship of the proletariat would be established to assist in the transformation to communism—the classless society that Marx considered the ultimate goal of all social evolution.

The fact that class conflict has not resulted in revolution in modern industrial societies has led most conflict theorists to abandon the idea of class conflict. Instead, they focus on the broad range of social factors that can produce conflict in societies. The work of Ralf Dahrendorf is representative of many modern conflict theorists.

Ralf Dahrendorf and Social Conflict. Ralf Dahrendorf, like all conflict theorists, agrees with Marx's belief that conflict is a central feature of all societies. He disagrees, however, with Marx's idea that class conflict is the moving force in human history. Instead, Dahrendorf holds that social conflict can take many forms. Conflict between racial or ethnic groups, religious or political groups, management and labor, males and females, the young and the old, and people with differing public opinions or self-interests all can lead to social change.

Dahrendorf also does not believe that revolution, or even violence, is the principal way in which conflicts are resolved in modern industrial society. In many instances, interest groups are able

In many areas of the world, such as the Middle East, Armenia, and Northern Ireland, the process of social change is becoming increasingly violent.

to institute social change through compromise and adaptation.

Critics of modern conflict theory note that it suffers from the same problem that troubles equilibrium theory—too narrow of an emphasis. By concentrating on conflict as the principal cause of social change, conflict theorists ignore changes that occur in the absence of conflict. Technological innovations, for example, generally do not arise in response to conflict. Nevertheless, they have a profound effect on society. In addition, conflict theory ignores those elements in society that serve to maintain the social order.

As we have noted, no single theory has proved to be up to the task of explaining all aspects of social change. And, given the complex nature of social change, it is very likely that no single theory could ever prove adequate. In recognition of this fact, many social scientists combine elements of the various theories in an attempt to gain a better understanding of the nature of social change.

SECTION 1 REVIEW

IDENTIFY Oswald Spengler, Pitirim Sorokin, Gerhard Lenski, Talcott Parsons, Ralf Dahrendorf

1. ***Contrasting Ideas*** **(a)** What is the cyclical theory of social change? **(b)** How did Oswald Spengler's and Pitirim Sorokin's views of social change differ?

2. ***Understanding Ideas*** How does modern evolutionary theory differ from early evolutionary theory in terms of how it views social evolution?

3. ***Summarizing Ideas*** **(a)** What is the equilibrium theory of social change? **(b)** According to Talcott Parsons, how is social equilibrium maintained in the case of evolutionary change?

4. ***Analyzing Viewpoints*** How does Karl Marx's view of social change differ from the view held by Ralf Dahrendorf?

2 MODERNIZATION

Many sociologists interested in social change focus on modernization. **Modernization** is the process by which a society's social institutions become increasingly complex as the society moves toward industrialization. Some sociologists interested in modernization concentrate on social change in less developed nations. Other sociologists turn their attention to analyzing the effects of modernization on social life and the natural environment in more developed nations.

In this section, we first will explore the process of modernization in less developed nations. We then will turn our attention to analyzing the positive and negative effects of modernization on the social and natural environments.

The Process of Modernization

Why have the more developed nations of the world—the United States, Canada, Western Europe, Australia, and Japan—modernized so much more quickly than have the less developed nations that make up much of Latin America, Africa, and Asia? Modernization theory and world-system theory offer two different explanations.

Modernization Theory. According to the view presented by **modernization theory,** the more developed nations of the world were the first to modernize because they were the first to industrialize. Once less developed nations begin to industrialize, they too will undergo modernization. As a result, less developed nations eventually will resemble the more developed nations in their social structure, norms, and values.

Many modernization theorists hold that less developed nations can modernize even in the absence of industrialization. According to this view, modernization primarily is dependent on the adoption of the political and social reforms characteristic of the more developed nations. Once these reforms are in place, modernization is guaranteed.

Like large cities in many less developed nations, Mexico City is a stark mixture of modern skyscrapers and poverty-stricken slums.

Tropical Deforestation

One of the consequences of modernization in many of the less developed nations has been the destruction of tropical rain forests. At one time, the earth contained about 4 billion acres of tropical forests. Today, fewer than 2.5 billion acres remain. Most of this deforestation has occurred over the past 45 years.

Environmentalists estimate that approximately 40 to 50 million acres of tropical rain forest are lost each year—an area roughly the size of Florida. Estimates indicate that if the destruction of tropical rain forests continues at the current rate, tropical forests will vanish from the earth within only 115 years.

Why are the tropical rain forests of the world disappearing? The causes of the disappearance primarily are economic in nature. The vast majority of tropical rain forests are located in the less developed nations of Latin America, Africa, and Asia. In their efforts to industrialize, these nations have been clearing large areas of forest.

Some acres have been cleared for cattle ranching. This is particularly true in Central and South America, where nearly two-thirds of the original rain forest has been lost to ranching. Other acres have been lost to logging. The tropical rain forests of the world contain nearly half of the live wood on earth. Unfortunately, the forests seldom are replanted when they are cleared of their trees. Thus the forests are permanently lost once they are logged. In contrast, logged forests in the more developed nations normally are replanted to provide trees for the future.

Most acres of tropical rain forests, however, have been cleared in an effort to ease the population problems faced by less developed nations. There now are more than 5 billion people living on the earth. Demographers estimate that this figure will grow to 10 billion over the next century. More than 90 percent of this growth will occur in the less developed nations of the world.

As the less developed nations fall victim to over-urbanization, increasing numbers of poverty-stricken people migrate to the rain forests in an effort to survive. They clear the land as their ancestors did—by using the "slash-and-burn" method. This method involves cutting and burning the wild vegetation and then using the ashes as fertilizer. Rain forests easily can accommodate this type of agriculture when population densities are low. The forests cannot, however, sustain the current rates of clearing. In Brazil, for example, scientists have reported as many as 6,000 slash-and-burn fires on a single day.

The problem is intensified by the fact that land cleared from the rain forest can be farmed only for a short time. The nutrients needed to grow vegetation in the rain forests are contained in the trees. When the trees are cut down and burned, their ashes provide nutrients only for a few years. Once these nutrients are used up, crops falter. Unless farmers can afford chemical fertilizers, the land quickly becomes barren. Thus the farmers must move on and clear new land.

The destruction of tropical rain forests also has global consequences. These forests generate approximately 20 percent of the world's oxygen. Also, seventy percent of the plants identified as containing cancer-healing properties can be found only in the rain forests. Moreover, countless species of life forms are being destroyed before scientists even have a chance to study them.

In addition, widespread slash-and-burn agriculture releases as much as one billion tons of carbon into the air each year. This carbon greatly contributes to acid rain and other environmental problems. Concern over the environmental consequences of destroying the world's tropical rain forests has led international development organizations, such as the World Bank, to begin considering environmental costs when funding economic development projects.

At the basis of modernization theory is the belief that modernization will produce the same social changes in less developed nations that it produced in more developed nations. According to modernization theorists, extended family structures will be replaced by the nuclear family as less developed nations modernize. Similarly, the role of religion in guiding social interaction will decrease. In addition, modern systems of medicine and mass education will arise. And, the majority of the population will move to the cities.

Modernization theory had a large following during the 1950s and 1960s. Modernization was seen as a cure for the poverty and illiteracy that plagued many less developed nations. Through modernization, less developed nations would be able to raise their standards of living and become full partners in the world economy. To speed up this process, many industrialized nations instituted assistance programs. Money, technology, and advisers flooded into the less developed nations.

Rather than narrowing, the gap in living standards between the less developed and the more developed nations has increased over the past three decades. As a result, support for modernization theory has weakened. Why were theorists wrong in their predictions? Critics of modernization theory argue that the theory was doomed to failure because it did not take into account that less developed nations face social conditions that are very different from those faced by the more developed nations during their modernization.

When the more developed nations of the world began to modernize, they had large amounts of land and resources and relatively self-sufficient economies. The less developed nations, on the other hand, have a long history of economic dependence on the West. This economic dependence results in large part from the fact that many of the less developed nations are former colonies of the world's major industrial powers. More developed nations such as the United States, Great Britain, France, Spain, the Netherlands, Germany, and Portugal used their colonies as sources of raw materials and cheap labor. While this helped the colonial powers to industrialize, it greatly slowed economic development in the colonies.

In addition, the population pressures faced by less developed nations are very different from the pressures faced by more developed nations during

their own period of modernization. The United States, for instance, had a relatively small population and a great deal of land. Thus population growth did not present a serious problem. Other nations, such as Great Britain and France, were able to ease their population pressures by sending people to various colonies.

Less developed nations, on the other hand, are beginning the modernization process with already large populations, which are made still larger by industrialization. As we noted in Chapter 17, as less developed nations begin to industrialize, the introduction of modern medicine causes their death rates to drop much more quickly than was the case in Western Europe. Because birth rates remain high while death rates decline, the population grows at an alarming rate. As a result, the modernization process in these nations is slowed. Modernization slows because most of the economic gains produced by industrialization must be used to maintain the existing standard of living for an expanding population.

Modernization also is slowed in many less developed nations by antimodernization sentiments. In many Islamic nations, for instance, modernization is seen as a threat to traditional social and religious values. The revolution that brought about the overthrow of the Shah of Iran, for example, partially was a reaction to the Shah's support of modernization based on a Western model.

World-System Theory. A different explanation for why societies modernize at varying rates is offered by world-system theory. First proposed by Immanuel Wallerstein in the early 1970s, **world-system theory** views societal development in terms of the world economy.

According to world-system theory, the spread of capitalism has resulted in an international division of labor. This division of labor is between more developed nations such as the United States, Canada, Western Europe, and Japan and the less developed nations that make up much of Latin America, Africa, and Asia. According to this view, the more developed nations control the factors of production, while the less developed nations provide cheap labor and raw materials.

To emphasize the fact that the more developed nations of the world are at the center of the global economy, world-system theorists refer to

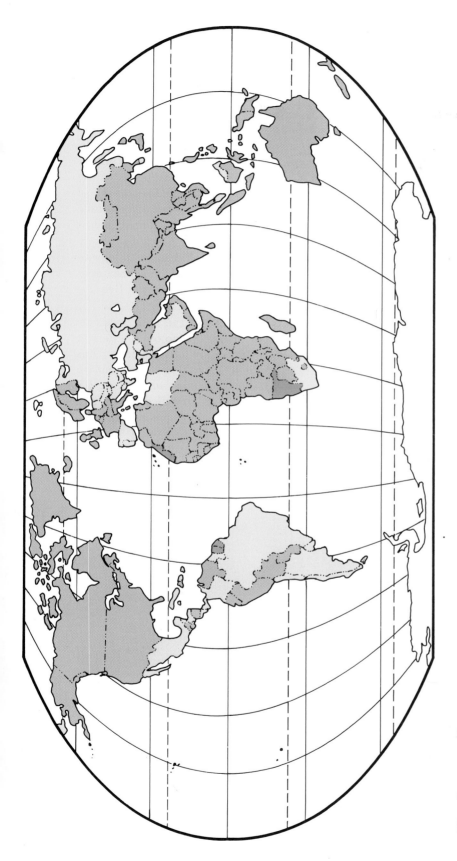

The Status of
Human Welfare

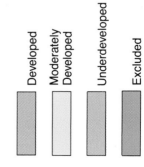

■ Developed

☐ Moderately
Developed

▨ Underdeveloped

▨ Excluded

Social scientists generally distinguish between more developed and less developed nations on the basis of economic development. Economic development is not, however, the only feature that can be used to determine developmental status. Social scientists Robert J. Tata and Ronald R. Schultz, for instance, have created a developmental status index based on human welfare.

Tata and Schultz's index, which they call the Index of Developmental Status, rates nations on the basis of four variables: (1) *physical characteristics* (the value of industrial output and the number of people per square kilometer of farmable land); (2) *economic characteristics* (the monetary value of the products produced each year); (3) *social characteristics* (the number of infant deaths per 1,000 live births, the percentage of the adult population that has attended college, and the percentage of the population

living in rural areas); and (4) *political characteristics* (the amount of money the government spends on each citizen, the level of political freedom, and the number of radios per 1,000 population). Based on these variables, Tata and Schultz assign a human welfare score to each nation. This score then is used to determine whether a nation is developed, moderately developed, or underdeveloped. The above map indicates how the nations of the world rank based on the Index of Developmental Status. Note that French Guiana, Morocco, and Namibia have been excluded from the analysis.

Source: Based on data from Robert J. Tata and Ronald R. Schultz, "World Variations in Human Welfare: A New Index of Developmental Status," *Annals of the Association of American Geographers*, 78(4), 1988, pp. 580-593.

these nations as **core societies.** They refer to less developed nations, on the other hand, as **peripheral societies** to emphasize that these nations are economically dependent on the core societies. According to world-system theorists, core societies have been able to gain worldwide control of the factors of production because they were the first nations to industrialize. Thus they have strong economies and therefore are able to export money and technology to other nations.

On the surface, the international division of labor appears to be a positive arrangement for all of the societies involved. By locating production facilities in peripheral societies or by purchasing raw materials from these societies, businesses in core societies are able to lower their production costs. Peripheral societies, on the other hand, receive technological and economic assistance in return for cooperating with the core societies.

In spite of apparent benefits, world-system theorists argue that the international division of labor has serious negative side effects for peripheral societies. Among the negative side effects are a lack of economic diversity, a dependence on exports and foreign assistance, and increased economic stratification.

The lack of economic diversity in peripheral societies is a serious problem because it slows economic growth. For economic growth to occur, the number and variety of goods and services produced in a society must increase. This increase, in turn, is dependent on a society's work force having a wide variety of skills. When core societies are heavily involved in the economy of a peripheral society, economic activity tends to be concentrated in those areas that meet the needs of the core societies. In most instances, this results in the majority of a peripheral society's work force being employed in a narrow range of unskilled or semiskilled positions.

Export dependency and reliance on foreign financial assistance result from the concentration of economic activity in peripheral societies. Because most economic activity in a peripheral society is tied to meeting the needs of the core societies, the society seldom produces enough goods and services to make its economy self-sufficient. Thus the society's economic survival is dependent on exporting goods or raw materials to the core societies. When world demand for these goods and raw materials declines, the peripheral society's economy suffers greatly.

Many of the world's largest corporations have production facilities in less developed nations.

Dealing with Debt in Less Developed Nations

Nations Ever Revising Loan Payments			Nations Ever Defaulting on Loan Payments
Guatemala	Congo	Ivory Coast	Mexico
Honduras	Angola	Ghana	Venezuela
Nicaragua	Zaire	Togo	Guyana
Costa Rica	Zambia	Mali	Surinam
Panama	Mozambique	Niger	Peru
Cuba	Madagascar	Chad	Bolivia
Dominican Republic	Malawi	Tanzania	Chile
Jamaica	Morocco	Burundi	Gambia
Colombia	Mauritania	Somalia	Nigeria
Ecuador	Senegal	Sudan	Uganda
Brazil	Guinea-Bissau	Egypt	Iraq
Argentina	Guinea	Turkey	North Korea
Central African Republic	Sierra Leone	Thailand	Philippines
Gabon	Liberia	Vietnam	

To prevent economic collapse, the peripheral society often must turn to the core societies for loans and other types of financial assistance. Without economic growth, however, peripheral societies find it difficult to repay the loans. Thus they remain in debt to the core societies. The chart on this page lists some of the less developed nations that have at one time or another defaulted on loans (that is, have failed to meet the terms of their loan repayments) or have revised the terms of their loan repayments to avoid default.

According to world-system theorists, these factors work together to increase the level of social stratification found in peripheral societies. In the absence of a diversified economy, money becomes concentrated in the hands of a few people who have close ties to the core societies. These people have a vested interest in maintaining the system. As a result, most less developed nations remain at a low level of modernization.

Many of the critics of world-system theory admit that the theory is useful in explaining why many of the less developed nations of Latin America and Africa have low levels of economic growth. These critics point out, however, that the theory is unable to explain why the formerly communist nations of Eastern Europe also have experienced low levels of economic growth and modernization. These nations, unlike the less developed nations of Latin America and Africa, have never been under colonial rule.

World-system theory also is unable to explain why some less developed nations are following a modernization path similar to the one followed by the more developed nations of the West. Critics note that a few nations—Hong Kong, South Korea, Singapore, and Taiwan, for example—have been so successful in their rate of industrialization and modernization that they are presenting the industrial powers of the West with serious economic competition.

Modernization theory and world-system theory share one important characteristic. Both theories recognize that the nations of the world are becoming increasingly interdependent. So great is this interdependence that some social scientists have adopted the term *global village* to describe the world of the twenty-first century. According to these social scientists, the nations of the world are much like the members of a village—if the group is to survive, all members must work together to achieve common goals.

Nowhere in the home is the effect of modernization more apparent than in the kitchen.

The Granger Collection, New York

The Consequences of Modernization

Regardless of the reasons why a society modernizes or at what rate, the process of modernization has both positive and negative consequences for social life and the natural environment. The most notable of the positive consequences of modernization is an increase in the standard of living in a nation. Modernization brings with it longer life expectancies, lower birth rates, higher rates of literacy, a decrease in economic and social inequality, and more personal comforts.

There are, however, costs to modernization. The very same technological innovations that improve the standard of living and prolong life in modern societies also give rise to problems. The family and religion, for instance, lose some of their traditional authority in modern society. The government, on the other hand, takes on a larger role in directing the lives of the members of society. Because people move more frequently in modern societies, social relationships tend to be weaker than they are in traditional societies. Thus feelings of social isolation are more common. In

Over the years, technological innovations have reduced the size of computers while increasing their capabilities.

FOX TROT © 1988 *Universal Press Syndicate.* Reprinted with permission. All rights reserved.

addition, people often find themselves faced with conflicting norms and role expectations.

Modern technology also gives rise to moral and ethical issues. At what point, for instance, should doctors give up the fight to keep terminally ill patients or severely deformed infants alive through the use of modern medical technology? Or, now that humans have the ability to destroy the world through nuclear warfare, what steps should be taken to prevent such warfare? These questions, and thousands like them, must be dealt with in modern society.

The effects of modernization on the natural environment also cannot be ignored. Modernization has brought with it the problems of soil, water, and air pollution. The use of pesticides in agriculture and the use of chemicals in manufacturing have created serious environmental and health problems, most of them unanticipated. Industrial societies now are faced with finding safe ways to dispose of millions of tons of hazardous wastes each year.

In the United States, for example, the Environmental Protection Agency (EPA) estimates that 198 million tons of hazardous waste are produced each year. The Office of Technology Assessment (OTA) places the figure at as high as one billion tons. At present, the United States is spending $74 billion a year on hazardous waste disposal, with industries picking up two-thirds of the cost. In addition, the government is faced with paying for the cleanup of thousands of hazardous waste dumps that are releasing toxic substances into the environment.

Water pollution also is a significant problem in industrial societies. Clean-water legislation has resulted in the cleanup of many polluted lakes and rivers in industrialized nations. The Cuyahoga River in Ohio, for example, was at one time so badly polluted that it burst into flames. Today, after extensive cleanup efforts, the river once again can support fish. The cleanup of contaminated groundwater, however, presents a more serious challenge. Over the years, chemicals have

Text continues on page 476.

Dealing with the effects of water pollution costs businesses and taxpayers over $36 million annually.

APPLYING SOCIOLOGY

An Environmental Prediction

What might happen to our environment if we do not learn to control pollution? Can people continue to withstand the addition of harmful chemicals to their food and water?

Biologist Rachel Carson painted a gloomy picture of what the earth might be like if we keep dumping pesticides and other chemicals into our air, soil, and rivers. In her book *Silent Spring,* Carson predicted that the uncontrolled use of chemicals will bring about the destruction of all living things, including people.

Although this book was written over 30 years ago, many of Carson's fears still are very strong concerns of environmentalists today. In the following excerpt from *Silent Spring,* Carson paints a picture of what might someday happen to the world if we fail to take steps to curb chemical pollution.

There was once a town in the heart of America where all life seemed to live in harmony with its surroundings. The town lay in the midst of a checkerboard of prosperous farms, with fields of grain and hillsides of orchards where, in spring, white clouds of bloom drifted above the green fields. In autumn, oak and maple and birch set up a blaze of color that flamed and flickered across a backdrop of pines. Then foxes barked in the hills and deer silently crossed the fields, half hidden in the mists of the fall mornings.

Along the roads, laurel, viburnum and alder, great ferns and wildflowers delighted the traveler's eye through much of the year. Even in winter the roadsides were places of beauty, where countless birds came to feed on the berries and on the seed heads of the dried weeds rising above the snow. The countryside was, in fact, famous for the abundance and variety of its bird life, and when the flood of migrants was pouring through in spring and fall people traveled from great distances to observe them. Others came to fish the streams, which flowed clear and cold out of the hills and contained shady pools where trout lay. So it had been from the days many years ago when the first settlers raised their houses, sank their wells, and built their barns.

Then a strange blight crept over the area and everything began to change. Some evil spell had settled on the community: mysterious maladies swept the flocks of chickens; the cattle and sheep sickened and died. Everywhere was a shadow of death. The farmers spoke of much illness among their families. In the town the doctors had become more and more puzzled by new kinds of sickness appearing among their patients. There had been several sudden and unexplained deaths, not only among adults but even among children, who would be stricken suddenly while at play and die within a few hours.

There was a strange stillness. The birds, for example—where had they gone? Many people spoke of them, puzzled and disturbed. The feeding stations in the backyards were deserted. The few birds seen anywhere were moribund; they trembled violently and could not fly. It was a spring without voices. On the mornings that had once throbbed with the dawn chorus of robins, catbirds, doves, jays, wrens, and scores of other bird voices there was now no sound; only silence lay over the fields and woods and marsh.

On the farms the hens brooded, but no chicks hatched. The farmers complained they were unable to raise any pigs—the litters were small and the young survived only a few days. The apple trees were coming into bloom but no bees droned among the blossoms, so there was no pollination and there would be no fruit.

The roadsides, once so attractive, were now lined with browned and withered vegetation as though swept by fire. These, too, were silent, deserted by all living things. Even the streams were now lifeless. Anglers no longer visited them for all the fish had died.

In the gutters under the eaves and between the shingles of the roofs, a white granular powder still showed a few patches; some weeks before it had fallen like snow upon the roofs and the lawns, the fields and streams.

No witchcraft, no enemy action had silenced the rebirth of new life in this stricken world. The people had done it themselves.

From this excerpt, you can see that chemical pollution is clearly a serious problem we all must face. Because the world is a single ecological system, any damage or destruction to one part of it can cause a breakdown in the entire system. Based on this information and on the reading, consider the following questions:

1. Some people have argued that chemical insecticides give us larger crop yields and really are not harmful at all. How would you respond to this argument?

2. What steps can we take to ensure the survival of plants and animals, assuming that pesticides may have harmful effects?

3. Do you think this reading exaggerates the dangers to our environment? Why or why not?

seeped into the groundwater in many areas, contaminating the water supply. Once contaminated, groundwater is extremely difficult to clean up. The EPA estimates that as many as three-quarters of the known hazardous waste sites may be leaking toxic chemicals into the groundwater.

Industrialized nations also are faced with cleaning up their air. Although some progress is being made, air pollution still is a serious problem. Scientists fear, for instance, that air pollution will permanently damage the earth's ozone layer. Ozone, which is a rare form of oxygen found only at very high altitudes, is responsible for absorbing ultraviolet radiation. Ultraviolet radiation is dangerous because it can cause cancer and blindness, in addition to destroying plant life. As the ozone layer is destroyed, increasing amounts of ultraviolet radiation are reaching the earth.

Acid rain is another significant problem related to air pollution. Acid rain is believed to result from the burning of fossil fuels such as coal and gasoline. The burning of these fuels releases sulfur and nitrogen oxides into the air. Once in the air, these oxides mix with the moisture in clouds and form acids that fall back to the earth as rain or snow. Acid rain has been responsible for destroying many species of trees and killing the fish and plant life in countless lakes and streams.

Since 1980, oil spills have resulted in the release of more than one million tons of oil into the world's waters.

Realization of the effects of pollution on the natural environment and human life is not a recent phenomenon. Over 30 years ago, biologist Rachel Carson wrote of the effects of chemical pollution in her book *Silent Spring*. An excerpt from the book is presented in the Applying Sociology feature on pages 474–475. *Silent Spring* did much to bring the concerns of **ecology**—the science that studies the relationship between living organisms and their environment—to the attention of the general public. Ecologists note that modernization is of little use if it results in the destruction of the natural environment.

Finally, modernization is giving rise to concerns over resource depletion. The industrial nations of the world are using up natural resources at an alarming rate. The United States, for instance, uses approximately 24 percent of the world's energy. Canada and the United States together use 30 percent of the world's petroleum and 31 percent of its natural gas. This has led some less developed nations to express fears that the reserves of natural resources will run out before these nations have a chance to fully industrialize.

Pollution is not the only environmental problem associated with modernization. Modernization also has placed many animals in danger of extinction.

SECTION 2 REVIEW

DEFINE   modernization, core societies, peripheral societies, ecology

1. **Contrasting Ideas   (a)** How do modernization theory and world-system theory differ in their views of the modernization process in less developed nations? **(b)** What criticisms have been leveled against each theory?

2. **Comprehending Ideas**   What are some of the positive and negative consequences of modernization?

CHAPTER 18   SUMMARY

Sociologists define social change as alterations in various aspects of society over time. Sociological theories of social change can be grouped into four broad categories: cyclical theory, evolutionary theory, equilibrium theory, and conflict theory.

Cyclical theories of social change view change from a historical perspective. Societies are seen as moving back and forth between stages of development. Evolutionary theories, on the other hand, view change as a process that moves in one direction. Although early evolutionary theories have been discredited, modern evolutionary theories enjoy continued support.

According to equilibrium theory, change results from a society's attempt to maintain stability. When stability is disrupted by change in one part of the system, all parts of the system must change slightly to restore equilibrium. Conflict theory, on the other hand, sees change as resulting from con-

flicts between social groups with competing interests. Conflict theory is rooted in the class-based theories of Karl Marx. Modern conflict theorists, however, take a broader view of conflict than did Karl Marx.

Many sociologists who are interested in social change focus on the process of modernization in less developed nations. The two major theories of modernization are modernization theory and world-system theory.

Other sociologists who are interested in social change focus on the effects of modernization on the social and natural environments. Among the positive effects of modernization is an increase in the standard of living. Negative effects include a loss of traditional values, feelings of social isolation, an increase in the number of moral and ethical issues facing members of society, and serious environmental problems.

DEVELOPING SOCIOLOGICAL

WRITING ABOUT SOCIOLOGY: Composing a Comparative Essay

You already have learned the skill of composing an essay in Chapter 3. Students of sociology sometimes are required to compose a special type of essay called a comparative essay. A comparative essay notes the similarities and differences between multiple points of view, courses of action, or issues. Following is an example of a directive for a comparative essay.

ESSAY DIRECTIVE: Compare the views of modernization theorists and world-system theorists concerning modernization in less developed nations.

How to Compose a Comparative Essay

Review the steps for composing an essay on page 62. Instead of using a structured overview,
however, you now will learn how to use an outline and a chart to organize your essay.

Applying the Skill
Read and respond to the following directive.

ESSAY DIRECTIVE: Contrast the views of social change presented by early evolutionary theorists with those presented by modern evolutionary theorists.

Now, study the chart on this page. This chart organizes the information to be used in the essay. The outline on page 479, which is developed from the information contained in the chart, shows the basic parts of the essay. A sample essay based on the outline appears on page 479.

Two Evolutionary Views of Social Change		
Points of Contrast	**Early Evolutionary Theories**	**Modern Evolutionary Theories**
Direction of change	All societies progress through distinct stages of social development.	Societies have a tendency to become more complex over time. But change can come from many sources.
Nature of change	Each new stage of development brings with it improved social conditions and increased complexity.	Change does not always produce progress.
View of progress	Western society is the ideal toward which all societies are moving.	What is considered progress differs from society to society.
Basis of social evolution	According to Herbert Spencer, social evolution is a process of natural selection—the strongest societies survive. Thus the domination of weak societies by strong societies is a natural part of social development, just as is social inequality within societies.	According to Gerhard Lenski, social evolution takes place because of changes in a society's economic base. As a society changes its form of subsistence, all other social institutions are changed to some degree. Each new level of development forms the basis for future changes.
Weaknesses in argument	Early theories have an ideological bias—Western societies are seen as the ideal toward which all other societies are moving. Theories also do not explain *why* change takes place.	Modern theories correct some of the problems of early theories. Nevertheless, modern theories still have only limited explanatory power. They cannot, for example, explain war or short-term change.

IMAGINATION

I. Introduction

II. Contrasts in the Two Theories

    A. Direction of change

    B. Nature of change

    C. View of progress

    D. Basis of social evolution

    E. Weaknesses in argument

III. Conclusion

Practicing the Skill

Reread the essay directive in column one on page 478. On a separate sheet of paper, complete the following exercises.

1. List the informational and performance terms in the directive.

2. Develop a chart with three columns headed "Points of Comparison," "Modernization Theory," and "World-System Theory."

3. Prepare an outline based on the chart and then write a comparative essay.

SAMPLE ESSAY

INTRODUCTION

All evolutionary theories of social change view change as a process that moves in one direction—toward increasing complexity. As members of society attempt to adapt to their environment, they push the society forward in development.

DIRECTION OF CHANGE

Although all evolutionary theorists see change as moving in one direction, early and modern evolutionists differ in their views on the path of that change. Early evolutionists saw societies as progressing through distinct stages of development. Modern evolutionists see societies as having a *tendency* to become more complex over time. But change can come from many sources and can take many paths.

NATURE OF CHANGE

Early and modern evolutionists also differ in their views on the nature of change. Early theorists argued that each higher stage of development brings with it improved social conditions and increased complexity. Modern theorists argue that change does not always produce progress.

VIEW OF PROGRESS

Early and modern evolutionists also differ on what is meant by progress. For early evolutionists, progress was measured against the ideal of Western society. Modern theorists believe that the definition of progress differs from society to society.

BASIS OF SOCIAL EVOLUTION

Early and modern evolutionists also differ on what they see as the basis of social evolution. Herbert Spencer saw social evolution as a process of natural selection—the strongest societies survive. Modern evolutionist Gerhard Lenski, on the other hand, argues that social evolution takes place because of changes in a society's economic base. As a society changes its form of subsistence, all other social institutions are changed to some degree.

WEAKNESSES IN ARGUMENT

Early evolutionary theories fell out of favor for two reasons. First, the theories were ideologically biased in that they viewed Western society as the ideal toward which all societies are moving. Second, the theories did not explain *why* change takes place. Modern evolutionary theories avoid some of these problems. Nevertheless, they still have only limited explanatory power. They cannot, for example, explain war or short-term changes.

CONCLUSION

Thus early and modern evolutionary theorists differ greatly in their views on social change.

Reviewing Sociological Terms

On a separate sheet of paper, supply the term that correctly completes each sentence.

1. _____ is the science that studies the relationship between living organisms and their environment.

2. The process by which a society moves toward industrialization is called _____.

3. An _____ _____ is a culture that contains both ideational and sensate characteristics.

4. _____ _____ is the alterations in various aspects of a society over time.

Thinking Critically about Sociology

1. *Understanding Ideas* According to world-system theory, in what way is the relationship between core societies and peripheral societies like an international division of labor?

2. *Seeing Relationships* *(a)* What is the cyclical theory of social change? *(b)* Why are cyclical theories of social change appealing during periods of extreme social turmoil?

3. *Expressing Viewpoints* Prepare a brief summary of Ralf Dahrendorf's view of social change. Be sure to explain why he disagrees with the view of social change presented by Karl Marx.

4. *Analyzing Ideas* How do modern evolutionary theories attempt to avoid the criticisms leveled against early evolutionary theories of social change?

5. *Using Sociological Imagination* *(a)* Describe the view of modernization presented by modernization theory. *(b)* Describe the view of modernization presented by world-system theory. *(c)* How might modernization theorists and world-system theorists differ in the way in which they view the relationship between modernization and the fate of individuals within less developed societies?

6. *Developing a Structured Overview* Prepare a structured overview of the positive and negative consequences of modernization.

7. *Summarizing Ideas* *(a)* According to Pitirim Sorokin, between what two extreme forms of culture do all societies fluctuate? *(b)* What are the characteristics of these two forms of culture? *(c)* Why do societies shift from one form of culture to the other?

Exercising Sociological Skills

1. *Extending Ideas* Reread the Applying Sociology feature on pages 474–475. Then research the problems presented by the disposal of hazardous nuclear waste. Based on your research information, write a story, similar to the one written by Rachel Carson, describing a world contaminated by nuclear waste.

2. *Drawing Conclusions* According to the Case Study on page 467, what are the causes and consequences of the destruction of tropical rain forests in Latin America, Africa, and Asia?

3. *Composing a Comparative Essay* Reread the Developing Sociological Imagination feature on pages 478–479. Using the steps outlined in the feature, write a comparative essay contrasting the view of social change presented by equilibrium theory with the view presented by conflict theory.

Extending Sociological Imagination

1. Prepare a brief report on the Peace Corps, the World Bank, or some other organization designed to assist the modernization efforts of less developed nations.

2. Read Alvin Toffler's *The Third Wave* and prepare a brief book report to share with the class.

3. Create a bulletin board containing pictures of animals that are in danger of extinction.

INTERPRETING PRIMARY SOURCES
The Environmental Costs of Communism

The transition from communism to democracy in the former Soviet Union has brought new freedoms, but it has also brought new problems. Decades of communist rule have left the former Soviet Union not only with an economy in ruins, but also with an environmental crisis of mammoth proportions. In this excerpt from the article "Toxic Wasteland," which appeared in the April 13, 1992, issue of *U.S. News & World Report*, Douglas Stanglin explores the environmental legacy of communism. While reading the excerpt, consider why the environment of the former Soviet Union became so damaged and why this damage will be difficult to repair.

Communism has left the 290 million people of the former Soviet Union to breathe poisoned air, eat poisoned food, drink poisoned water and, all too often, to bury their frail, poisoned children without knowing what killed them. Even now, as the Russians and the other peoples of the former U.S.S.R. discover what was done to them in the name of socialist progress, there is little they can do to reverse the calamity: Communism also has left Russia and the other republics too poor to rebuild their economies and repair the ecological damage at the same time, too disorganized to mount a collective war on pollution and sometimes too cynical even to try. . . .

A confidential report prepared by the Russian (formerly Soviet) Environment Ministry for presentation at the Earth Summit in Rio de Janeiro this summer blames the country's unparalleled ecological disaster primarily on a policy of forced industrialization dating back to the 1920s. The report . . . notes the "frenetic pace" that accompanied the relocation of plants and equipment to the Urals and Siberia during World War II and their rapid return to Europe and Russia after the war. This, the report says, created a "growth-at-any-cost mentality." . . .

Not surprisingly in a nation obsessed with national security and secrecy, another culprit was the military-industrial complex, which the Environment Minister's report says "has operated outside any environmental controls." In 1979, some 60 people died in a mysterious outbreak of anthrax near a defense institute in Sverdlovsk (now renamed Ekaterinburg). After years of Soviet denials of any link with defense matters, the Presidium of the Supreme Soviet voted in late March to compensate the victims of the incident and conceded that it was linked to "military activity."

At the same time, the report says, communism's reliance on central planning and all-powerful monopolies produced an "administrative mind-set" that created huge industrial complexes that overtaxed local environments. . . . Nor did Soviet industries, shielded from competition, feel any need to improve efficiency or switch to cleaner, more modern technology. . . .

A pervasive secret police force, meanwhile, ensured that the people seldom found out about the horrors visited on them in the name of progress and that, if they did, they were powerless to stop them. It took Soviet officials more than 30 years to admit that an explosion had occurred in a nuclear storage site near Chelyabinsk in 1957. The blast sent some 80 tons of radioactive waste into the air and forced the evacuation of more than 10,000 people. . . .

Even now, with the fall of the Communist Party and the rise of more-democratic leaders, there is no assurance that communism's mess will get cleaned up. Its dual legacy of poverty and environmental degradation has left the new political leaders to face rising demands for jobs and consumer goods, growing consternation about the costs of pollution and too few resources to attack either problem, let alone both at once.

Source Review

1. How did communist rule lead to environmental problems in the former Soviet Union?

2. Why will it be difficult for the former Soviet Union to solve its environmental crisis?

ACROSS SPACE AND TIME

The Women's Movement of the 1800s

Many people believe that the women's movement had its origins in the turbulent decade of the 1960s. In actuality, however, efforts toward changing women's status in American society began in the early 1800s. Enormous changes were taking place in the United States during this time, many of which led people to realize that a number of inequalities existed between the sexes.

Women first experienced the income inequality of the labor market when industrialization took many of them out of the home and into the factory. The opening of colleges to women, beginning with Oberlin College in 1833, gave women the opportunity to interact on an intellectual basis with others and to attend lectures given by liberal speakers of the time. These two factors helped lay the groundwork for the early women's movement.

It was the abolitionist movement of the 1830s, however, that provided the strongest push toward women's rights. Although slavery was an accepted practice in some states during this time, many people considered it to be inhumane and fought strongly to abolish it. Involvement in the abolitionist movement taught many women how to be effective public speakers. Some women, however, found that they were barred from abolitionist meetings and from public speaking simply because they were women.

Elizabeth Cady Stanton and Lucretia Coffin Mott were two women who were very involved in the abolitionist movement. In spite of their involvement, they found that they were barred from participating in the London World Anti-Slavery Convention in 1840. Although they protested being excluded from the convention, Stanton and Mott were told that only men could participate. Incidents such as this soon led women to realize that there were similarities between the treatment of slaves and the treatment of women in society. Stanton, Mott, and others continued their efforts toward the abolitionist cause, but now they also began to speak out on behalf of women's issues.

In 1848, Stanton and Mott decided to hold the first Women's Rights Convention, in Seneca Falls, New York. They placed an advertisement in the newspaper announcing the meeting, but they expected little response. To their surprise, over 300 men and women arrived, prepared to discuss the social, legal, and economic position of women. Two days of meetings and speeches produced the Declaration of Sentiments, based on the Declaration of Independence. The declaration stated that "all men and women are created equal." The declaration also contained a number of resolutions, among which were women's suffrage (the right to vote) and the elimination of legal discrimination against women. The right of women to vote was considered the most radical issue, and much heated debate occurred before the resolution was passed.

Although great effort was made to secure legislative enactment of these resolutions, most people of the day did not believe in women's rights. Thus little change was made in the years following the convention. When the Civil War began in 1861, women's rights activists were urged to give up their cause and join the war effort. Following the war, activists once again took up their cause. This time, however, almost all of their efforts were concentrated on a single issue—that of gaining suffrage for women.

A number of groups, including the Women's Trade Union League and the Women's Christian Temperance Union, joined forces to work for women's suffrage. The goal took years to accomplish. Many women were ridiculed, beaten, and jailed for speaking out. Finally, in 1920, 72 years after it first became an issue, the Nineteenth Amendment to the Constitution became effective and women gained the right to vote.

UNIT 5 REVIEW

Reviewing Sociological Ideas

1. **(a)** What is a social movement? **(b)** Describe the life cycle of a social movement.

2. **(a)** Define population. **(b)** What factors affect the size and structure of populations? **(c)** How do sociologists measure these factors?

3. **(a)** What is collective behavior? **(b)** What preconditions are necessary for collective behavior to occur?

4. **(a)** What are the two main strategies that have been used in recent years to control population growth? **(b)** What are some of the problems associated with each of these strategies?

5. **(a)** What is urban ecology? **(b)** Describe the three models of urban ecology.

6. **(a)** What is modernization? **(b)** What are some of the positive and negative consequences of modernization?

7. **(a)** What is a collectivity? **(b)** Describe the three factors that distinguish collectivities from social groups.

Synthesizing Sociological Ideas

1. **Making Comparisons** Compare and contrast the views of collective behavior presented by contagion theory and emergent-norm theory.

2. **Seeing Relationships** **(a)** Trace the evolution of cities. **(b)** Why is urbanization such a recent phenomenon?

3. **Summarizing Ideas** Describe the characteristics of each of the types of collectivities discussed in Chapter 16.

4. **Analyzing Ideas** **(a)** What is social change? **(b)** What views of social change are presented by cyclical theory, evolutionary theory, equilibrium theory, and conflict theory?

5. **Contrasting Ideas** **(a)** Describe the characteristics of urban anomie theory, compositional theory, and subcultural theory. **(b)** How do the theories differ in their view of city life?

6. **Understanding Ideas** **(a)** According to Malthusian theory, what factors lead to population change? **(b)** According to demographic transition theory, what causes a society's population to change and through what three stages does each society pass?

7. **Organizing Ideas** Construct a chart describing the four types of social movements discussed in Chapter 16. In column 1, list each type of social movement. In column 2, provide a definition for each type of social movement. In column 3, list the characteristics of each type of social movement.

8. **Expressing a Viewpoint** **(a)** Describe the views of social movements presented by deprivation theory and by resource-mobilization theory. **(b)** Which theory do you believe presents the most logical view of social movements? Why?

Applying Sociological Imagination

1. Choose a less developed nation in Latin America, Africa, or Asia. Research the economic and social conditions found in the nation you have chosen. Next, analyze the nation from the perspective of modernization theory and then again from the perspective of world-system theory.

2. Write a brief research report on a current environmental problem, such as acid rain, nuclear waste, or water pollution.

3. Prepare a chart that lists and describes the characteristics of each of Herbert Blumer's four types of crowds.

4. Locate a magazine article that describes the current problems of the American inner city. Summarize the article, concentrating on the problems discussed and the proposed solutions to these problems. Evaluate the effectiveness of the solutions. If you do not agree with the suggested solutions, propose alternative courses of action.

APPENDIX
Sociological Research Methods

We have defined sociology as the science that studies human society and social behavior. Because sociology is a science, it seeks answers to questions through empirical research. **Empirical research** is research that relies on the use of experience, observation, and experimentation to collect facts. In scientific terms, these facts are called **data.** [Although the word *data* sometimes is treated as a singular noun, it actually is the plural form of *datum.* Thus when speaking of data, scientists generally say "the data are. . . ."] If something can be seen, smelled, tasted, touched, or heard, it is considered to be empirical.

Sociologists, like most scientists, collect empirical data by using the scientific method. The **scientific method** is an objective, logical, and systematic way of collecting empirical data and arriving at conclusions. Researchers who use the scientific method (1) try to prevent their own notions, values, and biases from interfering in the research process; (2) use careful and correct reasoning in drawing conclusions from their data; and (3) carry out research in an organized and methodical manner.

The Characteristics of Social Research

Sociological research covers a wide range of topics. This is evident from your textbook's Table of Contents. Nevertheless, most research shares certain basic characteristics. Among these characteristics are the types of research issues that are of interest to sociologists and the importance placed on determining causation and correlation.

Issues of Interest. The main interest of most sociologists lies in examining the structure and function of various features of society. Sociologists are, for example, concerned with the structure and function of groups. This interest leads sociologists to examine how groups are organized and the consequences that group actions have for society. Sociologists also are interested in rates of behavior— how often particular behaviors occur under specific conditions. Unlike psychologists, who are interested in individual behavior, sociologists are interested in how groups of people with similar characteristics are likely to act under given circumstances. Finally, sociologists are interested in stability and change. They seek to understand how and why certain features of society change over time, while other features remain relatively stable.

Crowd behavior is a topic of interest to most sociologists.

Causation and Correlation. Like all scientists, sociologists want to uncover the causal connections between events. Things do not just happen. There is a cause behind each occurrence. Whether we are talking about biological growth, riots, atomic fission, or wars—all events have causes.

Sociologists study cause and effect by examining the relationships among variables. A **variable** is a characteristic that can differ from one individual, group, or situation to another in a measurable way. Anything that can vary in amount or quality from case to case can be considered a variable. Age, race, income, level of education, and marital status are just a few of the things that can serve as sociological variables. A **causal relationship** exists when a change in one variable causes a change in another variable.

When examining cause and effect, sociologists distinguish between two types of variables: independent variables and dependent variables. An **independent variable** is a variable that causes a change in another variable. A **dependent variable,** on the other hand, is the variable that is changed by the independent variable. In a study of teenage drug use, for instance, the level of drug use might be the dependent variable, while the independent variables might include school grades or teenage attitudes toward drug use. In this instance, sociologists might be interested in determining if the level of drug use is influenced by grades in school or attitudes toward drug use. Is drug use, for example, lower among students who are on the honor roll at school?

The first step in determining cause and effect is to establish whether a correlation exists between two variables. A **correlation** exists when a change in one variable is regularly associated with a change in another variable. Correlations may or may not be causal. In addition, correlations may be either positive or negative. In the case of a **positive correlation,** both variables change in the same direction. Cigarette smoking, for example, is positively correlated with diseases such as lung cancer. The higher the rate of cigarette use, the higher the rate of lung cancer. In the case of a **negative correlation,** the variables change in opposite directions. As individuals age, for example, they need fewer hours of sleep.

In some instances, variables appear to be correlated, but the relationship actually is spurious. A **spurious correlation** exists when variables appear to be related but actually are being affected by the existence of a third variable. Hospitalization and death, for example, appear to be highly correlated. This does not mean, however, that hospitalization causes death. It is more likely that a third variable—serious illness—is responsible for the high correlation. Thus, hospitalization and death are spuriously correlated.

Sociologists determine whether variables are causally related, correlated, or spuriously correlated through the use of controls. In sociological terms, **controls** are ways of excluding the possibility that outside variables are affecting the relationship between the two variables under investigation. Suppose, for example, that a group of sociologists find that the level of government spending on social

Socioeconomic status is a common independent variable in sociological research.

programs and the level of voter participation are positively correlated in most nations of the world. To determine whether increased government spending causes higher rates of voter participation, the sociologists might control for the level of economic development in each nation. If the sociologists find that both the level of government spending and the level of voter participation are related to the level of economic development in a nation, they will conclude that the correlation between government spending and voter participation is spurious.

The Research Process

Sociologists generally follow a series of seven steps when conducting empirical research. These steps include defining the problem, reviewing the literature, forming a hypothesis, choosing a research design, collecting the data, analyzing the data, and presenting conclusions. Emile Durkheim's classic 1897 study of the social causes of suicide provides the earliest example of the application of these steps to a sociological problem.

Defining the Problem. The first step in the research process involves selecting a topic for study and developing operational definitions of key concepts. An **operational definition** is a definition that is stated in terms of measurable characteristics. For example, Emile Durkheim wished to study the effect of social integration on suicide rates among various groups of individuals. In order to do this, he had to define suicide and social integration in terms that would enable him to measure both concepts.

Reviewing the Literature. Good sociological research is conducted within the context of an existing body of knowledge. In order to determine how others have approached a particular research problem and what conclusions they have reached, sociologists review the published reports of studies that have a bearing on their research interests. This not only provides researchers with valuable insights that help guide their work, it also prevents the unnecessary duplication of research efforts.

Thus when Emile Durkheim began his study of suicide, he examined the existing literature to determine how other researchers explained the phenomenon. In addition, Durkheim reviewed the available statistics on suicide. What he found led him to dismiss the psychological explanations that were popular in the literature and to concentrate his attention on social factors.

Forming a Hypothesis. Once the existing literature has been reviewed, sociologists develop testable hypotheses. A **hypothesis** is a statement that predicts the relationship between two or more variables. Emile Durkheim, for example, hypothesized that suicide rates within groups vary inversely with the degree to which group members are integrated into society. In other words, Durkheim

---

The Research Process

STEP 1
Define the Problem

↓

STEP 2
Review the Literature

↓

STEP 3
Form a Hypothesis

↓

STEP 4
Choose a Research Design

↓

STEP 5
Collect the Data

↓

STEP 6
Analyze the Data

↓

STEP 7
Present Conclusions

Methods

predicted that the more family, religious, and community bonds group members have, the less likely they are to commit suicide.

Choosing a Research Design. The next step in the research process involves selecting a research design. A **research design** is a plan for collecting, analyzing, and evaluating data. Not all research problems lend themselves to every data collection technique. Selecting the correct research design therefore is extremely important. Most of the data collection methods used by sociologists fall into four categories: surveys, experiments, observational studies, and the analysis of existing sources.

Once the data are collected, many sociologists employ some form of statistical analysis to evaluate their findings. Emile Durkheim, for example, statistically analyzed existing sources—official suicide records from various European nations—to test his hypotheses. The basic methods used to collect and analyze sociological data are presented in the Applying Sociology feature on pages 14–15.

Collecting the Data. Once they have developed a research design, sociologists must follow the design in collecting their data. Different research designs require taking different factors into consideration. Regardless of the method being used, however, information must be carefully recorded. Careless data collection can affect the accuracy of the research findings.

Analyzing the Data. The analysis of data is a very important step. Even if the proper research design has been used and data have been carefully collected, the accuracy of findings can be affected by how the data are analyzed. Researchers must be careful to maintain their objectivity and not read more into the data than is there. Research findings are only as good as the methods used to collect and analyze the data.

The purpose of data analysis is to determine whether the data support the research hypotheses. When Durkheim analyzed his data on suicide, he found that rates varied among different groups within society. He found, for example, that Catholics had lower rates of suicide than did Protestants and that married people, particularly those with children, were less likely than single people to commit suicide. He attributed these findings to the weakness of social bonds among Protestants and single individuals. Durkheim reasoned that the importance of individual actions in the religious values and practices of Protestantism would lead Protestants to rely on themselves rather than on others in times of crisis. Similarly, he reasoned that unmarried individuals generally have fewer people on whom to rely for support. These findings led Durkheim to confirm his hypothesis that suicide rates vary inversely with the degree of social integration.

Presenting Conclusions. The last step in the research process involves drawing conclusions from the data and presenting the

The introduction of computers into the research process has changed the nature of sociological data collection and analysis.

research findings to others. Sociologists generally report their findings in professional journals, in scholarly books, and at professional meetings. By reporting their research findings, sociologists add to the body of sociological knowledge. They also make it possible for other sociologists to evaluate the data and the research process. When sociologists do not supply enough information to allow their research to be repeated by other sociologists, the findings often are viewed as suspicious.

Basic Research Methods

Although we presented an overview of research methods in the Applying Sociology feature in Chapter 1 (pages 14–15), two areas warrant addition discussion. These two areas are survey methods and statistical analysis.

Survey Methods.   As we noted in the Applying Sociology feature, the survey method allows sociologists to collect data on attitudes and opinions from large numbers of people. The two techniques most commonly used to gather survey data are questionnaires and interviews.

A **questionnaire** is a list of questions or statements to which people are asked to respond in writing. Questionnaires can be administered in person or they can be sent through the mail. Because questionnaires can be administered to many people at the same time, this research method has the advantage of allowing sociologists to collect a great deal of information in a relatively short period of time. The questionnaire method also is a relatively inexpensive way to collect large amounts of data.

An **interview** is much like a questionnaire, except that people are asked to respond orally to questions. Interviews can be administered in person or over the telephone. The interview technique solves a problem that often arises when questionnaires are used to collect data. When sociologists collect data through questionnaires, they cannot be certain that the people answering the questionnaires have understood the questions. In the case of interviews, researchers can ask for clarifications and can look for any signs of confusion on the part of those people responding to the surveys.

Regardless of whether sociologists choose to use questionnaires or interviews, they must first select the people they wish to question. Sociologists refer to the people who respond to surveys as **respondents.** Unless a population is very small, it is impractical to have everyone in the population respond to a survey. Thus, sociologists generally survey a sample of a population. A **sample** is a small number of people drawn from a larger population.

For a sample to be useful, it must be representative of the population from which it was drawn. To help ensure representativeness, sociologists generally rely on random samples. A **random sample** is a sample chosen in such a way that every member of the population has an equal chance of being included in the sample.

A famous example of the consequences of not using a random sample is provided by the presidential election poll conducted by the *Literary Digest* in 1936. The *Literary Digest* wished to predict the outcome of the presidential election between Republican Alfred E. Landon and Democrat Franklin D. Roosevelt. The magazine selected its respondents from telephone directories and automobile registration lists. The results of their survey of over 2 million Americans indicated that Landon would beat Roosevelt by a margin of 15 percentage points. The magazine was quite embarrassed when Roosevelt won by a landslide.

Why was the magazine's survey so far off the mark? The reason rests in how the sample was selected. During the Depression years, only members of the middle and upper classes could afford telephones and automobiles. Members of the middle and upper classes were mostly Republican in the 1930s. Thus, Republicans were vastly overrepresented in the sample. Members of the much larger working class, on the other hand, were not included in the survey. It was the working class, most of whom were Democrats, that was responsible for electing Roosevelt as president.

Statistical Analysis. Once data are collected, they must be analyzed. Sociologists use a wide range of statistical methods, many of them very complicated. Students of sociology, however, can interpret a great deal of sociological information if they have a basic understanding of a few statistical concepts. The most important of these concepts are the three measures of central tendency: the mode, the mean, and the median.

When sociologists speak of a **measure of central tendency,** they are referring to a statistical average—a single value—that describes the data under consideration. Measures of central tendency can be calculated on any set of data as long as the data can be translated into numbers.

The same data will produce different averages depending on which of the three measures of central tendency are being used. The **mode** is the number that occurs most often in the data. The **mean,** on the other hand, is the measure obtained by adding up all of the numbers in the data and dividing that number by the total number of cases. This is the measure that we most often think of when we think of averages. The **median** is the number, or value, that divides the range of data into two equal parts.

We can illustrate the differences between mode, mean, and median using the following set of data on the prices of nine different makes of compact cars:

A faulty research design led the *Literary Digest* to predict incorrectly that Alfred E. Landon would be elected president by a landslide in 1936.

$11,500	$10,000	$13,000
$12,500	$15,000	$14,000
$ 9,000	$11,000	$13,000

To calculate the mode on the above set of figures, we simply need to look for the price that occurs most often. In this case, the price that occurs most often is $13,000. To calculate the mean, we must add up all of the prices and divide the total by nine. This procedure yields a mean of approximately $12,111. Finally, to calculate the median, we need to rank the prices from low to high and pick out the price that is in the middle. In the above set of data, the median is $12,500. As you can see, each measure of central tendency produces a different average of the data.

Ethics and Social Research

Scientific research is an important part of sociology. Without research, sociologists could not extend our knowledge of society and human behavior. The fact that social research often focuses on people presents sociologists with many special research problems. Often these problems involve ethical issues.

Ethics are the moral principles that guide our behavior. They are based on group values—the shared beliefs about what is good or bad, right or wrong, desirable or undesirable. Ethical principles in science help to ensure that research is directed toward achieving worthwhile goals.

Every scientist is bound by a set of universal ethical principles when conducting research. All scientists, for example, must conduct their research competently, report their findings accurately, and accept responsibility for their actions. Scientists who study people have the added responsibility of protecting the welfare of participants. For sociologists, the protection of participants is a very important ethical consideration.

In sociology, the ethical treatment of *subjects*—the term sociologists use for human research participants—involves ensuring that they are never intentionally harmed. Potential risks include such things as physical, emotional, or moral endangerment, the loss of personal rights, and monetary losses. Consequently, certain types of research—such as research that would require confining subjects over long periods of time or depriving them of basic necessities—cannot be conducted by sociologists.

Informed consent also is an important ethical consideration for sociologists. Unfortunately, the nature of social research sometimes makes it impractical or impossible to inform subjects that they are participating in a research project. This is particularly true in observational studies. In many cases, if individuals knew that they were being studied, they would alter their behavior, either intentionally or unintentionally.

Whenever possible, however, subjects should be given full knowledge of the research project, including its goals and the intended use of the findings. Armed with this information, subjects should then be allowed to volunteer for the study or decline to participate. Subjects also should be allowed to withdraw their participation at any time. It is highly unethical for a researcher to force people into participating in a study, either by offering unrealistic rewards or by pressuring them psychologically.

Although sociologists might fantasize about studying social behavior in a controlled environment, ethical and practical concerns place limits on the ways in which research can be conducted.

Closely tied to the issue of informed consent are the problems of privacy invasion and the use of deception. These problems are particularly likely to arise when subjects have not been informed that they are being studied, such as in the case of observational research. Sociologists therefore must always attempt to draw the line between legitimate research methods and methods that involve the invasion of privacy or deception.

Finally, sociologists must deal with the ethical issue of value neutrality. It is impossible to be totally value-neutral. The personal values of social scientists affect what they choose to study and how they choose to gather information. Researchers should not, however, attempt to impose their values on others or alter their subjects' behavior. In addition, social scientists should attempt to guard against letting their values influence their interpretation of findings. It is extremely unethical for a sociologist, or any social researcher, to manipulate the data so that these data will support a predetermined set of values.

These issues are so crucial to the research process that the American Sociological Association has published a code of ethics to which all sociologists are expected to adhere. An excerpt from the American Sociological Association's *Code of Ethics* can be seen beginning on page 548.

References

Babbie, Earl. *The Practice of Social Research,* 3rd ed. Belmont, Cal.: Wadsworth, 1983.

Bart, Pauline, and Frankel, Linda. *The Student Sociologist's Handbook,* 3rd ed. Chicago, Ill.: Scott, Foresman, 1981.

Berger, Peter. *Invitation to Sociology.* New York: Anchor Books, 1963.

Durkheim, Emile. *The Rules of Sociological Method.* New York: Free Press, 1938.

Durkheim, Emile. *Suicide.* Glencoe, Ill.: Free Press, 1964. Originally published in 1897.

Kohl, Jeanne, and Reisman, Jane. *Social Research Challenges.* Los Angeles, Cal.: Roxbury Publishing Company, 1992.

Nisbet, Robert A. *The Sociological Tradition.* New York: Basic Books, 1966.

Nisbet, Robert A. *The Sociology of Emile Durkheim.* New York: Oxford University Press, 1974.

Reece, Robert D., and Siegal, Harvey A. *A Primer in the Ethics of Social Research.* Macon, Ga: Mercer University Press, 1986.

Reinharz, Shulamit. *Social Research Methods: Feminist Perspectives.* New York: Oxford University Press, 1992.

CAREERS IN SOCIOLOGY

Planning for a career is one of the most important steps a student can take to plan for the future. Careers in Sociology has been designed to describe some career options in fields related to sociology and what you can do now to help you receive training in sociology. For further information, you might wish to consult the latest edition of the *Occupational Outlook Handbook,* published by the United States Department of Labor. The *Handbook* contains detailed descriptions of a variety of jobs, including working conditions, qualifications, current salaries, and job outlooks.

Majoring in Sociology

After having completed your course in sociology, some of you may find that you would like to further your study of the subject in college. Some of you even may decide to make sociology your major course of study. The following guidelines contain some of the things you can do now to help you gain admittance to a college or university in which you might pursue your goals.

■ *Learn* basic English and mathematical skills while in high school. Many colleges and universities require their applicants to take and pass entrance examinations. Acquiring English and mathematical skills while in high school will help you to pass these examinations. These skills also will serve you throughout the entire course of your college life and beyond.

■ *Discuss* your decision to go to college and major in sociology with your sociology teacher and with the career counselor in your high school. These people can give you valuable insights into such things as how to apply for college, what colleges to apply to, how to learn about scholarships, grants, and financial assistance, and what college life is like. These people also can supply you with valuable information concerning possible careers available in the area of sociology.

■ *Read* the *Directory of Departments of Sociology,* which is published by the American Sociological Association, and college catalogues.

These resources are available in your high school library or in a public or university library near you. If you need help locating these materials, speak to your high school career counselor or a librarian. Reading all you can about various colleges and universities will help you find the one most suited to your needs.

■ *Decide* which colleges and universities you are interested in attending. Make a list of these places, noting their addresses, telephone numbers, and the department or person to whom you should write. Discuss with your parents the advantages and disadvantages of each college and university.

■ *Write* to all of the colleges and universities on your list, requesting catalogues, applications, and supplementary information concerning housing and financial assistance. Read and discuss these materials with your parents, sociology teacher, and career counselor. Make a final list of the colleges and universities that you would like to attend.

■ *Complete* the applications for those colleges and universities on your final list. If you are unsure how to proceed, seek assistance from your parents or from your career counselor. Follow all instructions on the applications very carefully and supply all of the information that is requested. Be sure to mail your applications before the deadline dates given. If possible, make plans to visit some college campuses.

Following this list of guidelines will help you get started on your way toward a future career in sociology. While in college, you will find that sociology gives you a valuable background with which you may pursue a wide range of career opportunities.

Careers in Sociology

Although a bachelor's degree in sociology does not prepare you to become a professional sociologist, an undergraduate major in sociology provides you with a strong liberal arts education. This background will prepare you for many entry-level positions in a wide range of areas.

Graduates with a bachelor's degree in sociology may be hired, for example, as assistants or trainees in business, industry, and government. Coursework in the areas of complex organizations, industrial sociology, and statistics are helpful for careers in these areas. Courses such as these also are helpful if you are seeking employment with a research organization as an interviewer or research assistant.

Many students of sociology are interested in pursuing careers in social welfare agencies. If this is your career goal, courses in the areas of marriage and the family, ethnic and racial relations, stratification, and urban sociology would give you a strong background. A number of students in sociology complete the requirements for a teaching certificate and go on to become secondary school teachers. Other career possibilities open to students with a bachelor's degree in sociology include sales, personnel management, probation and parole work, community planning, marketing and public relations, and writing and editing.

Becoming a professional sociologist typically requires graduate training, either at the master's degree level or the Ph.D. level. The master's degree usually takes between one and three years of study past the bachelor's degree. Some departments of sociology also require master's-level students to write a thesis, or major research report.

People with master's degrees in sociology may seek teaching positions in community colleges, liberal arts colleges, and some universities. Master's degree-level persons also may find careers in government work, corporations, industrial firms, and research organizations. A recent survey by the American Sociological Association found that almost half of all people with a master's degree in sociology are employed by government agencies, either on the federal, state, or local levels.

The Ph.D. (Doctor of Philosophy) in sociology typically requires at least four to five years of study beyond the bachelor's degree. This is the highest degree awarded in the field of sociology. Doctoral degree recipients must complete a dissertation, which is a book-length project in some area of original research.

A Ph.D. typically is required for teaching and research at the university level. This level of training also is required for high-level careers in government agencies, private corporations, and research institutes.

Some professional sociologists choose to work in specialized fields. Following is a description of some of these fields.

Criminology. The criminologist specializes in investigating the causes of crime and methods of crime prevention. Somewhat related to criminology is *penology,* which concentrates on the investigation of punishments for crime, the management of penal institutions, and the rehabilitation of criminal offenders. Many criminologists work with police departments, the courts, and prisons in assessing problems and setting policies.

Demography. The demographer is a specialist in the area of population. Demographers collect and analyze statistics related to population size and population change, such as births, deaths, and marriages. Some demographers help businesses plan their marketing and advertising programs. Others help nations assess population problems and set population policies.

Gerontology. Gerontologists study the processes and phenomena of aging. Most sociologists who specialize in gerontology focus on the social, rather than physical, aspects of aging. Gerontology is a rapidly growing area of specialization in sociology, accompanying the aging of the population. Gerontologists assist in setting

Careers

policies for the aged and in assessing the needs of an aging population. Related to the field of gerontology is the growth in the allied health fields and service industries geared toward the needs of the elderly.

Urban sociology. Urban sociologists investigate the origin, growth, structure, composition, and population of cities. These sociologists specialize in studying the social and economic patterns of living that are common in the city environment. Many urban sociologists work as urban planners, helping cities plan for the needs of urban populations in areas such as housing, commerce, parks, and transportation. Somewhat related to urban sociology is rural sociology. Rural sociologists study the way of life in rural communities and the contrasts between rural and urban living.

Industrial sociology. Industrial sociologists specialize in the area of work and the professions. They are particularly interested in analyzing the social relationships within an industry or institution. These specialists typically are employed by businesses and corporations to analyze and assess the needs and problems of workers and management.

Medical sociology. Medical sociologists investigate the social factors that affect health care. These specialists concentrate on patient and practitioner behavior, the delivery of health care, and the rate and control of disease. Many medical sociologists are employed by hospitals, governmental agencies, and medical schools.

Social welfare research. Social welfare research workers investigate social problems in order to plan and carry out social welfare programs. These specialists collect and analyze statistics and write reports from their findings. Many social welfare research workers are employed in governmental social welfare agencies, community welfare councils, and schools of social work.

These, then, are some of the opportunities open to students with an interest in the field of sociology. No matter where your interests lie, however, it is important to remember that success in your chosen field requires preparation, dedication, and hard work.

THE SOCIOLOGIST'S BOOKSHELF

The Sociologist's Bookshelf contains a listing of the materials used in the preparation of this textbook and additional sources that will prove helpful to the student of sociology. This list contains both contemporary and classic works in the field of sociology.

 The Sociological Point of View

Avineri, Shlomo. *The Social and Political Thought of Karl Marx.* Cambridge: Cambridge University Press, 1968.

Babbie, Earl. *The Practice of Social Research,* 3rd ed. Belmont, Cal.: Wadsworth, 1983.

Berger, Peter. *Invitation to Sociology.* New York: Anchor Books, 1963.

Birnbaum, Norman. *Social Structure and Social Thought.* New York: Oxford University Press, 1993.

Collins, Randall. *Sociological Insight: An Introduction to Non-Obvious Sociology.* New York: Oxford University Press, 1992.

Coser, Lewis A. *Continuities in the Study of Social Conflict.* New York: Free Press, 1967.

Coser, Lewis A. *Masters of Sociological Thought,* 2nd ed. New York: Harcourt Brace Jovanovich, 1977.

Durkheim, Emile. *The Rules of Sociological Method.* New York: Free Press, 1938.

Hawthorn, Geoffrey. *Enlightenment and Despair: A History of Sociology.* Cambridge: Cambridge University Press, 1976.

Levin, Jack. *Sociological Snapshots: Seeing Social Structure in Everyday Life.* Newbury Park, Cal.: Sage Publications, 1992.

Mills, C. Wright. *The Sociological Imagination.* New York: Oxford University Press, 1959.

Nisbet, Robert. *The Sociology of Emile Durkheim.* New York: Oxford University Press, 1974.

Nisbet, Robert. *Sociology as an Art Form.* New York: Oxford University Press, 1976.

Padover, Saul K., ed. *The Essential Marx.* New York: New American Library, 1978.

Reece, Robert D., and Siegal, Harvey A. *A Primer in the Ethics of Social Research.* Macon, Ga: Mercer University Press, 1986.

Turner, Jonathan H. *The Structure of Sociological Theory,* 4th ed. Chicago, Ill.: The Dorsey Press, 1986.

Wrong, Dennis, ed. *Max Weber.* Englewood Cliffs, N.J.: Prentice-Hall, 1970.

2 Cultural Diversity

Birenbaum, Arnold, and Sagarin, Edward. *Norms and Human Behavior.* New York: Praeger, 1976.

Black, Donald. *Social Structure of Right and Wrong.* San Diego, Cal.: Academic Press, 1993.

Chagnon, Napoleon A. *Yanomamö: The Fierce People,* 3rd ed. New York: Holt, Rinehart and Winston, 1983.

Harris, Marvin: *Cannibals and Kings: The Origins of Cultures.* New York: Random House, 1977.

Harris, Marvin. *The Sacred Cow and the Abominable Pig: Riddles of Food and Culture.* New York: Simon & Schuster, 1985.

Bookshelf

Kingston, Maxine Hong. *The Woman Warrior: Memoirs of a Childhood among Ghosts.* New York: Vintage Books, 1976.

Macionis, John. *Society: The Basics.* Englewood Cliffs, N.J.: Prentice-Hall, 1991.

Mead, Margaret. *Sex and Temperament in Three Primitive Societies.* New York: Dell, 1935.

Miner, Horace. "Body Ritual Among the Nacirema." *American Anthropologist* 58, 1956.

Murdock, George P. "World Ethnographic Sample." *American Anthropologist* 59, 1957.

Rabin, A.I., and Beit-Hallahmi, Benjamin. *Twenty Years Later: Kibbutz Children Grown Up.* New York: Springer, 1982.

3 Cultural Conformity and Adaptation

Bell, Daniel. *The Coming of Postindustrial Society.* New York: Basic Books, 1973.

Goffman, Erving. *The Presentation of Self in Everyday Life.* Garden City, N.Y.: Doubleday Anchor, 1959.

Harris, Louis. *Inside America.* New York: Vintage Books, 1987.

Harris, Marvin. *The Sacred Cow and the Abominable Pig: Riddles of Food and Culture.* New York: Simon & Schuster, 1985.

Klein, Joe. "Whose Values?" *Newsweek,* June 8, 1992.

Knottnerus, J. David. "Status Attainment Research and Its Image of Society." *American Sociological Review* 52, 1987.

Kramer, B.J. "The Dismal Record Continues: The Ute Indian Tribe and the School System." *Ethnic Groups* 5, 1983.

Lasch, Christopher. *The Culture of Narcissism.* New York: Basic Books, 1979.

Linton, Ralph. *The Study of Man: An Introduction.* Englewood Cliffs, N.J.: Prentice-Hall, 1964.

Williams, Robin M., Jr. *American Society: A Sociological Interpretation,* 3rd ed. New York: Knopf, 1970.

Yankelovich, Daniel. *New Rules: Searching for Self-Fulfillment in a World Turned Upside Down.* New York: Random House, 1981.

4 Social Structure

Blau, Peter. *The Dynamics of Bureaucracy.* Chicago: University of Chicago Press, 1963.

Chagnon, Napoleon A. "Life Histories, Blood Revenge, and Warfare in a Tribal Population." *Science* 26, 1988.

Deal, Terrence E., and Kennedy, Allan A. *Corporate Cultures: The Rites and Rituals of Corporate Life.* Reading, Mass.: Addison-Wesley, 1982.

Durkheim, Emile. *The Division of Labor in Society.* Glencoe, Ill.: Free Press, 1964. Originally published in 1893.

Homans, George C. *Social Behavior: Its Elementary Forms,* rev. ed. New York: Harcourt Brace Jovanovich, 1974.

Kanter, Rosabeth Moss. *Men and Women of the Corporation.* New York: Basic Books, 1977.

Lenski, Gerhard, and Lenski, Jean. *Human Societies,* 5th ed. New York: McGraw-Hill, 1987.

Peter, Laurence J., and Hull, Raymond. *The Peter Principle.* New York: William Morrow, 1969.

Steuve, Ann. "The Elderly as Network Members." *Marriage and Family Review* 5, 1982.

Tiger, Lionel, and Fox, Robin. *The Imperial Animal.* New York: Dell, 1971.

Tönnies, Ferdinand. *Community and Society.* East Lansing, Mich.: Michigan State University Press, 1957. Originally published in 1887.

Weber, Max. Translated and edited by H.H. Gerth and C. Wright Mills. *From Max Weber: Essays in Sociology.* New York: Oxford University Press, 1946.

Bookshelf

Whyte, William F. *Social Theory for Action: How Individuals and Organizations Learn to Change.* Newbury Park, Cal.: Sage Publications, 1991.

5   Socializing the Individual

Bandura, Albert. *Social Learning Theory.* Englewood Cliffs, N.J.: Prentice-Hall, 1977.

Beck, Melinda. "The Young and the Gifted." *Newsweek,* June 28, 1993.

Bettelheim, Bruno. *The Uses of Enchantment: The Meaning and Importance of Fairy Tales.* New York: Vintage Books, 1977.

Burkitt, Ian. *Social Selves: Theories of the Formation of Personality.* Newbury Park, Cal.: Sage Publications, 1992.

Cooley, Charles Horton. *Human Nature and the Social Order.* New York: Scribner's, 1902.

Curtiss, Susan. *Genie: A Psycholinguistic Study of a Modern-Day "Wild Child."* New York: Academic Press, 1977.

Davis, Kingsley. "Extreme Social Isolation of a Child." *American Journal of Sociology* 45, 1940.

Erikson, Erik H. *Childhood and Society*, anniversary ed. New York: W.W. Norton, 1986.

Mead, George Herbert. *Mind, Self, and Society: From the Standpoint of a Social Behaviorist.* Chicago: University of Chicago Press, 1934.

Spitz, Rene. "Hospitalism: An Inquiry into the Genesis of Psychiatric Conditions in Early Childhood." In Anna Freud et al., eds. *The Psychoanalytic Study of the Child.* New York: International Universities Press, 1945.

Tiger, Lionel, and Fox, Robin. *The Imperial Animal.* New York: Dell, 1971.

Watson, John B. *Behavior.* New York: W.W. Norton, 1924.

Wilson, Edward O. *Sociobiology: The New Synthesis.* Cambridge, Mass.: Harvard University Press, 1975.

6   The Adolescent in Society

Bachman, Jerald G., Johnston, Lloyd D., and O'Malley, Patrick M. *Monitoring the Future: Questionnaire Responses from the Nation's High School Seniors.* Ann Arbor, Mich.: University of Michigan Press, 1992.

Billy, John O.G., and Udry, J. Richard. "The Influence of Male and Female Best Friends on Adolescent Sexual Behavior." *Adolescence* 20, 1985.

Durkheim, Emile. *Suicide.* Glencoe, Ill.: Free Press, 1964. Originally published in 1897.

Elkind, David. *The Hurried Child: Growing Up Too Fast Too Soon.* Reading, Mass.: Addison-Wesley, 1981.

Farley, Dixie. "Eating Disorders Require Medical Attention." *FDA Consumer* 26, 1992.

Goodstadt, Michael S. "Prevention Strategies for Drug Abuse." *Issues in Science and Technology,* Winter 1987.

Hayes, Cheryl D. *Risking the Future: Adolescent Sexuality, Pregnancy, and Childbearing.* Washington, D.C.: National Academy Press, 1987.

Kantrowitz, Barbara. "Teenagers and AIDS." *Newsweek,* August 3, 1992.

Korman, Sheila K. "Nontraditional Dating Behavior." *Family Relations* 32, 1983.

Lamar, Jacob V. "Kids Who Sell Crack." *Time,* May 9, 1988.

Lester, David. "One Theory of Teen-age Suicide." *Journal of School Health* 58, 1988.

Lewitt, Eugene M. "Teenage Childbearing." *The Future of Children* 2, Winter 1992.

Neiger, Brad L., and Hopkins, Rodney W. "Adolescent Suicide: Character Traits of High-Risk Teenagers." *Adolescence* 23, 1988.

Schwartz, Gil. "Playing the Prom Game." *Seventeen,* March 1988.

Waller, Willard. "The Rating and Dating Complex." *American Sociological Review* 2, 1937.

Bookshelf

White, Sharon D., and DeBlassie, Richard R. "Adolescent Sexual Behavior." *Adolescence* 27, 1992.

Willis, Judith Levine. "Acne Agony." *FDA Consumer* 26, 1992.

Worsnop, Richard L. "Teenage Suicide." *CQ Researcher,* June 14, 1991.

7 The Adult in Society

Bielby, William T., and Baron, James N. "Men and Women at Work: Sex Segregation and Statistical Discrimination." *American Journal of Sociology* 91, 1986.

Farrell, Michael P., and Rosenberg, Stanley D. *Men at Midlife.* Boston, Mass.: Auburn House, 1981.

Frieze, Irene H., Parsons, Jacquelynne E., Johnson, Paula B., Ruble, Diane N., and Zellman, Gail L. *Women and Sex Roles: A Social Psychological Perspective.* New York: W.W. Norton, 1978.

Giele, Janet Zollinger, ed. *Women in the Middle Years.* New York: John Wiley and Sons, 1982.

Levinson, Daniel. *Seasons of a Man's Life.* New York: Knopf, 1978.

Morgan, Leslie A. "The Financial Experience of Widowed Women." *The Gerontologist* 26, 1986.

Neugarten, Bernice L. *Middle Age and Aging: A Reader in Social Psychology.* Chicago: University of Chicago Press, 1968.

Pampel, Fred C., and Park, Sookja. "Cross-national Patterns and Determinants of Female Retirement." *American Journal of Sociology* 91, 1986.

Sheehy, Gail. *Passages: Predictable Crises of Adult Life.* New York: Bantam Books, 1976.

Terkel, Studs. *Working: People Talk About What They Do All Day and How They Feel About What They Do.* New York: Random House, 1974.

8 Deviance and Social Control

Becker, Howard S. *Outsiders: Studies in the Sociology of Deviance.* New York: Free Press, 1963.

Black, Donald J. "The Social Organization of Arrest." *Stanford Law Review* 23, 1971.

Clark, Charles S. "Youth Gangs." *CQ Researcher,* October 11, 1991.

Crime Victimization in City, Suburban, and Rural Areas. U.S. Department of Justice, June 1992.

Erikson, Kai T. *Wayward Puritans: A Study of the Sociology of Deviance.* New York: John Wiley, 1966.

Farrington, David P., Ohlin, Lloyd E., and Wilson, James Q. *Understanding and Controlling Crime: Toward a New Research Strategy.* New York: Springer, 1986.

Gest, Ted. "The Prison Boom Bust." *U.S. News & World Report,* May 4, 1992.

Goffman, Erving. *Stigma: Notes on the Management of Spoiled Identity.* Englewood Cliffs, N.J., 1963.

Hirschi, Travis. *Causes of Delinquency.* Berkeley, Cal.: University of California Press, 1969.

Hugick, Larry, "Public Sees Crime Up Nationally." *The Gallup Poll Monthly,* March 1992.

Hull, Jon D. "No Way Out." *Time,* August 17, 1992.

Juvenile Justice, 1991 Annual Report. U.S. Department of Justice, 1991.

Lemert, Edwin M. *Human Deviance, Social Problems, and Social Control.* Englewood Cliffs, N.J.: Prentice-Hall, 1967.

Link, B. "Mental Patient Status, Work and Income: An Examination of the Effects of Psychological Labeling." *American Sociological Review* 47, 1982.

Merton, Robert K. "Social Structure and Anomie." *American Sociological Review* 3, 1938.

Sutherland, Edwin H. *Principles of Criminology.* Philadelphia: Lippincott, 1939.

Bookshelf

Thompson, Terri, Hage, David, and Black, Robert F. "Crime and the Bottom Line." *U.S. News & World Report,* April 13, 1992.

Wright, Erik Olin, and Martin, Bill. "The Transformation of the American Class Structure, 1960–1980." *American Journal of Sociology* 93 1987.

9 Social Stratification

Avery, Robert B., and Elliehausen, Gregory E. "Financial Characteristics of High-Income Families." *Federal Reserve Bulletin* 72, 1986.

Bingham, Richard D., Green, Roy E., and White, Sammis B., eds. *The Homeless in Contemporary Society.* Newbury Park, Cal.: Sage Publications, 1987.

Blumberg, Paul. *Inequality in an Age of Decline.* New York: Oxford University Press, 1980.

Bottomore, T.B. *Classes in Modern Society.* New York: Pantheon Books, 1966.

Davis, Kingsley, and Moore, Wilbert E. "Some Principles of Stratification." *American Sociological Review* 10, 1945.

Dreier, Peter, and Appelbaum, Richard. "American Nightmare: Homelessness." *Challenge,* March/April 1991.

Frazier, E. Franklin. *Black Bourgeoisie: The Rise of a New Middle Class.* New York: Free Press, 1957.

Freedman, Robert. *The Mind of Karl Marx: Economic, Political, and Social Perspectives.* Chatham, N.J.: Chatham House, 1986.

Kozol, Jonathan. *Rachel and Her Children: Homeless Families in America.* New York: Crown, 1988.

Quigley, Eileen. "The Homeless." *CQ Researcher,* August 7, 1992.

Rose, Stephen J. *Social Stratification in the United States: The American Profile Poster.* New York: New Press, 1992.

Veblen, Thorstein. *The Theory of the Leisure Class.* New York: New American Library, 1953. Originally published in 1899.

Weber, Max. *The Protestant Ethic and the Spirit of Capitalism.* New York: Scribner's, 1958.

10 Racial and Ethnic Relations

Brown, Dee. *Bury My Heart at Wounded Knee: An Indian History of the American West.* New York: Bantam Books, 1970.

Duckitt, John. *The Social Psychology of Prejudice.* Westport, Conn.: Greenwood Press, 1992.

Edmonston, Barry, and Passel, Jeffrey S. "U.S. Immigration and Ethnicity in the 21st Century." *Population Today,* October 1992.

Gelman, David. "Black and White in America." *Newsweek,* March 7, 1988.

Griffin, Rodman D. "Hispanic Americans." *CQ Researcher,* October 30, 1992.

Hirschman, Charles, and Wong, Morrison G. "Socioeconomic Gains of Asian Americans, Blacks, and Hispanics." *American Journal of Sociology* 90, 1984.

Jost, Kenneth. "Hate Crimes." *CQ Researcher,* January 8, 1993.

Kitano, Harry H.L. *Race Relations,* 3rd ed. Englewood Cliffs, N.J.: Prentice-Hall, 1985.

Markides, Kyriakos S., and Levin, Jeffrey S. "The Changing Economy and the Future of the Minority Aged." *The Gerontologist* 27, 1987.

Marrus, Michael R. *The Holocaust in History.* New York: New American Library, 1987.

Matthiessen, Peter. *In the Spirit of Crazy Horse.* New York: Viking Press, 1983.

Merton, Robert K. *Social Theory and Social Structure,* 3rd ed. New York: Free Press, 1968.

Myrdal, Gunnar. *An American Dilemma.* New York: Harper & Row, 1944.

Ostrander, Susan A. *Women of the Upper Class.* Philadelphia: Temple University Press, 1984.

Bookshelf

Pettigrew, Thomas F., *Prejudice.* Cambridge, Mass.: Harvard University Press, 1982.

Rowan, Carl T. *Dream Makers, Dream Breakers: The World of Thurgood Marshall.* Boston, Mass.: Little, Brown, 1992.

Scott, Hilda. *Working Your Way to the Bottom: The Feminization of Poverty.* Boston, Mass.: Routledge & Kegan Paul, 1984.

Thomas, Melvin E., and Hughes, Michael. "The Continuing Significance of Race: A Study of Race, Class, and Quality of Life in America, 1972–1985." *American Sociological Review* 51, 1986.

Van Dijk, Teun A. *Communicating Racism: Ethnic Prejudice in Thought and Talk.* Newbury Park, Cal.: Sage Publications, 1987.

Weyr, Thomas. *Hispanic U.S.A.: Breaking the Melting Pot.* New York: Harper & Row, 1988.

Williams, Bruce B. *Black Workers in an Industrial Suburb: The Struggle Against Discrimination.* New Brunswick, N.J.: Rutgers University Press, 1987.

Worsnop, Richard L. "Native Americans." *CQ Researcher,* May 8, 1992.

11 Gender, Age, and Health

Anglim, Christopher, and Gratton, Brian. "Organized Labor and Old Age Pensions." *International Journal of Aging and Human Development* 25, 1987.

Berheide, Catherine White. "Women's Work in the Home: Seems Like Old Times." *Marriage and Family Review* 7, 1984.

Brownmiller, Susan. *Femininity.* New York: Ballantine Books, 1984.

Castro, Janice. "Paging Dr. Clinton." *Time,* January 18, 1993.

Congressional Quarterly. *Aging in America: The Federal Government's Role.* Washington, D.C.: CQ Press, 1989.

Ergas, Yasmine. "The Social Consequences of the AIDS Epidemic." *Social Science Research Council* 41, 1987.

Etzioni, Amatai. "Spare the Old, Save the Young." *The Nation,* June 25, 1988.

Foster, Carol D., ed. *AIDS.* Wylie, Tex.: Information Plus, 1992.

Friedl, Ernestine. *Women and Men: An Anthropologist's View.* New York: Holt, Rinehart and Winston, 1975.

Goldberg, Gertrude S., and Kremen, Eleanor. "The Feminization of Poverty: Only in America?" *Social Policy,* Spring 1987.

Gorman, Christine. "Invincible AIDS." *Time,* August 3, 1992.

Griffin, Rodman D. "The Disabilities Act." *CQ Researcher,* December 27, 1991.

Griffin, Rodman D. "Women in the Military." *CQ Researcher,* September 25, 1992.

Hager, George. "Proposal to Freeze COLA Stirs Up Old Debates." *Congressional Quarterly,* February 6, 1993.

Hasson, Judi. "Opposition Lies in Wait for Health-Care Reformers." *USA Today,* February 22, 1993.

Horner, Matina. "Fail: Bright Women." *Psychology Today,* 1969.

Hugick, Larry. "American Unhappiness with Health Care Contrasts with Canadian Contentment." *The Gallup Poll Monthly,* August 1991.

Kurtz, Richard A., and Chalfont, Paul. *Sociology of Medicine and Illness.* Needham Heights, Mass.: Allyn and Bacon, 1991.

Lord, Mary. "Away with Barriers." *U.S. News & World Report,* July 20, 1992.

Mead, Margaret. *Sex and Temperament in Three Primitive Societies.* New York: Dell, 1935.

Millett, Kate. *Sexual Politics.* New York: Ballantine Books, 1970.

Opie, Iona, and Opie, Peter, eds. *The Oxford Dictionary of Nursery Rhymes.* London: Oxford University Press, 1952.

Podolsky, Doug, and Silberner, Joanne. "How Medicine Mistreats the Elderly." *U.S. News & World Report,* January 18, 1993.

Ruggles, Patricia, and Moon, Marilyn. "The Impact of Recent Legislative Changes in Benefit Programs for the Elderly." *The Gerontologist* 25, 1985.

Tavris, Carol, and Offir, Carole. *The Longest War: Sex Differences in Perspective.* New York: Harcourt Brace Jovanovich, 1977.

"U.S. AIDS Cases Reported Through September 1992." *HIV/AIDS Surveillance,* October 1992.

12 The Family

Adams, Bert N. *The Family: A Sociological Interpretation,* 4th ed. San Diego, Cal.: Harcourt Brace Jovanovich, 1986.

Ahlburg, Dennis A., and DeVita, Carol J. "New Realities of the American Family." *Population Bulletin* 47, August 1992.

Amato, Paul R. "Parental Divorce and Attitudes Toward Marriage and Family Life." *Journal of Marriage and the Family* 50, 1988.

"As Family Leave Is Enacted, Some See End to Logjam." *Congressional Quarterly,* February 6, 1993.

Blumstein, Philip, and Schwartz, Pepper. *American Couples.* New York: William Morrow, 1983.

Booth, Alan, and Edwards, John N. "Age at Marriage and Marital Stability." *Journal of Marriage and the Family* 47, 1985.

Callan, Victor J. "The Personal and Marital Adjustment of Mothers and of Voluntarily and Involuntarily Childless Wives." *Journal of Marriage and the Family* 49, 1987.

Clark, Charles. "Work, Family and Stress." *CQ Researcher,* August 14, 1992.

Crosby, Faye J., ed. *Spouse, Parent, Worker: On Gender and Multiple Roles.* New Haven, Conn.: Yale University Press, 1987.

Glazer, Sarah. "Violence Against Women." *CQ Researcher,* February 26, 1993.

Glenn, Norval D., and Weaver, Charles N. "The Changing Relationship of Marital Status to Reported Happiness." *Journal of Marriage and the Family* 50, 1988.

Kantrowitz, Barbara, "How to Protect Abused Children." *Newsweek,* November 23, 1987.

Kolko, David J. "Characteristics of Child Victims of Physical Violence." *Journal of Interpersonal Violence* 7, June 1992.

Leslie, Gerald R., and Korman, Sheila K. *The Family in Social Context*, 7th ed. New York: Oxford University Press, 1989.

Mancini, Jay A., and Orthner, Dennis K. "The Context and Consequences of Family Change." *Family Relations* 37, 1988.

"Single Parents." *American Demographics Desk Reference,* July 1992.

Steinberg, Laurence, and Silverberg, Susan B. "Influences on Marital Satisfaction During the Middle Stages of the Family Life Cycle." *Journal of Marriage and the Family* 49, 1987.

Straus, Murray, and Gelles, Richard J. "The Costs of Family Violence." *Public Health Reports* 102, 1987.

Straus, Murray, Gelles, Richard J., and Steinmetz, Suzanne K. *Behind Closed Doors: Violence in the American Family.* Garden City, N.Y.: Anchor Books, 1980.

Sussman, Marvin B., and Steinmetz, Suzanne K., eds. *Handbook of Marriage and the Family.* New York: Plenum Press, 1987.

Weiss, Robert S. *Going It Alone: The Family Life and Social Situation of the Single Parent.* New York: Basic Books, 1979.

Weitzman, Lenore. *The Divorce Revolution: The Unexpected Social and Economic Consequences for Women and Children in America.* New York: Free Press, 1985.

Bookshelf

13 The Economy and Politics

Asher, Herbert. *Polling and the Public: What Every Citizen Should Know.* Washington, D.C.: CQ Press, 1988.

Barrett, Laurence I. "Perot-Noia." *Time,* November 9, 1992.

Birnbaum, Norman. *The Crisis of Industrial Society.* New York: Oxford University Press, 1969.

Christy, Carol A. *Sex Differences in Political Participation: Processes of Change in Fourteen Nations.* New York: Praeger, 1987.

Clements, John. "World Scene." *Clement's International Report,* January 1993.

Fineman, Howard. "The Torch Passes." *Newsweek,* November/December 1992.

Fromm, Erich. *Escape From Freedom.* New York: Avon Books, 1969.

Galbraith, John Kenneth. *The Affluent Society.* New York: New American Library, 1984.

Garreau, Joel. *The Nine Nations of North America.* New York: Avon Books, 1982.

Gomory, Ralph E., and Shapiro, Harold T. "A Dialogue on Competitiveness." *Issues in Science and Technology* 4, 1988.

Graber, Doris A. *Mass Media and American Politics.* Washington, D.C.: CQ Press, 1988.

Griffin, Rodman D. "Aid to Russia." *CQ Researcher,* March 12, 1993.

Hume, Scott. "Perot Wins! Or at Least His Ads." *Advertising Age,* November 2, 1992.

Keefe, William J. *Parties, Politics, and Public Policy in America.* Washington, D.C.: CQ Press, 1987.

Mills, C. Wright. *The Power Elite.* New York: Oxford University Press, 1956.

"Multinationals: Back in Fashion." *The Economist,* March 27, 1993.

Nasar, Sylvia. "What Governments Should Be Doing." *Fortune,* March 14, 1988.

Reinarman, Craig. *American States of Mind: Political Beliefs and Behavior among Public and Private Workers.* New Haven, Conn.: Yale University Press, 1987.

Spanier, John. *Games Nations Play.* Washington, D.C.: CQ Press, 1987.

Weber, Max. Translated and edited by H.H. Gerth and C. Wright Mills. *From Max Weber: Essays in Sociology.* New York: Oxford University Press, 1946.

Young, Amy. "Lobbyists Descend on the Statehouse." *Common Cause Magazine,* Winter 1992.

14 Education and Religion

Antin, Mary. *The Promised Land.* Boston, Mass.: Houghton Mifflin, 1940.

Beck, Melinda. "Thy Kingdom Come." *Newsweek,* March 15, 1993.

Becker, Howard S., Geer, Blanche, Hughes, Everett C., and Strauss, Anselm. *Boys in White: Student Culture in Medical School.* Chicago: University of Chicago Press, 1961.

Bellah, Robert N., and Hammond, Phillip E., eds. *Varieties of Civil Religion.* New York: Harper & Row, 1980.

Berger, Peter L. *The Sacred Canopy: Elements of a Sociological Theory of Religion.* Garden City, N.Y.: Anchor Books, 1969.

Boyer, Ernest L. *High School: A Report on Secondary Education in America.* New York: Harper & Row, 1983.

Bromley, David G., and Shupe, Anson D., Jr. *Strange Gods: The Great American Cult Scare.* Boston, Mass.: Beacon Press, 1981.

Comer, James P. "Educating Poor Minority Children." *Scientific American,* September 1988.

Dunn, William. "Educating Diversity." *American Demographics,* April 1993.

Bookshelf

Durkheim, Emile. *The Elementary Forms of Religious Life.* Glencoe, Ill.: Free Press, 1954. Originally published in 1912.

Fantini, Mario D. *Regaining Excellence in Education.* Columbus, Ohio: Charles C. Merrill, 1986.

Gardner, David. "A Nation Still at Risk." *Newsweek,* April 19, 1993.

Glazer, Sarah. "Violence in Schools." *CQ Researcher,* September 11, 1992.

Goodlad, John I. *A Place Called School.* New York: McGraw-Hill, 1983.

Hertzke, Allen D. "The Role of Religious Lobbies." In Charles W. Dunn, ed. *Religion in American Politics.* Washington, D.C.: CQ Press, 1989.

Kozol, Jonathan. *Illiterate America.* New York: New American Library, 1985.

McGroaty, Mary. "The Societal Context of Bilingual Education." *Educational Researcher* 21, March 1992.

Meacham, Jon. "What the Religious Right Can Teach the New Democrats." *The Washington Monthly,* April 1993.

National Commission on Excellence in Education. "A Nation at Risk." In Beatrice Gross and Ronald Gross, eds. *The Great School Debate.* New York: Simon & Schuster, 1985.

Oakes, Jeannie. *Keeping Track: How High Schools Structure Inequality.* New Haven, Conn.: Yale University Press, 1985.

Rohlen, Thomas P. *Japan's High Schools.* Berkeley, Cal.: University of California Press, 1983.

Roof, Wade Clark, and McKinney, William. *American Mainline Religion: Its Changing Shape and Future.* New Brunswick, N.J.: Rutgers University Press, 1987.

15 Science and Sport

Acosta, Vivian, and Carpenter, Linda. "Women in Athletics: A Status Report." *Journal of Physical Education, Recreation, and Dance* 56, 1985.

Beardsley, Tim. "Teaching Real Science." *Scientific American,* October 1992.

Berger, Peter, and Luckmann, Thomas. *The Social Construction of Reality.* Garden City, N.Y.: Anchor Books, 1967.

Cole, Jonathan R. *Fair Science: Women in the Scientific Community.* New York: Columbia University Press, 1987.

Coleman, James S., Hoffer, Thomas, and Kilgore, Sally. *High School Achievement: Public, Catholic, and Private Schools Compared.* New York: Basic Books, 1982.

Crane, Diana. *Invisible Colleges: Diffusing Knowledge in Scientific Communities.* Chicago: University of Chicago Press, 1988.

Desertrain, Gloria Solomon, and Weiss, Maureen R. "Being Female and Athletic: A Cause for Conflict?" *Sex Roles* 18, 1988.

Fisher, Arthur. "Why Johnny Can't Do Science and Math." *Popular Science,* September 1992.

Gruneau, Richard. *Class, Sports, and Social Development.* Amherst, Mass.: University of Massachusetts Press, 1983.

Jerome, Fred. "A Retreat—and an Advance—for Science and TV." *Issues in Science and Technology* 4, 1988.

Jones, Gregg A., Leonard, Wilbert M., II, Schmitt, Raymond L., Smith, D. Randall, and Tolone, William L. "Racial Discrimination in College Football." *Social Science Quarterly* 68, 1987.

Kahn, Lawrence M., and Sherer, Peter D. "Racial Differences in Professional Basketball Players' Compensation." *Journal of Labor Economics* 6, 1988.

Kane, Mary Jo. "The Female Athletic Role as a Status Determinant Within the Social Systems of High School Adolescents." *Adolescence* 23, 1988.

Klatell, David A., and Marcus, Norman. *Sports for Sale: Television, Money, and the Fans.* New York: Oxford University Press, 1988.

Bookshelf

Koch, James V., and Vander Hill, C. Warren. "Is There Discrimination in the 'Black Man's Game'?" *Social Science Quarterly* 69, 1988.

Kuhn, Thomas S. *The Structure of Scientific Revolutions*, 2nd ed. Chicago: University of Chicago Press, 1970.

McCormack, Jane B., and Chalip, Laurence. "Sport as Socialization." *The Social Science Journal* 25, 1988.

Manning, Steven. "Battling Down the Barriers." *Scholastic Update,* May 1, 1992.

Marsa, Linda. "Scientific Fraud." *Omni Magazine,* 1992.

Merton, Robert K. "Priorities in Scientific Discovery: A Chapter in the Sociology of Science." *American Sociological Review* 22, 1957.

Merton, Robert K. "The Matthew Effect." *Science* 159, 1968.

Merton, Robert K. *Sociology of Science: Theoretical and Empirical Investigations.* Chicago: University of Chicago Press, 1973.

Morse, Susan L. "Women and Sports." *CQ Researcher,* March 6, 1992.

Sagdeev, Roald Z. "Science and Perestroika: A Long Way to Go." *Issues in Science and Technology* 4, 1988.

Schrof, Joannie M. "Pumped Up." *U.S. News & World Report,* June 1, 1992.

Star, Susan Leigh. "Introduction: The Sociology of Science and Technology." *Social Problems* 35, 1988.

Teeter, Ruskin. "Scientific Origins of Adolescent Sport." *Adolescence* 22, 1987.

Wrisberg, Craig A., Draper, M. Vanessa, and Everett, John J. "Sex Role Orientations of Male and Female Collegiate Athletes from Selected Individual and Team Sports." *Sex Roles* 19, 1988.

"Why Isn't Popular Science More Popular?" *American Scientist,* September/October 1988.

16 Collective Behavior and Social Movements

Blumer, Herbert. "Collective Behavior." In Alfred McLung Lee, ed. *New Outline of the Principles of Sociology.* New York: Barnes & Noble, 1951.

Brunvand, Jan Harold. *The Baby Train and Other Urban Legends.* New York: W.W. Norton, 1993.

Koenig, Fredrick. *Rumor in the Marketplace: The Social Psychology of Commercial Hearsay.* Dover, Mass.: Auburn House, 1985.

Lacayo, Richard. "Tower Terror." *Time,* March 8, 1993.

LeBon, Gustave. *The Mind of the Crowd.* New York: Viking, 1960. Originally published in 1895.

Mathews, Tom. "The Siege of L.A." *Newsweek,* May 11, 1992.

Nock, Steven L., and Kingston, Paul W. *The Sociology of Public Issues.* Belmont, Cal.: Wadsworth, 1990.

Oxford, Edward. "Night of the Martians." *American History Illustrated* 23, 1988.

Rubin, Beth A. "Class Struggle American Style: Unions, Strikes and Wages." *American Sociological Review* 51, 1986.

Smelser, Neil J. *Theory of Collective Behavior.* New York: Free Press, 1962.

Terkel, Studs. *American Dreams: Lost and Found.* New York: Ballantine, 1980.

Turner, Ralph H., and Killian, Lewis M. *Collective Behavior,* 2nd ed. Englewood Cliffs, N.J.: Prentice-Hall, 1972.

17 Population and Urbanization

Burgess, Ernest W. "The Growth of the City." In Robert E. Park and Ernest W. Burgess, eds. *The City.* Chicago, Ill.: University of Chicago Press, 1925.

Bookshelf

Ehrlich, Paul R. *The Population Bomb.* New York: Ballantine Books, 1978.

Fischer, Claude S. "Toward a Subcultural Theory of Urbanism." *American Journal of Sociology* 80, 1975.

Gans, Herbert J. *The Urban Villagers.* New York: Free Press, 1962.

Gottdiener, M., and Feagin, Joe R. "The Paradigm Shift in Urban Sociology." *Urban Affairs Quarterly* 24, 1988.

Harris, Chauncy D., and Ullman, Edward L. "The Nature of Cities." *The Annals of the American Academy of Political and Social Science* 242, 1945.

Hawley, Amos H. *Human Ecology.* Chicago: University of Chicago Press, 1986.

Hoyt, Homer. *The Structure and Growth of Residential Neighborhoods in American Cities.* Washington, D.C.: Federal Housing Authority, 1939.

Linden, Eugene. "Megacities." *Time,* January 11, 1993.

Morris, Robert. "Concluding Remarks: Consequences of the Demographic Revolution." *The Gerontologist* 27, 1987.

Mumford, Lewis. *The City in History.* New York: Harcourt, Brace and World, 1961.

Spates, James L., and Macionis, John J. *The Sociology of Cities,* 2nd ed. Belmont, Cal.: Wadsworth, 1987.

Tien, H. Yuen. "China's Demographic Dilemma." *Population Bulletin* 47, 1992.

Wirth, Louis. "Urbanism as a Way of Life." *American Journal of Sociology* 44, 1938.

18 Social Change and Modernization

Adler, Jerry. "Stretched to the Limit." *Newsweek,* July 11, 1988.

Berger, Peter. *Facing Up to Modernity: Excursions in Society, Politics, and Religion.* New York: Basic Books, 1977.

Bergeson, Albert, ed. *Crises in the World System.* Beverly Hills, Cal.: Sage Publications, 1983.

Carson, Rachel. *Silent Spring.* Boston, Mass.: Houghton Mifflin, 1962.

Chirot, Daniel. *Social Change in the Modern Era.* New York: Harcourt Brace Jovanovich, 1986.

Dahrendorf, Ralf. *Class and Class Conflict in Industrial Society.* Berkeley, Cal.: Stanford University Press, 1959.

Hammond, Allen, ed. *The 1993 Information Please Environmental Almanac.* Boston, Mass.: Houghton Mifflin, 1993.

Kidron, Michael, and Segal, Ronald. *The New State of the World Atlas.* New York: Simon & Schuster, 1987.

Lenski, Gerhard, and Lenski, Jean. *Human Societies,* 5th ed. New York: McGraw-Hill, 1985.

Parsons, Talcott. *Societies: Evolutionary and Comparative Perspectives.* Englewood Cliffs, N.J.: Prentice-Hall, 1966.

Schneider, Claudine. "Hazardous Waste: The Bottom Line Is Prevention." *Issues in Science and Technology* 4, 1988.

Sorokin, Pitirim A. *Social and Cultural Dynamics.* New York: American Books, 1937.

Spengler, Oswald. *The Decline of the West.* New York: Knopf, 1962. Originally published in 1918.

Stanglin, Douglas. "Toxic Wasteland." *U.S. News & World Report,* April 13, 1992.

Stone, Roger D. "The Global Stakes of Tropical Deforestation." *USA Today,* March 1988.

Tata, Robert J., and Schultz, Ronald R. "World Variation in Human Welfare: A New Index of Development Status." *Annals of the Association of American Geographers* 78, 1988.

"The Burning Jungle." *U.S. News & World Report,* October 31, 1988.

Volti, Rudi. *Society and Technological Change,* 2nd ed. New York: St. Martin's Press, 1992.

Wallerstein, Immanuel. *The Modern World System.* New York: Academic Press, 1974.

GLOSSARY

The Glossary contains many of the terms you need to understand as you study sociology. After each term, there is a brief definition or explanation of the meaning of the term as it is used in the textbook. The page number in parentheses after each definition refers to the page in the textbook where the boldfaced term can be found.

The definitions in the Glossary do not always provide all the information about these terms as they currently are used by sociologists. Therefore, you may find it useful to turn to the page(s) listed in the parentheses to read more about any of the terms. You also may consult a more comprehensive work in sociology, a dictionary, or your teacher.

A

absolute deprivation situation in which people lack one or more social rewards. **(421)**

absolute monarchy authoritarian type of government in which the hereditary ruler holds absolute power. **(335)**

accommodation state of balance between cooperation and conflict. **(81)**

achieved status status acquired by an individual on the basis of some special skill, knowledge, or ability. **(69)**

acquired immune deficiency syndrome (AIDS) fatal disease caused by a virus that attacks an individual's immune system, leaving the person vulnerable to a host of deadly infections. **(280)**

adolescence period between the normal onset of puberty and the beginning of adulthood. **(122)**

ageism belief that one age category is by nature superior to another age category. **(270)**

agents of socialization specific individuals, groups, and institutions that provide the situations in which socialization can occur. **(112)** *See also* **socialization.**

aggregate group of people gathered in the same place at the same time who lack organization or lasting patterns of interaction. **(71)**

agricultural society type of society characterized by the use of draft animals and plows in the tilling of fields. **(77)**

Alzheimer's disease organic condition that results in the progressive destruction of brain cells. **(165)**

animism belief system in which spirits are active in influencing human life. **(364)**

anomie situation that arises when the norms of society are unclear or are no longer applicable. **(182)**

anthropology comparative study of various aspects of past and present cultures. **(6)**

anticipatory socialization learning of the rights, obligations, and expectations of a role in preparation for assuming that role at a future date. **(127)**

antinatalism official policies designed to discourage births. **(443)**

aptitude capacity to learn a particular skill or acquire a particular body of knowledge. **(103)**

ascribed status status assigned according to standards that are beyond a person's control. Age, sex, family heritage, and race are examples of ascribed statuses. **(68)**

assimilation blending of culturally distinct groups into a single group with a common culture and identity. **(59, 242)**

authoritarianism type of government in which power rests firmly with the state. **(335)**

authority legitimate power. **(330)**

B

baby-boom generation collective term for the approximately 76 million children born in the United States from 1946 through 1964. **(271)**

barter practice of exchanging one good for another. **(77)**

bilateral descent descent system in which kinship is traced through both parents. **(297)**

bilingual education system of education in which non-English-speaking students are taught in their native languages until they can attend classes taught in English. **(359)**

bilocality residential pattern in which a newly married couple is allowed to choose whether they will live with the husband's parents or the wife's parents. **(297)**

birth rate annual number of live births per 1,000 members of a population. **(430)**

bourgeoisie (boor-ZHWAH-zee) owners of the means of production in a capitalist society. **(208)**

bureaucracy ranked authority structure that operates according to specific rules and procedures. **(83)**

C

capitalism economic model in which the factors of production are owned by individuals and that is regulated by the forces of profit and competition. **(323)**

caste system system in which scarce resources and rewards are distributed on the basis of ascribed statuses. **(207)** *See also* **class system.**

causal relationship relationship in which a change in one variable causes a change in another variable. **(486)**

charismatic authority power that is legitimated on the basis of the personal characteristics of the individual exercising the power. **(331)**

city permanent concentration of relatively large numbers of people who are engaged mainly in nonagricultural pursuits. **(445)**

class system system in which scarce resources and rewards are determined on the basis of achieved statuses. **(207)** *See also* **caste system.**

coercion power that is exercised through force or the threat of force. **(331)**

collective behavior relatively spontaneous social behavior that occurs when people try to develop common solutions to unclear situations. **(406)**

collectivity collection of people who have limited interaction with each other and who do not share clearly defined, conventional norms. **(408)**

communism political and economic system in which property is communally owned. **(325)**

competition interaction that occurs when two or more persons or groups oppose each other to achieve a goal that only one can attain. **(80)**

compositional theory theory of city life that examines the ways in which the composition of a city's population influences life in the city. According to this theory, individuals are able to protect themselves from the anonymity of the city by forming primary groups with others who are like themselves. **(451)**

concentric zone model model of urban structure proposed by Ernest W. Burgess in which the typical industrial city is said to spread outward from the center in a series of circles within circles. **(449)**

Glossary

conflict   deliberate attempt to control by force, oppose, harm, or resist the will of another person or persons. **(80)**

conflict perspective   theoretical perspective that focuses on those forces in society that promote competition and change. **(13)**

constitutional monarchy   type of government in which the ruler, or monarch, is nothing more than the symbolic head of state. Constitutional monarchies are considered democratic because the ultimate power rests with elected officials. **(334)**

contagion theory   theory of collective behavior proposed by Gustave LeBon in which the hypnotic power of a crowd is said to encourage people to give up their individuality to the stronger pull of the group. Individuals then become anonymous, with no will power or sense of responsibility. **(413)**

controls   ways of excluding the possibility that outside variables are affecting the relationship between the two variables under investigation. **(486)**

control theory   theory of deviant behavior in which deviance is seen as a natural occurrence and conformity as the result of social control. **(184)**

cooperation   interaction that occurs when two or more persons or groups work together to achieve a goal that will benefit many people. **(81)**

core societies   according to the world-system theory of modernization, those more developed nations that are at the center of the world economy and upon which less developed nations are economically dependent. **(469–470)** *See also* **peripheral societies.**

corporation   business organization that is owned by stockholders and is treated by law as if it were an individual person. **(326)**

corrections   sanctions—such as imprisonment, parole, and probation—used to punish criminals. **(192)**

correlation   change in one variable is regularly associated with a change in another variable. **(486)**

counterculture   group that rejects the values, norms, and practices of the larger society and replaces them with a new set of cultural patterns. **(38)**

crime   any act that is labeled as such by those in authority, is prohibited by law, and is punishable by the government. **(187)**

crime syndicate   large-scale organization of professional criminals that controls some vice or business through violence or the threat of violence. **(192)**

crowd   temporary collection of people who are in close enough proximity to interact. **(408)**

cult   religious group founded on the revelations of a person believed to have special knowledge. **(365–366)**

cultural lag   situation in which some aspects of the culture change less rapidly, or lag behind, other aspects of the same culture. **(60)**

cultural pluralism   policy that allows each group within society to keep its unique cultural identity. **(242)**

cultural relativism   belief that cultures should be judged by their own standards. **(37)**

cultural-transmission theory   theory that views deviance as a learned behavior transmitted through interaction with others. **(179)**

cultural universals   common features that are found in all human cultures. **(32)**

culture   shared products of human groups. These products include both physical objects and the beliefs, values, and behaviors shared by the group. **(24)** *See also* **material culture; nonmaterial culture.**

culture complex   cluster of interrelated culture traits. **(30)**

culture pattern   combination of a number of culture complexes into an interrelated whole. **(30)**

culture trait individual tool, act, or belief that is related to a particular situation or need. **(30)**

cyclical theory of social change historical view of social change in which societies are seen as rising and then falling or as continuously moving back and forth between stages of development. **(460)**

D

data information collected through scientific research. Although the word *data* sometimes is treated as a singular noun, it actually is the plural form of *datum*. Thus when speaking of data, most scientists say "the data are . . . ." **(14, 485)**

de facto segregation segregation based on informal norms. **(243)**

de jure segregation segregation based on laws. **(243)**

death rate annual number of deaths per 1,000 members of a population. **(431)**

democracy type of government in which power is exercised through the people. **(331)**

democratic socialism combination of a democratic government and a socialist economy. **(334)**

demographic transition theory theory of population in which population patterns are said to be tied to a society's level of technological development. Theoretically, a society's population progresses through three distinct stages. **(439)**

demography scientific study of human populations. **(430)**

denomination well-established religious organization in which a substantial portion of the population are members. **(365)**

dependency shift from being an independent adult to being dependent on others for physical or financial assistance. **(166)**

dependent variable variable that is changed by the independent variable. **(486)**

deprivation theory theory of social movements in which social movements are said to arise when large numbers of people feel economically or socially deprived of what they think is necessary for their well-being. **(421)**

deviance behavior that violates significant social norms. **(176)**

dictatorship authoritarian type of government in which power is in the hands of a single individual. **(335)**

differential association proportion of associations a person has with deviant versus nondeviant individuals. **(179)**

diffusion spread of culture traits (ideas, acts, beliefs, and material objects) from one society to another. **(57)**

discovery when people recognize new uses for existing elements in the world or begin to understand them in new ways. **(56)**

discrimination denial of equal treatment to individuals based on their group membership. **(236)**

division of labor specialization by individuals or groups in the performance of specific economic activities. **(74)**

doubling time number of years necessary for a population to double in size, given its current rate of growth. **(435)**

drug any substance that changes mood, behavior, or consciousness. **(138)**

dyad group with two members. **(72)**

dysfunction negative consequence an element has for the stability of the social system. **(13)**

E

early adulthood first era of adulthood, spanning ages 17 through 39. **(151)**

ecclesia type of religious organization in which all people in the society are members by virtue of their birth. **(365)**

ecology science that studies the relationship between living organisms and their environment. **(476)**

economic institution system of roles and norms that governs the production, distribution, and consumption of goods and services. **(320)**

economics study of the choices people make in an effort to satisfy their wants and needs. **(8)**

education system of roles and norms that ensures the transmission of knowledge, values, and patterns of behavior from one generation to the next. **(348)**

egalitarian system authority pattern in which authority is shared by both the mother and the father. **(298)**

emergent-norm theory theory of collective behavior proposed by Ralph Turner and Lewis Killian. According to this theory, the people in a crowd often are faced with a situation in which traditional norms do not apply. Gradually, new norms emerge when a leader initiates new behavior. **(416)**

empirical research research that relies on the use of experience, observation, and experimentation to collect data. **(485)**

endogamy marriage within one's own social category. **(207)**

Equal Rights Amendment (ERA) amendment approved by Congress in 1972 proposing equality for the sexes. Defeated when it did not receive ratification by the required number of states. **(265)**

equilibrium theory of social change Talcott Parson's view of social change in which society is likened to a living organism. Change in one part of the social system produces change in all other parts, as the system attempts to regain balance, or equilibrium. **(463–464)**

ethicalism belief system in which moral principles have a sacred quality. **(365)**

ethnic group individuals who share a common cultural background and a common sense of identity. **(233)**

ethnicity set of cultural characteristics that distinguishes one group from another group. **(233)**

ethnocentrism tendency to view one's own culture and group as superior to all other cultures and groups. **(36, 60)**

evolutionary theory of social change view of social change in which change is seen as a process that moves in one direction—toward increasing complexity. **(462)**

exchange individual, group, or societal interaction undertaken in an effort to receive a reward in return for actions. **(80)**

exchange theory theory that holds that people are motivated by self-interests in their interactions with other people. **(80)**

exogamy marriage outside of one's own social category. **(207)**

extended family family form that consists of three or more generations of a family sharing the same residence. **(295)**

F

factors of production resources that can be used to produce and distribute goods and services. **(320)**

fad unconventional thought or action that a large number of people are attached to for a very short period of time. **(411)**

family group of people who are related by marriage, blood, or adoption and who live together and share economic resources. **(295)**

family of orientation nuclear family into which a person is born. **(295)**

family of procreation nuclear family consisting of an individual, his or her spouse, and their children. **(295)**

Glossary

family planning conscious decision by married couples to have only the number of children that they want. **(443)**

fashion enthusiastic attachment among large numbers of people for a particular style of appearance or behavior. **(410)**

fecundity biological potential for reproduction. **(431)**

fertility actual number of births per 1,000 women of childbearing age in a population. **(431)**

folkways norms that do not have great moral significance attached to them—the common customs of everyday life. **(27)**

formal organization large, complex secondary group that has been established to achieve specific goals. **(83)**

formal sanction reward or punishment that is given by some formal organization or regulatory body, such as the government, the police, a corporation, or a school. **(53)**

free trade trade between nations that is unrestricted by trade barriers. **(328)**

function positive consequence an element of society has for the maintenance of the social system. **(12)** *See also* **dysfunction; latent function; manifest function.**

functionalist perspective theoretical perspective that views society as a set of interrelated parts that work together to produce a stable social system. **(13)**

G

Gemeinschaft (ga-MINE-shoft) societies in which most members know one another, relationships are close, and activities center on the family and the community. **(79)**

gender behavioral and psychological traits considered appropriate for males and females. **(260)**

gender roles specific behaviors and attitudes that a society establishes for men and women. **(261)**

generalized other internalized attitudes, expectations, and viewpoints of society that we use to guide our behavior and reinforce our sense of self. **(110)**

genocide extermination aimed at intentionally destroying an entire targeted population. **(243)**

gerontology scientific study of the processes and phenomena of aging. **(162)**

Gesellschaft (ga-ZELL-shoft) societies in which social relationships are based on need rather than on emotion, relationships are impersonal and temporary, and individual goals are more important than group goals. **(79)**

group set of two or more people who interact on the basis of shared expectations and who possess some degree of common identity. **(71)**

growth rate birth rate minus the death rate. **(434)**

H

heredity transmission of genetic characteristics from parents to children. **(100)**

heterogamy tendency for individuals to marry people who have social characteristics different from their own. **(302)**

hidden curriculum transmission by schools of cultural goals that are not openly acknowledged. **(351)**

history study of past events. **(8)**

homogamy tendency for individuals to marry people who have social characteristics similar to their own. **(131, 301)**

horizontal mobility type of social mobility in which the individual moves from one position in a social-class level to another position in that same social-class level. **(217)**

horticultural society type of society characterized by a reliance on vegetables grown in garden plots as the main form of subsistence. **(76–77)**

Glossary

hunting and gathering society type of society characterized by the daily collection of wild plants and animals as the main form of subsistence. **(76)**

hypothesis statement that predicts the relationship between two or more variables. **(487)**

I

I unsocialized, spontaneous, self-interested component of the personality and self-identity. **(111)**

ideal type description of the essential characteristics of some aspect of society. **(12)**

idealistic culture type of culture in Pitirim Sorokin's cyclical theory of social change that combines both ideational and sensate characteristics. **(461)** *See also* **ideational culture; sensate culture.**

ideational culture type of culture in Pitirim Sorokin's cyclical theory of social change in which truth and knowledge are sought through faith or religion. **(461)** *See also* **idealistic culture; sensate culture.**

ideology system of beliefs or ideas that justifies some social, moral, religious, political, or economic interests held by a social group or by society. **(55)**

incest taboo norm forbidding sexual relations or marriage between certain relatives. **(298–299)**

independent variable variable that causes a change in another variable. **(486)**

industrial society type of society in which the mechanized production of goods is the main economic activity. **(76)**

infant mortality rate annual number of deaths among infants under one year of age per 1,000 live births in a population. **(433)**

informal sanction spontaneous expression of approval or disapproval given by an individual or individuals. **(53)**

ingroup group that an individual belongs to and identifies with. **(74)** *See also* **outgroup.**

instinct unchanging, biologically inherited behavior pattern. **(101)**

institutionalized discrimination discrimination that is an outgrowth of the structure of society. **(236)**

interactionist perspective theoretical perspective that focuses on how individuals interact with one another in society. **(16)**

interest group organization that attempts to influence the political decision-making process. **(339)**

intergenerational mobility form of vertical mobility in which status differs between generations in the same family. **(217)**

internalization process by which a norm becomes a part of an individual's personality, thereby conditioning the individual to conform to society's expectations. **(52)**

interview much like a questionnaire, except that people are asked to respond orally to questions. **(489)**

invention use of existing knowledge to create something that did not previously exist. **(56)**

iron law of oligarchy tendency of organizations to become increasingly dominated by small groups of people. **(88)**

J

junta authoritarian type of government in which political power has been seized from the previous government by force. **(335)**

K

kibbutz collective farm or settlement in Israel. **(35)**

kinship network of people who are related by marriage, birth, or adoption. **(295)**

Glossary

L

labeling theory   theory that focuses on how individuals come to be labeled as deviant. **(184)**

labor force   all individuals 16 and older who are employed in paid positions or who are seeking paid employment. **(156)**

language   organization of written and spoken symbols into a standardized system. **(25)**

late adulthood   third and last era of adulthood, spanning ages 65 and over. **(151)**

latent function   unintended and unrecognized consequence of some element of society. **(13)**

law   written rule of conduct that is enacted and enforced by the government. By definition, the violation of these norms is considered a criminal act. **(27)**

law of demand   principle that states that the demand for a product increases as the price of the product decreases and demand decreases as price increases. **(324)**

law of supply   principle that states that producers will supply more products when they can charge higher prices and fewer products when they must charge lower prices. **(324)**

legal discrimination   discrimination that is upheld by law. **(236)**

legitimacy   right of those people in power to control, or govern, others. **(330)**

less developed nations   nations that have low levels of per capita income, industrialization, and modernization. **(433)**

life chances   likelihood individuals have of sharing in the opportunities and benefits of society. **(222)**

life expectancy   average number of years a person born in a particular can be expected to live. **(167, 222, 433)**

life span   maximum length of life that is biologically possible. **(433)**

life structure   combination of statuses, roles, activities, goals, values, beliefs, and life circumstances that characterize an individual. **(150)**

looking-glass self   interactive process by which we develop an image of ourselves based on how we imagine we appear to others. **(109)**

M

Malthusian theory   theory of population proposed by Thomas Malthus, in which population increases geometrically and the food supply increases arithmetically. Because the food supply cannot keep up with the expanding population, Malthus predicted widespread starvation would result. **(438)**

mandatory education   enforced schooling. **(350)**

manifest function   intended and recognized consequence of some element of society. **(13)**

marriage   set of norms that specify the ways in which family structure should be organized. **(296)**

mass hysteria   unfounded anxiety shared by people who are scattered over a wide geographic area. **(410)**

mass media   newspapers, magazines, books, television, radio, films, and other forms of communication that reach large audiences without personal contact between the individuals sending the information and those receiving it. **(113)**

master status   status that plays the greatest role in shaping a person's life and determining his or her social identity. **(69)**

material culture   physical objects created by human groups. Sociologists and anthropologists use the term *artifacts* to refer to the physical objects of material culture. **(24)**

matriarchal system   authority pattern in which the mother holds most of the authority. **(298)**

Glossary

matrilineal descent   descent system in which kinship is traced through the mother's family. **(297)**

matrilocality   residential pattern in which a newly married couple are expected to live near or with the wife's parents. **(297)**

Matthew effect   tendency for honors and recognition to go to those scientists who have already achieved recognition. On the other hand, they tend to be withheld from scientists who have not yet made their mark. **(381)**

me   part of the identity that is aware of the expectations and attitudes of society; the socialized self. **(111)**

mean   measure obtained by adding up all of the numbers in the data and dividing that number by the total number of cases. **(490)**

means of production   tools, buildings, and materials needed to produce goods and services. **(207)**

measure of central tendency   statistical average—a single value—that describes the data under consideration. **(490)**

mechanical solidarity   close-knit social relationships common in preindustrial societies that result when a small group of people share the same values and perform the same tasks. **(79)** *See also* **organic solidarity.**

median   number, or value, that divides the range of data into two equal parts. **(490)**

Medicaid   state and federally funded health-insurance program for people with little or no money. **(282)**

Medicare   government-sponsored insurance plan for the elderly and the disabled. **(273)**

megalopolis   area composed of a series of metropolises formed by the running together of central cities and their suburbs. **(448)**

mentor   someone who fosters an individual's development by believing in the person, sharing the person's dreams, and helping the person achieve those dreams. **(153)**

metropolitan statistical area (MSA) urban area—either a city or a central city and its suburbs—that has a population of 50,000 or more. **(448)**

middle adulthood   second era of adulthood, spanning the ages 40 through 59. **(151)**

middle-old   people aged 75–84. **(162)**

migration   movement of people from one specified area to another. **(433)**

migration rate   annual difference between in-migration and out-migration. **(433)**

minority group   category of people who share physical characteristics or cultural practices that result in the group being denied equal treatment. **(235)**

mob   emotionally charged collectivity whose members are united by a specific or violent goal. **(409)**

mode   number that occurs most often in the data. **(490)**

modernization   process by which a society's social institutions become increasingly complex as the society moves toward industrialization. **(466)**

modernization theory   theory of modernization that argues that the more developed nations of the world were the first to modernize because they were the first to industrialize. **(466)**

monarchy   type of government in which one person rules. In a monarchy, the ruler comes to power through inheritance. **(334)**

monogamy   marriage of one man to one woman. **(296)**

monotheism   belief in one god. **(365)**

more developed nations   nations that have high levels of per capita income, industrialization, and modernization. **(433)**

mores   (MORE-ayz) norms that have great moral significance attached to them. **(27)**

Glossary

mortality number of deaths in a society. **(431)**

multiple-nuclei model model of urban structure proposed by Chauncey Harris and Edward Ullman in which the city is said to have a number of specialized centers devoted to different types of land use. **(451)**

N

narcissism extreme self-centeredness. **(51)**

negative correlation variables change in opposite directions. **(486)**

negative sanction sanction in the form of a punishment or the threat of punishment. **(53)** *See also* **sanction; positive sanction.**

neolocality residential pattern in which a newly married couple is free to set up their residence apart from both sets of parents. **(297)**

nonmaterial culture abstract human creations, such as language, ideas, beliefs, rules, skills, family patterns, work practices, and political and economic systems. **(24)**

norm of communalism norm that states that all scientific knowledge should be made available to everyone in the scientific community. **(380)**

norm of disinterestedness norm that states that scientists should seek truth, not personal gain. **(380)**

norm of organized skepticism norm that states that no scientific finding or theory is immune to questioning. **(380)**

norm of universalism norm that states that scientific research should be judged solely on the basis of quality. **(380)**

norms shared rules of conduct that tell people how to act in specific situations. **(26)**

novice phase term proposed by Levinson and his colleagues for the first three stages of the early adulthood era. **(153)**

nuclear family family form that consists of one or both parents and their children. **(295)**

O

objective method technique used to rank individuals according to social class in which sociologists define social class in terms of factors such as income, occupation, and education. **(214)**

old-old people aged 85 and older. **(162)**

oligopoly situation that exists when a few people control an industry. **(327)**

operational definition definition that is stated in terms of measurable characteristics. **(487)**

organic solidarity impersonal social relationships, common in industrial societies, that arise with increased job specialization. **(79)** *See also* **mechanical solidarity.**

outgroup any group that an individual does not belong to or identify with. **(74)** *See also* **ingroup.**

overurbanization situation in which more people live in the city than the city can support in terms of jobs and facilities. **(447)**

P

panic spontaneous and uncoordinated group action to escape some perceived threat. **(410)**

paradigm set of shared concepts, methods, and assumptions that make up the scientific reality at any point in time. **(385)**

pastoral society type of society characterized by a reliance on domesticated herd animals as the main form of subsistence. **(76)**

patriarchal system authority pattern in which the father holds most of the authority. **(297–298)**

Glossary

patrilineal descent   descent pattern in which kinship is traced through the father's family. **(297)**

patrilocality   residential pattern in which a newly married couple is expected to live with or near the husband's parents. **(297)**

peer group   primary group composed of individuals of roughly equal age and social characteristics. **(112)**

peripheral societies   according to the world-system theory of modernization, those less developed societies that are economically dependent on the core, or more developed, societies. **(470)** *See also* **core societies.**

personality   sum total of behaviors, attitudes, beliefs, and values that are characteristic of an individual. **(100)**

phenomenon   observable fact or event. **(4)**

plea bargaining   process of legal negotiation that allows an accused person to plead guilty to a lesser charge in return for a lighter sentence. **(192)**

pluralist model   model in which the political process in the United States is said to be controlled by interest groups that compete with one another for power. **(341)**

political institution   system of roles and norms that governs the distribution and exercise of power in society. **(330)**

political party   organization that seeks to gain power in the government through legitimate means. **(336)**

political science   study of the organization and operation of governments. **(8)**

polyandry   form of polygamy in which a woman is permitted to marry more than one man at a time. **(296)**

polygamy   marriage with multiple partners. **(296)**

polygyny   form of polygamy in which a man is permitted to marry more than one woman at a time. **(296)**

polytheism   belief in a number of gods. **(365)**

population   number of people living in an area at a particular time. **(430)**

population pyramid   graphic representation of the age and sex distribution of a population. **(435)**

positive correlation   both variables change in the same direction. **(486)**

positive sanction   sanction in the form of a reward. **(52)** *See also* **negative sanction; sanction.**

postindustrial society   type of society in which economic activity centers on the production of information and the provision of services. **(76)**

poverty   standard of living that is below the minimum level considered decent and reasonable by society. **(219)**

poverty level   minimum annual income needed by a family to survive. **(219)**

power   ability to control the behavior of others, with or without their consent. **(209, 330)**

power-elite model   model in which political power in the United States is said to be exercised by and for the privileged few in society. **(341)**

preindustrial society   type of society in which food production—carried out through the use of human and animal labor—is the main economic activity. **(74)**

prejudice   unsupported generalization about a category of people. **(236)**

prestige   respect, honor, recognition, or courtesy an individual receives from other members of society. **(210)**

primary deviance   nonconformity undetected by authority in which the individuals who commit deviant acts do not consider themselves to be deviant, and neither does society. **(186)** *See also* **deviance; secondary deviance.**

Glossary

primary group   small group of people who interact over a relatively long period of time on a direct and personal basis. **(72–73)** *See also* **secondary group.**

primary sector   sector of the economy that deals with the extraction of raw materials from the environment. **(320–321)** *See also* **secondary sector; tertiary sector.**

principle of immanent change   according to Pitirim Sorokin's cyclical theory of social change, the natural tendency of a society's structure to swing back and forth between an ideational and a sensate culture. **(461)** *See also* **ideational culture; sensate culture.**

profane   anything considered to be part of the ordinary world and thus commonplace and familiar. **(361)**

profession   high-status occupation that requires specialized skills obtained through formal education. **(156)**

proletariat   workers in a capitalist society who sell their labor in exchange for wages. **(208)**

propaganda   organized and deliberate attempt to shape public opinion. **(413)**

protectionism   use of trade barriers to protect domestic manufacturers from foreign competition. **(328)**

psychology   science that deals with the behavior and thinking of organisms. **(6)**

puberty   physical maturing that makes an individual capable of sexual reproduction. **(122)**

public   group of geographically scattered people who are interested in and divided by some issue. **(412)**

public goods   goods and services that the government provides for everyone in society. **(329)**

public opinion   collection of differing attitudes that members of a public have about a particular issue. **(412)** *See also* **public.**

Q

questionnaire   list of questions or statements to which people are asked to respond in writing. **(489)**

R

race   category of people who share inherited physical characteristics and who are perceived by others as being a distinct group. **(232)**

racism   belief that one's own race or ethnic group is naturally superior to other races or ethnic groups. **(238)**

random sample   sample chosen in such a way that every member of the population has an equal chance of being included in the sample. **(489)**

rational-legal authority   power that is legitimated by formal rules and regulations. **(331)**

rationalization   process by which every feature of human behavior becomes subject to calculation, measurement, and control. **(83, 388)**

recidivism   repeated criminal behavior. **(193)**

reciprocal roles   corresponding roles that define the patterns of interaction between related statuses. **(69)**

reciprocity   idea that if you do something for someone, they owe you something in return. **(80)**

reference group   any group with whom individuals identify and whose attitudes and values they often adopt. **(73)**

reform movements   type of social movement, the goal of which is to improve some part of society through social change. **(418)**

regentrification   upgrading of specific neighborhoods in an attempt to encourage the middle and upper classes to relocate to the cities. **(448)**

relative deprivation   situation in which people have a lesser portion of social rewards compared to other people or groups. **(421)**

religion   system of roles and norms organized around the sacred realm that binds people together in social groups. **(361)**

religiosity   importance of religion in a person's life. **(367)**

reputational method   technique used to rank individuals according to social class. This is done by asking individuals in the community to rank other community members based on what they know of their characters and life-styles. **(214)**

research design   plan for collecting, analyzing, and evaluating data. **(488)**

resistance movements   type of social movement, the goal of which is a return to traditional ways of acting and thinking. **(417)**

resocialization   break with past experiences and the learning of new values and norms. **(115)**

resource mobilization   organization and effective use of resources. **(422)**

resource-mobilization theory   theory of social movements that states that even the most ill-treated group with the most just cause will not be able to bring about change without resources. **(422)**

respondents   people who respond to surveys. **(489)**

revolutionary movements   type of social movement, the goal of which is a total and radical change of the existing social structure. **(418)**

riot   crowd that erupts in generalized destructive behavior, the purpose of which is social disorder. **(410)**

ritual   established pattern of behavior through which a group of believers experience the sacred. **(363)**

role   behavior—the rights and obligations—expected of someone occupying a particular status. **(68)**

role conflict   situation that occurs when fulfilling the expectations of one role makes it difficult to fulfill the expectations of another role. **(70)**

role expectations   socially determined behaviors expected of a person performing a role. **(69)**

role performance   actual behavior of a person performing a role. **(70)**

role set   different roles attached to a single status. **(70)**

role strain   situation that occurs when a person has difficulty meeting the expectations of a single role. **(70)**

role-taking   taking or pretending to take the role of others. **(110)**

rumor   unverified piece of information that is spread rapidly from one person to another. **(411)**

S

sacred   anything that is considered to be part of the supernatural world and that inspires awe, respect, and reverence. **(361)**

sample   small number of people drawn from a larger population. **(489)**

sanctions   rewards or punishments used to enforce conformity to norms. **(52)** *See also* **formal sanction; informal sanction; negative sanction; positive sanction.**

scapegoating   practice of placing blame for one's troubles on an innocent individual or group. **(239)**

schooling   instruction by specially trained teachers who follow officially recognized policies. **(348)**

science   pursuit of knowledge through systematic methods. **(376)**

Glossary

scientific method objective, logical, and systematic way of collecting empirical data and arriving at conclusions. **(485)**

secondary deviance nonconformity that results in the individuals who commit acts of secondary deviance being labeled as deviant and accepting that label as true. **(186)** *See also* **deviance; primary deviance.**

secondary group group in which interaction is impersonal and temporary in nature. **(73)** *See also* **primary group.**

secondary sector sector of the economy that concentrates on the use of raw materials to manufacture goods. **(321)** *See also* **primary sector; tertiary sector.**

sect relatively small religious organization that typically has split off from a denomination because of doctrinal differences. **(365)**

sector model model of urban structure proposed by Homer Hoyt in which the growth of a city is said to occur in wedge-shaped sectors that extend outward from the center to the edge of the city. **(450)**

secularization movement away from the realm of the sacred to the realm of the profane. **(386)**

segregation physical separation of a minority group from the dominant group. **(243)**

self conscious awareness of possessing a distinct identity that separates us from other members of society. **(109)**

self-fulfilling prophecy prediction that results in behavior that makes the prediction come true. **(237)**

self-fulfillment commitment to the full development of one's personality, talents, and potential. **(51)**

sensate culture type of culture in Pitirim Sorokin's cyclical theory of social change in which people seek knowledge through science. **(461)** *See also* **idealistic culture; ideational culture.**

sexism belief that one sex is by nature superior to the other. **(268)**

shamanism belief system in which spirits communicate only with one person acknowledged as a specialist. **(364)**

significant others specific people, such as parents, brothers, sisters, other relatives, and friends, who have a direct influence on our socialization. **(110)**

slavery ownership of one group of people by another group. **(243)**

small group group with few enough numbers that everyone is able to interact on a face-to-face basis. **(72)**

social category group of people who share a common trait or status. **(71)**

social change alterations in various aspects of a society over time. **(460)**

social class grouping of people with similar levels of wealth, power, and prestige. **(208)**

social control enforcing of norms through either internalization or sanctions. **(54)**

social Darwinism perspective that holds that societies evolve toward stability and perfection. **(11)**

social gerontology subfield of gerontology that studies the nonphysical aspects of aging. **(162)**

social inequality unequal sharing of social rewards and resources. **(206)**

social institution system of statuses, roles, values, and norms that is organized to satisfy one or more of the basic needs of society. **(70, 294)**

social integration degree of attachments people have to social groups or to society. **(141)**

social interaction how people relate to one another and influence each other's behavior. **(4)**

social mobility movement between or within social classes or strata. **(217)**

social movement long-term conscious effort to promote or prevent social change. **(55, 417)**

social network web of relationships that is formed by the sum total of an individual's interactions with other people. **(74)**

social psychology study of how an individual's behavior and personality are affected by the social environment. **(6)**

social sciences related disciplines that study various aspects of human social behavior. **(6)**

social stratification ranking of individuals or categories of people on the basis of unequal access to scarce resources and social rewards. **(206)**

social structure network of interrelated statuses and roles that guides human interaction. **(68)**

socialism economic model in which the factors of production are owned by the government, which regulates all economic activity. **(323)**

socialization interactive process through which individuals learn the basic skills, values, beliefs, and behavior patterns of society. **(109)**

society group of mutually interdependent people who have organized in such a way as to share a common culture and feeling of unity. **(24–25)**

sociobiology systematic study of the biological basis of all social behavior. **(102)**

socioeconomic status (SES) rating that combines social factors such as level of education, occupational prestige, and place of residence with the economic factor of income in order to determine an individual's relative position in the stratification system. **(209)**

sociological imagination ability to see the connection between the larger world and our personal lives. **(6)**

sociology science that studies human society and social behavior. **(4)**

sociology of science sociological perspective that examines how scientific knowledge develops. **(376)**

sport competitive games that are won or lost on the basis of physical skills and are played according to specific rules. **(386)**

spurious correlation variables appear to be related but actually are being affected by the existence of a third variable. **(486)**

stacking tendency to assign people to central or noncentral athletic positions on the basis of race or ethnicity. **(391)**

state primary political authority in society. **(330)**

status socially defined position in a group or in a society. **(68)** *See also* **achieved status; ascribed status; master status.**

stereotype oversimplified, exaggerated, or unfavorable generalization about a category of people. **(238)**

stigma mark of social disgrace that sets the deviant apart from the rest of society. **(177)**

structural-strain theory theory of deviant behavior that views deviance as the natural outgrowth of the values, norms, and structure of society. **(182)**

subcultural theory theory of city life in which the characteristics of the city are said to encourage rather than discourage the formation of primary group relationships. **(452)**

subculture group with its own unique values, norms, and behaviors that exists within a larger culture. **(37)**

subjective method technique used to rank individuals according to social class in which the individuals themselves are asked to determine their own social rank. **(214)**

subjugation maintaining of control over a group through force. **(243)**

subsistence strategy way in which a society uses technology to provide for the needs of its members. **(74)**

suburb politically independent community that is next to or near a city. **(448)**

Glossary

symbol anything that stands for something else and has a shared meaning attached to it. Language, gestures, images, sounds, physical objects, events, and elements of the natural world can serve as symbols as long as people recognize that they convey a particular meaning. **(16, 25)**

symbolic interaction interaction between people that takes place through the use of symbols. **(16)**

T

technology knowledge and tools people use to manipulate their environment for practical purposes. **(56)**

terrorism use of threatened or actual violence in the pursuit of political goals. **(419)**

tertiary sector sector of the economy that concentrates on the provision of services. **(321)** *See also* **primary sector; secondary sector.**

theism belief in a god or gods. **(365)**

theoretical perspective general set of assumptions about the nature of phenomena. In the case of sociology, a theoretical perspective outlines certain assumptions about the nature of social life. **(12–13)**

theory systematic explanation of the relationship among phenomena. **(12)**

total institution setting in which people are isolated from the rest of society for a set period of time and subjected to the control of officials of varied ranks. **(115)**

totalitarianism most extreme form of authoritarian government. Under totalitarianism, government leaders accept few limits on their authority. **(335)**

totemism belief in a kinship between humans and animals or natural objects. **(365)**

tracking assignment of students to different types of educational programs. **(354)**

traditional authority power that is legitimated by long-standing custom. **(330)**

transfer payments principal way in which the government attempts to reduce social inequality by redistributing money among various segments of society. **(223)**

triad three-person group. **(72)**

U

unemployment situation that occurs when people do not have jobs but are actively seeking employment. **(156)**

unemployment rate percentage of the civilian labor force that is unemployed but actively seeking employment. **(156)**

urban anomie theory theory of city life in which the city is seen to be an anonymous and unfriendly place that carries serious negative consequences for those who live there. **(451)**

urban ecology approach that examines the relationship between people and the urban environment. **(447)**

urban legends stories that are untrue but that seem realistic and teach a lesson. **(412)**

urban renewal programs designed to provide adequate housing for low-income families and to rebuild the economies of central cities. **(448)**

urbanization concentration of the population in cities. **(78, 445)**

utopian movements type of social movement, the goal of which is the creation of an ideal society apart from the existing social structure. **(418)**

V

values shared beliefs about what is good or bad, right or wrong, desirable or undesirable. **(26)**

variable characteristic that can differ from one individual, group, or situation to another in a measurable way. **(15, 486)**

Verstehen   empathetic understanding of the meanings others attach to their actions. **(12)**

vertical mobility   movement between social classes or strata in which the individual moves from one social-class level to another. **(217)**

voluntary association   nonprofit association formed to pursue some common interest. **(85)**

voluntary childlessness   conscious choice to remain childless. **(310)**

W

wealth   most obvious dimension of social stratification because it is made up of the value of everything the person owns and money earned through salaries and wages. **(209)**

white-collar crime   crime that is committed by an individual or individuals of high social status in the course of their professional lives. **(191)**

white ethnics   collective reference to immigrants from the predominantly Catholic countries of Ireland, Italy, France, Poland, and Greece. **(252)**

world system theory   theory of modernization, by Immanuel Wallerstein, in which the spread of capitalism is seen as producing an international division of labor between more developed and less developed nations. According to this view, the more developed nations control the factors of production and the less developed nations serve as sources of cheap labor and raw materials. **(468)**

Y

young-old   people aged 65–74. **(162)**

Z

zero population growth   point at which nearly equal birth and death rates produce a growth rate of zero. **(442)**

Glossary

INDEX

Page numbers in *italics* that have a *c* before them refer to charts, graphs, or tables. Page numbers in *italics* that have a *p* before them refer to photographs.

Index

B

Index

Index

E

Index

Index

Index

Index

Index

Index

N

Index

Index

Index

Index

Index

Index

Index

Index

THE SOCIOLOGIST'S CODE OF ETHICS

Research is an important part of the work pursued by sociologists. This research adds to our body of knowledge concerning human behavior. Like all scientists, sociologists are bound by a set of ethical principles when they conduct their research. In fact, ethical concerns are of such importance to sociologists that the American Sociological Association (ASA) has published a code of ethics to which all sociologists are expected to adhere. An excerpt from the ASA *Code of Ethics* is reproduced here.

Objectivity and Integrity. Sociologists should strive to maintain objectivity and integrity in the conduct of sociological research and practice.

1. Sociologists should adhere to the highest possible technical standards in their research, teaching, and practice.
2. Since individual sociologists vary in their research modes, skills, and experience, sociologists should always set forth *ex ante* [beforehand] the limits of their knowledge and the disciplinary and personal limitations that condition the validity of findings which affect whether or not a research project can be successfully completed.
3. In practice or other situations in which sociologists are requested to render a professional judgment, they should accurately and fairly represent their areas and degrees of expertise.
4. In presenting their work, sociologists are obligated to report their findings fully and should not misrepresent the findings of their research. When work is presented, they are obligated to report their findings fully and without omission of significant data. To the best of their ability, sociologists should also disclose details of their theories, methods and research designs that might bear upon interpretations of research findings.
5. Sociologists must report fully all sources of financial support in their publications and must note any special relations to the sponsor.
6. Sociologists should not make any guarantees to respondents, individuals, groups or organizations—unless there is full intention and ability to honor such commitments. All such guarantees, once made, must be honored.
7. Consistent with the spirit of full disclosure of method and analysis, sociologists, after they have completed their own analyses, should cooperate in efforts to make raw data and pertinent documentation collected and prepared at public expense available to other social scientists, at reasonable costs, except in cases where confidentiality, the client's rights to proprietary [privately owned] information and privacy, or the claims of a fieldworker to the privacy of personal notes necessarily would be violated. The timeliness of this cooperation is especially critical.
8. Sociologists should provide adequate information and citations concerning scales and other measures used in their research.
9. Sociologists must not accept grants, contracts or research assignments that appear likely to require violation of the principles enunciated [specified] in this Code, and should dissociate [separate] themselves from research when they discover a violation and are unable to achieve its correction.

10. When financial support for a project has been accepted, sociologists must make every effort to complete the proposed work on schedule, including reports to the funding source.

11. When several sociologists, including students, are involved in joint projects, there should be mutually accepted explicit agreements at the outset with respect to division of work, compensation, access to data, rights of authorship, and other rights and responsibilities. Such agreements may need to be modified as the project evolves and such modifications must be agreed upon jointly.

12. Sociologists should take particular care to state all significant qualifications on the findings and interpretations of their research.

13. Sociologists have the obligation to disseminate [share] research findings, except those likely to cause harm to clients, collaborators and participants, or those which are proprietary under a formal or informal agreement.

14. In their roles as practitioners, researchers, teachers, and administrators, sociologists have an important social responsibility because their recommendations, decisions, and actions may alter the lives of others. They should be aware of the situations and pressures that might lead to the misuse of their influence and authority. In these various roles, sociologists should also recognize that professional problems and conflicts may interfere with professional effectiveness. Sociologists should take steps to insure that these conflicts do not produce deleterious [harmful] results for clients, research participants, colleagues, students and employees.

Disclosure and Respect for the Rights of Research Populations. Disparities in wealth, power, and social status between the sociologist and respondents and clients may reflect and create problems of equity in research collaboration. Conflict of interest for the sociologist may occur in research and practice. Also to follow the precepts [rules] of the scientific method—such as those requiring full disclosure—may entail adverse consequences or personal risks for individuals and groups. Finally, irresponsible actions by a single researcher or research team can eliminate or reduce future access to a category of respondents by the entire profession and its allied fields.

1. Sociologists should not misuse their positions as professional social scientists for fraudulent purposes or as a pretext for gathering intelligence for any organization or government. Sociologists should not mislead respondents involved in a research project as to the purpose for which the research is being conducted.

2. Subjects of research are entitled to rights of biographical anonymity.

3. Information about subjects obtained from records that are opened to public scrutiny cannot be protected by guarantees of privacy or confidentiality.

4. The process of conducting sociological research must not expose respondents to substantial risk of personal harm. Informed consent must be obtained [from respondents] when the risks of research are greater than the risks of everyday life. Where modest risk or harm is anticipated, informed consent must be obtained.

5. Sociologists should take culturally appropriate steps to secure informed consent and to avoid invasions of privacy. Special actions may be necessary where the individuals are illiterate, have very low social status, or are unfamiliar with social research.

6. To the extent possible in a given study sociologists should anticipate potential threats to confidentiality. Such means as the removal of identifiers, the use of randomized responses and other statistical solutions to problems of privacy should be used where appropriate.

7. Confidential information provided by research participants must be treated as such by sociologists, even when this information enjoys no legal protection or privilege and legal force is applied. The obligation to respect confidentiality also applies to members of research organizations (interviewers, coders, clerical staff, etc.) who have access to the information. It is the responsibility of administrators and chief investigators to instruct staff members on this point and to make every effort to insure that access to confidential information is restricted.

8. While generally adhering to the norm of acknowledging the contributions of all collaborators, sociologists should be sensitive to harm that may arise from disclosure and respect a collaborator's wish or need for anonymity. Full disclosure may be made later if circumstances permit.

9. Study design and information gathering techniques should conform to regulations protecting the rights of human subjects, irrespective of source of funding, as outlined by the American Association of University Professors (AAUP) in "Regulations Governing Research On Human Subjects: Academic Freedom and the Institutional Review Board," *Academe,* December 1981: 358–370.

10. Sociologists should comply with appropriate federal and institutional requirements pertaining to the conduct of research. These requirements might include but are not necessarily limited to failure to obtain proper review and approval for research that involves human subjects and failure to follow recommendations made by responsible committees concerning research subjects, materials, and procedures.

Continued from page iv

CREDITS

KEY: (t) top, (l) left, (c) center, (r) right, (b) bottom.

PHOTOGRAPHS

UNIT 3: 202-203, Pete Saloutos/Tony Stone Images; 203(t), John Aikins/Uniphoto; 203(ct), Charles Gupton/Stock, Boston; 203(cb), HBJ Photo by Rodney Jones; 203(b), Juan Ortega.

CHAPTER 9: 204, Andrew Holbrooke/Black Star; 207(t), Isac Jo/Artstreet; 207(b), Ed Simpson/Tony Stone Images; 208(l), Joseph Nettis/Photo Researchers; 208(r), Frank Fisher/Tony Stone Images; 210, D.R. Thompson/Tony Stone Images; 213(t), Blair Seitz/Seitz & Seitz; 213(c), David Stone/Berg & Assoc.; 213(b), Richard Dunoff/The Stock Market; 215(tl), Burt Glinn/Magnum Photos; 215(tr), William Strode/Woodfin Camp & Assoc.; 215(bl-br), Craig Aurness/Woodfin Camp & Assoc.; 216, Jon Riley/Tony Stone Images; 218, Mary Lee Edwards; 220(t,bl), Richard Choy/Peter Arnold, Inc.; 220(br), C. Vergara/Photo Researchers; 223(t), UPI/Bettmann Newsphotos; 223(l), AP/Wide World Photos; 223(r), AP/Wide World Photos; 224(t), Superstock; 224(b), Tom McHugh/Photo Researchers; 225, Bob Daemmrich/Stock, Boston.

CHAPTER 10: 230, James H. Karales/Peter Arnold, Inc.; 233(l), Will & Deni McIntyre/Photo Researchers; 233(c), Richard Hutchings; 233(r), David R. Frazier Photolibrary; 234(tl), Randall Hyman/Stock, Boston; 234(tr), Lowell Georgia/Photo Researchers; 234(c), Craig Aurness/Woodfin Camp & Assoc.; 234(bl), Freda Leinwand; 234(br), Catherine Ursillo/Photo Researchers; 237, John Marmaras/Woodfin Camp & Assoc.; 238(t), AP/Wide World Photo; 238(b), National Geographic Society, Courtesy of The Supreme Court Historical Society; 239(t), The Bettmann Archive; 239(b), UPI/ Bettmann Newsphotos; 241(l), Jim Anderson/Woodfin Camp & Assoc.; 241(c), Donald Dietz/Stock, Boston; 241(r), Mark Reinstein/Gamma Liaison; 242(l), Lenore Weber; 242(r), Bill Anderson/Monkmeyer Press; 244(l), Culver Pictures; 244(r), AP/Wide World Photos; 248, Lawrence Migdale; 250(t), UPI Bettmann Newsphotos; 250(b), Jean Louis Atlan/Sygma; 252(t), Woolaroc Museum, Bartlesville, Oklahoma; 252(b), R. Vroom/Miller Services/Photo Researchers.

CHAPTER 11: 258, Comstock; 261, John Chiasson/Gamma Liaison; 262(t), Jay Dickman/Gamma Liaison; 262(b), AP/Wide World Photos; 265, Jon Riley/Tony Stone Images; 267(l), Dan Weinberg/The Image Bank; 267(c), Michael Salas/The Image Bank; 267(r), Dennis Hallinan/FPG International; 268, Dennis Brack LTD/Black Star; 269(tl), Photo World/FPG International; 269(c), Charles Gupton/Stock, Boston; 269(b), Stephanie Maze/Woodfin Camp & Assoc.; 269(tr), Kolvoord/TexaStock; 270, David Austin/Stock, Boston; 273(l), John Ficara/Woodfin Camp & Assoc.; 273(tr), David Stone/Berg & Assoc.; 273(br), Michelle Bridwell/Frontera Fotos; 274, David Strickler/Monkmeyer Press; 275, Charles Gupton/Stock, Boston; 276, William Strode/Woodfin Camp & Assoc.; 277, Dr. A. Farquhar/Valan Photos; 278(l), Hank Morgan/Photo Researchers; 278(r), Gerhard Gscheidle/Peter Arnold, Inc.; 281, Jeffrey Markowitz/Sygma; 282, Hank Morgan/Photo Researchers.

UNIT 4: 290-291, Pete Turner Inc./The Image Bank; 291(t), Stanislaw Fernandes/The Image Bank; 291(ct), Larry Lee/Westlight; 291(cb), Owen Franken/Stock, Boston; 291(b), Steve Weber/Uniphoto.

CHAPTER 12: 292, L. Powers/H. Armstrong Roberts; 295(l), Tony Freeman/PhotoEdit; 295(r), Katrina Thomas/Photo Researchers; 296, Tony Howarth/Woodfin Camp & Assoc.; 297, David Binder/Black Star; 298(l), Jeffry Myers/Stock, Boston; 298(r), Lisa Davis; 298(b), Chuck Fishman/Woodfin Camp & Assoc.; 299(t), Michal Heron/Woodfin Camp & Assoc.; 299(b), Peter Garfield/Tony Stone Images; 301(t), Alon Reininger/Contact Press Images; 301(c), John Wang/Shostal Assoc./Superstock; 301(b), Obremski/The Image Bank; 304, National Committee for Prevention of Child Abuse; 305, Freda Leinwand/Monkmeyer Press; 307(l), Peter Papadopolous/The Stock Market; 307(r), Bob Daemmrich/Stock, Boston; 309(b), Steve McCurry/Magnum Photos; 310, Joseph Nettis/Stock, Boston; 311(l), Henley & Savage/The Stock Market; 311(r), Liane Enkelis/Stock, Boston; 312, Michelle Bridwell/Frontera Fotos.

CHAPTER 13: 318, R. Kord/Allstock; 321(t), Robert Caputo/Stock, Boston; 321(c), Ulrike Welsch/Photo Researchers; 321(b), David Pollack/The Stock Market; 322(r), Frank Fisher/Tony Stone Images; 324, Stuart L. Craig, Jr./Bruce Coleman, Inc.; 325(l), Jonathan T. Wright/Bruce Coleman, Inc.; 325(r), Frank Fisher/Tony Stone Images; 326-327, Catherine Ursillo/Photo Researchers; 327(tr), George Jones III/Photo Researchers; 327(br), Jon Feingersh/The Stock Market; 328(l,r), Len Berger/Berg & Assoc.; 328(b), Michael Guest/Berg & Assoc.; 330, AP/Wide World Photos; 334, Adam Woolfit/Woodfin Camp & Assoc.; 335(t), William Gentile/Picture Group; 335(b), Novosti Press Agency/Gamma Liaison; 339, Paul Conklin/Monkmeyer Press.

CHAPTER 14: 346, Charles Gupton/Stock, Boston; 349(l), D. Degnan/H. Armstrong Roberts; 349(r), Ian Berry/Magnum Photos; 351(l), Richard Kalvar/Magnum Photos; 351(r), AP/Wide World Photos; 354(l), Kevin Horan/Stock, Boston; 354(r), Alex Webb/Magnum Photos; 356(l), Arnold Kaplan/Berg & Assoc.; 356(r), Katrina Thomas/Photo Researchers; 360, Daniel J. Schaefer; 361(l), Owen Franken/Stock, Boston; 361(r), Cary Wolinsky/Stock, Boston; 361(b), Miro Vintoniv/Stock, Boston; 364(l), Jonathon T. Wright/Bruce Coleman, Inc.; 364(tr), Kal Muller/Woodfin Camp & Assoc.; 364(br), Henry D. Meyer/Berg & Assoc.; 366, UPI/Bettmann Newsphotos; 368, Steve McCurry/Magnum Photos.

CHAPTER 15: 374, Bruce Curtis/Peter Arnold, Inc.; 379(t), Dick Luria/Tony Stone Images; 379(b), John Zoiner/Peter Arnold, Inc.; 384(t), Robert Frerck/Tony Stone Images; 384(b), Bill Gallery/Stock, Boston; 387(t), David Kent Madison/Bruce Coleman, Inc.; 387(bl), AP/Wide World Photos; 387(br), Miro Vintoniv/Stock, Boston; 388(all), AP/Wide World Photos; 389(t), Reuters/UPI/Bettmann Newsphotos; 389(b), Bob Daemmrich/Stock, Boston; 392, Jim Zerschling/Photo Researchers; 393, UPI/Bettmann Newsphotos; 394(tl), Bob Daemmrich/Stock, Boston; 394(tr), UPI/Bettmann Newsphotos; 394(b), Tony Duffy/Woodfin Camp & Assoc.

UNIT 5: 402-403, Walter Bibikow/The Image Bank; 403(t), Tom McHugh/Photo Researchers; 403(ct), Michelle Bridwell/Frontera Fotos; 403(cb), Gregory Heisler/The Image Bank; 403(b), Chad Slattery/Tony Stone Images.

CHAPTER 16: 404, Al Francekevich/The Stock Market; 407, David Butow/Black Star; 409(l), Michael Alexander/Black Star; 409(b), Kim Newton/Woodfin Camp & Assoc.; 416, AP/Wide World Photos; 417(l), Photo Researchers; 417(r), Carol Halebian/Gamma Liaison; 420, The Bettmann Archive; 421(l), Bill Foley/Woodfin Camp & Assoc.; 421(r), Owen Franken/Stock, Boston; 422(l), Ginger Chih/Peter Arnold, Inc.; 422(r), UPI/Bettmann Newsphotos.

CHAPTER 17: 428, Brownie Harris/The Stock Market; 431, Michel Tcherevkoff/The Image Bank; 434(t), George Haling